READER'S DIGEST
50th Anniversary Treasury

�֍

*A selection of the best of 50 years
from The Reader's Digest*

THE READER'S DIGEST ASSOCIATION, INC.,
PLEASANTVILLE, NEW YORK

INTERNATIONAL BOOK YEAR

Contents

5

A "Swift Power to Illuminate"

By Edward Weeks

Editor of *The Atlantic Monthly,* 1938-66

[Foreword]

DeWITT WALLACE, in cre-
ating The Reader's Digest, devised a technique to bring home
unexpected truths, American humor and aspiration, science,
faith-in-being, and the human adventure to the largest reader-
ship the world has ever known. It is an accomplishment for
which every editor salutes him. His initiative and taste have
shaped the character of this Treasury, which in its variety of

7

subject matter, in its liveliness and swift power to illuminate represents what is best in The Reader's Digest during its first half century.

To understand the originality of his technique one must recall the magazine world as it was when the 20-year-old Wallace was first experimenting. Editors took pride in being exclusive, and their readers were segregated. The intelligentsia subscribed to "the Quality Group": seven literary monthlies, some illustrated, of which only two, *Harper's* and the *Atlantic,* survive. The middlebrows, of which I was one, held a family loyalty to either *The Saturday Evening Post* or *Collier's,* rarely both. For women there were magazines of fashion and home-making which featured fiction; for the quizzical reader, eager for muckraking, there was *McClure's,* while the *National Geographic* nourished those with wanderlust. Then there were the *Literary Digest,* designed for teachers and clergymen, and *Littell's Living Age,* which digested the foreign press and periodicals for a precarious circulation of 15,000 copies. That was the scope, in 1910, and no one knew how many millions it left untouched.

As a young and hungry reader Wallace kept a file of the magazine articles that interested him and with impatience penciled out the superfluous verbiage to get at the heart of the matter. After writing promotion for a textbook publisher in hometown St. Paul, he put his savings into a booklet, *Getting the Most Out of Farming,* an annotated guide to free agricultural bulletins. With this idea of serving the reader by making the best practical advice accessible—perhaps doing it for a general audience—he felt he was on the track of something good. The war decided him: in France in 1918 he spent four months in hospital recovering from shrapnel wounds received at Meuse-Argonne and reading every magazine he could get his hands on. By now his habit of cutting had become a precision tool. After his discharge, he printed on his own a pocket-size sample of 31 magazine articles, picked and rigorously cut to his liking, and this prototype of the Digest he submitted to a number of publishers. No one would even nibble; Hearst thought it too serious for a mass market.

So with no backers, during the depression of 1921, DeWitt laid out the first issue of The Reader's Digest on capital ($1800) mostly borrowed from his father and brother. To help him he had his bride, Lila Acheson—her outside job paid their rent that first year in New York. Since the first issue of February 1922, the Digest has been endowed with the faith and talent of them both. The growth from an initial printing of 5000 to a worldwide sale of 29 million copies a month, in 13 languages, is an achievement without parallel.

In the citation conferring the Medal of Freedom on both DeWitt and Lila Wallace, President Nixon praised them "for creating a feeling of idealism in this country and among people abroad." To the conservative Midwest philosophy inherited from his father, a preacher and president of struggling little Macalester College, DeWitt added his own priorities. He is an editor who believes, not doubts. He believes absolutely in the individual, and in the concept of self-help, or "one-man power" —that man is not a passive, helpless creature, but is capable of influencing his own fate. This belief is central in the Digest.

Insatiably curious about America and the world, Wallace has gone gunning for the problems that baffle us all. He avoided "the literary," bypassed poetry, ruled out the exploitive sex and melancholy which have obsessed much of modern fiction. He was confident that an expert's word would be accepted without tedious documentation. He enjoys action, biography and, pre-eminently, the excitement of new ideas. In the 1930s, with growing confidence and financial resources, the Digest itself began commissioning articles, placing some, printing others as "originals," and drawing at greater length from books.

If in this anthology the contributions over the last four decades are of deeper perception and concern than those of the early years, it is because we as a people have grown more conscientious. Consider the circumstances of the inspiriting lead piece, "Bold Men, Bold Dreams," by Catherine Drinker Bowen. Invited by *Sports Illustrated* for an issue celebrating "bold sportsmen," it was written during the peril of the Cuban crisis and inspired by Bacon's phrase that Columbus had made hope reasonable: could the United States now sustain that hope? Consider "Racism in White America," by Whitney Young, the strongest statement by an American black the Digest has ever published: it could not have been taken seriously before the Decision of 1954.

It is not our desire to live dangerously, but we do. Which is why we must remember *Time's* tense, poignant reporting, "Death in Dallas"; why we must grieve over the mystery and the waste of "Hippie or Schoolgirl," which came straight out of the columns of the New York *Times* and was awarded a Pulitzer Prize; why we must "Pray for Barbara's Baby"; and why elders, denouncing the use of marijuana by their young, are brought up short by the probing of "Alcohol and Your Brain." No man in this century had so many lives depending on his judgment as Gen. Dwight Eisenhower in that critical hour when he ordered the invasion of Europe, a time for greatness so superbly recounted by Cornelius Ryan in "The Longest Day." Respond to the shock of "—And Sudden Death," which had its inception in Wallace's conversation with a wayside mechanic. It has proved to be the most quoted and I believe influential magazine piece of our time.

"One-man power" is most strikingly illustrated in this Treasury by a woman: "The Extraordinary Story of Helen Keller" demonstrates a memorable triumph of spirit over physical disability. Faith-in-being, as I call it, comes from the excerpt from Winston Churchill's autobiography, in which the boy at the bottom of his class at Harrow blesses the man who taught him English; it comes from Eleanor Roosevelt recalling her not always patient submission to her mother-in-law; and from James Michener's "You Never Stop Learning"—the perfect blend for a commencement address, short but stirring.

The Digest seems to find at least one illuminating piece on health for every issue—an emphasis which at times has been parodied. Yet the magazine ranks as a pioneer of popular but responsible medical journalism. A prime example is "Facts Behind the Cigarette Controversy," the lead-off article in a 14-year series that brought home as never before the association between smoking and lung cancer. No other periodical has so altered the public's attitude toward cigarettes.

The science in this Treasury is in human terms. It begins with a description of man's first flight into lunar orbit, an achievement that thrilled earthbound television watchers with their first close view of the moon, and it ranges from Wolfgang Langewiesche's interpretive reading of each layer of the Grand Canyon, to "The Secret World of the Unborn," a woman doctor's beautiful clarification of life within the womb.

In this book home truths come to us from many directions: from an Air Force physician with his authoritative program for exercise ("How to Feel Fit at Any Age"); from John Gunther, one of the great fact-gatherers for the Digest, with his searching assessment of the Russian people; from Stanley High in "I Go to Church" and Donald Culross Peattie in "The Wonder of Wood"; from Charles Lindbergh depicting his sense of release and humility while walking in an Indonesian jungle; from the insight of William James on "Making Habits Work for You"; and in her wise charming way from Marya Mannes in "The

11

Power Men Have Over Women." Amen say I, let's keep it.

The naturalists here have a story to tell those who, like myself, are distressed about our vanishing wildlife. The revival of the Pribilof seals ("Seal Islands—Treasure Islands") sets an example which might save the Atlantic salmon. One shudders at the electronic extermination of leviathans (". . . And God Created Great Whales"), and in an ingenious Yellowstone National Park expedition we witness how and when the great grizzlies go to bed.

DeWitt Wallace has always remembered that people read for enjoyment as much as for enlightenment. Such Digest departments as "Life in These United States" and "Quotable Quotes" are funny because they are so true. So is that glorious characterization, "God and My Father," by Clarence Day. And from the heart out come "Corporal Hardy," that evocation of loyalty by Richard Ely Danielson, and "When Hannah Var Eight Yar Old," a classic from the days when many stories were in dialect. I prize that true-to-life affair, "84, Charing Cross Road"—and of all memorable characters in this Treasury I choose that Down East erratic of laughter and tears, "My Quicksilver Uncle" by Robert P. Tristram Coffin.

Wallace has said that "the Digest opens windows on the world." Yes, and what the world sees through them are people—striving, progressing, cheery, and, in the main, American.

Edward Weeks has long been a commanding presence on the American literary scene. He established himself with the Atlantic Monthly Press, in Boston, during the late 1920s as a brilliant book editor. Then for almost three decades he edited the august pages of The Atlantic Monthly, maintaining its prestige while giving it new breadth and vigor.

His own books include "The Open Heart," "In Friendly Candor," and "This Trade of Writing."

Reader's Digest

50th
Anniversary Treasury

Bold Men, Bold Dreams

Catherine Drinker Bowen

[July 1965]

THEY were bold from the first. A man stood on the shores of Portugal and looked westward, nearly five centuries ago. From the way the winds blew, from the seasonal steadiness of them and the direction, the man conjectured there might be land behind these winds. A mariner might sail, and by dead reckoning—by the log, by the compass— he might find this land.

A wild thought, a bold dream, yet it came true. The ships embarked, captained by freemen, adventurers. At the end of voyage, at the end of struggle, endurance and high gamble, a New Continent was found. On a perilous horizon America took shape, and was realized. Columbus had made hope reasonable.

The years passed, and the generations. Not Columbus now but America herself made hope reasonable. Put it in terms of government: "We the people of the United States, in order to form a more perfect Union . . . do ordain and establish this Constitution for the United States of America."

Europe laughed. "We the people." What kind of phrase was that? A government erected on the proposition that all men are by nature equally free and independent? Preposterous statement, subverting the established order! Nor did Americans pause to argue it. They simply declared certain "truths" to be "self-evident." *"Novus Ordo Seclorum,"* they wrote on their Great Seal: A new order for the ages.

Was ever a country, young or old, so brash? How serious, asked Europe, were these Americans? How long could they sustain this impudent program? Europe laid traps, offered bribes, hoping to divide these united states and bring them low. A federation so large, embracing such diversified regions and interests, would surely fail, disintegrate, slip and slide of its own weight in one quarter or another.

In the Old World only an occasional statesman saw into the future. Edmund Burke in the House of Commons said, "America, which at this day serves for little more than to amuse you with stories of savage men and uncouth manners, yet shall, before you taste of death, show itself equal to the whole of that British commerce which now attracts the envy of the world."

Threats from without only helped to solidify the Union. Ours was a country founded in a religious era by men of fierce fighting piety and dogma; religion could have divided us. But we had seen the religious wars of Europe and we were forewarned. From the first, Americans made a profoundly significant separation of church and state, giving citizens a scope and a hope which nowhere else were entertained. Thomas Jefferson, a man who could not put pen to paper without leaving a trace of fire, wrote the Virginia *Statute of Religious Liberty*: "Whereas Almighty God hath created the mind free . . . our civil rights have no dependence on our religious opinions, any more than our opinions in physics and geometry."

Nowhere had the documents and declarations mentioned "the individual." Yet by this government and this system the American individual was freed exactly as if fetters had been struck from him. The U.S. Constitution provided for neither class nor privilege. A man could move up or he could slip down. It was a wholly unprecedented departure. Neither the Declaration of Independence nor the Constitution claimed to make timid men courageous, lazy men active or stupid men bright. But these documents allowed bold men to be bold; they unlocked doors, let Americans walk through, each to his destiny.

Take it in terms of those men who opened up our western territory. Trappers, fur traders, Lewis and Clark, the Long Hunters and the Mountain Men. The Mormons carried fiddles across the plains, and there was dancing within the circle of wagons below the dry western mountains. Bold men and women; scared, hungry, sick, yet surmounting. Daniel Boone. . . . Other countries possessed virgin lands, timber, rivers, mines, rich plains, yet could Daniel Boone be imagined anywhere but in America? *"All power is vested in, and consequently derived from, the people."* The impact of such ideas, entered upon unitedly, can send a man on a very far journey.

It was union which gave us power; it was the federal idea which gave us scope. Nevertheless, the doubters still spoke out. National federation on such a scale was impossible, they said; the country had grown too big for union. In 1828 Harvard College had a debate: "Can one man be President of the United States when it is eventually settled from Atlantic to Pacific?" The no's were victorious.

Thirteen states became 20, became 34. Through the terrible years, 1861-65, the Union held. "I have often inquired of myself," said Lincoln, "what great principle or idea kept this federation so long together. It was that which gave promise that in due time the weights should be lifted from the shoulders of all men, and that all should have an equal chance."

When Richmond fell and the Civil War was over, citizens celebrated. In Boston, New York, Philadelphia, men stood on soapboxes to orate. "The United States," they said, like a refrain. Tears poured down men's faces. "Yes, sir!" they shouted. "You bet! The U-nited States of America!"

A federation needs, above all, communication, interchange of commerce. It was the year 1865, with a transcontinental railway to be laid. Two companies contracted for the work, Union Pacific and Central Pacific: the one to start laying track at Omaha, the other in California, and the tracks to meet eventually at Promontory Point, Utah. The project became a race and a competition, unequaled for magnitude in sporting or business circles before or since. It was a game, an epic, an American legend.

Thousands of Chinese laborers from the West, Irish laborers from the East, competed as to which gang could lay the most track, matched skill and endurance, even fought it out on occasion with charges of dynamite. Snow in the Sierras, higher than a man's head. Night storms on the hot Nebraska plains, the water foul to drink. By May 1869 the two companies were within a dozen miles of meeting. The whole country watched, getting the news by telegraph where it could. On May 10 the track came together, the last spike was hammered. In the cities cannon boomed, firebells rang, citizens paraded. Nobody remembered who had won—they only knew the goal was reached.

Competition! The great, reckless, expensive American game had begun.

Followed now the captains of industry: steel kings, oil kings, railroad manipulators—promoters. A rich land lay ready to hand and they took it over: Astors, Vanderbilts, Rockefellers, bold men who for the most part came from plain beginnings, men whose imagination was limitless, who worked the country for what it was worth, using and discarding human material as they chose, and who built America into the greatest industrial productive system the world has ever seen.

Over against them rose the labor leaders, Americans made bold in their turn by desperation. Uriah S. Stephens and Terence V. Powderly of the Knights of Labor; Samuel Gompers and, much later, the towering, scowling, well-nigh symbolic figure of John L. Lewis. Pushing along with them came the bold men and women of moral protestation, fighting corruption in business and politics. Ida Minerva Tarbell, Jane Addams, Jacob Riis, Susan B. Anthony, Lucy Stone, Carry Nation. Saints or crackpots, America had room for them all.

The quiet men, the thinkers, writers, philosophers who knew how to express the American spirit—these also proved bold. Emerson, Thoreau, Mark Twain; William James, John Dewey, Robert Frost; each name conveys an American era.

Consider also the builders, the innovators who altered the face of our cities. Louis Henri Sullivan, father of the skyscraper. We see him as a youth step from an eastern train to the open shed of the Chicago station after the great fire of 1871. He looks toward the city, ruined and in ashes. He raises a hand, stamps his foot among the crowd and cries out loud, "This is the place for me!"

We remember, too, the Roeblings, father and son, engineers

for the Brooklyn Bridge. Washington Augustus Roebling, the son, at 35 was carried out unconscious from the caissons beneath the East River, suffering from the bends. He did not fully recover; yet for 11 years he directed work from his room overlooking the river, struggling against illness and against the corruption of contractors and politicians who sought to defeat the bridge. Roebling saw his work completed, saw the cable swing from tower to tower and fireworks zoom across the sky on the night the bridge was opened.

Through two world wars the system has held; the Union has held, and the vision. Under it our country has grown so great that we find ourselves apologetic. We stoop our head like a man too tall for a doorway; we talk ourselves down.

America's role is global, now. The United States has won to a sophistication the world finds surprising; yet we have not lost our good provinciality, the qualities which make our strength and which define the genius of our independence. Not long ago a New York museum sent an exhibition of "The New American Painting" to eight countries in Europe. The critics might have been writing not of painting but of skyscrapers, or of Charles Lindbergh, or Henry Ford the first: "Americans possess an enormous daring . . . the quality of adventure, a pioneering sense of independence and vitality . . . that climate of unconstraint which never fails to strike anyone traveling to the United States for the first time."

The bold men still go their way, and the "climate of unconstraint" still prevails.

Two hundred years ago this climate was deliberately created and confirmed by men brave enough to launch a revolutionary government, men wise enough to create a Constitution expedient, workable, elastic—a government under which the bold American still finds scope.

᠂᠊᠊ *What This Country Needs Is* . . . family trees that produce more lumber, fewer nuts (*Parts Pups*) . . . a car muffler that will last as long as a beer can (Door County, Wis., *Advocate,* quoted in *The National Observer*) . . . a good, five-cent bumper-sticker remover (Don MacLean)

Man's Epic First Flight
to the Moon

*It was a 147-hour odyssey, made during Christmas week of 1968.
In the spacecraft called Apollo 8, three men—Frank Borman, James
Lovell and William Anders—left earth for a breathtaking voyage
into lunar orbit and return. It marked the beginning of the payoff
for a massive, ten-year, 33-billion-dollar space effort. Within
months, other U.S. astronauts would actually set foot on the moon.
But no drama is likely to eclipse that of man's first soaring escape
from this planet.*

[March 1969]

A SCANT decade ago, man
was making his first tentative probes into near space. Now, his
eye fixed on the moon, that cold and lifeless globe with its borrowed light, he was poised to soar beyond earth's atmosphere
into a vast and trackless void.

It began flawlessly. On Pad 39A at Cape Kennedy, Borman,

Lovell and Anders lay strapped in the 13-foot command module, perched atop a 278-foot Saturn 5 rocket. With a deafening bellow, the rocket inched upward on a rising pillar of smoke and flame, then spurted off into earth orbit. During its second turn around the planet, it accelerated from 17,400 m.p.h. to 24,200 m.p.h.—enough to escape earth's gravitational embrace and send Apollo 8 on the road of night that would lead to the moon.

About 69 hours after lift-off—and 230,000 miles farther away from home than any humans had ever before traveled—the three astronauts made their historic rendezvous. Below them, less than 70 miles away, lay a desolate, pockmarked landscape. In the black sky above hung a half-disk—the earth—its blue-and-brown surface mottled by large patches of white. Thus, incredibly, they were there, precisely where the mission planners had predicted, finally living the dreams of untold generations. And, from orbit around the moon, their telecasts gave earthbound viewers an unforgettable astronaut's-eye view.

"The moon is essentially gray, no color," Lovell reported. "Looks like plaster of paris, or sort of a grayish deep sand. We can see quite a bit of detail. Langrenus is quite a huge crater. It's got a central cone to it. The walls of the crater are terraced, about six or seven terraces on the way down."

On Christmas Eve, during their ninth circuit of the moon, the astronauts presented the longest and most impressive of the mission's six telecasts. "This is Apollo 8 coming to you live from the moon," reported Borman, focusing the TV camera on the lunar surface drifting by below. "The moon is a different thing to each of us. My own impression is that it's a vast, forbidding-type expanse of nothing. It looks rather like clouds and clouds of pumice stone. It would not appear to be a very inviting place to live or work."

Lovell: "The loneliness up here is awe-inspiring, and it makes you realize just what you have back there on earth. The earth from here is a grand oasis in the great vastness of space."

Anders: "The horizon is very, very stark. The sky is pitch-black, and the moon is quite light. The contrast between the sky and the moon is a vivid dark line."

As the Apollo spacecraft sped toward the terminator (the

continuously moving line that divides the day and night hemispheres of the moon), the sun dropped from directly overhead toward the horizon, lengthening shadows and bringing out more surface detail. Anders observed that the Sea of Crises was "amazingly smooth as far as the horizon."

Now Apollo was nearing the terminator, which showed as a sharply defined front of darkness. To conclude their telecast, the astronauts took turns reading aloud the first ten verses of Genesis: "In the beginning God created the heaven and the earth. . . ." Accompanying the final views of the primordial lunar landscape below, it was impressive.

The entire presentation was appropriate for the men of the Apollo 8 crew. They are deadly serious men, cool under pressure, each with an intense sense of mission and purpose. Borman, the spacecraft commander, and Lovell are active Episcopalians; Anders is a civic-minded Roman Catholic.

The mission's most important decision had come earlier, on December 24 when Apollo was approaching the moon. It was whether to allow the spacecraft simply to whip around the moon and head back toward earth, or to fire the Service Propulsion System (SPS) engine and place the craft in orbit. As time for the decision neared, both the astronauts and their Houston controllers fell strangely silent. Only essential communications were exchanged, monosyllabic and tension-filled.

Finally, as Apollo raced unerringly on a course that would bring it at one point within 70 miles of the moon, ground controllers decided that all spacecraft systems were in perfect working order. A terse message was radioed: "This is Houston at 68:04 [68 hours 4 minutes after launch]. You are go for LOI [lunar orbit insertion]."

Borman responded: "O.K., Apollo 8 is go."

"You are riding the best bird we can find," the communicator assured the astronauts.

"Two minutes and 50 seconds away from LOS [loss of signal]," came the report as Apollo began to curve around the back side of the moon, where its radio communication with earth would be blocked. Then from Houston, "One minute. All systems go. Safe journey, guys."

"Thanks a lot, troops," replied Anders. "We'll see you on the other side."

Then all was silent. Apollo would be behind the moon and out of contact for 45 minutes. Until it emerged, no one on earth would know if the little, 3½-foot-long SPS engine had fired on schedule (about ten minutes after LOS) or fired long enough to place the craft in orbit. If it cut off during one crucial 30 seconds, Apollo would be left in an unstable orbit and might crash into the moon. And if it did not restart after orbiting the moon, the astronauts would be left stranded in space, without hope of rescue.

Finally from Houston came the message everyone awaited: "We've acquired a signal. We are looking at engine data, and it looks good. We've got it! Apollo 8 is in lunar orbit."

"Good to hear your voice," said astronaut Lovell, breaking the long silence. Wild cheering filled the Houston control room.

Once safely in orbit, the astronauts had their work cut out for them. During their second circuit of the moon, they briefly fired the SPS engine to change their orbit from a 70-by-194-mile-high ellipse to a near-perfect 70-mile circle. They shot movie and still pictures of the lunar landscape and of the distant earth. With sextant and scanning telescope, they took star sightings and pinpointed lunar landmarks—to enable navigators on future flights to find their landing sites more easily.

Lovell later reported a lunar phenomenon that piqued Houston's curiosity. "Before the sun came above the limb [horizon]," he said, "definite rays could be seen coming from it. It was a uniform haze, apparently where the sun was going to rise." This suggested that the moon might have a slight atmosphere after all, a possibility to be investigated in future flights.

At one point, when Borman inquired about the weather in Houston, a communicator reported that there was "a beautiful moon out there tonight." Replied Borman: "Now, we were just saying that there's a beautiful earth out there."

Another time Lovell observed: "I keep imagining I am some lonely traveler from another planet. What should I think about the earth, at this altitude? Whether it would be inhabited or not."

As Apollo began its tenth revolution, tension rose again. During their final pass behind the moon, the astronauts were scheduled to restart the SPS engine to increase velocity from 3625 m.p.h. to 5980 m.p.h.—enough to propel them out of lunar orbit and back toward the earth. This time there were no final *bon voyages,* no quips and no sentiment. "All systems are go, Apollo 8," the controller reported. From Borman, a terse "Roger." As the spacecraft passed into radio silence, the world waited. Although it was Christmas Day in Houston, the controllers avoided any exchange of greetings, awaiting word that Apollo 8 was safely on its way home.

That word came 37 minutes later as Apollo re-emerged. "Please be informed," Jim Lovell said, "that there *is* a Santa Claus."

Compared with the drama of flight near the moon, the outward-bound and return trips were uneventful. Accelerated by the earth's own gravity, the spacecraft hurtled at increasing speed toward its last great challenge—re-entry of earth's atmosphere. Finally, jettisoning the service module and its trusty SPS engine, the astronauts pitched their cone-shaped command module until its blunt end was forward, and then plunged into the outer atmosphere at 24,629 m.p.h.—some 7000 m.p.h. faster than the re-entry speed of previous missions. Apollo roared down into the thickening atmosphere within a sliver of the planned angle of 6.43°. The spacecraft had to re-enter at an angle no greater than 7.4° nor less than 5.4°. If re-entry were too steep, deceleration forces might cause "a structural breakup, loss of spacecraft and crew." But if Apollo hit the atmosphere at too shallow an angle, it could bounce off like a flat stone skipping on water, and sail into a large elliptical orbit around the earth. The astronauts would have insufficient oxygen and electrical power to survive the hours it might take to return to the atmosphere and land.

The spacecraft shot in over Peking and Tokyo, the temperature of its heat shield rising to 5000° Fahrenheit. Flying over the Pacific, a jetliner pilot saw its fiery track: an astonishing 5 miles wide and 100 miles long.

After a tense three-minute silence (re-entry heat ionizes the atmosphere around the capsule, and temporarily blocks radio communications), the spacecraft's parachutes deployed on schedule and floated Apollo to a splashdown in the Pacific about 5000 yards from the U.S. Navy aircraft carrier *Yorktown.* There recovery helicopters spotted the capsule's beacon flashing in the pre-dawn darkness. It was 10:51 a.m. (E.S.T.), just seconds ahead of the predicted splashdown time, and precisely 147 hours after Apollo 8's spectacular launch.

Apollo 8's safe return prompted announcement of the scheduling of the next three space flights—including the lunar landing mission, now set for July or August. [Apollo 11 was in fact launched on July 16, 1969, and the lunar module containing astronauts Neil Armstrong and Edwin "Buzz" Aldrin touched down on the moon July 20 at 4:17:43 p.m. E.D.T.]

"This is not the end but the beginning," said Dr. Thomas Paine, acting administrator of NASA. "We are just at the onset of a program of space flights that will extend through many generations. We're looking forward to manning space stations, conducting lunar exploration and, in the distant future, blazing a new trail out to the planets."

Brothers in the Eternal Cold

Archibald MacLeish

[*March 1969*]

Men's conception of themselves and of each other has always depended on their notion of the earth. When the earth was the World—all the world there was—and the stars were lights in Dante's heaven, and the ground beneath men's feet roofed Hell, they saw themselves as creatures at the center of the universe, the sole, particular concern of God—and from that high place they ruled and killed and conquered as they pleased.

And when, centuries later, the earth was no longer the World

25

but a small, wet, spinning planet in the solar system of a minor star off at the edge of an inconsiderable galaxy in the immeasurable distances of space—when Dante's heaven had disappeared and there was no Hell (at least no Hell beneath the feet)—men began to see themselves not as God-directed actors at the center of a noble drama, but as helpless victims of a senseless farce where all the rest were helpless victims also, and millions could be killed in worldwide wars or in blasted cities or in concentration camps without a thought or reason but the reason—if we call it one—of force.

Now, in the last few hours, the notion may have changed again. For the first time in all of time, men have *seen* the earth: seen it not as continents or oceans from the little distance of a hundred miles or two or three, but seen it from the depths of space; seen it whole and round and beautiful and small, as even Dante—that "first imagination of Christendom"—had never dreamed of seeing it; as the 20th-century philosophers of absurdity and despair were incapable of guessing that it might be seen. And seeing it so, one question came to the minds of those who looked at it. "Is it inhabited?" they said to each other and laughed—and then they did not laugh. What came to their minds a hundred thousand miles and more into space—"halfway to the moon" they put it—what came to their minds was the life on that little, lonely, floating planet, that tiny raft in the enormous, empty night. "Is it inhabited?"

The medieval notion of the earth put man at the center of everything. The nuclear notion of the earth put him nowhere—beyond the range of reason even—lost in absurdity and war. This latest notion may have other consequences. Formed as it was in the minds of heroic voyagers who were also men, it may remake our image of mankind. No longer that preposterous figure at the center, no longer that degraded and degrading victim off at the margins of reality and blind with blood, man may at last become himself.

To see the earth as it truly is, small and blue and beautiful in that eternal silence where it floats, is to see ourselves as riders on the earth together, brothers on that bright loveliness in the eternal cold—brothers who know now they are truly brothers.

God and My Father

Clarence Day

[*August 1940*]

THE religious ideas of my strong-minded, conservative father were straightforward and simple. From boyhood he accepted churches as a natural part of his surroundings. He would never have invented such things himself. But they were here and he regarded them as unquestioningly as he did banks. They were substantial structures, respectable, decent, and frequented by the right sort of people.

On the other hand he never allowed churches—or banks—to dictate to him. He gave each the respect due it, from his point of view; but he also expected from each the respect he felt due to him. Above all, the one thing a church should not tamper with was a man's soul—after all a man's soul was his own personal affair. And when our rector talked of imitating the saints, it seemed drivel to Father. Father regarded himself as a more all-around man than the saints. From his point of view they had neglected nine tenths of their duties—they had no business connections, no families, they hadn't even paid taxes.

My mother, who more than made up for the piety Father lacked, once wrote in my plush-covered autograph album, "Fear God and keep His commandments," but the motto that Father wrote was, "Do your duty and fear no one." Father's code was definite and indisputable. It was to be upright, fearless and honorable, and to brush your clothes properly; and, in general, always to do the right thing in every department of life. The right

27

thing to do for religion was to go to some good church on Sundays.

Father never doubted the existence of God. On the contrary, God and Father had somehow achieved a strange but harmonious relationship. He seemed to envisage a God in his own image —a God who had small use for emotionalism and who prized strength and dignity, although he could never understand why God had peopled the world with "so many damn fools and Democrats." God and Father seldom met: their spheres were so different. But they had perfect confidence in each other and, Father thought, saw eye to eye in most things.

For example, God must feel most affectionately toward my mother, just as he did. God knew she had faults, but He saw she was lovely and good—despite some mistaken ideas she had about money. Naturally God loved Mother, as everyone must. At the gate of Heaven, if there was any misunderstanding about his own ticket, Father counted on Mother to get him in. That was her affair.

Unlike Mother, Father never had any moments of feeling "unworthy." This was a puzzle to Mother. Other people went to church to be made better, she told him. Why didn't he? He replied in astonishment that he had no need to be better—he was all right as he was. It wasn't at all easy for Father to see that he had any faults; and if he did, it didn't even occur to him to ask God to forgive them. He forgave them himself. In his moments of prayer, when he and God tried to commune with each other, it wasn't his own shortcomings that were brought on the carpet but God's.

Father expected a good deal of God. Not that he wanted God's help; far less His guidance. But Father was always trying to bring some good thing to pass, only to meet with obstacles. Wrathfully he would call God's attention to them. He didn't actually accuse God of inefficiency, but when he prayed his tone was loud and angry, like that of a dissatisfied guest in a carelessly managed hotel.

I never saw Father kneel in supplication. He usually talked with God lying in bed. On those nights the sound of *damns* would float up to my room—at first tragic and low, then loud and exasperated. At the peak of these, I would hear him call "Oh, God?" over and over, with a rising inflection, as though demanding that God should present himself instantly. Then when Father felt that God was listening, he would recite his current botheration and begin to expostulate in a discouraged but strong voice, "Oh, God, it's too much. Amen. . . . I say it's too damned much. . . . No, no, I can't stand it! Amen." After a pause, if he didn't feel better, he would suspect that God might be trying to sneak back to Heaven without doing anything, and I would hear him shout warningly, "Oh, God! I *won't* stand it! A-a-men." Sometimes he would ferociously bark a few extra Amens, and then, soothed and satisfied, peacefully go to sleep.

Father's behavior in church was often a source of sorrow to Mother. He usually started at peace with the world, settled contentedly in his end seat. The Episcopal service in general he didn't criticize—it was stately and quiet—but the sermon was always a gamble. If bad, his expression would darken as he struggled to control himself. At such times Mother, who had been anxiously watching him out of the corner of her eye, would say, "Clare, you mustn't." To which Father would reply, "Bah!"

One day a visiting rector went too far. Ending his sermon he drew a fanciful picture of a businessman at the close of day. This hardheaded man sat surrounded by ledgers, and after studying them for hours he chanced to look out of his window at the light in God's sky, and it came to him that money and ledgers were dross. Whereat, as twilight spread over the city, this strange businessman bowed his head, and with streaming eyes resolved to devote his life to Far Higher Things.

"Oh, damn!" Father burst out, so explosively that the man across the aisle jumped, and I heard old Mrs. Tillotson, in the second pew behind, titter.

Aside from the untruth of such a picture of business, to Father the whole attitude was pernicious. Anyone dreamy enough to think of money as "dross" was bound to get in hot water.

When hymns were sung Father usually stood as silent as an eagle among doves, leaving others to abase themselves in sentiments that he didn't share. "Cover my defenseless head, with the shadow of thy wing." How could Father sing that? His head was far from defenseless, and he would have scorned to ask shelter. As he stood there, high-spirited, resolute, I could imagine him marching with that same independence through space—a tiny speck masterfully dealing with death and infinity.

It was Father's custom to put one dollar in the contribution plate weekly. It bothered Mother dreadfully to see him give so little. Father's reply was that a dollar was a good handsome sum, and that it would be better for Mother if she could learn this. He had a great deal to say on this point. But after a while Mother made him feel that it was beneath his dignity not to give more. Even then he didn't surrender; he compromised: before starting for church he put his usual dollar in his right-hand waistcoat pocket, but in the left-hand pocket he put a new five-dollar bill. And he stated that from now on he would make a handsome offer: let the rector preach a decent sermon and he would give him the five.

When the rector entered the pulpit we boys watched with a thrill, as though he were a racehorse at the barrier. He usually either robbed himself of the prize in the very first lap by getting off on the wrong foot—or after a blameless beginning, he would run clear off the course that Father had in silence marked out for him, and gallop away unconsciously in some other direction. It gave a boy a sobering sense of the grimness of fate.

One day the rector began talking about the need for what he called a New Edifice. Father paid little attention to this until he realized that he too would have to subscribe. Then he became roused. He said he might have known it was just a damn scheme to get money.

He was still more upset when Mother said that, since he had a good pew, they would expect him to give a big sum. This was like an earthquake. Father barricaded himself every evening in the library and declared he wouldn't see any callers. Later, however, when he had cooled down a bit, Mother told him he'd at least have to see the committee.

He waited, fretful and uneasy. One night Mother heard sounds in the library. Father was doing all the talking, stating his sentiments in his usual strong round tones. He got more and more shouty. Mother began to fear the committee mightn't like being scolded. But when she peeked in, there was no one there but Father, thumping his hand with a hammerlike beat on his newspaper. "In ordinary circumstances," he was saying to the imaginary committeemen, "I should have expected to subscribe to this project. But recently my investments" (thump, thump on the newspaper) "have shown me heavy losses." Here he thought of the New Haven Railroad and groaned. "*Damned* heavy losses!" he roared. "Who the devil's that? Oh, it's you, Vinnie. Come in, dear Vinnie. I'm lonely."

In the end he gave liberally—as befitted his status in the church. Our pew had cost Father $5000, and though he hated to invest all that money in a mere place to sit, he could sell out again someday. Pews were like seats on the stock exchange, fluctuating in price as the demand rose or fell. Father used to ask Mother periodically for the current quotation. When she came home with the news that the last sale had been for $3200, Father said she had led him into this against his better judgment and now the bottom was dropping out of the market. He swore if that damn pew ever went up again he would unload it.

When Mother married Father she had naturally supposed him a good churchman. But one day she chanced to find out from Grandpa that Father had never been baptized. I doubt if I can even imagine what a shock this was to my devout mother. She hurried home with her terrible news, supposing that as soon as Father heard it he would be baptized at once. But he flatly refused.

"If you won't be baptized," Mother wailed, "you aren't a Christian at all."

"Why, confound it, of course I'm a Christian," Father roundly declared. "A damned good Christian, too. A lot better Christian than those psalm-singing donkeys at church!"

Father's general position seemed to be that he didn't object to baptism. It was all right for savages, for instance. But among civilized people it should come only when one was young.

For months Mother waged an unsuccessful campaign to get Father baptized. Then at long last it seemed that she might prevail. She had a bad illness, which worried Father so much that when she kept begging him to do this thing for her he said he would. But when she was well again he said flatly he had no recollection of having agreed to it, that probably her fever had made her misunderstand him.

Finally, under Mother's constant attacks, Father went into the whole matter as thoroughly as a railroad report. He asked just how wet would a man have to get. Exactly what rigmarole would he have to go through? He said if it wasn't too complicated, perhaps he'd consider it, just to please her.

He was startled to learn that he couldn't have an accommodating parson baptize him quietly some morning at the house, after breakfast; no, the performance would have to take place in a church; and, worse, there would have to be others present. Father declared that he certainly wasn't going to be made a fool of in that way.

At last Mother discovered a distant parish, set in thick, quiet woods. Mr. Morley, the rector, agreed to make everything as easy for Father as possible.

Father agreed, and the great day arrived. He came down to breakfast in a good temper that morning, and the bacon and eggs suited him for once. Mother gave a happy, tender look at this soul she was saving. The dining room seemed full of sunshine, and the whole world lighthearted. But when Mother said the cab was waiting, Father demanded what cab. He listened to her answer in horror and sprang up with a roar.

It was as though an elephant which had been tied up with infinite pains had trumpeted and burst every fetter. Mother stood up to him, armed with God's word and also, as she despairingly reminded him, with his own Sacred Promise. When these arguments failed, Mother fell back on her last weapon: the waiting cab. Wasting money on cabs was simply unheard of in our family. When we ordered a cab we did not keep it waiting. This cab, now at the door, reached those depths of Father's spirit which God couldn't.

As we drove out of the city, Father's wrath became increasingly bitter. When we reached the church he glowered like a bull in the ring, waiting to charge the reverend toreador. Father felt hurt, outraged and lonely. His whole private life had been pried into, even his babyhood. Mr. Morley, a shy, earnest man, approached our little group trustingly, to shake Father's hand, but he got such a look that he turned to me instead and patted me on the head several times.

When Mr. Morley came to the part in the service—"Dost thou renounce the devil and all his works, the vain pomp and glory of the world?"—Father looked as though he might have been an annoyed Roman general, participating much against his will in a low and barbaric rite.

At last the great moment came for the actual baptism. I remember how Father stood, grim and erect, in his tailed morning coat; but when I saw Mr. Morley dip his hand in the water and make a pass at Father's forehead, I shut my eyes tightly at this frightful sacrilege. And whether he actually landed or not I never knew.

When the service was over, we stood awkwardly for a moment. Then Mr. Morley began piously to urge Father to "mortify all his evil affections." But Father broke in, saying abruptly, "I shall be late at the office," and strode down the aisle.

As we drove off, Mother sank back into her corner of the cab, quite worn out. Father was still seething as though his very soul was boiling over. He got out at the nearest Elevated station, thrust his red face in the cab window, and with a burning look at Mother said, "I hope you are satisfied." Then this new son of the church took out his watch, gave a start, and Mother and I heard him shout "Hell!" as he raced up the stairs.

Pen Sketches

ᐳᐤ "If flowers could walk," writes Nina Epton, "they would no doubt walk like Japanese ladies in kimonos, who give the impression that they have been plucked off a stalk and are still a little unsure how to advance."   *Seedweed for Breakfast* (Dodd, Mead)

ᐳᐤ "His face was knobby and gnomish," writes Pamela Frankau of a character in her novel *Sing for Your Supper,* "and he wore a stiff collar, rather high, suggesting that if you took off his head there might be chocolates inside."   Published by Random House

Good-By, America!

Henry W. Nevinson

[November 1923]

THE great ship slides down the river. Good-by, most beautiful of modern cities! Good-by to glimmering spires and lighted bastions, dreamlike as the castles and cathedrals of a romantic vision though mainly devoted to commerce and finance! Good-by to heaven-piled offices, so clean, so warm, where lovely stenographers, with silk stockings and powdered faces, sit leisurely at work! Good-by, New York! I am going home. I am going to an ancient city of mean and mouldering streets, extended monotonously over many miles; of grimy smoke clinging closer than a blanket; of smudgy typists who know something of powder but little of silk, and less of leisure. Good-by, New York! I am going home.

Good-by to beautiful "apartments" and "homes"! Good-by to windows looking far over the city as from a mountain peak! Good-by to central heating and radiators, to frequent and well-appointed bathrooms, the glory of America's art! Good-by to suburban gardens running into each other without hedge or fence to separate friend from friend or enemy from enemy! Good-by to shady verandas where rocking chairs stand ranged in rows, ready for reading the voluminous Sunday papers and the *Saturday Evening Post*. Good-by, America! I am going home. I am going to a land where every man's house is his prison—a land of open fires and chilly rooms and frozen waterpipes, of washing stands and slop pails, and one bath per household at the most; a land of fences and hedges and walls, where people sit aloof, and see no reason to make themselves seasick by rocking upon shore. Good-by, America! I am going home.

Good-by to the long stream of motors. Good-by to the deliberate appearance of hustle and bustle in business, however little is accomplished. Good-by to outside staircases for escape from fire! Good-by to scrappy suburbs littered with rubbish of old boards, tin pails, empty cans, and boots! Good-by to standardized villages and small towns, alike in litter, in ropes of electric wires along the streets, in clanking "trolleys," in chapels, stores, railway stations, Main Streets, and isolated wooden houses flung at random over the countryside. Good-by to miles of advertisement imploring me in ten-foot letters to eat somebody's codfish ("No Bones"!), or smoke somebody's cigarettes ("They Satisfy"!) or sleep with innocence in the "Faultless Nightgown"! Good-by to the long trains where one smokes in a lavatory, and sleeps at night upon a shelf screened with heavy green curtains and heated with stifling air, while over your head or under your back a baby yells and the mother tosses moaning, until at last you reach your "stopping-off place," and a porter sweeps you down with a little broom, as in a supreme rite of unction! Good-by to the house that is labeled "One Hundred Years Old," for the amazement of mortality! Good-by to fields enclosed with casual pales and lengths of wire! I am going to a land where the horse and bicycle still drag out a lingering life; a land of persistent and silent toil; a land of old villages and towns as little like each other as one woman is like the next; a land where trains are short, and one seldom sleeps in them, for in any direction within a day they will reach a sea; a land of vast and ancient trees, of houses time-honored three centuries ago, of cathedrals that have been growing for a thousand years, and of village churches built while people believed in God. Good-by, America! I am going home.

Good-by to the multitudinous papers, indefinite of opinion, crammed with insignificant news, and asking you to continue a first-page article on page 23 column 5! Good-by to the weary platitude, accepted as wisdom's latest revelation! Good-by to the docile audiences that lap rhetoric for sustenance! Good-by to politicians contending for aims more practical than principles! Good-by to Republicans and Democrats, distinguishable only by mutual hatred! Good-by to the land where Liberals are thought dangerous, and Radicals show red! A land too large for concentrated indignation; a land where wealth beyond the dreams of British profiteers dwells, dresses, gorges and luxuriates emulated and unshamed! I am going to a land of politics violently divergent; a land where even Coalitions cannot coalesce; where meetings break up in turbulent disorder, and no platitude avails to soothe the savage breast; a land fierce for personal freedom, and indignant with rage for justice; a land where wealth is taxed out of sight, or for very shame strives to disguise its luxury; a land where an ancient order of feudal families is passing away—and Labor leaders whom Wall Street would shudder at are hailed by Lord Chancellors as the very fortifications of security.

Good-by to prose chopped up to look like verse! Good-by to the indiscriminating appetite which gulps lectures as opiates, and "printed matter" as literature! Good-by to the wizards and witches who claim to psychoanalyze my complexes, inhibitions and silly dreams! Good-by to the exuberant religious or fantastic beliefs by which unsatisfied mankind still strives desperately to penetrate beyond the flaming bulwarks of the world! Good-by, Americans! I am going to your spiritual home.

The Feminine Negative

When a masked man entered the Western National Bank in Casper, Wyo., and demanded money, Mrs. Thelma Anderson, the bank's newest cashier, had a ready answer. "Don't bother me," she replied. "I'm just a beginner." UPI

A woman who drove up for gasoline at our station exclaimed when I started to raise the hood, "Don't look under there, it's too messy!"
H. Miller in *Gasoline Retailer*

Asked by a reporter to reveal her age, actress Greer Garson answered: "I do wish I could tell you, but it's impossible. My age keeps changing all the time." Lloyd Shearer in *Parade*

The Secret World
of the Unborn

Margaret Liley, M.D., with Beth Day

*A practicing pediatrician in New Zealand,
Dr. Margaret Liley has herself given birth to
five children. Her husband is Dr. William
Liley, the obstetrician who developed the medical practice of fetology—diagnosing and treating babies still in the womb.*

[November 1965]

I⁣T WAS long thought that the
unborn must have the nature of a plant: static in habit, and
growing only in size. This is far from true. By the third month
of his mother's pregnancy, the unborn baby is a perfectly
formed little creature about the size of a man's thumb. He is an
aquatic animal—a sort of combination astronaut and underwater swimmer—living in a balloon of fluid.

The fluid, which at this stage completely surrounds him, acts
as a shock absorber as well as providing a constant temperature.
Falls or knocks sustained by his mother affect him little. After
the first three months his mother could have her ovaries removed or be unconscious from a brain or spinal injury and he
would go right on developing inside her, since he manufactures
quite enough hormones to sustain the pregnancy for them both.
And, as the astronaut, he has the further advantage of "weight-
lessness," with little gravitational draw.

The balloon of fluid is large in proportion to the tiny body, and the unborn of three months is buoyant and active. His movements, to and fro, around and around, up and down, have the wonderfully relaxed grace we see in films of life under-water. Although he is so small—a scant three inches long—that his mother is not yet aware of his activities, he is really a very busy little creature, moving around in his own private space capsule, developing the proficiencies and arts he will need for survival when he is finally thrust into the outside world.

Until quite recently, we have seen our little Tom Thumbs only in an aborted state, removed from their watery environ-ment. Their magical beauty is instantly lost, like that of a sea anemone snatched from its rocky pool, and they appear mis-shapen and shriveled. The fluid that surrounds the human fetus at three, four, five and six months is essential to both its growth and its grace. The unborn's structure at this early stage is highly liquid and, although his organs are developed, he does not have the same bodily proportions as a newborn baby. The head, hous-ing the miraculous brain, is large in proportion to the remainder of the body, and the limbs are still relatively small. Within his watery world, however (where we have been able to observe him in his natural state through a sort of closed-circuit X-ray television set), he is quite beautiful, perfect in his fashion, ac-tive and graceful.

He is neither a quiescent vegetable nor a witless tadpole, as some have in the past conceived him to be, but rather a tiny individual human being, as real and self-contained as though he were lying in a crib with a blanket, instead of his mother, wrapped around him.

Contrary to popular belief, the womb is not silent, nor do we know that it is completely dark. The unborn's eyes open and shut about the eighth month, and at birth his eyes, nearly adult size, are able to distinguish between light and shadow. If the womb is even dimly lit—as for example when the mother stands unclothed in sunlight—then the unborn baby would be able to see. The visual stimuli would, however, be confined to the rods of the retina: that part of the eye used in seeing at night and in distinguishing brightness rather than detail. We find that the newborn will reach for the shiniest toy, long before shape has any meaning for him.

Since his nose is underwater until he is born, the unborn does not have a chance to develop a sense of smell. There are, however, stimuli for the development of his sense of hearing. The womb, in fact, can be a noisy place. Especially if the mother hasn't got too plump, a great many outside noises come through to the baby quite clearly—street noises, crashes and bangs, music. His mother's heartbeat, the rumblings of her intestines are constantly with him.

Mothers often express concern because someone has told them that if they are bad-tempered, or scream, their emotions will adversely affect their baby. It is true that the unborn will "leap in its mother's womb" as a response to a loud noise—but not because he shares his mother's emotion. Once we watched on a recorder the heartbeat of a six-month-old fetus when his mother was frightened. The baby's heartbeat first slowed down and then accelerated violently. This was because when she experienced fear, endocrine changes in her blood affected him too. The baby experienced the *physical* response without experiencing the emotion itself. A mother's scream of rage or fright means no more to the unborn than a dropped saucepan.

Another worry common to many mothers is that, in his movements, the baby may get tangled in his cord and strangle. This is quite unlikely, since the cord, while in the intra-uterine state, is filled full of blood and is therefore stiff and erectile. When the baby encounters it, he can usually disengage himself quite easily, since it is not sufficiently flexible to loop around him. It is only after he is born, and the cord no longer contains its burden of blood, that it appears slack and ropelike.

Between the third and seventh month of his intra-uterine life the unborn baby grows faster than he ever will again. There may be as much as a 12-inch increase in his length. His physical activity becomes more vigorous. After the fifth month, strong movements will be felt as knocks against the maternal abdominal wall, and the mother, at long last, will feel the "quickening"— as the Bible calls it—within her.

As the unborn comes to occupy more and more of the available space within the enlarging womb, the surrounding fluid is diminished in proportion. The uterus changes from globular to pear shape, with the maximum space at the top. The largest single part of the baby is his head, but when he curls up, the area composed of his buttocks, thighs, legs and feet is larger. Thus 97 percent of all babies, to be comfortable, lie head down in the uterus in late pregnancy and are born headfirst. The occasional unborn individual who is most comfortable with his legs over his shoulders will select the breech position. It is usually useless to attempt to change him. If the doctor turns him, the baby will turn right back again.

The awareness of comfort and discomfort becomes a reality for the unborn as his body fills the available uterine space. One of the most uncomfortable ledges he encounters is his mother's backbone. If he is lying so that his own backbone is across hers, there is no fleshy padding between the two bony areas, and it is like lying on a bed of rocks. This is the reason that, late in pregnancy, when the tired mother lies down on her back to sleep, her baby, who is not yet civilized into gallantry, objects strenuously and kicks and turns and twists. Until he has found a better napping ground for himself, she has no hope of sleep.

We have evidence, in X rays, that by the time he is 14 weeks old the unborn baby is drinking his surrounding fluid in small quantities. He is, even at this Tom Thumb stage, practicing the art of sucking and swallowing. (We have X rays that show unborn babies of various ages sucking their thumbs.) Very hungry or greedy babies may drink as much as six to eight pints of fluid per day by the eighth or ninth month, the equivalent calorically of 3½ ounces of milk. Some babies, because their esophagus is blocked, cannot drink, and they are always smaller at birth.

When he's been hurt, an unborn baby protests just as violently as does a baby lying in his crib, by flailing out his tiny arms, wriggling his entire body—and crying. Although the watery environment in which he lives presents small opportunity for crying, which requires air, the unborn knows how to cry and, given a chance, will. One doctor in South America, who was attempting to locate the placenta in a patient, injected an air bubble into the amniotic sac and took X rays. At one position in which he had the mother, the air bubble covered the baby's head. The whole procedure had no doubt given the little fellow an uncomfortable joggling, and the minute he had air to breathe, they heard a faint protesting wail emitting from the uterus.

A mother's birth pains are minor compared with what the baby goes through when he is brutally ejected from his safe, warm, weightless world. He may protest with every means at his command: his arms and legs wave about; his blood pressure and temperature shoot up; when he gets some air, he promptly sets up the loud *wanh wanh* cry of distress. When he emerges he is exhausted, badly hurt, dazed by the harsh light. The kindest thing you can do for the battered, weary little fellow is to give him a warm cuddling and reassurance as quickly as possible.

But the change from the uterine to the outside world is not, in many ways, as dramatic as people have long imagined. The newborn is not really so "new." Food and sound are already familiar to him. He has for months been busily champing, sucking, drinking, feeling, kicking, listening, sleeping. The experience of birth is a momentary trauma—intense but soon forgotten. Once rested from the ordeal, he is ready to face the world.

Teed Off

As we waited to tee off on the 18th hole, a man in the foursome ahead drove three successive balls into the water. In a fury he picked up his golf bag and hurled it into the lake, then stamped off toward the clubhouse.

We weren't surprised to see him sheepishly return a few minutes later, roll up his pants, take off his shoes and wade in after the clubs. It was what we'd expected. But to our amazement, he fished out the bag, unzipped the pocket, took out his car keys, flung the clubs back into the water again and stalked off. — Louis H. Williams

When some golfers have a temper tantrum on the course, they throw golf clubs. Not Pam Barnett, one of the women pros. She rips off her wig and slams it to the ground. — John G. Rogers in *Parade*

Death in Dallas

[January 1964]

O VER Nob Hill and the Harvard Yard, across Washington's broad avenues and Pittsburgh's thrusting chimneys, in a thousand towns and villages the bells began to toll. In Caracas, Venezuela, a lone Marine sergeant strode across the lawn of the U.S. embassy while a soft rain fell, saluted the flag, then lowered it to half-mast. At U.S. bases from Korea to Germany, artillery pieces boomed out every half hour from dawn to dusk in a stately, protracted tattoo of grief.

It was the kind of feeling that words could hardly frame. At Boston's Symphony Hall, conductor Erich Leinsdorf laid down his baton, raised it again to lead his orchestra in the funeral march from the *Eroica*. On a Washington street corner, a blind Negro woman plucked at the strings of her guitar, half-singing, half-weeping a dirge: "He promised never to leave me . . ."

Later the words came, torrents of them in official messages of condolence, in formal statements from government leaders, in black-bordered newspaper editorials. But two words said all there was to be said. A Greek-born barber said them in his Times Square shop: "I cry." A woman said them in a different way on London's Strand: "My God!" Jacqueline Kennedy said them as her husband pitched forward, dying: "Oh, no—" And a Roman Catholic priest said them, with irrevocable finality, outside the Dallas hospital where he had just administered the last rites to John Fitzgerald Kennedy: "He's dead."

42

In the U.S. Senate, Chaplain Frederick Brown Harris mounted the rostrum and placed a single sheet of scrawled notes before him. "We gaze at a vacant place against the sky," he said, "as the President of the Republic goes down like a giant cedar." Then he recalled the words that Ohio Representative James A. Garfield spoke on the morning that Abraham Lincoln died in 1865. "Fellow citizens," said Garfield, who was to die by assassination himself 16 years later, "God reigns, and the government at Washington still lives."

So it does. In such circumstances the change of power is cruel but necessary. Ninety-eight minutes after Kennedy was pronounced dead, Lyndon Baines Johnson, 55, was sworn in as 36th President of the United States. And even as the Presidential jet, Air Force One, winged over the sere plains of Texas and the jagged peaks of the Ozarks, over the Mississippi and the Alleghenies, bearing not only the new President but the body of the one just past, the machinery of government was still working.

In the West Wing of the White House, Presidential Aide McGeorge Bundy began drafting briefing papers for the new President. Hurrying to the capital after a flight from Hawaii, Secretary of State Dean Rusk paused just long enough to say, "We have much unfinished business." In his office, House Speaker John W. McCormack conferred with Democratic leaders.

ON THE morning of his last day of life, John Fitzgerald Kennedy arose early, left his Fort Worth hotel, walked with buoyant stride through a slight mist to a nearby parking lot, where several thousand Texans were waiting behind barricades to see him. Explaining why Jackie had not accompanied him, the President laughed. "Mrs. Kennedy," he said, "is busy organizing herself. It takes a little longer, you know, but then she looks so much better than we do." And indeed she looked lovely when, wearing a pink wool suit and pillbox hat, she joined her husband at a breakfast sponsored by the Fort Worth Chamber of Commerce.

Next on the President's schedule was Dallas, and during the

flight there he put the finishing touches on a speech he meant to deliver at noon. Its concluding words:

We in this country, in this generation, are—by destiny rather than choice—the watchmen on the walls of world freedom. We ask therefore that we may be worthy of our power and responsibility—that we may exercise our strength with wisdom and restraint—and that we may achieve in our time and for all time the ancient vision of 'peace on earth, goodwill toward men.' That must always be our goal—and the righteousness of our cause must always underlie our strength. Or, as was written long ago: 'Except the Lord keep the city, the watchman waketh but in vain.'

At Dallas airport, nearly 5000 people were waiting. The President, in a dark-blue suit, stepped from his plane, smiling happily. He and Jackie were met by a committee that gave her a bouquet of red roses. Their car was ready to leave, but Kennedy had to shake hands with some voters. Jackie, her roses cradled in her left arm, also touched the outstretched hands. After a few minutes she started to walk away, but, noticing that her husband was still at it, smiled fondly and returned.

Finally, at 11:50 a.m., they entered the President's Lincoln, its bubbletop off, and began to drive into Dallas.

To President Kennedy, popularity was the breath of life— and now he was breathing of it deeply. Texas was supposed to be a hostile political land, but for 23 hours he had been acclaimed there. Conservative Dallas was supposed to be downright dangerous, but he had just come from a warm airport welcome and along much of his motorcade route in the downtown district he had basked in waves of applause from crowds lined 10 and 12 deep. What was about to happen must have been the farthest thing from his mind.

Next to him sat Jackie. In front of them, on jump seats, were Texas' Democratic Governor John Connally and his wife, Nellie. As the President's car approached an underpass near the intersection of Elm, Main and Commerce streets, Nellie Connally turned to Kennedy and said laughingly, "You can't say that Dallas isn't friendly to you today." The President started to reply.

That reply was stilled by a shot. It was 12:30 p.m. C.S.T., and in a split second a thousand things happened. The President's body slumped to the left; his right leg shot up over the car door. A woman close by at the curb saw it. "My God!" she screamed. "He's shot!" Blood gushed from the President's head as it came to rest in Jackie's lap. "Jack—" she cried. "Oh, no—no—"

John Connally turned—and by his turning probably saved his own life. There were two more shots, and a bullet pierced his back, plowed down through his chest, fractured his right wrist and lodged in his left thigh. A photographer looked up at a seven-story building on the corner—the Texas School Book Depository, a warehouse for textbooks—and caught a glimpse of a rifle barrel being withdrawn from a window on the sixth floor.

There was a shocked, momentary stillness, a frozen tableau. Then Kennedy's driver cried, "Let's get out of here quick!" He automatically pulled out of the motorcade—the set procedure in emergencies. The Secret Service agent next to him grabbed the radio telephone, called ahead to the police escorts and ordered them to make for the nearest hospital. Jackie bent low, cradling the President's head in her lap, and the Lincoln bolted ahead as if the shots themselves had gunned the engine into life. Spurting to 70 m.p.h., it fled down the highway, rounding curves on two wheels. A Secret Service man, who had jumped onto the rear bumper of the car, flung himself across the trunk, and in his anger and frustration pounded it repeatedly with his fist.

The next car in line, an open touring sedan containing agents bristling with weapons, followed swiftly. In the third car, an open convertible carrying the Lyndon Johnsons and Texas' Democratic Senator Ralph Yarborough, security agents yelled for the passengers to duck low, and that car followed in wild pursuit.

Five minutes later the cars arrived at the emergency entrance of Parkland Memorial Hospital on Harry Hines Boulevard. The agents ran inside to get stretchers. John Connally was still conscious. The President had never known what hit him. Jacqueline Kennedy, even then proving that she had courage, calmly continued to cradle her husband. Stretchers were brought out, and both men were placed on them. Jackie, her skirt and stockings blotched by blood, helped get the President out of the car and, her hand on his chest, walked into the hospital beside him.

Policemen surrounded the entrance as the crowds thickened. A guard was set up around the Lincoln as Secret Service men got a pail of water and tried to wash the blood from the car. They left the sprays of red roses and asters that Jackie and Nellie Connally had been given at the airport lying forlorn on the floor.

Inside the hospital, John Connally was quiet and calm in his pain as surgeons prepared to operate. "Take care of Nellie," he told his aide, Bill Stinson.

For four hours the doctors worked, cleaning the wounds, removing bone splinters from the governor's chest cavity, stitching a hole in one lung, treating the wounds in his thigh and wrist. At week's end doctors said his condition was satisfactory.

But the President never regained consciousness. In Emergency Room No. 1, Dr. Kemp Clark, chief of Parkland's neurosurgical department, examined a large wound in the President's head and another smaller wound—from the second of the three shots—in his throat. Clark and eight other doctors worked over him for 40 minutes, but the President was already as dead as though he had fallen on a battlefield in mortal combat. The doctors gave him oxygen, anesthesia, performed a tracheotomy to help breathing; they fed him fluids, gave him blood transfusions, attached an electrocardiograph to record his heartbeat.

When heart action failed to register, they tried closed-chest massage. But, said the doctors, "it was apparent that the President was not medically alive when he was brought in. There was no spontaneous respiration. He had dilated, fixed pupils. By using vigorous resuscitation, intravenous tubes and other measures, we were able to raise a semblance of a heartbeat." There were some "palpable pulses," said one doctor, but "to no avail."

While the doctors worked, Jackie waited. The look in her eyes, said a young medical student who saw her, "was like an animal that had been trapped, like a little rabbit—brave, but fear was in the eyes."

At 12:45, two Roman Catholic priests went swiftly into the

emergency room. A policeman came out. "How is he?" a reporter asked. "He's dead," came the reply. Assistant Press Secretary Malcolm Kilduff appeared. To a deluge of questions, he screamed, "I can't say, I just can't say—"

But the President was dead. It was about 1 p.m. The Very Rev. Oscar L. Huber drew back a sheet that covered the President's face, and anointed John Kennedy's forehead with oil. He gave him conditional absolution—tendered when a priest has no way of knowing the victim's mind or whether the soul has yet left the body. In Latin, Father Huber said, "I absolve you from all censures and sins in the name of the Father, and of the Son and of the Holy Spirit. Amen."

Jacqueline Kennedy stood next to the President's body, and with a clear voice prayed with the others: "Our Father, Who art in Heaven . . ." and "Hail, Mary, full of grace. . . ."

Lyndon Johnson, guarded by contingents of agents, was hurried away from the hospital to the airport. Press aide Kilduff came out at 1:36. His eyes red-rimmed, his voice barely controlled, he said, "President John F. Kennedy died at approximately 1 p.m. Central Standard Time, here in Dallas. He died of a gunshot wound in the brain. I have no other details of the assassination."

Soon, a white hearse drew up before the entrance and a simple bronze casket was taken inside the hospital. Jackie removed the wedding band from her left hand and slipped it on the President's finger, then the casket was closed.

Mrs. Kennedy wanted to return immediately to Washington. The casket, with Jackie walking alongside, her hand on its burnished surface, was carried outside. At Love Field, the Presidential plane was waiting. Inside Air Force One, trembling with the vibration of its idling engines, Jackie joined a shaken group waiting for Lyndon Johnson to take his oath of office.

The plane's sweltering, gold-carpeted "living room" was crowded with 27 people. At Johnson's right was his wife, Lady Bird. Behind them ranged White House staff members: Larry O'Brien and Kenneth O'Donnell were in tears; the shirt cuffs of Rear Adm. George Burkley, President Kennedy's personal physician, bore bloodstains. Federal District Judge Sarah T.

Hughes, a trim, tiny woman of 67 whom Kennedy had appointed to the bench, pronounced the oath in a voice barely audible over the engines. Johnson, his left hand on a small black Bible, his right held high, repeated firmly: *I do solemnly swear that I will faithfully execute the office of President of the United States. . . .*

The President leaned forward, kissed Lady Bird on the forehead. Mrs. Johnson turned to Jackie, held her hand and said, "The whole nation mourns your husband." Dallas Police Chief J. E. Curry stepped up and advised the widow: "God bless you, little lady, but you ought to go back and lie down." Replied Jackie, "No, thanks, I'm fine." Minutes later Johnson gave his first order as President of the United States. "Now," he said, "let's get this thing airborne."

The ceremony in Air Force One occurred at 2:38 p.m., just 98 minutes after John Kennedy was officially declared dead. Technically, Johnson had become President the moment that Kennedy died. But with that ceremony President Johnson seemed to realize for the first time that the transfer of responsibility was real. And as the blue-and-white plane sped through clear skies toward Washington, the President, as a President must, began to think about his country.

Apt Comparisons

— There are some people whose idea of adventure is to sit home like great puddings with the sauce of television pouring over them.
Gene Rhéaume, quoted by Alan Donnelly, CP

— Our car-crazy 16-year-old was explaining to a friend why a girl in a certain commercial held his attention. "It's her voice," he said. "She sounds like she's in low, just fixing to go into second." Mrs. J. J. Banks

— Once when illustrator Paul Laune was traveling by train in Italy, he sat opposite a reserved middle-aged Englishwoman. The train passed through innumerable tunnels, popping out of one into the light only to be plunged almost immediately into the gloom of the next. Finally the woman leaned over and said, "Rather like traveling through a flute, isn't it?" *Art Digest*

Making Habits Work for You

William James

[*August 1937*]

"HABIT a second nature?
Habit is *ten times* nature," the Duke of Wellington exclaimed;
and the degree to which this is true no one can appreciate so
well as a veteran soldier. Daily drill and years of discipline
make a man over in most of his conduct.

Habit is the flywheel of society, its most precious conserving
agent. The great thing, then, is to make our nervous system our
ally instead of our enemy. We must make automatic and habitual, as early as possible, as many useful actions as we can, and
guard against growing into ways that are disadvantageous as
we guard against the plague. The more details of our daily life
we can hand over to the effortless custody of automatism, the
more our higher powers of mind will be set free for their proper
work. There is no more miserable person than one in whom
nothing is habitual but indecision, and for whom the lighting
of every cigar, the drinking of every cup, the time of rising and
going to bed every day, and the beginning of every bit of work,
are subjects of deliberation. Half his time goes to deciding or
regretting matters which ought to be so ingrained as practically
not to exist for his consciousness at all.

In the acquisition of a new habit, or the leaving off of an old
one, there are four great maxims to remember: First, *we must
take care to launch ourselves with as strong an initiative as
possible*. Accumulate all possible circumstances which reinforce

the right motives; make engagements incompatible with the old way; take a public pledge, if the case allows. In short, envelop your resolution with every aid you know. This will give you such momentum that the temptation to break down will not occur as soon as it otherwise might—and every day it is postponed adds to the chances of it not occurring at all.

Second, *never suffer an exception to occur till the new habit is securely rooted in your life.* Each lapse is like letting fall a ball of string which one is carefully winding up; a single slip undoes more than a great many turns wind up again. Continuity of training is the great means of making the nervous system infallibly act right.

Success at the outset is imperative. Failure is apt to dampen the energy of all future attempts, whereas past successes nerve one to future vigor. The question of tapering off in abandoning a habit is therefore one about which experts differ. In the main, however, expert opinion would agree that abrupt acquisition of the new habit is the best way, *if there be a real possibility of carrying it out.* We must be careful not to give the will so stiff a task as to ensure defeat at the outset; but, *provided one can stand it,* a sharp period of suffering, and then freedom, is the best thing to aim at, whether in giving up a habit like drinking or in simply changing one's hour of rising. It is surprising how soon a desire will die if it be *never* fed.

"One must learn to proceed firmly before one can begin to make oneself over again," writes Dr. Bahnsen. "He who every day makes a fresh resolve is like one who, arriving at the edge of the ditch he is to leap, forever stops and returns for a fresh run. Without *unbroken* advance there is no such thing as accumulation of positive forces."

The third maxim is: *Seize the first possible opportunity to act on every resolution you make.* It is not in the moment of the resolution's forming but in the moment of its producing *motor effects* that the new "set" is communicated to the brain. No matter how full a reservoir of maxims one may possess, and no matter how good one's sentiments, if one has not taken advantage of every concrete opportunity to *act,* one's character may remain entirely unaffected for the better. With mere good intentions hell is proverbially paved. And this is an obvious consequence of the principles laid down.

"Character," as J. S. Mill says, "is a completely fashioned will." And a will, in the sense he means it, is an aggregate of tendencies to act in a firm, prompt and definite way upon all the principal emergencies of life.

The tendency to act becomes ingrained in us only in proportion to the frequency with which such actions actually occur, and the brain "grows" to their use. When a resolve or a fine glow of feeling is allowed to evaporate without bearing practical fruit, it is worse than a chance lost; it works so as positively to hinder the discharge of future resolutions and emotions. There is no more contemptible human character than that of the nerveless sentimentalist and dreamer, who spends his life in a weltering sea of sensibility and emotion but never does a manly concrete deed. The weeping of the Russian lady over the fictitious personages in the play, while her coachman is freezing to death outside, is the sort of thing that happens everywhere on a less glaring scale.

If we let our fine emotions evaporate, they get into a way of evaporating. Similarly, if we often flinch from making an effort, before we know it the effort-making capacity is gone. And if we suffer the wandering of our attention, presently it will wander all the time. As the fourth practical maxim, then: *Keep the faculty of effort alive in you by a little gratuitous exercise every day.* That is, be systematically ascetic or heroic in little unnecessary points, do every day or two something for no other reason than that you would rather not do it, so that when the hour of dire need draws nigh, it may find you nerved and trained to stand the test.

Asceticism of this sort is like the insurance a man pays on his house. The tax does him no good at the time and may never bring a return. But if the fire does come, his having paid it will be his salvation. So with the man who has daily inured himself to habits of concentrated attention, energetic volition and self-denial. He will stand like a tower when everything rocks around him, and when his softer fellow mortals are winnowed like chaff in the blast.

The hell to be endured hereafter, of which theology tells, is no worse than the hell we make for ourselves in this world by —habitually—fashioning our character in the wrong way. If we realized the extent to which we are mere walking bundles of habits, we would give more heed to those habits' formation. We are spinning our own fates, good or evil, and never to be undone. Every smallest stroke of virtue or of vice leaves its ever-so-little scar. The drunken Rip van Winkle in Jefferson's play excuses himself for every fresh dereliction by saying, "I won't count this time!" Well, he may not count it, and a kind Heaven may not count it; but it is being counted nonetheless. Down among his nerve cells and fibers the molecules are counting it, registering it, and storing it up to be used against him when the next temptation comes.

The fact that nothing we ever do is, in strict scientific literalness, wiped out of course has its good side as well as its bad one. As we become permanent drunkards by so many separate drinks, so we become saints in the moral sphere, and experts in the practical and scientific spheres, by so many separate acts and hours of work.

Let no one have anxiety about the upshot of his education. If he keep faithfully busy each hour of the working day, he may safely leave the final result to itself. He can with perfect certainty count on waking up some fine morning to find himself one of the competent ones of his generation, in whatever pursuit he may have singled out.

Personnel Problems

&~ Trying to determine why production had declined in a plant in Maine, an efficiency expert asked the company's personnel director, "How many of your employes are approaching retirement age?"

"Well," replied the personnel director, "we haven't got any going the other way."

John M. Geise

&~ The personnel man received a questionnaire which asked, among other things: "How many people do you have, broken down by sex?" His answer: "Liquor is more of a problem with us."

Hugh Park in Atlanta Journal

A Family for Freddie

Abbie Blair

[December 1964]

I REMEMBER the first time I saw Freddie. He was standing in his playpen at the adoption agency where I work. He gave me a toothy grin. "What a beautiful baby," I thought.

His boarding mother gathered him into her arms. "Will you be able to find a family for Freddie?" she asked.

Then I saw it. Freddie had been born without arms.

"He's so smart. He's only ten months old, and already he walks and talks." She kissed him. "Say 'book' for Mrs. Blair."

Freddie grinned at me and hid his head on his boarding mother's shoulder. "Now, Freddie, don't act that way," she said. "He's really very friendly," she added. "Such a good, good boy."

Freddie reminded me of my own son when he was that age, the same thick dark curls, the same brown eyes.

"You won't forget him, Mrs. Blair? You will try?"

"I won't forget."

I went upstairs and got out my latest copy of the Hard-to-Place list.

> Freddie is a ten-month-old white Protestant boy of English and French background. He has brown eyes, dark-brown hair and fair skin. Freddie was born without arms, but is otherwise in good health. His boarding mother feels he is showing signs of superior mentality, and he is already

walking and saying a few words. Freddie is a warm, affectionate child who has been surrendered by his natural mother and is ready for adoption.

"He's ready," I thought. "But who is ready for him?"

It was ten o'clock of a lovely late-summer morning, and the agency was full of couples—couples having interviews, couples meeting babies, families being born. These couples nearly always have the same dream: they want a child as much like themselves as possible, as young as possible, and—most important—a child with no medical problem.

"If he develops a problem after we get him," they say, "that is a risk we'll take, just like any other parents. But to pick a baby who already has a problem—that's too much."

And who can blame them?

I wasn't alone in looking for parents for Freddie. Any of the caseworkers meeting a new couple started with a hope: maybe they were for Freddie. But summer slipped into fall, and Freddie was with us for his first birthday party.

"Freddie is so-o-o big," said his boarding mother, stretching out her arms.

"So-o-o big," said Freddie, laughing. "So-o-o big."

And then I found them.

It started out as it always does—an impersonal record in my box, a new case, a new "Home Study," two people who wanted a child. They were Frances and Edwin Pearson. She was 41. He was 45. She was a housewife. He was a truck driver.

I went to see them. They lived in a tiny white frame house in a big yard full of sun and old trees. They greeted me together at the door, eager and scared to death.

Mrs. Pearson produced steaming coffee and oven-warm cookies. They sat before me on the sofa, close together, holding hands. After a moment Mrs. Pearson began: "Today is our wedding anniversary. Eighteen years."

"Good years." Mr. Pearson looked at his wife. "Except—"

"Yes," she said. "Except. Always the 'except'." She looked around the immaculate room. "It's too neat," she said. "You know?"

I thought of my own living room with my three children. Teen-agers now. "Yes," I said. "I know."

"Perhaps we're too old?"

I smiled. "You don't think so," I said. "We don't either."

"You always think it will be this month, and then next month," Mr. Pearson said. "Even when you begin to guess the truth, you don't want to accept it."

"We've tried everything," Mrs. Pearson said. "Examinations. Tests. All kinds of things. Over and over. But nothing ever happened. You just go on hoping and hoping, and time keeps slipping by."

"We've tried to adopt before this," Mr. Pearson said. "One agency told us our apartment was too small, so we got this house. Then another one said I didn't make enough money. We had decided that was it, but this friend told us about you, and we decided to make one last try."

"I'm glad," I said.

Mrs. Pearson glanced at her husband proudly. "Can we choose at all?" she asked. "A boy for my husband?"

"We'll try for a boy," I said. "What kind of boy?"

Mrs. Pearson laughed. "How many kinds are there? Just a boy. My husband is very athletic. He played football in high school; basketball, too, and track. He would be good for a boy."

Mr. Pearson looked at me. "I know you can't tell exactly," he said, "but can you give us any idea how soon? We've waited so long."

I hesitated. There is always this question.

"Next summer maybe," said Mrs. Pearson. "We could take him to the beach."

"That long?" Mr. Pearson said. "Don't you have anyone at all? There *must* be a little boy somewhere."

"Of course," he went on after a pause, "we can't give him as much as other people. We haven't a lot of money saved up."

"We've got a lot of love," his wife said. "We've saved up a lot of that."

"Well," I said cautiously, "there *is* a little boy. He is 13 months old."

"Oh," Mrs. Pearson said, "just a beautiful age."

"I have a picture of him," I said, reaching for my purse. I handed them Freddie's picture.

"He is a wonderful little boy," I said. "But he was born without arms."

They studied the picture in silence. He looked at her. "What do you think, Fran?"

"Kickball," Mrs. Pearson said. "You could teach him kickball."

"Athletics are not so important," Mr. Pearson said. "He can learn to use his head. Arms he can do without. A head, never. He can go to college. We'll save for it."

"A boy is a boy," Mrs. Pearson insisted. "He needs to play. You can teach him."

"I'll teach him. Arms aren't everything. Maybe we can get him some."

They had forgotten me. But maybe Mr. Pearson was right, I thought. Maybe sometime Freddie could be fitted with artificial arms. He did have nubs where arms should be.

"Then you might like to see him?"

They looked up. "When could we have him?"

"You think you might want him?"

Mrs. Pearson looked at me. "Might?" she said. *"Might?"*

"We want him," her husband said.

Mrs. Pearson went back to the picture. "You've been waiting for us," she said. "Haven't you?"

"His name is Freddie," I said, "but you can change it."

"No," said Mr. Pearson. "Frederick Pearson—it's good together."

And that was it.

There were formalities, of course; and by the time we set the day Christmas lights were strung across city streets and wreaths were hung everywhere.

I met the Pearsons in the waiting room. There was a little snow on them both.

"Your son's here already," I told them. "Let's go upstairs, and I'll bring him to you."

"I've got butterflies," Mrs. Pearson announced. "Suppose he doesn't like us?"

I put my hand on her arm. "I'll get him," I said.

Freddie's boarding mother had dressed him in a new white suit, with a sprig of green holly and red berries embroidered on the collar. His hair shone, a mop of dark curls.

"Going home," Freddie said to me, smiling, as his boarding mother put him in my arms.

"I told him that," she said. "I told him he was going to his new home."

She kissed him, and her eyes were wet.

"Good-by, dear. Be a good boy."

"Good boy," said Freddie cheerfully. "Going home."

I carried him upstairs to the little room where the Pearsons were waiting. When I got there, I put him on his feet and opened the door.

"Merry Christmas," I said.

Freddie stood uncertainly, rocking a little, gazing intently at the two people before him.

They drank him in.

Mr. Pearson knelt on one knee. "Freddie," he said, "come here. Come to Daddy."

Freddie looked back at me for a moment. Then, turning, he walked slowly toward them; and they reached out their arms and gathered him in.

Good Sisters

~ A young nun had not seen her twin brother, a bomber pilot on wartime duty overseas, for over two years, and prayed each day for his safe return. One day Sister X was told that a visitor awaited her in the reception room. As she descended a stairway, her brother stepped out into the lobby. With a scream of surprise and delight, she rushed forward and embraced him with something more than ordinary fervor.

At that moment three older nuns crossed the lobby. There was no pause in their progress, no impairment of poise, just a slight raising of eyebrows. But as they went on their way, there was this *sotto voce* comment by one of them: "She must know him." The Rev. Rufus Esser

~ A priest's description of nuns at confession: "It's like being stoned to death with popcorn." Pat O'Brien on "Tonight Show," NBC-TV

QUOTABLE QUOTES

A BIRD in the hand is a certainty. But a bird in the bush may sing.   Bret Harte

IF YOU are out to describe the truth, leave elegance to the tailor.   Albert Einstein, quoted in *Think*

MAN IS a slow, sloppy and brilliant thinker; the machine is fast, accurate and stupid.   William M. Kelly, quoted in
Notes, Quotes & Anecdotes, Canada

NEXT TO the wound, what women make best is the bandage.
Barbey d'Aurevilly

JEALOUSY is the most radical, primeval and naked form of admiration—admiration in war paint, so to speak.
Robert Louis Stevenson

AN OUNCE of "keep your mouth shut" beats a ton of explanation.   *The American Citizen*

PEOPLE differ. Some object to the fan dancer, and others to the fan.   Elizabeth W. Spalding in
Bardstown *Kentucky Standard*

A CONSULTANT is a man who borrows your watch and tells you what time it is, then sends you a bill.   Carl Ally

BY THE streets of "by and by" one arrives at the house of "never."   Spanish proverb

THE TROUBLE with people who have broken a habit is they usually have the pieces mounted and framed.   Ivern Boyett

CHANCE is the pseudonym of God when He did not want to sign.   Anatole France

The Desert,
Land of Surprises

Edward Abbey

[February 1967]

HE AIR is so dry here I can
hardly shave in the mornings. The water and lather dry on my
face as I reach for the razor: aridity. The inch of snow that falls
during a stormy night in the middle of May has all disappeared an hour after sunrise, except in shaded places, and an
hour after the snow melts, the surface of the desert is again
bone-dry.

It seldom rains. The geography books credit this portion of
Utah with nine to ten inches of precipitation per year but this
is merely an average. Actual rainfall and snowfall vary widely
from year to year. There are a few perennial springs hidden in
secret places, known only to the deer and the coyotes, to myself
and a few friends, but the water does not flow far before vanishing into the air and under the ground. Even the rain, when
it comes, does not always fall to the ground but can often be
seen evaporating halfway down—curtains of blue rain dangling
out of reach, torture by tantalizing.

If he lives long enough in the desert, a man, like other animals, can learn to smell water. Learn, at least, the smell of
things associated with water—the odor of the cottonwood tree,
for example, which out here might well be called the tree of
life. In this wilderness of naked rock, there is no vision more

59

pleasing than the acid-green leaves of this venerable tree, signifying not only water but shade.

The cottonwood means water, but it may be too far underground to be of any use. If you have what is called a survival problem and try to dig for this water during the heat of the day, the effort may cost you more in sweat than you will find to drink, for it is difficult to satisfy your thirst with moist sand. I have tried it. Better to wait for nightfall, when the cottonwood trees and other plants along the wash seem to release some of the water they have taken in during the day and a potable trickle may rise to the surface of the sand. If it does not, you are then welcome to march onward until sooner or later you find a spring or at least a seep on the canyon wall. On the other hand, you might not. The desert is a land of surprises, some of which are terrible. Terrible as derived from terror. When out for a walk bring your own water—not less than a gallon a day.

More surprises. In places you will find clear, flowing streams, as in the Salt Wash of the Arches, where the water looks beautifully drinkable but is too saline to swallow. You might think, dying of thirst, that any water however salty would be better than none at all, but this is not true. Small doses will not keep you alive, and a deep drink will force your body to expend water in getting rid of the excess salt, with the result a net loss of body moisture and a hastening of dehydration. Dehydration first enervates, then prostrates, then kills.

Nor is blood, your own or a companion's, a substitute for water; blood is too salty. The same is true of urine. If it's your automobile which has failed you, you'd be better off tapping the radiator. If this resource is not available and water cannot be found in the rocks or sand, and you find yourself too tired and discouraged to go on, crawl into the shade and wait for help. If no one is looking for you, write your will in the sand and let the wind carry your last words east to the borders of Colorado and south to the mountains of the moon. Someday, never fear, your bare, elegant bones will be discovered and marveled at.

A great thirst is a great joy when assuaged in time. On my first walk down into Havasu Canyon, which is a small hidden branch of the Grand Canyon, never mind exactly where, I took with me only a one-quart canteen, thinking that would be enough water for a 14-mile downhill hike on a warm day in August. On the rim of the canyon the temperature was a tolerable 96 degrees, but it rose about one degree for each mile down and forward. Like a fool I rationed my water, drank sparingly, and could have died of sunstroke. When late in the afternoon I finally stumbled—sun-dazed, blear-eyed, parched as an old bacon rind—upon that blue stream which flows like a mirage across the canyon floor, I was too exhausted to pause and drink soberly from the bank. Dreamily, deliriously, I slogged into the waist-deep water and fell on my face. Like a sponge I soaked up moisture through every pore, letting the current bear me along beneath a canopy of willow trees. I had no fear of drowning in the water—I intended to drink it all.

Other surprises. Northeast of Moab, Utah, in a region of gargoyles and hobgoblins, a landscape left over from the late Jurassic period, is a peculiar little waterhole named Onion Spring. A few wild onions grow in the vicinity but more striking, in season, is the golden princess plume, an indicator of selenium, a mild poison often found in association with uranium, a poison not so mild. In addition to the selenium, the water of Onion Spring contains arsenic. Taste it, see for yourself.

What else is odd about this little spring? Well, the water is too clear. There's no life in it. No bugs. When in doubt about drinking from an unknown spring, look for life. If the water is scummy with algae, crawling with worms, tadpoles, flukes and scales, be reassured, drink hearty, you'll get nothing worse than dysentery. But if it appears innocent and pure, beware.

There are rumors that when dying of thirst you can save soul *and* body by extracting water from the barrel cactus. This is a dubious proposition. It might be possible in the low desert of Arizona where the barrel cactus will often grow as high as a man and big around as a beer keg. But in Utah a similar species grows no more than a foot up and bristles with needles curved like fishhooks. To even get close you need leather gloves and a machete. Slice off the top and you find inside not a little tun of precious water but only the green pulpy core of the living plant. To get a few drops of liquid from that you would have to hack the cactus into manageable chunks and wring what water you could from each piece. Meanwhile, you are sweating badly from the labor and the exasperation, dehydrating rapidly, doomed anyway. You'd be better off to stay at home with the TV and a case of beer. If this happy thought arrives too late, relax and enjoy your demise as best you can; it's your only one.

In July and August, here on the high desert, come the thunderstorms. The mornings begin clear and dazzling bright, the sky as blue as the Virgin's cloak, unflawed by a trace of cloud from the Book Cliffs on the north to the Blue Mountains 80 miles to the south, from the Sierra La Sal on the east to the notched reef of the San Rafael 100 miles west. By noon, though, clouds are beginning to form over the mountains, coming it seems out of nowhere, out of nothing, a special creation. They merge and multiply, cumuli nimbi piling up like whipped cream, like mashed potatoes, building upon one another into a second mountain range greater than the terrestrial range below. The massive forms jostle and grate, ions collide, and the sound of thunder is heard on the sun-drenched land.

At my observation point on a sandstone monolith, the sun is blazing down as intensely as ever, the air crackling with dry heat. But the storm clouds are taking over the sky and, as they approach, the battle breaks out. Lightning streaks among the clouds like gunfire; volleys of thunder shake the air. So long as the clouds exchange their bolts with one another no rain falls, but now they begin bombarding the ridgetops and buttes below. Forks of lightning, like illuminated nerves, link heaven and earth. The wind is rising.

Above me the clouds roll in, smoking billows in malignant violet, dense as wool. Most of the sky is lidded over, but the sun remains clear, halfway down the west, shining beneath the storm. Over my head the clouds thicken, then crack and split with a roar like that of cannonballs tumbling down a marble staircase; their bellies open—too late to run now!—and suddenly the rain comes down.

Comes down: not softly, not gently, with no quality of mercy, but like heavy water in buckets, raindrops like lead pellets smashing and splattering on the flat rock, knocking the berries off the juniper, plastering my shirt to my back, drumming on my hat like hailstones, running like a waterfall off the brim. The pinnacles and arches of sandstone, glazed with water but still exposed to the sun, gleam like old gray silver in the holy—no, unholy—light that slants in under the black ceiling of the storm.

For five minutes the deluge continues, then trails off quickly, diminishes to a shower, to nothing, while the clouds, moving off, rumble in the distance. A fresh golden light breaks through and now, in the east, a double rainbow appears, with one foot in the canyon of the Colorado and the other far north in the Salt Wash Valley. The desert storm is over and through the sweet pellucid air the cliff swallows and the nighthawks plunge and swerve, with cries of hunger and warning and—who knows?—perhaps of exultation as well.

After the storm has passed and the streambeds are as dry as they were before, water still remains in natural cisterns and potholes carved by wind and weather into rimrock, canyon bench and mesa top. Some of these holes may contain water for days or weeks after rain, depending upon their depth and exposure to the sun. Often far from any spring or stream, these temporary pools attract doves, ravens and other birds for so long as they last, provide the deer and the coyotes with a short-lived water supply; you too, if you know where to look, may slake your thirst there, and fill your canteens.

The rainpools, set in monolithic rock, are usually devoid of plant life but not always of animal life. They may contain certain amphibians such as the spadefoot toad, which lives in the sediment in the bottom of the pothole. When rain comes, he emerges from the mud, singing madly, mates with the nearest female, and fills the pool with a swarm of tadpoles, most of them doomed to an ephemeral existence. With luck a few may survive to become mature toads, and as the pool dries up they, like their parents, make themselves a burrow in the mud, which they seal with mucus to preserve the moisture necessary to life. They wait down there, patiently, hopefully, indefinitely, for the next rain. If it comes soon, the cycle can be repeated; if not, the colony is reduced to dust, a burden on the wind.

A strange and stirring sight, to come on a pool at night, after a little rain, and see the toads and frogs clinging to the edges of their temporary pond, bodies immersed in the water but heads in the air, all of them croaking away in tricky counterpoint. Why do they sing so joyfully? They are not hunting or fighting or mating with each other; they are not moving about in search of love. Since the zoologist has no good explanation, I'll settle for the answer implied in the question: they are singing for joy, for joy in the coolness and wetness after weeks of desert heat, for joy in their music, for joy in life, however brief that life may turn out to be.

Has joy any survival value in the operations of evolution? It certainly does. Behold the jolly toads belching musically in their slimy, shrinking, sun-doomed home. Meanwhile rattlesnakes and whipsnakes, attracted by the uproar, are gliding close in quest of supper; some of the musical amphibians will continue their metamorphosis via the nerves and tissues of a reptile, in which process the joy of the toad is transmuted into the contentment of the snake. Perhaps nothing is lost, then, except the individual consciousness, which some philosophers maintain is only an illusion anyway.

Water, water—there really is no shortage of water in the desert. There is, in fact, exactly the right amount, a perfect ratio of water to rock, ensuring a decent, habitable spacing among plants and animals, and human inhabitants also. Even so, only the boldest of travelers, seeking visions, will stay for long in the strange country of the standing rock, where the spadefoot toads bellow madly on the edge of a rainpool, where the arsenic spring awaits the thirst-crazed traveler, where the thunderstorms blast the pinnacles and cliffs, and the quiet deer walk at evening up glens of sandstone through tamarisk and sage toward hidden springs of sweet, cool, clear, unfailing water.

ॐ A young Finn who worked in my brother's office announced he was going to be married. Everyone wanted a description—was the girl blond or brunette, thin or fat, etc. "She is not what you would say fat or thin," he replied. "But she is very complete."   Mrs. O. M. Hopper

The Disrobing of Flapper Jane

Bruce Bliven

[November 1925]

JANE is a flapper of 19. Let us take a look at this young person as she strolls across the lawn of her parents' suburban home, having just put the car away after driving 60 miles in two hours. She is, for one thing, a very pretty girl. Beauty is the fashion in 1925. She is, frankly, heavily made up, not to imitate nature but for an altogether artificial effect—pallor mortis, poisonously scarlet lips, richly ringed eyes— the latter looking not so much debauched (which is the intention) as diabetic. Her walk duplicates the swagger supposed by innocent America to go with the female half of a Paris Apache dance. And there are, finally, her clothes.

These were estimated the other day by some statistician to weigh two pounds. Probably a libel; Jane isn't wearing much this summer. If you'd like to know exactly, it is: one dress, one step-in, two stockings, two shoes.

A step-in, if you are ignorant, is underwear—one piece, light, exceedingly brief but roomy. Her dress is also brief. It is cut low where it might be high, and vice versa. The skirt comes just an inch below her knees, overlapping by a faint fraction her rolled stockings. The idea is that when she walks in a breeze, you shall now and then observe the knee (which is *not* rouged—that's just newspaper talk) but always in an incidental, Venus-surprised-at-the-bath sort of way. This is a bit of coyness which hardly fits in with Jane's general character.

Jane's haircut is also abbreviated. She wears of course the very newest thing in bobs, even closer than last year's shingle. Because of this new style, one can confirm a rumor heard last year: Jane still has ears.

The corset is as dead as the dodo's grandfather. The petticoat is even more defunct. The brassiere has been abandoned since 1924. While stockings are usually worn, in hot weather Jane reserves the right to discard them, just as all the chorus girls did in 1923. As stockings are only a frantic, successful attempt to duplicate the color and texture of Jane's own sunburned slim legs, few but expert boulevardiers can tell the difference.

The clothes which I have described are not merely a flapper uniform. They are The Style, Summer of 1925, Eastern Seaboard. These things and none other are being worn by all of Jane's sisters and her cousins and her aunts. In our larger cities the baggage-transfer companies one and all declare they are being forced into bankruptcy. Ladies who used to go away for the summer with six trunks can now pack 20 dainty costumes in a bag.

This year's styles have gone quite a long step toward genuine nudity. Nor is this merely sensible dressing as everyone ought to in hot weather. Last winter's styles weren't so dissimilar, except you got the full effect only indoors. Next year's styles, from all one hears, will be, as they are already on the continent, even More So.

Where will it all end? No one can say. Nudity has been the custom of many countries over long periods of time. No one who has read history can be very firm in saying that It Never Can Happen Again.

Few anymore are so naïve as not to realize that there are fashions in morals. And costume, of course, is A Moral. You can get a rough measure of our Great Disrobing Movement if you look at the theater and see how the tidemark of tolerance has risen. For instance:

1904—Performance of *Mrs. Warren's Profession* halted by police.

1919—Mrs. Warren okay. Town roused to frenzy by *Aphrodite,* in which one chorus girl is exposed for one minute in dim light and a union suit.

1923—Union suit okay. Censors have conniption fits over chorus girls naked from waist up.

1925—Nudity from waist up taken for granted. Excitement caused by show in which girls wear only fig leaves.

Projecting the curve into the future, it is easy to see that complete nudity in the theater in this country will be reached on March 12, 1927. Such displays have long been familiar in the theaters of several European capitals.

The recent history of the movement can be checked up in another way by looking at bathing costumes. There are still a few beaches near New York City which insist on more clothes than anyone can safely swim in, and thereby help to drown several young women each year. But in most places a girl is now compelled to wear no more than is a man.

"Jane," say I, "why do all of you dress the way you do?"

"The old girls are doing it because youth is," says Jane. "Everybody wants to be young now—though they want all us young people to be something else. Funny, isn't it?

"In a way, it's just honesty. Women have come down off the pedestal lately. They are tired of this mysterious-feminine-charm stuff. Maybe it goes with independence, earning your own living and voting and all that. There was always a bit of the harem in that cover-up-your-arms-and-legs business.

"Women still want to be loved," goes on Jane, "but they want it on a 50-50 basis, which includes being admired for the qualities they really possess. Dragging in this strange-allurement stuff doesn't seem sporting. It's like cheating in games.

"I read this book whaddaya-call-it by Rose Macaulay, and she showed where they'd been excited about wild youth for three generations anyhow—since 1870. I have a hunch maybe they've always been excited.

"It's funny," says Jane, "that just when women's clothes are getting scanty, men's should be going the other way!"

Do morals go with the clothes, or are they independent? Generally speaking, it is safe to say that as regards the wildness of youth there is a good deal more smoke than fire. Anyhow, the new Era of Undressing, as already suggested, has spread far beyond the boundaries of Jane's group. The fashion is followed by hordes of unquestionably monogamous matrons, including many who join heartily in the general ululations as to what young people are coming to.

The fact is, as Jane says, that women today are shaking off the shreds and patches of their age-old servitude. "Feminism" has won a victory so nearly complete that we have even forgotten the fierce challenge which once inhered in the very word. Women have resolved that they are just as good as men, and intend to be treated so. They don't intend to be debarred from any profession or occupation which they choose to enter. They clearly mean (even though not all of them yet realize it) that in the great game of sexual selection they shall no longer be forced to play the role, simulated or real, of helpless quarry. If they want to wear their heads shaven, as a symbol of defiance against the fate which for three millenniums forced them to dress their heavy locks according to male decrees, they will have their way.

ᢣᐅ There is an ancient and decorous men's shop in New York which derives secret pride from the fact that it made Abraham Lincoln's clothes. When the manager confided this fact to me one day, I asked, "Why don't you use that in your advertisements?"

His scowl was withering as he replied, "Mr. Lincoln wore them so badly."　　　Richardson Wright, *Another Gardener's Bed-Book* (Lippincott)

Sione in Two Worlds

Nardi Reeder Campion

[July 1968]

In the tiny Polynesian king-
dom of Tonga—150 islands dotting 270 square miles in the vast
South Pacific—a competitive exam was given in 1965 to all
high-school students. One of the high scorers was 16-year-old
Sione Toupouniua. The Putney School, a small preparatory
school in faraway Vermont, U.S.A., offered a scholarship to
this boy who had never used a knife or fork, never eaten from
a plate, never worn a pair of shoes. Within weeks he bade his
parents, two sisters and six brothers a tearful good-by and sailed
on the monthly passenger-freighter from his home island of
Tongatapu to Fiji, where he boarded a plane. His experiences in America dramatize the classic confrontation between
an innocent culture and modern civilization.*

Sione's plane arrived over San Francisco at night, and when
the boy from Tonga saw the great blaze of light he thought the
city was on fire. Dazzled, open-mouthed, he stepped down the
gangway. His baggy gray suit was too big and very wrinkled.
He had no idea how to tie a necktie, so he had wound it loosely
about his neck. His bushy hair stood straight up, and he wore
socks but no shoes. He had bought a pair in Fiji—triple-E width,
the widest made—but they proved so painful that now he simply carried them.

Transportation had been arranged to take Sione from the airport to a hotel. The youth tried to communicate. Although he

had studied English, all he could say comfortably was "hello," "good-by," "please" and "thank you." The hotel manager took one look at the gesticulating boy with the wild hair and moved rapidly to whisk him out of sight.

He shoved a key into Sione's hand, put him in the self-service elevator and told him to get off at the tenth floor. Sione's recollection of what happened next is vivid: "The door slid shut, the box went up, and I got airplane stomach again. Then the box stopped at the ninth floor. What to do? I figured, nine and one make ten, so if I push ONE I should go up to TEN."

He pushed ONE, and when the door opened he was back in the lobby. The manager shouted, "What are you doing down here?" He grabbed a bellboy and said, "Take this—er—gentleman up to his room, and put him *inside* it."

The bellboy smiled and Sione grinned back, relieved to find that Americans *could* smile. The bellboy showed Sione to his room, turned on the shower to warm the water, and left. It never occurred to him that a traveler might not know what a shower was, much less what H and C taps stood for.

Soon steam was everywhere, and the room became blistering hot. Sione took off his clothes; it felt good to be naked again. The steam seeped under the bedroom door and out into the hall. A man passing by saw it and rang the fire alarm. People came running into Sione's room, shouting. The manager shouted loudest of all, his face scarlet.

Sione just stood there, naked and speechless. The manager threw a towel at him and yelled, "For heaven's sake, cover yourself up!"

Firemen with helmets charged through the steam. Sione did not know what was going on; he supposed it was some strange American custom. One of the firemen discovered the shower running. He turned it off, and they all laughed—even the nervous manager. *We laughed together,* Sione remembers. *I felt good. In Tonga we laugh a lot. When you laugh with people you're not strangers anymore.*

Sione rode east on the bus all the next day, popeyed with excitement but weak from hunger. When the bus stopped he eagerly followed a fellow passenger into a restaurant. The waitress placed a menu on his plate. In Tonga, banana leaves are used as plates, and extra leaves are placed on top to keep the food hot. Sione looked under the menu to see the food. Nothing. Then he tried to peel off the paper, thinking it might be something to eat. Finally, the waitress opened the menu for him, and he pointed at random.

Now Sione examined the silver and napkin, trying to figure out what to do with them. But when the waitress put a dish in front of him, he couldn't swallow one bite—it was a plate full of white worms! Weeks later he learned that this food was called spaghetti.

Outside the restaurant, Sione ran into a fruit vendor and bought oranges, bananas, a pineapple, a coconut. He smashed the coconut and began to pick out the meat. The other bus passengers gathered around to watch. Sione grinned and the others grinned back.

That's nice, he thought, *they're friendly. It's so sad to see all these people just sitting there silent. At home everyone would be joking and laughing and having a good time on a trip, whether they knew each other or not. In Tonga we think it is rude not to talk, and politeness to strangers is instilled in us from childhood.*

When at last his bus pulled into Putney, where he was met by his American "parent," Edward Dodd, Sione was so exhausted that he slept for 36 hours. When he awoke, 8000 miles from home, his strange situation struck him like a blow in the face, and tears started. Everything was so foreign. He didn't even dare use the bathroom: it was too clean. In Tonga, most people simply went to an outhouse.

Mr. and Mrs. Dodd did all they could to make their forlorn guest feel at home. They even held a pig roast for him, and introduced him to several boys his age. They helped him with his English, which quickly improved. They took him to his first church service in America. Sione eagerly looked forward to it. Methodist missionaries had converted the Tongans in the early 19th century, and religion is so important that even fishing is forbidden on Sunday. But Sione was sadly disappointed.

Only a handful of people were there. I thought the others

*were late, but they didn't come at all. Our church is packed
every Sunday. Everybody wears white, and the service is full of
joy. Here everybody wore black, and it was as if someone had
died. The music made me homesick. I thought about the beautiful hymns my father composes, and I cried all during the service. We cry a lot at home. It helps you get rid of bad feelings;
then you get up and go on. The Bible says Jesus wept—why
should American men be embarrassed to cry?*

When Putney opened, the other students were puzzled by
the new boy's woebegone expression and odd ways. Luckily
there was a soccer game that first week. Sione had never seen
soccer, but like most Tongans he is a natural athlete—and was
the star of the game even in his bare feet. From then on, all the
students felt warmer toward him, and his feelings of strangeness
started to dissolve. Sione's sense of humor and natural openness
soon made him many friends.

Those first months in the United States were booby-trapped
with strange devices like clocks (*My mother would tell us, "Try
to be home by the time the sun gets below the mango tree"*),
and locks (*If someone wants something badly enough to steal,
we say let him have it*). The feeling of isolation was hardest to
adjust to. Privacy is unknown in the open houses and grass huts
of Tonga; in the United States, people seem to prefer going it
alone. *Here, helping others is only an obligation. In Tonga,
helping others is the joy that gives life its meaning.*

The greatest thrill in Sione's new life came from learning.
He had always taken the Tongan school lightly, often skipping
classes altogether to swim or fish. Now, all at once, the world of
the mind was open to him. He learned quickly, and the excitement of learning propelled him into more learning.

*Everything I was exposed to was new. The discovery of the
test tube and the microscope and history and maps and typewriters and films and all those books was so sudden for me. I
read, read, all the time. Only two books have been published in
Tongan—the Bible and a hymnal. Now I could read book after
book in English! I began with Melville's stories of my own
South Seas, and kept going. American kids have grown up with
the tools of knowledge, so the excitement of discovery escapes*

them. The trouble with being sophisticated is that you lose the joy of surprise.

This adventure in learning was remarkably successful: after two years at Putney, Sione Tupouniua of Tonga sailed into Harvard College with a full scholarship. He is now an honors student there, on the dean's list, president of his club, and captain of the varsity rugby team. Summers he has spent working as a carpenter. "Sione's natural joyousness inspires the others here," says a Harvard housemaster. "Without even knowing it, he seeds this place with ideas of how to live."

Many things about America still puzzle Sione. He does not understand young people's lack of respect for their elders; nor their love of loud music that prevents communication; nor their fear of getting fat. (Tongans admire great weight. King Tupou IV is envied because he weighs 300 pounds.)

Some aspects of student social life bother Sione. *American boys and girls get too serious too soon. They start thinking ahead instead of rejoicing in the present. And I don't understand the continuous debate about morality. To us, morality is not how much of the body is covered up or how much joy you deny yourself. Morality is how you treat people. If you are kind and loving to them, that is moral. If you are mean and selfish to them, that is immoral.*

As much as he loves this country Sione plans to return to Tonga to live. He would like to start a college. (There is none there now.) He doesn't want Tongans to lose their loving, natural ways; but he would like to pass on to them some of America's ability to counter the destructive forces of nature: weather, insects, disease. And American know-how—the experience of organizing difficult jobs and getting them done.

Back in Tonga I know I will miss books and libraries; films, plays and concerts; the change of seasons; snow and the thrill of skiing; and most of all, friends. I don't think I'll miss modern conveniences and physical comforts, like television and hot baths, and I know I won't miss the uncomfortable clothes, the crowds, the noise, the polluted air, the traffic jams, and the people who half-run, half-walk.

I have a goal: to give my people a deep appreciation of what we have in Tonga—something you can discover only by going away. We have nothing, really, and yet we have so much. We have ofa. "Ofa" is a Tongan word meaning respect, kindness, sympathy and love—all the things of the heart. It is the most important word in our vocabulary. In America, success is measured by what you produce or what you possess. In Tonga, success is measured only in terms of your relationships with other human beings.

*   *   *

After Harvard, Sione went on to Oxford University. Today back in Fiji, he teaches political science and economics at the South Pacific University while completing work on his doctoral thesis. He still has every intention of returning to Tonga.

Cartoon Quips

Wife to husband: "I took one of those compatibility tests in a magazine today, and you flunked."   Leo Garel in *The Wall Street Journal*

Wakened out of deep sleep, man answering phone: "You have the wrong idiot, you number!"   Chon Day in *Look*

Attractive secretary, counting slips from suggestion box, to boss: "You got two, and I got 26."   Thaves, King Features

Youngster, explaining poor report card, to father: "My teaching machine is a lemon."   Salo, Chicago Tribune-New York News Syndicate

Man to waiter: "We'll have the businessman's luncheon. Very dry."   Leonard Dove in *The Saturday Evening Post*

Woman watching soap opera on TV: "The trouble with real life is there's no plot."   Bernhardt in *The Kiwanis Magazine*

Doctor to plump patient: "Let me put it this way—you're an addict, and your grocer is a pusher."   S. Harris in *Hospital Physician*

Woman motorist to another at filling station: "I don't mind gasoline, but I think oil is a racket."   Don Tobin, McNaught Syndicate

Financier's wife to guests: "Speak softly, Edward always says, but carry a big portfolio."   Weaver in *The Wall Street Journal*

Can a Scientist Believe in God?

Warren Weaver

[July 1955]

$\mathcal{S}$CIENCE and religion. Science is the activity whereby man attempts to gain understanding and control of nature. I don't feel the need to qualify this statement by saying: This is *my* kind of science or this is what science means to *me*.

Religion, on the other hand, is a highly personal affair. I can tell you only what it means to me: first, a guide to conduct; second, the theory of the moral meaning of our existence.

Science tries to answer the question "How?" How do cells act in the body? How do you design an airplane that will fly faster than sound? Religion, by contrast, tries to answer the question "Why?" Why was man created? Why ought I to tell the truth?

Science attempts to analyze how things and people and animals behave; it has no concern whether this behavior is good or bad. Religion is precisely the quest for such answers.

How do you define God? When I am troubled or afraid or deeply concerned for those I love, when I listen to the hymns which go back to the loveliest memories of my childhood, then God is to me an emotional and comforting God—a protecting Father.

When I am trying to work out a problem of right and wrong, then God is a clear and unambiguous voice, an unfailing source of moral guidance. I do not understand how these things happen; but I know perfectly well, if I listen to this voice, what is the right thing to do. I have many times been uncertain as to what course of action would best serve a certain *practical* purpose; but I cannot think of a single instance in my life when I asked what was the really *right* thing to do and the answer was not forthcoming.

These two statements cover my everyday relation with God. I do not find it necessary to try to analyze them in logical terms. They state facts of experience. You can no more convince me that there is no such God than you can convince me that a table or a rock is not solid—in each case the evidence is simple, direct and uniform.

As a scientist familiar with detailed explanations of the atomic structure of, say, the table and the rock, it does not disturb me that these everyday concepts of God do not offer me a detailed logical explanation. God on an intellectual plane (corresponding to the theoretical plane of the physicist) is something else, and, just as a scientist would expect, abstract. And it gratifies me that, in addition to the everyday way, I am able to think about God in ways intellectually satisfying and consistent with the thinking I try to do along scientific lines.

God is, to me, the name behind a consistent set of phenomena, which are all recognizable in terms of moral purpose and which deal with the control of man's destiny.

Can a scientist believe in God? Scientists are precisely the persons who believe in the unseeable, the essentially undefinable. No scientist has ever *seen* an electron. "Electron" is simply the name for a consistent set of things that happen in certain circumstances. Yet nothing is more "real" to a scientist than an electron. Chairs, tables, rocks—these are not very "real" to him, if he thinks deeply. A table, viewed with the precise tools of the atomic physicist, is a shadowy, swirling set of electric charges, in themselves vague and elusive. So viewed, the table completely loses its large-scale illusion of solidity.

The scientist is the last to expect that an "ultimate explanation" is going to involve familiar ideas. He is just the one who should *not* say that an abstract concept of God results in an "unreal" God. To him, the real is what is *universally experienced.* He raises a basic question: "Does this definition *work* successfully?" "Electron" is only the name behind a set of phenomena, but essentially all physicists agree as to what these electron phenomena are. If there is this kind of consistency, then a definition "works"—and the scientist finds it acceptable and satisfying. Man has not attained the same agreement for what can be called God phenomena, yet I accept the abstract and intellectual idea of God for three reasons:

First, in the total history of man, there has been an impressive amount of general agreement about the existence of "God." This agreement is not so logically precise as the agreements about electrons; but far, far more people believe and have believed in God than believe or have ever believed in electrons.

Second, I know I cannot think through the realm of religious experience as satisfactorily as I can through less important problems. But the nuclear physicist today has only incomplete and contradictory theories. Yet the theories work pretty well and represent the best knowledge we have on the subject.

Third, I accept two sets of ideas of God—the everyday concept of an emotional and intuitive God, and the intellectual concept of an abstract God—for the very good reason that I find both of them personally satisfying. It does not at all worry me that these are two rather different sets of ideas. Scientists think of electrons as being both (or either) particles and waves; if an electron can be two wholly inconsistent things, it is a little narrow to expect so much less of God.

Can a scientist believe the Bible? I think that God has revealed Himself to many at many times and in many places. Indeed, He continuously reveals Himself to man today: every new discovery of science is a further "revelation" of the order which God has built into His universe.

I believe that the Bible is the purest revelation we have of the nature and goodness of God. It seems to me inevitable that the human record of divine truth should exhibit a little human frailty along with much divine truth. It seems to me quite unnecessary to be disturbed over minor eccentricities in the record. The reports of miraculous happenings are to me understandable as poetic exaggeration, or as ancient interpretations of events which we would not consider miraculous today.

Seal Islands—Treasure Islands

Edison Marshall

[*July 1943*]

On JUNE 29, 1786, while cruising in the fogbound void of Bering Sea, a Russian navigator named Gerasim Pribilof heard a most peculiar sound. That same sound, when I heard it 141 years later, seemed to me like the full-throated roar of a crowded stadium when the home team makes a touchdown.

The hardy captain set sail toward the uproar. After an hour or more he discovered, through rifts in the fog, four islands. Two of them were no more than big rocks. The ear-blasting noise was caused by a herd of two million fur seals blackening the shores and roaring, coughing and bleating all at once.

Loading his ship with skins, Pribilof sailed to Siberia and sold his catch to Chinese mandarins for what even today would be a fancy price. But when his agent returned for another load in October, the islands were silent as a tomb, the beaches empty and desolate.

The bold captain tried again the following summer. Again the seas were black with swimming mother seals, long reaches of the beach were a solid mass of fighting bull seals, the sand dunes were crawling with young bachelor seals, and the wild wheat was alive with idle bull seals that hadn't been able to snaffle any mates and were hanging about the harems in the hope of achieving that very thing. All were yelping and bellowing as noisily as before.

The Pribilof Islands have made history ever since. When Secretary of State Seward in 1866 wished to persuade a penny-pinching Congress to buy Alaska from the Russians, the argument that clinched the deal was its value as the breeding ground of the fur seals, yielding then about 100,000 skins a year. Except for this treasure trove the historic deal would have fallen through.

At first we wasted this treasure in scandalous fashion. Almost free slaughter was permitted until the herd was three-fourths killed. Then to maintain the yield we permitted sealers to lie off the islands and kill the matkas (mother seals) as they came out to fish. By this practice for every skin three lives were taken—the mother, her unborn pup, and her nursling pup left on shore to starve. When the herd was finally reduced to a paltry 150,000 and the beaches were littered with the wasted bodies of baby seals, our government took bold steps: prohibited pelagic sealing and prescribed the number of surplus males that could be killed each season. The herd increased to nearly two million again.

Naturally, other nations coveted this treasure of glossy fur. During Theodore Roosevelt's Presidency, Japanese poachers landed on the beaches and were unceremoniously shot by U. S. guards. Since then our Coast Guard vessels have patrolled the foggy, roaring coasts.

What interests me most about these fabulous islands is not the 50,000 prime skins that our Department of Fisheries harvests every year, soft and beautiful and still an aristocrat among furs, but the social order of the seals themselves, developed a million years before the first human being spread a sail in the Smoky Seas.

The fur seal is not to be confused with the sea lion that performs in circuses, or with the hair seal found off Newfoundland. He is distantly related to the bear, and he moves like one. Unlike any other seal, he can run on land nearly as fast as a man. The pups are not born swimmers; they must learn the hard way and many of them drown in the attempt. But the fur seals become the most beautiful and versatile of swimmers, and in speed are in a class with porpoises.

Along in May, when the wild wheat begins to sprout on the

Pribilofs, and the lichens drip with the spring rains, the bull seals haul themselves up on the naked beaches by the hundred thousand. They weigh five or six hundred pounds apiece, and are fat from good fishing in the seas of all the world. It is good that they are, because many busy months will pass before they go again to sea, or even taste food or drink.

At once there begins the biggest free-for-all fight in the whole animal kingdom. The giant bulls tear into one another, each to hold a certain little area of beach that has taken his fancy. Before long the best bulls have established their claims, but only by right of fang and flipper; and if they relax their guard for one minute even in the dead of night, the homeless bulls waiting in the grass will seize their homesteads.

Yet the bulls do not usurp the entire beach. By an incredible arrangement among themselves, certain strips are left vacant to provide safe passage for young male seals—as yet too young and weak to seize and control harems—between their interior playgrounds and the sea.

In June comes the bulk of the herd, a million or so females and a swarm of young bachelors, or holluschickie. The latter go up the aisles to the sand dunes and the grass, there to romp and loaf the summer through, with occasional trips to sea after belly cargoes of fish. But the poor little cows, scarcely a fifth the weight of the massive bulls, are in for trouble. The courtship that follows makes the famous visit of the Sabine women to Rome seem a Sunday-school picnic.

The bulls rush down to the surf and seize the approaching matkas by the scruffs of their necks and drag them to the harem grounds. Often two or three bulls make a rush for the same cow, and how she avoids being torn to pieces in the brawl that follows was never clear to me. Every bull is determined to get as many cows as he possibly can, but he pays for his greed throughout a busy summer. His wives are utterly amoral, calmly accepting nature's mandate that to the victor belong the spoils. The sight of an old bull endlessly rounding up his harem, roaring defiance at would-be wife thieves, torn and bleeding from wounds, without food or drink or rest for weeks on end, makes one understand why polygamy is not widely adopted by humans.

The cows are heavy with young when they arrive at the islands, and in a few days they drop their pups. Almost immediately the new mothers are again impregnated, at which fact many a medical man has expressed disbelief. In no other mammal can pregnancy occur during the first few weeks of lactation. In other creatures that bear young every year, the gestation period is nine months or less, leaving an interval for nature to prepare the womb for another inmate and for the baby to get a good start. In the fur seal, the gestation period is ordinarily just under a full year. The explanation of this mystery is that the matka has a double womb and uses one side of it at a time.

The old bull understands that his wives must leave him every few days to go forth to sea, catch fish and manufacture milk for their babies. Thus thousands of females are either going to sea or hauling themselves out every moment of the day. And since by the middle of July there are some hundreds of thousands of pups crawling about the beaches, or sleeping in the pale sunlight, or learning to swim in the combers, how can any mother find her own child?

I don't know how she does it, but she does. She seems to come straight toward him, in tremendous haste and flurry, knocking aside any neighbor children in her way. Sometimes a little waif tries to snitch a dinner as she goes by, but she will have none of him.

Meanwhile the young bachelors are passing by the hundreds through the aisles left for them. When they are not out fishing they assemble in droves in the grass, sometimes climbing the sand dunes with apparently no motive other than the fun of shuffling down them. It is these bachelors that furnish ladies their sealskin coats. Sealers come to drive them to the killing grounds, to club and skin them, and because they have never learned to fear men, they do not try to escape.

The bachelors are careful to avoid the harems. Not so some of the mature but idle bulls that lurk at the edge of the beaches. Occasionally one of these goes berserk and charges the rookeries in a frantic effort to steal a wife. Sometimes he succeeds, though often an outraged husband tears into him, bites and pummels him, and then with incredible strength hurls him out of his harem into the private grounds of a neighbor bull. There he is again attacked, then knocked about from harem to harem, in what appears an outburst of moral indignation on the part of all the settled husbands, until he is torn to pieces.

However, the greater number of the idle bulls keep their skins, and near summer's end they have their inning—truly one of the greatest marvels in the whole marvelous life story of the seals. Up out of the sea come the virgin females, a hundred thousand or more. By now the harem masters are exhausted, and these sleek and sprightly maidens fall easy victims to the waiting "wolves."

The latecomers drop their pups the following summer at the same time as the bulk of the cows, although they have carried them only nine months instead of nearly twelve. Why should a mother's first baby seal have a shorter gestation period than the second? Apparently the fetus develops faster when the mother is not nursing other young; and it seems a thrilling instance of nature's care for her species—staggering the breeding season so that the young may have fit fathers.

Soon after this, in September, the great outbound migration begins. The yearlings have by now learned to swim. With their mothers bearing unborn pups, and with swarms of young bachelors, they take off from the beaches and head southward through the Aleutian Islands into the trackless immensity of the Pacific. The old bulls linger a while, heaven knows why except that they seem too tired to move, and then they too waddle down to the surf and disappear. The Aleut hunters retire to their smoky huts, the blue foxes feed on the carcasses of the slain, and the wind shrills across forsaken beaches. But the rocks, by their glasslike smoothness, bespeak the herds assembling here for the past million years. As surely as the green of spring they will come again.

ε≫ Discussing a politician, one man observed, "I don't think they could put him in a mental hospital. On the other hand, if he were already in, I don't believe they'd let him out."

Charles van Kriedt, quoted by Herb Caen in San Francisco *Chronicle*

Hippie or Schoolgirl—
Which Was "the Real Linda"?

J. Anthony Lukas

[December 1967]

T HE windows of Dr. Irving
Sklar's reception room at 2 Fifth Avenue, New York City, look
out across Washington Square—from it a patient can watch
pigeons circling Stanford White's dignified Washington Arch,
children playing hopscotch on the square's wide walkways. Dr.
Sklar has long been the family dentist of the Irving Fitzpatricks, who live in a 30-room home a mile from the Greenwich, Conn., Country Club, and for them "the Village" has
always been the Henry James scene they saw out his windows.
But for their 18-year-old-daughter, Linda—at least in the last
ten weeks of her life—the Village was a different scene whose
ingredients included crash pads, acid trips, freaking out, witches
and warlocks.

If the Fitzpatricks' knowledge of the Village stopped at
Washington Square, their knowledge of their daughter stopped
at the unsettling but familiar image of a young, talented girl
overly impatient to taste the joys of life. Reality in both cases
went far beyond. In mid-October, a week after Linda's murder,
the Fitzpatricks were still unable to believe what their daughter
had gone through in her last days.

Which was "the real Linda"—the Linda of Greenwich,
Conn., or the Linda of Greenwich Village? As the New York

Times investigated, it found her a mixture so tangled that Linda herself probably did not know.

The forces at work on young people like Linda are the source of puzzlement for many other parents, and of studies by social workers and psychologists. Until a few months ago, Linda—or "Fitzpoo," as she was known to family and friends—seemed a happy product of wealthy American suburbia. "Linda is a well-rounded, fine, healthy girl," her mother, a well-groomed woman in a high-collared chocolate-brown dress, said during the three-hour *Times* interview in which she often used the present tense in talking of her daughter.

Born in Greenwich, Linda attended Greenwich Country Day School, where she excelled in field hockey, swimming and riding. She went on to Oldfields, a four-year college-preparatory school in Glencoe, Md. A blonde tending to pudginess, she never quite matched the striking good looks of her mother or of her elder sister, Cindy. At country-club dances she often sat in the corner and talked with one of her half brothers; but, apparently more interested in sports and painting than dancing, she never seemed to mind very much.

Last June Linda returned from Oldfields and, after several weeks in Greenwich, she left with the family for a month in Bermuda. "We always do things as a family," said Irving Fitzpatrick, tall, athletic-looking, a wealthy spice importer.

The family included seven children—Linda and 9-year-old Melissa (Missy) from this marriage; Perry, 32; Robert, 30; Carol, 27; and David, 25, from Fitzpatrick's previous marriage, which ended in divorce; and Cindy from Mrs. Fitzpatrick's first marriage, which also ended in divorce. But this time only Linda and Missy accompanied their parents to Bermuda, while Cindy and her husband joined them later for ten days.

As the Fitzpatricks remember it, Linda spent "a typical Bermuda vacation"—swimming in the ocean; beach parties; hours of painting; occasional shopping expeditions to town.

On July 31 the family returned to Greenwich, where Linda spent most of August. Again, the family insists she was "the girl we knew and loved." They say she spent most of her time painting in the studio in the back of the house. But she found plenty of time for swimming with friends in the large robin's-egg-blue pool. If Linda went to New York during August, it was "just a quick trip in and out—just for the day."

Linda's friends in the Village have a different story of her summer.

"Linda told me she took LSD and smoked grass [marijuana] many times during her stay in Bermuda," recalled Susan Robinson, a small, shy hippie who ran away last May from her home on Cape Cod, Mass. "She talked a lot about a fellow who gave her a capsule of acid [LSD] down there and how she was going to send him one."

The two-room apartment of Susan and her husband, David, served last summer as a "crash pad"—a place where homeless hippies could spend the night. "Linda first showed up one evening early in August with a guy named Pigeon," Susan said. "She'd just bought Pigeon some acid. She stayed maybe a couple of hours and then took off.

"A few nights later she came back with a kid from Boston. She turned him on, too [gave him some LSD]. She was always doing that. She'd come into the city on weekends with $30 or $40 and would buy acid for people who needed some."

David Robinson, a gentle, black-bearded young man who worked in a brassiere factory, recalled how Linda turned him on, on August 22. "We went to this guy who sold us three capsules for $10 apiece," he said. "She put one away to send to the guy in Bermuda, gave me one and took one herself. We were out in Tompkins Park and we dropped it [swallowed it] right there. Around midnight we walked over to Cooper Union Square where we had a very good discussion with a drunk. By then we were really flying. She was very, very groovy. At 8 a.m. Linda took the subway up to Grand Central and got on the train to Greenwich. She must still have been flying when she got home."

That weekend Mrs. Fitzpatrick was getting Linda ready for school. "We bought her almost an entire new wardrobe," she recalled, "and Linda even agreed to get her hair cut."

For months Fitzpatrick had complained about Linda's hair, which flowed down over her shoulders, but Linda didn't want to change it. Then at the end of August she agreed. "We went to Saks Fifth Avenue and the hairdresser gave her a blunt cut, short and full. She looked so cute and smart. Hardly a hippie thing to do."

The first day of school was only 11 days off when Linda went to New York on September 1. Next day she told her mother she didn't want to go back to Oldfields—she wanted to live and paint in the Village. "We couldn't have been more surprised," Mrs. Fitzpatrick said.

"We talked about it all through the weekend," Fitzpatrick added. "Finally, on Sunday night, we gave her our reluctant permission, though not our approval."

"After all," her mother said, "Linda's whole life was art. She had a burning desire to be something in the art world. I knew how she felt. I wanted to be a dancer or an artist when I was young, too.

"Linda told us that she was going to live at the Village Plaza, a very nice hotel on Washington Place, near the university. 'I'll be perfectly safe, Mother,' she kept saying. 'It's a perfectly nice place, with a doorman.' She said she'd be rooming with a girl named Paula Bush, a 22-year-old receptionist from a good family. That made us feel a lot better."

Linda left for New York the next morning. The family never saw her alive again.

The Village Plaza has no doorman. The stooped desk clerk said, "Sure, I remember Linda." And riffling through a pile of thumb-marked cards, he came up with one that had Linda's name inked at the top in neat schoolgirl penmanship. Below it in pencil was written: "Paul Bush. Bob Brumberger."

"Yeh," the clerk said. "She moved in here on September 4, Labor Day, with these two hippie guys. They had Room 504. She paid the full month's rent—$120—in advance. Of course she had lots of other men up there all the time. Anybody off the street—the dirtiest, bearded hippies she could find.

"I kept telling her she hadn't ought to act like that. She didn't pay me any attention, but she never answered back real snappy like some of the other girls. She had something, I don't know—class. The day she checked out—oh, about September 20—she

said, 'I guess I caused you a lot of trouble,' and I said, 'Oh, it wasn't any trouble, really.' You want to see the room?"

The elevator was out of order. The stairs were dark and narrow, heavy with the sweet reek of marijuana. A knock, and the door to 504 swung open. A bearded young man took his place again on the swaybacked double bed that filled half the room. He and three girls were plucking chocolates out of a box. On the mirror above the dresser with one drawer missing was scrawled, "Tea Heads Forever" [a tea head is a marijuana smoker], and in lighter pencil, "War Is Hell." Red plastic flowers hung from an overhead light fixture.

"Would you like to see Linda's room?" her mother asked. On the third floor Mrs. Fitzpatrick opened the red curtains in the large room. "Red and white are Linda's favorite colors," Mrs. Fitzpatrick said, taking in the red-and-white-striped wallpaper, the twin beds with red bedspreads, the red pillow with white lettering, "Decisions, Decisions, Decisions."

On the shelves, between a ceramic collie and a glass Bambi, were Edith Hamilton's *The Greek Way* and Agatha Christie's *Murder at Hazelmoor*. Nearby was a stack of records. In the bright bathroom hung ribbons from the Oldfields Horse Show and the Greenwich Riding Association Show. "As you can see, she was such a nice, outgoing, happy girl," her mother said. "If anything's changed, it's changed awfully fast."

The Fitzpatricks said they had been reassured about Linda's life in the Village because she said she had a job making posters for a company called Poster Bazaar at $80 a week.

The records show Linda worked for $2 an hour selling dresses at a shop called Fred Leighton's Mexican Imports, Ltd. On the third day she was discharged. "She was always coming in late," a salesgirl said.

David Robinson said Linda supported herself from then on by panhandling on Washington Square. "She was pretty good at it," he said. "She always got enough to eat." Yet "she had a thing about money. Once she told me she wanted to get a job with Hallmark cards drawing those little cartoons. She said she'd make $40,000 a year, rent a big apartment on the Upper East Side and then invite all her hippie friends up there."

"Linda was very shy," her mother said. "When a boy got interested in her, she'd almost always lose interest in him. She got a proposal in August from a very nice boy from Arizona. She told me, 'I like him, but he's just too anxious.' The boy sent flowers for the funeral. That was thoughtful."

The Robinsons and her other friends in the Village said there were always men in Linda's life there: first Pigeon, then the boy from Boston, then Paul Bush, who carried a live lizard named Lyndon on a string around his neck. Bush, now in San Francisco, was interviewed by telephone.

"I met Linda at the Robinsons' about August 18—a few days after I got to town," he recalls. "We wandered around together. She said her parents bugged her, always hollered at her. So I said I'd get a pad with her and Brumberger, this kid from New Jersey.

"She said she'd tell her parents she was living with a girl named Paula Bush. That was okay with me. I only stayed a week anyway, and Brumberger even less. Then she brought in some other guy—tall, with long hair and a beard."

This may have been Ed, a tall hippie the Robinsons saw with Linda several times in mid-September. Later came James L. (Groovy) Hutchinson, the man with whom—in less than a month—she would be killed.

Toward the end of September, Susan Robinson says, Linda told her she feared she was pregnant. "She was very worried about the effect of LSD on the baby, and since I was pregnant too we talked about it for quite a while."

"I don't believe Linda really had anything to do with the hippies," her father said. "I remember during August we were in this room watching a CBS special about the San Francisco hippies. I expressed my abhorrence for the whole thing, and her comments were much like mine. I don't believe she was attracted to them."

Her friends say Linda was fascinated by the San Francisco scene. Susan recalls that suddenly on October 1 Linda turned up at her pad and said she had been to Haight-Ashbury. "She said she stayed out there only two days and that it was a really bad scene; that everybody was on speed [a powerful drug called methedrine]. She said she got out and drove back, with two warlocks [male witches] she met out there. They could snap their fingers and make light bulbs pop.

"This didn't surprise me," Susan said. "Linda told me several times she was a witch. She discovered this one day sitting on a beach when she wished she had some money, and three dollar bills floated down from heaven."

One of Linda's self-styled warlock friends, who calls himself Pepsi, is in his late 20s, with long, sandy hair, a scruffy beard, heavily tattooed forearms, wire-rim glasses and high suede boots. "My buddy and I ran into Linda in a club in Indianapolis called the Glory Hole," Pepsi said. "You could see right away she was a real meth monster [methedrine user]. We were two days driving back. We got in on October 1, and she put up with me and my buddy in this pad on Avenue B. She was supposed to keep it clean, but all she ever did all day was sit around. She had this real weird imagination, but she was like talking in smaller and smaller circles. She was supposed to be this great artist, but it was just teeny-bopper stuff.

"It sounds like I'm knocking her. I'm not. She was a good kid, if she hadn't been so freaked out on meth. She had a lot of, what do you call it—potential. Sometimes she was a lot of fun to be with. We went out on the Staten Island Ferry one day at dawn, and surfing once on Long Island."

Pepsi saw Linda at 10 p.m. on October 8 standing in front of the Cave on Avenue A with Groovy Hutchinson. She said she'd taken a grain and a half of speed and was "high." Three hours later she and Groovy were dead—their nude bodies stretched out on a boiler-room floor, their heads shattered by bricks. The police charged two men with the murders and were continuing their investigation.

"It's too late for the whole thing to do *us* much good," her brother, Perry, said after he had been told of her life in the Village. "But maybe somebody else can learn something from it."

꙯ The brook would lose its song if we removed the rocks.

Parts Pups

89

The Violent Sun

Herbert Friedman

[March 1966]

A T 2:37 P.M. on November 12, 1960, astronomers in Michigan detected a brilliant explosion on the face of the sun. Six hours later, a gigantic cloud of solar hydrogen gas—ten million miles across and still trailing halfway back to the sun, 93 million miles away—collided with earth at a speed of 4000 miles a second.

Though inaudible and invisible, the collision started a violent chain of disturbances on and around the earth, an electrical and magnetic storm of mammoth proportions. Compass needles wavered erratically. For hours all long-distance radio communications were blacked out. Teletypes printed gibberish. Overhead, sheets of flaming-red northern lights flashed in the night sky, bright enough to be seen through overcast and clouds. In farmhouses, electric lights flickered as if a thunderstorm raged, yet the air and sky were clear and silent.

For more than a week such chaotic conditions continued. They were clearly the results of our sun on a rampage. Yet, let me assure you, such a storm amounts to no more than a tiny ripple in the usual steady flow of solar energy.

The sun's power staggers the imagination. In one *second* this star of ours (and the sun is, after all, a star—just one of an estimated *100 billion* in the Milky Way) radiates more energy than man has used since the beginning of civilization! It delivers to us in a few days as much heat and light as would be produced by burning the earth's entire oil and coal reserves, and all the wood of its forests. Yet what earth receives is only one half of one billionth of the sun's total radiant energy!

What makes the sun shine so brilliantly? The now accepted answer: atomic energy. The nuclei, or cores, of hydrogen atoms collide, and unite—to form helium nuclei. As the union is accomplished, bursts of energy are given off.

This nuclear fusion goes on at, atomically speaking, a slow pace. The sun may be considered as a very slow-burning hydrogen bomb. Only because it is so large is its total production of energy so enormous. *Pound for pound,* the sun actually produces less energy than the human body—two calories per pound daily, while the average human body generates about ten.

Man's study of the sun was long seriously hampered by the earth's murky, shimmering atmosphere, which distorts light beams and blots out the sun's X rays as well as much of its ultraviolet and infrared radiation. But in 1946 rockets became available to carry telescopes and spectrographs above the atmosphere. (I currently direct the solar rocket astronomy program at the U. S. Naval Research Laboratory in Washington, D.C.) Now satellites point instruments steadily at the sun. Huge radar transmitters bounce beams off the swollen outer atmosphere of the sun to probe its structure and movement. Meanwhile, with the optical spectroscope, we can analyze light arriving from 93 million miles away and tell what the sun is made of, just as accurately as if we had a sample in the laboratory.

Triangulating with other celestial objects, astronomers have gauged the size of the sun accurately. It has a diameter of 864,000 miles—compared with earth's 8000. It could hold 1,300,000 earths!

The spectrum shows that the sun consists principally of hydrogen. Hydrogen atoms are roughly ten times as abundant there as helium, 1000 times as abundant as carbon, nitrogen or oxygen, which are so common on earth. Except for this overabundance of hydrogen and helium, the chemical composition of the solar atmosphere is much the same as that of earth's crust.

Although the density at its center must be about 11.4 times that of lead, the sun remains entirely gaseous. That is, the atoms are free to move about, unlike those in a solid, which are fixed in a regular pattern. Spots on the sun show us that it rotates from east to west, and in a very peculiar way: different parts spin at various speeds. A spot close to the equator, for example, completes a rotation in 25 days; the polar zone may take 34 days. Most of the changing features observed on the surface of the sun must be related in some way to this contortion.

When astronomers examine the sun with a solar telescope, its edge appears sharp, as if it marked a definite surface. This apparent surface is in fact a transparent, highly luminous layer of gas about 200 miles thick, called the photosphere. From it comes most of the light we get. Outside lie two other layers—a region of flamelike outbursts of gas, called the chromosphere, and an almost endless outer atmosphere called the corona.

The surface temperature is about 5700° C. But we have good reason to believe that at the sun's center, close to half a million miles deep, pressure reaches 100 billion atmospheres, and to produce such pressure, gas must be heated to about 16,000,000°. A pinhead of material at that temperature would emit enough heat to kill a man 100 miles away.

In this nuclear furnace most of the fantastically hot, dense gas is invisible, since nearly all its radiation is X rays—produced by nuclear reactions and the collisions of fast-racing nuclei and electrons. The path of an X ray as it escapes from the core resembles the zigzagging track of the steel ball in a pinball machine. Even though the rays travel at the speed of light, the devious trip to the sun's surface takes about 20,000 years. Meanwhile, each time an X ray is deflected, the frequency of its vibration is reduced slightly and its wavelength is increased. In time, the X rays turn into ultraviolet and visible light.

Most of what we know of the sun's outer atmosphere comes from studies of solar eclipses. During an eclipse in 1842, astronomers noted the very faint outer atmosphere of the sun. As the moon blocked out the brilliant disc, a pearly-white corona with delicate streams and curved arches stood revealed. Closer to the black edge of the moon, a reddish ring could be seen encircling the sun, giving rise to the name "chromosphere."

Pictures of the rim show thousands of tongues of gas, called spicules, springing fountainlike above the sun's surface. They surge up and fall back in five to ten minutes, rising as high as 6000 miles. At any instant as many as 100,000 spicules may be in action. Also, huge streamers of bright gas, called prominences, often loop as high as 100,000 miles into the corona, then dip back as much as half a million miles away.

But these dramatic activities of a quiet sun pale into insignificance beside the explosive phenomenon known as a solar flare. A large flare can erupt in an hour's time with the force of a billion hydrogen bombs. It was such a flare that disrupted communications in November 1960.

Nevertheless, the sun is a very ordinary star—a yellow dwarf, midway between the largest and the smallest and between the hottest blue stars and the coolest red stars. To earth-based observers, it is brighter than any other star—though Rigel, for example, is 15,000 times more luminous. And 36 million suns could be fitted into Antares, a red supergiant!

In time, the sun's core will deplete its hydrogen: some calculations indicate the proportion has decreased from two thirds to one third in the past five billion years. With the core spent, the zone of thermonuclear reaction will spread out closer to the surface where unused hydrogen still exists. As this happens, the tremendous nuclear heat now at the core will also move outward, forcing the sun to expand. The sun will then become a giant red star like Antares. It will blow up to a monstrous ball of extremely rarefied, red-hot gas, large enough to engulf the four nearest planets—Mercury, Venus, Earth and Mars.

When will the sun reach this stage? No cause for immediate concern—it may take another five billion years!

Finally, when all its hydrogen has been converted to helium, the sun will cool and shrink. Ultimately it will become a white dwarf, no bigger than the earth but weighing several tons per cubic inch.

Meanwhile, the sun is our bridge to the stars—the only star whose surface and atmosphere we can study in fine detail.

꒰꒱ The "amen!" of nature is always a flower.   Oliver Wendell Holmes

The Secret Life of Walter Mitty

James Thurber

[*January 1943*]

"WE'RE going through!" the commander's voice was like thin ice breaking. He pulled his heavily braided cap down rakishly over one cold gray eye. "Throw on the power lights! Rev her up to 8500! We're going through!" The pounding of the cylinders increased: ta-pocketa-pocketa-*pocketa-pocketa.* The commander stared at the ice forming on the pilot window, then walked over and twisted a row of complicated dials. "Switch on No. 8 auxiliary!" he shouted. The crew, bending to their various tasks in the huge eight-engined Navy hydroplane, looked at one another and grinned. "The Old Man'll get us through," they said. "The Old Man ain't afraid of hell!" . . .

"Not so fast! You're driving too fast!" said Mrs. Mitty. "What are you driving so fast for?" "Hmmm?" said Walter Mitty. He looked at his wife in the seat beside him with shocked astonishment. She seemed grossly unfamiliar, like a strange woman who had yelled at him in a crowd. "You were up to 55," she said.

Walter Mitty drove toward Waterbury in silence, the roaring of the Navy SN202 through the worst storm in 20 years fading in the remote, intimate airways of his mind. He stopped the car in front of the building where his wife went to have her hair done. "Remember to get those overshoes while I'm having my hair done," she said. "You're not a young man any longer." He raced the engine a little. "Why don't you wear your gloves?" Mitty hastily pulled on his gloves. He drove past the hospital on his way to the parking lot.

. . . "It's the millionaire banker, Wellington McMillan," said the pretty nurse. "Yes?" said Walter Mitty, removing his gloves slowly. "Who has the case?" "Dr. Renshaw and Dr. Benbow, but there are two specialists here, Dr. Remington from New York and Dr. Pritchard-Mitford from London. He flew over." A door opened and Dr. Renshaw came out, distraught and haggard. "Hello, Mitty," he said. "We're having the devil's own time with McMillan, the millionaire banker and close personal friend of Roosevelt. Obstreosis of the ductal tract. Tertiary. Wish you'd take a look at him." "Glad to," said Mitty.

In the operating room there were whispered introductions: "I've read your book on streptothricosis," said Pritchard-Mitford, shaking hands. "A brilliant performance, sir." "Thank you," said Walter Mitty. "Didn't know you were in the States, Mitty," grumbled Remington. "Coals to Newcastle, bringing Mitford and me here for a tertiary." "Very kind," said Mitty. A huge, complicated machine connected to the operating table began to go pocketa-pocketa-pocketa. "The new anesthetizer is giving way!" shouted an intern. "No one in the East knows how to fix it!"

"Quiet, man!" said Mitty in a low, cool voice. He sprang to the machine, which was now going pocketa-pocketa-*queep*. He began fingering delicately a row of glistening dials. "Give me a fountain pen!" he snapped. Someone handed him a fountain pen. He pulled a faulty piston out of the machine and inserted the pen in its place. "That will hold for ten minutes," he said. "Get on with the operation." A nurse hurried over and whispered to Renshaw. Mitty saw the man turn pale. "Coreopsis has set in," said Renshaw nervously. "If you would take over, Mitty?" Mitty looked at him, at the grave, uncertain faces of the two great specialists. "If you wish," he said. They slipped a white gown on him; he adjusted a mask and drew on thin gloves; nurses handed him shining . . .

"Back it up, Mac! Look out for that Buick!" Walter Mitty jammed on the brakes. "Wrong lane, Mac," said the parking-lot attendant, looking at Mitty closely. "Gee. Yeh," muttered Mitty. "Leave her sit there," said the attendant. "I'll put her away." The attendant vaulted into the car, backed it up with insolent skill, and put it where it belonged.

They're so damned cocky, thought Walter Mitty, walking along Main Street; they think they know everything. He kicked at the slush on the sidewalk. "Overshoes," he said to himself, and he began looking for a shoe store.

When he came out into the street again, with the overshoes in a box under his arm, Walter Mitty began to wonder what the other thing was his wife had told him to get. He hated these weekly trips to town—he was always getting something wrong. Kleenex, he thought, Squibb's, razor blades? No. Toothpaste, toothbrush, bicarbonate, carborundum, initiative and referendum? He gave it up. But she would remember. "Where's the what's-its-name?" she would ask. "Don't tell me you forgot the what's-its-name." A newsboy went by shouting something about the Waterbury trial.

. . . "Perhaps this will refresh your memory." The District Attorney thrust a heavy automatic at the quiet figure on the witness stand. "Have you ever seen this before?" Walter Mitty took the gun and examined it expertly. "This is my Webley-Vickers 50.80," he said calmly. An excited buzz ran around the courtroom. The Judge rapped for order. "You are a crack shot with any sort of firearms, I believe?" said the District Attorney, insinuatingly.

"Objection!" shouted Mitty's attorney. "We have shown that the defendant could not have fired the shot. We have shown that he wore his right arm in a sling on the night of the 14th of July." Walter Mitty raised his hand briefly and the bickering attorneys were stilled. "With any known make of gun," he said evenly, "I could have killed Gregory Fitzhurst at 300 feet *with my left hand.*" Pandemonium broke loose in the courtroom. A woman's scream rose above the bedlam, and suddenly a lovely, dark-haired girl was in Walter Mitty's arms. The District Attorney struck at her savagely. Without rising, Mitty let the man have it on the point of the chin. "You miserable cur!" . . .

"Puppy biscuit," said Walter Mitty. The buildings of Waterbury rose up out of the misty courtroom and surrounded him again. A woman who was passing laughed. "He said 'puppy biscuit,'" she said to her companion. Walter Mitty hurried on. He went into an A&P. "I want some biscuit for small, young dogs," he said to the clerk. "Any special brand, sir?" The greatest pistol shot in the world thought a moment. "It says 'Puppies Bark for It' on the box," said Walter Mitty.

His wife would be through at the hairdresser's soon. She would want him to be waiting for her as usual in the hotel lobby. He found a big leather chair facing a window, and he put the overshoes and the puppy biscuit on the floor beside it. He picked up an old copy of *Liberty* and sank down into the chair. "Can Germany Conquer Through the Air?" Walter Mitty looked at the pictures of bombing planes and ruined streets.

. . . "The cannonading has got the wind up in young Raleigh, sir," said the sergeant. Captain Mitty looked up at him through tousled hair. "Get him to bed," he said wearily, "I'll fly alone." "But you can't, sir," said the sergeant anxiously. "It takes two men to handle that bomber, and Von Richtman's circus is between here and Saulier." "Somebody's got to get that ammunition dump," said Mitty. "I'm going over. Spot of brandy?" He poured a drink for the sergeant and one for himself. There was a rending explosion and splinters flew through the room. "A bit of a near thing," said Captain Mitty carelessly. "The box barrage is closing in," said the sergeant. "We only live once, sergeant," said Mitty, with his faint, fleeting smile. "Or do we?" He poured another brandy, tossed it off, then stood up and strapped on his Webley-Vickers automatic. "It's 40 kilometers through hell, sir," said the sergeant. Mitty finished one last brandy. "After all," he said softly, "what isn't?" The rat-tat-tatting of machine guns increased and from somewhere came the menacing pocketa-pocketa-pocketa of the new flame-throwers. Walter Mitty walked to the door of the dugout humming *Auprès de ma blonde*. He turned and waved to the sergeant. "Cheerio!" he said. . . .

Something struck his shoulder. "I've been looking all over this hotel for you," said Mrs. Mitty. "Why do you have to hide in this old chair? How did you expect me to find you?" "Things close in," said Walter Mitty vaguely. "What?" Mrs. Mitty said. "Did you get the what's-its-name? The puppy biscuit? What's in that box?" "Overshoes," said Mitty. "Couldn't you have put them on in the store?" "I was thinking," said Walter Mitty. "Does it ever occur to you that I am sometimes thinking?" She looked at him. "I'm going to take your temperature when I get you home," she said.

They went out through the revolving doors that made a faintly derisive whistling sound when you pushed them. At the corner drugstore she said, "Wait here for me. I forgot something. I won't be a minute." She was more than a minute. Walter Mitty lighted a cigarette. It began to rain. He stood up against the wall of the drugstore, smoking. . . .

He put his shoulders back and his heels together. "To hell with the handkerchief," said Walter Mitty scornfully. He took one last drag on his cigarette and snapped it away. Then, with that faint, fleeting smile playing about his lips, he faced the firing squad: erect and motionless, proud and disdainful, Walter Mitty, the Undefeated, inscrutable to the last.

❧ As a personnel interviewer, I read many employment applications in a day. Often the answers to form questions are quite similar. Recently, however, an applicant came up with an unusual twist—and the best answer yet—in response to the request, "Describe yourself in 25 words or less."

He wrote simply: "Concise."   R.S.

I Am Fifty—
And It Doesn't Hurt

Dorothy Canfield Fisher

[*May 1929*]

Do you remember the little girl who asked if it didn't feel queer for a few days after you grew up? I think of her when people ask me how I feel about being middle-aged. The answer is, "You don't feel anything sensational. You just go on living."

Of course I realize that I am no exception to the laws which make all women around 50 very different from what they were at 20. To take first the most obvious change, and one that has always provided a theme for melancholy poems—the inexorable passing of the smooth-skinned, bright-haired radiance of youth. Why have I been so little troubled by this change?

The war taught me a lesson on that point. I spent much time in France, in contact with the direst needs. We, who were doing what we could to help, desperately needed reinforcements. To be of any use, our reinforcements must be capable of endurance, perseverance, self-forgetfulness. We came to distrust bright eyes and gleaming young hair. These pretty signs of physical youth became associated with childishness, fickleness, lack of conscience. We could not always provide the "something exciting" without which they would not stick at a long, tiresome job. Would not? Apparently could not. For dependability is a quality almost impossible to youth, but natural to the middle-aged taste.

Remembering the heartfelt liking we had in our war work for the plain, middle-aged faces of the women who could be counted on to stick it out, no matter what came, I do not, now that I am a plain, middle-aged woman, feel desolately that the world has no more welcome for me.

A young poet would, of course, be horrified at my resigned satisfaction. But bring to mind the fact that 99.5 percent of good lyric poetry always has been written by young people who are brilliantly improvising on a subject they know nothing about.

Being middle-aged is a nice change from being young. Honestly, I mean it. One of the traits of human nature about which there is unanimity of opinion is its love for change. When I was a young lady—that is what we *were* 30 years ago—I was anything but superior to the pleasures of young ladyhood. I adored opening the long pasteboard box which meant a bouquet from an admirer. I loved maple-nut sundaes to distraction, and there never was a girl, I am sure, who more heartily delighted in West Point hops. But suppose that by some miracle I should now look young again, and should be invited to dance once a week for the rest of this session at West Point, as I used to do. I'd rush into it as enthusiastically as I should carry out a sentence to play ing for an hour a day.

I still quite naturally enjoy playing tennis, riding horseback, skating and mountain climbing. It is true I don't engage in these sports as ferociously as I did at 20, and for a good reason. I don't need to, or care to. At 20 I was like nearly everybody else of that age, frightfully uncertain—half of the time at least—of deserving to be in the world at all, and frightfully anxious to prove my worth to myself in the only way youth knows—by beating somebody else at something.

Here is one of the pleasures of middle age of which nobody breathes a word to you beforehand: the deliciousness of outgrowing that neuralgia of youthful pain at being surpassed at anything! This change is not due to greater magnanimity—rather to the fact that moderately successful, healthy-minded older people have found an excuse for existence, in some job that the world seems to want done, which after a fashion they seem competent to do.

My gentle old uncle, when the cat had settled down to sleep in his favorite soft chair, used always to leave her there and sit upon a hard chair till she woke up and went away. When we remonstrated with him, he answered, "A cat has so few pleasures compared with those open to me." I have something of the same feeling about the boy who beats me in a race on the ice. He does *so* enjoy beating somebody. And there is so much else that I can enjoy of which he doesn't dream. For one thing, I can consciously, disinterestedly relish the physical delights of the exercise, the miraculous knife-edge poise, the gliding speed, the tingling air, the beauties of the frosty trees. I enjoy these things far more than he does, or than I did at his age, freed as I am now from his single reason for being on the ice: either beating, or learning to beat, somebody else.

Understand me, I do not make the claim that I enjoy my corner of the pond *more* than that magnificent, long-legged kid out there, racing from one end of the hockey field to the other in eagle-like swoops. He is enjoying a wild, physical intoxication which gets considerably dimmed by the years. But as far as that goes, his physical intoxication is not so wild as that of a group of quite little children who, with faces of pure joy, are merely scuffling along on a slide at one end of the pond. The point is that we are all, in different ways suitable to our ages, having a glorious time, and that the young couple who swing dreamily around and around, hands clasped, are not the only ones to enjoy the ice.

I use skating, of course, as a convenient symbol for the way life is taken at different ages. Now you will note that of all those age groups on the ice, I, being the oldest, am the only one who has any notion that *everybody* is having a good time. Although the 14-year-old kid may be amused by "the kids without even any skates," he is not sorry for them, because he remembers that ages ago he used to enjoy sliding. But it is real pity he feels for the poor fish who's got tied up with a girl and has to steer her around. And probably his pity is even greater for the gray-haired woman who seems to think that cutting circles is skating. The young couple know, of course, that the hockey-playing boys who have not yet found their mates are having some sort of childish good time, but they are convinced that it must be awful to be so old as to have gray hair, with your first love far behind you.

The trouble, you see, is that they don't trust the future. Young people seldom do. They are afraid to. They are so impressed with the present that what they can't get now this instant seems lost forever.

Is it true, as people say, that youth is naturally happier than age because the one lives on hopes, the other on memories, and that while you can change hopes to suit yourself, memories persist in staying more or less the way they actually happened? Stuff and nonsense! Hope's always left, no matter what afflictions have come out of Pandora's box. It's not a question of an age limit. From cradle to grave the favorite slogan of every mother's son and daughter is always: "I know I used to be a dub, but I've learned my mistakes. Hereafter everything I tackle is going to go over big."

The fear of approaching old age? Having arrived at an age which seemed to me at 20 as forlorn as 80 does to me now, and perceiving that a change of tastes and desire has gone along with a change in age, I cannot help guessing that if I continue to yield myself naturally to the rhythm of the years, I shall find the inner timetable making as close and accurate a connection for me then as now.

&⤳ A Pittsburgh executive received this letter from a friend and former business associate:

"Would you keep an eye open for a job that might be suitable for our young David this summer? I know such jobs are hard to find nowadays, but that's all right, so is David most of the time.

"Dave is 16½, but dumb for his age. He is very strong, with a powerful right arm which comes from combing his hair in front of a mirror for hours at a time. He is a very persuasive talker, having convinced his mother that the U marks all over his report card stand for 'Unexcelled.'

"At dinner the other evening he said, 'Pass the potatoes.' His mother said, '*Please* pass the potatoes.' David said, 'I asked first.'

"What more would any prospective employer want? Don't write, Mac—telegraph." Charles F. Danver in Pittsburgh *Post-Gazette*

LIFE IN THESE UNITED STATES

An ATLANTA lawyer has a reputation for always crossing every "t" and dotting every "i." One afternoon on a crowded road another car banged into his. Immediately he jumped out and, with his Polaroid camera, made pictures from several angles. He then began dictating into his tape recorder: "This is . . . I am on the Northeast Expressway at 5:29 p.m. on Monday, July 29, 1968. My car has just been struck from the rear by a car driven by . . ." and he handed the microphone to the other driver.

"Good heavens!" she gasped. "I've hit James Bond!"

Avanelle S. McHan, *Atlanta, Ga.*

As HE walked through a dismally rundown city neighborhood, thinking of its effect on youthful character, a friend of mine was horrified to see a small boy sitting on the steps of an old apartment building calmly cutting a worm in half with the top of a tin can. Then he drew closer—and heard the child say, leaning solicitously over his victim, "There, now you have a friend." Patricia McGauley, *Worcester, Mass.*

THE WOMEN of our church had a handsome 30-inch-tall papier-mâché stork, which was used frequently for baby showers. The last time they got it out for one of these occasions, however, they couldn't use it—someone had wrung the bird's neck. Orville A. Cochran, *Sierra Vista, Ariz.*

AFTER a trip to Texas, a friend told about one view of the Lone Star State he'll never forget. South of Lubbock, toward Houston, he passed a great field knee-high in richly green clover. Grazing in the clover was the finest herd of white-faced Hereford cattle he had ever seen. And all alone in the center of the field stood the magnificent herd bull—scratching his neck on an oil derrick. Jack Webb, *La Habra, Calif.*

It was Monday afternoon and there were few shoppers in our local grocery store. I took my time sauntering down the aisles. At the vegetable counter I dug into the lettuce bin, examining each head carefully. Finally on the very bottom layer I found one that suited me. I put it in my basket and was about to move on when a masculine voice behind me said politely, "Madam, would you kindly tell me which is the *second* best head?" Mrs. Hugh McLafferty, *McAllen, Texas*

I was on a flight from St. Louis to Indianapolis. As we landed in Terre Haute for a short stop, the entire crew piled out and began a close inspection of the nose wheel. I joined them to ask what the trouble was. "Oh, no trouble at all, sir," a stewardess explained. "Just before we leave St. Louis, we chalk five numbers on this tire. The person whose number lands on the bottom in Terre Haute buys ice cream for the rest of the crew." L. O'Day, *San Diego, Calif.*

Some important papers which I kept in a loose-leaf binder had torn loose from the rings, and I decided to repair them with gummed reinforcements. Turning to my elderly maiden aunt, I asked if she knew what I had done with my reinforcers.

"Jack," she replied, "I don't think there's a drop left in the house." John T. Parks, *Galesburg, Ill.*

Shortly after the advent of the automatic washing machine, I found my brother sitting on his kitchen floor surrounded by nuts, bolts and other parts of a well-worn conventional machine. His wife was hovering, offering suggestions to her baffled handyman on how to put it together again.

As I was leaving she walked to the car with me. "I really hate to see him work so hard at this," she confessed sweetly. "But I need a new washer badly, and if he fixes this one again I'll never get it. Poor guy! I knew he'd discover it if I took some parts away, so I just *added* a few extra little things."

Several days later I dropped in to see her new automatic washer. Mrs. LeRue E. Thurston, *Orem, Utah*

When the Doctor Examines You

Warren R. Young

[February 1963]

‖T IS AN oddly shaped machine, only a few feet long, rather spongy on the surface and warm to the touch. Within its soft shell uncounted thousands of parts, many as brittle as glass or fragile as moth wings, are fitted together in the most intricate pattern known. Sturdy little pulleys and ropes of unique design move its girders and beams this way and that. Pumps and bellows spew precise amounts of liquid or vaporous chemicals through its maze of pipes and chambers. Electrical networks branching like trees carry incessant messages from a computer-like command post to the rest of the apparatus. When all of its delicately balanced parts are performing as they should, the owner of the machine rarely gives a thought to the precarious complexity upon which he so depends. The wondrous machine is the human body.

Like the prudent owners of any precision equipment, a good many people take their bodies to their physician once each year for a preventive inspection. While a 15-minute appraisal may be adequate to obtain an insurance policy or a job, a complete study of a patient, by a conscientious doctor who has not previously examined him, takes at least *one full hour*. It can be the most important hour of a person's life.

As the doctor performs the necessary series of procedures, it also becomes a time filled with fearful tension. While the physician gently pokes and pinches the patient as if he were a fattening calf, thumps him as he would a ripening melon, listens to him as he might to a broken watch, fixing him all the while with a suspecting eye, the patient's mind dwells darkly upon the mysteries within. If the doctor confines himself to an occasional, ominous "Hmmm!" the patient naturally wonders: "What can he possibly learn from these simple maneuvers? What is going on in his mind?" The answers, for the most part, can be easily understood.

What follows is in effect a panoramic tour through one adult patient, over the age of 35, who is not aware of having any grave condition. Every checkup takes different turns, but there are some unchanging principles.

First comes the all-important "history taking," the searching interview which includes questions relating to each system in the body. Just the way a person stands, sits, walks and talks may give the doctor some first clues, and mention of a known pain, malfunction or abnormality will of course focus the physician's attention on areas to which he should give special emphasis. Then, his medical history duly recorded, the patient must take off his clothes for a step by step detailed appraisal of the body from head to toe.

During this examination the doctor depends primarily not on a battery of gadgets or laboratory tests—useful as they are—but on his relatively unaided senses. First of all, on simple visual inspection. Posture and bony structure are appraised. The doctor can see at a glance such things as irregularities in the spine that may foretell back trouble, the stooping, tensely held shoulders and barrel chest that may mean chronic asthma or emphysema, or an abnormally held leg that hints at tuberculosis (or congenital deformity) of the hip. A groove across the chest may have been left long ago by rickets; if the patient is a woman it raises doubts about her ability to give birth without a Caesarean, since the pelvic bones may also have been affected. Multiple deformations of bones can be the sign of calcium-metabolism difficulties.

The doctor also scrutinizes the skin. Do loose folds of tissue suggest recent and drastic weight loss? Are there sores or rashes that may be due to improper diet? Wrinkles in a young person may connote a loss of elasticity that needs to be explained. Abnormal skin dryness may have a variety of causes, ranging from a deficiency in thyroid function to diabetes.

Variations in skin color convey their own signals. A pale lemon-yellow hue, for example, flashes a suggestion of pernicious anemia or bacterial endocarditis. Slightly raised scarlet marks which look like spiders—with round bodies surrounded by thin, crooked, leglike lines—are swollen capillaries. When they appear during pregnancy they usually mean nothing. But this "spider angioma" can also be a mark of cirrhosis of the liver.

The physician will also take a look at the hand. It may have the knobby knuckles of rheumatoid arthritis, or the weak grip which may mean bursitis of the shoulder or some nerve or muscle impairment. A hand that is cold but dry makes the doctor suspect circulation troubles. Cold and moist, it may mean arthritis or simply emotional tension. The hand of a person with liver disease may be a mottled red, a sign known as "liver palm."

If everything looks all right, the doctor may write on his chart: "Well developed, well nourished and apparently healthy." He has already arrived at a wealth of opinion about the patient's health—in far less time than it takes to read about it.

Now the overt activity accelerates. The doctor weighs the patient, places a thermometer in his mouth, wraps a blood-pressure cuff around his arm. "Normal" pressure varies with the individual. Abnormal readings, depending upon degree, suggest a wide number of possibilities to be looked into. As for the temperature reading, interpreting it is not always simple. There is a range for normalcy (between 96.5° and 99° F.) rather than a fixed point (98.6°)—a fact which, if more generally known, could avert many needless "emergency" calls.

Next the physician reaches for his otoscope and inspects the ear canal and eardrum. He is looking for compacted wax, which can interfere with hearing, and for bulging or redness of the drum membrane, which could mean infection.

Now the doctor places two fingers on the wrist to take the

pulse. He may consider the rate normal at anywhere from 60 to 75 beats a minute for a man, 70 to 80 for a woman. He also notes whether it jumps wildly or flutters gently. Some normal pulses miss beats, usually because of anxiety. But skipped beats can also be caused by intermittent blockage of stimulus to the heart.

While taking the pulse the doctor usually can feel whether the artery is hardened. In some cases of arteriosclerosis, calcium deposits make the arteries in the arm feel as lumpy as a string of beads. The doctor may also check the pulse in the ankles, especially if he suspects widespread disease of the arteries.

Next the physician investigates the patient's breathing. A quick rate of respiration—more than 18 each minute—may be caused by hunger for air. Something could be wrong with oxygen delivery through the windpipe into the lungs, and from the lungs' air sacs into the bloodstream—or something could be wrong with the red blood cells which deliver oxygen to the tissues. Abnormally slow breathing, shallow inspirations, gasping, or rasping, barking, crowing and whistling air-intake patterns—each connotes a possibility of malfunction. The patient's breath may also convey a meaningful odor. The sweetish smell of new-mown hay or of rotting apples, for example, denotes acetone, which may be produced in diabetes or dehydration.

Now the doctor looks the patient in the eye. In certain cases of goiter he may find the entire eyeball pushed forward. With the lid closed, he will gently feel each eyeball to see if it is unusually hardened—a sign of glaucoma. If the cornea, the transparent outer covering of the eye, is cloudy or marred by an opaque ring, it may be due to various diseases—among them tuberculosis and arteriosclerosis. The iris, the colored area ringing the pupil, may appear dulled, discolored and swollen if the patient has infected teeth or tonsils, diabetes or certain types of arthritis. The whites of the eyes are turned yellow by jaundice or pernicious anemia, and a peculiar blue-tinged pearl color in most other cases of anemia.

For the most revealing part of the eye inspection the doctor uses a flashlight-size instrument, the ophthalmoscope. He peers through the magnifying lenses set in its illuminated, concave mirror. Now he can clearly see the retina, on which are inscribed plain clues to the patient's health. The retina resembles a bright red-orange curtain a little larger than a nickel, with a whitish circle, the optic-nerve head, approximately at its center. Crisscrossing the scarlet fabric are dark-red, threadlike lines—veins and arteries, which can be seen more directly here, without surgical operation, than in any other place in the body.

In high blood pressure the retinal arteries become narrowed and look like copper wires. Leukemia produces a telltale retinal pattern of yellowish, red-ringed spots. With certain types of brain tumor and in various other diseases the optic nerve itself swells, pales or changes shape.

Next the physician looks into the mouth, nose and throat. Their inner appearance can indicate a virus infection of which the patient is unaware. Blocked nasal passages may be caused by polyps or small tumors—or more often by allergic reaction or infection, in which cases the sinuses are likely to be tender and may appear opaque rather than illuminated when a light is held inside the mouth.

The request to say "Aaah" is far from an outmoded ritual. Should the protruded tongue be tremulous, the doctor thinks of an excess of thyroid hormone; if enlarged, he considers a deficiency in thyroid function. The tongue's normal color scheme is a complex of red dots on a field of pink; variations may indicate certain diseases or diet deficiencies.

Before turning his attention to the main trunk of the body, the examiner feels just beneath the Adam's apple for the thyroid gland, an important regulator for the body. If afflicted with goiter, the gland is usually enlarged. It may pulsate and emit a persistent hum which sounds through the stethoscope like a beehive, sure signs that the patient is in effect racing his motor.

Now for the patient's heart and lungs. A multitude of sounds comes through the doctor's stethoscope from the interior of the human chest, and the physician must know them all and be able to detect the one sour note. There is the clean, loud "lub-*dub* . . . lub-*dub*" of normal heart valves clinking delicately into position, sometimes varied by the faint rumbling or whistling murmurs of scarred or swollen valves as they leak blood. Pistol-shot sounds suggest that the aorta is regurgitating blood back into the heart. Sometimes the heartbeats sound strangely far away. This could mean that the pericardium, the sac around the heart, is thickened or filled with blood or fluid, and it calls for further tests.

The doctor, however, does not rely entirely on his stethoscope. He feels the chest wall near the heart. If the valves are sufficiently scarred, a vibration or "thrill" can be detected. He also employs percussion, thumping different spots. A solid substance gives a different note from that of an air-filled container, and since the heart lies in a pneumatic cushion of surrounding lung, the doctor can thus outline its size and shape—in the same way that a house carpenter locates the studs in a wall.

Looking at the whole chest, the doctor determines whether both of the patient's lungs expand equally. Tapping again reveals the outlines of the hollow lungs, and any areas filled with congestion. The physician listens also to the lungs through the stethoscope. Various malfunctions produce sounds like shifting autumn leaves or crunching snow, a hacksaw, or the cooing of a pigeon. And while he is in the chest area, the doctor explores the breasts, of men as well as women, for possible lumps.

Next he turns to the liver and spleen, organs normally tucked far under the ribs. He palpates (feels with the fingertips) for them: if they are diseased they may be enlarged and have lumps or hardened edges that can be felt. His probing fingers go on to the area above the kidneys, stomach and intestines, searching for undue tenderness or abnormality. While the patient lies on the table the stethoscope is used again: healthy peristalsis, the action of the intestinal tract, utters a characteristic gurgle, which changes in cases of intestinal obstruction to a tinkle or no sound at all. The doctor also looks for hernias, placing a finger on the groin and asking the patient to cough.

"This is the part I don't like," the discomfited patient says as the doctor prepares to examine the rectum and sigmoid portion of the lower bowel. But here is where some 70 percent of the cancer of the large intestine can be found. So in addition to palpation of the rectum, and in men the prostate—a gland shaped like a small apple which should have no irregular bumps—a thorough doctor inserts a sigmoidoscope. This is a tubular device with its own light bulb with which he can search visually for polyps or pre-cancerous growths. The procedure may be uncomfortable, but it is painless.

The central nervous system remains. To check every aspect of it would take far more than an hour, but some hints of nerve afflictions are seen even without special tests. So the patient who has shown no related problem may merely be tapped on the knee with a rubber hammer and scratched with a sterile pin, to verify that the specialized nerve fibers are properly transmitting both sensory and motor messages.

Finally, to round out the physical examination, the doctor will routinely call for a few basic laboratory tests—a chest X ray for tuberculosis and lung cancer, blood tests for diabetic sugar and for signs of general infection, a urine test for diabetes, an electrocardiogram for further information about the heart. With women a smear test for uterine cancer is standard. There are hundreds of other lab tests available, but they are largely to confirm conditions which the doctor has by now suspected; by themselves they would not tell him as much as the physical examination he has just completed.

As the doctor has gone through the checkup, sights and sounds have been pouring into his mind to form an ever clearer pattern. He has changed direction, discarded some tentative opinions, constantly fitted his fragmentary, unspoken thoughts together. No single clue has been so important to him as the company of other clues it keeps. And finally the doctor has discovered the distinctive pattern of this particular individual's health. The human body, as expressive as if made of glass, tells all its secrets to the man who knows how to read the signs.

౭❧ Soon after a London baker hung up a sign advertising "Vienna Rolls," someone added, "London Swings."   *Evening Standard,* London

౭❧ Above the washbasin in my husband's office, the boss had put a large "THINK!" sign. Directly below, someone hung a small hand-lettered sign saying: "THOAP!"   Patricia E. Crump

Savage Dog

J. L .Wolff

[August 1932]

THE TEAM jogged along the hard clay surface of a northern Kansas road as we approached a lone farmhouse. At the driveway my horses turned in. They were thirsty.

I unfastened their checkreins. But they seemed to have forgotten their thirst. They were nervous. Afraid.

I too sensed danger close at hand and looked quickly toward the barn. Every door closed—not a sign of life. In each window of the house a faded curtain hung all the way down. It was eerie. I wanted to run.

Then I saw. A tremendous dog of mastiff breed just inside the house gate, straining powerfully against a heavy chain, trying to reach the intruder. Bloodshot eyes fixed upon mine. Wanting to kill.

Several minutes I looked at this ferocious specimen, whose shoulders stood better than three feet high. The chain seemed secure. Slowly I walked toward him, talking all the while in a low tone. He neither barked nor growled. He merely stood, straining every muscle of his mighty body to snap the leash.

Approaching the gate and this apparition of frozen hate, a chill tingled down my spine.

Still talking, I opened the latch and very slowly walked toward this formidable guardian. Not by the faintest quiver did he show any movement other than with his burning red eyes which followed mine. I talked about the weather, the size of his doghouse, the weight of his chain, the terrific strain against his collar. And this latter I was exceedingly careful to examine before gradually, inch by inch, settling to my haunches with his head but two feet from my own.

Ten minutes must have passed. Never for an instant did I stop talking. I began to wonder if this huge beast wasn't utterly devoid of friendliness. Minute followed minute. Almost imperceptibly the chain commenced to slacken. On and on I talked. "It's a shame to be left alone on this Kansas prairie, where the nearest house is miles away; it must be lonesome to be a savage dog whom everyone is afraid of—to have them walk in wide circles around you, to have no one say one kind word to such a magnificent animal as you are. Your heart, if it's in proportion to your body, must be gigantic. How long has it been since any man or any child has played with you, has stroked your fur or tickled you behind your ears?"

As I continued to sympathize with him, he gradually relaxed, loosening his chain. Our eyes never parted. Neither moved—until carefully I lifted my hand and reached gradually toward his nose. A foot, eight inches, five, two—barely one inch! Not by the slightest twitch of his nostrils did he show any interest.

"Why don't you smell my hand. Don't you want to be friends?"

My arm was commencing to ache and I began to think my overtures were doomed to failure. And then his head moved slightly toward my fingers as gently he strained against his chain, trying to reach them. Softly I stroked the side of his nostrils. Now he was looking at me with only a questioning gaze, all viciousness gone. Farther and farther back along the side of his face my fingers scratched, until his jaws could easily have crushed my wrist.

My legs were falling asleep. So, patting his head, I arose cautiously. The great animal swung his rear quarters over toward me and I scratched his shoulders. For a long time we stood thus, while I kept up my low-voiced conversation—and my fingers never rested. But I was ready instantly to jump out of reach.

Ever so imperceptibly I edged closer until his shoulder rested against my side. All thought of danger disappeared and I was filled with compassion for this majestic creature. He never looked up, his tail never wagged—he was content to lean against me, to be stroked, to hear my sympathetic voice.

But this could not go on. There were miles ahead of us and the afternoon was getting late. Yet I hated to leave him, after friendship so laboriously gained. And his surrender to the delight of my fingertips was complete.

As I moved away he looked up in wonder. As I reached for the latch he whined—just a little, and looked at me pleadingly. I couldn't run out on him this way. Quickly I returned and without hesitation dropped to my knees and put my arm around his neck. Softly he rubbed his nose against my cheek. I no longer talked—merely stroked and patted his neck and shoulders.

It almost broke my heart when once more I started for the gate, this time going through resolutely, not even turning to look back. I got in the buggy and swung the horses around. As I drove past he was whining—whining. I couldn't leave him so. Again I jumped down and ran back.

His immense tail slowly moved from side to side as eagerly he put his head against me and looked into my eyes. It was unbearable to think of his lonesomeness, the utter loneliness that belongs to a savage dog, scolded and cursed, whose longing for a friendly gesture no one can guess.

In his deep brown eyes, looking understandingly into my own, I saw a newborn loyalty. Steadfast. Eternal.

Tears streamed down my cheeks as I left him, straining to follow me, his whines cut short by the collar that was choking him. As my horses clogged down the road he howled—

Many years have passed. I can't even remember the town from whose livery stable came the team. But every detail of that friendship is seared deep in my memory.

&~ "Chivalry," said a little boy after studying knighthood in school, "is going around releasing beautiful maidens from other men's castles and taking them to your own castle."

Sydney J. Harris, Publishers Newspaper Syndicate

THE LONGEST DAY

Cornelius Ryan

THE LONGEST DAY

*In recent years The Reader's Digest has commis-
sioned a number of books. Among them is "The
Longest Day," by Cornelius Ryan, now a Roving Editor
for the magazine. A vividly detailed reconstruction of
the Allied invasion of Hitler's Europe, the book became
one of the most popular ever written about World
War II. In producing the research for works of this
sweep and range, the Digest's character as an international magazine with local resources in many countries has proved of particular value.*

*Two sections of "The Longest Day" appeared in the
magazine. Reprinted here is the first.*

THE VILLAGE was silent in the damp June morning. Its name
was La Roche-Guyon and it had sat undisturbed for nearly 12
centuries roughly midway between Paris and Normandy. For
years it had been just a place that people passed through on
their way to somewhere else. Its only distinction was its castle,
the seat of the dukes of Rochefoucauld.

But now the village had attained a distinction of another
kind. For behind its pastoral front La Roche-Guyon was really
a prison—the most occupied village in all of occupied France.
For every one of the 543 villagers there were more than three
German soldiers. One of these soldiers was Field Marshal Erwin
Rommel, commander in chief of Army Group B, the most powerful force in the German West. From his headquarters in
the castle, in this crucial fifth year of World War II, Rommel
was preparing to fight the most desperate battle of his career.

Although Rommel did not know it, that battle—against the

Allied invasion—would begin in 48 hours. For this was Sunday, June 4, 1944.

Under Rommel's command more than half a million troops manned defenses along a tremendous length of coastline—stretching almost 800 miles, from the dikes of Holland to the Atlantic-washed shores of the Brittany peninsula. His main strength, the 15th Army, was concentrated about the Pas-de-Calais, at the narrowest point of the Channel between France and England.

Night after night, Allied bombers hit this area. Bomb-weary veterans joked bitterly that the place for a rest cure was in the zone of the Seventh Army, in Normandy. Hardly a bomb had fallen there.

For months, behind a fantastic jungle of beach obstacles and mine fields, Rommel's troops had waited. But the blue-gray English Channel had remained empty of ships. Nothing happened. From La Roche-Guyon, on this gloomy and peaceful Sunday morning, there was still no sign of the Allied invasion.

IN THE ground-floor room he used as an office Rommel was alone, working by the light of a single desk lamp. Although he looked older than his 51 years, he remained tireless as ever. This morning as usual he had been up since before four. Now he waited impatiently for six o'clock. At that time he would breakfast with his staff, and then depart for Germany—his first leave at home in months.

The decision to go had not been easy to make. On Rommel's shoulders lay the enormous responsibility for repulsing the Allied assault the moment it began. Hitler's Third Reich was reeling from one disaster after another. Day and night, thousands of Allied bombers pounded Germany. Russia's massive forces had driven into Poland. Allied troops were at the gates of Rome. Everywhere the Wehrmacht was being driven back and destroyed. Germany was still far from beaten, but the Allied invasion would be the decisive battle—and no one knew it better than Rommel.

Yet this morning he was going home. For months he had hoped to spend a few days in Germany the first part of June.

Also, he wanted to see Hitler. There were many reasons why he believed he *could* leave now. And, although he would never have admitted it, he desperately needed rest.

Only one person really knew the strain that Rommel was under. To his wife, Lucie-Maria, he confided everything. In less than four months he had written her more than 40 letters.

On April 6 he wrote: "Here the tension is growing from day to day. It will probably be only weeks that separate us from the decisive events."

On May 6: "Still no signs of the British and Americans. Every day, every week we get stronger. I am looking forward to the battle with confidence. Perhaps it will come on May 15, perhaps at the end of the month."

On May 15: "I can't take many more big inspection trips because one never knows when the invasion will begin."

On May 19: "I am wondering if I can spare a few days in June to get away from here. Right now there isn't a chance."

But there was a chance after all. Among the reasons for Rommel's decision to leave at this time was his own estimate of the Allies' intentions. Before him on the desk was Army Group B's weekly report—due to be sent the following day to Field Marshal Gerd von Rundstedt's headquarters at St.-Germain, outside Paris—and from there to Hitler's headquarters, OKW (*Oberkommando der Wehrmacht*). The estimate noted that the Allies had reached a "high degree of readiness" and that there was an "increased volume of messages going to the French Resistance." But, it went on, "according to past experience this is not indicative that an invasion is imminent."

Rommel had guessed wrong again.

Now that May had passed—and it had been a month of perfect weather for the Allied attack—Rommel had reached the conclusion that the invasion would not come for several more weeks. He now reasoned—as did Hitler and the German High Command—that the invasion would take place either simultaneously with the Red army's summer offensive or shortly thereafter. The Russian attack, they knew, could not begin until after the late thaw in Poland, *i.e.*, not until after mid-June.

In the west the weather had been bad for several days, and it promised to be worse. The 5 a.m. report for June 4, prepared by the Luftwaffe's chief meteorologist in Paris, predicted increasing cloudiness, high winds and rain. Even now, a 20- to 30-m.p.h. wind was blowing in the Channel. To Rommel, it seemed hardly likely that the Allies would dare launch their attack during the next few days. He opened the door of his office and went down to have breakfast with his staff.

The bell in the village church sounded the Angelus. Each note fought for its existence against the wind. It was 6 a.m.

ROMMEL had been in France since November 1943. To the humiliation of Von Rundstedt, the aristocratic 68-year-old commander in chief, West, responsible for the defense of all western Europe, Rommel had arrived with a *Gummibefehl*, an "elastic directive," ordering him to inspect the coastal fortifications—Hitler's much publicized "Atlantic Wall"—and then report directly back to the Führer's headquarters.

The Atlantic Wall was one of Hitler's relatively new obsessions. Up to 1941 victory had seemed so certain to the Führer and his strutting Nazis that there was no need for coastal fortifications. After the collapse of France Hitler expected the British to sue for peace. They didn't; and as time passed the situation changed. With U. S. help Britain began staging a slow but sure recovery.

Hitler, by now deeply involved in Russia—he had attacked the Soviet Union in June 1941—saw that the coast of France was no longer an offensive springboard but a soft spot in his defenses. And in December 1941, after America entered the war, the Führer ranted to the world that "a belt of strongpoints and gigantic fortifications runs from Kirkenes (on the Norwegian-Finnish frontier) to the Pyrenees, and it is my unshakable decision to make this front impregnable against every enemy." It was a wild, impossible boast. Discounting the indentations, this coastline stretches over 3000 miles.

Gen. Franz Halder, then chief of the German High Command, well remembers the first time Hitler outlined his fantastic scheme. Halder, who would never forgive Hitler for refusing to invade England, was cool to the whole idea. He ventured the opinion that fortifications "if needed" should be constructed "behind the coastline, out of range of naval guns"; otherwise troops might be pinned down. Hitler dashed across the room to a table on which there was a large map and for a full five minutes threw an unforgettable tantrum. Pounding the map with his clenched fist, he screamed, "Bombs and shells will fall here . . . here . . . here . . . and here . . . in front of the Wall, behind it and on it . . . but the troops will be safe in the Wall! Then they'll come out and fight!"

Halder said nothing, but he knew, as did the other generals, that despite all the Reich's intoxicating victories the Führer already feared a second front—an invasion.

Still, little work was done on the fortifications. In 1942, as the tide of war began to swing against the Germans, Hitler thundered at his generals that the Wall must be completed at top speed. Construction was to be rushed "fanatically."

It was. Thousands of slave laborers worked night and day to build fortifications. Millions of tons of concrete were poured—so much that all over Hitler's Europe it became impossible to get concrete for anything else. Staggering quantities of steel were ordered, but this commodity was in such short supply that the engineers were often forced to do without it. Parts of the old French Maginot Line and Germany's frontier fortifications, the Siegfried Line, were cannibalized for materials and equipment. Still by the end of 1943, although half a million men were working on it, the Wall was far from finished.

Hitler now was faced with another great problem: finding the divisions to man his growing defenses. In Russia, division after division was being chewed up. In Italy, knocked out of the war after the invasion of Sicily, thousands of troops were still pinned down. So, by 1944, Hitler was forced to bolster his garrisons in the west with a strange conglomeration of replacements—old men and young boys, the remnants of divisions shattered on the Russian front, impressed "volunteers" from occupied countries. Questionable as these troops might prove to be in combat, they filled out the gaps. Also, Hitler still had a hard core of seasoned troops and panzers. By D Day German strength in the west would total a formidable 58 divisions. Not all these divisions would be up to full strength, but Hitler was still relying on his Atlantic Wall—that would make the difference.

What Rommel saw when he inspected the Wall in November 1943 appalled him. In only a few places were the fortifications completed, and at some places work had not even begun. True, even in its present state, the Wall was a formidable barrier. Where finished, it fairly bristled with heavy guns. But there were not enough of them, or of anything, to suit Rommel. He denounced the Atlantic Wall as a farce, a "figment of Hitler's *Wolkenkuckucksheim* (cloud cuckoo-land)."

Von Rundstedt heartily concurred—probably the only time he completely agreed with Rommel on anything. The wise old Von Rundstedt never believed in fixed defenses. He had masterminded the attack outflanking the Maginot Line in 1940 that led to the collapse of France. To him Hitler's Atlantic Wall was an "enormous bluff . . . more for the German people than for the enemy." It would "temporarily obstruct" the Allied attack, but nothing, Von Rundstedt was convinced, could prevent the initial landings from being successful. His plan to defeat the invasion was to hold the great mass of his troops back from the coast and to attack *after* the Allied troops had landed.

With this Rommel disagreed. He was positive there was only one way to smash the attack: meet it head-on.

Capt. Helmut Lang, his 36-year-old aide, well remembers a day when Rommel summed up his strategy. They stood on a deserted beach and Rommel, a short, stocky figure in a heavy greatcoat with an old muffler around his throat, stalked up and down waving his "informal" marshal's baton, a two-foot-long, silver-topped black stick with a red, black and white tassel. He pointed to the sands and said, "The war will be won or lost on the beaches. We'll have only one chance to stop the enemy, and that's while he's in the water struggling to get ashore. Reserves will never get up to the point of attack and it's foolish even to consider them. The *Hauptkampflinie* (main line of resistance) will be here. Everything we have must be on the coast. Believe me, Lang, the first 24 hours of the invasion will be decisive. For the Allies, as well as Germany, it will be the longest day."

Hitler had approved Rommel's plan in general, and from then on Von Rundstedt became merely a figurehead. In a few short months Rommel's ruthless drive changed the whole picture. On every beach where he considered a landing possible he ordered crude anti-invasion obstacles erected. These obstacles —jagged triangles of steel; sawtoothed, gatelike structures of iron; metal-tipped wooden stakes and concrete cones—were planted just below high- and low-tide watermarks. Strapped to each one were explosives.

Rommel's strange inventions (he had designed most of them himself) were both simple and deadly. Their object was to impale and destroy troop-filled landing craft or obstruct them long enough for shore batteries to zero in. More than half a million of these lethal underwater obstacles now stretched along the coastline.

Still Rommel, the perfectionist, was not satisfied. In the sands, in bluffs, in gullies and pathways leading off the beaches, he ordered mines laid—all varieties, from the large pancake type capable of blowing off a tank's tracks, to the small S mine which when stepped on bounded into the air and exploded level with a man's midriff. Over five million of these mines now infested the coast. Before the attack came, Rommel hoped to have another six million planted along Omaha Beach alone. He aimed for a total of 50 million.

Overlooking the coastline, back of this jungle of mines and obstacles, Rommel's troops waited in pillboxes, concrete bunkers and communication trenches, all surrounded by layers of barbed wire. From these positions every piece of artillery the Field Marshal had been able to lay hands on looked down on sands and sea, already sighted in to give overlapping fields of fire.

Rommel took advantage of every new technique or development. Where short of guns, he positioned batteries of rocket launchers or multiple mortar throwers. At one place he even had miniature robot tanks called Goliaths. These devices, capable of carrying half a ton of explosives, could be guided by remote control from the fortifications down onto the beaches and detonated among troops or landing craft.

Never before in the history of warfare had a more deadly

array of defenses been prepared for an invading force. Yet Rommel was not content. He wanted more pillboxes . . . more beach obstacles . . . more mines . . . more guns and troops. Most of all he wanted the massive panzer divisions which were lying in reserve far from the coast. But now at this crucial moment, the Führer insisted on holding these armored formations under his personal authority. There was only one way to get them: Rommel had often told Lang, "The last man who sees Hitler wins the game." On this leaden morning, as he prepared to leave for Germany and the long drive home, Rommel was more determined than ever to win the game.

At 15th Army headquarters, 125 miles away near the Belgian border, one man was glad to see the morning of June 4 arrive. Lt. Col. Hellmuth Meyer sat in his office, haggard and bleary-eyed. He had not had a really good night's sleep since June 1. But the night that had just passed had been the worst yet; he would never forget it.

Meyer had a frustrating, nerve-racking job. He headed the only counterintelligence team on the invasion front. The heart of his setup was a 30-man radio-interception crew whose job was to listen, nothing more. But each man was an expert who spoke three languages fluently and there was hardly a word, hardly a single stutter of Morse code whispering through the ether from Allied sources that they did not hear.

Meyer was good at his job. Several times a day he sifted through sheaves of monitored reports, always searching for the suspicious, the unusual—even the unbelievable. And during the night his men had picked up the unbelievable. The message, a high-speed press cable, had been monitored just after dark. It read: URGENT PRESS ASSOCIATED NYK FLASH EISENHOWER'S HQ ANNOUNCES ALLIED LANDINGS IN FRANCE.

Meyer was dumfounded. His first impulse was to alert headquarters. But he paused and calmed down. The message had to be wrong, for two reasons. First, there was a complete absence of any Allied radio traffic along the invasion front. (He would have known immediately if there had been an attack.) Second, in January Adm. Wilhelm Canaris, then chief of German intelligence, had given Meyer the details of a two-part signal which he said the Allies would use to alert the underground prior to the invasion.

Coded sentences were commonly read out to the underground after the regular BBC news broadcasts. Most of the messages—given in French, Dutch, Danish and Norwegian—were meaningless: "The Trojan War will not be held." "Molasses tomorrow will spurt forth cognac." "John has a long mustache." Canaris had warned that the Allies would broadcast hundreds of such messages in the months preceding the attack. Only a few would actually relate to D Day; the remainder would be fake, to mislead and confuse. But Meyer was to monitor them all in order not to miss the important one.

At first Meyer had been skeptical. It seemed madness to him to depend entirely on only one message. But following the 9 p.m. BBC news on the night of June 1, it came through—exactly as described by Canaris. "Kindly listen now to a few personal messages," said the voice in French. Instantly Sgt. Walter Reichling switched on a wire recorder. There was a pause, and then: *"Les sanglots longs des violons de l'automne"* ("The long sobs of the violins of autumn").

Reichling rushed out of the bunker and burst into Meyer's office. "Sir, the first part of the message—it's here!"

Together they returned to the radio bunker where Meyer listened to the recording. There it was—the first phrase of *Chanson d'Automne* by Paul Verlaine. According to Canaris' information, this line was to be transmitted on the "first or 15th of a month, and will represent the first half of a message announcing the Anglo-American invasion."

The last half of the signal would be the following phrase of the Verlaine poem, *"Blessent mon coeur d'une langueur monotone"* ("Wound my heart with a monotonous languor"). When this was broadcast it would mean "the invasion will begin within 48 hours, the count starting at midnight of the day of transmission."

Meyer at once informed the 15th Army's chief of staff. "The first message has come," he said. "Now something is going to happen." Immediately the alarm was given to alert the army.

Meyer meanwhile sent the message by Teletype to Hitler's headquarters (OKW). Next he telephoned Von Rundstedt's headquarters (OB West) and Rommel's headquarters (Army Group B).

At OKW the message was delivered to Gen. Alfred Jodl, chief of operations. The message remained on Jodl's desk. He did not order an alert; he assumed Von Rundstedt had done so. But Von Rundstedt thought Rommel's headquarters had issued the order. Rommel must have known about the message, but from his estimate of Allied intentions it is obvious that he discounted it. So along the invasion coast only one army was placed on readiness: the 15th. The Seventh Army, holding the coast of Normandy, heard nothing about the message and was not alerted.

On the nights of June 2 and 3 the first part of the message was again broadcast. It was within the hour after the repeat on June 3 that the AP flash regarding the Allied landings in France was picked up. If the Canaris warning was right, Meyer knew, the AP report must be wrong. (The flash turned out to be the weirdest kind of security leak. During the night an AP Teletype operator in England had been practicing on an idle machine in an effort to improve her speed. Through an error the perforated tape carrying her practice flash somehow preceded the usual nightly Russian communiqué. It was corrected after only 30 seconds, but the word was out.)

After his first moment of panic, Meyer had bet on Canaris. Now on Sunday morning he was weary but elated. The coming of the dawn and the continued peacefulness along the front more than proved him right. Now there was nothing to do but wait for the last half of the vital alert, which might come at any moment.

As MEYER settled down to wait, the commander of Army Group B was preparing to leave for Germany. At 7 a.m. the Field Marshal's car, with Rommel in the seat beside the chauffeur, drove through the village of La Roche-Guyon and turned left onto the main Paris road.

Leaving on this particular dismal Sunday morning suited

Rommel fine. The timing of the trip could not have been better. Beside him on the seat was a cardboard box containing a pair of handmade gray-suede shoes, size 5½, for his wife. There was an especial and very human reason why he wanted to be with her on Tuesday, June 6. It was her birthday.

IN ENGLAND it was 8 a.m. (there was one hour's difference between British Double Summer Time and German Central Time). In a house trailer in a rain-washed wood near Portsmouth Gen. Dwight D. Eisenhower, Allied Supreme Commander, was sound asleep after having been up nearly all night.

Although he could have moved into the more comfortable quarters of the naval headquarters at big, sprawling Southwick House two miles away, Eisenhower had decided against it. He wanted to be as close as possible to the ports where his troops were loading.

Eisenhower's trailer, a long, low 3½-ton caravan, had three small, sparsely furnished compartments serving as bedroom, living room and study. From this trailer he commanded almost three million Allied troops. More than half of his immense command was American: roughly, 1,700,000 soldiers, sailors, airmen and coast guardsmen. British and Canadian forces together totaled around one million, and in addition there were Free French, Polish, Czech, Belgian, Norwegian and Dutch contingents. Never before had an American commanded so many men from so many nations or shouldered such an awesome burden of responsibility.

Four months before, in the directive appointing him Supreme Commander, the Combined Chiefs of Staff in Washington had spelled out his assignment in one precise paragraph. It read: "You will enter the continent of Europe and, in conjunction with the other United Nations, undertake operations aimed at the heart of Germany and the destruction of her armed forces."

Intensive military planning for the invasion had been going on for more than a year, but men had been thinking about the assault almost from the time of Dunkirk. A small Anglo-American group of officers under Britain's Lt. Gen. Sir Frederick Morgan had long been laying the groundwork. Ultimately their studies, enlarged and modified into the final plan (code-named Overlord) after Eisenhower took over, called for more men, ships, planes and matériel than had ever been assembled for a single military operation.

Even before the plan reached its final form an unprecedented flow of men and supplies began pouring into England. Soon there were so many Americans in the small towns and villages that the British who lived in them were often outnumbered, and by May southern England looked like a huge arsenal. Hidden in the forests were mountainous piles of ammunition. Stretching across the moors, bumper-to-bumper, were more than 50,000 tanks, half-tracks, armored cars, trucks, jeeps and ambulances. In the fields were long lines of howitzers and anti-aircraft guns, great quantities of prefabricated materials, from Nissen huts to airstrips. The most staggering sights of all were the valleys filled with long lines of railroad rolling stock: almost 1000 brand-new locomotives and nearly 20,000 tanker cars and freight cars, which would be used to replace shattered French equipment.

There were also strange new devices of war. There were tanks that could swim, and others equipped with great chain flails that beat the ground in front of them to explode mines. Perhaps strangest of all were two man-made harbors that were to be towed across to the Normandy beaches. The harbors, called Mulberries, consisted, first, of an outer breakwater made up of great steel floats. Next came 145 huge concrete caissons in various sizes which were to be sunk butt-to-butt to make an inner breakwater. The largest of these caissons had crew quarters and anti-aircraft guns, and when being towed it looked like a five-story apartment building lying on its side. Within these man-made harbors, freighters as large as Liberty ships could unload into barges ferrying back and forth to the beaches. Smaller ships like coasters or landing craft could dump their cargoes at massive steel pierheads, where waiting lorries would run them to shore over floating pontoon-supported piers. Beyond the Mulberries a line of 60 concrete blockships was to be sunk. In position off the invasion beaches, each harbor would be the size of the port of Dover.

All through May, men and supplies moved down to the ports and the loading areas. In cities of Nissen huts and tents men slept in bunks stacked three and four deep. Showers and latrines were usually several fields away and the men had to queue up to use them. Chow lines were sometimes a quarter of a mile long. There were so many troops that it took some 54,000 men, 4500 of them newly trained cooks, just to service American installations. The last week in May, troops and supplies began loading onto the transports and the landing ships. The time had finally come.

EISENHOWER and his commanders had done everything to ensure that the invasion would have every possible chance of success at the lowest cost in lives. But now, after all the years of military and political planning, Operation Overlord lay at the mercy of the elements. The weather was bad. Eisenhower was helpless. All he could do was wait and hope that conditions would improve. On Sunday, June 4, no matter what happened, he would be forced to make a momentous decision: to go—or to postpone the assault. The success or failure of Operation Overlord might depend on that decision. And nobody could make it for him. The responsibility would be his alone.

Eisenhower was faced with a dreadful dilemma. On May 17 he had decided that D Day would have to be one of three days in June—the 5th, 6th or 7th. Meteorological studies had shown that two of the vital weather requirements for the invasion could be expected for Normandy on those days: a late-rising moon and, shortly after dawn, a low tide.

The paratroopers and gliderborne infantry who would launch the assault—some 22,000 men of the U.S. 101st and 82nd divisions and the British Sixth Division—needed moonlight. But their surprise attack depended on darkness up to the time they arrived over the dropping zones. Thus their critical demand was for a late-rising moon.

The seaborne landings had to take place when the tide was low enough to expose Rommel's beach obstacles. On this tide the timing of the whole invasion would depend. And to complicate the calculations further, follow-up troops landing much later in the day would also need a low tide—and it had to come before darkness set in. These two critical factors, moonlight and tide, shackled Eisenhower. Tide alone reduced the number of days for the attack in any one month to six—and three of those were moonless.

There were many other factors. First, all the services wanted long hours of daylight and good visibility. They wanted light to be able to identify the beaches; for the Navy and Air Force to spot their targets; and to reduce the hazard of collision when the mass of ships began maneuvering almost side by side in the Bay of the Seine. Second, a calm sea was required. Apart from the havoc a rough sea might cause to the fleet, seasickness could leave the troops helpless long before they even set foot on the beaches. Third, low winds, blowing inshore, were needed to clear the beaches of smoke so that targets would not be obscured. And finally, the Allies would require three more quiet days after D Day for the quick build-up of men and supplies.

Nobody at Supreme Headquarters expected perfect conditions on D Day, least of all Eisenhower. In countless dry runs with his meteorological staff he had schooled himself to recognize and weigh all the factors which would give him the minimum acceptable conditions for the attack. But the chances were about ten to one against Normandy's having, on any one day in June, weather meeting even the minimums.

Of the three possible days for the invasion Eisenhower had chosen the 5th, so if there was a postponement he could launch the assault on the 6th. But if he ordered the landings for the 6th and then had to cancel them again, the problem of refueling the returning convoys might prevent him from attacking on the 7th. There would then be two choices. He could postpone D Day until the next period when the tides were right—June 19. But June 19 was moonless. The alternative was to wait until July—and that long a postponement, as he was later to recall, "was too bitter to contemplate."

So terrifying was the thought of long postponement that many of Eisenhower's most cautious commanders were prepared to risk attack on the 8th or 9th instead. They did not see how a quarter of a million men—more than half of them already briefed—could be kept isolated and bottled up for weeks on ships, in embarkation areas and on airfields without having the secret of the invasion leak out. For everybody the prospect of a postponement was grim.

On Sunday, June 4, at 5 a.m.—about the time that Rommel got up at La Roche-Guyon—Eisenhower made one fateful decision: because of unfavorable weather conditions the Allied invasion would be postponed 24 hours. If conditions improved, D Day would be Tuesday, June 6.

AT DAWN, Sunday, June 4, Comdr. George D. Hoffman, 33-year-old skipper of the destroyer U.S.S. *Corry*, looked through his binoculars. A long column of ships was plowing steadily across the English Channel behind him. They were on course and exactly on time. The crawling convoy, following a circuitous route and moving slowly, had sailed more than 80 miles since leaving Plymouth. At any moment now Hoffman expected trouble—U-boats, aircraft attacks, mine fields, or all three—for as every minute passed they were sailing farther into enemy waters. France lay ahead, now only 40 miles away.

The young commander was immensely proud to be leading this magnificent convoy. But as he looked at it through his glasses he knew it was a sitting duck for the enemy.

Ahead were the mine sweepers—six small ships spread out in a diagonal formation like one side of an inverted V. Behind the mine sweepers came the lean, sleek shapes of the "shepherds," the escorting destroyers. And behind them, stretching as far as the eye could see, came a great procession of lumbering, unwieldy landing ships carrying thousands of troops, tanks, guns and vehicles, and ammunition. Multiplying the total number of ships by the distance separating one from the next, Hoffman figured that the tail end of this fantastic parade must still be back in England, in Plymouth harbor.

And this was only *one* convoy. Dozens of others had been due to sail at the same time or during the day. That night all of them would converge on the Bay of the Seine. By the morning of June 5, according to plan, an immense fleet of 2700 ships would stand off the invasion beaches of Normandy.

Hoffman could hardly wait to see it. His convoy was part of a massive American force—the Fourth Division—destined for a place that most Americans had never heard of before—a stretch of wind-blown sand on the eastern side of the Cherbourg peninsula that had been given the code name Utah. Twelve miles to the southeast, in front of the seaside villages of Vierville and Colleville, lay the other American beach—Omaha, a crescent-shaped strip of silvery strand where the men of the First and 29th divisions would land.

Suddenly the *Corry's* bridge telephone buzzed. Hoffman picked up the receiver. "Bridge," he said. "This is the captain." He listened for a moment. "Are you quite sure?" he asked. "Has the message been repeated?" He listened a moment longer, then replaced the receiver on its cradle. It was unbelievable: the whole convoy had been ordered back to England. What could have happened? Had the invasion been postponed? No reason had been given.

Hoffman's job and that of the other destroyers now was to wheel this monstrous convoy around—and quickly. Because he was in the lead, his immediate concern was the flotilla of mine sweepers several miles ahead. He could not contact them by radio because a strict radio silence had been imposed—and they had to be swung around first. "All engines ahead full speed," Hoffman ordered. "Close up on the mine sweepers. Signalman on the light."

As the *Corry* raced forward, he looked back and saw the destroyers behind him wheel and swing around the flanks of the convoy. Now, with signal lights blinking, they began the tremendous job of turning the convoy around.

IN THE huge Operations Center at Allied Naval Headquarters in Southwick House, they waited for the ships to come back. The long, high room with its white-and-gold wallpaper was the scene of intense activity. One entire wall was covered by a gigantic chart of the English Channel. Every few minutes two WRENS, working from a traveling stepladder, plotted the new positions of each returning convoy. Staff officers from each of the Allied services watched in silence as each new report came in. Outwardly they appeared calm, but there was no disguising the strain that everybody felt. Not only must the convoys wheel about, almost under the very noses of the enemy, and return to England along specific, mine-swept tracks; they were now faced with the threat of another enemy—a storm at sea. Already the wind in the Channel was blowing up to 30 m.p.h., with waves up to five feet—and due to get worse.

As the minutes passed, the face of the chart reflected the orderly pattern of the recall. There were streams of markers backtracking up the Irish Sea, clustered in the vicinity of the Isle of Wight, and huddled together in various ports and anchorages along the southwest coast of England. It would take some of the convoys nearly all day to put back to port, but there was hope that they would make it.

And now, as the hours slipped by and the weather steadily worsened, the greatest airborne and amphibious force ever assembled waited for General Eisenhower's decision. Would Ike confirm June 6 as D Day? Or would he be compelled because of Channel weather—the worst in 20 years—to postpone the invasion once again?

In the fading light of the afternoon the Supreme Commander occasionally came to the door of his trailer and gazed up through the wind-swept treetops at the blanket of clouds that covered the sky—a solitary figure, shoulders slightly hunched, hands rammed deep into his pockets.

Shortly before 9:30 that night of June 4, Eisenhower's senior commanders and their chiefs of staff—altogether 12 officers—gathered in the library of Southwick House. Standing in little groups, they talked quietly. Near the fireplace Eisenhower's chief of staff, Maj. Gen. Walter Bedell Smith, conversed with the pipe-smoking Deputy Supreme Commander, Air Chief Marshal Sir Arthur Tedder. Only one officer was dressed informally. The peppery Bernard Law Montgomery, who would be in charge of the D-Day assault, wore his usual corduroy slacks and roll-neck sweater.

At exactly 9:30 the door opened and Eisenhower, neat in his dark-green battledress, strode in. There was just the faintest flicker of the Eisenhower grin as he greeted his old friends, but the cloud of worry quickly returned to his face as he opened the conference. There was no need for a preamble: everybody knew the seriousness of the decision that had to be made. Almost immediately the three senior Overlord meteorologists, led by Group Capt. J. N. Stagg of the RAF, came into the room.

There was a hushed silence as Stagg opened the briefing. Quickly he sketched the weather picture of the previous 24 hours, and then he said quietly, "Gentlemen, there have been some rapid and unexpected developments in the situation." And he presented the anxious-faced Eisenhower and his commanders with a slender ray of hope.

A new weather front had been spotted which, he said, would move up the Channel within the next few hours and cause a gradual clearing over the assault areas. These improving conditions would last throughout the next day and continue up to the morning of June 6. After that the weather would begin to deteriorate again. During this promised period of improved weather, the winds would drop appreciably and the skies would clear—enough at least for bombers to operate on the night of the 5th and throughout the morning of the 6th. By noon the cloud layer would thicken and the skies would become overcast again. In short, a barely tolerable period of fair conditions, far below the minimal requirements, would prevail *for just a little more than 24 hours.*

For the next 15 minutes Eisenhower and his commanders deliberated. The urgency of making a decision was stressed by the fiery Allied Naval Commander, Adm. Sir Bertram Ramsay. The American task force for Omaha and Utah beaches would have to get the order within a half hour if Overlord was to take place on Tuesday.

Eisenhower now polled his commanders one by one. General Smith thought that the attack should go in on the 6th—it was a gamble, but one that should be taken. Tedder and the Allied Air Commander, Air Chief Marshal Sir Trafford Leigh-Mallory, were both fearful that even the predicted cloud cover would prove too much for the air forces to operate effectively. It might mean that the assault would take place without adequate air support. They thought it was going to be "chancy."

Montgomery stuck to his judgment of the night before when the June 5 D Day had been postponed: "I would say—go."

It was now up to Ike. The moment had come for decision. There was a long silence as he weighed all the possibilities. General Smith watched, struck by the "isolation and loneliness" of the Supreme Commander as he sat, hands clasped before him, looking down at the table. The minutes ticked by. Some say two minutes passed, others as long as five. Then Eisenhower, his face strained, looked up. Slowly he said, "I am quite positive we must give the order. I don't like it, but there it is. I don't see how we can do anything else."

Eisenhower stood up. He looked tired, but some of the tension had left his face. Tuesday, June 6, would be D Day.

It was about 10 p.m. when Pvt. Arthur B. "Dutch" Schultz of the 82nd Airborne Division decided to get out of the crap game. The game had been going on ever since the announcement that the airborne assault was off for at least 24 hours. It had begun behind a tent, moved under the wing of a plane, and now was going full blast in the hangar which had been converted into a huge dormitory.

Dutch was one of the big winners. How much he'd won he didn't know, but he guessed that it came to over $2500—more money than he'd seen at any one time in all his 21 years.

Physically and spiritually he had done everything to prepare himself for the jump. In the morning, services for all denominations had been held on the airfield, and Dutch, a Catholic, had gone to confession and received communion. Now, he mentally figured out what he was going to do with his winnings. He would leave $1000 with the adjutant's office: he could use that on pass when he got back to England. Another $1000 he planned to send to his mother in Philadelphia, telling her to keep half for him and half for herself—she sure could use it. As for the remainder—that would go on a helluva blowout when his outfit, the 505th, reached Paris.

The young paratrooper felt good; he had taken care of everything. . . . But had he? At mail call that morning he had received a letter from his mother, and enclosed with it was a rosary. Now the thought of the rosary suddenly gave rise to an uneasiness. *What was he doing gambling at a time like this?*

He looked at the folded and crumpled bills. At that moment he *knew* that if he pocketed all this money, he would surely be killed. Dutch decided to take no chances. "Move over," he said, "and let me get at the play." He glanced at his watch and wondered how long it would take to lose $2500.

As night closed in, the invasion forces all over England continued to wait. Keyed up by months of training, they were ready to go, and the postponement had made them jittery. It was now about 18 hours since the stand-down, and each hour had taken its toll of the patience and readiness of the troops. They did not know that D Day was barely 26 hours away; it was still much too early for the news to filter down. And so, on this stormy Sunday night, men waited—in loneliness, anxiety and secret fear—for something, anything, to happen.

They did precisely what the world expects men to do under such circumstances: they thought of their families, their wives, their children, their sweethearts. And everybody talked about the fighting that lay ahead. What would the beaches really be like? Would the landings be as rough as everybody seemed to think? Nobody could visualize D Day, but each man prepared for it in his own way.

A few men, nerveless and cool, slept soundly. At a British 50th Division embarkation area one such man was Company Sgt. Maj. Stanley Hollis. Evacuated from Dunkirk, he had fought with the Eighth Army in North Africa and had landed in Sicily. Among the millions of troops in Britain that night Hollis was a rarity. He was looking forward to the invasion: he wanted to get back and kill more Germans.

It was a personal matter with Hollis. He'd been a dispatch rider at the time of Dunkirk, and in the town of Lille during the retreat he had seen a sight which he'd never forgotten. Cut off from his unit he had taken a wrong turn in a part of the town the Germans had apparently just passed through. He found himself in a cul-de-sac filled with the still-warm bodies of over 100 French men, women and children. They had been machine-gunned. Embedded in the wall behind the bodies and littering the ground were hundreds of spent bullets. From that moment Stan Hollis had become a superb hunter of the enemy. His score was now 90. At D Day's end, he would notch his Sten gun with his 102nd victory.

On the U.S. transport *New Amsterdam* anchored near Weymouth, 2nd Lt. George Kerchner of the Second Ranger Battalion was occupied with a routine chore. He was censoring his platoon's mail. It was particularly heavy tonight; everybody seemed to have written long letters home. The Second and Fifth Rangers had been given one of the toughest D-Day assignments. They were to scale the almost sheer 100-foot cliffs at a place called Pointe du Hoc and silence a battery of six long-range guns—guns so powerful they could zero in on Omaha Beach *or* the transport area of Utah Beach. The Rangers would have just 30 minutes to do the job.

Casualties were expected to be heavy—some thought as high as 60 percent—unless the air and naval bombardment could knock out the guns before the Rangers got there. Either way, nobody expected the attack to be a breeze—nobody, that is, except Staff Sgt. Larry Johnson, one of Kerchner's section leaders.

The lieutenant was dumfounded when he read Johnson's letter. None of the mail would be sent out until after D Day—whenever that would be—but this letter couldn't be delivered through ordinary channels even then. Kerchner sent for Johnson. "Larry," he said drily, "you better post this yourself—after you get to France." Johnson had written a girl asking for a date early in June. She lived in Paris.

The troops who suffered most during the waiting period were the men in the recalled convoys. All day they had ridden out the storm in the Channel. Waterlogged and weary, they glumly lined the rails as the last of the straggling convoys dropped their anchors. By 11 p.m. all the ships were back.

Outside Plymouth harbor, Commander Hoffman of the *Corry* stood on his bridge looking at the long lines of dark shadows, blacked-out landing ships of every size and description. It was cold and Hoffman was weary. On their return to port, they had learned the reason for the postponement. Now they had been warned to stand to once again.

Below decks the news spread quickly. Radioman Third Class Bennie Glisson heard it as he prepared to go on watch. He made his way to the mess hall and when he got there he found more than a dozen men having dinner—turkey with all the trimmings. Everybody seemed depressed. "You guys," he said, "act like you're eating your last meal." Bennie was nearly right. At least half of those present would go down with the *Corry* a few minutes before H Hour on D Day.

At midnight Coast Guard cutters and naval destroyers began the huge job of reassembling the convoys. This time there would be no turning back.

MONDAY, June 5, 1944. In the early-morning light the beaches of Normandy were shrouded in mist. The intermittent rain of the previous day had become a steady drizzle, soaking everything. Beyond the beaches lay the ancient, irregularly shaped fields over which countless battles had been fought—and over which more would be fought.

For four years the Normans had lived with the Germans on their soil. This bondage had meant different things for different people. In the three major cities—Le Havre, Cherbourg and Caen—the occupation was a harsh and constant fact of life. Here were the headquarters of the Gestapo and the SS. Here were the reminders of war—the nightly roundups of hostages, the never-ending reprisals against the underground, the welcome but fearful Allied bombing attacks.

Beyond the cities—particularly between Caen and Cherbourg—lay the hedgerow country: the little fields bordered by great mounds of earth, each topped with thick bushes and saplings that had been used as natural fortifications by invaders and defenders alike since the days of the Romans. Dotting the countryside were the timbered farm buildings with their thatched or red-tiled roofs, and here and there stood towns and villages like miniature citadels, nearly all with square-cut Norman churches surrounded by centuries-old gray-stone houses. To most of the world their names were unknown: Vierville . . . Colleville . . . La Madeleine . . . Ste.-Mère Eglise . . . Chef-du-Pont . . . Ste.-Marie-du-Mont . . . Arromanches . . . Luc . . .

Here, in the sparsely populated countryside, caught up in a kind of pastoral backwash of the war, there was nothing the Norman peasant could do but adjust to the occupation. Thousands of men and women were shipped out of the towns and villages as slave laborers, and those that remained were forced to work part-time in labor battalions for the coastal garrisons. But the fiercely independent peasants did no more than was absolutely necessary. They lived from day to day, hating the Nazis with typical Norman tenaciousness, stoically watching and waiting for the day of liberation.

In his mother's house on a hill overlooking sleepy Vierville, a 31-year-old lawyer, Michel Hardelay, stood at the living-room windows, his binoculars focused on a German soldier riding a large farm horse down the road to the seafront. On either side of his saddle hung several tin cans. The German was never late: he always brought the morning coffee down to the Vierville exit at exactly 6:15 a.m. The day had begun for the gun crews in the cliffside pillboxes and camouflaged bunkers at this end of the beach—a peaceful-looking, gentle curving strip of sand that within 24 hours would be known to the world as Omaha Beach.

Every morning the trooper rode three kilometers. Hardelay had watched the ritual many times—and it always struck him as amusing that the much vaunted technical know-how of the Germans fell apart when it came to a simple job like supplying men in the field with morning coffee.

But his was a bitter amusement. For some months Hardelay had watched German troops and conscripted labor battalions digging, burrowing and tunneling all along the bluffs. He had watched as, with methodical thoroughness, they demolished the line of pretty pink, white and red summer cottages and villas below the bluffs along the seafront. Now, out of 90 buildings, only seven remained. The others had been destroyed not only to give the gunners clear arcs of fire, but because the Germans wanted the wood to panel their bunkers. Of the seven houses still standing, one belonged to Hardelay. A few days before, he had been officially told that it too would be destroyed. But in some matters the Germans were unpredictable. He'd know for certain within 24 hours: he had been told the house would come down tomorrow—Tuesday, June 6.

Farther down the beach, near the Colleville exit, 40-year-old Fernand Broeckx was doing what he did every morning: he sat in his dripping barn, spectacles askew, head tucked down by the udder of a cow, directing a thin stream of milk into a pail. His farm, lying alongside a narrow dirt road, topped a slight rise barely a half mile from the sea. He hadn't been down that road or onto the beach in a long time—not since the Germans closed it off.

He had been farming in Normandy for five years. In the first World War Broeckx, a Belgian, had seen his home destroyed. He never forgot it. In 1939, when the second World War began, he promptly gave up his job in an office and moved his wife and daughter to Normandy, where they would be safe.

Fifteen miles away in the cathedral town of Bayeux his pretty 19-year-old daughter, Anne Marie, prepared to set out for the school where she taught kindergarten. She was looking forward to the end of the day, for then summer vacation began. She planned to spend her holidays on the farm, and intended to cycle home tomorrow. There was no way for her to know that tomorrow a tall, lean American from Rhode Island whom she had never met would land on the beach almost in line with her father's farm. Nor was there any way for her to know that one day she would marry him.

All along the coast people went about their usual daily chores. The farmers worked in the fields, tended their apple orchards, herded their white-and-liver-colored cows. In the little villages and towns the shops opened. For everyone it was just another routine day of occupation.

In the little hamlet of La Madeleine, back of the dunes and the wide expanse of sand that would soon be known as Utah Beach, Paul Gazengel opened up his tiny store and café as usual, although there was almost no business.

There had been a time when Gazengel made a fair living. But now the entire coastal area was sealed off. The families living just behind the seashore and all along this side of the Cherbourg peninsula had been moved out. Only those who owned farms had been permitted to remain. The café keeper's livelihood now depended on seven families that remained in La Madeleine and a few German troops in the vicinity whom he was forced to serve.

Gazengel would have liked to move away. As he sat in his café waiting for the first customer, he did not know that within 24 hours he would be making a trip. He and all the other men in the village would be rounded up and sent to England for questioning.

MONDAY was quiet and uneventful for the Germans too. Nothing was happening and nothing was expected to happen: the weather was so bad that in Paris, at the Luftwaffe's headquarters, Col. Prof. Walter Stöbe, the chief meteorologist, told staff officers they could relax. He doubted that Allied planes would even be operational this day. Anti-aircraft crews were promptly ordered to stand down.

Next, Stöbe telephoned Von Rundstedt's headquarters in St.-Germain. Von Rundstedt slept late that day as usual, and it was almost noon before he conferred with his chief of staff and approved OB West's "Estimate of Allied Intentions" so it could be forwarded to Hitler's headquarters, OKW. The estimate was another typical wrong guess. It read: "The systematic and distinct increase of air attacks indicates the enemy has reached a high degree of readiness. The probable invasion front still remains the sector from the Schelde in Holland to Normandy, and it is not impossible that the north front of Brittany might be included. But it is still not clear where the enemy will invade within this total area. Concentrated air attacks on the coast defenses between Dunkirk and Dieppe may mean that the main Allied invasion effort will be made there. But imminence of invasion is not recognizable."

With this vague estimate out of the way—an estimate covering almost 800 miles of the invasion coast—Von Rundstedt and his son, a young lieutenant, set out for the Field Marshal's favorite restaurant, the *Coq Hardi* at Bougival nearby. It was a little after one o'clock; D Day was 12 hours away.

All along the chain of German command the continuing

bad weather acted like a tranquilizer. The various headquarters were quite confident there would be no attack in the immediate future. Careful evaluations had been made of the Allied landings in North Africa, Italy and Sicily, and meteorologists had noted that the Allies never attempted a landing unless the prospects of favorable weather were almost certain—particularly for covering air operations. To the methodical German mind there was no deviation from this rule: the weather had to be just right or the Allies wouldn't attack. And the weather wasn't just right.

At Army Group B headquarters the work went on as though Rommel were still there; but the chief of staff, Maj. Gen. Dr. Hans Speidel, thought it was quiet enough to plan a little dinner party. He invited several guests, among them Ernst Juenger, the philosopher and author. The intellectual Speidel was looking forward to the dinner. He hoped they'd discuss his favorite subject: French literature. There was something else to be discussed: a 20-page manuscript that Juenger had drafted and secretly passed on to Rommel and Speidel. Both of them fervently believed in the document: it outlined a plan for bringing about peace—after Hitler had been either tried by a German court or assassinated.

In St.-Lô, at the headquarters of the 84th Corps, Maj. Friedrich Hayn, the intelligence officer, was making arrangements for a party for the corps commander, Gen. Erich Marcks. His birthday was June 6.

They were holding the surprise birthday party at midnight because Marcks had to leave for the city of Rennes in Brittany at daybreak. He and all the other senior commanders in Normandy were to take part in a big map exercise that was to begin early on Tuesday morning. Everyone thought the *Kriegsspiel* would be interesting: it dealt with a theoretical "invasion" which was supposed to take place in Normandy.

The *Kriegsspiel* worried the Seventh Army's chief of staff, Brig. Gen. Max Pemsel. It was bad enough that his senior commanders in Normandy and the Cherbourg peninsula would be away from their commands all at the same time. But it might be dangerous if they were away overnight. Rennes was a long way off for most of them, and Pemsel was afraid that some might be planning to leave the front before dawn. He believed that if an invasion ever came in Normandy the attack would be launched at first light. He decided to Teletype an order: "Commanding generals and others scheduled to attend the *Kriegsspiel* are reminded not to leave for Rennes before dawn on June 6." But it was too late. Some had already left.

One by one, senior officers had left the front on the very eve of the battle. All had reasons, but it was almost as though a capricious fate had manipulated their departure. Rommel was in Germany. So was his operations officer, Col. Hans George von Tempelhoff. Maj. Gen. Heinz Hellmich, commanding the 243rd Division, holding one side of the Cherbourg peninsula, departed for Rennes. So did Maj. Gen. Karl von Schlieben of the 709th Division. Brig. Gen. Wilhelm Falley, of the tough 91st Air Landing Division that had just moved into Normandy, prepared to go. Col. Wilhelm Meyer-Detring, Von Rundstedt's intelligence officer, was on leave. The chief of staff of one division was off hunting with his French mistress and could not be reached.*

At this point, with the officers in charge of beachhead defenses dispersed all over Europe, the German High Command decided to transfer the Luftwaffe's last remaining fighter squadrons in France far out of range of the Normandy beaches. The fliers were aghast.

The principal reason for the withdrawal was that the squadrons were needed for the defense of the Reich, which for months had been coming under increasingly heavy round-the-clock Allied bombing attack. Under the circumstances it just did not seem reasonable to the High Command to leave these vital planes on exposed airfields in France where they were

---

* After D Day the coincidence of these multiple departures from the invasion front struck the Germans so forcibly that there was actually talk of an investigation to see whether British secret service could possibly have had anything to do with it! The fact is that Hitler himself was no better prepared for the great day than were his generals. The Führer was at his Berchtesgaden retreat in Bavaria with his mistress, Eva Braun, entertaining a number of Nazi dignitaries and their wives.

being destroyed by Allied fighters and bombers. Hitler had promised his generals that 1000 Luftwaffe planes would hit the beaches on the day of invasion. Now that was patently impossible. On June 4 there were only 183 day fighter planes in the whole of France; about 160 were considered serviceable. Of the 160, one wing of 124—the 26th Fighter Wing—was being moved back from the coast this very afternoon.

At the headquarters of the 26th at Lille, Col. Josef "Pips" Priller, one of the Luftwaffe's top aces (he had shot down 96 planes), stood on the airfield and fumed. Priller had a reputation for telling off generals, and now he telephoned his group commander. "This is crazy!" he yelled. "If we're expecting an invasion, the squadrons should be moved *up!* And what if the attack comes during the transfer? You're all crazy!"

"Listen, Priller," said the group commander. "The invasion is out of the question. The weather is much too bad."

Priller slammed down the receiver. He walked out onto the airfield. There were only two planes left—his and one belonging to Sgt. Heinz Wodarczyk, his wingman. "What can we do?" he said to Wodarczyk. "If the invasion comes, they'll probably expect us to hold it off all by ourselves. So we might as well start getting drunk now."

OF ALL the millions who watched and waited throughout France, less than a dozen men and women actually knew the invasion was imminent. They went about their affairs calmly and casually as usual. Being calm and casual was part of their business: they were the leaders of the French underground. Most of them were in Paris. From there they commanded a vast and complex organization so secret that leaders rarely knew each other except by code names, and never did one group know what another was doing.

This great secret Resistance army of men and women had been fighting a silent war for more than four years—a war that was often unspectacular, but always hazardous. Thousands had been executed, thousands more had died in concentration camps. But now, although the rank and file didn't know it yet, the day for which they'd been fighting was close at hand.

In the previous days the underground's high command had picked up hundreds of coded messages broadcast by the BBC. A few of these had been alerts warning that the invasion might come at any moment. One was the first phrase of the Verlaine poem, *Chanson d'Automne*—the same alert that Lieutenant Colonel Meyer's men at the German 15th Army headquarters had intercepted on June 1. Canaris had been right.

Now, like Meyer, but much more excited, the underground leaders waited for the second phrase of the poem. For the underground at large, however, the real tip-off would come when the Allies ordered the prearranged sabotage plans to go into effect. Two messages would trigger the attacks. One, *"It is hot in Suez,"* would put into effect the Green Plan—the sabotaging of railroad tracks and equipment. The other, *"The dice are on the table,"* would call for the Red Plan—the cutting of telephone lines and cables. All regional, area and sector leaders had been warned to listen for these two messages.

On this Monday evening, the eve of D Day, one message was broadcast by the BBC at 6:30 p.m. The announcer said, *"The dice are on the table. . . . Napoleon's hat is in the ring. . . . The arrow will not pass."* The other came minutes later.

Everywhere now, Resistance groups were quietly told the news by their immediate leaders. Each unit had its own plan and knew exactly what had to be done. Albert Augé, the stationmaster at Caen, and his men were to destroy water pumps in the yards, smash the steam injectors on locomotives. André Farine, a café owner from Lieu Fontaine near Isigny, had the job of strangling Normandy's communications: his 40-man team would cut the massive telephone cable feeding out of Cherbourg. Yves Gresselin, a Cherbourg grocer, had one of the toughest jobs of all: his men were to dynamite a network of railway lines between Cherbourg, St.-Lô and Paris. Everywhere along the invasion coast, from Brittany to the Belgian border, men prepared.

In the seaside resort town of Grandcamp, almost centered between Omaha and Utah beaches, sector chief Jean Marion had vital information to pass to London. He wondered how he'd get it there—and if he had time. Early in the afternoon his men had reported the arrival of a new anti-aircraft-battery group in the area. Marion had casually cycled over. He knew he'd get through: among the many fake identification cards he had for such occasions was one stating that he was a construction worker on the Atlantic Wall.

Marion was shaken by the size of the unit and the area it covered. It was a motorized Flak Assault Group with heavy, light and mixed anti-aircraft guns. Their crews were toiling feverishly to emplace the guns, almost as if working against time.

Although Marion did not know it, the guns covered the precise route the planes and gliders of the 82nd and 101st paratroopers would take within a few hours. Yet, if anybody in the German High Command had any knowledge of the impending attack, they hadn't told Col. Werner von Kistowski, hard-boiled commander of Flak Assault Regiment 1. He was still wondering why his 2500-man flak unit had been rushed up here. But Kistowski was used to sudden moves. His outfit had once been sent into the Caucasus Mountains all by themselves. Nothing surprised him anymore.

OFF THE French coast a little before 9 p.m. a dozen small ships appeared. They moved quietly along the horizon, so close that their crews could clearly see the houses of Normandy. The ships went unnoticed. They finished their job and then moved back. They were British mine sweepers—vanguard of the mightiest fleet ever assembled.

For now, back in the Channel, plowing through the choppy gray waters, a phalanx of ships bore down on Hitler's Europe—the might and fury of the free world unleashed at last. They came, rank after relentless rank, ten lanes wide, 20 miles across, 2727 ships of every description. There were fast new attack transports, slow rust-scarred freighters, small ocean liners, channel steamers, hospital ships, weather-beaten tankers, coasters and swarms of fussing tugs. There were endless columns of shallow-draft landing ships—great wallowing vessels, some of them almost 350 feet long. Many of these and the other heavier transports carried smaller landing craft for the actual beach assault: more than 2500 of them.

Ahead of the convoys were processions of mine sweepers, Coast Guard cutters, buoy-layers and motor launches. Barrage balloons flew above the ships. Squadrons of fighter planes weaved below the clouds. And surrounding this fantastic cavalcade of ships packed with men, guns, tanks, motor vehicles and supplies was a formidable array of more than 700 warships.

There was the heavy cruiser U.S.S. *Augusta,* leading the American task force—21 convoys bound for Omaha and Utah beaches. Nearby, steaming majestically with all their battle flags flying were the battleships: H.M.S. *Ramillies* and *Warspite;* U.S.S. *Texas, Arkansas* and the proud *Nevada* which the Japanese had sunk and written off at Pearl Harbor.

Leading the 38 British and Canadian convoys bound for Sword, Juno and Gold beaches was the cruiser H.M.S. *Scylla.* And close by was one of Britain's most famous cruisers—H.M.S. *Ajax,* one of a trio which had hounded the *Graf Spee* to her doom in Montevideo harbor. There were many famous cruisers: the U.S.S. *Tuscaloosa* and *Quincy,* H.M.S. *Enterprise* and *Black Prince,* France's *Georges Leygues*—22 in all.

In lines along the edges of the convoys were a variety of ships: sloops, corvettes, powerful gunboats—like the Dutch *Soemba*—anti-submarine patrol craft, fast PT boats, and everywhere sleek destroyers. Besides the scores of American and British destroyer units there were Canada's *Qu'appelle, Saskatchewan* and *Restigouche;* Free Norway's *Svenner;* and even a contribution from the Free Polish forces—the *Piorun.*

Slowly, ponderously, this great armada moved across the Channel. It followed a staggered minute-by-minute traffic pattern of a kind never attempted before. Ships poured out of British ports and, moving down the coasts in two-convoy lanes, converged on the assembly area south of the Isle of Wight. There they sorted themselves out and joined with the forces heading for the beach to which they had been assigned. Out of the assembly area, which was promptly nicknamed Piccadilly Circus, the convoys headed for France along buoy-marked lanes. And as they approached Normandy these five paths, like a network of highways, split up into ten channels—two for each beach: one for fast traffic, the other for slow. Up front near

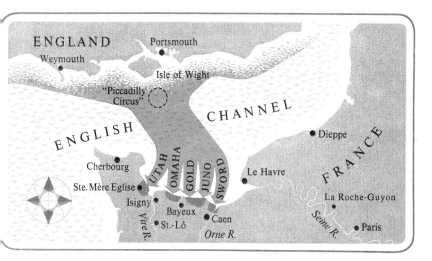

the head of these dual channels and lying behind the spearhead of mine sweepers, battleships and cruisers were the command ships—five attack transports bristling with radar and radio antennas. These would be the nerve centers of the invasion.

Everywhere there were ships, and to the men aboard, this historic armada was the most impressive, unforgettable sight they had ever seen. It was good to be on the way at last—despite the discomforts and dangers ahead. Men were still tense, but some of the strain had lifted. Now, everybody simply wanted to get the job over and done with.

On the landing ships and transports men wrote last-minute letters, played cards, joined in long bull sessions, and as Maj. Thomas Dallas recalls, "Chaplains did a land-office business."

One of them on a jam-packed landing craft, Capt. Lewis Fulmer Koon, found himself pinch-hitting for all denominations. A Jewish officer, Capt. Irving Gray, asked Chaplain Koon if he would lead his company in prayer "to the God in whom we all believe, whether Protestant, Roman Catholic or Jew, that our mission may be accomplished and that, if possible, we may be brought safely home again."

Before they had been in the Channel very long, many men

who had spent hours worrying about their chances of survival couldn't wait to reach the beaches. Seasickness had struck through the 59 convoys like a plague, especially in the rolling and heaving landing craft. Each man had been supplied with anti-seasickness pills, also an article of equipment which was listed in the loading sheets with typical Army thoroughness as "Bag, Vomit, One."

Some men tried to read. Cpl. Alan Bodet began the book *Kings Row,* but found it difficult to concentrate because he was worrying about his jeep. Would the waterproofing hold out when he drove it into three or four feet of water? Chaplain Lawrence E. Deery on the transport H.M.S. *Empire Anvil* was amazed to see a British naval officer reading Horace's *Odes* in Latin. Deery himself, who would land on Omaha Beach in the first wave, spent the evening reading Symonds' *Life of Michelangelo.* Nearby on a landing craft Capt. James Douglas Gillan, a Canadian, to quiet his own nerves and those of a brother officer, opened his Bible at the 23rd Psalm and read aloud, "The Lord is my shepherd; I shall not want. . . ."

It was a little after 10:15 p.m. when Lieutenant Colonel Meyer, the German counterintelligence officer, rushed out of his office. In his hand was probably the most important message the Germans had intercepted throughout the whole of World War II. He now knew that the invasion would take place within 48 hours—and with this information the Allies could be thrown back into the sea. The message picked up from a BBC broadcast to the French underground was the second phrase of the Verlaine poem: *"Blessent mon coeur d'une langueur monotone."*

Meyer burst into the dining room where Gen. Hans von Salmuth was playing bridge with his chief of staff and two others. "General!" he said breathlessly. "The message, the second part . . . it's here!" Von Salmuth thought a moment, then gave the order to put the 15th Army on full alert. As Meyer hurried out of the room, Von Salmuth was again looking at his bridge hand. "I'm too old a bunny," he recalls saying, "to get too excited about this."

LIKE HIS fellow paratroopers, Pvt. Dutch Schultz of the 82nd Airborne was ready, waiting on the airfield: he was in his jump suit, with a parachute, unfastened, hanging over his right arm. His face was blackened with charcoal, his head shaven except for a narrow tuft of hair running back the center of his scalp which made him look like an Iroquois. All around him was his gear. Dutch felt good, for he had succeeded in losing his winnings. All he had left were the rosary beads his mother had sent him. Suddenly someone yelled, "Okay, let's go!" Then the trucks began to move across the airfield toward the waiting planes.

All over England the Allied airborne armies boarded their planes and gliders. The pathfinder planes had already left. Over at the 101st Airborne Division's headquarters at Newbury, General Eisenhower, with a small group of officers and four correspondents, watched the first planes get into position for take-off. He had spent more than an hour talking to the men. He was more worried about the airborne operation than any other phase of the assault. Some of his commanders were convinced that the airborne assault might result in upward of 75-percent casualties.

Eisenhower stood watching now as the planes trundled down the runways and lifted slowly into the air. One by one they followed each other into the darkness. Above the field they circled as they assembled in formation. Eisenhower, his hands deep in his pockets, gazed up into the night sky. As the huge formation of planes roared once more over the field and headed toward France, the NBC correspondent looked at the Supreme Commander. Eisenhower's eyes were filled with tears.

Minutes later, over the Channel, the men of the invasion fleet heard the roar of the planes, too. It grew louder by the second as wave after wave passed overhead. The formations took more than an hour to pass. Then the thunder of their engines began to fade. On the decks of the ships the men gazed up into the darkness. Nobody could say a word. And then as the last formation flew over, an amber light blinked down through the clouds on the fleet below. Slowly it flashed out in Morse code three dots and a dash: V for Victory.

The Shock of Happiness

George Kent

[*March 1966*]

For eight months the girl lay in a Swiss tuberculosis sanatorium making virtually no progress. One day her father arrived, and after a worried look at her departed for a talk with the physician in charge. A half hour later a horse-drawn sleigh, jingle bells and all, was at the door. The girl was bundled in blankets and carried down—and away they went, up and down the snow-covered mountain roads, with a stop for chocolate and cakes, another for a gape at an Alpine valley, then off again for another 20 minutes.

No miracle happened, but it is on the record that from that moment recovery started. Less than a year later, the girl was home, well along the road to normal health.

This is as good an example as I know of what may be called cure by the shock of happiness. Webster defines a shock as "a sudden and violent agitation of the sensibilities." In other words, a brusque upsetting of routine, a rock tossed through the gray window of boredom. Let the upset be joyous. The old wives have always known that happiness is a medicine. Administered sharply and dramatically, it can work wonders.

The business of living calls for an occasional squeal of delight, and that comes only from being brought up short by something we may have dreamed about but certainly did not expect. We all tend to get into ruts. Gifts on birthdays, anniversaries, Christmas—of course! But the present that shakes awake the sagging spirit is one offered for no reason at all except tenderness, and on any old ragamuffin of a day.

And why not turn a simple surprise into a jolt of joy by making the gift dramatically different or outsize? Calling on a woman friend, a man I know brought a bucket of freesias, enough to adorn and perfume the house for weeks. They are still remembered. On another occasion he came bearing a box of candy with a single white orchid caught in the twine. The rule about giving is to give more than expected. Knock the postman, the waiter, the cleaning woman off their feet with a haymaker of a tip. You won't go bankrupt, and you'll get the money back in smiling service. And ditto for gifts to anyone at any time. The annual necktie from Aunt Emma always got a thank-you note, but the Christmas she sent a hydraulic jack the house was lit up by the sparkle in Papa's eyes, and instead of a letter she received a telephone call that rang with hosannas.

An evening out that follows a sudden impulse is worth a dozen carefully planned affairs. One night a friend, a business executive, telephoned his wife: "I'm waiting for you in the lobby of the St. George Hotel. We're having dinner out—I've found a swell new steak house." You could almost hear her stammer, "But the dinner—it's all ready." "Stick it in the icebox; we'll eat it tomorrow," said the brute.

The woman was rocked by vertigo, but secretly happy; it was as if they were back in the old days of courtship when nothing mattered except being together. And after dinner, instead of a sedate dancing spot, they went to a discothèque where, in shock abandoned, they rocked and twisted, imitating the youngsters about them. At one o'clock the husband moaned with a grin, "Oh, my aching back!" "Oh, my darling!" said the lady, and the glow of the moon was in her eyes.

"Every evening should have its menu," said Balzac. It may be an hour of skating under the moon. It may be exotic food. Instead of a show, why not go to a political meeting and get up and express your opinion? Explore the possibilities—they are as varied as your wit and imagination.

And let the daring young man remember to keep doing this after marriage. Once joined in wedlock, he usually falls off the trapeze; the inventor of surprise and tingling forgets what made him a hero. At work he will still pummel his brains, but home becomes for him a place for *not* thinking. Not thinking can become a habit. Brilliance too is a habit, and can be cultivated. If you create high-voltage shocks at home, you are more likely to shine at the office.

For some men and women, lack of self-confidence is almost pathological: the man who freezes when asked to address an audience, the woman who falls to pieces when there are more than four for dinner. For such persons, the simple shock of sudden change may be better than shock treatment by electricity.

I have in mind a timid soul who lived in a small house in the suburbs with two children and a wife who peevishly ruled him. His job as accountant gave him a knowledge of all aspects of the company he worked for; one day, safe in the routine of memo-passing, he sent in a suggestion. It was a good idea, but it required investigation, and so our Mr. Milquetoast was asked to pack his bag and tackle it. He wanted passionately to refuse but, standing on the executive carpet, he did not dare.

The news that this mild creature of routine was going on an unexpected trip was like the explosion of a bomb. The shock waves spread as he settled in his seat on an airplane, put up at a good hotel, made telephone calls and appointments. Overnight our man became a man of the world. Life in the suburbs was never the same again. He bought a new car and gradually assumed command of his home. His wife brightened up and rediscovered the joy of laughter.

It is possible for all of us to create, by our own efforts, the shock that can change our lives. It may take a little courage to shake oneself out of the pajamas of habit. But it can be done. In Finland, one rushes from the superheated sauna bath for a plunge into the icy waters of a lake. Stop to think and you won't do it—ever. Dive in without hesitancy, and after the shock you feel more wonderful than ever before.

The idea is to make greater use of the power that drives us—our emotions—by agitating them in a wise but ruthless fashion. Franz Kafka once said, "We need an ice ax to break the frozen sea within us." The best ax is a shock of happiness.

How to Save Money Buying a Car

Robert O'Brien

[September 1967]

WHEN is it time to think seriously about buying another car—new or used? That's not always easy to decide. "A new car," says a top Detroit executive, "is a highly deferrable purchase. While most automobiles are traded in before they are four years old, the average one being *scrapped* is 13 years old and has run 120,000 miles."

Let's say that your present car is four or five years old, with 60,000 miles on the odometer. That it's burning oil. That it could use a new battery, seat covers, a couple of tires. Nevertheless, it chugs along faithfully. Does it make sense to sell it?

Quite possibly not. You've already absorbed two thirds or more of its depreciation, and if you're thinking of replacing it with a used model, you know *your* car's condition better than you'll know the condition of anything on a used-car lot.

So, if you're interested in saving money, age and superficial defects don't, by themselves, necessarily indicate that it's time for a replacement. The really compelling questions are:

1) Is your car costing more to operate than you can properly afford? 2) Does it need a major repair job, estimated at 25 percent or more of your equity in it? 3) Is it no longer adequate to your real needs? 4) Do you worry about its safety?

If the answer to any one of these questions is "Yes," you

should start shopping for a replacement, and the sooner the better. Here are some basic tips on how to go about it.

• Know what you want. "Most customers have little idea of what they really want in a car," says a top Chrysler saleswoman in New Jersey. "The salesman then has the opportunity to help them make the big decision." If he's conscientious, fine. But if he's more interested in pushing a sale than in your welfare, you may drive off in an expensive mistake. So, before heading for a showroom, answer these questions:

1. What are your needs? How many people must the car accommodate? Think ahead: a sports car may be a joy when you're just married, but where are you going to put that first baby? Perhaps you'll be taking elderly relatives for drives; if so, a two-door car is apt to prove inconvenient. With children and an active suburban life, you'll probably need a station wagon.

2. How much can you afford to pay? Do you count on borrowing? In that case, suppose you can pay $75 a month for two years. (A three-year contract naturally costs more in interest charges; it's wise to avoid, if possible.) At this payment rate and 12-percent annual interest, you'll get a loan of nearly $1600. Let's say the wholesale value of your present car is about $600. This means you have some $2200 to work with.

So, now, your next car begins to take shape. If it will fit your needs, the most economical buy in your price range will be a new compact. If this won't do, then a used car, one or two years old, may be the best buy for your $2200.

If you're in doubt about buying a new car as opposed to a used car, remember this rule: A small new car is a more economical buy than a big used car. Depreciation will be higher, but it will be cheaper to maintain. You'll have longer, fuller warranty coverage. Insurance will cost less. And you'll save on gasoline, oil and tires with every mile you drive.

Shop around for your purchase loan and most favorable interest rate *before* selecting your car. Loan interest is an integral part of car cost, just like tires or brake drums. Keep it to a minimum by making the biggest possible down payment.

• Study performance reports and prices. Read the automobile buyers' guides and price books for general ideas on costs; you can find them at most newsstands for less than two dollars. Study road-test reports in auto magazines. Talk to friends. Remember that the "factory suggested" prices on the stickers include the dealer's hoped-for markup—from some 15 percent on compacts to 22 percent on luxury cars—and that no one pays these list prices. How much you get knocked off may depend on anything from the weather to the dealer's overhead.

If you're trading in an old car, keep your eye on the "cash difference"—the final, net amount the dealer is charging you. He may offer a high trade-in value, and make up for it by a smaller discount; or, he may compensate for an attractive discount by giving less for your trade-in. Your bartering objective, of course, should be the most favorable "cash difference."

• Choose your options. If you can afford more than the "stripped down" model, family-car options are recommended in this order:

Get an automatic transmission. If you have from about $125 to $180 extra, and a wife who drives your car, order an automatic transmission. You'll get much of the cost back at resale. Will it use more gas? Not enough to matter.

Get a four-door. Because of the side posts, a four-door model is stronger, less prone to rattle, easier to get in and out of. Don't worry about the children opening the rear doors at the wrong time; you can buy inexpensive rear-door locks that can be opened only from the outside. Most four-door models cost only $50 to $70 more than two-door models, and you get most of that back when you trade or sell.

Get a V-8 over a 6. The V-8 delivers more horsepower than the 6, gives faster pickup, smoother handling. It's not so important if you're buying a compact, but in the intermediates, and particularly in the heavier standards, the V-8 is a sound investment. Slightly lower gas mileage—if, indeed, there is any difference—will be offset by higher value at trade-in time. Some V-8s come in two or more sizes: for economy get the smallest—and one that uses "regular" gasoline.

As to other options, it's a question from here on of special use, and ability to pay. Undercoating, costing about $17 to $35, is a must if you live where salt or other chemicals are applied to icy roads in winter. Power steering? On heavy cars, yes; try driving a model without it to see.

• Inspect—and drive—before you buy. Don't make up your mind until you've carefully examined and compared at least three different lines of cars in the size and price range you're after. Test-drive each car to see how it handles: how it starts, stops, accelerates and corners; how it *feels* to you on the road.

Before you take delivery of a car, new or used, see that the gauges, warning lights, windshield wipers and washer, radio, heater, seat belts and everything else work. Check the spare tire and tools. Details, yes; but it's likely to be easier to get adjustments before you drive away than later.

• Buy in bad weather. Selling cars is a seasonal business. In good temperate weather, business is brisk. But in cold weather, or muggy summer weather, business is slow—and dealers welcome you with open arms and larger discounts.

What about buying a year-end leftover, still in stock after the new models have gone on sale? The moment you drive home in it, it's already a year old. It may be a good buy, but only if you plan to keep it for four or five years. Unless you get a *very* large discount, it will take you that long to make up for your initial depreciation loss.

• Seek a dealer who wants you as a regular customer. A sound, reliable dealer is sure to be a respected member of the business community, with a reputation for follow-up service and satisfied customers. He won't advertise cars for "no money down" or as "fantastic steals." He won't turn glib, high-pressure salesmen and "closing" experts loose on you. He'll be more interested in selling integrity—of product *and* service. He'll talk like the dealer who advertises, "We want a customer to buy his next car here, too—and the next ones after that."

That makes sense for all concerned.

꙳ A friend of mine was grooming his horse one Sunday as the pastor walked by on his way to church. "You know, parson," he remarked, "they say cleanliness is next to godliness." "Yes," the pastor said thoughtfully. "Maybe the horse will make it."   Trescott T. Abele

I Remember Hyde Park

Eleanor Roosevelt

[June 1963]

I FIRST remember going to the big house when I was a timid young girl not yet engaged to Franklin Delano Roosevelt; he had brought me there to meet his mother's relatives. I remember our honeymoon there a year later—ten days, alone in the house (still closed for the winter) except for the Scots laundress-maid, Elsie, who cooked our meals for us. I remember going back every spring and autumn with our growing family. I particularly recall being there for part of the year when Franklin, at 39, was stricken with polio. And I remember returning on April 15, 1945, when my husband was laid to rest in the rose garden, close to the house where he was born and which he loved so well for all his 63 years.

But I remember too that it was my mother-in-law's Hyde Park. It was indeed her home, and she made every decision concerning it. For over 40 years I was only a visitor there. My mother-in-law did *all* the housekeeping. She directed the activities of her seven indoor servants and her five outdoor men, and when we brought extra servants to help with the children and the enormous collection of guests—as we did when Franklin was governor and later, President—she always told our servants what to do. My mother-in-law allowed household participation by anyone else in only one way: when the telephone bills became really terrific, she permitted Franklin to pay them.

Her house, like the other big establishments on the Hudson River, was run like an English manor house. There were great breakfasts, which you served yourself from the sideboard: chafing dishes filled with oatmeal, scrambled eggs, an assortment of sausage, ham and bacon, and a variety of hot breads. Then there was a big formal luncheon, starting with soup and ending with dessert, and always tea in the late afternoon, to which she expected everyone to come.

An hour before dinner a big Chinese gong beside the hall staircase was rung, as a reminder to wash and dress. Franklin used to invite everyone into his study half an hour before dinner for cocktails—an invitation that was invariably turned down by his mother, who thoroughly disapproved of drinking. In the dining room we all had set places. The young children sat at a table in the alcove. At the main table my husband sat at one end, Mama at the other and I at the side.

After dinner we usually went into the enormous library-living room with its two fireplaces, one at either end. Here too we had our special seats. After my husband's two terms as governor, he had been given the two high-backed brown-leather chairs he had used in office, as is the custom. These chairs were on either side of one fireplace. Franklin always sat in the 1929–1930 chair, usually working on his stamps in the evening. His mother occupied the 1931–32 chair, either reading or knitting. I sat anywhere, also knitting or reading, and sometimes I read aloud to them. Because of my custom of reading to the children after lunch and after tea each day, in order to keep them quiet,

I had learned to read very dramatically, as you must to hold the attention of small children. Apparently my dramatics were also appreciated by the not-so-small.

Life at Hyde Park, however, was not always serene. After Franklin had polio, several changes were made in household arrangements. Until then he and I had shared a bedroom in the new wing, directly over the big library-living room; after his illness I took the small neighboring room, and his mother made the sitting room of our suite into a bedroom for herself. A ramp for his wheelchair was built over part of the stairs leading into the living room, and the large dumbwaiter in the kitchen wing became a lift for Franklin.

As I suppose must always be the case when there are two women under one roof, my ideas and those of my mother-in-law often differed sharply. She had been opposed to Franklin's marrying me, because she felt he was too young to marry and because she thought he could have made a more worldly and social match. Then, when she knew it was going to happen anyway, she determined to bend the marriage the way she wanted it to be. She wanted to hold onto Franklin and his children. As it turned out, Franklin's children were more my mother-in-law's children than they were mine.

Undoubtedly this was partly my fault, since for a great many years she completely dominated me, and I permitted it. I never dreamed that my mother-in-law could be wrong about anything at all. Let me explain how this could be possible.

After Franklin and I married we lived in a hotel apartment while he finished law school, so I had no chance to learn housekeeping. When we were ready to settle in New York City while he practiced law, his mother had a fully furnished house waiting for us. Here were born my daughter Anna and my son James—and my mother-in-law engaged nurses for them. I was not allowed to take care of the children, nor had I any sense of how to do it. As I was terribly inexperienced about taking responsibility of any kind, I was frightened to death of the nurses and obeyed every rule they made.

Later Mama decided that the house was too small for us. She built two houses side by side on East 65th Street—one for herself, the other for us. There were three connecting doors between the houses, joining the dining-room floor, the living-room floor, and the fourth floor at the boys' room. You were never quite sure when she would appear, day or night. Even when we moved to Albany for the four years Franklin was a state senator, my mother-in-law came with us at first to engineer our getting settled and to give our first reception.

It was not until the last two children arrived—Franklin, Jr., and Johnny—that I developed enough initiative to start trying to handle my children's lives myself. And I cannot help but think that the two youngest had far better childhoods than the first three children.

But asserting myself was one thing and being effective was another. My mother-in-law judged people almost solely by their social position, and she continually tried to teach my children to do the same. She found it extremely difficult to get on with Al Smith and many other politicians of the New York City type, and while only people who knew her well could tell when she was being really rude, my children were among those who knew her well.

She had the most carrying whisper I have ever heard, and occasionally during a luncheon at which Franklin was entertaining an important politician we would hear her piercing whisper: "Who is that dreadful person sitting next to my son?" Every time there was a big Democratic meeting her lawn was ruined, and she was miserable about it for days.

However, in our life at Hyde Park, there were also many occasions of family unity and pleasure, even in the period directly after Franklin got polio. Earlier I'd given up attempting to drive a car. After Franklin's illness I just had to learn, and soon I was organizing large picnics to which I drove all of us. One time, I will admit, by error I backed a station wagon containing the entire family right down an embankment.

Our only wedding at Hyde Park was a lovely one. It was when our daughter Anna married Curtis Dall. To this event came all the dozens of Roosevelts on both sides, and friends from everywhere. We entertained almost as expansively for a succession of prominent guests. Our most publicized social event was the 1939 visit of the King and Queen of England, the present Queen Elizabeth's parents. Their stay was studded with a series of comic and embarrassing incidents.

Their Majesties, together with a large party, were to arrive in time for dinner Saturday night. In preparation we had collected all our most valuable china, and had even borrowed dishes from Franklin's stepbrother, "Rosie" Roosevelt, and his wife, who lived next door. Further, we had brought some of the White House butlers to serve—a fact that so outraged Mama's English butler that he left for a vacation in England.

While we waited for our royal guests, Mama and Franklin sparred about the familiar subject of cocktail drinking. My mother-in-law said firmly, "I'm sure that, being English, they will prefer tea." Seated in the library with the cocktail tray ready in front of him, Franklin could hardly wait to say to His Majesty, "My mother thinks you would rather have a cup of tea after your tiring trip, but I wonder if you'd like a cocktail?" His Majesty smiled at them both before answering, "My mother would say exactly the same thing. I'd frankly prefer a cocktail."

The first really embarrassing episode occurred in the middle of dinner. Behind a screen hiding the kitchen door, the extra china for upcoming courses had been piled on an old-fashioned table with a middle pedestal and leaves. Suddenly, as we were all dining and chatting, there was a horrible crash. The table, off balance, had fallen to the floor. We all paused, stunned, and then my stepsister-in-law said to Mama in a clearly heard aside, "I do hope that wasn't *my* china."

After dinner, Franklin, who was usually wheeled from the dining room to the library-living room, chose to walk beside the King, leaning on Jimmy's arm and using his cane. They were almost to the door of the living room, with the rest of us behind them, when we received our second shock. The head butler from the White House had forgotten to send glasses and liqueurs ahead of us. Now, carrying a gigantic tray loaded with glasses, bowls of ice and liqueur bottles, he hurried past us— to stumble on the steps beside Franklin's ramp and fall full-length on the living-room floor. For the remainder of her life, my mother-in-law was to remark, with complete conviction,

"If *my* butler had been used instead of those White House people, none of these things would have happened."

I am sure Their Majesties were relieved next day when they were finally back on their train. But they must have felt the same pang I did when their special cars pulled out. People stood thick on both banks of the Hudson River, and suddenly the air was filled with thousands of voices singing "Auld Lang Syne." We all knew that the King and Queen were returning home to face a war, and I still think that the sound of those singing voices was the most moving thing I have ever heard.

During the 40-odd years that we came and went at Hyde Park there were many changes in all of us. My husband had suffered the most demoralizing blow that can strike a vigorous man—and had four times been paid the highest honor an American can receive from his countrymen. My children had been born, grown and married. I had slowly done what every human being must eventually do: I had learned the lessons of adaptability and adjustment, then of self-reliance.

After Franklin's death, the Secretary of the Interior accepted full title to Hyde Park and its surrounding grounds, and it was opened to the public in 1946 as a National Historic Site. Today, it looks much as it did when we lived there: I see the same furniture, china, bric-a-brac and paintings, and I look at such intimate reminders of our life as the leash and blanket of Franklin's dog Fala, and my husband's glasses lying on his study desk. But now there are additions: the crowds of people moving quietly along the hallways, the uniformed guards, the gated fences blocking the doorways to all the rooms that had become so familiar during the years. And of course there are subtractions, all of them people: my husband, my five children, Mama, and our assorted friends. It is of them that I really think when I remember Hyde Park.

&⧫ A man in San Rafael, Calif., trained his boxer to chase a flashlight beam. Now he sits at a window and waves the flashlight back and forth, while the dog gets his exercise chasing it all over the backyard.

Don Vaughan, quoted by Bill Kennedy in Los Angeles *Herald-Express*

The Heart—Wondrous and Courageous Organ

Henry Morton Robinson

[February 1948]

Don't worry too much about your heart, as so many healthy people seem to be doing nowadays; rejoice, rather, that nature has placed in your breast one of her most delicate yet durable marvels, an organ of surpassing patience, flexibility and strength. Rejoice, and try to understand how it works. It will work all the better for being understood.

Borrow a doctor's stethoscope and listen to the beating of your own heart. In its steady rhythm—lubb-*dup*, lubb-*dup*—you will hear the sound of life itself as blood courses through the valves and chambers of this inimitable pump. For the heart, mechanically speaking, is just that—a pressure pump which forces the blood, with its freight of oxygen, food or waste, through the vessels of the body. If ever this stream should cease to deliver oxygen, the body cells would quickly perish.

Driven by the heart, the five or six quarts of blood in the average human body make a round trip about once every minute. In 24 hours the heart receives and pumps out again some 10,000 quarts of blood, and expends enough energy to raise a 150-pound man to the height of the Empire State Building. In a life span of the Biblical three score years and ten, the heart lubb-*dups* some two and a half billion times, without a single shutdown for repairs. And—so it seems—without a rest.

Yet without rest no muscle can endure, and the heart is a muscle. Though brief, the pauses between *"dup"* and the next "lubb" are rest enough. The normal heart, like man himself, spends twice as much time relaxing as it does at work. Besides, the heart draws extra rations. Though it weighs but 1/200 of the body's weight, it requires 1/20 of the blood in circulation for itself.

Your heart is about the size of your fist, and snugly enclosed in a tough protective covering, the pericardium. Attached to the body only by the great blood vessels stemming from its base, it hangs within your chest, pointing diagonally downward toward your left breast. It is divided into two parts, right and left, by a bloodtight wall. Each part forms a separate pump.

And each of these two pumps, in turn, has two interacting chambers: the auricle, which receives blood into the heart from the veins, and the ventricle, which forces it out again into the body through the arteries. The heart's specialized muscles are so cunningly layered and interwoven that they can squeeze, twist and literally wring out the contents of their chambers at every "lubb"—in other words at every contraction of the pump.

What causes the heart to beat? This question, asked 1700 years ago by the anatomist Galen, was not answered until about 1890, when investigators began to suspect electrochemical energy. They were right. We now know that a kind of electrical timing apparatus called the pacemaker normally generates, 70 times a minute, a tiny electrical impulse which sweeps down and across the muscle fibers, causing them to contract.

The heart, then, is a kind of electromuscular pump, contrived by millions of years of evolution, for the purpose of keeping the blood circulating in two main circuits. One, starting from the left chamber of the heart, is the great systemic circuit, which the blood makes through the entire body for the purpose of maintaining the body's tissues. A shorter, independent circuit goes from the right chamber of the heart to the lungs to let the blood discharge its freight of carbon dioxide and pick up life-renewing oxygen. This is known as the pulmonary circuit.

In order to fully understand the action of the heart, let us trace more precisely the course of the blood. Dark venous blood,

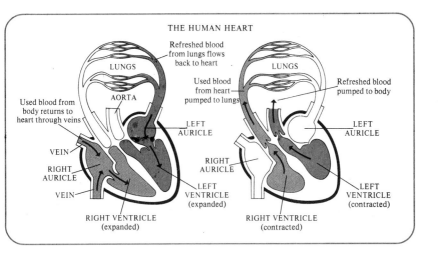

THE HUMAN HEART

laden with carbon dioxide and waste matter picked up in its progress through the body's veins, is drawn into the right auricle as the auricle lies momentarily relaxed. When the auricle is filled, the valve in its floor opens downward and the blood pours into the ventricle below.

When the ventricle is full, its smooth pumping pressure closes the valve, which bellies out like a parachute. This same pressure simultaneously *opens* another set of valves (half-moon shaped) and forces the blood out of the ventricle into the artery that leads directly to the lungs. In the thin-walled network of the lungs the dark blood is purified by exchanging its load of carbon dioxide for oxygen from the outer air. Thus freshened, the blood returns bright crimson to the heart—and the marvel of pulmonary circulation has been accomplished, in less than ten seconds.

Meanwhile the left chamber of the heart, more powerful than the right, carries on the next phase in rhythmic unison with the first. Fresh from the lungs, the blood enters the left auricle. When the auricle is full, the valve opens and the ventricle begins to fill. A fraction of a second later the ventricle contracts, pushing its cupful of blood into the aorta, the huge artery that leads out from the base of the heart. When the pressure in the aorta exceeds the pressure from the ventricle, the half-moon valves between them close. The brisk *dup* that you hear is the sound of the valves slamming shut.

From the aorta, widest of the rivers of life, the red flood branches out, ever more slowly through arteries and arterioles and tiny capillaries, to every cell in the body.

The heart repeats this process of contracting and relaxing, of systole and diastole, lubb-*dup*, lubb-*dup*, day after day, year in, year out, in disease and health, through sleep, love and battle, with the enduring constancy of time itself, with an efficiency not equaled by any of man's inventions and a courage that passes all understanding.

ᶜ᠍⧽ *This prayer was a favorite of Thomas E. Dewey's, the onetime governor of New York. He often quoted it. The author is a Mother Superior who prefers to remain anonymous.*

Lord, Thou knowest better than I know myself that I am growing older, and will some day be old.

Keep me from getting talkative, and particularly from the fatal habit of thinking I must say something on every subject and on every occasion.

Release me from craving to try to straighten out everybody's affairs.

Keep my mind free from the recital of endless details—give me wings to get to the point.

I ask for grace enough to listen to the tales of others' pains. Help me to endure them with patience. But seal my lips on my own aches and pains—they are increasing and my love of rehearsing them is becoming sweeter as the years go by.

Teach me the glorious lesson that occasionally it is possible that I may be mistaken.

Keep me reasonably sweet; I do not want to be a saint—some of them are so hard to live with—but a sour old woman is one of the crowning works of the devil.

Make me thoughtful, but not moody; helpful, but not bossy. With my vast store of wisdom, it seems a pity not to use it all—but Thou knowest, Lord, that I want a few friends at the end.

Stowaway!

Armando Socarras Ramírez,
as told to Denis Fodor and John Reddy

[January 1970]

T̶HE JET engines of the Iberia
Airlines DC-8 thundered in earsplitting crescendo as the big
plane taxied toward where we huddled in the tall grass, just off
the end of the runway at Havana's José Martí Airport. For
months a friend and I had been planning to stow away in a
wheel well on this flight, No. 904—Iberia's once-weekly, nonstop run from Havana to Madrid. Now, in the late afternoon
of last June 3, our moment had come.

We realized that we were pretty young to be taking such a
big gamble; I was 17, my friend Jorge Pérez Blanco was 16. But
we were both determined to escape from Cuba, and our plans
had been carefully made. We knew that departing airliners
taxied to the end of the 11,500-foot runway, stopped momentarily after turning around, then roared at full throttle down
the runway to take off. We wore rubber-soled shoes to aid us
in crawling up the wheels and carried ropes to secure ourselves
inside the wheel well. We had also stuffed cotton in our ears as
protection against the shriek of the four jet engines. Now we
lay sweating with fear as the massive craft swung into its about-
face, the jet blast flattening the grass. "Let's run!" I shouted.

We dashed onto the runway and sprinted toward the left-
hand wheels of the momentarily stationary plane. As Jorge began to scramble up the 42-inch-high tires, I saw there was not

room for us both in the single well. "I'll try the other side!" I shouted. Quickly I climbed onto the right wheels, grabbed a strut and, twisting and wriggling, pulled myself into the semi-dark well. The plane began rolling immediately, and I grabbed some machinery to keep from falling out. The roar of the engines nearly deafened me.

As we became airborne the huge double wheels, scorching hot from takeoff, began folding into the compartment. I tried to flatten myself against the overhead as they came closer and closer; then in desperation I pushed at them with my feet. But they pressed powerfully upward, squeezing me terrifyingly against the roof of the well. Just when·I felt I would be crushed, the wheels locked in place and the bay doors beneath them closed, plunging me into darkness. So there I was, my five-foot-four-inch, 140-pound frame literally wedged in amid a spaghetti-like maze of conduits and machinery. I could not move enough to tie myself to anything.

Then before I had time to catch my breath, the bay doors suddenly dropped open again and the wheels stretched out into their landing position. I held on for dear life, swinging over the abyss, wondering if I had been spotted, if even now the plane was turning back to hand me over to Castro's police.

By the time the wheels began retracting again I had seen a bit of extra space among all the machinery where I could safely squeeze. Now I knew there *was* room for me, even though I could scarcely breathe. After a few minutes, I touched one of the tires: it had cooled off. I swallowed some aspirin tablets against the head-splitting noise, and wished I had worn something warmer than my light shirt and green fatigues.

Up in the cockpit of Flight 904, Capt. Valentín Vara del Rey, 44, had settled into the routine of the overnight flight, which would last 8 hours and 20 minutes. Takeoff had been normal, with the aircraft and its 147 passengers, plus crew of ten, lifting off at 170 m.p.h. But right after lift-off something unusual had happened. One of the three red lights on the instrument panel had remained lighted, indicating improper retraction of the landing gear.

"Are you having difficulty?" the control tower asked.

"Yes," replied Vara del Rey. "There is an indication that the right wheel hasn't closed properly. I'll repeat the procedure."

The captain relowered the landing gear, then raised it again. This time the red light blinked out.

Dismissing the incident as a minor malfunction, the captain turned his attention to climbing to assigned cruising altitude. On leveling out, he observed that the temperature outside was −41 degrees F. Inside, stewardesses began serving dinner.

Shivering uncontrollably from the bitter cold, I wondered if Jorge had made it into the other wheel well, and began thinking about what had brought me to this desperate situation. I wondered what my parents and my girl, María Esther, would think when they heard.

My father is a plumber, and I have four brothers and a sister. We are poor, like most Cubans. Our house in Havana has just one large room; 11 people live in it—or did. Food was scarce and strictly rationed. About the only fun I had was playing baseball and walking with María Esther along the seawall. When I turned 16, the government shipped me off to vocational school in Betancourt, a sugarcane village in Matanzas Province. There I was supposed to learn welding, but classes were often interrupted to send us off to plant cane.

Young as I was, I was tired of living in a state that controlled *everyone's* life. I dreamed of freedom. I wanted to become an artist and live in the United States, where I had an uncle. I knew that thousands of Cubans had got to America and done well there. As the time approached when I would be drafted, I thought more and more of trying to get away. But how? I knew that two planeloads of people are allowed to leave Havana for Miami each day, but there is a waiting list of 800,000 for these flights. Also, if you sign up to leave you are a *gusano*—a worm —and life becomes even less bearable.

My hopes seemed futile. Then I met Jorge at a Havana baseball game. We got to talking. Jorge too was disillusioned. "The system takes away your freedom—forever," he said.

Jorge told me about the weekly flight to Madrid. Twice we went to the airport to reconnoiter. Once a DC-8 took off and flew directly over us; the wheels were still down and we could see into the well compartments. "There's enough room in there for me," I remember saying.

These were my thoughts as I lay in the freezing darkness more than five miles above the Atlantic Ocean. By now we had been in the air about an hour, and I was getting lightheaded from lack of oxygen. Was it really only a few hours earlier that I had bicycled through the rain with Jorge and hidden in the grass? Was Jorge safe? I drifted into unconsciousness.

The sun rose over the Atlantic like a great golden globe, its rays glinting off the silver-and-red fuselage of Iberia's DC-8 as it crossed the European coast high over Portugal. With the end of the 5563-mile flight in sight, Captain Vara del Rey began his descent toward Madrid's Barajas Airport. Arrival would be at 8 a.m. local time, the captain told his passengers over the intercom, and the weather in Madrid was sunny and pleasant.

Shortly after passing over Toledo, Vara del Rey let down his landing gear. As always, the maneuver was accompanied by a buffeting as the wheels hit the slipstream and a 200-m.p.h. turbulence swirled through the wheel wells. Now the plane went into its final approach; now, a spurt of flame and smoke from the tires as the DC-8 touched down at about 140 m.p.h.

It was a perfect landing—no bumps. After a brief post-flight check, Vara del Rey walked down the ramp steps and stood waiting for a car to pick him up, along with his crew.

Nearby, there was a sudden soft plop as the frozen body of Armando Socarras fell to the concrete apron beneath the plane. A security guard was first to reach the crumpled figure. "His clothes were frozen stiff as wood," the guard said. "All he did was make a strange sound, a kind of moan."

"I couldn't believe it at first," Vara del Rey said. "He had ice over his nose and mouth. And his color . . ." As he watched the unconscious boy being bundled into a truck, the captain kept exclaiming, "Impossible! Impossible!"

The first thing I remember after losing consciousness was hitting the ground at the Madrid airport. Then I blacked out again and woke up later at the Gran Hospital de la Beneficencia in downtown Madrid, more dead than alive. When they took my temperature, it was so low that it did not even register on the thermometer. "Am I in Spain?" was my first question. And then, "Where's Jorge?" (Jorge is believed to have been knocked down by the jet blast while trying to climb into the other wheel well, and to be in prison in Cuba.)

Doctors said later that my condition was comparable to that of a patient undergoing "deep freeze" surgery. They called my survival a "medical miracle." In truth I feel lucky to be alive.

A few days after my escape I was up and around the hospital, playing cards with my police guard and reading stacks of letters from all over the world. I especially liked one from a girl in California. "You are a hero," she wrote, "but not very wise." My uncle, Elo Fernández, who lives in New Jersey, telephoned me to come to the United States to live with him. The International Rescue Committee arranged my passage.

I am fine now. I live with my uncle and go to school to learn English. I still hope to study to be an artist. I want to be a good citizen and contribute something to this country, for I love it here. You can smell freedom in the air.

I often think of my friend Jorge. We both knew the risk we were taking and that we might be killed in our attempt to escape Cuba. But it seemed worth the chance. Even knowing the risks, I would try to escape again if I had to.

A vice president of the Douglas Aircraft Co. which makes the DC-8 reports there is "one chance in a million" that a man would not be crushed when the plane's huge double wheel retracts. "There is space for a man in there," he says, "but he would have to be a contortionist to fit himself in."

Armando should also have died from both the lack of oxygen and extreme cold. At the altitude of Flight 904 (29,000 feet), the oxygen content of the air was about half that at sea level, and the temperature was 41 degrees below zero. An expert at Brooks Air Force Base School of Aerospace Medicine says at that altitude, in an unpressurized, unwarmed compartment, a man would normally retain consciousness for only two or three minutes, and live only a short while longer.

Perhaps a Spanish doctor summed up Armando Socarras' experience most effectively: "He survived with luck, luck, luck— many tons of luck."

Pray for Barbara's Baby

Kristin Hunter

[January 1969]

Tʜɪs is the story of a failure. My failure, my friends' failure, society's failure—everybody's. Which means, in some sense, yours.

I first met the girl I will call Barbara in the spring of 1966 when she was going on 15, a sophomore at a high school in the slums of North Philadelphia. A neighbor, a substitute teacher, had brought her home from school, ostensibly to help with housework. However, this well-intentioned young white woman's real purpose was to help a promising pupil escape the trap that seems to lie in wait for most teen-agers in the ghetto. She invited me over that day, hoping that I too would be persuaded to offer Barbara work now and then.

The moment I saw this pretty, mahogany-colored child with wide frightened eyes, a wild mop of hair, and a shy intelligence planted in a painfully underdeveloped body, I knew that something must be done to help her. Another voice, a kindly cynic's, should have intervened at that point with "Forget it. Nothing *can* be done."

But who would have listened? Not the teacher, not I, not any of the other kind-and-guilty hearts who became involved with Barbara and her troubles over the next two years.

A, the teacher, tutored Barbara; B, a businessman, gave her an after-school job; C, a salesman, provided clerical work. I, a black writer, offered—in addition to good pay for light housework—a sympathetic ear, frequent gifts and loans, and efforts at "common sense" advice.

For about two months Barbara moved dreamily through our lives, a sweet enigmatic shadow, smiling gently, replying to everything with soft "Yes ma'ams" and "No sirs." She provided an obligingly blank surface on which we could project our fondest middle-class hopes—college, or nursing school, or business training and an office job at the very least—but thought her own thoughts and went her own way. She was perhaps too considerate to reveal the stark truth of what she knew would be her future. But I think she knew it all along—that nothing any of us said or did would have any effect whatever.

When she visited me last month, ragged, dirty, pregnant, abused, and all but homeless at 16, I decided to go up to North Philadelphia to find out why.

The first thing you notice about the street Barbara lives on is children—running, stumbling, falling, screaming, fighting, climbing rubbish heaps, riding rattletrap wheeled toys, crashing into dilapidated walls and fences. The adults are invisible. But there is no escaping children.

Children are also the most noticeable feature of the house where Barbara lives. There isn't much else to notice: a scarred front door that doesn't close properly, a living room with an ancient suite of greasy gray furniture, a dismal kitchen ridiculously small for the 13 people who eat there. Barbara, unrelated to the Browns, the current occupants of the house, lives with them simply because she lived in the house before they did. Last summer it was her aunt's house, until the weekend that Barbara went off to visit a girl friend and returned to find the house vacated. (She later received a note saying that her aunt had moved to North Carolina.) When the Browns moved in, Barbara stayed.

The staggering problems that have afflicted Barbara's brief life climaxed on this street, but they did not begin there. They had their seeds, like most Northern ghetto troubles, in the South—specifically, in a small village in North Carolina, where 43 years ago Barbara's grandmother, age 15, gave birth to a daughter sired by her own father.

From all accounts, Barbara's mother was of mild demeanor and harmless enough as a girl, and she managed to grow up, marry and produce nine children before her worsening lunacy came to the attention of the authorities. Her first mental hospitalization occurred in Philadelphia in 1964, when Barbara was 12. Before then—and afterward, too, since her mother rejoined the family in spite of official prohibitions—Barbara led a rootless back-and-forth existence: when her mother encountered difficulty in Philadelphia, she returned to North Carolina with her children; when North Carolina palled, she brought them north again. As a result, the family lived in Philadelphia for 15 years officially—but never actually stayed there for more than two months at a time.

To make matters worse, this already disoriented woman fell under the spell of a charlatan who convinced her—for a healthy share of her household money—that she was capable of talking to God. Meanwhile, Barbara's father, who had the distinction among ghetto men of being steadily employed (in a furniture factory), adjusted as best he could through the series of separations and reunions with this incompetent and increasingly unworldly woman. It is perhaps understandable that he formed an additional liaison, which, over the years, resulted in eight more children.

Though Barbara was failing several subjects in school, the concerned teacher who had brought her home the day I met her reasoned that, in the light of her seesaw existence, the fact that she had reached tenth grade at all was a tribute to her intelligence. I would attribute it also to the school's indifference, since my neighbor was the first to alert officials there to the fact that her mother was keeping Barbara out of school more days than she was permitting her to attend.

A couple of months went by, as is the way with so many bureaucratic procedures, before a truant officer was dispatched to the house. There he was told by Barbara's mother that he was speaking to God and had better mind his manners. An investigation followed. As a result Barbara's mother was re-hospitalized, the father was decreed incapable of raising the children alone, and Barbara was placed in a foster home.

The period that followed was hopeful. The home was poor but nice; the foster mother believed in the benefits of education, and she had a teen-age daughter who encouraged Barbara to make something of herself. Barbara was transferred to another high school, where for the first time she was given academic subjects that engaged her mind. And she went every day. (At this point, A, B, C and I began behaving like a cheering section as its favorite quarterback nears the goal line.)

It all lasted exactly two months. Then Barbara's father rebelled against the payments imposed by the court to maintain Barbara in the foster home. Without any investigation he was allowed to remove Barbara from the home and board her free with the aunt who later abandoned her.

The last time I visited the house on Barbara's street, a wild group of children was in full possession of it—not just Mrs. Brown's five minor children and her grown daughter's two, but several others who had apparently found their way through the always-open door. Watching the energetic youngsters at their unrestrained "play," I smiled at the naïveté of social planners who think that improved housing is all that is needed to turn a ghetto into a model community. No one is going to provide money for nice fresh paint and hardwood floors and brand-new furniture anyway; but if someone did, this juvenile army of house-wreckers would turn it all into rubble in a week.

Yet in a house without other valuables, babies become the valued objects. How unimaginative are middle-class people who believe that poor women have babies for the sole purpose of increasing their relief checks. Poor women have babies because, in their bleak world, babies are the only dependable source of happiness. In the ghetto, men are transient, and older children are trouble. As babies grow up, they too rapidly become problems—noisy, dirty, aggressive. Therefore it is necessary always to have another infant in the house—a warm, cuddly, consoling creature who will accept all your devotion and do nothing in return to bring you anguish.

Ghetto babies must be the most thoroughly loved in the world; they are passed from loving arms to loving arms, cradled, cuddled, tickled, endlessly discussed and admired. Lip service is paid to the larger society's notion that illegitimacy is wrong, but everything points to the real attitudes of the community: that sex is as natural as eating and sleeping, that babies are a desirable product of this activity, and that females from the age of 14 on are expected to produce them. There is evidence that, in some quarters of North Philadelphia, something is considered wrong with girls if they don't.

Pressure was on Barbara to become pregnant long before she actually did. Last year when all her girl friends were pregnant she held out heroically, determined to defy the relatives and friends who had predicted long before that she would turn out exactly like her three older sisters—all mothers at 16. We, her middle-class cheering section, told her that the damning voices echoing constantly in her ears didn't have to be accurate, that she could easily prove them wrong.

But it wasn't to be. And, given the facts of her environment, it is surprising that Barbara remained virginal as long as she did.

The Browns are a fairly typical welfare family. The children are all legitimate, but Mr. Brown is an intermittent figure in the household because his employment is unstable and his wife needs the welfare checks that are available only to separated mothers and to wives whose husbands do not work.

The matriarchal family is practically the only kind of family existing in the hard-core ghetto. Where large families are the rule, children tend to dominate the adults by sheer numbers anyway. But when in addition society and its instrument, the welfare system, decree that there can be no husband or other employable man in the house, and adult authority resides only in the person of a tired, overworked and indulgent mother, victory of the children is assured. Chaos and anarchy take over— usually for good.

When Mrs. Brown took possession of the house, her two oldest daughters—Virginia, 22, who is separated from her husband, and Dorrie, 19, a widow—moved in with her. Mrs. Brown did her best to supervise the bulging household. "She didn't let us stay out late," says Barbara. "And there was no carrying on in the house when she was home." But Mrs. Brown was pregnant as a result of one of her husband's occasional visits, and her pregnancy brought on medical complications.

On the very day that Mrs. Brown was hospitalized, each of the daughters moved a boy friend into the house, and the boy friends thoughtfully brought along a friend for Barbara. A continuous party went on throughout Mrs. Brown's hospital stay —liquor flowing, music, visitors wandering in and out—and in this voluptuous atmosphere Barbara finally became pregnant.

Now, at last, Barbara belongs. She is a part of the group in the living room—including a 38-year-old grandmother and four 16-year-old mothers—all women together and equals, discussing teething and infant weight gains and other maternal concerns. Her middle-class supporters were asking her to do something almost excruciatingly difficult: to forgo immediate approval in her present world for the sake of some vague, far-off achievement in some unimaginable future world. Too polite and considerate to tell us, she knew we were asking the impossible.

What will happen to her now?

Her teen-age girl friends who prodded her to imitate them all have parents to back them up, make decisions, provide for them and their young—and a good thing it is, too. For these girls, despite their surface competence with maternity, are still children with children's minds and interests.

But Barbara, for all practical purposes, is parentless. Her mother died last summer in a North Carolina hospital. Her father, brothers and sisters have their own troubles. And her middle-class friends, after observing the futility of their efforts, have deserted her one by one.

Marriage? This is a subject that no one Barbara's age wants to think about, let alone discuss. Barbara and her friends use the phrase "my baby's father" to describe a relationship that has no other meaning for them. All of them have received, and refused, proposals from these remote figures. The reasons they give for shying away from marriage include "I'm not sure," "I'm not ready," "I've seen too many bad marriages in my family."

So what *will* become of Barbara? All she knows is that she will not go along with the Browns when they move to New

Jersey next month. She will get her own apartment instead. How she will pay for it, when she is now so destitute that she must borrow a quarter for carfare every time she visits me, is a problem mercifully blotted out for the time being by the confidence of youth and the notorious beatitude of pregnancy.

Her baby's father, she says blandly, will support her until she can get a job. If he fails to demonstrate this remarkable sense of responsibility for a 19-year-old, will she take him to court? No, that won't be necessary. See? He has already shown his good faith by buying her the new maternity dress she is wearing today—blinding turquoise rayon, even now showing a gaping rip in the shoulder seam which cannot be repaired because there is no seam allowance.

"I don't want my baby to know all the hard things I've had to know," Barbara says. And no one dares point out to her how little likelihood there is of her preventing it. That her child will also be a *person*—a human being with increasingly complex and expensive needs—she only dimly perceives, perhaps because she has never had a chance to become a person herself. And, again, no one dares interrupt her dream with realistic considerations. Least of all I.

But then, no one has to. The inexorable processes of nature will do it for us. Next month, at a city hospital, Barbara will have her baby, and will take it—where? To what?

&bw; A suburban Detroiter, after a heavy snow, had decided not to attempt to dig himself out, but he felt a surge of guilt when he saw his neighbor across the street come out, survey the scene, and then contact neighbors on either side. All three fell to—digging out the driveway, bulling the First Neighbor's car to the street and on to the plowed thoroughfare, where he took off with a jaunty wave.

"There's a man who's really devoted to his work," thought the stay-at-home, hating himself. This feeling lasted for about 15 minutes, until First Neighbor's car returned and barreled into the driveway. He opened the rear deck, lifted out a case of beer and handed it to Helpful Neighbor 1. A second case went to Helpful Neighbor 2. Then First Neighbor toted a third case into his own home and was seen no more that day.

Mark Beltaire in Detroit *Free Press*

"Golfers,
Quit All That Thinking!"

Sam Snead

[September 1959]

F EVERYBODY had to play golf
barefoot, I figure I'd hardly ever lose a tournament. I learned to
play golf barefoot and it's more natural for me. It feels good out
there, wiggling your toes. When you step up to the ball, you're
connected with the earth and you almost feel the roots go down.
Besides, you don't swing so hard. If you do, your toes will get
all cockeyed and you're liable to take a spill. So what happens?
You swing nice and easy, just like the book says.

With shoes on, I sometimes get to thinking I'm King Kong
and try to hit that little ball eight country miles. I like to hear
the crowd go "Oooh!" when I really get ahold of one. But I pay
for it. It's been the cause of a lot of my trouble.

My second big trouble is that I get mad when I miss a shot.
I want to take the club and pitch it straight up in the air. When
you get mad you get tense, and when you get tense your coördination goes all to pieces. But who ever heard of anybody getting
mad with their shoes off?

My third big trouble is missing short putts—little bitty ones
like from here to there. There's only two things I'm really afraid
of on the golf course—and the other one is lightning.

You'd think that at least when I played in the U. S. Open,
like last June—that's the tournament I'm famous for never win-

ning—I'd have played barefoot. But I wore shoes. That's because golf nowadays is like visiting a city cousin: you get all dressed up and mind your manners and think about a lot of things you don't usually have to mess with. It was never like that back in Hot Springs, Va., when I was a kid.

Me and my brother Pete just couldn't wait until the first day of May to take our shoes off. Then we'd play golf. We'd get Piggie McGuffin and Horsehair Brinkley and walk two miles over to the "goat course." Sometimes on the way we'd see rattlesnakes. We used to practice our swings by fixing an old mashie head onto the end of a buggy-whip shaft and lop their heads off clean as a whistle.

Once we got to the course we'd have to hunt around until we found some balls. I got so I could knock a ball out 200 yards or more in my bare feet, using a club whittled out of a swamp maple. We never kept score on account of we hardly ever played two holes in succession. We'd have to putt out real quick and run because there was an old cop who chased us.

I played golf barefoot until I got into high school. Then I got a secondhand set of sticks for ten dollars and drove spikes into an old pair of street shoes. Right then the game started getting complicated for me. Instead of banging away at the ball without a thought in my head, I found myself thinking about what I was trying to do—and in golf that's first-degree murder.

Most people who play golf think too much. To get any real mileage out of this game you've got to sit on your imagination. Take me. I never think any more than I can help it. I just try to get a mental picture of what I'm going to do on each shot, telegraph it to my muscles, then narrow my thinking down to one thing.

I'd say that golf is about 75 percent mental. And of all the mental hazards that afflict golfers, being scared is the worst. All golfers get scared some time or other. When they get scared, they get tense. A handy trick for working up a good mental attitude is to imagine that par on most holes is one stroke more than it really is. Then you'll hit within yourself instead of trying to kill the ball, and you'll chop about six strokes off your score.

This won't work for everybody. Figuring out the right mental attitude is each golfer's private problem. I have my particular problem. When I miss a shot, steam comes out of my ears. I'm madder than a bear poked with a sharp stick. That's when the ball turns into a little demon, and that's when I have to turn myself into a mangy old hypocrite.

I give the ball some sweet talk. I tell it that this isn't going to hurt a bit. I'm a friend and all I'm going to do is give it a nice little ride. If the ball catches a bad lie, I look down at it and say, "Hey, you beautiful little white thing! What are you doing down in that hole?"

Of course, I don't always manage to say it exactly that way. Most of the time I mumble and grumble. But I play well when I'm grumbling. It helps me keep fired up to a competitive pitch.

Other players are different. Take Ben Hogan. He's old stone-face out there. He puts chains on his thoughts and never lets anyone see what's going on inside. But Hogan pays for it at night by gritting his teeth. We shared a room one time traveling, and I know.

At the other end of the line from Hogan you have Tommy Bolt. I call him Thunder because he's always building up a storm. He gets madder than any grown man I ever saw. But sometimes he's just putting it on. I watch his neck. When he's really mad his neck gets the color of tomato soup.

When you're not concentrating, every little thing irritates you. Then the old noggin buzzes with notions, and you have to fight them off like bees. This is when you drop your guard, and then the old pressure comes in and grabs you by the throat. I've seen it grab all of them at one time or another.

All tournaments are won or lost with a putter. It's where concentration counts double. You've got two things to think about: how hard to hit the ball and what line of direction to hit it on. You can't think about both at once. First I think about the direction. I set the face of the putter on it, then try to put it out of my mind. When I stroke the ball I'm thinking about only one thing: speed.

The idea in golf is to have an automatic swing that you don't have to think about. But 98 percent of all golfers don't. So they try to even it up by thinking. I had a pupil tell me he thought about seven things when he swung at a ball. He's worse off than the fellow who thinks about three things during that 1.7 seconds that it takes to swing a golf club. And the man who thinks about only *one* thing has them both beat.

How do you decide what one thing to think about? Well, you've got to experiment. Each professional has figured out what he's going to think about. He calls it his "key," and it's hardly ever the same with any two of them. Bobby Locke's key is moving his left shoulder back to the same position on every long shot. Bobby Jones thought about turning his head slightly to the right just before he started his backswing. Byron Nelson tried to see the clubhead flatten out the ball at the moment of impact. He never did, of course, but just *trying* kept him from moving his head.

I have two keys, depending on how I'm playing. If I'm hooking, the one thing I try to think about when I swing is locking my left shoulder along the line to the target. When I'm not hooking, my key is swinging within myself, using only about 85 percent of my power. That's because, like most golfers, I like to slug the ball.

The reason nobody ever gets this game 100 percent under control is that everything about it is different from what it seems. If you hit the ball easy, it goes far. You hit down and the ball flies up. Golf teases you into doing a lot of thinking, but the simpler you keep it the better. It's played mostly by city folks, but it's really a game for country kids—playing barefoot.

En Route

On a visit to Panama a few years ago, my sister was returning from a night spot with her husband in an open taxi. It was midnight, it was pouring rain, and the driver was speeding like a madman down a curving road. She called out loudly: "Stop! You are ruining my hat! What's the hurry? We have all night. Stop, I say!"

But none of her commands were heeded. When they reached the hotel she popped out and gave the driver a piece of her mind. He calmly shrugged his shoulders. "I'm sorry, madam," he said. "I thought you two were making love."   Daisine Smith

Slaves of the Machine?

Stuart Chase

[April 1929]

From pulpit, rostrum and editorial chair rises the song to the effect that man has become the slave of his machines, even as Dr. Frankenstein was overwhelmed by the monster he created.

Let me list some of the mechanisms that I personally encounter in a day's march. The first thing I hear in the morning is a machine—a patented alarm clock. In the bathroom I shave with one mechanism, and another showers me with water. Downstairs I look at an electric motor which blows petroleum into my furnace, a motor which runs the washing machine, and a motor which operates my refrigeration engine. Meanwhile an electric range is cooking my breakfast, and bread is being browned by a toaster which suddenly splits open when the correct shade of brown has been attained. Before I leave the house the whine of the vacuum cleaner is already in my ears.

I go to the garage, start explosions in a six-cylinder engine, and pilot it past automatic signal lights to the station. There I resign myself to another man's operation of an enormous machine, fed by a third rail from a water turbine at Niagara Falls. Arrived at the metropolitan terminal I buy a package of cigarettes by depositing a coin in a machine. I enter my office building, and a machine shoots me vertically toward the roof. A sputter of typewriters greets me at my door.

So far as I am aware, no permanent evil effects befall me

by virtue of this machine aid. I suffer from no prolonged monotonies, fatigues or repressions. I do not feel like a slave, though of course I may be one. No individual living in a social group is ever free, but I wonder if my mechanized hours have put more chains on me than are to be found on a remote aborigine in a society innocent of engines. I do not think so.

But probe deeper. Whether I go to my office by subway or in my car, I am employing a machine for transportation. Are the psychological effects the same? Indeed they are not. In the one case my role is entirely passive. In the other case I dominate my mechanism and my role is psychologically stimulating.

We touch here the roots of the whole problem of machinery and man. It is obvious that certain machine contacts are as lethal as others are invigorating. To control a powerful mechanism such as an automobile is to give the ego a joy ride, the reverse of the slave psychology. To make sweeping conclusions about any process so varied is downright nonsense.

Let us concentrate for a moment upon the case of the factory worker who tends a machine with no responsibility for its control, for it is here if anywhere that the gloomy talk of slavery is merited. Is a race of robots, sub-men, really being created?

As nearly as I have been able to estimate from the Census of Occupations, there may be some five million persons in the United States whose work entails complete submission to a machine. So our possible number of robots works out to about five percent of the total population, or 13 percent of those gainfully employed. Greece in her great days had five million freemen standing on the backs of 12 million slaved. I dare you to conclude that a population 70-percent slave is more wholesome than one possibly five-percent slave to the machine.

There are important additional considerations. Our factory population has been steadily declining since 1920. There were 1,250,000 fewer employes in factories in 1928 than in 1923. Also, the whole course of modern technical development is in the direction of more automatic machinery, and this tends to replace machine tenders and feeders with skilled inspectors.

But the fact that the robot ratio is small, and growing smaller, does not dispose of the case. One does not need to be a sentimentalist to recoil from the thought of working in the stokehole of a liner, or of knotting broken threads in a textile mill all day.

Ralph Borsodi gives us an excellent illustration of the many robot occupations which still surround us. In one great factory there is a room filled with punching machines. In front of each stands a worker, feeding it pieces of steel by hand. A lever is geared to the mechanism, and to this lever the man is chained by a handcuff locked to his wrist. As the punch comes down the lever moves back, taking the hand with it. To look down the long room is to see machines, levers and men in unison—feed, punch, jerk back. (Yet before the levers and handcuffs were installed, the workers were continually losing fingers and hands under the down thrust of the punch.)

But are all machine-tenders thus handcuffed, actually or figuratively? Here on the other hand is a "steel bird," the man who rivets skyscrapers together. He is restless, adventurous, courageous and gay. He earns big money, is a mighty spender. He may be killed, but while he lives he *lives*—and swaggers. The power age exalts his personality. Here is a locomotive engineer, indefatigably ministering to a vast black monster. The control of this beast is not always good for his health, but no finer body of men in the sense of character and dependability was ever grown. And here is Charles Lindbergh, minding a machine over 3000 miles of ocean. I have not heard him called a robot.

It is alleged that the modern worker of the robot class we are considering suffers from injury to the body and to the mind. It is true that the physical health of certain industrial groups, particularly those where the factor of dust is high, does not measure up to the community average. But the evidence is that the health of industrial workers as a class is improving with that of the rest of the population.

As for the central charge—the injurious effects of the machine upon the worker's mind—the evidence is scantier and less conclusive. Mental cases now require as many hospital beds as all other cases combined. This is serious, but it tells us little about *trend*. That great numbers are slightly mad is only too apparent; but how many were in similar sad condition in the Middle Ages, when the only engines were perpetual-motion toys that would not work? When monks and nuns, cut off from the most normal of all human relations, filled their own asylums and overflowed upon the countryside? When saints, devils, witches and magicians were as popular as the movies?

For some men no repetitive task, however monotonous, is felt as such. Fred Colvin of the *American Machinist* admits that he has wept for the soul-destroying effects of the machine, and has urged the shifting of men from one routine job to another "to save their tottering reason." When he tried it there was a riot. Here was a man lying on a cradle under the assembly line, screwing up a bolt. He had a comfortable position, an admirable rest for his head. If shifted, he threatened to quit. He was convinced he had the softest berth in the shop. A man of this type is apt to be one who has recourse to pleasant daydreaming.

Is it not reasonably evident then that there is no ground for writing off our so-called robots as psychologically a total loss? Does it not depend on the kind of man and the kind of machine? A large fraction *like* their jobs. Those who hate their work and cannot compensate constitute a real industrial tragedy, and no stone should be left unturned to free them. Fortunately, ingenious methods of studying and preventing fatigue are being tried in some factories. What we need is not poetic moonshine about Dr. Frankenstein, but specific information as to where, and how, we are being hurt.

One of the real dangers lies in accidents. Rather than wail about machinery enslaving all mankind, I suggest that any manufacturer who permits machines to mangle his workers—or who puts workers on them without first testing their ability to stand the rhythm—be strong-armed. All machines which by their basic design are overdangerous either to body or mind should forthwith be melted down. However efficient, they are too costly for society to tolerate.

&~ At a party in New York's garment district, a salesman noticed a tray of canapés being passed around. "Look," he said to a friend. "Dinner swatches." Robert Sylvester, Chicago Tribune-New York News Syndicate

LAUGHTER,
THE BEST MEDICINE

ONE OF the factory workers refused to sign up for group insurance. No policy could be issued until all employes signed, but he held out. The foreman begged him to sign; so did the shop steward, the plant superintendent, the general manager. Still no go. Finally, the owner of the factory took him aside and said, "Listen, you idiot. Unless you sign up, I'll fire you."

The worker grabbed the paper and signed immediately. "Now," asked the owner, "why didn't you sign this thing before?" "Because," the man replied, "no one explained it as clearly as you."   Matty Simmons in *The Diners' Club Magazine*

DEMONSTRATING in front of a department store, a Women's Libber cried out, "Free women! Free women!"

A male passerby, just emerging from the store, responded: "Marvelous! Do you deliver?"   George Lemont, quoted by
Herb Caen in San Francisco *Chronicle*

A MAN who had been out fishing for hours without a nibble started nipping at a bottle of whiskey to console himself. By late afternoon, he was loaded. As he was coming back to the dock, a big fish leaped out of the water and landed in the boat. The fisherman seized it and threw it back into the lake. "If you ain't gonna bite," he growled, "you sure ain't gonna ride!"

Raymond Shutt, quoted by Joe Creason in Louisville *Courier-Journal*

As SOON as space vehicles become common, no doubt someone will put in some parking meteors.
S.S. Biddle in *The Wall Street Journal*

I AWOKE at 3 a.m. to a stifling-hot bedroom—once again my husband had shut the windows and opened the heat register. I'd had enough of this hassle. I spent the rest of the night on the living-room couch.

Our four daughters were puzzled to find me there next morning, so I explained. That afternoon I learned, through a series of amused phone calls, that our youngest daughter had announced during "telling-time" at kindergarten: "Mommy is sleeping on the couch now cause Daddy makes it too hot for her in the bedroom."
Nancy J. Fraser

"What time is it?" a passerby asked a hippie on Boston Common. "Twelve o'clock," replied the hippie.

"Goodness," said the man, "I thought it was later than that."

"Man, it never gets later than that around here," said the hippie. "Like, when it reaches twelve o'clock, we start over again."
Harold Winerip in The American Legion Magazine

My daughter was at the kitchen sink when the phone rang. Someone asked for her mother. "I think she's in the shower," she answered. "Just a minute, I'll see." She reached over and turned on the hot-water faucet. Immediately a piercing scream came from the back of the house. Turning off the faucet, my daughter reported: "Yes, she's still in the shower."
Harvey C. McGee in Sonora, Calif., Union Democrat

A Hopkins, Minn., family lent its male hamster to a friend to mate with his female. After seven new hamsters resulted, the Hopkins man thought this was a good opportunity to explain life to his nine-year-old son. "Son," he said, "you probably have some questions about the hamsters and their new babies."

"Yes, I do," the boy replied. "Can I charge a stud fee?"
"Almanac" in Minneapolis Tribune

I announced to our house guests from Australia that I would make after-dinner coffee for anyone who wished. I had three kinds to offer: coffee with the caffeine removed, coffee with the acids removed and caffeine left in, or instant coffee. "I say," answered one of the Australians, "would you possibly have some coffee that hasn't been interfered with?"
Mrs. Paul S. Reis

There Is No Death

Norman Vincent Peale, D.D.

Norman Vincent Peale is one of the most effective preachers of his time, with a reach far beyond his own pulpit. His writings— many of which have appeared first in the Digest—are read eagerly by millions the world over. His book "The Power of Positive Thinking," from which this article is drawn, has become a byword, a standard of inspirational literature.

[October 1953]

For years I have been recording a series of incidents which bear out the conviction that life, not death, is the basic principle of our universe. From them I have gained the unshakable belief that there is no death, that here and hereafter are one. When I reached this conclusion, I found it to be the most satisfying and convincing philosophy of my entire life. Following are the experiences which convinced me that human spirits on both sides of death live in a fellowship that continues unbroken.

H. B. Clarke, an old friend of mine, was of a scientific turn of mind, restrained, factual, unemotional. I was called one night by his physician, who expected him to live only a few hours. His heart action was slow. He had no reflex action at all.

I began to pray for him, as did others. The next day his eyes opened and after a few days he recovered his speech. His heart action returned to normal. After he recovered strength he said, "At some time during my illness something very peculiar happened to me. It seemed that I was a long distance away, in the most beautiful and attractive place I have ever seen. There were lights all about me. I saw faces dimly revealed—kind faces, they were—and I felt peaceful and happy. In fact I never felt happier.

"The thought came, 'I must be dying.' Then it occurred to me, 'Perhaps I have died.' I almost laughed out loud, and asked myself, 'Why have I been afraid of death all my life? There is nothing to be afraid of in this.'"

"Did you want to live?" I asked.

He smiled and said, "It did not make the slightest difference. If anything, I think I would have preferred to stay in that beautiful place."

Hallucination? A dream? A vision? I do not believe so. I have spent too many years talking to people who have come to the edge of "something" and had a look across, who unanimously have reported beauty, light and peace, to have any doubt in my mind.

A member of my church, Mrs. Bryson Kalt, tells of an aunt whose husband and three children were burned to death when their house was destroyed by fire. The aunt was badly burned but lived for three years. When finally she lay dying, a radiance suddenly came over her face. "It is all so beautiful," she said. "They are coming to meet me. Fluff up my pillows and let me go to sleep."

Friends of mine, Mr. and Mrs. William Sage, lived in New Jersey and I was often in their home. Will Sage died first. A few years later, when Mrs. Sage was on her deathbed, the most surprised look passed across her face. It lighted up in a wonderful smile as she said, "Why, it is Will!" That she saw him those about her bed had no doubt whatsoever.

Arthur Godfrey tells of being asleep in his bunk on a destroyer when he was in the Navy. Suddenly his father stood beside him, put out his hand, smiled and said, "So long, son." Godfrey answered, "So long, Dad." Later he learned of his father's death. The time of his passing had been the precise period during which Godfrey in his sleep "saw" his father.

The late Rufus Jones, one of the most famous spiritual leaders of our time, had a son, Lowell, the apple of his eye. The boy became sick when Dr. Jones was on the ocean bound for Europe. The night before entering Liverpool, while lying in his bunk, Dr. Jones experienced an indefinable, unexplainable sadness. Then, he said, he seemed to be enveloped in the arms of God. A great feeling of peace and a sense of a profound possession of his son came to him.

Upon landing in Liverpool he was advised that his son had died; the death occurred at the exact moment when Dr. Jones had felt God's presence and the everlasting nearness of his son.

A boy serving in Korea wrote to his mother, saying, "The strangest things happen to me. Once in a while at night, when I am afraid, Dad seems to be with me." His father had been dead for ten years. "Do you think that Dad can actually be with me here on these Korean battlefields?"

Why not? How can we not believe that this could be true? Again and again proofs are offered that this universe is a great spiritual sounding house, alive and vital.

My mother was a great soul, and her influence on me will ever stand out in my life as an experience that cannot be surpassed. During my adult years whenever I had the opportunity I went home to see her. It was always an exciting experience.

Then came her death, and in the fullness of summertime we tenderly laid her body in the beautiful little cemetery at Lynchburg in southern Ohio, a town where she had lived as a girl.

It came autumn, and I felt that I wanted to be with my mother again. I was lonely without her, so I went to Lynchburg. The weather was cold and the sky overcast as I walked to the cemetery. I pushed through the old iron gates and my feet rustled in the leaves as I walked to her grave, where I sat sad and lonely. But of a sudden the clouds parted and the sun came through.

Then I seemed to hear her voice. The message was clear and distinct, stated in her beloved old-time tone: "Why seek ye the living among the dead? I am not here. I am with you and my loved ones always."

In a burst of inner light I became wondrously happy. I knew that what I had heard was the truth. I stood up and put my hand on the tombstone and saw it for what it was, only a place where mortal remains lay. But she, that gloriously lovely spirit, is still with us, her loved ones.

The New Testament teaches the indestructibility of life. It describes Jesus after His crucifixion in a series of disappearances and reappearances. This indicates He is trying to tell us that when we do not see Him it does not mean He is not there. Out of sight does not mean out of life.

The mystical appearances which some of us today experience indicate the same truth: that He is nearby. Did He not say, "Because I live, ye shall live also"? In other words, our loved ones who have died in this faith are also nearby, and occasionally draw near to comfort us.

The Bible gives us other insights into the great question, "What happens when a man leaves this world?" And it wisely tells us that we know these truths by faith. The surest way into truth, says Henri Bergson, the philosopher, is by perception, by intuition; by reasoning to a certain point, then taking a "mortal leap." You come to that glorious moment when you simply "know" the truth.

Of these deep and tender matters I have no doubt whatsoever. I firmly believe in the continuation of life after what we call death takes place. I believe there are two sides to the phenomenon known as death: this side where we now live, and the other side where we shall continue to live. Eternity does not start with death. We are in eternity now. We merely change the form of the experience called life—and that change, I am persuaded, is for the better.

The Mature Male

ᑫᔓ A sixtyish woman whose husband was overly attentive to the young ladies at a party explained to a neighbor: "He's like a puppy running after cars. He doesn't want to catch one—he just wants to bark at them a little." A. W. Quattlebaum in Zebulon, Ga., *Pike County Journal*, quoted by Olin Miller in Atlanta *Journal*

ᑫᔓ "What kind of husband do you have?" asked one old girl of another at a class reunion.

"Well," the second replied, "if he mentions Daisy in his sleep, he's talking about flowers."

L & N Magazine, quoted by Tom Sims, King Features

Riddle of the
Quick-Frozen Mammoths

Ivan T. Sanderson

[April 1960]

N OBODY, as far as I have
been able to ascertain, seriously wants to quick-freeze an elephant. But the idea seems to have piqued the curiosity of some
people in the frozen-foods industry since I started asking if they
could tell me how to do such a thing. The reason for my question is simply that we already have lots of quick-frozen elephants; the flesh of some has retained its full flavor, and I want
to know how the job was done.

About one seventh of the entire land surface of our earth,
stretching in a great swath around the Arctic Ocean, across
northern Siberia, Alaska and Canada, is permanently frozen.
Most of this territory is covered with a layer of muck; usually
composed of sand or silt, it also includes a high proportion of
loam, all bound together with frozen water.

The list of animals that have been thawed out of this muck,
whole and in fragments, would cover several pages. It includes
the famous woolly mammoths and woolly rhinoceroses, horses
like those still existing wild in Asia, giant oxen and a kind of
huge tiger. In Alaska it also includes giant bison, wolves and
beavers—and a quite ordinary lion. The riddle: When, why and
how did all these creatures get killed and quick-frozen?

When Western scientists first became aware of this matter,

they summarily dismissed it with the statement that "the animals fell into the ice." Those who murmured that one cannot fall into ice were hushed by dismal accounts of Swiss mountaineers falling into crevasses in glaciers.

It came to light, however, that there are not—and never were—any glaciers in Siberia except on the upper slopes of a few mountains, and that the animals are never found in mountains but always on level plains. Further, none of the animals has ever been found in ice. They are all in the muck.

It was then explained that the animals fell into rivers and were deposited miles away in deltas and estuaries under layers of silt. That sounded splendid at first, but then the next lot of riddles appeared. These animal remains are not in deltas or estuaries. Almost without exception they are stuck in the plateaus that occur all over the tundra. The animals could not have drowned, for many of them are perfectly fresh, whole and undamaged, *and still standing or kneeling.*

Next, several versions of the "mud theory" became popular. There are certain kinds of clays found on the tundra sticky enough to hold a man by the legs. Russian scientists suggested that a few feet of this substance could hold a mammoth until a gigantic blizzard blew up and froze him in the goo forever. But spoilsports pointed out that no such substance has ever been found holding or lying under any frozen animal.

Around the turn of the century a mammoth was found sticking headfirst out of a bank of the Beresovka River in northern Siberia. This Beresovka corpse was sort of squatting, raised on one foreleg in front, with the other held forward as if about to salute. Much of the head had been eaten down to the bone by wolves, but much of the rest was perfect. None of its two-foot-long shaggy fur was rubbed or torn off.

Most important, the lips, the lining of the mouth and the tongue were preserved. And on the tongue, as well as between the teeth, were portions of the animal's last meal which it had not had time to swallow. This meal was composed of delicate sedges and grasses and—most amazing—fresh buttercups.

Perhaps none of these things sounds very startling at first, but examined one at a time they add up to an incredible picture.

Freezing meat is not quite so simple a process as one might think. To preserve it properly it must be frozen *very* rapidly. If it is frozen slowly, large crystals form in the liquids in its cells. These crystals burst the cells, and the meat becomes dehydrated and unfit to eat.

At minus 40° Fahrenheit it takes 20 minutes to quick-freeze a dead turkey, 30 to preserve a side of beef. But these are mere bits of meat, not live mammoths clothed in fur, at a living temperature of about 98°. Unless we have *tremendous* cold outside, the center of the animal will remain comparatively warm for some time, probably long enough for decomposition to start. Meanwhile, the actual chilling of the flesh will be slow enough for large crystals to form within its cells. Neither event occurred with most of the mammoths, one of which has been proved by the radiocarbon dating method to be just over 10,000 years old. The flesh of many of the animals found in the muck is remarkably fresh. Frozen-food experts say they must have been frozen at well below minus 150°.

Further, several studies indicate that mammoths were not specially designed for the arctic; nor did they live in arctic conditions. The Indian elephant, which is a close relative of the mammoth and just about the same size, has to have several hundred pounds of food daily just to survive. For most of the year there is nothing for any such creature to eat on the arctic tundra. Yet there were tens of thousands of mammoths there.

Little flowering buttercups, tender sedges and grasses exclusively were found in the stomach of the Beresovka mammoth. Buttercups will not grow even at *plus* 40°. Therefore: either the mammoths made annual migrations north for the short summer, or that part of the earth was once warmer—or both.

Here, then, is the amazing picture: Vast herds of enormous, well-fed beasts placidly feeding in sunny pastures, delicately plucking flowering buttercups. Suddenly they are all killed without any visible sign of violence, and before they can so much as swallow. Then they are quick-frozen so rapidly that every cell is preserved, despite their great bulk and high body temperature. *What could possibly do this?*

Fossils of plants requiring sunlight every day of the year

have been found in Greenland and Antarctica. This proves that at some time in the past either the poles were not where they are now, or those portions of the earth's surface were once elsewhere. Astronomers and engineers agree that the axis of the earth itself cannot ever have shifted, because the earth is a vast flywheel and, if any force great enough could be found to so shift it, it would fly apart. Ergo, the crust of the earth, which is relatively thin (estimates run from 20 to 60 miles), must have shifted.

If the crust does come unstuck from the spinning body of the earth, parts of it will drift. However, the circumference of the earth is 42 miles longer around the equator than it is around the poles: so any portion of the crust heading for the equator is going to have to stretch; any moving toward a pole will have to contract. What must then happen?

The crust of the earth is like taffy in that it can be stretched slowly but will break if pulled too fast. If a part of the crust goes up over the rise of the equator too fast, it will crack. Both about the equator and toward the poles, where the crust is squeezed most, every available volcano may well be set off.

Volcanoes in eruption spew out not only lava but also masses of dust particles and gases. This sudden extrusion of dust and gases might be so heavy as to cut out sunlight altogether for days, weeks, months or even years if the crustal movements continued. Winds beyond anything known today would be whipped up, and cold fronts of vast lengths would build up with violent extremes of temperature on either side. There could be 40 days and nights of snow in one place, continent-wide floods in another, roaring hurricanes, seaquakes and earthquakes. But perhaps most important might be the gases which would probably have been shot into the upper atmosphere.

If these volcanic gases went up far enough, they would be violently chilled by the "cold of space." Then, as they spiraled toward the poles, as all the atmosphere does in time, they would begin to descend. Coming upon a warm layer of air, they would weigh down upon it and eventually, perhaps in great blobs, pour down through the weakest spot. These blobs would displace the air already there, outward in all directions with the utmost violence—and they might well be below minus 150°.

Consider now our poor mammoth placidly munching away in his meadow, perhaps even under a warm sun. In a matter of minutes the air begins to move in that peculiar way it does today at the end of the arctic summer, when the first cold front descends and the temperature may drop as much as 60 degrees in an hour. The mammoth feels a violent tingling all over his skin and a searing pain in his lungs; the air seems suddenly to have turned to fire. He takes a few breaths and expires, his lungs, throat, eyeballs, ears and outer skin already crystallized.

In a few hours he is a standing monument. Softly the snow comes to bury him. Later, floods of melt water bring down great quantities of silt which gradually dissolves the snow below and eventually envelops the quick-frozen mammoth.

In Alaska, just outside the area where the blob descends, his distant cousin is still chewing away. The sky here probably clouds over; it may even start to snow—something the animal has not before encountered in September when he is in the north on his summer migration. He starts to pad off for cover. But there comes a wind that rapidly grows in fury and explodes into something unimaginable. He is lifted off his feet and, along with bison, lion, beaver from ponds and fish from rivers, is hurled against trees and rocks, torn literally to bits and then bowled along to be flung into a seething caldron of water, mud, shattered trees, boulders, mangled grass, shrubbery and bits of his fellows. Then comes the cold that freezes the whole lot, and finally, when the catastrophe is over, the snow to cover it all. This is what we find in Alaska: mammoths and other animals actually shredded but still fresh.

Here then may be the answer to our riddle, and clues in solving a thousand other riddles, some of which are of vital importance to our own well-being and future. At the same time, they may be a warning of most unpleasant things to come—if a similar convulsion of nature should occur again.

꙰ Statistics don't lie, but they don't always sit too well, either.

Nuggets

Moscow Revisited

John Gunther

John Gunther's byline first showed up in the Digest in 1929, and repeated 55 times thereafter. An indefatigable traveler who reported all he saw with zest, authority and photographic clarity, he achieved great success with his "Inside Europe" in the mid-'30s. Seven more "Inside" books followed: most of them written on assignment for the Digest or with Digest help. Gunther was doing one more, "Inside Australia," when he died in 1970.

[January 1969]

Moscow, replete with contradictions, challenges, defiances and loaded secrecies, is still the central bastion of the Other World, the supreme epitome of Soviet power. Recently I spent a few weeks there, my fifth visit in 20 years. Once more I felt the durability, vitality, the sheer ruthless drive of the U.S.S.R. as focused in its capital city.

Moscow is a double capital—capital of the Soviet Union as a whole, and of its principal constituent part, the Russian Soviet Federated Socialist Republic. Situated at the junction of the Moskva River and the Moscow Canal which leads to the Volga, the city is built in large concentric rings around the Kremlin. It looks dull, flat and ash-colored, except for a handful of ornate white skyscrapers and the marvelous centerpiece of the Kremlin with Red Square beside it. The square contains Lenin's tomb and St. Basil's Cathedral—the latter seemingly made of peppermint sticks, striped turnips and brightly painted onions. A circular highway almost 70 miles long defines the city limits about ten miles from the Kremlin. Beyond the exterior boulevards is a "forest belt" much like the Green Belt of London.

On my last trip in 1956 I had found Moscow an exceptionally clean city, but with few trees, even on the wide, handsome boulevards. Russians, however, crave the sight of something green and living, so this is a great city for plants. Even in the roughest tenement districts you see plants or ferns in almost every window. Today Moscow plants 400,000 trees a year.

Russian men are short and squat, built like square corks. It is unusual to meet one taller than five-foot-eight. The Russians are a terrific, a tremendous, a magnificent people. In some respects they closely resemble Americans—in good humor, robustness, curiosity and gregariousness, as well as in their capacity for organization and inventiveness, their aptitude for technical skills. During my 1956 trip I never saw an unfriendly face.

Now, a dozen years later, I was eager to see what changes had occurred. I found, for one thing, a notable improvement in the standard of living, although the standard still comes nowhere near equaling ours. Citizens are better dressed, more consumer goods are available in the shops (but not enough), more money is being spent.

I found, second, a spectacular advance in housing. The drive into Moscow from the airport is startling to a returning visitor because the boulevards are solidly lined today with large new housing developments in what was virtually open country in the 1950s. The whole city seems convulsed with building; gaunt yellow cranes are visible almost everywhere—even on the periphery of Red Square. Effort is made to achieve pleasant living conditions. Still, most of the new apartment buildings are crudely built, and sag and crack after a year or two. Door handles pull off; hinges break. And in spite of all the progress, 40 percent of Moscow's citizens still live in "communal" flats—that is, they share kitchen and toilet facilities with other families. The shortage of space in this city of 6,500,000—sixth-largest in the world—is so acute that three, four or even more members of a family may be stuffed into two tiny rooms. Marriages are compromised by lack of privacy. Sometimes, for a divorce, a blanket is simply hung between the beds.

I found, too, a large increase in traffic. Moscow has entered the automobile age. It doesn't have traffic jams or serious parking problems yet, but there are about 300,000 cars in the city, and the hiss and gurgle of traffic outside one's hotel can keep a person awake at night. We drove out to Zagorsk, 45 miles away, to see its celebrated monastery, and our small Russian-made Volga had to thread its way in and out of solid lines of trucks the entire length of the route.

Moscow is still astonishingly clean, and has no smog. This is because the authorities have modernized or transferred some of the most insalubrious factories. The city's gas is piped in from the Ukraine and the Caucasus, or from Saratov, 450 miles away on the Volga. During winter the snow is removed from the streets by no fewer than 1500 trucks and other vehicles, together with thousands of street cleaners, many of them women, wielding rough, tousled brooms. Muscovites seem to have a passion for covering things up to keep them clean; parked automobiles are often protected by a large slipcover, like a raincoat, and on Soviet aircraft most passengers encase their luggage in removable fabric jackets.

This is a silent city. Drivers are forbidden to use horns except in an emergency, and such familiar American sounds as shrieking police whistles and the moan of sirens are unknown. Airports are situated so no aircraft pass over the city, and children do not yell on the streets. The silence is strange, almost eerie, because this is very much a city of crowds, where noise would normally be expected. Men and women fairly pullulate along the streets. As British essayist V. S. Pritchett wrote, "There seems to be no such person as a Russian alone."

On a homely level, the streets are fascinating, from the beds of red tulips in the Kremlin gardens to the lines of small prerevolutionary wooden homes, like dolls' houses, with brightly painted ornate door and window frames, in the outskirts. There are vending machines everywhere, discharging *kvass* (a thin, sour beer) and a carbonated fluid, called simply "water," flavored with syrup. Old men with gnarled, shaven heads gaze endlessly at copies of *Pravda* spread out under standing glass frames at street corners, and crowds of restless young folk line up at refreshment stands for lollipops, beer and hot dogs, two to a roll. Ice-cream cones and other frozen confections are on sale almost everywhere, even in the subway.

Roughly one third of the people get about by subway, the rest by buses, streetcars, taxis and private cars. The subway costs five kopecks—a little more than a nickel. Buses and streetcars cost between three and five kopecks. There are generally no ticket collectors on the buses; the passenger operates on the honor system and deposits his coin in a box at the rear of the bus, far from the driver. Taxis—11,000 in Moscow—are state-owned, and can be ordered from about 150 phone booths placed along the streets exclusively for that purpose.

Strangely, children are not much seen on the streets of Moscow; they go to state-supported kindergartens or schools and, during their holidays, to "pioneer" camps. Outside school hours they play in the *dvor*, a backyard or garden. The *dvors* of old Moscow are haunts of the grandparents as well, who fill in as guardians while parents are at work.

A wife, incidentally, often has a more important and better-paying job than her husband, but this does not seem to incite jealousy or resentment. I met one woman—an important government official—whose husband is a lathe worker. Conversely, I know one foreign ambassador whose Muscovite cook is married to a Russian lawyer; they maintain a comfortable *dacha* (villa) in the country.

Alcohol is still a problem—one which has recently become more acute. For a long time, authorities hoped that alcoholism would gradually disappear. Who, in a "perfect" classless society, would want to relieve tensions or blot things out with alcohol? A 25-percent rise in the sale of vodka (a government monopoly) was recorded a year or so ago, after introduction of the five-day week. Presumably, many workers found nothing much else to do in their increased leisure time. The city maintains "drunk tanks" to which police take the obviously intoxicated. There the citizen receives a "cure," and is cleaned up and released the next morning, having had to pay a substantial fee.

Juvenile delinquency appears to be a lesser problem than in many other large cities—for what I gather are two main reasons. First, school is taken very seriously by most youngsters, homework is arduous, and there is no time for loitering. Second, youngsters may join the Comsomols (communist youth organizations), which have 800,000 members in Moscow. The Comsomols act as a kind of voluntary militia after school hours, helping to police the streets.

Moscow has comparatively little crime, though I have noticed friends carefully remove the blades of their windshield wipers and stow them inside the parked car before locking. Less than one tenth of one percent of the municipal budget, I heard, goes to the local police. And anyone can wander around anywhere at night in perfect safety.

The telephone service is not as good as ours. For many years there were only a few telephone books—a major nuisance, prompted by considerations of security. When new books were issued, they were exhausted so quickly that many owners of telephones never received a copy. The result: it can be hard to track a person down.

We arrived in Moscow just in time for the May Day celebrations. This is one of the formidable sights of the world. My wife and I had to go through seven different police inspections in a quarter of a mile to reach our places in the grandstand. The ceremony began at 10 a.m. on the split second. The day was brisk and sunny, with a clean wind that made the multitudinous banners flap and snap.

After a speech by the Soviet minister of defense, Marshal Andrei A. Grechko, the parade began, led by various generals. Most were so fat it seemed impossible that they could march so briskly. Thereafter, about 30 different elements of the Soviet military establishment marched past. At the end came the weapons-carriers bearing giant silver rockets, like fat pencils.

Then came unending civilian delegations. The parade was still going on full blast at 4 p.m. Even so, the crowds remained enormous. What the show intended to demonstrate was, as always, Soviet power—to give citizens psychological confidence in the armed might of their officers, troops and weapons.

Almost invariably, the first question asked of a person returning from Moscow is, "Were you followed?" It is difficult to be categorical on this point. Russia is a notoriously complicated country, and there are no's to every yes, yes's to every no. Suitcases are practically never opened or looked at on arrival at a frontier, but my mail was certainly opened—very clumsily, too. Perhaps our room was bugged, perhaps not.

It is still difficult for foreigners to make real contact with Russian citizens, not because they are unfriendly but because the government does its best to keep contact with outsiders to a minimum. Most Muscovites still seem frightened of being seen too often with foreigners.

Moscow is, it should be remembered, the capital of a *closed* society. An atavistic fear of the secret police, of concentration camps and forced labor in Siberia is still balefully alive in the heart of almost every citizen.

Exciting Moscow may be—industrious, creative, durable, packed with power—but it is still a kind of automaton among cities, regulated to the uttermost inch. Its principal hallmark continues to be lack of freedom.

ß`Trial marriages? Whose isn't?   Lane Olinghouse

Jumped or Fell

Ted Robinson, Jr.

[September 1950]

Provincetown, Mass., in the days
of my childhood was a place offering great natural advantages to one who meant to become a professional daredevil and
perhaps the world's greatest human fly. I was the damn boy
who damaged people's roofs by falling onto them or off them.
I fell onto roofs from trees, or from high gables to lower gables
or into the gutters. Sometimes I fell off them into the harbor.
I fell into flower beds, into lawns, and once into a pile of fresh
horse manure. If it hadn't been for the property damage involved I would probably still be falling.

I had the misfortune once to fall with a chimney: I had my
arms inside it as I climbed around it along the ridge of a pitched
roof, and the whole chimney gave way. We rolled—the bricks
and I—off the roof and into the yard next door. The cost of repairs was six dollars, and I had to earn it by washing dishes at
a quarter a meal. That was discouraging.

I was never seriously horrified by the thought of falling because I had never seen anyone fall, and I had then no acquaintance with the facts of death. One bad fall might possibly have
made me wonder, but I think not. I once slipped from the ridge-
pole of a church under construction; I fell and slid the long,
steep length of the roof, flopped over the gutter, and landed on
all fours on a scaffold about six feet down. What cause was I
ever given to worry?

It never occurred to me that I enjoyed the sort of luck that creates legends. Not counting scratches and bruises, I was injured in a fall only once and that was off the back of a truck. Provincetown had no paved streets or sidewalks then, and wherever I landed it was bound to be grass or sand or water.

I don't know why I wasn't killed once when I took a running dive off the edge of a sand pit. It was a 20-odd-foot drop, the night was quite dark, and I had only a faint idea of what lay ahead of me. I ran and dived out into the dark, took one easy turn, and landed in the sand on my feet. I felt fine. Why did I jump at all? I anticipate the question now because I have lately discovered that there are people to whom such impulses are foreign—to whom *all* wild impulses are foreign. Oh, well. I dived into the sand pit because it was fun.

I used to dream of flying without a plane, and this was almost it. I dived in the dark because the darkness helped the illusion. I did a turn in the air on the way because I thought I was Douglas Fairbanks.

Boys are better at lots of things than grown men are. Otherwise I would certainly have been killed the day a friend and I climbed the peak of Provincetown's Pilgrim Monument. This is a pencil-like column a couple of hundred feet high, capped by four tall arches supporting a small roof which is ringed by a battlement of chunky stone posts. We swiped a carton of golf balls from a hardware store and took them up the monument to see how far they'd bounce. We dropped the golf balls, one at a time. As we kept watching a ball going down, it diminished to nothing; presently there it was again, coming up. It grew larger slowly. It hung there, and then retreated, diminished, and vanished. We never found any of them.

The eight stone posts ringing the roof stand so close together that jumping from one to the other was not hard; but there was not a lot of space to land on, and it was a long way down. We made the circuit. An adult would have found even sitting on the battlement distasteful. He'd have looked straight down the side of the shaft and seen it leaning as the world rolled, and he'd have wished he were flat in bed and tied down. I watched the world roll, and stopped it by looking up; afterward I thought no more about it—except when I wanted to make it roll and looked down to do it.

Not injuries, nor maturity, but the police finally put an end to my human-fly career. My family moved to Cleveland. This was during a building boom, and wherever a boy looked he was likely to see what was in effect a giant jungle gym. I walked the bare floor beams of uncounted apartment houses still abuilding, scaled their faces by toe and finger holds in the stonework on the corners, descended by scaffolds, rubble chutes, laundry chutes, chimneys, and floor-to-floor drops down unstaired stairwells.

One day I walked out on a railroad drawbridge over the Cuyahoga River and, wrapping my arms and legs around part of the track, rode the end of it up while a freighter passed through; the bridge tender made a lot of noise but he had to stick to his post, and I got away on the far bank when he let me down.

Then I got interested in trains. It was only a matter of a few weeks before I was a juvenile-court character. My punishment—for riding a freight—was merely a lugubrious "talking to" in the judge's private chambers, but I gathered that if I was ever nabbed at *anything* again it was reform school for me. I was sufficiently impressed to give up trespassing for good.

A friend and I, talking it over later, agreed that it was just unbeatable bad luck that got us into this trouble and into court. The detective didn't seem like a bad sort, and he gave signs of being willing to let us go, until he asked us what our fathers did for a living; then he abruptly turned ugly. It was just our joint misfortune that my father was a poet and my friend's was a maker of roller coasters.

꿈 While visiting in a very small Midwestern town, I struck up a conversation with an old gentleman sitting on the "loafers' bench" outside the general store. "I see you don't have much of a population problem here," I remarked.

"You're wrong, son," he replied. "Dang near every problem we ever had here's been caused by the population."   Ollie Hiebert

How to Feel Fit at Any Age

Kenneth H. Cooper, M.D.

[March 1968]

After one of my lectures to a group of physicians a few years ago, a listener stopped me in the corridor. "I always tell my inactive patients they should get more exercise," he said. "And I usually suggest something mild, like walking, to get them started. But when they ask me *how much* or *how long,* I'm stumped. I don't know how much is enough. Do you?"

I didn't, but the problem had bothered me too. I had specialized in exercise physiology after graduating from medical school, and the more I thought about it the more I felt that what we needed was a catalogue of all the popular forms of activity, reduced to measurable amounts, so one could pick and choose among them and know that *this* much exercise would produce exactly *that* amount of benefit.

It was the U.S. Air Force that finally gave me the opportunity to solve this problem. After entering the service, I was assigned to do research on exercise, especially as it affects pilots and astronauts. I had at my disposal the most modern and sophisticated testing equipment, including some inherited from space-age technology. I also had an almost unlimited supply of the most priceless research commodity of all, the human body.

At this writing we have evaluated more than 5000 subjects—officers and airmen, the active and inactive, the well and unwell, men and women—both in the field and in the laboratory.

The information about exercise we have collected since 1964 may be the most extensive in medical history. The breakthroughs made in these tests, and the refinements in existing data, have immeasurably increased our knowledge about the ways in which exercise—or the lack of it—affects the body.

In our program, all popular exercises have been scientifically measured for the amount of energy it costs the body to perform them. These amounts have been translated into points, and it has been firmly established that, to produce and maintain the essential health of your body, a basic minimum of 30 such points each week is necessary. Earn those 30 points by whatever assortment of exercises you like, and you will have answered the question, "How much?"

The best kind of fitness is what we call endurance fitness: the ability to do prolonged work without fatigue. It has to do with the body's *overall* health—health of the heart, lungs and entire cardiovascular system, and other organs, as well as muscles. And the key to the whole thing is oxygen.

In simplest terms, any activity—breathing, digesting, even the beating of the heart—requires energy. The body produces this energy by burning foodstuffs, and the burning agent is oxygen. The body can store food at each meal, using what it wants now and saving some of the rest for later. *But it can't store oxygen.* We breathe every minute of our lives to keep the supply coming in, for if it were suddenly cut off, the brain, the heart, everything would cease functioning.

But, you might argue, if we need more oxygen we can just breathe more, so what's the problem? The problem is to get enough oxygen, which is carried in the blood, to *all the areas* in the human body—the small, hidden, almost infinite number of areas—where food is stored. Only then can the two combine to produce energy as required.

Most people can produce enough energy to perform ordinary daily activities. As the activity becomes more vigorous, however, some of them can't keep up. This is because in their bodies *means for the delivery of oxygen* is limited. This is what separates the men from the boys, the fit from the unfit.

The best kind of exercise therefore is that which demands

oxygen and forces your body to process and deliver it. *Even if you've been inactive or sick, these exercises may be good therapy —but you must have your doctor's permission.* If you follow the point system and get enough of the right kind of exercise, our Air Force studies have shown, many wonderful changes will take place in your body. I call these changes the "training effect." Some highlights:

• The lungs will process more air with less effort.

• The heart grows stronger, pumps more blood with each stroke, reducing the number of strokes necessary. Thus a conditioned man may have a resting heart rate 20 beats per minute slower than a deconditioned man, saving as many as 10,000 beats in one night's sleep—or up to 30,000 beats every day of a man's life.

• The number and size of the blood vessels that carry the blood to the body tissue are increased. So is the total blood volume, by as much as a quart in some men!

• The tone of muscles and blood vessels is improved, and blood pressure is often reduced.

Now, let's get to the exercises. The best ones are running, swimming, cycling, walking, stationary running, handball, basketball and squash—in just about that order. Isometrics, weight lifting and most calisthenics don't even make the list. Why? Consider the three basic categories of exercise:

Isometric exercises generally tense one set of muscles against another, or against an immovable object. Examples: pushing against opposite sides of a doorjamb, or pulling up on the chair you're sitting on. Such exercises can increase the strength of skeletal muscles, but cause no appreciable increase in oxygen consumption. Consequently they have no significant effect on lungs, heart or blood system, or on overall health.

Isotonic exercises contract muscles to produce movement, but again without demanding much oxygen. Popular examples are calisthenics and weight lifting, and some of the mild participant sports like archery, bowling and horseshoes. These too are aimed almost entirely at the skeletal muscles, and cannot qualify as primary conditioners.

I get some arguments, of course, especially about calisthenics.

There are a few all-muscle calisthenics that will make your chest heave, your heart pound and your blood race. But the huffing and puffing end too soon to do you much good. (A notable exception is running-in-place, if kept up nonstop for a considerable length of time.) I do calisthenics myself, but I earn my points elsewhere.

Aerobic ("with oxygen") exercises are the foundation on which any exercise program should be built. These are exercises which demand oxygen and which you keep up long enough to start producing those wonderful training-effect changes in your body.

How much is "long enough"? When do the benefits actually begin?

Our research indicates that if the exercise is vigorous enough to produce a sustained heart rate of 150 beats per minute, the training-effect benefits begin about five minutes after the exercise starts and continue as long as it is performed. If the exercise is not that vigorous it must be continued considerably longer.

But how in the world can any man figure out his heart rate while in the act of exercising? That is the beauty of the point system: we've done all the figuring for you. We selected exercises that demand oxygen, measured them for the exact amounts they require, then translated these amounts into points. The only principles laid down are that you must maintain a minimum of 30 points a week, and exercise at least four times a week, or every other day. The benefits start dropping off if you fall below either minimum. Don't, for instance, try to earn 30 points in one day and then forget exercise for the next six. But the choice of how you earn the points is yours. Find the point value of each exercise you plan to do, and do enough to earn 30 points.

Before you start, however, you may want to know what kind of shape you're in now.

To determine this, in our Air Force tests we rely mainly on the power treadmill. The treadmill, combined with oxygen-measuring equipment, is the ultimate at this state of the art in measuring total fitness. It permits accurate measurement of a subject's maximum oxygen consumption, and correlates it with his heart rate and blood pressure. It also enables us to determine how many milliliters (ml.'s) of oxygen a body consumes per kilogram of body weight per minute of exercise—and this is the figure we have translated into points.

Scientific and thorough, the treadmill test is also expensive and time-consuming. So what we have done is translate it into a simple 12-minute run/walk test. All you need is a place where you can run a measured distance of up to two miles. *(If you are over 35 years of age or have any medical condition, you must get your doctor's permission before you try the test.)* Your local high school or YMCA may have track facilities. If not, use a nearby park or a quiet stretch of road. You can check the distance by using the odometer in your car. When you're ready to run, dress in loose clothing and bring a watch with a sweep second hand. The idea is to get as far as you can, comfortably, in 12 minutes. Many men enlist their wives as timers, to follow along in the car and toot the horn when time is up.

Try to run the whole time, at a pace you can maintain without excess strain. If your breath gets short, walk for a while until it comes back, then run some more. But keep going for the full 12 minutes. Then check your distance on this chart:

DISTANCE COVERED	FITNESS CATEGORY
Less than 1 mile	I. Very Poor
1 to 1¼ miles	II. Poor
1¼ to 1½ miles	III. Fair
1½ to 1¾ miles	IV. Good *
1¾ miles or more	V. Excellent

* For men over 35, 1.4 miles is Good; for women, 1.3.

If you fall into one of the first three categories, you fail the test. But don't be too discouraged; about 80 percent of the American population rates there, too.

The categories are important because they place you in different conditioning programs—a 16-week program for Category I, 13 weeks for Category II, 10 weeks for Category III. If test results place you in Categories IV or V, you're already fit. Keep up a 30-point week and you'll stay that way. (If you prefer to omit the test, simply put yourself in Category I and take the full course.)

For the conditioning period we've worked out six different, progressive courses, based on a variety of activities. (See charts on the following pages.) Select whichever activity you prefer and start in.

The running program (Chart 1), without equivocation, is the best. It's quick, sure and inexpensive. I can recommend it to anyone of any age, assuming there is no physical impairment. It exercises the arms and legs and has a firming effect on

To use this and other charts: Find your category (as determined by the 12-minute test) in one of the three columns at left. Under the category, find the appropriate week, then read across to see what you should do that week.

• • •

Note: Start program by walking. Then walk/run, or run, as necessary, to meet the changing time goals.

1. RUNNING PROGRAM

CATEGORY I	II	III	DISTANCE (miles)	TIME (mins.)	TIMES a wk.	PTS. a wk.
	WEEKS					
1st	1st	...	1	13:30	5	10
2nd	...	...	1	13	5	10
3rd	2nd	1st	1	12:45	5	10
4th	3rd	...	1	11:45	5	15
5th	4th	2nd	1	11	5	15
6th	5th	3rd	1	10:30	5	15
7th	6th	...	1	9:45	5	20
8th	...	4th	1	9:30	5	20
9th	7th	5th	1	9:15	5	20
10th	8th	...	{ 1, 1½	{ 9, 16	{ 3, 2	} 21
11th	9th	6th	{ 1, 1½	{ 8:45, 15	{ 3, 2	} 21
12th	...	7th	{ 1, 1½	{ 8:30, 14	{ 3, 2	} 24
13th	10th	...	{ 1, 1½	{ 8:15, 13:30	{ 3, 2	} 24
14th	11th	8th	{ 1, 1½	{ 7:55, 13	{ 3, 2	} 27
15th	12th	9th	{ 1, 1½, 2	{ 7:45, 12:30, 18	{ 2, 2, 1	} 30
16th	13th	10th	{ 1½, 2	{ 11:55, 17	{ 2, 2	} 31
To maintain fitness after completion of conditioning program, follow any one of these alternatives:			1	8	6	30
			1	6:30	5	30
			1½	12	4	30
			2	16	3	30

muscle groups throughout the body, notably the abdomen. Running can be done alone or in groups, indoors or out, at any time of day.

Swimming (Chart 2) is a close second. Swimming exercises most of the large muscle masses, especially the arms and legs, although not in the same way as running. You can't expect the same firming effect on the abdominal muscles.

The disadvantages with cycling (Chart 3) are that you need a bike, and that weather—icy streets, wind—can play havoc. Also, cycling doesn't benefit the muscles of the upper body as much as running and, especially, swimming; it does toughen up the legs and hips more. However, the aerobic benefits—the

2. SWIMMING PROGRAM

CATEGORY			DISTANCE (yards)	TIME (mins.)	TIMES a wk.	PTS. a wk.
I	II	III				
WEEKS						
1st	1st	. . .	100	2:30	5	6
2nd	. . .	. . .	150	3	5	7½
3rd	2nd	1st	200	4	5	7½
4th	3rd	. . .	250	5:30	5	10
5th	4th	2nd	250	5	5	10
6th	5th	3rd	300	6	5	12½
7th	6th	. . .	300	6	5	12½
8th	. . .	4th	400	8:30	5	17½
9th	7th	5th	400	8:30	5	17½
10th	8th	. . .	{ 400,	8	2	} 19
			500	10:30	3	
11th	9th	6th	{ 400,	8	2	} 22
			600	12:30	3	
12th	. . .	7th	{ 500,	10:30	3	} 24
			700	15:30	2	
13th	10th	. . .	{ 600,	12:30	3	} 25
			800	16:30	2	
14th	11th	8th	{ 600,	12:30	2	} 29½
			800	16	3	
15th	12th	9th	700	15	5	30
16th	13th	10th	1000	20:30	4	34
To maintain fitness after completion of conditioning program, follow any one of these alternatives:			500	8-12	8	32
			600	10-15	6	30
			800	13-20	5	32
			1000	17-25	4	34

Points here are calculated for the overhand crawl. The breaststroke is less demanding, and so is the backstroke. The butterfly is considerably more demanding.

213

training effect—for the internal organs are identical to those of running and swimming.

Walking (Chart 4) is the bottom half of running. It consumes more time, but it's quite valid. Its overwhelming advantage is that it can be done by anyone, anytime, anywhere—and it doesn't even look like exercise. Don't underestimate stationary running (Chart 6). It can be substituted for other exercises on rainy or cold days when you can't get outdoors. You can do it while watching the morning news on television; then shower, and you're through exercising for the day.

Handball, basketball and squash (Chart 5) are almost identical in their benefits. They have the advantage of competition.

Points are based on use of an American single-speed bike, following a course that is equally up hill and downhill, equal time with and against the wind. For a course that is constantly against a wind of 5 m.p.h. or more, add ½ point per mile. If using a racing bicycle, stay in highest gear as much as possible and deduct ½ point per mile.

3. CYCLING PROGRAM

CATEGORY			DISTANCE (miles)	TIME (mins.)	TIMES a wk.	PTS. a wk.
I	II	III				
WEEKS						
1st	1st	. . .	2	7:45	5	10
2nd	. . .	. . .	2	6:45	5	10
3rd	2nd	1st	2	6:15	5	10
4th	3rd	. . .	3	11	5	15
5th	4th	2nd	3	10	5	15
6th	5th	3rd	3	9:15	5	15
7th	6th	. . .	4	15	5	20
8th	. . .	4th	4	13:30	5	20
9th	7th	5th	4	12:30	5	20
10th	8th	. . .	4, 5	12:30 16:30	4 1	} 21
11th	9th	6th	4, 5	12:30 16	3 2	} 22
12th	. . .	7th	4, 6	12:15 19	3 2	} 24
13th	10th	. . .	4, 6	12:05 18:30	3 2	} 24
14th	11th	8th	5, 6	15:30 18:30	3 2	} 27
15th	12th	9th	6	19	5	30
16th	13th	10th	8	25:30	4	32
To maintain fitness after completion of conditioning program, follow any one of these alternatives:			5	15-20	6	30
			6	18-24	5	30
			8	24-32	4	32
			10	30-40	3	30

With all the basic conditioning courses, be prepared for sore muscles. This soreness is temporary, and only indicates that you're beginning to use muscle groups which have been dormant too long. Nevertheless, do not plunge headlong into a program convinced that you can speed up the process. The running program, for instance, starts with walking. To try to get going faster is likely to lead to trouble with the feet, the ankles and other joints. Stick to the charts verbatim. They've been tested and retested, and are safe as well as sure.

Once you've worked your way back into condition, the idea is to stay there. And the way to do it is with a 30-point weekly program consisting of any combination of aerobic exercises. As

4. WALKING PROGRAM

CATEGORY			DISTANCE	TIME	TIMES	PTS.
I	II	III	(miles)	(mins.)	a wk.	a wk.
WEEKS						
1st	1st	. . .	1	15	5	5
2nd	. . .	. . .	1	14	5	10
3rd	2nd	1st	1	13:45	5	10
4th	3rd	. . .	1½	21:30	5	15
5th	4th	2nd	1½	21	5	15
6th	5th	3rd	1½	20:30	5	15
7th	6th	. . .	2	28	5	20
8th	. . .	4th	2	27:45	5	20
9th	7th	5th	2	27:30	5	20
10th	8th	. . .	{ 2, 2½	27:30 33:45	3 2	} 22
11th	9th	6th	{ 2, 2½	27:30 33:30	3 2	} 22
12th	. . .	7th	{ 2½, 3	33:15 41:30	4 1	} 26
13th	10th	. . .	{ 2½, 3	33:15 41:15	3 2	} 27
14th	11th	8th	{ 2½, 3	33 40	3 2	} 27
15th	12th	9th	3	41	5	30
16th	13th	10th	4	55	4	32
To maintain fitness after completion of conditioning program, follow any one of these alternatives:			2	24-29	8	32
			3	36-43	5	30
			4	48-58	4	32
			5	60-72	3	30

long as you get 30 points a week, you can be assured that you are getting a scientifically measured minimum to keep in active and productive health. But 30 points is the *minimum* for any age above 10. The 90-year-old shouldn't earn fewer, but the 19-year-old should earn more. In fact, for teen-agers I recommend as many as 50. Fat people, too, should get more than the 30-point minimum. And they should diet.

For anyone who is serious about athletics, I'd recommend a bare minimum of 50 points per week during the off season. For those involved in endurance sports such as boxing, basketball or soccer, the minimum should be as high as 100. Distance runners score up to 500 points a week. Think of them if you're ever tempted to complain about your weekly 30. And what

5. HANDBALL, BASKETBALL, SQUASH PROGRAM

CATEGORY			DURATION	TIMES	POINTS
I	II	III	(mins.)	a week	a week
WEEKS					
1st	1st	...	10	5	7½
2nd	...	...	15	5	11¼
3rd	2nd	1st	15	5	11¼
4th	3rd	...	20	5	15
5th	4th	2nd	20	5	15
6th	5th	3rd	20	5	15
7th	6th	...	30	5	22½
8th	...	4th	30	5	22½
9th	7th	5th	30	5	22½
10th	8th	...	35	5	26¼
11th	9th	6th	35	5	26¼
12th	...	7th	{ 35, 40	3 2	} 27¼
13th	10th	...	{ 35, 40	3 2	} 27¼
14th	11th	8th	{ 30, 45	2 3	} 29¼
15th	12th	9th	40	5	30
16th	13th	10th	50	4	30
To maintain fitness after completion of conditioning program, follow any one of these alternatives:			40	5	30
			50	4	30
			70	3	30

"Duration" refers to time spent in continuous exercise. Do not include breaks or time-outs.

about women? Women used to cite as their argument for not exercising the fact that they outlive men. However, heart disease is increasing among the weaker sex, and inactivity probably shares the responsibility.

Some of the Women's Air Force contingent participated in

6. STATIONARY RUNNING PROGRAM						
CATEGORY			DURATION	STEPS per	TIMES	POINTS
I	II	III	(mins.)	min.	a wk.	a wk.
WEEKS						
1st	1st	...	2:30	70-80	5	4
2nd	...	...	2:30	70-80	5	4
3rd	2nd	1st	5	70-80	5	10
4th	3rd	...	5	70-80	5	10
5th	4th	2nd	7:30	70-80	5	11¼
6th	5th	3rd	7:30	70-80	5	11¼
7th	6th	..	10	70-80	5	15
8th	...	4th	10	70-80	5	15
9th	7th	5th	12:30	70-80	5	18¾
10th	8th	...	12:30	70-80	5	18¾
11th	9th	6th	15	70-80	5	22½
12th	...	7th	10 (in a.m.), 10 (in p.m.), 15	70-80, 70-80, 70-80	2, 3	25½
13th	10th	...	12:30 (in a.m.), 12:30 (in p.m.), 15	70-80, 70-80, 70-80	2, 3	28½
14th	11th	8th	12:30 (in a.m.), 12:30 (in p.m.), 15	70-80, 70-80, 70-80	2, 3	28½
15th	12th	9th	20	70-80	5	30
16th	13th	10th	20	80-90	4	32
To maintain fitness after completion of conditioning program, follow any one of these alternatives:			10 (in a.m.), 10 (in p.m.)	70-80, 70-80	5	30
			15	70-80	7	30
			15	80-90	5	30
			20	80-90	4	32

In counting number of steps, count only when left foot hits the floor. Feet must be brought at least 8 inches from the floor.

our research program. Before training, only 20 percent made it into the Good category. Afterward, 45 percent made it. They showed that women can cope with the point system as easily as men—they need between 25 and 30 points a week—and receive identical training effects. What pleased the girls most was the way they changed fat weight to lean weight, and lost inches off their waistlines, all the while improving their health.

Any discussion of the benefits of aerobic exercise must deal with the most important muscle in the human body—the heart. The figures are familiar but frightening:

• Some 18 million Americans suffer some form of heart disease.

• As many as 800,000 have heart attacks every year.

• More than one million die of cardiovascular illnesses annually, accounting for 55 percent of all U.S. fatalities.

Ironically, the heart usually works faster and less efficiently when you give it less to do. A conditioned man who exercises regularly will have a resting heart rate of about 60 beats per minute or less; the average office worker, about 80.

What's your rate? Sit still for five minutes, then take your pulse and count the beats per minute. If you're 80 beats or above, you are not in top condition. The thing to do is to get up off that chair and get to work exercising. You might save your heart some of those 20,000 to 30,000 extra beats you've forced on it every day.

As your heart grows stronger in response to training, more exertion is necessary to tire it. This will be quite noticeable. During the first few weeks or months of regular exercising you are likely to feel tired each time. But eventually you will be getting all the exercise you need (30 points) without feeling it.

One of the most remarkable effects of aerobic conditioning is vascularization: more blood vessels open up in the muscle tissues, creating new routes for delivering more oxygen. This vascularization is a vital factor in the health of the heart. When its tissue is saturated with healthy blood vessels, this considerably reduces the chance of cardiac failure. And even if such a failure should occur, the extra vessels can "go around" the stricken area, outflanking it to keep the surrounding tissue

POINT VALUES FOR OTHER ACTIVITIES		
		POINTS *
Golf	18 holes	3
Rope Skipping	5 minutes	1½
Skating	15 minutes	1
(ice or roller)		
Skiing	30 minutes	3
(snow or water)		
Tennis	1 set	1½
Volleyball	15 minutes	1
Football	30 minutes	3

* Based on caloric requirements.

healthy and improving the chances of a speedy recovery. So if you haven't done anything for your heart lately, start now. Exercise it.

A few final tips to remember:

Any time of the day is fine for exercise. But spend a few minutes with warm-up calisthenics first, and then don't sit down or stand motionless immediately after strenuous exercise. Give the body a chance to unwind by walking around slowly for three to five minutes.

Don't exercise right after a meal. Wait at least two hours. (On the other hand, exercising just before a light meal is a good way to combine exercise with diet.)

Be prepared for "going stale"—for a period when you begin to wonder why you ever started a training program. It happens to everyone. Just sweat it out. Go through the motions. Your enthusiasm will return. *Don't quit.*

As a doctor who has specialized in physical fitness, I'd like to see our nation reverse the consequences of an affluent society and its inbred inactivity. I'd like to see our basic fitness figures reversed—four out of five Americans *in* good aerobic condition, instead of *out of*. I'd like to see my country become again a nation of doers instead of spectators.

I hope this Aerobics program leads that revolution. And I hope you're one of the revolutionists.

Symptoms of Being 35

Ring Lardner

[September 1934]

T
HE other night one of my friends whose name is Legion got me on the telephone and wanted I should come over, but I said no that I was busy on a book which I had promised my publisher I would write it.

"What is it about," says Legion.

So I told him "How it feels to be 35."

"That guy must think you got a good memory," says Legion.

Well friends 35 is how young I am no matter how old I look, but I am so use to haveing smart Alex make wise cracks when I tell them my age that it don't have no more effect on me now than the 6 day bicycle race. Only I can't figure why they think I would lie about it like I was trying to pose as a boy chess marvel or something. When a man has got a legal wife and 4 and no one hundredths children what does he care if he is 35 or double that amt.

And don't judge a person by their hair gents. Many a man that can remember the first Ford has got more foliage on their egg than myself. Personly I am not sensitive about my plummage. When my features got to the decision that one of them would half to retract all I done was thank God they picked the forehead and not the chin. The only hardship connected with pyorrhea of the scalp is trying to act surprised when the barber says you are looseing your hair.

But at the present writeing I can at lease state that being 35 don't feel nothing like being under 30. For inst. when the telephone rings now days I am scared to death that its somebody asking us to go somewheres for dinner. Six yrs. ago I was afraid it wasn't. At 29 home was like they used to say on the vaudeville stage, a place to go when all the other joints was closed up. At 35 its a place you never leave without a loud squawk. Its where you can take off your shoes. Its where you can have more soup. Its where you don't half to say nothing when they's nothing to say. Its where you don't half to listen.

When you was 29 you didn't care for the band to play Home sweet Home. It was old stuff and a rotten tune any way. Now you hope they won't play it neither. Its a pretty tune but it makes you bust out crying.

Well it was 5 or 6 yrs. ago when I realized that I was past my nonages as they say. It come to me all of a sudden that the only compliments I had for a long wile was what a pretty tie you got or something. Like for inst. a few wks. back I was up in Boston where I got a young and beautiful sister in law. When it come time to part she kissed me 6 times which was suppose to be once for me and once apiece for the Mrs. and 4 kiddies. Well I thought it was pretty nice and got kind of excited about it till I looked at her husband to see how he took it. He took it without batting an eye. When I had left, instead of lepping at her with a terrible curse he probably says "Janey, you're a game gal," and she gave him a kiss that meant something.

Now an incidence like this would of spoilt my whole trip if I didn't look at it in a sensible way which is to say to yourself, "Well if I wasn't in the Sears and yellow I wouldn't of got them 6 kisses. And 6 kisses is ½ a dozen kisses in any language."

All in all when you get hardened to it they's many advantages in reaching your dottage. When they's 7 passengers for a seven passenger car its never you that has to take one of them little torture seats. When the Mrs. thinks it would be nice to have a fire in the fire place, you ain't the one that has got to ruin his clothes. Or when one of my young brother in laws is around the house and I come in the rm. and they are setting in the easy chair, why they jump up like food shot from guns and say "Here take this chair."

As for the gen. symptoms of 35 the following may interest science:

1. The patient sometimes finds himself and one lady the only people left at the table and all the others is danceing. They seems to be nothing for it but to get up and dance. You start and the music stops and the young buddies on the flr. claps their hands for a encore. The patient claps too but not very loud and hopes the leader will take it in a jokeing way.

2. In going through an old trunk the patient runs acrost a bunch of keep sakes like a note a gal wrote him in high school, a picture of himself in a dirty football suit, a program of the May festival in South Bend 17 yrs. ago and etc. "Why keep this junk" he says and dumps them all in the waste basket.

3. The invalid goes to a ball game and along comes the last ½ of the 14th. innings and the score is 1 and 1 and the 1st. guy makes a base hit. The patient looks at his watch and if he leaves the park right away he can make the 6:27 home where as if he waits a few min. he will half to take the 6:54. Without no hesitation he leaves the park right away.

4. The subject is woke up at 3 a.m. by the fire whistle. He sniffles but can't smell no smoke. He thinks well it ain't our house and goes back to sleep.

5. He sets down after breakfast to read the paper. The mail man comes and brings him 3 letters. One of them looks like it was a gal's writeing. He reads the paper.

In conclusion its customary in these intimate capital-I talks to throw in a paragraph of blurb about the little woman. What ever success a man has had he has got to pretend he owes it to Her. So if they's any glory to be gleaned out of my success in reaching 35 and looking even older why she can have it.

ᢒᴗ Father Robert Farrar Capon, Episcopal parish priest and gourmet cook, says in his book *The Supper of the Lamb*: "Women are like cheese strudels. When first baked they are crisp and fresh on the outside, but the filling is unsettled and indigestible; in age, the crust may not be so lovely, but the filling comes at last into its own."

Published by Doubleday

Rearing Children in Samoa

Margaret Mead

[October 1929]

W HEN I picked a tiny island in American Samoa and set out to study adolescent children in that primitive community, I asked myself this question: Are Samoan children torn by the conflicts, baffled by the spiritual doubts, and tormented by the vague ambitions which are always considered an unavoidable element in the lives of American children of the same difficult age?

The answer, I found, was emphatically no. The period of adolescence was unstressed. Girls changed without vexation from little girls whose main business was baby-tending to big girls who could be trusted with longer and more difficult tasks. No conflicts with their parents, no confusion about sex vexed their souls. Their development was smooth, untroubled, unstressed. What is there in South Sea society that makes the difference?

The first big difference is in the family. Our typical family, father, mother and children, is hardly ever found in Samoa. The Samoans live in great households of ten to twenty people— father and mother, aunts, uncles, grandparents, relatives-in-law, cousins—all housed in a cluster of round open houses, with high thatched roofs, no walls and no privacy. In such families there is no youngest child, not for long. Some sister or aunt or cousin will have a baby in the next few months. There is no only child, the spoiled indulged pet of a family of adults. Similarly, the sharp division between parents and children vanishes. A family is just a long series of people of different ages, all somehow related to one another, grading down from the grandfather to the new baby.

The importance and prestige of the real father and mother are shared and diminished by the presence of a lot of other grown-up people. Furthermore, the mother takes very little care of her own babies after they are about six months old. At that age they are handed over to children of six and seven, who trundle them about everywhere, astride their hips. As often as not, it isn't mother who dries the baby's tears nor father who spanks the little mischief makers. And so the setting for parent fixations vanishes; the relationship between Samoan parents and children is too casual to foster such attitudes.

In this the advantages are surely on the side of Samoa. In our civilization, the self-conscious parent is forever sheltering the child, from bad grammar, from the measles, from casual associates. The American parent needs to remember always that wholesome social intercourse is essential to the healthy development of a child.

Life and death and sex are no mysteries to the growing child in Samoa. The horror, the shock, the nauseated recoil of our protected, unsophisticated children is unknown. In Samoa, little toddlers peep under the midwife's arm at birth, hover about the group preparing a corpse, and make an evening game of spying upon wandering lovers. The amatory arts are freely discussed, and the whole village stands ready to mock the inept lover. Any untimely, precocious participation in adult affairs is the most heinous of crimes, but this applies to actions, not to knowledge. Samoan children are not confused by false teaching. Hence they grow up with the best equipment in the world against shock—experience.

In this armoring of the children's nerves, quite as important a factor as the actual experience is the attitude of the parents. The grown people regard the whole course of human life simply. They consider sex as natural, birth as unexceptional. The spectator children are surrounded by their parents' uncomplicated attitudes. The facts of life, learned young enough, do not stagger nor particularly interest the young child, but the affective tone which surrounds the moment may permanently influence his whole attitude.

Our society is organized upon the basis of rewards for the swift, the precocious. Samoa distrusts all precocity. The child who boasts of having performed some adult task is not praised. Instead he is roundly berated at home and his conduct is publicly deprecated. Our adolescent children are met upon all sides by demands that they choose between religious faiths, between careers, between political allegiances. Samoan children are told to get up early in the morning, to keep their mouths shut, to listen attentively, and to wait till they have more judgment. The danger in the Samoan method, of course, is that it can blunt the ambitions and blur the spontaneity of gifted children. On the other hand, backward children are greatly helped. Inferiority complexes do not flourish in such an atmosphere.

At about 16 or 17 the girl has passed through the most marked period of adolescence and is ready for a way of life which holds no mystery for her. Her ambition is simple: she wishes as a girl to have as many affairs and as few responsibilities as possible; then to marry near home and have many children.

Her love affairs begin. Although surrounded by the trappings which seem to us most romantic—moonlight, palm trees, the rhythmic beat of the surf, white with "coral milk," and the soft perfume of the frangipani blossoms, low-voiced protestations of love and flowery invocations of the stars and moon—these affairs are not love affairs as we conceive of them. Samoan amours are more like the petting conventions of our younger generation. Comeliness and technique are the two most important requisites. Friendship, appreciation of personality, passionate love with its strong feeling of fidelity and chivalry—all are lacking. To the Samoan, sex is an art, a play to be learned with care and practiced with discretion. The emphasis is all upon the proper note of casualness, upon the fleeting hour.

Later, the Samoan girl is to enter upon a marriage of convenience arranged by her parents. Should she learn the meaning of a strong attachment to one person, a conflict might ensue. But she does not. She meets young men as lovers for brief butterfly affairs. And she marries, not to satisfy vague, undefined desires, but because she is a little weary of the love that flits so lightly among the palm trees and wants the social position of a married woman and children of her own.

The experience and perfection of sex knowledge in Samoa makes for happiness, but the absence of strong personal ties can only be deplored. The indiscriminate lovemaking and its necessary suppression of any genuine emotion lead to a disregard of the importance of personal relations. We can appreciate, as the Samoans cannot, the value of personal relations.

We could not reproduce the Samoan conditions if we would. Our complicated society, which is coming to realize personality as a value and cherish individuality of thought, demands higher prices than are ever paid by the graceful young Samoans in their shady, peaceful villages. And these prices our youth have to pay. Their young days can never be as untroubled, as unpoignant as the days of the Samoans.

Ahoy, Mate

An old contract, unearthed in Edinburgh, was drawn up by a seafarer who clearly envisaged each mate's duties in a shipshape union:

Having read to her the Articles of War, I explained to her the conditions under which we were to sail in company on life's voyage, namely:

She is to obey signals without question when received.

She is to steer by my reckoning.

She is to stand by as a true consort in foul weather, battle or shipwreck.

She is to run under my guns if assailed by picaroons or privateers.

I am to keep her in due repair and see that she hath her allowance of coats of paint, streamers and bunting, as befits a saucy craft.

I am to take no other craft in tow, and if any be now attached to cut their hawsers.

I am to revictual her day to day.

Should she be blown on her beam ends by wind or misfortune, I am to stand by her and see her righted.

I am to set our course for the Great Harbor in the hope that moorings and ground to swing may be found for two well-built craft when laid up for eternity.

Arthur Conan Doyle, *Micah Clarke* (Murray)

A SHORT STORY

Corporal Hardy

Richard Ely Danielson

[*June 1961*]

IN THOSE days, during the hay-
ing season on our Connecticut farm, the farmhands were given
their "dinners" out in the fields. I always carried his victuals to
Mr. Hardy, because I liked to sit while he ate and listen to
his stories. He was a Civil War veteran. Congress had given
him a medal—of honor—and men regarded him with respect.

I'm sure Mr. Hardy never thought of himself as a hero. He
was poor, he lived alone, he was unsuccessful. But he would
accept no pension. "I'm able-bodied. I can work, can't I?" Alas,
he was not really able-bodied. He had been grievously wounded
several times, and in 1895, when I fetched and carried for him
and sat at his feet, it was pitiful to see his valiant efforts to fork
hay on the wagon or do the other farming tasks which require
muscular strength. He was thin and bent, but his face was
brown and clean and his blue eyes were bright and indomitable.

I remember the last day I served him. I was ten years old. I
brought his dinner in a basket to where he sat in the shade
of an oak tree, leaning against a stack of hay.

"Thanks, Jackie," he said. "I don't seem to be hungry today.
It's hot and this tree don't give much shade. Why, dammit, it's
like that mean little oak tree down to Chancellorsville."

I said, "Oh, Mr. Hardy, you've told me about Antietam and
the Wilderness, but you've never told me about Chancellorsville. What was it like?"

"I ain't never told nobody about Chancellorsville," he said slowly, "and I don't aim to tell nobody—grownup, that is. But I'd like to tell somebody, for the first and last time. You'll forget it, and it would kind of ease my mind." He hoisted himself a little higher and made a pretense of eating.

"CHANCELLORSVILLE," Mr. Hardy said, "was a bad battle, an awful bad battle. We didn't fight good and they was too many of them and I lost my captain."

"Who was he?" I asked.

"Why," he said, incredulously, "you oughta know that! He was Capt. William Armstrong, commandin' Company B, 39th Connecticut. His twin brother, Ezra, was lootenant. They never was two men as much alike—in looks, that is, for they was quite unlike inside. The lootenant was always stompin' around an' shoutin' an' wavin' his arms, an' the captain he was always quiet an' soft-spoken an' brave an' gentle. He was a good man. I guess he was the best man I ever knowed."

He paused and took a sip of his cold coffee. Then he said, "When we come to leave town to go in the cars to Hartford and then to Washington, their father—he was old Judge Armstrong who lived in that big place up on Armstrong Hill—come up to me. 'Nathan, you kind of keep an eye on my boys, for my sake,' he says. 'I will, Judge,' I says. 'I'll do my best.'"

"But tell me, Mr. Hardy," I broke in, "what happened at Chancellorsville?"

"It was a bad battle, as I said. Them Rebs come charging out of the woods, hollerin' and yellin' and helligolarrupin'. The lootenant, he kept stomping up and down, shouting, 'Never give ground, boys! Stay where you are! Never retreat!' But my captain—I was next to him—says, 'They're too many; we can't stop 'em. Tell the men to retreat slowly, firing as often as they can reload.' Just then it hit him right in the chest. *Thunk!* was the noise it made. I caught him as he fell, and the blood began to come out of his mouth. He tried to speak, but all he could do was make faces, and his lips said, 'Tell Elizabeth . . .' and then he died. I put him down and noticed we was under a mean little oak tree on the edge of our trenches.

"Then they was around us, hairy men with bayonets, stabbin' and shootin' and yellin', and the lootenant was shouting, 'Don't retreat, men!' He got hit in the knee and fell down; so I picked him up and put him across my shoulder and started for the rear. He kep' hittin' me in the face and swearing, 'You damn coward! You left my brother there and you're making me retreat!' I says to him, 'Ezra, be reasonable; I'm takin' you to an ambulance. You ain't fit to fight, and as soon as I can I'm goin' back to bury William. They ain't goin' to shovel him into no trench.'

"I was strong then, and I musta carried him a mile till we come to a place where surgeons was carving men up. I handed over the lootenant and stayed with him while they sawed his leg off. They havin' run out of chloroform, it took four of us to hold him. And when it was over he was unconscious, and they put him in a cart with some others and took him away.

"I went back to a house where some burial men was loafing. It was pretty ruined, but I found a shingle and I wrote on it:

CAPT. WILLIAM ARMSTRONG
COMMANDING CO. B., 39 CONNECTICUT
He was an awful good man

"Then I borrowed a spade from this burial party and started off toward the Rebel lines. It was gettin' late an' I decided I couldn't find the captain in the dark, so I set down and tried to sleep, for I was tuckered.

"When it come gray the next mornin', I went along till I was challenged by the Rebel sentries. I answered, 'Union burial detail. I'm comin' for to bury my captain.' They begun shootin' at me in the mist, and one bullet struck me in the left thigh and I fell down. I took my belt off and strapped it real tight over the wound, and I got up and went on.

"They stopped shootin' and a man with a bayonet said, 'Yank, you're my pris'ner.' I said, 'Not till I bury my captain.' And I held up my shingle and spade. He says, 'You may be crazy, Yank, or you may be a spy. Come with me to the captain.'

"So he tuk me away with his bayonet in my back and the blood was squilchin' in my boot, but I got along to where his captain was and the captain asked questions, and the Rebel soldier, he tol' all he knew, an' the captain says, 'Where's he lie?' An' I says, 'By a mean little oak, where our lines was yesterday mornin'.'

"An' the captain says, 'That ain't far away. I'll send a detail to bury him.' I says, 'Ain't nobody goin' to bury the captain but me,' I says. 'After that, I'll be your pris'ner.'

"Then the captain says, 'What is your name an' rank?'

" 'Corporal Nathan Hardy, Company B, 39th Connecticut,' I says. An' he says, 'Corporal, you and I an' these men,' turnin' to the five or six Rebs who was listenin', 'will go together to find your captain.'

"So we went and I found him, under that mean little oak tree. He was lyin' all sprangled out an' undignified an' the first thing I done was to brush him off and lay him out regular. Then I started diggin', an' it would have been easy if it hadn't been for my leg and all the blood in my boot. Six-foot-four or thereabouts it was, and three-foot deep—not as deep as I wanted, but I couldn't dig no deeper, I was so tuckered.

"Then I laid the captain in the grave. An' as I stood lookin' down at him lyin' there, I says to myself, 'Ain't nobody goin' to shovel no dirt on the captain's face!' So I took my coat off and laid it over him, coverin' up his face best I could.

"The Rebs pulled me out of the grave, real gentle and considerate. An' then I noticed they was a Rebel general there, settin' on a blood horse. He see I was wounded and peaked, and he says, stern an' hard, 'Captain, what's the meanin' of this? Do you force wounded men to bury the dead?'

"The captain went over to him and began talkin' low and earnest, all the time I was fillin' in the grave. An' when I had patted the mound even, and stuck the shingle in the new earth at the head of the grave, I come over to where the general was an' saluted, an' I says, 'General, I ain't a great hand at askin' favors, but I was raised Episcopal and so was the captain. I'd kind of like to say a prayer before I surrender. . . .'

"The general said, 'Corporal Hardy, I am an Episcopalian, too, and you shall say your prayer.'

"So he dismounted and took off his hat, and he and I kneeled down by the grave, and it was awful hard for me to kneel. I looked up for a minute and all them Rebs was standin' with their caps off and their heads bowed, nice and decent, just like Northern people. An' then I had a dreadful time, for to save my life I couldn't remember a prayer, not a line, not a word. My brains was all watery an' thin, like, an' I don' know how long 'twas till somethin' come driftin' into my mind. It wasn't from the burial service; 'twas somethin' we used to chant in Evenin' Prayer. So I says it, loud as I could, for I was gettin' awful feeble.

" 'Lord,' I says, 'now lettest Thou Thy servant depart in peace, according to Thy Word. . . .' An' I couldn't remember or say any more. The general, he helped me to my feet and, by creepers, they was tears in his beard. Soon as I could speak I says, 'General, you've been real good to me and I thank you. An' now I'm your pris'ner, wherever you want to send me.'

" 'Corporal Hardy,' he says, 'you will never be a pris'ner of our people as long as I command this corps. Captain, I want a detail of six men an' a stretcher an' a flag of truce to take this brave soldier an' Christian gentleman back to the Union lines; an' I want this message delivered to the commanding officer to be forwarded to the President.' He put a paper against his saddle and wrote for some time.

"All this while I was kind of waverin' around because I was feeble from losin' blood an' the battle an' buryin' the captain an' a kind of feverish feelin'. Things begun to spin around. I heard someone yell, 'Catch him!' An' the next thing I knowed I was in a bed of straw and they was probin' for the bullet in my leg. Then I don't remember nothin' till I woke up in a bed, a clean bed, with a nice-lookin' woman leanin' over me, wipin' my head with a cold, wet towel. I says, 'Where am I?'

"An' she says, 'You're in the hospital of the Sanitary Commission in Washington. An', oh, Corporal Hardy,' she says, 'I'm so glad you're conscious, for today the President is comin' to give you the Medal of Honor. Now you just drink this an' go to sleep for a while, an' I'll wake you when he comes.'

"When I woke up again there was the ugliest man I ever see, leanin' over and pinnin' something to my nightshirt, an' he says, 'Corporal Hardy, even the enemy call you a brave soldier and a good man. Congress has voted you this medal. God bless you,' he says."

Mr. Hardy closed his eyes, and leaned against the haystack.

"But, Mr. Hardy," I said, "what happened to the lieutenant, and who was Elizabeth?"

"Who?" he said. "The lootenant? Oh, Ezra come back and married Elizabeth and they went to live in Massachusetts."

Just then my father came up, looking worried. "You've had all the sun you need, Nathan," he said. "I'll send the wagon and they'll take you up to the house, where you can be cool and rest a while." And, for once, Mr. Hardy made no protest. Father took me aside. "Jackie," he said, "go tell Dr. Fordyce he's wanted. I don't like Nathan's looks."

So Mr. Hardy was put to bed in the spare room. For several days he alternated between unconsciousness and a mild delirium. He kept mumbling phrases: "Take that quid out o' your mouth. 'Tain't soldierly!" . . . "Ain't nobody goin' to bury the captain but me."

One day he opened his eyes and said, "Here I am and I'm real easy in my mind. Call the boy in. He knows what I want said. He's young and 'twon't hurt him and he'll forget." So Mother got me, and I said, "What can I do, Mr. Hardy?"

"You can say what I said for the captain when I knelt down with the general."

So I knelt down and, having the parrotlike memory of childhood, I said, "You knelt down and so did the general, and then you couldn't remember any of the words of the burial service, but you did remember something that was sung in the evening, and you said, 'Lord, now lettest Thou Thy servant depart in peace, according to Thy Word. . . .'" And I began to cry.

"That's right," he said very faintly. "That's it. Yes, Captain. . . ."

My mother gathered me up and took me out and held me very close, rocking back and forth with me while I wept out how I loved Mr. Hardy. And that was why I was sent to my aunt at New London where I could swim and fish and forget about Mr. Hardy. But I didn't forget.

CAMPUS COMEDY

A PROFESSOR addressing a Parents Weekend audience at Syracuse University gave this example of how life has changed on campus. A student, explaining why he had not handed in an assignment on time, said, "I left it in my other car."

Gerald Hoffman

WHEN ASKED by the bursar's office to pay a $20 incidental fee, a University of Minnesota coed replied, "How many incidents does that entitle me to?"

Minneapolis *Tribune*

WITH competition for admission to graduate schools so intense, a young scholar received a letter from Harvard: "Because of the large number of applicants, it has been necessary to assign each one an identification number. In future communications, please refer to the number printed below." An inch of digits followed.

Not long after, the Harvard admissions office received a letter from the student: "Because of the large number of applications I am making this year, I find it necessary to assign each institution an identification number. In future communications, please refer to the number printed below."

He was accepted.

Charles M. Super

MY DAUGHTER, an English major in her senior year of college, wrote that she was having a dreadful time getting ready for mid-term exams. It seems there was a boy who intrigued her enormously and she was trying to really "get somewhere" with him. "But," she wrote, "it looks virtuously impossible."

Mrs. S. A. Harvey

A MATHEMATICS professor, specializing in geometry, was heard to mutter, "I love my wife, but oh, Euclid!" •

John G. Fuller in *Saturday Review*

THE COACH at a midwestern university was discussing the loss of a key football player. "He'll be tough to replace," said one alumnus. "What happened?"

"Well," the coach replied, "he could do absolutely everything with a football—except autograph it." E. C. Murphy

To ANNOUNCE their presence in our girls' dormitory, it is customary for the maintenance men to yell: "Man aboard!" When a campus custodian, summoned to repair a bureau, failed to give advance warning recently, a scantily clad girl answered his rap on the door. Embarrassed, he hastened to explain the nature of his call. "I'm here," he said, "to fix those knobs on your chest." Maryann Grskovich

HUNTING for a place to live, a professor went to a local apartment house and asked to see a list of the residents. When he came to the name of a certain student, the professor said, "Put me down for that fellow's apartment, please. He'll be leaving town any day now. I just flunked him in English." Roy A. Brenner

NOTED on a poster advertising a student mixer at M.I.T.: "Guys 99¢, Gals 1¢. Judges' decisions are final." Roy Maxwell

AMONG the drowsy members of my 7 a.m. literature class, one bright-eyed coed stood out. After a full semester of seeing her arrive so wide-awake, I asked her how she managed to do this. "It's simple," she replied. "I just rinse my contacts in ice water every morning." Linda Coleman

IN PREPARATION for a quiz at the U.S. Naval Academy my roommate, having trouble with electrical formulas, was advised to memorize just one important equation from which many others could be derived. The key to it was the jingle: "Twinkle, twinkle, little star, POWER EQUALS I^2 R."

When the results were posted—failure! He had solved each problem with the magic formula: "Little star up in the sky, POWER EQUALS R^2 I." Lt. (jg) Richard Pariseau

When the Loan Shark Shows His Teeth

Fred J. Cook

[June 1968]

THEY call him "the Doctor." You will meet him, if such is your misfortune, in the swankiest nightclubs of Manhattan, where maître d's bow and scrape as he circulates like the lord of the manor, his curvaceous young bride on his arm. A man in his 50s, dressed like the owner of a million-dollar wardrobe, the Doctor is always most charming. It is hard to imagine that he is in reality one of the most vicious loan sharks in New York, a hybrid species of spider-vulture who spins a web to enmesh his victim so he can pick clean the bones.

Just a step down the ladder from Carlo Gambino, probably the most powerful of the city's five Mafia family chieftains, the Doctor has no visible means of support. He never "works," as other human beings know the term. But when stopped by police, he never has less than $7000 on his person. "You can never charge him with vagrancy," one prosecutor says with a sour smile.

Indeed, the popular conception of the loan shark as a two-bit hoodlum lending $5 one Monday and collecting $6 the next has virtually no relation to reality. Loan-sharking is a multibillion-dollar operation, the safest and most remunerative racket in the underworld. Testifying before the New York State Commission of Investigation in December 1964, Frank Rogers, assistant district attorney of New York County, said loan-sharking is so profitable that one mob boss pyramided $500,000 into $7,500,000 in about five years—and there were, in New York County alone, "at least ten men comparable to him." It is so safe that it almost defies prosecution—which is probably the reason that top mobsters have been more openly connected with it than with gambling and narcotics.

There are four operating levels in the loan-sharking pyramid. On top is the Mafia chieftain. Just beneath him are his principal lieutenants who funnel money to their own subordinates for investment. These third-echelon underlings lend out much of the money themselves and pass the rest down to the lowest level, the working bookie and street-corner hoodlum. Sgt. Ralph Salerno, the now-retired racket expert of New York City's Bureau of Criminal Investigation, describes how it works:

"A big racket boss invites ten trusted lieutenants to a Christmas party in his home. He distributes one million dollars in cash—$100,000 to each of these ten men. He doesn't have to keep any record of the names or amounts. All he says is, 'I want one percent a week. I don't care what *you* get, but *I* want one percent.' For the next year's Christmas party, the only problem is where to find five more men to hand out the half-million dollars he earned in the preceding year."

This usurious one percent is known in the trade as vigorish—or "the vig." Naturally, the interest rate goes up as the money is filtered through the various echelons. On the second level the vigorish may be 1.5 or 2 percent a week. On the lowest level, it can be 5 percent a week—260 percent a year.

The Doctor is one of those top-level lieutenants who would be invited to the big chief's Christmas party. In his case, though, he would probably be given something more like a million. Operating through as many as 30 underlings, he has hundreds of thousands of dollars working at any one time.

Life for the Doctor is one unvarying round of seemingly innocent social contacts. He may brunch with his bride, daughter of a Mafia chieftain, then stop at the small office that he maintains as an ostensibly legitimate front. (Though no real business is conducted there, detectives deduce that it is a contact point at which the Doctor picks up messages or cash that may have been left for him.) He regularly visits his favorite Italian social club, where he chats—and undoubtedly transacts important business—with cronies. Then it's off to the plush bistros, some of which are so deeply in hock to him that he is, in fact, the secret owner. There, says a detective who has camped on the Doctor's trail, "perhaps he wanders off to the men's room and, just by chance, one of his lieutenants follows. A word is dropped, or money changes hands. There is little you can do about it."

Professional people and substantial businessmen are the loan shark's favorite targets. The borrower is always at the mercy of the shark, for the latter makes up the rules as he goes along. And the victim finds that when he is over a barrel with a loan shark, he is over a barrel with the Mafia—which is being over a nasty barrel indeed.

In one case a businessman borrowed $6000, made three payments, then missed two. For this offense the loan shark decided that the $6000 would now be considered $12,000, with the accompanying double vigorish. When the hapless borrower could not begin to pay this suddenly doubled load, the shark upped the principal to $17,000, then $25,000.

Just by simple mandate from the loan shark, the situation rapidly deteriorates to the point of utter hopelessness, which is what the shark wants. At this point he may suddenly turn on a friendly smile and say magnanimously, "Look, we will swap even. I will forget the loan, you forget your business. It is now mine."

Not every borrower is so "lucky." An investigative unit recently came into possession of a pocket notebook containing the record of transactions of a bookie-shark on the lowest level of the Doctor's ring. One account dealt with a loan that started out at $11,600. The borrower made regular payments at the start, but then the burden obviously became too heavy. His payments lapsed for weeks. Penalties were assessed.

These and accumulations of vigorish boosted the indebtedness, despite what had been paid, to $16,898. There the account ends—permanently. The man was found murdered in an alleyway, and investigators theorize that he paid with his life for having had the bad judgment to cost the syndicate money.

Coupled with the shark's utter ruthlessness is a devilish cunning that is always devising new ways of getting people in his power—and then driving them right through a wall. There are an infinite number of entrapment techniques.

In one typical case, a steerer at a bar introduced the resident loan shark to the son of a wealthy businessman. The son had junior-executive status in his father's business, and it did something for his playboy ego to be seen in the company of such an eminent Prince of Darkness. The shark and Junior began to bet together on Saturday football games. They started at the $10 level. Then the shark suggested they move up to the $100 class, but Junior didn't have that kind of money. Kindly Shark, slapping him on the back, reassured him: "Okay, old buddy, I'll back you." Soon, Junior was gambling $4000 each Saturday with the bookie to whom Kindly Shark had introduced him.

The inevitable happened. Came a series of disastrous weekends, when all that Junior's teams could do was lose—and he had no money, of course, with which to pay the thousands he owed. Now Kindly Shark's teeth showed. "Pay up, old buddy—and damn quick," he said. In desperation Junior embezzled a large sum of money from his father's firm.

Worldly-wise individuals are also caught in this trap and forced into paths of crookedness. Ralph Salerno told the New York investigation commission of the case of a nationally known sports broadcaster who became involved with two loan sharks. "He ended up steering affluent people, who knew his reputation, to a crooked dice game in order to earn a percentage of what they would be fleeced of, to be applied against his indebtedness."

Such is the unsavory picture. What can be done about it?

There must be increased understanding of the problem. The public still seems to think of the loan shark as an accommodating fellow who is offering a valuable service. The New York State Commission of Investigation was told of a businessman who borrowed a million dollars for a construction project from a second-echelon shark. When the businessman began to list the collateral he could put up to guarantee the loan, the shark wasn't interested. "Your body is your collateral," he said coldly. The public must be made to understand, officials say, that when a man borrows from a loan shark there is indeed a lien on his life.

Prosecution of sharks is extremely difficult. The witness willing to testify against a loan shark, with the terrifying shadow of the Mafia looming behind him, is exceedingly difficult to find.

It sometimes happens that a victim is driven to such a degree of desperation that he flees into the arms of the law. One such rarity was Berthold Kahn, of Spring Valley, N.Y., who became hopelessly entangled with Brooklyn loan sharks. In fear of his life, he sought out Brooklyn District Attorney Aaron E. Koota, who has been waging a vigorous campaign against the underworld's infiltration of legitimate businesses.

Kahn arrived at Koota's office quaking with fear. He said he wanted to telephone his wife. What she told him only increased his terror. In his absence she had received a telephone call from some tough-talking characters who informed her that her husband had not kept an appointment with them. They were going to come out to his house that night to teach him a lesson.

This incautious announcement was all the authorities needed. Brooklyn detectives and state police staked themselves out in Kahn's home. At 3:30 a.m. three hoods pounded on the door, shouting to Kahn to open up and asking him if he wanted his arms and legs broken. Having heard all they needed, the detectives moved in and arrested the trio on extortion charges.

Though it may be a long time before the Kahns feel entirely safe, authorities say that once the law has interested itself in a particular case the loan sharks tend to stay away. After all, why risk bothering with a man on whom the police are probably keeping a protective eye when you can go out tomorrow and keep turning over five percent a week?

"Law-enforcement authorities are prepared to act any time we can get the help of the public," says Koota. "But we have to have coöperation. It is the only way we can stop this racket."

→ A classified advertisement in the Brown University *Daily Herald* read: "Will the person who borrowed my metronome please return it? I rely on the rhythm method."   *Brown Alumni Monthly*

An Open Letter to Students

Dwight D. Eisenhower

Few men have been held in such universal high esteem as was General Dwight D. Eisenhower after World War II. His warmth, directness and famous smile contributed to that popularity, along with his leadership qualities.

In the 1960s, after his White House years, President Eisenhower became a regular contributor to this magazine. His distinguished byline appeared in its pages 24 times, and 18 of those articles—including this one—were written expressly for the Digest. Each reflected the deep commitment to duty and country that was an integral part of the man.

[October 1948]

As president of Columbia University I receive many letters from young people. Mostly they ask a question that could be put like this: Shall I keep on with school, or shall I plunge right off into "life"?

I try to answer each according to the circumstances. But if I could write a general answer, I think I would say:

Dear Jack—or Margaret: You say you wonder if it is worthwhile for you to go on with school. You particularly wonder if it is worthwhile to enter and finish college. The tedium of study, nose buried in books, seems a waste of time compared with a job and the stimulus of productive work. This problem of yours is not a trifling one at all. Your decision will affect your whole life, and I know how deeply it must worry you. It worried me when I was your age.

In a small Kansas town, 40 years ago, a reasonably strong case could be put up in favor of leaving school early. Most of

us knew our lives would be spent on the farm, or in one of the local stores, or at the creamery or elevator. The quickest road to practical knowledge was to *do*. That was the way we might have argued—and rightly, if there were no more to successful living than plowing a straight furrow, wrapping a neat package, keeping a machine well oiled.

Fortunately, we came of stock that set the school on the same plane as the home and church. The value of education had been bred into us. Our families stinted themselves to keep us in school a while longer; and most of us worked, and worked hard, to prolong that while.

Today the business of living is far more complex. No one of us can hope to comprehend all its complexity in a lifetime of study. But each day profitably spent in school will help you understand better your own relationship to country and world. If your generation fails to understand that the individual is still the center, the sole reason for the existence of all man-made institutions, then complexity will become chaos.

Consequently, I feel firmly that you should continue your schooling—if you can—right to the end of college. You say you are "not too good at books." I got a moving letter from a young girl halfway through high school. She said that in her studies she seemed to be always trailing. But she concluded: "I still think I can learn to be a good American."

That's the vital point. School, of course, should train you in the two great basic tools of the mind: the use of words and the use of numbers. And school can properly give you a start toward the special skills you may need in a trade, business or profession. But remember: As soon as you enter an occupation, you will be strongly tempted to fall into the routine of it, to become just a part of that occupation, which is just one part of America. In school—from books, from teachers, from fellow students—you can get a view of the whole of America, how it started, how it grew, what it is, what it means. Each day will add breadth to your view and a sharper comprehension of your own role.

I feel sure I am right when I tell you: *To develop fully your own character you must know your country's character.* A plant partakes of the character of the soil in which it grows. You are a plant that is *conscious,* that *thinks.* You must study your soil —which is your country—in order that you may be able to draw its strength up into your own strength.

It will pay you to do so. You will understand your own problems better and solve them more easily if you have studied America's problems and done something toward their solution. You have to look out for yourself *and* your country. Self-interest and patriotism, rightly considered, are not contradictory ideas. They are partners.

The very earth of our country is gradually getting lost to us. One third of the fertile top layer of our soil has already been washed away into rivers and the sea. This must be stopped or someday our country will be too barren to yield us a living. That is one national problem crying for solution.

In our cities there are millions of people who have little between them and hunger except a daily job, which they may lose. They demand more security. If they feel too insecure, their discontent might someday undermine *your* security, no matter how successful you might be in your own working life. That's another problem, and there are innumerable others.

It is dangerous to assume that our country's welfare belongs alone to that mysterious mechanism called "the government." Every time we allow or force the government, because of our own individual or local failures, to take over a question that properly belongs to us, by that much we surrender our individual responsibility—and with it freedom. But the very core of what we mean by Americanism is individual liberty, founded on individual responsibility, equality before the law, and a system of private enterprise that aims to reward according to merit.

Yours is a country of free men and women, where personal liberty is cherished as a fundamental right. But liberty is easily lost; the price of its continued possession is untiring alertness.

Never let yourself be persuaded that any one Great Man, any one leader, is necessary to the salvation of America. When America consists of one *leader* and a population of millions of *followers,* it will no longer be America. Any needless concentration of power is a menace to freedom.

World War II was not won by one man or a few men. It was won by hundreds of thousands and millions of men and women of all ranks. Audacity, initiative, the will to try greatly and stubbornly characterized them. Great numbers of them, if for only a few minutes in some desperate crisis of battle, were leaders.

You will find it so in the fields of peace. America at work is not just a few Great Men at the head of government, of corporations or of labor unions. It is millions and millions of men and women who on farms and in factories and in stores, offices and homes are leading this country—and the world—toward better and better ways of doing and making things.

We have the world's best machines because we ourselves are not machines; because we have embraced the liberty of thinking for ourselves, imagining for ourselves, and acting for ourselves out of our own energies and inspirations. Our true strength is not in our machines, splendid as they are, but in the inquisitive, inventive, indomitable souls of our people.

To be that kind of soul is open to every American boy and girl; *and it is the one kind of career that the nation cannot live without.* To be a good American—worthy of the heritage that is yours, eager to pass it on enhanced and enriched—is a lifetime career, stimulating, sometimes exhausting, always satisfying.

Start on it now; take part in America's affairs while you are still a student. "Let no man despise thy youth," Paul the Apostle said to Timothy. These words apply to you as an American. Loyalty to principle, readiness to give of one's talents to the common good, acceptance of responsibility—in home, neighborhood, school: these are the measure of a good American, not his age in years. Alexander Hamilton—General Washington's aide in war, President Washington's Secretary of the Treasury in peace—was speaking before applauding crowds of his fellow New Yorkers on the political problems of the American Revolution when he was only 17 years old and still a student in King's College, now Columbia University. The same stuff of which he was made is in you.

Above all, while still at school, try to learn the "why" of your country. To assure each citizen his inalienable right to life, liberty and the pursuit of happiness: that was the "why" behind the establishment of this Republic, and is the "why" for its continued existence. What that means to you personally, what you must do toward its fulfillment, cannot be answered completely in a letter. But I repeat that the answer can be found in your school, if you seek it deliberately and conscientiously. And you need neither genius nor vast learning for its comprehension.

To be a good American is essentially nothing more than being a good member of your community, helping those who need your help, striving for a sympathetic understanding of those who oppose you, doing each new day's job a little better than the previous day's, placing the common good before personal profit. The American Republic was born to assure you the dignity and rights of a human individual. If the dignity and rights of your fellow men guide your daily conduct of life, you will be a good American.

&~ Radio Free Europe reports that, at a time when Warsaw was plastered with posters reading "Polish-Soviet Friendship Week," an unknown wit scribbled under one sign: "Okay—but not one second longer."   *America*

Put Your Best Voice Forward

Stephen S. Price

[April 1955]

H AVE YOU ever heard how your voice sounds to others? Try it on a tape recorder. Or go to a corner of the room, face closely into it, cup your ears and speak a few words. That stranger you hear talking is *you*.

It is this voice by which people in their minds have been labeling you. It labels you every time you meet someone at a party, greet a new customer, express an opinion at a meeting or talk on the telephone.

Is it a voice that gives warmth and assurance, that helps you make the right impression?

There is no one who cannot make his or her voice more appealing. In acting as voice counselor to thousands of people in the past 21 years, I have found five major vocal shortcomings. To check your own performance, ask yourself these questions:

"Is my speech slurred rather than clear?"

Do people frequently misunderstand you or ask you to repeat? Say this sentence aloud several times: "Leaves, frost crisped, break from the trees and fall." If it makes you feel a little tongue-tied you are probably lip lazy. Vowels are easy to say, but we get power and clarity into our speech with consonants. And to pronounce these properly you must use tongue, lips and teeth energetically.

A father asked me to help his 19-year-old daughter, whose speech was listless and mumbling. She was moody and unhappy. I encouraged her to spend 30 minutes each day in front of a mirror energetically repeating the alphabet, and five minutes whistling. Whistling is a good corrective for lip laziness. Within two months people began noticing a change, an improvement, in her.

If you need to make your enunciation clearer, practice talking through clenched teeth. This makes you work your tongue and lips harder. With teeth closed tightly, read aloud, slowly at first, then rapidly. Repeat such phrases as, "He thrust three thousand thistles through the thick of his thumb." You'll find you have to exert more power in your breath, and your speech will be more energetic.

"Is my voice harsh rather than agreeable?"

Shrill, grating or brassy voices stem from tension in the throat and jaw. Europeans often comment on the harsh voices of American women. (Tension shows up more in a woman's voice.)

To relax your throat muscles, slump forward in your chair. Let your head drop, your jaw sag and your arms flop. Slowly and gently roll your head in a circle. Continue circling three minutes. Yawn a few times, opening your mouth wide, and then say such words as "clock," "squaw," "gong," "claw."

For at least a few minutes every day concentrate on talking slowly and gently to people—as if talking to a baby or a puppy. Gradually, gentleness will pervade all your talk.

"Is my voice weak?"

Your diaphragm, the band of muscle a few inches above your midriff, is the bellows that blows fire into your speech and adds oomph to your personality. If your diaphragm is weak, you probably have a thin, uncertain, shy voice.

A young research expert with a wispy voice said to me, "In a group I rarely get a chance to finish a sentence. Someone always butts in." I put my hand on his diaphragm and asked him to say loudly, "Boomlay, boomlay, boomlay, boom!" His diaphragm muscle barely fluttered. A well-developed diaphragm will really bounce when you say "boom."

I prescribed boxing lessons and daily "deep-breathing walks." I also told him to lie on the floor breathing deeply, with a heavy book on his diaphragm. Then to shout several times, "Hay! He! Ha! Hi! Ho! Hoo!" Then to sit up, inhale and blow out through a tiny hole formed by pursed lips. After these exercises he was to pick up a newspaper and see how long he could read aloud with one breath. As his diaphragm strengthened he was able to read for 15, and later 20, seconds in one breath (25 is excellent).

But it is breath control, not mere lung capacity, that gives you an outstanding voice. To check your breath control, hold a lighted candle four inches from your mouth and say, "Peter Piper picked a peck of pickled peppers." If you blow out the flame you have poor breath control.

Whispering is an excellent way to develop breath control and voice power. Have a friend stand across the room, then whisper loudly to him. As soon as he can hear you clearly, have him move into another room, and then go as far away as your whisper can reach him.

"Is my voice flat rather than colorful?"

Many persons talk in a droning, boring monotone. A prim New England woman with a cold listless voice once came to me. I asked her if she knew anyone who got a big kick out of life. She said, "Yes, the man who helps with our gardening." She envied his exuberance. To help bring warmth to her voice, I suggested she spend a few hours each week doing garden work with him. I also instructed her to laugh out loud, up and down the musical scale—first using "ho," then "ha," "he" and "hoo." Slowly at first, then faster and faster. In two months her voice took on warmth and feeling.

A widespread cause of flatness is "talking through the nose" in a twangy manner, a common quality in American speech. To check for this, hold your nose and say "meaning." Notice how strangely muffled it sounds. Feel the vibration. That is because the sounds "m," "n," and "ng" (and only those three basic sounds) are resonated mainly in the nose. Say, "Father Manning." You should feel vibration in your nose only when you say "Manning." If any other letters sound muffled, you are probably nasal in your speech.

To stop talking through your nose and add richness to your

voice, use your mouth, throat and chest. The farther you open your mouth, the richer, fuller and lower the tones will be. Try saying "olive" by opening your lips only slightly. Now repeat it while really opening your mouth and see the difference. To add vibrance to your voice, hum your favorite songs at odd moments.

"Is my voice high-pitched?"

You cannot actually "lower" your voice. But you can increase the use of your lower register by practicing sounds that can be resonated in the chest, such as, "Alone, alone, all, all alone. Alone, alone on a wide, wide sea."

Say, "Hello, how are you?" The first time, put your hand on your forehead and pitch your voice toward your hand. Now put your hand on your chest and low-pitch your words to the chest. Notice the greater depth and richness? You also can develop the warm lower tones of your voice by breathing more deeply as you talk and striving to speak softly, even when under stress.

A few general suggestions: Join in group singing. Read classics aloud—for example, the King James Version of the Bible. This will improve your articulation and rhythm. After a month or so of regular practice, your new way of speaking will begin to be automatic. When you sound better you can't help feeling better. And you will enjoy increased respect not only from others but from yourself.

Words' Worth

With entrance into junior high school, seventh-graders feel quite grown-up, an attitude reflected in the pseudo-sophisticated language of their English compositions. This so wearied one teacher that for the next assignment she forbade the use of words with the "ish" suffix: no latish evenings, no coolish nights, no youngish people. One student titled his paper: "Engl Composition."   Malou Ostien

To my nine-year-old granddaughter, who aspires to be a writer, I pointed out that it isn't the best practice to use the same word twice in one sentence if a suitable synonym is available. So she brought home a design for a sampler she made in art class. It read: "Home Sweet House."   C. W. Howe

248

I Was a Male War Bride

Henri Rochard

[November 1947]

I T ALL started when I met a U. S. Army nurse. While serving as a liaison officer for the Belgian government at the German war-crimes trials, I was accidentally hit by a car and was taken to a U. S. Army hospital. There I met Catherine. Upon release from the hospital I obtained my discharge from the Belgian army and returned to Nuremberg as a civilian employe of the U. S. War Department. Catherine and I became engaged.

Our first problem was to obtain permission from U. S. Army Headquarters to marry. It's not like asking a father for his daughter's hand and getting an immediate yes or no. I had to type up five copies of my personal history, which, together with our formal marriage request, were sent to headquarters. Two months later the documents were returned, duly stamped: "Henri Rochard, being morally and physically fit, and the union not seeming to bring discredit upon the Armed Forces of the United States, this marriage is approved."

We planned to leave for the United States as soon as possible, so we made inquiries at the nearest U. S. consulate regarding conditions of my entry. Four months later we received a reply: "It is probable that you can be admitted into the United States under the provisions of Public Law 271, which regulates the entry of War Brides." With that my troubles began.

Armed with the letter, I went to my own headquarters and

asked for the necessary Army forms. People there were very sorry, but there was no mention of male war brides in Army regulations; my wife would have to procure the forms through *her* headquarters. "For this purpose the Army considers you your wife's dependent."

Catherine secured the necessary papers and forwarded them. Six weeks later this startling letter arrived, addressed to Mrs. Henri Rochard (*i.e.,* me), c/o Captain Catherine G. Rochard:

> Dear Madam: [me again!]
> Following application of your husband [that is, my wife] you are informed that your application to enter the United States as a War Bride has been accepted by this office. Please fill in attached form.

The form requested full information about my past and also wanted to know if I was pregnant. If so, how many months?

A fortnight later a letter addressed to Mrs. Henri Rochard directed me to report to Bremerhaven, War Brides Division.

When I arrived there, accompanied by my wife, I reported as ordered to the Dependents' Hotel. The only males in the hotel, I found, were small babies and full colonels. The officer in charge, however, checked his incoming list: 139 War Brides, 126 children of War Brides, 9 dogs of War Brides, 1 War Husband. My vanity was not inflated by being listed after the dogs, but at least my sex had been restored.

At this point I was told that I must return to Belgium to obtain a passport. This took two weeks. Upon my return I was greeted with the information that I needn't have made the trip after all, because P.L. 271 provides that no passport or clearance is required!

The Army now instructed me to go to the Staging Area, Building 11. The sergeant on duty at Building 11 said he could give me neither room nor bed because according to regulations these quarters were for "U.S. Officers" and, although I was a reserve officer of an Allied army, I was actually a dependent. He directed me to Building 10, assigned to female dependents. There the WAC sergeant on duty screamed when I entered. I explained that I was a male sometimes listed as a female because the Army had no regulations covering my case and the category in which I fitted best was War Brides.

The WAC decided that I should try Building 9. There the lieutenant in charge laughed at my story and let me have a bed.

About 1 a.m., a sergeant woke me and told me to "get the hell out of that sack!" This was a room for GIs and he didn't want any trouble with the inspector.

"Listen, sergeant," I said, not quietly, "you can go to bed with your regulations. I'm not moving." Interspersed were a few smoky English words I had picked up. I heard nothing more.

In the morning a master sergeant informed me that I could be court-martialed for refusing to obey orders. I asked testily if there were any German hotels in the neighborhood. "Yes," said the sergeant, "but you can't go there. You are under military law, and those places are off limits."

The friendly lieutenant entered at that moment and saved more unpleasantness. A bed was finally found for me.

When I had located my wife, we walked over to the dining room. There I had to sign the war brides' sheet, my wife the officers' sheet. My wife paid for her meal, but my money was refused: as a war bride, I was a guest of the government.

Finally the long-awaited day of departure came and I was directed to ride to the dock with the other war brides. The merry-go-round was starting again—I appeared on the shipping list as Mrs. Henri Rochard! As I climbed the ship's gangway, a naval officer grabbed me by the lapel, where a shipping tag indicated my name (Mrs.), forwarding address and age. "Sorry," he said, "you can't board. You're not military personnel; not a civilian employe; not a dependent."

There was nothing for me to do but turn back. At the other end of the gangway stood the Army lieutenant in charge of war brides. He sent me back up again. In a moment, Army and Navy were engaged in hostilities in the middle of the gangway, while I served as shock absorber.

Finally the facts of the case were more or less agreed on: Mrs. Henri Rochard was a male. She (or he) was the spouse of a returning servicewoman and was entitled to the same rights and privileges as war brides—including a bunk in a first-class stateroom. Because female war brides in these quarters might object, however, it was decided to bunk me with staff officers.

As our ship passed the cliffs of Dover, our troubles seemed to be over. My wife and I managed to have our meals together, and nothing more than fire drills broke the tranquillity.

Then on the fifth day the transport surgeon called over the public-address system for all war brides to report to the hospital. I decided not to report. It was an error. When the last bride had received her checkup, the PA system started screaming the name of Mrs. Henri Rochard. So I reported.

"Are you the husband of that war bride who didn't think it necessary to come down?" the physician greeted me. "You tell her if she isn't here in two minutes, I'll close the damn place up, and she can explain to the immigration authorities."

I tried to explain that I was not the husband, I was the bride.

"You're the bride? For God's sake, do you realize what a mess you've put the Army in? There are a lot of things mentioned on this sheet that you don't have."

Hesitantly I suggested: "But, captain, since it is impossible to change my sex to comply with Army report sheets, how about checking over the things I do have?" This, after contemplation, he decided to do.

As we approached New York, landing cards were doled out: every war bride but me received one. It took a day to straighten that out. Then, as our ship entered the harbor, debarkation orders were distributed, and only the Naturalization and Immigration Service interview remained. For this I had to line up with the war brides again. As I came before the immigration officer he asked: "Where is your wife? She has to appear herself."

"I'm sorry, sir," I mumbled. "There is no wife. That's me."

"This is most unusual," he said, eying me sternly. Then, resignedly, "Okay, here's your stamp."

As we walked down the gangway, and I was about to set foot on U. S. soil for the first time, a sergeant barked: "Hey, you, get the hell back on that ship!"

"But, sergeant," my wife said sweetly, "he is my war bride."

"Oh, I'm sorry, sir—uh, ma'am. Well, then, I guess it's all right. Go ahead, keep her."

KON-TIKI

Thor Heyerdahl

KON-TIKI

"WESTWARD HO!" we shouted as the sail of our rudely constructed raft, the *Kon-Tiki*, caught the wind. The sail quickly filled and the *Kon-Tiki* began to move. The six of us were off to our great adventure.

It was early in the morning of April 29, 1947, and we had just bade a ceremonious farewell to our friends on the Peruvian naval tug which had towed us out into the Pacific. As the tug steamed away we watched the black column of smoke dissolve over the horizon, then shook our heads and looked at one another.

Our chart showed that we were 50 sea miles from our starting point at Callao, Peru. If my calculations were correct, in three months—more or less—we would be carried by the current and prevailing winds, with only the help of our few crude sails, westward from the coast of South America 4000 miles to the islands of the South Sea.

The expedition was undertaken to explore a theory I had formed that the original settlers of the South Sea islands had come from South America and not, as is generally believed, from the Orient. Legends of mysterious white ancestors are current all over Polynesia, and I was convinced these could be none other than the race of *Kon-Tiki,* the high priest and sun-king of the legendary "white men" who, before the Incas, had left enormous ruins in Peru. Similar monumental ruins are found on Easter Island, the Marquesas and other South Sea islands. I believed the early South Americans had sailed or drifted there by taking advantage of the Humboldt Current, which sweeps upward along the coast of Peru and then swings westward just below the equator. To prove my theory possible, I determined to build a primitive balsa raft, such as they must have used, and cross the sea myself. Most of my scientific friends thought I was mad.

Nevertheless, friends in the New York Explorers Club helped me raise the necessary funds and I was joined in the venture by four fellow Norwegians—Herman Watzinger, an engineer; Erik Hesselberg, a painter who also knew how to use a sextant; two wartime radio operators, Knut Haugland and Torstein Raaby—and by Bengt Danielsson, a Swedish ethnologist. Within a few months we had built and equipped our balsa raft, which we named *Kon-Tiki* after the legendary sungod of the pre-Incas. We felled the balsa logs ourselves in the Ecuadorian jungles, and drifted them down to the Pacific by river exactly as had the Indians of old. And we faithfully copied the old vessels of Peru and Ecuador by lashing nine of the great logs together with hemp rope, using not a single spike, nail or wire rope in the whole construction. We then lashed thin balsa logs crossways over them, laid down a deck of split bamboos, and erected a small open cabin walled with plaited bamboo reeds and roofed with leathery banana leaves.

Experts who looked at the raft gave us little encouragement. The biggest balsa exporter in Peru said the porous balsa logs would become waterlogged and sink before we had covered a quarter of the distance across the sea. A Norwegian boatswain said the raft would not hold together for a fortnight before every single rope was worn through by the movement of the big logs rubbing against each other. If we totted up all that the different experts, each in turn, pointed out as the vital flaw, there was not a length of rope, not a knot, not a measurement, not a piece of wood in the whole raft which would not cause us to founder at sea. But our whole voyage was founded on the belief that, if balsa wood had floated and lashings had held for the race of *Kon-Tiki* in 500 A.D., they would do the same for us now.

By LATE afternoon of our first day out the jagged mountains of Peru had vanished into a dense cloud bank behind us. The wind was blowing at full strength, and it quickly stirred up the ocean into roaring seas which swept against us from astern. From now onward, we should never get another chance to turn back. We were in the path of the real trade winds, and every day would carry us farther and farther out to sea. The only thing to do was to go ahead under full sail; if we tried to turn homeward, we should only drift farther out to sea stern first.

As night fell, the troughs of the sea grew gradually deeper, and our first duel with the elements began. Each time we heard the sudden deafening hiss of a roller close by and saw a white crest come groping toward us out of the darkness, we held on tight and waited for the worst.

But each time the *Kon-Tiki* calmly swung up her stern and rose skyward unperturbed, while the masses of water rolled along her sides and out through the round logs as if through the prongs of a fork. Herein obviously lay the advantage of a raft: the more leaks the better. We rose up on the foaming ridges and then flattened them out beneath us like a steam roller. A cork steam roller—that was what our balsa raft amounted to.

Our biggest problem was steering. Our steering oar, 19 feet long, of mangrove-wood so heavy that it would sink if it fell overboard, rested between two tholepins on a large block astern, only loosely secured by ropes. When the seas drove against it, it took all our strength to hold it steady. Two men at a time took turns at the job; even so, when a really big sea came they had to leave their post hastily and cling to the cabin as the masses of water thundered in over them from astern. Then they had to fling themselves at the leaping oar again before the raft could turn around and the sail thrash about.

For the first 24 hours every man, in unbroken succession, had two hours at the helm and three hours' rest. We clung like flies, two and two, to the steering oar in the darkness and felt the fresh sea water pouring off our hair while the oar hit us till we were sore all over and our hands grew stiff with the exertion of hanging on. When at last the relief came, we crept half-dazed into the bamboo cabin, tied a rope around our legs, and fell asleep with our salty clothes on before we could get into our sleeping bags.

The next night was worse still; the seas grew higher instead of going down. Two hours on end of struggling with the steering oar was too long; a man was not much use in the second half of his watch and the seas got the better of us and hurled us round and sideways, while the water poured on board. Finally we had to shorten the watch to one hour, and Knut Haugland had to be let off altogether while he suffered silent agonies of seasickness in the cabin.

About midnight of the first night a ship's light passed in a northerly direction. At three another passed on the same course. We hailed them with flashes from an electric torch, but they did not see us and the lights passed slowly northward into the darkness and disappeared. This was the last trace of men we should see till we had reached the other side of the ocean.

The third night the sea suddenly became calmer. Stiff, sore and utterly exhausted, we furled the sail, everything on board was lashed fast, and all six of us crawled into the little bamboo cabin, huddled together, and slept like mummies. We did not wake till well on in the day. The wind was still blowing straight from the southwest, but moderately now, and the sun beating down on the yellow bamboo deck gave the sea all around us a bright and friendly aspect.

Erik took our position at noon and found that, in addition to our run under sail, we had made a big deviation northward along the coast. We still lay in the Humboldt Current just 100 sea miles from land. The great question was whether we would get into the treacherous eddies south of the Galápagos Islands. This could have fatal consequences, for up there we might be swept toward the coast of Central America. But, if things went as we calculated, we should swing west across the sea with the main current before we got as far north as the Galápagos. We hoisted the sail, turned the raft stern to the sea, and continued our steering watches.

We had already struggled through the hardest steering of the voyage. But not till weeks later did we discover the Incas' simple and ingenious way of steering a raft. In the chinks between the big logs we had lashed planks which served as centerboards. One day one of them broke loose, and through this accident we learned that by simply raising and lowering the centerboards we could effect changes of course and keep to them without touching the steering oar.

KNUT had now recovered from the torments of seasickness, and he and Torstein clambered up to the swaying masthead, where they experimented with mysterious radio aerials which they sent up both by balloon and by kite. Suddenly one of them shouted from the radio corner of the cabin that the naval station at Lima was calling us. They announced that the American ambassador's plane was on its way out from the coast to bid us a last good-by and see what we looked like at sea. Soon after, we obtained direct contact with the operator in the plane. We gave our position as exactly as we could and sent direction-finding signals for hours. The voice in the ether grew stronger or weaker as they circled, but it was not easy to find the low raft down in the trough of the seas, and we never did hear the drone of the engines or see the plane. It was the last time anyone tried to find us.

The sea ran high in the days that followed, but the waves came hissing along from the southeast with even spaces between them and the steering went more easily. The southeast trade wind and the Humboldt Current were sending us along so quickly that our daily average was 55 to 60 sea miles, with a record of 71 sea miles in one day.

Our main concern was the raft. It was easy to see that the balsa logs absorbed water. The aft crossbeam was worse than the others; we could press a fingertip into the soaked wood till the water squelched. Without saying anything I broke off a piece of the sodden wood and threw it overboard. It slowly vanished down into the depths. Later I saw two or three of the other fellows surreptitiously do the same—and watch somberly as the waterlogged piece of wood quietly sank.

We had noted the water line on the raft when we started, but in the rough sea it was impossible to see how deep we lay, for one moment the logs were lifted out of the water and the next they went down deep into it. But if we drove a knife into the timber, we saw to our joy that the wood was dry an inch or so below the surface, and we hoped that the sap further in would check the absorption.

Then there were the ropes. The *Kon-Tiki* was held together by about 300 separate lengths of hemp rope. And as the experts, including an admiral of the Peruvian navy, had predicted that every single rope would soon be worn through, it was alarming, as we lay in the cabin at night, to hear the ropes creaking and groaning. It was like one single complaining chorus around us in the dark, each rope having its own note according to its thickness and tautness. But so far we had not found the smallest sign of wear. Not till we were far out to sea did we find the explanation. The balsa wood was so soft that the ropes wore their way slowly into the wood and were protected, instead of the logs wearing the ropes.

THE very first day we were left alone on the sea we had noticed fish around the raft, but we were too much occupied with the steering to think of fishing. The second day we went right into a thick shoal of sardines, and soon afterward an eight-foot shark came along and rolled over with its white belly uppermost as it rubbed against the raft's stern, where Herman and Bengt stood barelegged in the seas, steering. It played around for a while but disappeared when we got the hand harpoon ready for action.

Next day we were visited by tunnies, bonitos and dolphins, and when a big flying fish thudded on board we used it as bait, and at once pulled in two large dolphins (dorados) weighing from 20 to 35 pounds each—ample food for several days.

The nearer we came to the equator, and the farther from the

coast, the commoner flying fish became. When at last we came out into the blue water where the sea rolled by majestically, sunlit and serene, ruffled by gusts of wind, we could see them glittering like a rain of projectiles which shot from the water and flew in a straight line till their power of flight was exhausted and they vanished beneath the surface.

If we set the little paraffin lamp out at night, flying fish were attracted by the light and, large and small, shot over the raft. They often struck the bamboo cabin or the sail and tumbled helpless on the deck. Sometimes we heard an outburst of strong language when a cold flying fish caught some man slap in the face, but on the whole we were thankful to be in a maritime land of enchantment where delicious fish dishes came hurtling through the air.

Our intimacy with the sea was closer than we at first fully realized. When Torstein Raaby, who slept with his head nearest the cabin door, woke one morning and found a sardine on his pillow he was inclined to take it philosophically. But a few nights later something happened which caused Torstein to find himself a sleeping place on top of the kitchen utensils in the radio corner.

At about four o'clock in the morning something came hurtling on board, knocking over the paraffin lamp which Torstein always put close by his head to keep the night watches from stumbling over him as they crept in and out. Taking the unseen visitor for another flying fish, Torstein felt for it in the darkness. He caught hold of something long and wet, which wriggled like a snake, and he let go as if he had burned himself. The intruder twisted itself away and over to Herman, who likewise woke with a start. Presently we were all aroused, and by the time we got the lamp lighted, we found Herman sitting up gripping a long thin fish which wriggled in his hands like an eel. The creature was over three feet long, as slender as a snake, with dull black eyes and a long snout with a greedy jaw full of long sharp teeth. Suddenly under Herman's grip, a large-eyed white fish, about eight inches long, emerged from the monster's stomach, and soon after up came another just like it.

Bengt, the last to be awakened by all the noise, sat up drowsily in his sleeping bag and, taking one look at our uninvited guest, said solemnly: "No, fish like that don't exist." Whereupon he turned over quietly and fell asleep again.

Bengt was not far wrong, for it appeared later that we were the first men known to have seen this fish alive. It was a snake mackerel, and up till now only a few skeletons had been found on the coast of South America and the Galápagos Islands.

THOSE who plow across the sea with roaring engines, and then come back and say there is nothing to see far out on the ocean, can have no conception of the surprises that await him who drifts along slowly on the surface. Not a day passed but we were visited by inquisitive guests who wriggled and waggled about us, and a few of them, such as dolphins and pilot fish, grew so familiar that they accompanied the raft across the sea and kept around us day and night.

When night had fallen and the stars were twinkling in the dark tropical sky, a phosphorescence flashed around us in rivalry with the stars, and single glowing pellets so vividly resembled live coals that we involuntarily drew in our bare legs when they washed around our feet at the raft's stern. When we caught them, we saw that they were little brightly shining species of shrimp.

On such nights we were sometimes scared when two round shining eyes suddenly rose out of the sea right alongside the raft and glared at us with an unblinking hypnotic stare. The visitors were often big squids which came up and floated on the surface with their devilish green eyes shining in the dark. But sometimes the shining eyes were those of deep-water fish which came up only at night. Several times, when the sea was calm, the black water around the raft was full of their round heads, two or three feet in diameter, lying motionless and staring at us with glowing eyes. On other nights balls of light three feet and more in diameter would be visible down in the water, flashing at irregular intervals.

One cloudy night, the helmsman caught sight of a faint illumination down in the water which slowly took the shape of a large animal. The glimmer down in the black water gave the ghostly creature obscure, wavering outlines. Finally there were three of these large shining phantoms wandering around in slow circles under us.

They were real monsters—fully 30 feet long. We all collected on deck and followed their ghost dance. The glimmer of light on their backs revealed that the beasts were bigger than elephants; but they were not whales, for they never came up to breathe. Were they giant ray fish which changed shape when they turned over on their side? We couldn't tell. They took no notice at all if we held the light right down on the surface to lure them up closer, and, like all proper goblins and ghosts, they sank into the depths before dawn broke.

THE ONLY possible explanation of the mystery was suggested by a visit we received a day and a half later in full midday sunshine. It was May 24 and we were drifting on a leisurely swell. About noon I heard a wild war whoop from Knut, who was sitting aft, and we all flocked astern.

Knut had been squatting there, washing his pants in the swell, and when he looked up for a moment he was staring straight into the biggest and ugliest face any of us had ever seen. It was the head of a veritable sea monster, huge and hideous. The head was broad and flat like a frog's, with two small eyes right at the sides, and a toadlike jaw which was four or five feet wide and had long fringes drooping from the corners of the mouth. Behind the head was an enormous body ending in a long thin tail with a pointed tail fin which stood straight up and showed that this sea monster was not any kind of whale. The body looked brownish under the water, but both head and body were thickly covered with small white spots.

The monster came quietly, lazily swimming after us from astern. It grinned like a bulldog and lashed gently with its tail. The sight was so completely fantastic that we thought we had all gone mad. Walt Disney himself could not have created a more hair-raising sea monster.

This was a whale shark, the largest shark and the largest fish known in the world today. It is exceedingly rare, but scattered specimens, averaging 50 feet in length and weighing 15 tons, are observed here and there in the tropical oceans. Ours was so large that, when it began to swim in circles around us, its head was visible on one side while its tail stuck out on the other. And so incredibly grotesque did it appear when seen full-face that we could not help shouting with laughter, although we realized that it could smash the raft to pieces if it attacked us.

We stood around the raft with harpoons ready for action, but they seemed like toothpicks in relation to the beast we had to deal with. There was no indication that the whale shark ever thought of leaving us; again and again it circled the raft.

After perhaps an hour, though it seemed like a whole day, Erik, encouraged by ill-considered shouts, raised the harpoon and thrust it with all his giant strength deep into the whale shark's gristly head. It was a second or two before the giant understood properly what was happening. Then in a flash the placid halfwit was transformed into a mountain of steel muscles.

With a swishing noise the harpoon line rushed over the edge of the raft, and a cascade of water arose as the giant stood on its head and plunged down into the depths. The three men standing nearest were flung head over heels, two of them flayed and burned by the line as it rushed through the air. As soon as the end of the thick line—strong enough to hold a boat—was reached, it snapped off like a piece of twine. A few seconds later a broken-off harpoon shaft came to the surface. But although we waited for the monster to come back, we never saw anything more of him.

THE WEEKS passed. We saw no sign either of a ship or of drifting remains to show that there were other people in the world. The whole sea was ours, together with an incredible sense of peace and freedom. To us on the raft the great problems of civilized man appeared false and illusory. Only the elements mattered. And the elements seemed to ignore us.

If a boat had cruised our way on any average day out at sea, it would have found us bobbing quietly over a long rolling swell covered with little white-crested waves, while the trade wind held the orange sail bent steadily toward Polynesia.

Those on board would have seen, at the stern of the raft, a

brown-bearded man with no clothes on, either struggling desperately with a long steering oar while he hauled on a tangled rope or, in calm weather, sitting on a box dozing in the sun, keeping a leisurely hold on the steering oar with his toes.

If this man happened not to be Bengt, the latter would be found lying on his stomach in the cabin door with one of the 73 sociological books he had brought along as almost his sole baggage. Herman might have been found anywhere at any time of the day—at the helm, underneath the raft with diving goggles, checking the ropes, or in tow in the rubber dinghy, busy with his meteorological observations.

Knut and Torstein were always doing something to keep their little radio station going. Every night they took turns sending reports and weather observations out into the ether, where they were picked up by chance radio amateurs who passed the reports on to Washington.

Erik was usually patching sails and splicing ropes. At noon every day he took the sextant to find out how far we had moved since the day before. I myself had enough to do with the logbook and reports, the collecting of plankton, and fishing and filming.

At no time was either food or water a serious problem. We had on board a plentiful supply of military-type rations we had agreed to test, and Bengt and Torstein, who did not care for marine food, restricted their diet to these, while the rest of us ate fish. We had allowed a good quart of water per man daily, and this ration was by no means always consumed. On very hot days, when our bodies craved salt, we found to our surprise that we could add 20 to 40 percent of salt sea water to our freshwater ration without ill effect. Later, when we entered a region of storms, we caught rain water to replenish our supplies.

An apparently limitless source of food was plankton. More than once persons have starved to death at sea while sailing in strongly diluted raw-fish soup. If they had had a utensil for straining it, they would have found a nourishing meal in the thousands of tiny organisms drifting about near the surface.

We towed behind the raft a fine-mesh net in which we caught an endless variety of creatures. Most of them were tiny shrimplike crustaceans, or fish ova, but there were also jellyfish, larvae of fish and shellfish, and curious miniature crabs in all colors. Some looked like fringed, fluttering spooks cut out of cellophane while others resembled tiny red-beaked birds with hard shells instead of feathers. There was no end to nature's extravagant inventions in the plankton world.

THE FISH which most of all attached themselves to the raft were dolphins and pilot fish. From the moment the first dolphins joined us in the current off Callao there was not a day on the whole voyage on which we did not have large dolphins wriggling around us. On bad days there might be two or three, but as many as 40 might turn up the day after. What drew them we do not know, but either there was a magical attraction in being able to swim in the shade with a moving roof above or there was food to be found in our garden of seaweed and barnacles that hung like garlands from the logs and steering oar. It began with a thin coating of smooth green, but then the clusters of seaweed grew with astonishing speed, so that the *Kon-Tiki* looked like a bearded sea god as she tumbled along among the waves. The barnacles, incidentally, were delicious. They grew in hundreds, especially on the lee side of the raft, and as fast as we put the old ones into the soup kettle new larvae took root and grew up.

The dolphin, a brilliantly colored tropical fish, must not be confused with the small, toothed whale also called dolphin. Sometimes four feet in length, the fish in the water shone blue and green like a bluebottle with a glitter of golden-yellow fins. But if we hauled one on board, we sometimes saw a strange sight. As the fish died it gradually changed color and became silver gray with black spots, and finally a quite uniform silvery white. This lasted for four or five minutes, and then the old colors slowly reappeared. Even in the water the dolphin occasionally changed color like a chameleon.

As a rule we warned the cook 20 minutes in advance if we wanted fresh fish for dinner. He tied a line to a short bamboo stick and put half a flying fish on the hook. The dolphin was there in a flash, plowing the surface with its head as it chased the hook, with two or three more in its wake. It was a splendid fish to play and, when freshly caught, its flesh was firm and delicious to eat, like a mixture of cod and salmon.

We had on board some 200 coconuts to provide refreshing drinks as well as exercise for our teeth. Several of the nuts began to sprout, when we had been a few weeks at sea, and presently we had half a dozen baby palms a foot high. The coconuts also attracted a species of small pelagic crab, about as large as a fingernail, which came floating in from the sea, often clinging to a feather from some sea bird. They made pleasant tidbits if we managed to catch them before they scurried away under the raft. One little crab, however, which lived in a little hole by the steering block, became quite tame. We named him Johannes, and he became a part of our community. Every man who came on watch had a bit of biscuit or fish for him, and we needed only to stoop down over the hole for him to come right out on his doorstep and stretch out his hands. He took the scraps out of our fingers with his claws and ran back into the hole, where he sat down in the doorway and munched like a schoolboy, cramming the food into his mouth.

One day we were sitting as usual on the edge of the raft, having a meal, when suddenly something behind us blew hard —like a swimming horse—and a big whale came up and stared at us, so close that we saw a shine like a polished shoe down through its blowhole. It was so unusual to hear real breathing out at sea, where all living creatures wriggle silently about without lungs and quiver their gills, that we really had a warm family feeling for our old distant cousin the whale, who like us had strayed so far out to sea. It was almost like having a visit from a jovial well-fed hippopotamus from a zoo. Sometimes we had a whole school of whales puffing and blowing around us, but they never bothered us.

FROM the beginning, sharks were an almost daily occurrence. Most often they took up a position in our wake just behind the steering oar, and there they lay without a sound, stealing from starboard to port and occasionally giving a leisurely wag of their tails to keep pace with the raft's placid advance. The blue-gray body of the shark looked brownish in the sunlight just below the surface, and it moved up and down with the seas so the dorsal fin stuck up menacingly.

To begin with, we had much respect for these great bundles of steel muscles, with their small green cat's eyes and the enormous jaws which could swallow footballs. When the man at the helm sounded the alarm, we all sprang to our stations with hand harpoons and gaffs. We soon found, however, that the gaffs bent like spaghetti when struck against the sandpaper armor of the shark's back; or the harpoon heads snapped off, and all we got was a hectic struggle in which the water boiled around us till the shark broke loose and was off.

We never lost our respect for the rows of razor-sharp teeth which lay in ambush for anything within range, but we gradually learned better ways to put these unpleasant creatures in their place. Often we put out a bit of fish or a bag with scraps from dinner on a line; then, just as the shark was going to close its jaws, we pulled on the rope. The cheated animal swam on with an unspeakably foolish, patient expression and opened its jaws again. It ended by the shark's coming right up to the logs and jumping up like a begging dog for the food dangling above its nose.

At this point, as the shark gave up and turned quietly to go under again, its tail flickered up above the surface. Pulling animals' tails is held to be an inferior form of sport, but that may be because no one had tried it on a shark. Just inside the upper point of the shark's sandpaper tail there is an indentation which might have been made solely to allow a good grip. Taking a hold there, we gave a jerk, and before the shark could collect itself, we had as much as possible of the tail pulled in tight over the logs. After a few desperate jerks, the surprised shark became quite crestfallen and apathetic, and, as the loose stomach began to sink down toward the head, it at last became completely paralyzed. But we seldom needed to get more than half the heavy fish up out of the water before it woke up and with violent jerks swung its head around and up onto the logs. Then all we had to do was to get well out of the way until it had ceased to thrash its tail and gnash its devilish teeth forever.

Marine experts in Peru had warned us especially against the monstrous octopuses which have their favorite resort in the Humboldt Current. With their long tentacles and deadly beaks they were said to be fully capable of making an end to a big shark. Not at all relishing the prospect of feeling cold arms around our necks dragging us out of our sleeping bags at night, we each slept with a saberlike machete knife handy.

One morning we found a baby octopus, the size of a cat, which had washed on board in the night and now lay dead on deck in a pool of thick, black, inky liquid. We wrote a page or two in the logbook with the cuttlefish ink, which was like India ink. It was soon usual after that to find a small squid or two among the flying fish about the deck in the morning. And they were young ones of the real devilish kind, with eight long arms covered with sucking disks, and two still longer with thornlike hooks at the end. But large squids never gave a sign of coming on board, though more than once we saw the shine of phosphorescent eyes drifting on the surface on dark nights, and once we saw the sea boil and bubble as something like a big wheel came up and rotated in the air while the dolphins broke water in a wild effort to escape.

Our most surprising discovery was that the cuttlefish can "fly." One sunny morning we all saw a glittering shoal of something which we took to be flying fish. But when they came near and some of them sailed over the raft at a height of four or five feet, one ran straight into Bengt's chest and fell slap on the deck. It was a small squid.

We discovered that young squids, which like all their kind ordinarily swim on the principle of the rocket-propelled airplane, by pumping sea water with great force through their body, can get up such a terrific speed that they can escape their pursuers by taking to the air in the same way as flying fish. We often saw them sailing along for 50 to 60 yards, singly and in twos and threes. This fact has been a novelty to all the zoologists we have met since.

WHEN the sea was not too rough, we were often out in our little rubber dinghy taking photographs. I shall never forget the lunatic impression it made on us the first time we saw our proud craft at a distance. The raft looked exactly like an old Norwegian hayloft lying helpless, drifting about in the open sea—a warped hayloft full of sunburned, bearded ruffians.

Yet it was most remarkable what a psychological effect that shaky bamboo cabin had on our minds. It measured 8 by 14 feet, and to diminish the pressure of wind and sea it was built so low that we could not stand upright under the ridge of the roof. This primitive lair, so entirely out of place in among the waves, nonetheless gave us a greater feeling of security than white-painted bulkheads and closed portholes would have given in the same circumstances. Even though its wall was only five feet from the unprotected edge of the raft and only a foot and a half above the water line, we felt as if we had traveled many miles away from the sea and occupied a jungle dwelling remote from the sea's perils once we had crawled inside the door.

It was always hazardous to go out in the dinghy for, though we never went very far away, if the wind and sea were higher than we supposed we had to row for our lives to catch up with the raft. There was always only one thought in the head of every man—we must not be separated. And we must not fall overboard, especially on a solitary night watch. The Kon-Tiki could never stop and wait or turn around and come back.

THE TWO radio operators had had a tough job in their corner since the first day they came on board. Dampness was a constant problem, and then for a long time we lay in a dead zone of the Andes in which the shortwave was as dumb and lifeless as the air in an empty soapbox.

Then one night the shortwave suddenly broke through, and Torstein's call signal was heard by a chance radio amateur in Los Angeles who was trying to establish contact with another amateur in Sweden. When he learned that Torstein was calling from a bamboo cabin on a raft in the Pacific, there were several peculiar clickings until the man could pull himself together.

Thereafter we were in contact with some radio amateur almost every night. Late one night Knut was sitting tinkering by lamplight in the radio corner when he suddenly shook me by the leg and said he had been talking to a fellow in Oslo. This was a bit of an amateur record, for our little shortwave transmitter did not send out more than six watts, about the same strength as a small electric torch. This was August 2, and we had sailed more than 60 degrees around the earth, so that Oslo was at the opposite end of the globe. King Haakon was 75 years old the next day, and we sent him congratulations direct from the raft; shortly afterward we got his reply, wishing us continued good luck and success on our voyage.

We had now entered a region of storms. In an incredibly short time the seas round about us would be flung up to a height of 15 feet, single crests often towering 20 to 25 feet above the trough of the sea. Tropical rain poured over us in horizontal squalls, and whipped the surface of the sea, invisible all around us, while at the height of the storm thousands of tons of water poured in astern, sometimes breaking on board with a deafening thunderclap, so that the helmsman stood in water up to his waist. Water streamed from our hair and beards as, naked and frozen, we scrambled about on deck bent double, and the wind shook the bamboo wall and whistled and howled in the rigging. Sometimes this went on for days.

One day Herman was out with his anemometer, measuring the wind velocity, which had already reached 50 feet and more per second, when suddenly Torstein's sleeping bag went overboard. Herman tried to catch it as it went, took a rash step, and fell over the side. We heard a faint cry for help amid the noise of the waves, and saw Herman's head and a waving arm in the water. Torstein and I were the first to perceive him, and we went cold with fear. We bellowed "Man overboard!" at the top of our lungs as we rushed to the lifesaving gear.

Herman was an excellent swimmer, and we had a fair hope that he would manage to crawl back to the edge of the raft before it was too late. But as he came on a level with the stern of the raft he was too far away, and just missed the end of the logs. His last hope was to crawl to the blade of the steering oar and hang onto it. He reached out for the oar blade, but it slipped away from him.

The wind was so strong that when the life belt was thrown it was simply blown back to the raft. Herman was already far astern, swimming desperately to keep up with the raft, while the distance increased with each gust of wind. Henceforth the gap would simply go on increasing. Bengt and I had now got the dinghy into the water. Without a towline, which acted as a brake, it might be possible to drive the rubber boat to meet the swimming man, but whether it would ever get back to the *Kon-Tiki* was another matter.

Then we suddenly saw Knut take off and plunge headfirst into the sea. He had the life belt in one hand and was heaving himself along. Every time Herman's head appeared on a wave back Knut was gone, and every time Knut came up Herman was not there. But then we saw both heads at once; they had swum to meet each other and both were hanging onto the life belt. All four of us took hold of the life-belt line and hauled for dear life, with our eyes fixed on the dark object which was visible just behind the two men. Only Herman knew then that this was not a shark or any sea monster, but an inflated corner of Torstein's watertight sleeping bag. But, a moment after we had hauled the two men safe and sound on board, the sleeping bag disappeared. Whatever dragged it down into the depths had just missed a better prey.

As a result of the storms the *Kon-Tiki* had become a good deal weaker in the joints. The strain of working over the steep wave backs had stretched all the ropes, which now had become so loose that it was dangerous to let one's foot slip down between two logs, for it could be crushed when they came together violently. Forward and aft, where there was no bamboo deck, we had to give at the knees when we stood with our feet wide apart on two logs at the same time. The logs aft were as slippery as banana leaves with wet seaweed, and it was no easy job to keep one's foothold when a sea struck the raft. On the port side one of the nine giants bumped and banged against the crossbeams with dull, wet thuds both by night and by day. There came also new and fearful creakings from the ropes which held the two sloping masts together. It was evident too that the logs had absorbed a great weight of water but, since the cargo had been lightened by the food supplies we had consumed, this was roughly canceled out. With luck we should float and hold together for the distance that remained.

For some time now there had been small but unmistakable signs that we were nearing land. Flocks of frigate birds, last seen when we were still within range of the South American coast, now reappeared, shooting down over the wave crests in search of flying fish; and one day when we hauled up a nine-foot shark it threw up from its stomach a large undigested starfish, which could only have come from some nearby shore.

Unfortunately, it appeared that we were at an almost equal distance from two groups of islands. We had now been blown out of the real South Equatorial Current, and the ocean currents were no longer behaving dependably. There was no telling where we would end up.

One day we detected a curious stationary cloud above the horizon. The other clouds were small feathery wisps of wool which came up in the south and passed across the vault of the sky with the trade wind till they disappeared over the horizon in the west. This one did not move; it just rose like a motionless column of smoke. Such clouds, as ancient mariners knew, denoted land, being formed by the hot air rising from burning tropical sands.

At daybreak the next morning Herman, on watch, clambered down from the creaking, swaying mast and shook me by the leg. "Come out and have a look at your island!"

The whole horizon was suffused with a ruddy glow, against which, far down to the southeast, could be seen a faint shadow, like a blue pencil line, drawn for a short way along the edge of the sea.

Land! An island! We devoured it greedily with our eyes and woke the others, who tumbled out drowsily and stared silently at the unaccustomed spectacle.

According to Erik's positions this island was Pukapuka, the first outpost of the Tuamotu group—at last a visible proof that we had really been moving in all these months and not just tumbling about in the center of the same eternal circular horizon. Even as we rejoiced at having actually reached Polynesia, however, we also noted we were in no position to make a landing; we would have to submit helplessly to seeing the island lie there like a mirage while we continued our eternal drift across the sea westward. At half-past eight Pukapuka sank into the sea astern. Bengt remarked wryly that he at least was glad for he still had three books to read.

The next morning we detected two new clouds rising up like the steam from two locomotives below the horizon. Choosing the nearest, which we identified from the map as Angatau, we set our course accordingly, confident that the journey would soon be over now, for this island was ideally placed.

A few mornings later we witnessed a strange phenomenon. As the sun rose straight up over the sky astern of us, we could see a clear green glimmer high up toward the misty sky over the island. It was the reflection of the still, green lagoon on the inside of the surrounding reef. Some of the low atolls throw up mirages of this kind for many thousand feet into the air, so that they show their position to primitive seafarers long before the island is visible above the horizon. Presently the island itself came into view.

But once again landing proved impossible. All day we searched in vain for an opening in the surrounding reef. By afternoon we were so close to the island that through a gap in the forest of palms ashore we saw right into a blue glassy lagoon, surrounded by swaying coconut palms and shining bathing beaches. There was a whole native village lying in among the palm trunks, and it was alive with activity.

The natives evidently had already spotted us, for presently a number of them paddled out to meet us in their outrigger canoes, crossing the reef through a passage which we had missed. The natives could speak no English, but they were very friendly and happily accepted our offer of cigarettes. When they understood that we wanted to make a landing, they attached ropes from the raft to four of the outriggers and, spread out in fan formation like a dog team, attempted to tow us in. But it was already too late; the current was too strong. And at last they gave up the attempt and returned to their island, while the *Kon-Tiki* went back to drifting over the open sea. It was a wrench to have to say good-by to the first human beings we had seen for over three months.

LATE ONE night, when we had been a hundred days at sea, I woke feeling restless and uneasy. There was something unusual in the movement of the waves. We knew we were drifting straight toward the ominous Takume and Raroia reefs, which together blocked up 40 to 50 miles of the sea ahead of us, but we hoped to pass safely to the south of them. I was continually out on deck and up the mast. Nothing but sea was visible. Still I could get no quiet sleep.

At dawn, just before six, Torstein came hurrying down from the masthead. He could see a whole line of small palm-clad islands ahead. They must be the coral islands which lay strewn like pearls on a string behind the Raroia reef, and the nearest was not more than four or five sea miles away. A new current must have hit us; we were drifting diagonally right in toward the reef.

We had all agreed on what should be done if shipwreck were imminent. Everything of value was carried into the cabin and lashed fast. Documents and papers were packed into watertight bags, along with films and other things which would not stand a dip in the sea. The whole bamboo cabin was covered with canvas, and strong ropes were lashed across it. Whatever happened, we must hang on tight on board and let the nine great logs take the pressure from the reef. If we jumped overboard we should become helpless victims of the suction which would fling us in and out over the sharp corals. Our rubber raft would capsize, or, with us in it, would be torn to ribbons against the reef. But the wooden logs would sooner or later be cast ashore, and us with them, if we only managed to hold fast.

Those were anxious hours in which we lay drifting helplessly sideways, step after step, in toward the reef. It was noticeably quiet on board; but the absence of nervousness showed that we had all gradually acquired an unshakable confidence in the raft. If it had brought us across the sea, it would also manage to bring us ashore alive.

Right up to the last minute Torstein sat in the radio corner, busily sending out signals. We were now over 4000 sea miles from our old base at Callao, and still farther from the United States, where we had had our regular radio contacts. But, as chance willed, we had on the previous day got in touch with a capable radio "ham" who had a set on Rarotonga in the Cook Islands. All the time we were drifting closer and closer in to the reef, Torstein was sitting tapping his key and calling Rarotonga.

The dull drone of the surf came near; it came from the whole reef and filled the air like thrilling rolls of the drum, heralding the exciting last act of the *Kon-Tiki*.

We let down an improvised anchor which rushed overboard and caught hold of the bottom, so that the *Kon-Tiki* swung around and turned her stern in toward the breakers. It held us for a few valuable minutes, while Torstein sat hammering like mad on the key. He had got Rarotonga now. The breakers thundered in the air and the sea rose and fell furiously. All hands were at work on deck, and now Torstein got his message through. He asked Rarotonga to listen in on the same wave length every hour. If we were silent for more than 36 hours, Rarotonga must let the Norwegian embassy in Washington know. Torstein's last words were: "Okay. Fifty yards left. Here we go. Good-by."

Then he closed down the station and crawled out on deck as fast as he could to join the rest of us, for it was clear now that the anchor was giving way.

The swell grew heavier and heavier, with deep troughs between the waves, and we felt the raft being swung up and down, up and down, higher and higher. We were now so near that we no longer heard the steady continuous roar from all along the reef. We now heard only a separate boom each time the nearest breaker crashed down on the rocks.

ALL HANDS stood in readiness, each clinging fast to the rope he thought the most secure. A sea rose straight up under us, and we felt the *Kon-Tiki* being lifted up in the air. The great moment had come; we were riding on the wave back at breathless speed, our ramshackle craft creaking and groaning as she

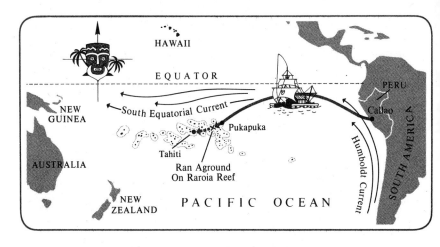

quivered under us. A new sea rose high up astern of us like a glittering green-glass wall. As we sank down it came rolling after us and in the same second in which I saw it high above me I felt a violent blow, and was submerged under floods of water. I felt the suction through my whole body, with such great power that I had to strain every single muscle in my frame and think of one thing only—hold on, hold on! Then I felt that the mountain of water was passing on and relaxing its devilish grip of my body.

In an instant hell was over us again, and the *Kon-Tiki* disappeared completely under the masses of water. The sea tugged and pulled with all the force it could bring to bear at the poor little bundles of human bodies. The second sea rushed over us, to be followed by a third.

Then I saw the next sea come towering up, higher than all the rest. We must have hit the reef that time. The whole submersion lasted only seconds, but it demanded more endurance than we usually have in our bodies. I determined that if I was to die I would die in this position, like a knot on the stay. The sea thundered on, over and past, and as it roared by it revealed a hideous sight. The *Kon-Tiki* was wholly changed; in a few seconds the vessel we knew had become a shattered wreck.

Two or three more seas rolled over us with diminishing force, and what happened then I do not remember, except that water foamed in and out. Then only crests of foam full of salt spray came whirling in, and I was able to work my way toward the after end of the logs which was highest up on the reef.

Knut sprang up onto the reef with a line which lay clear astern. While the backwash was running out he waded through the whirling water some 30 yards in and stood safely at the end of the line when the next sea struck. With each wave the raft was pushed a bit farther in, until soon it lay high up on the reef. All hands began the work of salvage.

Where we had stranded we had only pools of water and wet patches of coral about us; farther in lay the calm blue lagoon. The tide was going out, exposing more and more of the jagged reef which stretched north and south like a half-submerged fortress wall. Only 600 or 700 yards beyond lay a small island with palm tops rising into the sky and snow-white sandy beaches running out into the still lagoon. The whole island looked like a bulging green basket of flowers, or a little bit of concentrated paradise.

Herman stood beside me beaming all over his bearded face. He did not say a word, only stretched out his hand and laughed quietly with relief. The *Kon-Tiki* still lay far out on the reef with the spray flying over her. She was a wreck, but an honorable wreck. Everything above deck was smashed up, but the nine balsa logs from the Quevedo forest in Ecuador were as intact as ever. They had saved our lives.

I shall never forget that wade across the reef toward the heavenly palm island that grew larger as it came to meet us. When I reached the sunny sand beach, I slipped off my shoes and thrust my bare toes down into the warm, bone-dry sand. I went on, right in toward the center of the tiny island. Green coconuts hung under the palm tufts, and luxuriant bushes were covered with snow-white blossoms which smelled so sweet and seductive that I felt faint. In the interior of the island two quite tame terns flew about my shoulders, as white and light as wisps of cloud. Small lizards shot away from my feet, and large blood-red hermit crabs lumbered along in every direction.

I was overwhelmed. I sank down on my knees and thrust my fingers deep into the warm sand. The voyage was over.

A moment later Herman, always energetic, climbed up a small palm and pulled down a cluster of large green coconuts. We cut off their soft tops with our machete knives as if they were eggs, and poured down our throats the most delicious, refreshing drink in the world—sweet, cold milk from young and seedless palm fruit. On the reef outside resounded the monotonous drum beats from the guard at the gates of paradise.

"Purgatory was a bit damp," said Bengt, as we stretched ourselves luxuriously on the ground, "but heaven is more or less as I'd imagined it."

A FEW mornings later we saw some tiny white specks of sails coming toward us across the opal-blue lagoon. There was a native village on one of the islands across the lagoon, and from it the Polynesians had seen our fire. Now they had come in their outrigger canoes to fetch us.

With our salvaged radio equipment Torstein and Knut had succeeded in getting through to the man in Rarotonga. Before long a coasting steamer came to pick us up. Then later in Tahiti we transferred to a big Norwegian steamer.

We stood at the ship's rail as the whistle sounded over the palm-clad island. The ropes were cast off, the engines roared and the propeller whipped the water green as we slid sideways away from the quay. Soon the red roofs disappeared behind the palms, and the palms were swallowed up in the blue of Tahiti's mountains which sank like shadows into the Pacific.

Waves were breaking out on the blue sea. We could no longer reach down to them. White trade-wind clouds drifted across the blue sky. We were no longer traveling their way. We were defying nature now. We were going back to the 20th century, which lay so far, far away.

ु He is one of those who has had the wilderness for a pillow and called a star his brother. Alone. But loneliness can be a communion.

Dag Hammarskjöld, *Markings* (Knopf)

Racism in White America

Whitney M. Young, Jr.

[February 1970]

⊤HE AVERAGE white American
simply cannot fully understand what racism is. Most whites in-
terpret racism as joining lynching parties, not wanting Negroes
to sit beside them in a bus, or voicing racial slurs. But modern
racism is a good deal more subtle than that. It pervades our
society and infects everyone in it.

A black doctor I know is always being stopped by policemen
who see a black man behind the wheel of a car with MD plates
and assume it's stolen. Black professionals often find that when
they walk into a luxury apartment building, the doorman looks
them up and down as if Jack the Ripper were coming to violate
every tenant in the place. Similarly, while police brutality exists,
many more blacks feel the weight of what we might call police
humiliation—an overbearing manner, a refusal to show the least
politeness, an attitude of fear mixed with hostility that lets
black people know that this man with a uniform and a gun sees
them as somewhat less than human.

All these occurrences are part of the black experience in
White America, random evidence of our society's racism. *Racism, in fact, is the assumption of superiority, and the arrogance
that goes with it.*

It also takes another, equally condescending form: putting up
with outrageous behavior from a black man simply because he
is black. Early in 1968 the New Left held a convention in

Chicago, and a small group of blacks—perhaps ten percent of the delegates—organized themselves into a black caucus. The white radicals fell all over themselves trying to comply with their ridiculous demands. They gave the blacks half the convention votes, approved insulting resolutions, listened to wild talk that debased the purpose for which they had assembled. This itself was a subtle kind of racism, for the implicit assumption was that the blacks had to be humored; that no outrage was too great not to be accepted from the poor oppressed blacks.

I call this the "hit me again" guilt syndrome, and I've seen it countless times. I don't happen to think that the mission of black people in America is to play this kind of game.

Racism exists less in overt acts of brutality than in the silent complicity that preserves the status quo. If we understand that, it becomes clear that the federal government is the institution most responsible for its perpetuation. The laws passed in recent years, and the very real, determined efforts of recent administrations to break down the barriers of race and poverty, have been mere Band-Aids instead of the drastic surgery needed.

The budget for the Office of Economic Opportunity, whose programs are generally lumped together as the War on Poverty, was $1.9 billion in fiscal 1969. Contrast this with the $3.4 billion in subsidies for agriculture—a form of guaranteed annual income for cotton planters, tobacco growers, peanut growers, sugar growers and others. Direct federal subsidies to private industry were $6 billion a year, and indirect subsidies such as the oil-depletion allowance and tariff-protection laws bring the total to nearly $9 billion. I am not saying stop all these programs. I'm simply asking that this generosity be extended to those who need it most—America's 25 million poor.

The racial ghetto didn't just happen—it was created by the deliberate racism of the federal government and the private real-estate industry. In the 1930s and 1940s, Federal Housing Administration manuals stipulated as a condition of government mortgage backing that "properties shall continue to be occupied by the same social and racial group." The FHA recommended using restrictive covenants to "provide the surest protection against undesirable encroachment." It also "red-lined" areas not eligible for its services, supposedly because these areas were older and therefore more of an insurance risk. Most often the red-lined district perfectly coincided with the black ghetto—the very area most in need of FHA services.

At the same time, the federal government was helping to sponsor the massive white exodus to suburbia. FHA and the Veterans Administration financed $120 billion worth of new housing—only two percent of it to black families. The result has been to turn the cities into vast black ghettos in a sea of white suburbs. Middle-class suburbanites were further aided by a $40-billion subsidized road-building program, and by the fact that they can deduct expenses for financing their houses, while tenants in city apartments can't.

Moreover, programs designed to help low-income families have been used to benefit other segments of the population. In urban-renewal projects, nearly 400,000 housing units have been destroyed—replaced by about 100,000 new units. These include a mere 25,000 within the price range of the displaced low-income families, more than two thirds of whom were black.

Some of the country's top businessmen are taking the lead in opening up jobs for black people and in creating a non-discriminatory climate. But it is an uphill fight. Even the best companies—those that go into the ghetto to recruit workers, and those not satisfied with a token black face near the door—still lack sensitivity to the outlook of black workers. When the latter see no black foremen, no black supervisors, no black company officials, it becomes clear to them that they can't hope to get the promotions and raises that make a job worthwhile. Black workers have to see black people at the top, too.

To achieve a racially representative work force, especially at white-collar levels, is going to take time and effort. It will mean, among other things, working to recruit and train black people who never saw the inside of an office before.

Business has a responsibility to make the special effort, not only because its future prosperity depends upon it, but also because business, more than any other institution, created and profited from the ghetto. Business quietly tolerated school systems supported by its taxes which failed to train ghetto youngsters to function in the business world. It encouraged the housing segregation that keeps black workers concentrated in slums far from the jobs they need. It conscientiously pursued "white only" hiring policies. Every time progressive social legislation or civil-rights laws were proposed, business fought them tooth and nail. Because of this the cities—business's markets—are becoming poorer and blacker.

Even the strongest friends of labor, and I consider myself one, must reluctantly admit that as a whole the labor movement seems to have lost its passion for justice. It presents an image of a protective association, filled with middle-class people who, having advanced rather quickly, are preoccupied with maintaining the status quo and are increasingly hostile to efforts of minority groups to join them in their new-found prosperity.

Some of the unions most intent on freezing black workers out are those in the building trades and skilled crafts. Despite the efforts of civil-rights organizations, the Labor Department, Justice Department, courts, and the leadership of the AFL-CIO itself, these are still largely racially unrepresentative. In 1967, the Equal Employment Opportunity Commission (EEOC) examined the racial makeup of trainees in carpentry, plumbing and pipefitting, and electrical work in California, New York and Michigan. Out of 23,497 apprentices, only 951, or four percent, were Negroes. And less than one percent of the 1449 plumber-pipefitter trainees in California were black.

Overt bias today is rarely so blatant as an all-white provision in the union constitution. Sometimes it takes the form of negotiating seniority systems that place blacks in menial jobs, evading federal laws by accepting a few token members, using hiring halls and referral systems to keep blacks from bidding for jobs. When all else fails, some unions take refuge in tests that work against blacks with inadequate ghetto education. "Czolgosz is to Booth as McKinley is to (a) Lincoln, (b) Washington, (c) Roosevelt, (d) Garfield" is one such question on a test given applicants to a building-trades union.

America's schools have also helped to perpetuate racism. Black students get the worst schools, the least-trained teachers, the most inadequate equipment. They have to overcome not only the poverty and despair of the ghetto slums, but also the systematic destruction of their ability to learn, fostered by the hostility of many of their own teachers and counselors.

A Harvard psychology professor has proved that teachers' attitudes affect the performance of their students. In a San Francisco elementary school with a large Mexican-American enrollment, all students were given an I.Q. test. Then a random sampling of names was selected, and teachers were told that the test indicated these pupils would spurt ahead in achievement in the coming year. A year later the students were tested again. Sure enough, the ones picked at random actually did achieve better scores; in the earlier grades they scored I.Q. gains more than double those of other children.

Why? Because their teachers believed they would, and in hundreds of little ways conveyed that belief to the students, encouraging them to do better. For some children, it was the first time a teacher had really cared about their performance.

It is clear that among the black child's greatest obstacles in learning is the whole apparatus of an educational bureaucracy that doesn't believe that black kids are able to (or even ought to) learn. These attitudes need not be blatant—in fact, they often exist despite protestations of how much the child is loved and respected. But children can see in a raised eyebrow, in the tone of a voice, in a chance remark, a whole range of nuances that tells them they are unwanted and uncared for.

A society needs more than anything else to care. An ancient Greek scholar once was asked when justice would come to Athens. He replied, "When those who are not injured are as indignant as those who are." So shall it be here in America.

&⤳ A group of college freshmen went on a springtime spree and got arrested for hell-raising. In the police station, one of them, a pre-law student, stood on his legal right to make one phone call. Then they were all taken to their cells.

Soon after, a delivery boy arrived at the police station, approached the desk sergeant. "Okay," he said, "who ordered the pizza?"

Paul Light in St. Paul *Dispatch*

My Quicksilver Uncle

Robert P. Tristram Coffin

[*March 1943*]

U NCLES are a race apart, created to save children from growing up to be as dull as their parents. Uncles can afford to be natural, where a father can't. They can stuff nieces and nephews with candy and ice cream till their eyes bug out and their buttons pop, for uncles don't have to sit up nights with them. They can teach children to skip school and go to the fair. They don't have to sign the report cards next month.

They are the only creatures in the world, save milch cows and hound dogs, that have leisure. Parents don't have time for their children; they're too busy earning bread and butter or shoes. But uncles have time to sit down and tell stories while fathers sweat. Children don't respect uncles—but they love them.

Uncle Tim, who was my father's youngest brother, was always where life was the thickest, fastest and made the most noise. He was a scapegrace, a teller of tales, the life of every party, a dancer, a fiddler, the pepper and spice and the glory of the family.

My father brought him up after their father died. He tried to tame Uncle Tim to civilization, matrimony and business, but he might as well have tried to slip a halter on the northwest wind, or to hold a drop of quicksilver on a jackknife blade. Quicksilver is alive and changes its plans; it is here, there, everywhere, without warning, and it is gone suddenly into the grass where no one can ever find it again. Uncle Tim was like that.

The stars were against Uncle Tim's holding a job. When my father got him one in a gristmill, the mill burned to the ground from the cigar Tim always slept with. Father got him a place in the sawmill, but Tim crowded the saw with too big an oak log, and the saw split into a thousand pieces. Tim beat the fragments into the quiet woods and never returned to square accounts with his boss. He was forever getting into hot water and having to be got out, but he made his older brothers laugh, too.

Uncle Tim could dance anything from an Irish breakdown to a Saracen sword dance. He was double-jointed in his fingers and toes; he could move his shoes faster than sharp eyes could follow. A jig was in his joints and music in his marrow.

He could sing a clear tenor like a wood thrush educated to grand opera, and suddenly shift to a bass like a bullfrog in courting season. He had, too, the gift of whistling two notes at once. He bent in his chin, sparkled and rolled his eyes, did something mysterious with his throat muscles, and out came harmonious high and low notes side by side.

Uncle Tim could play any musical instrument. If there were reeds and tubes, his breath found its way around in them. When he got his mouth on a bass horn, he could make a tame horn player stare at the incredible arpeggios that came out of the brass morning glory. What he could do with a kitchen cup and a harmonica was something no organ player ever dreamed of. When he clamped his long black mustache, alive as a blacksnake, over the honeycomb of a harmonica's edge and played sad, it was like the surf on the last reef of a lost ocean.

He knew songs by the hundreds and made new ones as he went along. Some of his songs were not for she-ears and they made mustached men blush like a field of hawkweed, but Uncle Tim sang them with the innocent eyes of a boy of ten. He sang also of unrepentant prisoners on their way to the gallows; of girls like anemones, so pure they wilted and died if a man looked their way. His men were all buttocks and beer, his women all tears and true-love knots. And he sang hymn tunes as though they had never seen the inside of a church.

He was the town champion in everything that had legs or fists in it. His long legs could scissor over a five-foot fence with no start. He could throw a man twice his size. He could box an Irish rail-layer to a standstill, then beat an eel of a youth in a hundred-yard dash. He was forever taking off his shoes and shirt to show small boys how to turn seven cartwheels in a row, or do the giant swing.

My Uncle Tim's major calling in life was pranks. He tied a brick to Mr. Snodgrass's cow's tail so that Mr. Snodgrass could milk in peace without getting slapped on the cheek every few minutes. But when the cow swung her tail Mr. Snodgrass fell on the floor and lay in artificial peace for quite awhile.

Tim took the planks off the Widow Nye's dry well, so that when Peter Jordan came to walk out with her, as he had for 20 years, they fell in. They stayed down there all night, and folks talked so, they had to marry the very next day and set up house-keeping aboveground.

And it was Uncle Tim who thought up putting bourbon in the raspberry shrub at the Free-Will Baptist picnic. Crowds gathered thicker and thicker at the bowl. The word spread clear to town, and all denominations became Free-Willers for the day. Everybody voted it the best Free-Will Baptist picnic in half a century. It took half the night to collect the Baptists and temporary Baptists and herd them back, singing, to everyday living.

Uncle Tim kept his brothers' and sisters' children bright-eyed and in high animal spirits. He was an artist with a jackknife, and shocked his sisters and sisters-in-law with the jointed pine-wood dolls he made for his nieces. For he was a realist in his ideas of feminine beauty unclothed. The girls weren't allowed to play with the dolls, which were put away on a high shelf, and the small girls had to grow up into beautiful curves by accident rather than by imitation.

Uncle Tim taught his nephews how to get the best apples from the highest tree with the sternest farmer warding them, how to snake the biggest trout from under the deepest log, how to keep their temper in a fight. He kept people busy straightening out their households after he had paid a call. Their houses would be full of small imitative editions of him, getting their breeches dusted for having soaped the backstairs so that the hired man came down in a hurry.

The first time Uncle Tim ran away was to the Civil War. As far as I can make out from family tradition, it *was* a civil war until Uncle Tim got in it. But he got into so many side wars that no general craved having him in his army long.

Uncle Tim tried matrimony once. But he was not cut out for a house husband. Maybe if his firstborn son had lived, he might have been harnessed to providing the strain of quicksilver men the world so needs. But when the boy he loved died of diphtheria, he gave up family life. He parted with his wife after singing her to sleep with his guitar. He stole out quiet in the night and left the guitar—his best one—for her to remember him by. He did not leave his wallet. There was nothing in it.

One bright October day, Uncle Tim must have felt fall in his bones. Maybe he saw ahead long quiet evenings beside his brothers' stoves, they expecting him to dance the hornpipe for them and he with no hornpipe left in his legs. He slipped out of their lives when nobody was noticing that he had sobered for an instant. He slipped out with a last prank. Father had sent him to Falmouth with a load of mackerel. He sold the mackerel —*and* the sloop. With the dollars he never could keep from burning holes in his pockets, he headed into the blue unknown.

A pall fell upon his brothers. They discovered they were aging men. The ghosts of Uncle Tim's songs hung in the sound the Maine wind made around their houses. My father, delegated to bring him back, followed Uncle Tim's footsteps for nearly a year. Father found a print of his brother's feet once or twice. In a saloon on the Bowery someone from Down East had sung one night like a seraph, making hard men weep. That could be Tim. In a drab Philadelphia waterfront house, a board bill had been paid by stories that made the gray place a shining one. That sounded like Tim. In a lonely Kentucky shack, a family had sat spellbound for three days before such dancing as the nimble mountaineers had never laid eyes on. That might be Tim. The track led south. That would be like Tim: to head toward warmth as he felt his bones growing cool.

But the trail grew colder and colder. My father came back to his business a decade older. One terrible day, a newspaper described a Maine man who had died of smallpox in a shabby New Orleans house. My father telegraphed and wrote a dozen times. Finally a photograph was secured. It was not Tim. My father grew a decade younger.

The years crowded in fast. My father's hair grew whiter, and so did his brothers'. With no Tim to keep them companions they dropped away from one another. So at last most of them dropped into the earth. But the ones remaining remembered Tim's music, dancing and singing. Their sons remembered some of the songs. But none could sing Tim's way.

For my father, remembering Tim was like my remembering the jackknife I lost overboard one bleak November day. I saw it slanting down dimmer and dimmer into the dark water where no light ever comes. With it went a bright piece of my heart. It was Tim my father spoke of last, the night he died.

Quicksilver never stays. It runs off your jackknife into the grass. You can look for it among the grass-blades till your eyes hurt. It has gone back to the sun where it was born and where it belongs.

Truth or Error?

ᚱ Pittsfield, Mass., *Berkshire Eagle*: "The accident occurred shortly after 1 p.m. Pickett took his eyes from the road momentarily to look at a trick going in the opposite direction."

ᚱ Johnson City, Tenn., *Press-Chronicle*: "Tomorrow is slated to be mostly cloudy and mild with wisely scattered showers."

ᚱ London *Daily Telegraph and Morning Post*: "The government plans to relax regulations on boardinghouses to make more beds available for tourist sin late August and September."

ᚱ Huntington, W. Va., *Herald-Dispatch*: "We women tend to have more operations than men. We talk longer to recover from them."

ᚱ Personals column, Westlake, Ohio, *West Life*: "Josephine—please take me back. It was just a passing fanny. Your George."

—And Sudden Death

J. C. Furnas

This article is a landmark: the most quoted, most reprinted magazine piece of all time, and very probably the one that has had greatest impact on the public mind. It describes in graphic detail the results of highway accidents—a matter of continuing concern. (By 1970 the U.S. yearly totals had reached two million injured and 54,000 dead.) Commissioned originally by the Digest, the article has appeared in many anthologies. Six million reprints have been distributed by educators, judges and safety experts, who credit it with having "unquestionably" saved many lives.

[August 1935]

Publicizing the total of highway injuries—almost a million in 1934, with 36,000 deaths—never gets to first base in jarring the motorist into a realization of the appalling risks of motoring. He does not translate dry statistics into a reality of blood and agony.

Figures exclude the pain and horror of savage mutilation—which means they leave out the point. They need to be brought closer home. A passing look at a bad smash or the news that a fellow you had lunch with last week is in a hospital with a broken back will make any driver but a born fool slow down at least temporarily. But what is needed is a vivid and *sustained* realization that every time you step on the throttle death gets in beside you, waiting hopefully for his chance. That horrible accident you may have witnessed is no isolated horror. It happens every hour of the day, everywhere in the United States.

A judge now and again sentences reckless drivers to tour the accident end of a city morgue. But even a mangled body on a slab, waxily portraying the consequences of bad motoring judgment, isn't a patch on the scene of the accident itself. No safety-poster artist would dare depict that in full detail.

That picture would have to include motion-picture and sound effects, too—the flopping, pointless efforts of the injured to stand up; the queer, grunting noises; the steady, panting groaning of a human being with pain creeping up on him as the shock wears off. It should portray the slack expression on the face of a man, drugged with shock, staring at the Z-twist in his broken leg, the insane crumpled effect of a child's body after its bones are crushed inward, a realistic portrait of a hysterical woman with her screaming mouth opening a hole in the bloody drip that fills her eyes and runs off her chin. Minor details would include the raw ends of bones protruding through flesh in compound fractures, and the dark-red oozing surfaces where clothes and skin were flayed off at once.

THOSE are all standard, everyday sequels to the modern passion for going places in a hurry and taking a chance or two on the way. If ghosts could be put to a useful purpose, every bad stretch of road in the United States would greet the oncoming motorist with groans and screams and the educational spectacle of ten or a dozen corpses lying horribly still on the bloody grass.

Last year a state trooper of my acquaintance stopped a big red car for speeding. Papa was obviously a responsible person, obviously set for a pleasant weekend with his family—so the officer cut into Papa's well-bred expostulations: "I'll let you off this time, but if you keep on this way you won't last long. Get going—but take it easier." Later a passing motorist hailed the trooper and asked if the red car had got a ticket. "No," said the trooper, "I hated to spoil their party." "Too bad you didn't," said the motorist. "I saw you stop them—and then I passed that car again 50 miles up the line. It still makes me feel sick at my stomach. The car was all folded up like an accordion. They were all dead but one of the kids—and he wasn't going to live to the hospital."

Maybe it will make you sick at your stomach, too. But unless you're a heavy-footed incurable, a firsthand acquaintance with the results of mixing gasoline with speed and bad judgment ought to be well worth your while. If you have the nerve to drive fast and take chances, you ought to have the nerve to take the cure. You can't ride an ambulance or watch the doctor working on the victim in the hospital, but you can read.

The automobile is treacherous. As enthusiasts tell you, it makes 65 feel like nothing at all. But 65 miles an hour is 100 feet a second, a speed which puts a viciously unjustified responsibility on brakes and human reflexes, and can instantly turn this docile luxury into a mad bull elephant.

Collision, turnover or sideswipe, each type of accident produces either a shattering dead stop or a crashing change of direction, and, since the occupant—meaning you—continues in the old direction at the original speed, every surface and angle of the car's interior immediately becomes a battering, tearing projectile, aimed squarely at you—inescapable. There is no bracing yourself against these imperative laws of momentum.

Anything can happen in the split second of crash, even those lucky escapes you hear about. People have dived through windshields and come out with only superficial scratches. They have run cars together head on, reducing both to twisted junk, and been found unhurt and arguing bitterly two minutes afterward. But death was there just the same—he was only exercising his privilege of being erratic. This spring a wrecking crew pried the door off a car which had been overturned down an embankment, and out stepped the driver with only a scratch on his cheek. But his mother was still inside, a splinter driven four inches into her brain as a result of son's taking a greasy curve a little too fast. No blood—no horribly twisted bones—just a gray-haired corpse still clutching her pocketbook in her lap as she had clutched it when she felt the car leave the road.

On that same curve a month later, a light touring car crashed into a tree. In the middle of the front seat they found a nine-month-old baby surrounded by broken glass and yet absolutely unhurt. A fine practical joke on death—but spoiled by the baby's parents, still sitting on each side of him, instantly killed by shattering their skulls on the dashboard.

If you customarily pass without clear vision a long way ahead, make sure that every member of the party carries identification papers—it's difficult to identify a body with its whole face bashed in or torn off. Sometimes two drivers, going in opposite directions, swing out simultaneously at high speed. Too late they see each other and meet, almost head on, in a swirling, grinding smash that sends them caroming obliquely into others.

A trooper described such an accident—five cars in one mess, seven killed on the spot, two dead on the way to the hospital, two more dead in the long run. He remembered it far more vividly than he wanted to—the quick way the doctor turned away from a dead man to check up on a woman with a broken back; the three bodies out of one car so soaked with oil from the crankcase that they looked like wet brown cigars and not human at all; a man walking around and babbling to himself, oblivious of the dead and dying, even oblivious of the daggerlike sliver of steel that stuck out of his streaming wrist; a pretty girl with her forehead laid open, trying hopelessly to crawl out of a ditch in spite of her smashed hip. A first-class massacre of that sort is only a question of scale and numbers—seven corpses are no deader than one. Each shattered man, woman or child who went to make up the fatality statistics chalked up last year had to die a personal death.

A CAR careening and rolling down a bank, battering and smashing its occupants every inch of the way, can wrap itself so thoroughly around a tree that front and rear bumpers interlock, requiring an acetylene torch to cut them apart. In a recent case of that sort they found the old lady, who had been sitting in back, now lying across the lap of her daughter who was in front, each soaked in her own and the other's blood indistinguishably, each so shattered and broken that there was no point whatever in an autopsy to determine whether it was broken neck or ruptured heart that caused death.

Overturning cars specialize in certain injuries. Cracked pelvis, for instance, guaranteeing agonizing months in bed, motionless, perhaps crippled for life—broken spine resulting from sheer sidewise twist—the minor details of smashed knees and splintered shoulder blades caused by crashing into the side of the car as it goes over with the swirl of an insane roller coaster—and the lethal consequences of broken ribs, which puncture hearts and lungs with their raw ends. The consequent internal hemorrhage is no less dangerous because it is the pleural instead of the abdominal cavity that is filling with blood.

Flying glass—safety glass is by no means universal yet in 1935 —contributes much more than its share to the spectacular side of accidents. It doesn't merely cut—the fragments are driven in as if a cannon loaded with broken bottles had been fired in your face, and a sliver in the eye, traveling with such force, means certain blindness. A leg or arm stuck through the windshield will cut clean to the bone through vein, artery and muscle like a piece of beef under the butcher's knife, and it takes little time to lose a fatal amount of blood under such circumstances. Even safety glass may not be wholly safe when the car crashes into something at high speed. You hear picturesque tales of how a flying human body will make a neat hole in the stuff with its head—the shoulders stick—the glass holds—and the raw, keen edge decapitates the body as neatly as a guillotine.

Or, to continue with the decapitation motif, going off the road into a post-and-rail fence can put you beyond worrying about other injuries immediately when a rail pierces the windshield and tears off your head with its splintery end. Not as neat a job but just as efficient. Bodies are often found with shoes off and feet broken out of shape. The shoes are on the floor of the car, empty and with laces still neatly tied. That is the kind of impact produced by modern speeds.

But all that is routine in every American community. To be remembered individually by doctors and policemen, you have to do something as grotesque as the lady who burst the windshield with her head, splashing splinters all over the other occupants of the car, and then, as the car rolled over, rolled with it down the edge of the windshield frame and cut her throat from ear to ear. Or park on the pavement too near a curve at night and stand in front of the tail light as you take off the spare tire— which will immortalize you in somebody's memory as the fellow who was mashed three feet broad and two inches thick by the impact of a heavy-duty truck against the rear of his own car. Or snap off a nine-inch tree and get impaled by a ragged branch.

None of all that is scare-fiction; it is just the horrible raw material of the year's statistics as seen in the ordinary course of duty by policemen and doctors. The surprising thing is that there is so little dissimilarity in their stories.

It's hard to find an accident victim who can bear to talk. After you come to, the gnawing, searing pain is accounted for by learning you have both collarbones smashed, both shoulder blades splintered, your right arm broken in three places and three ribs cracked, with every chance of bad internal ruptures. Then as the shock begins to wear off, you realize you're probably on your way out. They shift you from the ground to the stretcher: your broken ribs bite into your lungs and the sharp ends of the collarbones slide over to stab deep into each side of your screaming throat. But when you've stopped screaming, it all comes back—you're dying, and you hate yourself for it.

And every time you pass on a blind curve, every time you hit it up on a slippery road, every time you step on it harder than your reflexes will safely take, every time you drive with your reactions slowed down by a drink or two, every time you follow the man ahead too closely, you're gambling a few seconds against this kind of blood and agony and sudden death.

Take a look at yourself as the man in the white jacket shakes his head over you, tells the boys with the stretcher not to bother and turns away to somebody else who isn't quite dead yet. And then take it easy.

&ᴥ Not long ago I found myself in a small prairie town and fell into conversation with a bright-eyed 70-year-old farmer who asked, "Where you from, son?"

I told him, "Washington."

"Washington, D.C.?"

"That's right."

"You've got some pretty smart fellas back there, ain't ya?" he asked. I nodded. "You've got some that ain't so smart, too, ain't ya?" Again, I agreed. "Damn hard to tell the difference, ain't it?" he concluded.
John B. Fisher

Queer People, These Americans

Stephen Leacock

[September 1938]

AMERICANS are queer people: they can't rest. They have more time, more leisure, shorter hours, more holidays and more vacations than any other people in the world. But they rush up and down across their continent as tourists; they move about in great herds to conventions; they invade the wilderness, they flood the mountains, they keep the hotels full. But they can't rest. The scenery rushes past them. They learn it, but they don't see it. Battles and monuments are announced to them in a rubberneck bus. They hear them, but they don't get them. They never stop moving.

Americans are queer people: they can't read. They have more schools and better schools than all Europe. But they can't read. They print more books in one year than the French print in ten. But they can't read. They buy eagerly thousands of new novels. But they read only page one. The last American who sat down to read died in the days of Henry Clay.

Americans are queer people: they can't drink. They have a fierce wish to be sober; and they can't. They pass fierce laws against themselves, shut themselves up, shoot themselves; and they can't stay sober and they can't drink. They got this mentality straight out of home life in Ohio, copied from the wild spree and the furious repentance of the pioneer farmer. The nation keeps it yet. It lives among red specters, broken bottles, weeping children, barrooms and broken oaths.

Americans are queer people: they can't play. They want their work as soon as they wake. It is a stimulant—the only one they're not afraid of. They eat all night, dance all night, build buildings all night, make a noise all night. They can't play. They try to, but they can't. They turn football into a fight, baseball into a lawsuit, and yachting into machinery. The little children can't play: they use mechanical toys instead—toy cranes hoisting toy loads, toy machinery spreading a toy industrial depression of infantile dullness. The grown-up people can't play: they use a mechanical gymnasium and a clockwork horse. They can't run: they use a car. They can't laugh: they hire a comedian and watch him laugh.

Americans are queer people: they don't give a damn. All the world writes squibs like this about them and they don't give a damn. Foreign visitors come and write them up; they don't give a damn. Lecturers lecture at them; they don't care. They are told they have no art, no literature and no soul. They never budge. Moralists cry over them, criminologists dissect them, writers shoot epigrams at them, prophets foretell the end of them; and they never move. Seventeen brilliant books analyze them every month; they don't read them. The Chinese look on them as full of Oriental cunning; the English accuse them of British stupidity; the Scotch call them close-fisted; the Italians say they are liars; the French think their morals loose; the Soviets call them ruthless.

But that's all right. The Americans don't give a damn; don't need to—never did need to. That is their salvation.

Character Reference

℣➜ The bridge-club members were discussing half-forgotten boy friends of years long gone. A name was mentioned. "What was he like?" "Well," said one, "I think you'll know when I tell you this. Sometimes a big gang of us would go on picnics to a remote beach area. We girls would solve the undressing problem by forming a circle around the one who was changing into her swimsuit, and take turns. We'd tell the boys to put their hands over their eyes and not peek. And Jack would *do* it." *KVP Sutherland Philosopher*

Abby, Her Farm

Margaret Buell Wilder

[*August 1941*]

IT BEGAN with a chance remark
at the age of seven, on a Sunday afternoon in the country.
"When I grow up, *I* shall have a farm." Her father and I
smiled, perceiving nothing ominous.

Thereafter, the references to a farm—ultimatums—came
with increasing frequency. About a year later, vaguely dis-
quieted, and thinking to take up the slack of our eight-year-old's
morbid rural yearnings, I bought her a Thoroughbred mare
and boarded it in one of those sweet-scented, spit-and-polish
Connecticut stables.

It worked—for about a week. Then one day, accusingly, she

led the animal up to me and exclaimed: "Just look at this horse's feet! Those shoes will hardly hold! Now if we had a *farm* . . ."

I groaned and looked away from those remorseless eyes that bored through my makeshift soul. "But darling, we *can't*," I began for the hundredth time. "We have a *lease*. Your father works in Wall Street. Have you any idea what *that* means?"

But somehow during the next few weeks a large dog, two rabbits and five cats were added unto us. Though otherwise extremely prudish, Abby did not quail before the facts of reproduction. Kittens aplenty, and frequently a-borning, were to be found anywhere from our best shoes to the kitchen sink. "That's all right," she would reassure us. "The mother will clean it up. But on the farm I may have to help the lambs get born."

"It would be nice if we had a pig—now," she said implacably.

Our zoning restrictions very definitely prohibited pigs. "But how would they know?" Abby argued reasonably. "The cops don't even catch kidnapers. How would they catch a pig?"

"By smell, if nothing else," I muttered. "Now for heaven's sake keep *still* about it! Pigs are *out*."

Scarcely were the words out of my mouth when the P.T.A. announced its annual party—with a greased pig to be given away to that male parent lucky enough to catch it barehanded.

The odds of 200-to-1 against Abby's father catching the pig must have challenged his spirit, for when the time came to loose the creature upon the school lawn he had organized a "pig circle" with all 200 fathers holding hands. Someone sprang the box lid, the frenzied shoat made a beeline for the nearest man, and Abby's next-to-fondest dream came true. She had a pig.

Burning with mother love, she husbanded the poor creature into its box, then shut it in our car. "You and Pop can go back to the party now," she said firmly. "You aren't enough like other parents as it is."

"But that greasy pig will get out on the upholstery! Besides, he's hurt—he's groaning. He should be killed at once!" Then, "What do you mean, I'm not like other mothers?"

Her eyes never left the boxful of pig. "Well, you aren't. You don't knit, you never make cookies and you haven't any bosom."

I threw up my hands and allowed myself to be led away, muttering, by her ribald father. When we got back the pig had been freed. "It had claustro—claustra—that thing you get in the subway," Abby explained. "Anyway—pigs are very nervous."

Stricken, we stared inside the car. It had indeed been very nervous—all over the upholstery. We considered the poor panting creature at bay on the back seat; then we considered Abby. "I think," said her father heavily, "it would be cheaper to trade her in for something civilized."

Christmas brought only one wistful request, for a female goat —ungranted. "But we could drink the milk and save money," she protested.

Her terrifying blend of logic and economy finally took its toll of our resistance. Every time the market went down, her father would gaze across the dinner table and say, "Abby, tell me about the farm. Could we live on silage?"

By New Year's he had left on a business trip and I was alone with Abby and the Rotation of Crops.

"What is that book you seem to be making?" I asked one night.

"My farm book." Hesitantly she brought it to me—a thin, cardboard affair tied with green yarn and illustrated with beautiful pink and black watercolors of Poland China hogs.

I stared at the first page and read: "In the beginning of the 20th century, Mr. Aaron Aaronsohn discovered a wild wheat growing on the dry and rocky slopes of Mt. Herman." Page two was solid with statistics about the yields one may expect from an acre of corn. The next page, in a fine spirit of *non sequitur,* bore only this avowal: "Nothing Will Be Bought From A Store. I Shall Weave My Clothes And Wear Long Hair."

"Abby!" I cried. "Is *this* why you won't have your hair cut? Is *this* why I go through hell and high water every day fixing those pigtails?" I peered sharply at her braids and remembered how she measured their weekly progress with a piece of string. "Will you have spring shearings with the sheep?" I asked.

"If you'll turn to the end of the book," she said, unmoved, "you'll see what the farm's going to be like. Then you won't worry so." Rebuked by her dignity, I turned to a sort of prose poem, entitled simply "My Farm."

I want the kind of farm where chickens run loose in the front yard, and a timid long-laged colt pokes his inquisartive nose out from his mother's back to stare at you in surprise.

I will hear the tinkling of bells made by the big brony Merion sheep as they drift slowly along, following their leader. I will see the big fat mother sow and her recent family grunting for food and enjoying the cool inviting mud.

Then I will go slowly through my filds of waveing corn to a low rambling farmhouse nestled among the lilac trees. I will enter. There will be a smell of good things in the air. I will see sausage broiling on the stove.

The sunbeams will find their way across the thick planked oaken floors to the pewter plates on the mantell. The flowers on the table will match the crazy patchwork quilt on my high wooden bed. The sheets will be old and fine; there will be a rag rug on the floor.

Yea, though I walk through the Valley . . . my mind subconsciously went on in the rhythm of those paragraphs. Then I closed the Farm Book and laid it down gently.

"I see I was wrong about those pigtails," I said. "They'll be *very* proper—if we can keep them out of the churn!"

With a wild whoop she was upon me, and the guerrilla warfare of two long years was wiped out with one tremendous hug. "Will you wire Pop right away—will you tell him to buy a farm?" she shrieked.

Clinging to reason with one enfeebled hand, I managed to push her off to bed without that final incriminating Yes.

An empty victory. Next morning I found on my desk this conclusive document in a familiar hand:

Dept. of Agriculture, Washington, D. C.
dear sirs,

My father is going to by a farm so I wish to be prepared to whatever might follow. Could you send me instructions for the care of theese certen domesticate animals.

a few cows of Guernsey breed, a few of the harder things about horses, goats (the best breed) sheep and where to by the best stock. p.s. right away.

I picked up the phone. "Western Union," I said. "And *hurry.*"

Socialism Doesn't Jibe With Human Nature

Max Eastman

Max Eastman was a poet, philosopher and political firebrand as early as pre-World War I. He helped to found, and edited, The New Masses and The Liberator, radical weeklies. Then in Russia from 1922 to 1924 he studied the "New Society" at first-hand. Result: disillusionment. He was among the first on the far left to announce that the revolutionary dream was dead, communism had failed.

Originally a professor of psychology and philosophy, Eastman wrote dozens of extraordinarily varied books—important works of literary criticism, poetry, fiction and humor, as well as political philosophy.

For 14 years he was a Digest Roving Editor.

[June 1941]

WHEN Hitler calls his hate-filled raid on civilization "socialist," and gets away with it, it seems as though words themselves must be going crazy.

The word "socialist" was born well over a hundred years ago in excited talk about the ideas of Robert Owen, a benign English gentleman who came to this country in 1825 and bought a whole town and 30,000 acres of land in Indiana on the banks of the Wabash. He issued a sweeping invitation to "the industrious and well disposed of all nations" to come there and live in coöperative peace and loving-kindness as Nature intended.

It sounded like a reckless scheme, but America was a reckless country then. Owen, moreover, was a shrewd businessman, a sort of larger-hearted Henry Ford, and America welcomed him with her most royal gift of publicity. The hall of Congress was turned over to him, and he explained socialism to an audience which included the President, a majority of both Houses of Congress, and most of the Justices of the Supreme Court.

"I am come to this country," he said, "to introduce an enlightened social system which shall gradually unite all interests into one, and remove all causes for contest between individuals."

That is the un-Hitlerish state of mind the word "socialist" was invented to describe.

It was a wonderful and dewy-minded bunch from all over the earth, including several well-known writers and scientists, who accepted Robert Owen's invitation to "New Harmony," Indiana. Their ramshackle paradise held together only so long as Owen bossed it. Left to themselves, its thousand-odd members fell to chiseling and snitching and indulging in rather more slander, if you can imagine it, than is usual. After two years they "divvied up" in a cool mood and quit. Owen thought it was because "the habits of the individual system" prevailing in the rest of the world were too strong.

Notwithstanding this dismal and swift failure, Owen's idea—that if *business* were run on coöperative principles, life in general would be friendly and harmonious—became dominant among radical minds the world over. It gave birth to a whole litter of variations: syndicalist, communist, guild-socialist, bolshevik, anarchist. Even those who could not subscribe to it as a practical measure have assumed that this idea pointed the way of civilization's highest hopes.

The word "socialism," in passing from Robert Owen's kindly dream—which took for granted belief in moral decency, in scientific truth, in sympathetic understanding—to Hitler's ruthless tyranny, pursued a course that can teach us something.

Two really big things happened to that dream during its hundred years of life. Around the middle of the century an intellectual genius named Karl Marx undertook to prove that, although it had failed dismally in Indiana, it was inevitably coming true throughout the world. Marx was personally more impractical, more like what you'd call a crank, than Owen. While telling a planet how its future business was to be run, he threw up his hands at the comparatively simple task of earning his own living. He had to be supported throughout life like a baby, and as though to compensate he grew an enormous beard which spouted to the four winds from every corner of his face and made him look like the grandfather of God Almighty. But Marx had a brain like a locomotive; when he set out to prove a thing, there was nothing for practical considerations to do but get out of the way. Marx made his proof so comprehensive and so cloudy, and wound up so much true science with romantic metaphysics, that he convinced the best radical minds of three generations that Robert Owen's dream *was* inevitably coming true.

It was coming because the whole of present-day society was going to split violently in half like a growing acorn. In irresistible revolutionary class war the under half was going to grab the land and industries, and *impose* this dream on the upper half. The whole capitalist class was to disappear. No more little postcard utopias on the banks of the Wabash! And no more trust in benevolent gentlemen! Hard-headed, hard-fisted proletarians were going to put the thing across. The owners of the world didn't *want* a New Harmony—that's why Robert Owen failed. Well, they were going to get a New Harmony whether they wanted one or not. And—to translate Karl Marx into plain American—they were going to get it in the neck.

The second big thing that happened was that such an upset actually occurred, in Russia. It occurred largely because another great man, Lenin, gave his life to Owen's dream.

Lenin, like Robert Owen, combined selfless idealism with the canny gift for getting things done. He had more love for people than Karl Marx had. He looked like an able executive who had lost his hair, though none of his vigor, sitting at a desk bossing a big industry.

Lenin believed religiously in the whole Marxian system. He never questioned a syllable in that five-foot shelf of books. Yet he was flexible, cunning, alive to new developments—an experimental scientific intelligence if there ever was one.

In the name of Marx, Lenin led an actual revolution to victory, and set going on the scale of the Russian empire the same experiment that Robert Owen had failed with on the banks of the Wabash 90 years before. The results were not better but far worse. To know how much worse, you have only to compare 30,000 acres of land with the Russian empire, and scandal, negligence and inefficiency with state-planned murder.

In his speeches before he seized power, Lenin promised even more wonderful things than Robert Owen had:

> Democracy from below! Democracy without an officialdom, without police, without a standing army. The state itself will wither away as, freed from the innumerable absurdities and infamies of capitalist exploitation, people gradually become accustomed to observing the elementary rules of social life without constraint, without the special apparatus for compulsion called the State!

That was the promise. And you know the result: Officialdom gone mad, officialdom erected into a new and merciless exploiting class which literally wages war on its own people; the "slavery, horrors, savagery, absurdities and infamies of capitalist exploitation" so far outdone that men looked back to them as to a picnic on a holiday; bureaucrats everywhere, and behind the bureaucrats the secret police; death for those who dared protest; death for theft—even of a piece of candy.

People who still insist that this is a New Harmony are for the most part dolts or mental cowards. It is clear that Lenin's experiment, like Robert Owen's, failed.

It failed, however, in a different way. It did not drop naturally apart because the boss went home and let it run itself. The boss stayed all too firmly on the job. It failed because it was *prevented* from dropping naturally apart, by military force—by massacre, machine guns, spies, concentration camps and engineered starvation. It failed as a libertarian and humane hope because as a going concern it survived. It survived long enough to show what was in it—tyranny, and the totalitarian state.

And the name survived with it—Socialism!

Hitler did not set out to produce socialism. On the contrary, he set out to stop it with a totalitarian state. But he found that totalitarian control leads toward socialization almost as impetuously as socialization toward totalitarian control. Whether you call it "National Socialism" or "Socialism in One Country" makes no deep difference. The word is lost in either case to civilized mankind. The dream of Robert Owen, made plausible by the pseudo science of Karl Marx, and dynamic by the engineering genius of Lenin, is ended.

Why did the monumental efforts of these three great men and tens of millions of their followers, consecrated to the cause of human happiness—why did they so miserably fail? They failed because they had no science of human nature, and no place in their science for the common-sense knowledge of it. Both Owen and Karl Marx did their thinking before psychology as we know it was born.

In October 1917, after Kerensky's government fell, Lenin appeared at a meeting of the Workers and Soldiers Soviet of Petrograd and, when the long wild happy shouts of greeting had died down, said: "We will now proceed to the construction of a socialist society"—as simply as though he were proposing to put up a new cowbarn. But in all his life he had never asked: How is this newfangled contraption going to fit in with the instinctive tendencies of the animals it was made for?

Lenin actually knew less about the science of man than Robert Owen did a hundred years earlier. Owen had described human nature, fairly well for an amateur, as "a compound of animal propensities, intellectual faculties and moral qualities." He had written into the preamble of the constitution of New Harmony that "man's character is the result of his formation, his location, and of the circumstances within which he exists."

It seems incredible, but Karl Marx, with all his talk about making socialism "scientific," took a step back from this elementary notion. He dropped out the factor of man's hereditary nature altogether. He dropped out *man* altogether, so far as he might present an obstacle to social change. "The individual," he said, "has no real existence outside the milieu in which he lives." By which he meant: Change the milieu, change the so-

305

cial relations, and man will change as much as you like. That is all Marx ever said on this primary question. And Lenin said nothing.

That is why they failed. They were amateurs—and worse, mystics—in the subject most essential to their success.

Unfortunately, the science of human behavior is still in its infancy. But let me mention a few verified concepts which I think largely explain why, instead of the New Harmony he expected, Lenin produced the horrors of a totalitarian state.

To begin with, man is the most plastic and adaptable of animals. He truly can be changed by his environment, and even by himself, to a unique degree, and that makes extreme ideas of progress reasonable. On the other hand, he inherits a set of emotional impulses or instincts which, although they can be trained in various ways in the individual, cannot be eradicated from the race. And no matter how much they may be repressed or redirected by training, they reappear in the original form—as sure as a hedgehog puts out spines—in every baby that is born. Civilization is not transmitted in heredity, but has to be acquired anew by every individual.

One of these instincts is an aggressive or pugnacious tendency. Whenever the human animal is frustrated in any of his impulses, he is likely to get an impulse to lambaste somebody. And as all of us in the nature of things are a good part frustrated all the time, there is always plenty of pugnacity lying around. This, I think, is what made Marx's doctrine so much more popular than Robert Owen's. The two men had the same ultimate goal of peace and harmony, but in the meantime Marx gave his followers a chance to fight. They were going to arrive at the goal by way of a sort of grand historic universal knock-down-and-drag-out, known as the revolutionary class struggle.

I hope I do not sound frivolous, for I am saying the most important thing I know how to say about socialism. It has been more myth than science. Its aim has been escape from reality rather than adjustment to it. Instead of trying to "remove all causes for contest between individuals," as Owen did, or even between classes as Marx did, we ought to recognize that contest forms a large part of what keeps mankind healthy and interested. Progress must consist in elevating the level and humanizing the terms on which the vital contests are fought. This takes perhaps a little of the flame out of the heart of the revolutionist, but it will keep a light shining in his head.

Another trait of man that socialism has ignored, or rather misunderstood, is his gregarious drive. It is not mere social goodwill, but a disposition, which enables distinct and wayward individuals to cohere in a crisis and act as a unit. To this end each individual had to be capable of adopting toward his neighbor, with impetuous sincerity, an attitude either of dominance or submission. It is this confusing and yet neat pair of attributes that socialists most fatally ignored. Particularly the submissive side has been ignored—the veritable passion that both men and women have for regimentation and discipleship, for being led, for obeying and conforming and belonging to.

Men have, then, in their hereditary nature a good-sized dose of belligerence, and a disposition—not an acquired taste—both to submit to others and to boss them. Their appreciation of independence and equality, as well as their coöperativeness, is thus qualified by very strong drives of a contrary kind. And Owen's experiment did not fail merely because of the "habits of the individual system." It failed primarily because of the instincts of the social animal prevailing in its members. The idea of producing a Society of the Free and Equal by socializing property and production assumed a greater self-dependence and a more peaceable disposition than these human animals are born with, or capable in large numbers of acquiring.

It seems obvious to me now—though I have been slow, I must say, in coming to the conclusion—that the institution of private property is one of the main things that have given man that limited amount of free-and-equalness that Marx hoped to render infinite by abolishing this institution. Strangely enough Marx himself was the first to see this. He is the one who informed us, looking backward, that the evolution of private capitalism with its free market had been a precondition for the evolution of all our democratic freedoms. It never occurred to him, looking forward, that if this was so, those other freedoms might disappear with the abolition of the free market.

That, however, is exactly what happened in Russia—with astounding speed. I cannot believe the "backwardness" of the country explains this. Russia's backwardness can hardly explain why collectivization made her more backward. Nor do I think the "capitalist encirclement"—so much like Owen's excuse!—explains it. It cannot be explained without a reference to the facts which Marxists, out of loyalty to their antique doctrine, refuse to think about: the hereditary as against the acquired nature of man; the fact that we still have the same taste for fighting as tribal savages.

Particularly in time of stress and danger, men instinctively gang up under a leader and fight. And in that union all those "moral qualities," the reasonableness and justice, candor and magnanimity which Owen counted on, and Marx and Lenin after him, tend to give way before the deeper-lying instincts. Thus the very party of revolutionists consecrated to bringing the free society to birth in Russia became the nucleus of a blind fighting gang. As soon as Lenin's own moderating hand was withdrawn, they stamped to death with shrill yells of rage every individual who dared stand out for his promises, or for any other thing but hatred and obedience. Instead of producing a higher civilization, the turmoil of "complete collectivization" swept away whole sections of the acquired fabric of civilization altogether, and left the technique of modern industry and education at the mercy of the naked instincts of a vengeful gang.

"Primitive communism," socialists used to say, proves that such a system is suitable to human nature and will work. It did not occur to us that in reverting to the economics of savagery we might revert to its crude level of culture.

So an honest, bold, noble attempt to produce through common ownership a Society of the Free and Equal produced instead a tyrant and a totalitarian state; there sprang up in its wake, borrowing its name and imitating its political procedures, other tyrants and totalitarian states; the whole world was plunged into war. And no one who has lived a thinking life these twenty years will deny that Lenin's experiment in socialism broke the dam and dug the political channels in which the whole flood has been running. It is not enough therefore to pick flaws in the tactics of Lenin; his basic undertaking must be questioned.

I think any wise socialist, viewing the sequence in the light of what we know about human nature, will be inclined to reconsider his assumptions. In his further efforts toward a world in which science shall have conquered poverty and superstition, and made a rich life possible to all, he will be cautious about the extent to which common ownership and state control may be carried. The more "radical" he is—in the sense of intelligently caring about liberty and justice and a chance at life for the wage workers—the more cautious he will be. Of that I am firmly convinced. Socialism was amateur; we must learn to be expert.

℞ for Romance

ॐ When I met Sandra I was taking meprobamate, one tablet before each meal and two at bedtime. By coincidence she was also on tranquilizers, same dosage. On our first date we fell calmly in love. Before long I was down to one tablet twice daily, and she only had to take a half tablet every now and then, as needed, for relaxation.

When our romance grew more feverish I began taking a multivitamin capsule once daily before breakfast, and she went back on tranquilizers, one tablet before each meal and two at bedtime.

Every weekend I wined and dined her—she grew chubby and my ulcer flared up. She began taking an appetite suppressant, one capsule daily, and I an antacid gel, two tablespoons one hour after each meal.

On a skiing weekend we both caught deep chest colds, and the resort doctor placed us on an elixir of terpin hydrate compound, one teaspoon every four hours, as indicated, for cough. It was great sitting around the fire in the lodge, sipping terpin hydrate, dreaming our little dreams.

At Christmas we exchanged pillboxes. We announced our engagement in February. Two days before the wedding, she got into a terrible argument with her mother over the invitation list and broke out in the worst case of hives her doctor had ever seen. He prescribed an antihistamine capsule every eight hours and renewed her tranquilizer prescription, one tablet before each meal and two at bedtime. The next day she disappeared. I received a postcard from her a week later stating that she had eloped with her pharmacist.

I am now taking an antidepressant, two tablets before each meal and three at bedtime. So far they haven't worked. Oscar London in *Look*

309

How Your Prayers
Are Answered

The Rev. Earl A. Blackman

[June 1948]

A CHILD came to me with a dime in his hand. "Look what God gave me," he said.

"God doesn't give little boys dimes," I replied in reproof.

"Well," he said gravely, "He gave me this one. I asked God for a dime to buy food for my pet turtle, and kept on asking Him, until suddenly, as I was walking across the park, I saw a dime lying in the grass, right where God had dropped it."

Frankly I was awed, the boy was so simple and convincing.

Everybody I have known has told me he prayed at some time or another. In frustration or danger or in the presence of a problem more formidable than we can overcome, we call back to the source of our being for renewed strength. But as they grow older, many persons are less inclined to pray because they do not see the immediate answer lying, like the little boy's dime, shining in the grass. One must be able to recognize the answer to a prayer.

A parishioner of mine almost went mad when the doctors told him his wife was dying of cancer. He came to my house every night and together we prayed for her recovery even though her condition was too serious for any hope.

The poor woman died. Later I asked him whether the death of his wife in the face of our prayers had weakened his faith.

"Certainly not," he said. "It strengthened my faith. I thought I could not bear to lose her, but God gave me strength to accept the inevitable. My prayer was answered in a larger way than I asked it." The way to get your prayers answered is to pray for strength to answer them yourself.

People have asked me whether there is any prescribed attitude of prayer more efficacious than another. I do not think so. One of my most devout friends told me he did most of his praying while driving his car. I told him that, considering the way he drove, it probably was the best time to pray. But he was quite serious about the matter. He said there was something about driving that brought from the subconscious the half-articulated desires and the forgotten sins.

I have always done most of my private praying at night in bed, between waking and sleeping. Airplane pilots have told me that they feel most prayerful when in flight, poised between heaven and earth, and intensely aware of their own insignificance. Any setting or attitude that relaxes tense minds and muscles seems to me most desirable.

I know one man who writes letters to God on the typewriter. He is not conventionally religious and looks upon prayer as a kind of mental hygiene. He thinks that by writing out his prayers he is better able to analyze his half-formed desires and even, as he defines them, his faults and his sins.

While it is most efficacious to talk to God in prayer, it is very important that we listen to Him, too. If you talk all the time you can't learn anything, and so the calm silences, fraught with childlike faith, are as necessary in prayer as is a continued beseeching.

When I am in trouble, and pray for a long period, guidance never fails to come—usually in the form of some self-decision. The decision may be extremely painful to me, but ultimately I find that it is the best thing for everybody concerned.

A prayer need not be uttered to be said. Many of my friends feel that their ineffable yearnings, their sense of beauty, rightness and hope are themselves prayers. Pearl Buck, the novelist, and the late George Washington Carver, the famous Negro chemist and educator, both told me that their prayers were seldom if ever articulated. Yet both had their unuttered prayers richly answered. Donald W. Douglas, of the Douglas Aircraft Company, says that his idea of prayer is a constant attitude of the individual toward the world in which he lives.

"This attitude should be one of expectancy of good, free of personal judgment or criticism," he says. "It should strive to be continuously friendly and helpful. It should have enough faith in the plan under which we live to be thankful for triumphs, yet to embrace disaster calmly with a wish to make the bitter lesson a stairway to happy surroundings, rather than a decline into hopelessness and despair."

My favorite prayer was written by St. Francis of Assisi:

"Lord, make me an instrument of Thy peace. Where there is hatred, let me sow love; where there is doubt, faith; where there is despair, hope; where there is darkness, light; and where there is sadness, joy.

"O Divine Master, grant that I do not so much seek to be consoled as to console, to be understood as to understand, to be loved as to love; for it is in giving that we receive, it is in pardoning that we are pardoned, and it is in dying that we are born to everlasting life."

I like this prayer because it places full responsibility for its answer upon him who says it. We may pray for friendship when we are lonely, but we receive friendship only when we give it. That prayer is not only good religion but also good psychiatry.

Once formed, the habit of prayer becomes as natural as breathing and as beneficial to one's life.

ᓃ *Primed for Action.* I had offered to drive my new neighbor, a widow in her early 70s, to the supermarket. She came out of her house dressed as stylishly as though going to a tea party. Surprised, I complimented her on her appearance.

She said, "I'm merely following the advice my mother gave me many years ago. She loved to ride and her motto was: 'Always wear your spurs—you never know when you may meet a horse!' "

Eileen M. Hunter

It Might Be Verse

Once in a philosophic mood Ogden Nash wrote, ". . . if you are the mother of a poet, don't gamble on the chance that future generations will crown him. Follow your original impulse and drown him." Even his own mother ignored the advice. As master of the offbeat meter and contortionist rhyme, Ogden Nash knew no equal. Language lovers find delight in his uncurbed doggerel, as sampled here.

THE GUPPY

Whales have calves,
Cats have kittens,
Bears have cubs,
Bats have bittens.
Swans have cygnets,
Seals have puppies,
But guppies just have little guppies.   —*Versus*

THE PEOPLE UPSTAIRS

The people upstairs all practice ballet.
Their living room is a bowling alley.
Their bedroom is full of conducted tours.
Their radio is louder than yours.
They celebrate week ends all the week.
When they take a shower, your ceilings leak.
They try to get their parties to mix
By supplying their guests with pogo sticks,
And when their orgy at last abates,
They go to the bathroom on roller skates.
I might love the people upstairs wondrous
If instead of above us, they just lived underus.   —*Versus*

PIANO TUNER, UNTUNE ME THAT TUNE

I regret that before people can be re-
    formed they have to be sinners,
And that before you have pianists in
    the family you have to have beginners.   —*Versus*

313

A girl who is bespectacled
Don't even get her nectacled,
But safety pins and bassinets
Await the girl who fascinets.   *—Hard Lines*

NO, *YOU* BE A LONE EAGLE

I find it very hard to be fair-minded
About people who go around being
      air-minded . . .
I know the constant refrain
About how it's safer up in God's
      trafficless heaven than in an
      automobile or a train
But—
My God, have you ever taken a good
      look at a strut? . . .
At least when I get on the Boston
      train I have a good chance of
      landing in the South Station
And not in that part of the daily
      press which is reserved for
      victims of aviation.
Then, despite the assurance that
      aeroplanes are terribly com-
      fortable I notice that when
      you are railroading or auto-
      mobiling
You don't have to take a paper bag
      along just in case of a funny feeling.
It seems to me that no kind of
      depravity
Brings such speedy retribution as
      ignoring the law of gravity.
Therefore nobody could possibly
      indict me for perjury
When I swear that I wish the Wright
      brothers had gone in for silver
      fox farming or tree surgery.   *—Hard Lines*

Poets aren't very useful,
Because they aren't very consumeful or
      very produceful.   *—The Saturday Evening Post*

Wise Animals I Have Known

Alan Devoe

[July 1954]

Most of my life has been spent in getting to know animals. When I was five or six the animal was an ol' houn'-dawg—one of the wisest persons in the world I thought at the time. I may have been right. Later it was rabbits, guinea pigs, white mice. Then in my adult life as a naturalist it has been deer, coons, skunks, foxes and a long parade of other wild animals observed in close intimacy outdoors. If I live to be 80 and still greet the mornings with a praise like prayer, it will not be from anything I have read in books of philosophy. It will be because I knew animals.

They are very close, said Saint Francis, to the paternal heart of God. I think they must be. By instinct an animal puts infinite trust in life.

This morning at sunrise I watched Thomas, our cat, greet the new day. Thomas is now (in human terms) going on for 80. Every morning I share daybreak with him. It is great medicine. First there is his rush up the cellar stairs, lithe and springy as a tiger, from the place where he sleeps by the furnace. While I fix his food I watch him. He always begins with the ritual of strr-*etch*-ing. Nothing trivial or hasty, mind you, but a leisurely, carefully relished luxury that does him as much good as a vacation. Left front paw, right front paw, now both hind legs, now a long bend of the back . . . *aaah!* A brisk shake; the big green eyes open wide; the ears perk up.

He dashes to the French window, rears up with forepaws on the glass, and peers out all quivering and tail twitching with excitement. Sunshine! Trees! Great heaven, there is a leaf blowing hop-skip across the lawn! Thomas has looked out through this same pane hundreds of mornings, but every time it is fresh and challenging and wonderful.

And so with breakfast. You'd think he had never seen this old chipped dish before. He pounces on his food like a man finding uranium. Then, when the last bit has been neatly licked from the plate, comes the ecstatic moment for going out to the new day.

Thomas never just goes through the doorway. (Animals don't take these moments lightly.) First he glides *half*way through, then stands drinking in the sounds, scents, sights out there. Another inch or two and he stands again. At last, very slowly, he slips over the threshold. If so much wonder were to hit Thomas all at once he could hardly stand it.

Now he rushes to the middle of the lawn and there this octogenarian performs a riotous caper. He takes a flying jump at nothing in particular, then zigzags after nonexistent mice. He leaps in the air and claps his paws on invisible butterflies. Then some quick flip-flops, rolling over and over, all four paws waving. In a minute it is finished and he steps gravely off to his day's adventures.

What better lesson in living could one have? Here is joy in every moment, an awareness of the electric excitement of the earth and all that's in it. One further lesson from Thomas: when he sleeps, he *sleeps*. He curls up in a ball, puts one paw over the top of his head and turns himself over to God.

All animals give themselves wholeheartedly to the joy of being. At dusk in my woods flying squirrels play aerial roller-coaster. I have seen an old fox batting a stick in absorbed rapture for half an hour. Children react thus simply to the world about them, before reason steps in to complicate their lives.

One summer dusk I watched a buck deer browsing along a pasture hedgerow. His whole being was given over to the taste of the earth-cool grass, the caress of the slanting evening sun on his tawny flanks. He was as relaxed as putty. Nature was saying to him, "Taste, and enjoy yourself, old man," and he was doing just that.

Suddenly a snake wriggled almost under his nose. In a flash the buck became a taut, fighting fury. "Get it!" said Nature, and he plunged to answer. Slash! Thwack! The sharp, cutting hoofs flailed and in a moment it was over. Then the voice said to him, "Back to your peace and your browsing, old man." All knots of fight and fear were gone out of the buck's body; again free and relaxed he sauntered up the pasture hill, and the soft dark of evening wrapped around him like an arm.

If animals can be said to have a philosophy, it is as simple as this: When Nature says, "I give you the glory of the senses and of awareness, and the splendor of earth," surrender yourself to these things, not worrying if it looks undignified to turn somersaults at 80. When the word is "Fight!" pitch in and fight, not weighing hesitant thoughts about prudence.

"Rest," says your monitor. "Play." "Sleep." "Feed and breed and doze in God's green shade by the brookside," each in its season. Heed the voice and act. It is a simple philosophy. It holds the strength of the world.

Animals do not know worry. What bird could raise a family if it worried about the problems to be overcome, the impossible number of feeding trips in a day to keep those clamoring mouths stilled with food? That is not the way birds or animals respond to life. Nature says "Feed them!" and the mother bird goes ahead and does it. Between dawn and sunset a tiny wren must make hundreds of such round trips to feed her brood.

An animal doesn't know what brotherhood means, but when it hears the call "Help!" it answers instinctively. If a prairie dog is shot, the others in the prairie-dog village come tumbling out, not giving a hang for gunfire, and haul their fallen fellow underground. Big-game hunters have seen elephants, disregarding danger, lift a wounded comrade to his feet with their tusks and, supporting him by one member of the herd on each side, help him walk to the forest depths.

Even small birds work miracles of valiance. I once nearly had the daylights beaten out of me by a pair of phoebes, of all things. I had spied their nest on the underside of an old wooden bridge across a stream and was working my way from boulder to boulder in the rushing water to have a close look at the nestlings. Suddenly mother phoebe shot past me only an inch from my nose. I had hardly recovered from my dodge of surprise when she turned and flew straight at my eyes. I jumped sideways and one leg went into the water. At that moment father phoebe dive-bombed, and his wings knocked my glasses off. These parents were not concerned about impossible odds; they were acting on the message "Get him!" They did. I came out from under that bridge as if bears were after me.

Not only do the wild things meet life in all its aspects wholeheartedly; they greet death the same way. "Sleep now, and rest," says Nature at the end. When my old dog Dominie died he lay down in a favorite corner, gave a long sigh and was gone. I remember an old woodchuck that died in my pasture. As I watched him he stretched out on a sun-warmed stone, breathed his last and surrendered himself to what Nature was saying to him. To do that could not have seemed strange to him—he had been doing it all his life. In animals shines the trust that casts out fear.

Next Question?

> "Why," a man asked a friend, "do you always answer a question with a question?" Replied the friend, "Why not?"

George T. Simon in New York *Herald Tribune*

> On Long Island a group of housewives attended a lecture on "A Happy Sex Life." At the conclusion there were questions and answers. Finally the lecturer asked, "Are there any more questions?" From the back of the room came: "Are there any more answers?"

Robert Sylvester, Chicago Tribune-New York News Syndicate

> In her nightclub act, Carol Channing sometimes invites the audience to ask her personal questions. One evening, a man at a ringside table strode up to her and asked, "Do you remember the most embarrassing moment you ever had?"

"Yes, I do," Miss Channing answered. "Next question?"

Bill Adler, *My Favorite Funny Story* (Four Winds)

The Extraordinary Story of Helen Keller

Ishbel Ross

[July 1950]

H ELEN KELLER, at age 70, has an ageless quality about her—inherent even in her looks—in keeping with her amazing life story. Blind, deaf and mute from early childhood, she rose above her triple handicap to become one of the best-known characters in the modern world, an inspiration to both the blind and the seeing everywhere.

Although warmed by the interest in her, she has no wish to be set aside from the rest of mankind. She believes the blind should live and work like their fellows, unremarked and with full responsibility. In the inner quiet of her own dark castle she builds up strength. Each decade brings her fresh wisdom, and some accentuation of her highly developed powers.

Those closest to her observe that her articulation improved noticeably in her 60s. She frequently makes recordings, and the voice of Helen Keller—which in itself represents one of the chief areas of effort in her life—is heard across the world. Her mastery of speech has been called "the greatest individual achievement in the history of education."

Helen, at ten years old, already was reading Braille avidly and could communicate by means of the manual alphabet. That spring of 1890 she learned of a deaf, dumb and blind Norwegian girl who had been taught to talk. Helen burned with ambi-

319

tion. Like lightning she spelled into Anne Sullivan's hand: "I must speak." Miss Sullivan took her to Sarah Fuller, principal of the Horace Mann School for the Deaf in Boston. Miss Fuller went to work at once, passing Helen's hand lightly over the lower part of her face, and putting Helen's fingers into her mouth to feel the position of the teacher's tongue, teeth and the movement of the lower jaw.

Miss Fuller then set her tongue in position and, with Helen's forefinger against her teeth, another finger on her throat, repeated the sound of *i* as in *it* several times. As soon as she had ceased, Helen's "fingers flew to her own mouth and throat and after arranging her tongue and teeth, she uttered a sound so nearly like what I had made that it seemed an echo of it."

They practiced the vowels *a* and *o*, which Helen repeated distinctly, then tried the two-syllable words *mama* and *papa*. After a few repetitions, *mama* and *papa* came correctly and with "almost musical sweetness from her lips."

Going home in the streetcar after her seventh lesson, Helen turned to Miss Sullivan and said in "hollow, breathy tones": *I am not dumb now.* This was her first real use of words in conveying a thought, and it came within a month after her first lesson in articulation.

"We have a lesson to learn from this child," Alexander Graham Bell said. His own skepticism had been washed away earlier when he paid Helen an unexpected visit after receiving a letter from her so beautifully written and well composed that he could not believe the deaf, dumb and blind child was its author. However, he found her alone in a room, writing to someone else with equal skill and fluency. He became her close friend, and remained so to the end of his life.

Helen took 11 lessons from Miss Fuller, but this was only the beginning of her lifelong tussle with speech. Week after week, year after year, she labored to improve enunciation. She repeated words and sentences for hours, using her fingers to catch the vibrations of Miss Sullivan's throat, the movement of her tongue and lips, the expression of her face as she talked.

"I have only partially conquered the hostile silence," Helen says. "My voice is not pleasant, I am afraid, but I have clothed

320

its broken wings in the unfailing hues of my dreams. My struggle for it has strengthened every fiber of my being, and deepened my understanding of all human strivings and disappointed ambitions."

She became adept at reading lips by vibration—placing her middle finger on the nose, forefinger on the lips and thumb on the larynx. She found Franklin D. Roosevelt an ideal subject. She caught Mark Twain's best jokes by vibration. With her fingers on his lips Enrico Caruso "poured his golden voice" into her hand. Feodor Chaliapin shouted the "Volga Boat Song" with his arm encircling her tightly so that she could feel every vibration of his mighty voice. Jascha Heifetz played for her while her fingers rested lightly on his violin. She has read Carl Sandburg's verses from his lips and folk songs from the rim of his banjo. With her hand resting on a piano she detects "tiny quavers, returns of melody and the rush that follows." She gets some small response by vibration from radio, too.

BORN in the little Alabama town of Tuscumbia, Helen Keller was a normal baby up to 19 months. Then she was stricken with a "fever of brain and stomach." She was desperately ill, but the fever subsided almost as suddenly as it had begun.

Soon her mother noticed that Helen's eyes did not close when she bathed the child. She took her to an oculist and learned that Helen was blind. Next she noticed that the child did not respond to the loud ringing of a bell. Helen was deaf, too. Inevitably, by the age of three she was also mute, and such words as she had babbled at 18 months were forgotten.

Helen grew fast and was physically strong and well formed, but her good nature dissolved in frantic tantrums. Her failure to make herself understood was followed by wild gusts of rage. She would fling herself on the grass and give way to uncontrollable fits of screaming. Her table manners were appalling. She would not wash her face or button her shoes.

There was great power in Helen instead of the apathy that usually rests heavily on the triply handicapped child. Here lay the germ of her future success. But Mrs. Keller was close to despair when she read of Laura Bridgman, the deaf, mute and blind girl in New England whose mind had been reached by Samuel Gridley Howe. Helen was taken to Michael Anagnos, who had succeeded Dr. Howe as head of the Perkins Institution. He recommended as tutor an Irish girl, just graduated: Anne Sullivan.

Anne's own childhood had a Dickensian touch. Her drunken father beat her. She was starved, bruised, neglected, and finally abandoned to the almshouse. She entered Perkins in 1880, blind from trachoma. Two operations restored most of her sight, although she had trouble with her eyes all her life.

Anne Sullivan, arriving in Alabama in 1886, was struck by Helen Keller's fine bearing and intelligent face. The six-year-old rushed at her as she stepped from the carriage, felt her dress and face, repulsed a caress, tried to open Miss Sullivan's bag, and staged a scene when Mrs. Keller attempted to take it from her. Miss Sullivan produced a doll sent by the Perkins children. Helen, quickly beguiled, played with it for some time and then Miss Sullivan spelled into her hand the letters *d-o-l-l*. The child's attention was arrested by this unfamiliar maneuver and she tried to imitate the finger motions.

When Miss Sullivan took away the doll a tussle began—the first of many. The new teacher moved Helen away from her distracted parents to an adjoining cottage. A herculean battle of wills raged for several days. It was a physical as well as a mental struggle, but Miss Sullivan won, even though she had to hold Helen down by force for two hours at a time to quell her fierce resistance. "Her restless spirit gropes in the dark," Teacher commented. "Her unsatisfied hands destroy whatever they touch—they do not know what else to do with things."

She noticed that the child already had sundry ways of indicating her wishes. If she longed for ice cream she turned the handle of an imaginary freezer. For bread and butter she went through the motions of cutting and spreading. To symbolize her father she pretended to put on glasses. She took to rocking the new doll, making a monotonous chanting sound with her lips. But she also learned to spell words by the manual language— *pin, hat, cup* and verbs like *sit, stand, walk*—without comprehending that they had any meaning.

Within two weeks a gleam of light dawned. Miss Sullivan took her to the pump house and drew water. As it flowed into the mug and over the child's right hand she spelled *w-a-t-e-r* into the other. "The word, coming so close upon the sensation, seemed to startle her," Miss Sullivan wrote. "She dropped the mug and stood as one transfixed."

Helen's own recollection is: "Somehow the mystery of language was revealed to me. I knew then that *water* meant the wonderful cool something that flowed over my hand. That living word awakened my soul; gave it light, hope, joy; set it free!"

Helen returned to the house in a fever of excitement, touching everything as she moved, visibly seeking its name. Within a few hours she added 30 new words to her vocabulary. From that point on, her education proceeded with uncanny speed. "The eagerness with which she absorbs ideas is delightful," Miss Sullivan related.

Miss Sullivan taught her to read with little sentences slipped into a frame, after each separate word—raised on cardboard—had been placed beside its object, like *doll is on bed*. "When her fingers light on words she knows, she fairly screams with pleasure. I gave her my Braille slate to amuse her and the little witch soon was writing letters. I had no idea she knew what a letter was."

At the end of three months Helen knew 400 words and many idioms. That summer they studied outdoors and in, and everything that could "hum or buzz or sing or bloom" was part of Helen's education. She felt the downy peaches in the orchard, squeezed the bursting cotton bolls, caught an insect in a plucked flower. She learned to distinguish mountain laurel from honeysuckle, a pig from a hen. Miss Sullivan made raised maps in clay, with strings and orange sticks for equator, meridians and poles. She taught Helen to count by stringing beads in groups, and by arranging kindergarten straws for addition and subtraction. It was the only subject the child disliked. Her pencil writing soon was excellent. Within a month after trying it, she wrote a correctly spelled and legible letter to her cousin.

By the end of August Helen knew 625 words. But after a year's instruction she had become extremely pale and thin.

Everyone thought her overtaxed and driven. This charge was to be made later when Helen was preparing for Radcliffe, but the teacher's immediate comment was: "So far nobody seems to have thought of chloroforming her, which is, I think, the only effective way of stopping the natural exercise of her faculties."

Miss Sullivan took Helen to Perkins Institution when she was eight, and a whole new world opened up for her. She had Braille books to read and she could associate with other children who knew the manual alphabet. She soon displayed sensational abilities. Miss Sullivan let her browse from book to book, picking out words at random, long before she could actually read them. She systematically studied arithmetic, geography, zoology, botany and reading, toiling over every aspect of her work, refusing to leave a task unfinished. When urged to rest she would say: "It will give me strength if I finish it *now*."

These were days of great mental growth for Helen. As she and her teacher traveled, Teacher spelled into her hand fluent descriptions of the passing scene—the hills and rivers, the hamlets and cities, the way people looked and what they wore. They summered on Cape Cod and Helen learned to swim, but her first splash into the sea brought a great surprise. No one had thought to tell her there was salt in the ocean! She learned to row and sail, to ride and use a tandem bicycle.

The intellectuals of Boston were taking stock of this brilliant girl. Oliver Wendell Holmes wept when she recited Tennyson's "Break, break, break" to him in halting sentences. John Greenleaf Whittier told her he could understand every word she said, which made Helen happy. She corresponded with famous men, writing to them in both French and English. By this time she was tall and graceful and showed charm and humor.

With Miss Sullivan always by her side to read the lectures into her hand, Helen entered the Gilman School for Young Ladies in Cambridge and was intensively tutored. In 1900 she enrolled at Radcliffe, the first individual with a triple handicap to enter an institution of higher learning.

But college was a disappointment to Helen. She did well, but felt the lack of time for meditation. She could not take notes during lectures because her hands were "busy listening." She jotted down what she could remember when she got home. Examinations were a nightmare. Still she enjoyed some of her classes and she and Teacher worked with their usual whole-hearted concentration.

She was graduated in 1904, taking special honors in English. Helen was 24 years old. Already requests were flowing in for appearances and for magazine articles. She prepared to lecture by taking special voice lessons. At times her voice would dive down or go soaring up beyond her control. Rain, wind, dust or excitement affected its pitch. But in 1913 she made her first public-speaking appearance.

"My mind froze," Helen said. She prayed. Words rose to her lips, but she could not utter a syllable. At last she forced out a sound that felt to her like a cannon going off. Later she was told it was only a whisper.

But after this Miss Keller and Teacher made many appearances in public. In 1914 they set out on the first of a number of transcontinental speaking tours. By this time a brisk and capable young Scottish girl, Polly Thomson, had joined them as secretary and manager. They went to Hollywood to make the film *Deliverance*. Then they embarked on a dignified vaudeville act, Miss Keller causing a sensation at the Palace in New York. Helen loved it. She found vaudeville full of life, color and variety. She "felt the breath of the audience in her face."

Helen Keller was known now around the world. Her books were published in many languages, as well as Braille. She went repeatedly to Europe, then to the Orient, interested always in the blind, talking for the blind, raising money for the blind. She received honorary degrees and decorations in many lands.

But Teacher's health was failing. She was almost blind. She died in 1936, shortly after the last of a long series of eye operations. That year the Roosevelt medal for Coöperative Achievement of Unique Character and Far-Reaching Significance was awarded to this remarkable pair.

TODAY Miss Keller and Miss Thomson live in a graceful rambling house set in the Connecticut woods near Westport. A stone Japanese lantern, eight feet high, stands in one corner of the lawn with a constantly burning light—not to go out while Helen Keller lives. A winding path leads from her garden to the woods, and here she likes to stroll and meditate, alone except for her dogs, moving along with her hand lightly touching a rustic handrail. She looks extraordinarily young for 70, her face unlined, her hair only lightly streaked with gray. Her eyes are alive and expressive: not the lackluster eyes of the blind.

Miss Keller spends long hours sitting tall and straight at the typewriter in her study, filling requests for messages addressed to the blind—and the sighted—from all over the world. Around the walls are her Braille books, which she reads until the fingertips that have traveled over so many miles of Braille have to be bound with silk for protection. Her Braille Bible is her most valued possession. She knows great stretches by heart.

She reads in the dark or the daylight, like all the blind, who sleep poorly and do not know night from day. Miss Thomson reads her the news at breakfast. Articles that closely touch her interests are sometimes Brailled for her.

Miss Keller can smell the woods and flowers beyond her windows. She knows when it rains or snows, when the sun shines or the day is gray, when the early grass comes up, the roses bloom, the leaves wither and smoke trails from autumn bonfires. She has her own suite shut off from the rest of the house and there she functions in complete independence. She tidies her own bathroom, makes her own bed, keeps her papers in place. She and Miss Thomson garden at dawn when the weather is right. She likes to cut grass, to weed and rake leaves.

Helen Keller is deeply spiritual. Her faith sustains her in the quiet hours when she retreats from her busy life into the deep silence that only the deaf can know. Around her shines the steady flame of character, purpose and hard work.

"I look forward to the world to come," she says, "where all physical limitations will drop from me like shackles; where I shall again find my beloved Teacher, and engage joyously in greater service than I have yet known."

*   *   *

The symbolic flame was extinguished in June 1968. Helen Keller had died just days before her 88th birthday.

Who Made That
Kidnap Ladder?

Arthur Koehler, as told to Boyden Sparkes

[June 1935]

Aᴆᴛᴇʀ the Lindbergh baby
had been kidnaped I read about that homemade ladder left behind by the kidnaper and I grew excited. I thought it might be
possible to trace its wood so as to compromise the man involved.
You see, I have spent many years studying wood—its growth,
cellular structure and identification; I work on it all day with
microscopes, calipers and even X rays in the U. S. Government
Forest Products laboratory at Madison, Wis.

When, in May 1932, I was asked to look at slivers taken from
the fateful ladder, I recognized some as second-growth North
Carolina pine. The ladder itself had cleats—cross pieces—instead
of rungs. One edge of each of these, and one of the side rails,
had been dressed with a dull plane, which left a signature in
ridges. Magnified, these stood up almost as prominently as the
steel rails of a railroad track.

The ladder was made in three sections. There were significant
nail holes in a side rail of the top section. They were square
holes made by old-fashioned cut nails. There was no trace of
rust. This told me that the board had previously been used in a
place sheltered from the weather. I worked out that nails of a
size to fit these holes could be driven into 10,000 places in that
board without duplicating holes. By the laws of chance it would

take a world much vaster than ours to provide a coincidence of those four nail holes matching accidentally four other nail holes with which they had no connection.

The two rails of the bottom section showed no sign of previous usage. Their grain matched end to end, showing they had been cut from the same strip of what the lumber trade calls one-by-four common. That kind of North Carolina pine grows in many states other than the Carolinas, from Texas to New Jersey. I detected some marks of the machine planing that these boards had received in some unidentified mill. At regular intervals of precisely .86 of an inch along a corresponding edge of both rails there was a faint mark, the track of some machine's unique behavior. It was just a series of shallow intermittent grooves, so faintly scarring the surfaces that it was visible only in the shadow-making glare of light cast obliquely along the surface. That defect is called a "revolution mark": a rough spot on a blade scores the surface each time the cutter makes a revolution. Then I scrutinized the knife cuts on the faces of the boards, and I found another slight irregularity every eighth knife mark. I measured with the utmost care. Eight knives had touched the board face every time the board proceeded through the planer .93 of an inch.

My problem was to figure out, from these distinctive markings, the characteristics of the planer that had dressed those boards. Then, to locate the mill which planed those boards, the dealer to whom they were shipped, the man who bought them.

I kept on working day by day and often late at night. At last, checking with manufacturers of planers, I was able to say: the machine that dressed the ladder rails had six knives in each edge cutter and eight knives in each face cutter; the edge cutters revolved faster than the face cutters; moreover, it was a fast-feed machine. They told me that such planers are comparatively rare in Eastern mills.

I knew cheap lumber of this kind had not been shipped far. Even so, there were some 1600 pine mills in the section—the Atlantic coast states—out of which I was sure those boards had come. I wrote each mill asking if it had any planers answering my description. Only 25 mills reported yes and forwarded samples of their one-by-four material. I checked every piece, and at last found it: a sample board dressed by cutters that made eight knife cuts every .93 of an inch on both faces. I checked the edges of the sample and found six knives had made a revolution every .86 of an inch. These samples came from the Dorn mill at McCormick, S. C.

Of course, these did not show exactly the same shallow intermittent groove as appeared on the ladder rails. Mill men do not leave dull knives in their planers, and that specific marking had vanished when the planer's blades were sharpened.

I won't set down the details of my 2000-mile odyssey trying to locate, aided by Dorn shipping records, stock of one-by-four common with that specific marking, although for years to come, on tired nights in dreams, I'll still be tracking through a score of cities and their environs.

Finally we came to the National Lumber & Millwork Co. in Bronx Borough, New York City. The foreman said that he had made some bins out of that Dorn stock. One look was enough! The marks on the edge were the same. The same spacing and in precisely the same location as on the ladder rails. But when we asked to see his retail ledgers we got a dreadful disappointment.

"We sell for cash alone," the foreman said. "There's not a record on our books of what we did with the rest of that stock."

That was a blow. After all my months of searching I was looking at a high blank wall laid right across my path, just when I was getting close to that man who made the ladder.

Well, then the police got him. He changed, just once too often, a bill from his deftly hidden cache of ransom money. Questioned about his employment he made what to me always will be his first confession. "I worked," Bruno Richard Hauptmann volunteered, "for the National Lumber & Millwork Co., right here in the Bronx."

Another scanning of the lumber-company records uncovered a sales slip showing that employe Hauptmann, late in December 1931, bought $9 worth of lumber. The Dorn mill shipment had arrived December 1. As far as I'm concerned that completes the journey of the North Carolina pine from mill to the hands of Bruno Hauptmann. But there was more.

Recall that brand left on one rail and one edge of every cleat of the ladder by some hand plane. In the garage where they found the money hidden was Hauptmann's plane. I fixed a board in a workbench vise and cut a shaving off. Next I put a sheet of paper on the board and rubbed a pencil lead back and forth over the plane's pathway. Then I made a similar tracing of the plane marks on the ladder. The many scratch lines matched in an overwhelming sequence of coincidences. That plane had written a label no one could misread.

With Hauptmann under lock and key, a detective and I explored his house. One board at the edge of the one-inch flooring in the attic had been cut in half, sawed off between the joists. There were nail holes in the joists where formerly that board had extended all the way across the attic just like its fellows. We had with us the one-inch ladder rail with the four cut nail holes. I had figured early in my search that if ever we should find four holes to match the four in our ladder rail, the chance of being wrong would be as one in 10,000,000,000,000,000. There simply is not such a chance in human experience. I placed the ladder rail down on the joists and one by one I fitted cut nails into each of the holes, lightly tapping them in.

Just one thing is left that seems important. Every tree within itself has written all its individual history in its growth rings. The end of the piece of flooring that had been robbed to make a ladder showed its rings quite clear, and so did the ladder rail. A gap of 1⅜ inches had been trimmed, yet the rings matched.

And there was more proof. A board is cut lengthwise of a tree, so the rings of small second-growth stuff are curved and several rings expose their edges along a board in what we call the grain. It is a pattern that is always varied, and yet the pattern of the grain in ladder rail and floor board matched as perfectly as if etched within the tree just to be a trap for anyone who dared so to misuse wood as to form it into a kidnap ladder.

᠀ "I didn't come here to be told I'm burning the candle at both ends," said a patient to his doctor. "I came for more wax."
Bulletin of Brookwood Rotary Club, quoted by Leo Aikman in Atlanta *Constitution*

Marriage—
Unsafe at Any Speed

Jean Kerr

[May 1970]

KNOW what I wish Ralph
Nader would investigate next. Marriage. It's not safe—it's not
safe at all.

Do you realize that every day the unwary and the unready
leap into an arrangement that has no guarantee, no warranty,
no money back? It's time we faced up to the fact that it is harder
to get a driver's license than a marriage license. In most states
prospective drivers have to take an eye test, a written test and a
road test. Now surely it would help if persons about to be married were required to undergo an eye test. They should have to
prove to some qualified official that they really did see what
they saw in each other.

It would be harder, I know, to arrange a road test for marriage that would duplicate the actual traffic conditions, but it
could be done. An engaged couple could be asked to live for one
week in a third-floor walk-up apartment with four children
under ten (two of whom have colds), a sink that's stopped up,
and a puppy that isn't housebroken. This would prove an eye
opener.

Lastly, there absolutely must be a written test. Psychiatrists
say that the chief causes of trouble in marriage are money, sex
and in-laws. But it has been my observation that it isn't what

people *do* in these major areas that's so important; it's what they *say*. So, just as potential drivers must indicate their awareness that one never parks in front of a fire hydrant, the about-to-be-married ought to have to show that they are aware that one never asks, "How did you ever get out of high school without learning to add?" or, "Is this the lamb we had three nights ago?"

Admittedly, I don't know *every* wrong statement that can be made in a marriage (my husband would dispute this), but I know *some* of them. And I have made up my own little multiple-choice test to weed out the unmarriageable. As it is barely out of the blueprint stage, I am making things easier by placing the correct answer *last* in every case.

For Men

What is the proper answer when the little woman makes the following observations? (Check one answer only.)

▷ *I suppose you wish I were as good a cook as Emmy.*
  (a) Or even half as good.
  (b) I'm sure you could cook as well as Emmy does if you were willing to put in the same amount of time.
  (c) Oh, I'd get pretty sick of all that rich food day after day. And they say Bill's getting a liver condition.
▷ *Do you love me as much as the day we were married?*
  (a) Yeah.
  (b) Oh, God, not again.
  (c) If you have to ask that question, honey, it must be my fault. I mustn't be showing all the love I really feel.
▷ *Will you lower that damn ball game?*
  (a) If I do, all I'll hear is you screaming at the kids.
  (b) When you're listening to Ol' Dave or Ol' Walter, I can hear it as I step off the train.
  (c) Oh, sorry. Why don't I go up to the bedroom and watch it on the portable. You'll be coming up, won't you?
▷ *Have I been a help to you in your work?*
  (a) Please, don't make dumb jokes.
  (b) Undoubtedly. If I didn't have you and the kids, I'd be a beachcomber today. And very happy.

(c) Honey! Could I ever have got to teach third grade without you right here beside me?

▷ *You never talk to me.*
   (a) I don't talk to you because the only topics that interest you are Billy's rotten report card, your rotten dishwasher, and that rotten milkman who keeps tracking up your linoleum.
   (b) Of course I talk to you. What am I doing now—pantomime?
   (c) And here I was, sitting here and thinking how beautiful you are and how lucky I am and how peaceful it was.

For Women

What is the proper answer when hubby makes these observations? (Check one answer only.)

▷ *What happens to all my clean handkerchiefs?*
   (a) I eat them.
   (b) You don't have clean handkerchiefs because you don't put them in the wash. You leave them all scrunched up in your slacks, which are on the floor of the closet.
   (c) Here's a clean one of mine. We'll fold it so the lace doesn't show.

▷ *Don't you think Abe's new wife is attractive?*
   (a) Everybody's new wife is attractive. Your problem is that you're stuck with your old one.
   (b) Yes, but I think she might do something about that little mustache.
   (c) I think *all* of Abe's new wives are attractive.

▷ *When you write a check, will you, for God's sake, please write down the amount somewhere? Anywhere?*
   (a) Why do you carry on like a madman? The checks never bounce.
   (b) Okay—you're J. Paul Getty; you make out the checks.
   (c) Yes.

▷ *Ye gods—does that kid have to eat that way?*
   (a) No. I coach him to eat that way because I know it drives you crazy.

(b) That kid just also happens to be your kid, and anytime you want to give him your famous lecture on table manners, I'll be rooting for you all the way.

(c) Darling, I *want* to reprimand him, but he's so exactly like you I just melt.

▷ *Oh, Lord—you're crying again! What is it this time?*

(a) I spent three hours stuffing the veal, and you never even said it was good. I had my hair done, and you didn't notice. It rained all day, and the kids were like maniacs. And you never, never, never offer to do anything to help me.

(b) Because I want to marry Aristotle Onassis and live on the island of Skorpios and have a hundred servants and my own airline.

(c) Oh, because I'm silly and I don't count my blessings. Here—give me a little squeeze and take out the garbage, and I'll be through here in no time.

Perhaps I should add a final cautionary note: Those persons who found themselves anticipating the correct answer *in each instance* are probably so perfect that they would drive any other human being bonkers. I suggest that they remain single.

Vendetta

§➤ An automatic ticket machine in an underground station in London failed to deliver a ticket in exchange for my shilling. I tried shaking it, but nothing happened. Then a huge army sergeant who had been waiting stepped forward and, swinging a mighty booted foot, almost uprooted the machine. It promptly produced my ticket.

"There you are, ma'am," said my burly helper. "A little affection, that's all it wanted."

Heather Dennison

§➤ When a vending machine malfunctions, some customers take it personally. A craneman in a steel mill, who had put a quarter in without result, hooked his hitch onto the vending machine, lifted it 50 feet into the air and dropped it. Then he came down from his crane, went through the mess and retrieved the quarter the machine owed him.

Bill Cornelius, quoted by Joe Browne in Pittsburgh *Post-Gazette*

The Wild West—
Fact or Fantasy?

Bernard De Voto

[September 1954]

URING a full century while
it was being explored and settled, the West cast over the rest of
the United States a spell of strangeness and wonder, of spectacle and adventure. It was seen through a mist of enchantment, a residue of which exists still in the minds of Easterners
and Westerners alike.

Here is a country of hard and restless men who tamed a continent—of fur traders in buckskin pants, gold-rushers off to Cali-
for-ni-ay, prospectors driving a burro across the desert in search
of another Last Chance Gulch but destined to die of thirst short
of the bonanza. It is the country of the covered wagon, the pony
express, the overland stage, the Pacific Railroad, of Sitting Bull,
Geronimo, the Little Big Horn.

Finally, it is the country of the open range, the thundering
herd and the cowboy.

This last cluster of symbols has become the center of the
Western myth. Today dude ranches abound not only in the
West but on Long Island, in the Berkshires and practically
everywhere else. Your local newsstand stocks 20 pulp magazines
devoted exclusively to cowboys wrecking barrooms, slugging
sheriffs, shooting rustlers and saving the fair damsel from the
stampede. Your television station averages at least a dozen horse

operas a week. Small fry in Hopalong Cassidy outfits chase others in Lone Ranger outfits down your block.

Here is make-believe on a national scale. So far as it relates to reality at all, it dates back to a time period which lasted little more than 20 years and ended forever before 1890.

The period called the Cattle Kingdom began just after the Civil War, when herds of Texas longhorns were driven north to the new railroads that were building across Kansas. Other herds went on to the untouched ranges in Wyoming and Montana, New Mexico and Arizona. No matter what the ostensible date of a horse opera may be, its plot, emotions, conventions and clichés all relate to this brief time.

Nature rang down the curtain on this era when the winter of 1886–87 killed hundreds of thousands of cattle, bankrupted innumerable outfits and changed the stock business forever. But homesteaders (the "nesters" of the pulps) and barbed wire were already strangling the Cattle Kingdom when the winter of the big freeze came. It had been able to exist only because of the open range, which belonged to the people of the United States; and they were now taking it away from the barons and bronzed horsemen.

No one can explain why the United States has chosen this aspect of the West to romanticize into a myth. True, there was abundant gunfire (though hardly a tenth part of what goes out by coaxial cable every evening), but it was no more romantic than any other business method, which is what it was. The big outfit shot up the little outfit to get rid of competition for the range. Big and little outfits ganged up to shoot sheepmen, who had no damned right to the range which the bronzed horsemen were stealing from the government. The gunmen—the Robin Hoods of the balladry, were hired thugs, indistinguishable from metropolitan hoods of today and equally repulsive.

The cowboy's trade required skill, courage and endurance—but so did all frontier occupations, whether felling white pine in Wisconsin or taking a broadhorn down the Ohio. His life was dangerous and full of hardship—but life was that way in all frontier environments. (For squalor and unregarded suffering, take the first few winters at any mining camp from Bannack to

Leadville, with the rat-gnawed corpses of drunks and paupers dragged from canvas huts only when the snows melted.)

The cowboy seems an illogical choice as a master symbol of the West. If the symbol is to stand for wilderness skill, the Rocky Mountain trapper of an earlier day would have served better, for his was the most complex skill ever exercised on this continent. If importance for the future makes a culture hero, then it should have been the homesteader, who brought the country in and created the West of today. Finally, the cowboy image is in great part phony, a counterfeit, and concentration on it obscures the rich diversity of the West. Past or present, there is a lot more to the West than a cow outfit.

"THE WEST" encompasses 40 percent of the area of the United States—a great variety of landscapes and of people. What, for instance, have Miles City and Santa Fe in common?

Miles City was settled in the late 1870s in the high plains where Tongue River reaches the Yellowstone. Vastness is on all sides of it; it is immensely western, an explosion of trees planted to make a refuge for minds strained by sun and wind and vacancy. It is surrounded by cattle country, wheat country, oil country and badlands.

Santa Fe, also typically western, is set in a mountain basin 7000 feet high and ringed with higher peaks. It was a Spanish town ten years before the *Mayflower* anchored in Plymouth harbor. Mexican Spanish is heard as commonly as English on its streets, and the Pueblo Indian tongues almost as often. Cattle ranching means little to it and oil wells less, but silversmiths, anthropologists, poets and painters are dirt-common.

Abundant contrast and yet only two towns. Now bring in Denver, the Salt Lake Tabernacle, San Diego, the Top of the Mark, Portland's skid road, great wheat ranches, the atomic secrecies of Hanford, the cotton fields along the Gila and the wetbacks who work them, 425,000 acres of orchards in California's Central Valley. Can any pattern be traced? Easily enough, but you must take paradox in stride.

In the West it is always a long way from here to there, and only a little way from here to wilderness—to mountains or desert. The scale is so large that Westerners have developed a new sense of space and time. In Santa Fe a woman looks up from the Denver *Post* with a gleam in her eyes and says that Denver Dry Goods is having a sale on blouses. It is 367 miles to Denver but a one-day round trip to save $1.19 is nothing. Los Angelenos drive 290 miles to Las Vegas for a whirl at the tables. Wyoming trout streams are populous with San Franciscans.

The cult of the sun has been most publicized in Southern California—"Great, tall, empty, sunburned blondes," a resented poem runs—but it exists everywhere. In the Sierra and every other range, adolescents and grandparents burn their skins black, fishing, hunting, the men bare to the waist, the girls just about. Thus Westerners retain what was once the birthright of all Americans: a full awareness of the forms and processes of nature, the weather, the growing seasons, the web of life.

Western life is maintained as a precarious victory over an enemy who always has heavy armor in reserve. This is a country of droughts, blizzards, sandstorms, cloudbursts, twisters. This year you get a bonanza crop, buy a Cadillac, spend the winter in San Diego. Next year there is no rain, and the sun is a sickly green disc behind a cloud of dust three miles high. Dust piles around fence posts in rippled cones; a crop is just a few brown shoots sticking through it; you throw some bedding in a truck and the bank takes over.

Down a gulch that has been dry for a decade comes a 40-foot wall of water from a cloudburst 40 miles away, with somebody's corral posts and drowned steers floating on top of it. Or the cloudburst hits an overgrazed spot on a mountainside, the mountainside slides into a creek, which becomes a river of thick mud. It pours out of the canyon and buries fields and orchards under ten feet of gravel and boulders that weigh up to 300 tons.

Violence and chance have necessarily been the themes of the West's way of life. Every effort was a gamble. The government bet you a quarter section that you couldn't live on it for five years. You bet your pile and, not infrequently, your life that there was gold in the gravel. That you would strike water before the drill broke, or oil before you went broke. That the price of wheat or cattle would hold.

It is the gambler's buoyancy that the Easterner sees as western breeziness. There were never any servants in the West, no caste barriers except such as are erected by the West's dreariest rich. (The waitress calls your wife "honey" and is genuinely eager to please you. The bellboy consults you about his problems as a pre-medic at State U.)

Here is one part of the country that is not sunk in anxiety about the end of the world. It is the United States as we knew it in a more vigorous time. Or a more youthful time.

WHAT MAY escape observation at first is the Westerner as schizophrenic. Never did the pillar of cloud move so constantly before Moses as the vision of El Dorado before the West. The boomer is a man who looks at a solitary water tank or grain elevator beside a railroad track and sees a metropolis-to-be, who glances from a sagebrush flat to the snowy peaks on the horizon whence water might be brought and sees the garden of the world flowering at his feet. The other half is the boom going bust—the dry well, the blue-sky promotion, the salted claim. The collapse of the boom is the very essence of western experience—and yet the essence of the western character has always been the conviction that tomorrow is another day. Last time the vein pinched out, or the locusts came. But next time . . .

Since the mid-1920s enormous dams and gigantic systems of water distribution have literally remade the West and launched it on its greatest boom. At the same time the West has become more suave. The practice of the arts, for generations tolerated only in San Francisco and Carmel, has proliferated amazingly. There are painters everywhere now, not merely at Taos. And ceramists, symphony orchestras, chamber-music groups. Every second Westerner is writing a novel.

Such are the stresses and ferments at work on the West. They account for the vivacity and volatility of an engaging people, whose spirit is a blend of pure credulity, pure cynicism, and illusion. But there enters in, too, awareness of almost incredible achievement.

Properly speaking, the West was uninhabitable. And yet there it is in plain view, the garden of the world. Westerners have done what was clearly impossible—therefore rejoice, but therefore also be wary. For who knows whether the hills at the horizon are real or a mirage?

They are self-assured because they have subdued the unsubduable, so that the best symbol for them is the big dam which stores the water which creates life. And they are skeptical because the dam is a frail thing and will be no more substantial than the mirage if the rains fail. It is an old saying that Americans love a hard country. But the West must be loved as you love a woman you know you cannot trust.

Or maybe, since so much of their country is fabulous, the right word for Westerners is fable. Space, you learn out West, has color. The color of space is deep blue turning lavender and darkening to violet. You can see it any autumn morning in any mountain range, any evening in any desert, or at any hour in any of the chasms of which the Grand Canyon is the best known. A blue gauze is drawn across the rock shapes and they change, or the color changes, and you aren't seeing what you lately saw, or you saw what wasn't there.

Maybe the West has provided its own best fable. It is older than the white man's West; it has been told in many Indian tongues about many streams. If you drink of Fountain Creek, which issues from big springs called Manitou in a gulch above Colorado Springs, it has been said, the spell is on you. Wherever you go, you will come back to drink that water again.

The Alchemy of Woman

In the original Sanskrit, the creation of woman by Tvashtri—the Vulcan of Hindu mythology—is described thus: "He took the lightness of the leaf and the glance of the fawn, the gaiety of the sun's rays and the tears of the mist; the inconstancy of the wind and the timidity of the hare, the vanity of the peacock and the softness of the down on the throat of the swallow. He added the harshness of the diamond, the sweet flavor of honey, the cruelty of the tiger, the warmth of fire and the chill of snow. He added the chatter of the jay and the cooing of the turtle dove. He melted all this and formed a woman. Then he made a present of her to man."

Neal O'Hara in Boston *Traveler*

Alcohol and Your Brain

Albert Q. Maisel

[June 1970]

I T IS A fact of life in present-day America that 85 million adults—about 79 percent of all men and 63 percent of all women—drink alcoholic beverages. One drinker in 18 (more than 4,800,000 Americans) is an outright alcoholic. Four to five million more are "heavy" drinkers —meaning their consumption is enough to cause serious personal problems. That leaves 75 million of us moderate or social drinkers. We may take a cocktail or two before dinner, wine with a meal or a few beers at a cookout, but we seldom, if ever, come anywhere near getting drunk.

Until quite recently, such occasional imbibers were believed to suffer no permanent ill effects. Even when they did get "high," physiologists were convinced, their slurred speech and slowed-up reactions evidenced only a transitory effect upon the brain and nervous system. Now, however, strong evidence indicates there is no guaranteed "safe" level of drinking.

Let's look at what happens when we drink. Whether we swallow beer or wine or whiskey or vodka, the substance that affects us is ethyl alcohol. It is extremely soluble in the water that is the principal component of almost all the tissues of our bodies. It is so soluble, in fact, that a part of every sip of alcohol you take is absorbed right through your tongue and gums before you have time to swallow it!

Nor is the rest of it broken down or digested like ordinary

foods. Instead, it is absorbed directly into your bloodstream through your stomach's walls or the lining of your small intestines—so rapidly that on an empty stomach fully 90 percent of it may enter your bloodstream within an hour. It is quickly carried to every organ of your body—especially those which, like the brain, have a high water content and a rich blood supply.

Physiologists have established a direct relationship between the quantity of alcohol and the area of our brain it affects. If, for example, a 150-pound man consumes two bottles of beer on an empty stomach, the level of alcohol dissolved in his blood will reach about .05 percent. Normal activity of the cortex, or outer layer of the brain—particularly in the centers concerned with worry or anxiety—will be affected. The drinker will feel falsely "lifted up," because the inhibitions that usually hold him steady have, in effect, been paralyzed.

If he drinks enough to raise his blood alcohol level to about .1 percent, activity in the motor centers at the back of his brain will be depressed. He'll begin to lose the ability to control his muscles. If his blood alcohol level rises to .2 percent, the deeper portions of his mid-brain will become affected and he'll become increasingly sleepy. Should the level pass .5 percent, the respiratory centers in the lowest part of his brain may become paralyzed and the drinker will pass from stupor to death.

Just how does alcohol exert these successive effects? Over the last three decades, increasing numbers of physiologists have come to believe that alcohol acts indirectly upon the brain's various layers by depriving them of the oxygen essential for cell function. This theory derives its strong support from the fact that a direct deprivation of oxygen—such as that experienced by mountain climbers or aviators—produces exactly the same sequence of effects. (If a flier without an oxygen mask climbs over 9000 feet he begins to experience a sense of exhilaration that closely parallels that of a drinker after a cocktail or two. Should he rise above 18,000 feet, his respiratory centers will stop functioning and he will die.)

Yet only recently has the mystery of *how* alcohol deprives the brain of oxygen been solved—by a brilliantly simple series of experiments conducted by Prof. Melvin H. Knisely and two young associates, Drs. Herbert A. Moskow and Raymond C. Pennington, at the Medical University of South Carolina.

In a healthy individual the heart pumps the blood through a series of ever-smaller arteries until it reaches the minute capillaries that spread through every tissue of the body. In these tiny, narrow blood vessels the red cells yield up their oxygen, thus maintaining the life of the surrounding cells. For reasons not yet completely clear, many disease conditions bring about the production of a substance that coats the red cells and makes them stick together in clumps. As these bits of "sludge" reach a capillary, they pile up into a wad that may plug it. When sludging is extensive and many capillaries become plugged, cells in entire areas of an organ will starve for oxygen.

To observe this sludging directly, as far back as the early 1940s Dr. Knisely was illuminating the eyeball, where numerous capillaries lie just below the transparent surface. He thus observed through a microscope all the variations of sludging and capillary-blocking that occur in more than 50 human diseases—from malaria to typhoid fever. For his investigations he needed a sludge-causing substance that, given in controlled quantities to laboratory animals or student volunteers, would permit him to create and observe any desired degree of sludging. Alcohol proved perfect for his purpose.

The experimenters quickly discovered that they could detect sludging of the blood in the eye capillaries of students who had consumed as little as one large glass of beer. They went on to study every intoxicated person admitted to one private sanitarium over a 17-month period. They found that with every increase in blood alcohol concentration, wads of red cells also increased, and the rate of blood flow slowed. In patients with higher blood alcohol levels, they observed an increasing number of fully plugged capillaries. At the highest concentrations, a substantial number of the capillaries had been ruptured, producing microscopic hemorrhages.

One key question remained: Were the capillaries in other organs affected in the same way as in the eye? Dr. Pennington gave alcohol to rabbits and then examined a wide range of internal organ tissues. In each test animal he found sludged blood plugging capillaries in *every organ and tissue* that could be properly illuminated for microscopic study. Having determined this, the researchers felt justified in concluding that they had discovered the mechanism by which alcohol injures and destroys cells throughout the body.

The drinker who consumes enough alcohol to reach a stuporous state will thus incur a substantial number of small brain hemorrhages and an even larger number of plugged brain capillaries. Around each of these minute points, some brain cells will die for lack of oxygen. Our bodies are incapable of creating new brain cells. But the average adult brain contains more than 17 billion individual cells, so the destruction of even a few thousand in a single drinking bout leaves the heavy drinker with his brain powers apparently intact.

Gradually, however, the accumulation of such losses will show up as the slowed wits and impaired judgment of the alcoholic. And when he dies—probably some years sooner than if he had been a non-drinker—an autopsy of his brain will reveal enormous numbers of small areas of atrophy in which brain cells have been destroyed. Dr. Knisely has observed entire convolutions of the brain so shrunken that the loss of tissue can be seen the moment the brain is exposed to view.

But what of the moderate or occasional drinker? He, too, the South Carolina researchers suspect, might incur some loss of irreplaceable brain cells every time he drinks. The only real difference between his loss of brain tissue and that of the heavy drinker is one of degree.

This same capillary-clogging, cell-killing action may well be a significant factor in cirrhosis of the liver (eight times as frequent in alcoholics as in non-alcoholics). But the liver, unlike the brain, can produce new cells, so degeneration can be stopped if drinking stops. For heart-disease victims, liquor was once advised as a medication to help dilate the blood vessels that nourish heart muscle. It may actually damage these tissues. Cardiologists no longer prescribe it.

What should all this mean to the millions who are moderate or social drinkers? Obviously, each of us will come to his own conclusions.

What Really Killed
Marilyn Monroe?

Clare Boothe Luce

[November 1964]

HE SUICIDE of Marilyn Monroe in August 1962 was splashed across the front pages of the world. Editorialists, critics, fellow artists, friends and foes seemed obsessed by the question of why this woman, possessing beauty, fame and money in such abundance, had so feared or hated life that she could no longer face it.

While views differed as to who or what had executed her, one villain was the most favored: Hollywood. But the easy acceptance of this view has obscured whatever meaning and moral her life and death may have. Hollywood brought her fame, money, adulation, two respected and well-known husbands (Joe DiMaggio and Arthur Miller), and the help, however belatedly sought, of competent psychiatrists. But for all these, Marilyn might have gone to her death in her 20s instead of her 30s. Indeed, fame gave her the only form of sustained emotional security she knew, or perhaps was capable of understanding.

She believed that her extraordinary power to project sex was her great gift. Her despair at the end, when she reached out for her last and lethal dose of barbiturates, was perhaps akin to that of a painter who discovers he is going blind. The mob worship of her for her pure sexuality could last only a few years longer. She was 36, and her mirror had begun to warn her.

A girl entering her teens has intense, secret, often lengthy encounters with a looking glass. They are a legitimate manifestation of concern for her future as wife and mother. The more mature and emotionally secure a woman becomes, the less she turns to the looking glass for self-confidence and a sense of her own personhood. But for a movie star, the narcissistic approach to the mirror is a continuing, ever more urgent professional necessity. Her daily, often hourly encounters with "mirror, mirror on the wall," however satisfying and reassuring in the beginning, become summit meetings with her archenemy—time.

After Marilyn passed 30, her sessions with her studio mirror must have been increasingly agonizing experiences. The growing hostility and aggressiveness she began to show, the endless changes of clothes and protracted primpings in her dressing room, the vomiting just before the cameras began to grind—all these may have foreshadowed her terror of that hour when the wolf-whistling men and oohing-and-aahing women would desert her. What then would make her valuable? Who *was* Marilyn Monroe if not that delectable creature on the screen?

"I feel as though it's all happening to someone right next to me," she said in one of her triumphant hours. "I'm close—I can feel it, I can hear it, but it isn't really *me*." Marilyn knew who the "real me" was. But it was an admission she sought to escape. For this "real me" was one of the saddest and most frightened little girls ever born—Norma Jeane Mortenson.

An ugly congeries of evil fairies—insanity, infidelity, illegitimacy, ignorance and poverty—presided over her cradle. Her mother, Mrs. Gladys Baker, was a pretty, red-haired 24-year-old Hollywood film cutter whose husband had deserted her, taking their two children with him. She then met Marilyn's father, an itinerant baker. When the child of this casual union was born on June 1, 1926, in Los Angeles, the father was not present: he disappeared the day Gladys told him she was pregnant.

After the first few years, her mother began to give evidence of violent mental disturbance and was committed to an institution. For the next four or five years Norma Jeane was farmed out by the County Welfare Agency to a series of foster parents who were paid $20 a month. She was sent for a while to an orphanage. There she earned nickels by washing dishes and cleaning toilets. Compared with this rootless little orphan of the City of the Angels, the fairy-tale Cinderella sweeping ashes from the hearth lived a normal, protected, happy life.

"I always felt insecure and in the way," she once said. "But most of all I felt scared."

At the age of seven or eight, in one of the foster "homes," Norma Jeane was seduced by an elderly star boarder, who gave her a nickel "not to tell." When she did tell, her foster mother severely punished her for making up lies about the "fine man." The unhealthy and confused emotional correlations she made all through her life among sex, money and guilt may have stemmed in part from this ugly encounter.

In her early teens Norma Jeane discovered, to her great delight, her one dazzling gift—an exuberant, vital capacity to project her sexuality. "My arrival in school started everybody buzzing," she recalled. "The boys began screaming and groaning."

She married in 1942, when she was barely 16. But she and her husband separated in 1944, apparently without tears. Never having known the face of love, she was certainly incapable of giving what she herself had not experienced. Years later, during her marriage to Arthur Miller, Marilyn said, "Now for the really first time, I feel I'm not alone anymore. I have a feeling of being sheltered. It's as if I have come in out of the cold. . . ."

Young Norma Jeane was always trying to avoid the cold. Despising marriage, deeply distrustful of both men and women but nevertheless hungry for admiration, affection and acceptance, she sought "love" with what must have been a fever-pitch promiscuity. Indeed, by the time she was entering womanhood

347

a miracle was needed to save her from a life of overt or covert prostitution. That miracle happened: Hollywood.

In 1945 she found employment as a photographer's model, bleached her hair a golden blond and played a bit part in a 20th Century-Fox movie. Then at 22, her name changed to Marilyn Monroe, she got the lead in an obscure B picture *Ladies of the Chorus,* shot in 11 days. The movie magazines recorded a "romance" with a musical director. The failure of this romance revealed that she was already flirting with another escort—death; she made one of her several attempts at suicide. Rejection could not have failed to trigger and intensify the feelings of unwantedness ingrained in her by her miserable childhood.

A big movie break came when Arthur Hornblow, Jr., and John Huston were casting a minor role in *The Asphalt Jungle* that called for an angel-faced blonde with a wickedly curvaceous figure. Marilyn was tested for the part.

"As soon as we saw her we knew she was the one," Hornblow recalls. Hollywood was looking for a quality that would at once touch the heart, evoking tenderness, and race the blood, stirring all the senses. This was the quality of innocent depravity, and it can be found only in a female "juvenile delinquent." Marilyn had that quality. Hollywood simply recognized it.

But the picture that really made her famous was a calendar photograph of her in the nude for which she had cheerfully posed a year earlier. The public became aware of the fact that the calendar girl was Marilyn, just as her film *Clash by Night* was about to be released. The Fox brass blew their tops and threatened to drop her. Facing the old pattern of rejection and punishment for a misdemeanor involving sex, Marilyn once more talked of suicide. But this time the "howling mob" came to her rescue. The public clamored to see more of her. Thus it was she and the public, not Hollywood, who launched her career as a Love Goddess and started her off on her years of stardom.

A year and a half after her suicide, the question of "What killed Marilyn?" was revived by her third husband, playwright Arthur Miller. In his autobiographical and self-defensive play, *After the Fall,* he holds that Marilyn wrought her own destruction by insisting on seeing herself as the utterly helpless victim of her parents, her lovers and husbands, her profession and her friends—a victim who could be "saved" only by a "limitless love." One of the themes of the play is that no man can give "limitless love," not even to the loveliest and neediest of women.

There is no reason to dispute Miller's self-exculpation for the tragedy of this woman to whom for four troubled years he sincerely tried to give enough of his mind and heart to make any normal woman feel "sheltered." She was not, of course, a normal, mature woman. She was still the orphan child—the child seeking a permanent home where warmth and tenderness would always be given unconditionally by the "grownups," in this case by Arthur Miller. He encouraged her to seek psychiatric help and to bolster her self-esteem by developing whatever gifts she believed she might have as an actress.

Miller has accurately identified some of the problems that led to her three divorces, to her many troubles with her studio, and eventually to her suicide: the insatiable demands for "limitless love"; the moodiness and depressions; the orgies of self-recrimination alternated with orgies of recrimination of others; the clearly self-destructive urges always boiling and seething under the mask of careless, vibrant happiness that she tried to project to the public.

Marilyn died on a Saturday night. This "love object" of millions of unknown lonely males had no date that evening. She was suffering physically and mentally, but she evidently neither loved nor trusted anyone enough to seek help. For above all, Marilyn was profoundly suspicious of the motives of everyone in her own regard. She had an almost psychopathic fear of being "used"—financially, as she had first been used by the foster parents who tolerated her only for the $20 board money; sexually, as she was used by the star boarder; professionally, by producers and agents.

For all its "corn," the simplest lesson of Marilyn's life is that children need parents, or parent substitutes, who not only love them but who love and respect each other. Without this greatest of cradle gifts—a happy home—it is all but impossible in adulthood to deal with either failure or success.

How to Sell an Idea

Elmer Wheeler

[December 1948]

Have you ever approached your boss with a red-hot idea for increasing efficiency—only to have him become resentful instead of enthusiastic? Have you ever offered your wife or the neighbors "good advice"? If you have, you know what I mean when I say that people resent having other people's ideas forced on them.

When someone approaches us with a new idea, our instinctive reaction is to put up a defense against it. We feel that we must protect our individuality; and most of us are egotistical enough to think that our ideas are better than anyone else's.

There are three tested rules for putting your ideas across to other people so as to arouse their enthusiasm. Here they are:

Rule One: Use a fly rod—not a feeding tube. Others won't accept *your* idea until they can accept it as *their* idea.

It was said during World War I that Colonel House was the most powerful man in the world because he controlled the most powerful man in the world—Woodrow Wilson. "I learned that the best way to convert him to an idea," explained House, "was to plant it in his mind casually, to get him thinking about it on his own account."

When you want to sell someone an idea, take a lesson from the fisherman who casts his fly temptingly near the trout. He could never ram the hook into the trout's mouth. But he can entice the trout to come to the hook.

Don't appear too anxious to have your ideas accepted. Just bring them out where they can be seen.

"Have you considered this?" is better than "This is the way." "Do you think this would work?" is better than "Here's what we should do."

Let the other fellow sell himself on your idea. Then he'll stay sold.

Rule Two: Let the other fellow argue your case. He instinctively feels called upon to raise some objection to save his face. Give him a chance to disagree with you—by presenting your own objections!

"The way to convince another," said wise old Ben Franklin, "is to state your case moderately and accurately. Then say that of course you may be mistaken about it; which causes your listener to receive what you have to say and, like as not, turn about and convince you of it, since you are in doubt. But if you go at him in a tone of positiveness and arrogance you only make an opponent of him."

Franklin used this technique, against great opposition, in his sale of the idea of adopting the Constitution of the United States. "I confess," he began, "that I do not entirely approve of this Constitution; but, Sir, I am not sure I shall never approve it; for having lived long, I have experienced many instances of being obliged by better information or fuller consideration to change opinions, even on important subjects, which I first thought right. I cannot help expressing a wish that every member of the convention who may still have objections to it would with me on this occasion doubt a little of his own infallibility, and, to make manifest our unanimity, put his name to this instrument."

Abraham Lincoln used the same technique in selling his ideas to a jury. He argued both sides of the case—but there was always the subtle suggestion that his side was the logical one. An opposing lawyer said of him: "He made a better statement of my case to the jury than I could have made myself."

Another technique is to sell the other fellow the idea as his, not yours. "You gave me an idea the other day that started me thinking," you begin.

Tom Reed, for many years Speaker of the House, was an adroit persuader. At a committee hearing he would remain silent until everyone had had his say, making notes of all objections. Then, when everyone else was argued out, Reed would say, "Gentlemen, it seems to me that what has been said here can be summarized as follows . . ." Reed would then present *his* ideas—and sell them.

Once Dudley Nichols, the movie director, wasn't satisfied with a scene in one of his pictures. To remedy the situation he said to Rosalind Russell, the star, "Wonderful, wonderful. But I could see, Miss Russell, when you hesitated that brief instant, that you were thinking about the possibility of playing the scene down just a trifle more. Shall we try it once the way you were thinking?"

Rule Three: Ask—don't tell. Patrick Henry, another famous idea salesman, was a political unknown when first elected to Virginia's House of Burgesses—but every resolution he introduced was passed. Listen to him in his famous Liberty or Death speech and see how he uses questions to get his ideas across:

"Our brethren are already in the field—why stand we here idle?"

"Shall we lie supinely on our backs?"

"What is it that gentlemen wish? What would they have? Is life so dear or peace so sweet as to be purchased at the price of chains and slavery?"

Try saying the same thing in positive statements and see how much antagonism it would invoke.

When you put your ideas across with questions, you give the other fellow a share in the idea. You don't tell him—you ask him for the answer. You're giving him a chance to sell himself.

Try these rules the next time you want to put an idea across to your boss, your family or the neighbors.

ે✥ Personal notice in the Washington *Star:* "I will not be responsible for six live fresh lobsters being shipped from scenic New Hampshire by my wife at a cost of $32 plus postage, which I am supposed to pick up at the airport after a hard day at the office. Robert H. Rhoads."

PERSONAL GLIMPSES

BENNY GOODMAN, the "King of Swing," lives only for his clarinet. One night, before Benny was married, we gave a party for him and invited a good-looking girl along for him. The boys in the band had never seen him dance before, and they collapsed with laughter when they noticed that Benny's right hand was unconsciously playing the clarinet fingering of the tune up and down the girl's spine.

Robin Douglas-Home, *Sinatra* (Grosset & Dunlap)

EDWARD M. KENNEDY at age 30 landed in the U.S. Senate after a race in which his mother, Rose Fitzgerald Kennedy, was perhaps his best campaigner. That fragile-looking but indomitable matriarch hit the street corners of Massachusetts in support of her boy. Her pitch was an exquisite blend of politics and religion.

In answer to the charge that he was too young, she said, "You're right about Teddy. He is too young for that old Senate. As a matter of fact, I wanted him to enter the priesthood. I've always regretted not having a priest in the family. I thought for a time that Teddy would become one," she'd say with a catch in her voice that moved her audiences. "But he wanted to start out as a bishop," she would finish—bringing down the house.

Bob Considine, Hearst Headline Service

BASEBALL umpire Eddie Hurley takes a dim view of umpires who aren't mean, nasty and antisocial. "When I'm nice," he says, "I'm acting." Morris Siegel in Washington *Star*

STRIP-TEASE artist Gypsy Rose Lee made several appearances in Milwaukee, but some old-time newsmen will never forget her visit to the Milwaukee Press Club. She was wearing a long dress with a high neckline and long sleeves. She was introduced and talked briefly, but no one remembers what she said, because, as she talked, she slowly unbuttoned three buttons at the wrist of each sleeve. Then she ended her talk with a demure bow.

There are some who say it was the sexiest performance they ever saw. Raymond E. McBride in Milwaukee *Journal*

WHEN Herbert Bayard Swope was city editor of the old New York *World* he sat on a dais in the city room and took a beguilingly possessive attitude toward the news. "Who is covering my subway accident?" he would shout. "Who is covering my murder?"

Once he looked out of a window on a wintry day, frowned and barked at an assistant, "Who is covering my snowstorm?"
E. J. Kahn, Jr., *The World of Swope* (Simon & Schuster)

ONCE when Toscanini was rehearsing Debussy's *La Mer* he wanted to achieve a highly evanescent effect in one spot. At a loss for words to describe what he wanted, he took from his breast pocket a large white-silk handkerchief. He threw it high into the air and every man in the orchestra was hypnotized as it floated softly, sensuously, to the floor. "There," the Maestro smiled happily, "play it like that."
Milton Katims in New York *Times Magazine*

"WHEN I was very young and the urge to be someplace else was on me," wrote John Steinbeck, "I was assured by mature people that maturity would cure this itch. When years described me as mature, the remedy prescribed was middle age. In middle age I was assured that greater age would calm my fever, and now that I am 58 perhaps senility will do the job. Nothing has worked. Four hoarse blasts of a ship's whistle still raise the hair on my neck and set my feet to tapping. The sound of a jet, an engine warming up, even the clopping of shod hooves on pavement brings on the ancient shudder, the dry mouth and vacant eye, the hot palms and the churn of stomach high up under the rib cage. In other words, I don't improve; in further words, once a bum always a bum. I fear the disease is incurable." *Travels With Charley* (Viking)

I Go to Church

Stanley High

[March 1958]

I HAVE SAT in my quota of hard pews, heard my share of "volunteer" choirs and listened to enough uninspired and uninspiring sermons to last a lifetime. But I still go to church. I go to the church at the end of the street in the little town where I live.

I was raised a Methodist and at one time was a Congregationalist. The church at the end of the street happens to be Presbyterian. My wife belongs to the guild. We both like the preacher. It is convenient. But it lays claim to no special distinction. We have good music but it is no better than the Sunday-morning music I could get on the radio. The preacher is better than average. But his renown is pretty much limited to our town.

My church, in short, is like 10,000 other small churches, with no more to offer and no less. But I enjoy it. I feel that I have missed something when I do not go.

I grant that habit may have something to do with it. My Methodist parents laid great store by churchgoing, and so, as a boy, did I. It would be difficult to shake the influence of that early training. About half-past ten on Sunday mornings, the old youth-bred inclination lays hold of me. If I stay at home, I do it in the face of an internal protest. I suppose if I stayed home often enough I would get over that feeling. But I generally go.

I go to church for the same reason that I go to the theater—

because I get something out of it. What I get is different. But it is something that I want and I have not found any other place where I can get it.

For one thing, at church I generally get some perspective—often not so much as I would like, but always a little. That little is more than I can be sure of getting anywhere else. And I am glad to have it. The rest of the week I am addicted to all those devices by which the average American is led to believe that a thing is important only if it is recent; that the biggest news is, *ipso facto,* the latest news. I read several daily papers; I listen to the news flashes on the radio and television, and every week buy three news magazines.

Then, on Sunday, I go to church. We sing the doxology, "Praise God From Whom All Blessings Flow." Some form of doxology has been sung by men and women at worship for at least 21 centuries. The hymns do not go back that far. But they go back far enough to be out of the running for the radio's Song Hits of the Week. I sang them on Sunday mornings when I was a boy. My father and mother sang them, and their parents before them. I like them for more than their age, but I do like them for that.

The minister reads the Old Testament lesson. That goes back farther than either the hymns or the doxology. It may go back 30 centuries—a thousand years before Christ. He reads the New Testament lesson, preferably in the King James Version. There is nothing new enough in what he reads to make the headlines. I heard the same passages in my youth. Men and women not very different from those in our church have heard them, generation before generation into the past. My children and their children will hear them generations into the future. They are more to me than a bridge to the past or the future. But they are that.

And before the preacher begins his sermon, I find that I have become consciously aware of something which the rest of the week is no more than a hunch. I realize that people like myself, with problems like mine, have been here a long time; that yesterday's newspapers did not say the first word and tomorrow's newspapers will not say the last word on anything. I know that tomorrow is another day. But I can say to myself: "Why so hurried, my little man?"

That is what I mean by perspective. I get that—a few minutes of it, at least—when I go to church. And that is more of it than I get anywhere else I go.

For another thing, I go to church because I like to be in a place, once in a while, where men take their hats off. I know all the places where, customarily, men's hats come off. What I mean is something more than custom. I suppose that "reverence" is the word for it. It may be just another survival from my youth, but I still find in my surroundings an atmosphere and in myself a sense of reverence when I go to church. I am glad that I do.

I think it is important to have something to revere—a banner, or a cause, or a person that is bigger than we are and better than we are when we are at our best; some place where, now and again, we can climb down from our high horses, and are in proportion. Bumptiousness is no virtue, despite its prevalence among intelligent people.

I have reservations, of course, when I go to church. I cannot, for example, go down the line word for word with the Apostles' Creed. For that matter, I do not take the church itself in my stride, as I once did. I have seen the ecclesiastical wheels go round, and I know that they are very much like any other wheels. Nevertheless, when I go to church I meet up with a great deal that I can still revere—more, in fact, than I meet up with anywhere else.

A few of my friends are intellectuals—ultra-ultras. They say that in an intelligent man's universe "there is no room for God." I never argue with them. But when I ask them what their "intelligent man's universe" does have room for, I stand in awe before the things that they admit nobody knows. On the next Sunday morning, therefore, I go to church. I go reverently, because I believe in God. But if I did not believe in Him, I would go anyway—out of reverence for the size of the mystery with which the little we know is surrounded.

Then, too, I go to church because the big idea back of what goes on there is to encourage whatever in me is good. My preacher does not go in very much for politics and economics. He just keeps hammering away on right and wrong. Sometimes I think he hammers away at me. But he is almost always right, and I take it.

It is very much like having an annual physical overhauling or seeing your dentist twice a year. Except that in the area where the church operates, I think most of us need to be over-hauled oftener than that. I go to church because, after having sized things up all week by more or less selfish standards, I am ready for an hour in which they are sized up by moral standards. I can generally tell what I want to do without calling in any outside help. When it comes to deciding what is *right* to do, I can afford to have some counsel and advice.

The things that I get from my church are not offered any-where else. And I have been going long enough to be sure, in my own mind, that I get along better with those things than without them.

Connoisseurs

In his book of French-Canadian reminiscences, *The Happy Time,* Robert Fontaine tells of his Uncle Desmonde, who once said that he wished during his last meal on earth to drink great wines and to have with him the six most beautiful girls in Canada, wearing black net stockings, long gloves, picture hats, and nothing else. "Is this a good thing or an evil thing?" Robert's father asked the priest.

"It all depends," Father Sebastian replied, "on the choice of wines."
Published by Simon and Schuster

Lucius Beebe, a famed *bon vivant* and connoisseur of wines, had an attack of acute appendicitis. As they were about to take him to the hospital a friend leaped into the ambulance and insisted on going along. Why? He explained, "I want to make sure they open him at room temperature."
Jerome Beatty, Jr., in *Saturday Review*

Stories are told of the strength and longevity of ivy and of its ability to hold up masonry walls, but here's a story of its cunning. A root of the ivy growing on the walls of Magdalen College in Oxford groped its way into the wine cellar, made its way into the cork of a bottle—and drank all the port inside.
The National Observer

"Hurricane Coming!"

Thomas Gallagher

[September 1962]

n September 11, 1961, one of the biggest (350 miles in diameter) and most violent (90 times as much energy as a 50-megaton bomb) hurricanes in recorded weather history whirled in from the Gulf of Mexico to blast the coast of Texas. Pushing 40 billion tons of water before her, Hurricane Carla left 30,000 Texans homeless and destroyed hundreds of millions of dollars' worth of property.

Thousands of persons might well have lost their lives. But for two days preceding, sheriffs in Texas coastal communities— urged to action by U. S. Weather Bureau forecasts—had been warning: "Hurricane coming! Get out or drown!" So more than 500,000 persons, in the greatest mass exodus in U. S. history, boarded up their homes, packed their cars and headed upstate to Red Cross shelters or to the homes of relatives or friends.

When Carla struck the Texas coastline, her fullest force was aimed directly at the little town of Port O'Connor on a neck of land between Galveston and Corpus Christi. Here is the story of 11 who remained behind—and saw 98 percent of the town swallowed up before their eyes.

Port O'Connor lay waiting tensely. An old fishing town, it was a summer resort as well, with imported palm trees, a marina, motel, trailer camp, and many cottages whose lawns were matted with fine white sand from the beach. Devastated by hurricanes four times since the turn of the century, it was a town where there were as many barometers as coffeepots.

On Saturday, September 9, when the U.S. Air Force ordered its planes and personnel evacuated from the base on Matagorda Island only six miles away, the residents of Port O'Connor began to leave. Chris Clarich, an old merchant seaman and shrimp fisherman, whose house was a quarter-mile from the beach, would have left with them if he had not promised to look after the six Almanzar children while their mother visited her doctor in nearby Port Lavaca.

"I don't think the storm will come here," he said to his 77-year-old wife, who had the youngest child, a five-month-old infant, in her arms. "But there's still time. We'll all leave as soon as Mrs. Almanzar returns." What Chris Clarich didn't know was that Mrs. Almanzar was at that moment undergoing an emergency appendectomy in Port Lavaca.

Ten blocks farther inland from the beach were three brothers —Edgar, Whip and William Munsch—who had no intention of leaving Port O'Connor. For half a century they had never left to escape a hurricane. "You don't leave a place," they said. "You take precautions, but you don't leave."

In 1950, Edgar had taken every precaution by building a house the like of which had never been seen in Port O'Connor. "There are more struts and braces in this house than in any three other houses put together," Whip said to me afterward. "Edgar used extra-long nails, too, and bent each one over at the end. Why, you couldn't *pull* this house apart."

In honor of his 25 years in the U. S. Coast Guard, Edgar had also constructed a glassed-in, five-foot-square lookout at the apex of the roof, with a view in every direction. In front of the house lay a field of live-oak thickets, a tight mass of wooden arms strong enough to catch and hold the uprooted trees, piles and telephone poles that could become battering-rams against houses during a hurricane. Whip, the Port O'Connor weatherman, had always advised his fellow townsmen to allow the thickets on their property to grow, but most people had had them uprooted and replaced by lawns or summer-rental cottages. The only house in Port O'Connor protected by thickets was Edgar Munsch's.

It was in this house that the three brothers, no more aware of Chris Clarich's presence in town than he was of theirs, awaited developments.

WATER began to trickle into the Clarich yard that evening. Chris watched patch after patch of sand "melt like sugar" around his doorstep. When the electricity went off, he decided to leave town with his wife and the six children without waiting longer for Mrs. Almanzar.

After putting on hip boots and carrying his wife and the infant to the car, he drove to the Port O'Connor schoolhouse four blocks away, where the older children were playing. He left his motor running and sloshed through the yard to the auditorium where the children had said they'd be. He rounded them up—but in those few minutes the water had risen to cover the car's exhaust. Was the road to Port Lavaca already washed out?

"Children, go back to the auditorium," he said. "Hurry!"

When all were safely inside the sturdy brick building, he ran to the principal's office to telephone for help. The line was dead.

THE NEXT morning, Sunday, the Munsch brothers saw from their lookout that the water was advancing on the town from three directions—from Matagorda Bay, San Antonio Bay and the Intracoastal Waterway. It came inquiringly, over roads that might have been the decks of a slowly sinking ship.

"I began to feel small and humble," William Munsch, a yacht captain, told me later. "The air became tense and felt almost too heavy and wet to breathe. And the sky turned hazy and yellow in a way that made everything look unreal."

Birds and animals seemed alive to what was happening, too, for the brothers could see black skimmers and Caspian terns hugging windbreaks in an effort to rest before flying inland. At one point Whip saw a possum rushing so frantically up a telephone pole that when it reached the top it kept right on going— up into the air and then down into the water again.

In the evening the wind increased with steady persistence. This was the rim of the hurricane and, as it blew through the town, electric and telephone wires ripped like cat-o'-nine-tails through air already filled with broken glass, car license plates, pails, clothing and bits of lumber.

"WHEN the storm struck, it was the worst thing I've ever experienced," Chris Clarich said. "The tide had to be at least 20 feet above normal for the town—which is 7 to 12 feet above sea level—to be that covered. The auditorium looked like a swimming pool."

The night before, after trying in vain to phone for help, Clarich had rushed home for mattresses, blankets, food, water, an oil lamp and a single-burner stove. Now out of stacked tables, benches and chairs he built an island on the auditorium stage, piled the bedding and equipment on top and lifted his wife and the children up.

There was a square opening in the ceiling above the stage leading to the attic, and as Chris worked he kept scanning it. If things got much worse he planned to pile one table on top of another, climb through the opening to the attic and, with a knotted blanket, pull his wife and the children to safety.

Meanwhile, from a backstage window to which he kept running, he could see the piled-up masses of water rushing past, the twisted and broken spines of boats, and sometimes the swollen bodies of dead cattle. There were terrible impacts of debris and jarrings of air, vicious rushes of wind in which all the atmosphere seemed concentrated, and then, above the steady roar, rending shrieks like air-raid sirens.

During hurricanes at sea, Chris recalled, there had been a monstrous kind of harmony between the raging waves and the struggling ship. Here on land everything that happened was unlike what it happened to. Sedentary objects—sofas and TV sets—flew by like grotesque things with wings. A trailer, emptied of furnishings, its metal skin ribboning off the framework in the wind, sailed by looking like a discarded sardine tin.

"By Monday morning," Chris said later, "I wanted to stop what I was doing and just listen, because I couldn't believe my ears anymore. If ten jet planes had been in the auditorium with us, they could not have made more noise than that wind."

As dawn was coming up, Chris's eyes wandered to the auditorium windows high above the water level on the lee side, and what he saw suddenly made cereal of his body's fiber. The glass was smashed, and coiled in and around the narrow sashes were more than a dozen rattlesnakes and water moccasins. The wind and water had chased them from their lairs on Matagorda Island, swept them across the bay, and thrown them against the trees and buildings of Port O'Connor.

Chris knew that the storm had torn shingles and even planks off the roof, leaving gaping holes. Had snakes crawled through into the attic—the only place left for his group to go? This possibility haunted him as the water rose and he tried to distract the children and make their island of safety higher.

AT THE Munsch house, Whip was urging his brothers to follow his example and put on life preservers. Whip's car in the garage, like the others parked in the yard, had disappeared under the churning waters. On the first floor the piano, refrigerator, sofa and chairs were all either covered or afloat.

Yet the destruction of their belongings shrank to insignificance beside the sheer vastness of the destruction they could see from the lookout. They saw the whole roof of a house poised on a blast of air, then tossed half a block as one might toss a book. They saw trees, trucks, butane tanks rising and rolling with the masses of water rushing past. If it had not been for the live-oak thicket directly in front of them, this wreckage would have ripped their house to pieces.

"The barn's moving!" Whip shouted suddenly to his brothers. He was passing through the hallway when he noticed that the view from its window had changed. He wasn't supposed to see the barn through this window, but there it was—and it was moving! Even more astounding, it was moving *against* the wind.

"I was taking a barometric reading at the time," Edgar said later. "The reading was 27.68, I remember. Just then there was a rumble through the house, and I could hear the branches being ripped off the mulberry tree in the yard and the windows crashing on that side of the house. 'That ain't the barn moving!' I shouted to Whip. 'It's us!' You see, the bottom of the house is sealed with marine plywood and rests on concrete blocks four feet from the ground. When the water and wind came in a rush like that, the whole house just pulled loose from the blocks and became a boat." Broad and solid, the house floated serenely backward to where trees, 150 feet away, brought it to a halt.

THE STORM had now reached its height. In the school auditorium, Chris and his seven were all up on the island in the middle of the stage, on their knees praying. Mrs. Clarich, cradling the infant in one arm, held a crucifix.

"I knew that if the wind kept up there would not be a brick left in the building," Chris said. "But when I prayed I began to hope. After a few minutes I remember standing up and shouting, 'God has answered our prayers!' It was like a dream. The wind stopped all of a sudden, and the water started going down just like when the stopper is pulled in a bathtub."

At the Munsch house, just before this calm, the brothers saw a four-by-ten-foot workbench of Edgar's come floating out of the garage. Loaded with tools, nails and boxes of screws, it passed beyond them out of sight to be destroyed, they thought, and become part of the storm's debris. No sooner did the water begin to recede, however, than the bench reappeared, minus the tools, nails and screws, and headed straight back toward the garage from which it had come. "If it had made the trip all the way back," Whip said, "I think I'd have given up. Hurricanes do funny things, but that would have taken the cake."

THE "EYE" or calm center of Hurricane Carla, 25 miles in diameter, came at 2:40 p.m. on Monday, September 11, and remained until 4 p.m. Outside the eye, the winds were still tearing along at more than 150 miles an hour, but in Port O'Connor itself five candles could have been lighted in the open air with a single match. As the water receded to below the motor level of Edgar Munsch's pickup truck, a short circuit developed in the wires connected to the horn. Suddenly the horn started to blow in the absolute silence of the calm.

"You couldn't even have heard the noise during the storm," Edgar said. "But with the eye over the town it was more than I could stand. I waded out and disconnected the wires."

The Clariches and Munsches knew that the wind was going to return suddenly from the opposite direction, so no one ventured far out of doors. "While we were in the eye, the auditorium was almost dry for about 40 minutes," Chris said. "Then when the wind shifted the auditorium filled up again, and the water began rushing past even faster than it had the first time. It was going downhill now, back into the Gulf. Things flew by so fast you couldn't even identify them."

When on Tuesday morning the hurricane had passed, more than 98 percent of Port O'Connor had been destroyed. A terrible stench filled the air, mostly from the mud and muck and seaweed. The carcasses of hundreds of snakes and cattle lay caught in barbed-wire fences or hidden under debris and seaweed in fields. In front of the Munsch house, a boat, blown from a town 35 miles away, stood tilted on its keel in mud.

A YEAR later, the Clarich house, completely destroyed, had been replaced by the Red Cross. The Munsch house had been moved back onto its blocks. And all of Port O'Connor was alive with the hammering and sawing of new lumber.

At lunchtime, carpenters and masons could be found listening to the jukebox at either the new Stryker's Café (of Stryker's old place all that had been left was a beer-can opener) or Hurricane Junction, a totally new restaurant. Ed Payne's Fishing Headquarters and Tourist Courts, completely rebuilt, were doing a better business than ever, with fishermen from all over coming to try for the Gulf's sailfish, tarpon and other game fish.

Meanwhile, Chris Clarich and the Munsch brothers discovered an interesting thing. When the evacuees returned, they stood weeping on the ground where their houses had once been, their bereavement unalleviated by the fact that their lives had been spared—since their lives were never threatened. Chris and the Munsches, though also losers, concentrated on their gain—and were thankful. They were still alive!

ॐ The cure for anything is salt water—sweat, tears or the sea.

Isak Dinesen

365

Beware
the Phony Price-Tag "Bargain"

Don Wharton

[December 1958]

A TWO-PAGE advertisement in a trade magazine this year made retail stores one of the most brazen propositions I've ever seen in print. The ad, by a watch wholesaler and importer (not a manufacturer), pictured watches priced from $9.50 to $14.90 wholesale. At the bottom was an order blank to be filled in by the dealer: "I want these free resale tags with my order: ☐ 16.95 ☐ 19.95 ☐ 24.95 ☐ 29.95 ☐ 39.95 ☐ 49.95."

In other words, the distributor was offering to put any printed price tag on the watches that the retailer wanted, so the retailer could then discount this "list price" and appear to be offering customers a great bargain.

Such loaded price tags are the backbone of phony bargains offered us every day. In recent years nearly one third of all complaints and corrective orders issued by the Federal Trade Commission involved fictitious pricing. The Association of Better Business Bureaus reports that questionable price claims account for more complaints from competitors than any other kind of advertising abuse.

On my worktable now is a tawdry imitation-pearl bracelet-necklace-earring set, bought in Savannah by a Better Business Bureau investigator. The glistening price tag in the box says

$27.50. The investigator purchased the set for $1.75. It's possibly worth 59 cents. Before me is a folder picturing another set—watch, cuff links, tie bar and matching money clip—carrying a price tag of $71.50. A Chicago firm peddles this junk to merchants at $4.50 and will supply "any desired price tag."

Jewelry is by no means the only merchandise involved in phony pricing. Here is a huge ad in a national trade paper, headlined "Look at my fantastic price structure." It tells dealers of a 19-inch lawn mower: "Suggested list $109.95. Can retail with full markup for only $59.95."

Sometimes considerable ingenuity is used to make the fictitious price appear genuine. One firm advertised a perfume in a national women's magazine: "$18.50 per ounce at better shops." The firm then by-passed the better shops, sold the perfume at 50 cents an ounce to retailers. Each ounce bottle carried a sticker imprinted "$18.50." And with each shipment went a copy of the magazine ad, blown up for window display. Customers buying at $4.95 a bottle thought they were getting a bargain. Actually they were paying a markup of 990 percent!

Manufacturers and distributors refuse to take sole blame. A mattress maker, caught in phony pricing last year by the Pittsburgh BBB, wrote: "The high retail price tag is something every manufacturer in the country regrets, but it is a national practice and the retailers all demand it." The president of Horrocks-Ibbetson Co., one of the top makers of fishing tackle, publicly stated: "In the last few years we have been getting requests from retailers to mark a $20 rod $40—and then they sell it for $19.95. We refuse even if we lose that business."

Usually what's called the "bargain price" is simply the "regular price" of merchandise of that quality. The Chicago BBB recently investigated 23 "bargains" in appliances—washers, gas ranges, refrigerators and such. If a family bought one of each, the advertised or implied "savings" would total $2112.59. The investigation showed you actually would have spent $49.71 *more* buying these "bargains" than buying the identical items at the regular price in other stores.

The fictitious list price isn't steep enough for some stores. In my files is a vacuum-cleaner ad which says: "Originally sold for as much as $99.50." Actually the manufacturer's list price on this model was $54.95, and $99.50 was never the "original" or "recommended" price. Recently in Cleveland a discount house advertised a TV set: "Retail Price $189.95. Our Price $128.75." The BBB discovered the manufacturer's suggested retail price had been jacked up $31.95.

Are shoppers really taken in by fictitious pricing? Several years ago a study by the Duquesne University business school showed that two thirds of those questioned did believe comparative-price claims in men's wear, appliances, women's wear and household furnishings. Over half believed them in bedding, furniture, rugs, carpets and TV sets, and nearly a third in furs and jewelry. The St. Louis BBB says women "do not really have to get a bargain, but they want the illusion." Fictitious pricing creates that illusion. Probably few men or women buying a "$39.95" electric fry pan for $12.95 think it was really worth $39.95, but that fake figure gives many the illusion that it was worth more than $12.95.

What can the consumer do about it?

First, it is wise to buy the products of manufacturers who have established reputations.

Second, it is important to remember that the test of value is not what an article *used to* cost but how much it costs today, compared with similar articles at other stores. Disregard such phrases as "formerly," "made to sell for," "reduced from." Shop around before making any major purchase; find out the actual market price.

Third, we can help fight this evil. FTC officials give this advice:

1. If duped by a fictitious-pricer, don't remain silent and thereby help him victimize others. Write the facts of your case to your local Better Business Bureau or chamber of commerce.

2. Send copies of your letter to the newspaper or broadcasting station that carried the ad.

3. If the offending firm sells products across state lines, send the facts to the Federal Trade Commission, Washington, D.C. Enclose a copy of the misleading ad. Your name will be held in complete confidence.

Your Mind Can Keep You Well

John A. Schindler, M.D.

[December 1949]

WHAT one thing contributes most to unhappiness? As a doctor I can answer: a long period of illness. It is a little frightening, because this human clay is heir to a thousand different ailments. But one of them is as common as the other 999 put together. Fifty percent of all the people going to doctors in the United States today are victims of this one disease. Many would put the figure higher. Of 500 consecutive admissions to the Ochsner Clinic in New Orleans, 386—or 77 percent—were sick with this one disease. Persons of any age, in any walk of life, can contract it. Furthermore it is a terrifically expensive disease to diagnose and treat.

It used to be called psychoneurosis. Now it is known as psychosomatic illness. And don't get any misconceptions: it is *not* a disease in which the patient just *thinks* he is sick. The pain you get is often just as severe as the pain you get with a gall-bladder colic.

Psychosomatic illness isn't produced by a bacterium, or by a virus, or by a new growth. It is produced by the circumstances of daily living. I have tried to find one word for it, but it takes three, each meaning about the same thing but in different degrees. They are: *cares, difficulties, troubles.* Whenever one has such a thick, impenetrable layer of c.d.t. that he can't get up above it into a realm of joy and pleasure occasionally, he gets a psychosomatic illness.

There are three general groupings of people who suffer from c.d.t. In the first group are the people who are habitually crabby. A friend of mine has a beautiful farm. I drove past his farm one summer day and I thought to myself, "Those oats ought to make Sam happy." So I drove in and I said, "Sam, that's a wonderful field of oats," and Sam said, "Yes, but the wind will blow it down before I get it cut." He got it cut all right, he got it threshed, and he got a good price for it. Well, I saw him one day and I said, "Sam, how did the oats turn out?" And he said, "Oh, it was a good crop, and I guess the price was all right, but you know a crop like that sure takes a lot out of the soil."

People like Sam invariably get a psychosomatic illness, and when they get it they get it hard. As a rule they are invalids for the rest of their lives. There is nothing you can do about it.

The second group, where most of us belong, are the people who all day long manage to be concerned, to be anxious, to be worrying about something. If there's nothing around home or the business, they worry about Mrs. Smith down the street. Why doesn't she get her daughter in before 11 o'clock at night? Something is going to happen to her!

The third group is made up of those who have an acute but temporary case of c.d.t. Maybe they have got themselves into some kind of mess—financial ruin or domestic trouble, perhaps. They are usually easier to treat than the second group, as the latter are easier to treat than the first group.

How does this c.d.t. bring on illness? To understand that, we must consider what thinking is and what emotion is. Thinking, we ordinarily suppose, is something that goes on solely in the brain, but that is quite wrong. Thinking involves the entire body in a series of correlated nerve impulses that center in the brain. Particularly is this true when an emotion colors our thinking. The psychologist William James gave us the best definition we have of emotion when he said it is the state of mind that manifests itself by a perceptible change in the body.

One emotion we all recognize is anger. You don't have to be told when a man is angry. His face either gets white or it gets red; his eyes widen; his muscles tighten up so that he trembles.

That is a state of mind manifesting itself by a perceptible change in the body.

Another emotion is embarrassment. A person who blushes certainly doesn't have a disease of the skin. In his case embarrassment produces a dilation of the blood vessels in the face.

A third example is vomiting or fainting at sight of blood. The sight of blood leads to such painfully disagreeable thinking that the stomach does the things that result in vomiting. Or the heart and the blood vessels leading to the brain do the things that result in fainting.

Now, how does all this bring about a disease? Very simply. Most of our disagreeable emotions produce muscle tightness. Suppose that all day long your thinking is acutely disagreeable. You are tightening up muscles. Take your fist and hold it loosely; it doesn't hurt. But hold it tight for a long time and it begins to hurt. The squeeze produces pain.

One of the first places to show tension is the group of muscles at the back of the neck. Another group that come into play very early are the muscles at the upper end of the esophagus. When they squeeze down you feel a lump. It is difficult to swallow. If the muscles in the lower esophagus contract, then it's more serious: much more commonly the stomach is involved. And when the muscles of the stomach begin to squeeze down you are conscious of a heavy, disagreeable pressure inside. When the muscles squeeze down hard, then it hurts. And it hurts just as bad as any ulcer.

This same kind of muscle spasm can occur in any part of the colon. Many persons who complain of a pain exactly like gall-bladder pain don't have gall-bladder trouble at all. They're dissatisfied, and the upper colon is squeezing down. And believe me, their suffering is real. If the pain happens to be lower down in the colon, it will seem just like appendicitis. And then it takes a smart doctor not to open that abdomen.

Other muscles besides those in the intestinal tract respond to emotional stimuli, particularly the muscles of the blood vessels. A good many of the people who have a headache severe enough to cause them to go to a doctor have that headache because some blood vessel inside or outside the skull is squeezing down so hard from nervous excitation that it produces pain.

And a third of all skin diseases treated by dermatologists are produced by blood vessels in the skin reacting to anxiety, worry, disgust and so on. Each time certain individuals become upset or irritated or peeved, serum is actually squeezed out through the wall of the blood vessel and into the skin. The tissue becomes thickened with it. Finally the serum is pushed up through the surface of the skin where it becomes scaly, crusty and itchy, and the patient has a neurodermatitis.

One favorite place for nervous tension is the muscles in the upper left part of the thorax. People rarely come to see us doctors because they have a pain on the right side. It's almost always on the left. If it's on the right—pshaw!—it doesn't amount to anything. If it's on the left—ah!—could be heart trouble! Then they start watching for it. And merely watching for it can bring the pain on.

Another way symptoms are produced in a psychosomatic illness is through the effect emotion has on the endocrine system. Most of you have driven down a street too fast when suddenly somebody backed out from a side road. You started to breathe deeply, your heart started to pound, you got a little faint. Acute fear in your mind produces these bodily changes. An impulse is sent to the adrenal glands, which squeeze adrenalin into the bloodstream. When that adrenalin hits the heart, the heart starts to thump. When it hits the blood vessels going into the brain, they narrow down and you feel woozy.

There are other organic effects in psychosomatic illness. If it happens to be the blood vessels on your heart that squeeze down every time you get excited or angry, it is serious. John Hunter, the English physiologist, had that kind of heart, and he always said, "The first scoundrel that gets me angry will kill me." And that's exactly what happened. He got up in a medical meeting to refute something, and anger produced such a contraction of the blood vessels on his heart that he fell dead.

Many victims of psychosomatic illness are up and around. Many are in hospitals. Thousands have been in bed at home for years. To avoid psychosomatic illness, you must learn to think right. It would be idiotic for me to say that you can be pleasant and cheerful all the time. Of course you can't. But I can offer certain suggestions which will help you to think right about yourself.

First, quit looking for a knock in your motor. Don't be analyzing your feelings all the time, looking for trouble.

Second, learn to like to work. One of the things you will escape is the tension that comes to those who look upon work as something to be gotten over with.

Third, have a hobby. A hobby is an important element in getting your mind off work tension. During the day when you are hurrying and worrying, just relax for 30 seconds by thinking briefly about that thing you're making in the basement, that community project you're interested in or that fishing trip you're taking next weekend.

Fourth, learn to like people. Carrying a grudge or dislike can have disastrous bodily effects. We had a man in the hospital who got there because he had to work in an office with a man he didn't like. He said, "I don't like the way he combs his hair; I don't like the way he whistles through his teeth; I don't like the way he always starts a sentence with 'Listen!'" On questioning the patient I found he never liked anybody—his mother or his father or any member of his family. But you have to meet people. You've got to live with them, so learn to like them.

Fifth, learn to be satisfied when the situation is such that you can't easily change it. A young woman was in a hospital with a psychosomatic illness because she had become dissatisfied with her life. She had been a secretary, had held a war job in Washington. There she married an Army captain. After the war she found herself living in a trailer, raising three children. She didn't like to live in a trailer, didn't like to raise children in a trailer, wasn't sure she liked to live with her husband in a trailer. She wanted to be a secretary back in Washington.

I didn't tell her what her trouble was. I just advised her to get the four Pollyanna books and read them. She did, and returned to live in the trailer and like it. She had to learn that it is just as easy under most conditions to be satisfied as it is to be dissatisfied, and it is much more pleasurable.

Sixth, learn to accept adversity. In this life you're going to meet some adversity, and may meet a lot. Try not to let it bowl you over. I had a patient who hadn't worked for a year. Then his wife died. A month later his son was killed. And he sat around thinking "How unfortunate I am—why did this have to happen to *me!*" He became very sick. A lot of people start a psychosomatic illness after an adversity.

Seventh, learn to say the cheerful, humorous thing. Never say the mean thing, even if you feel like doing so. Saying the pleasant thing will make you feel better.

Finally, learn to meet your problems with decision. About the worst thing to do is to have a problem and to mull it over and over in your mind. Decide what you are going to do about it and then quit thinking about it.

These are some of the things you have to learn if you want to escape the most common disease of all. The key is: *I'm going to keep my attitude and my thinking as pleasant and as cheerful as possible.* There isn't any better definition for happiness.

Speak Up

𝒞❧ The electronic age has gone too far—another machine keeps calling my telephone-answering machine. The caller drones on for its allotted time about the virtues of some product while my machine obediently gives it instructions on how to leave a message. Then come the tone signals from each machine, and silence while each waits for an incoming message. There is none. The operators of the machine on the other end have obviously chalked me up as a "no response" and have programmed their machine to call me again.

At least that's what I think has happened. Or could it be that the machines are attracted to one another? You see, my machine has a male voice recording, theirs has a female.   Bruce Peasley

𝒞❧ A cleaning woman was dusting a desk in a Milwaukee office where electronic phone-answering equipment had just been installed. When the phone rings and no one is around, the device automatically picks up the receiver, and a tape-recorded message is "spoken" into the mouthpiece. Well, the phone rang, the device went into action and the message was repeated. The surprised cleaning woman became so frightened that she beat the machine with her dust rag until it shut up.

Roland Sibley, quoted by Doyle K. Getter in Milwaukee *Journal*

Exploits of Charles

Shirley Jackson

[*March 1950*]

HE DAY my son Laurie started kindergarten he renounced corduroy overalls with bibs and began wearing blue jeans with a belt; I watched him go off the first morning with the older girl next door, seeing clearly that an era of my life was ended, my sweet-voiced nursery-school tot replaced by a long-trousered, swaggering character who forgot to stop at the corner and wave good-by to me.

He came home the same way, the front door slamming open, his cap on the floor, and the voice suddenly become raucous shouting, "Isn't anybody *here?*"

At lunch he spoke insolently to his father, spilled his baby sister's milk, and remarked that his teacher said we were not to take the name of the Lord in vain.

"How *was* school today?" I asked, elaborately casual.

"All right," he said.

"Did you learn anything?" his father asked.

Laurie regarded his father coldly. "I didn't learn nothing. The teacher spanked a boy, though. For being fresh," he added, his mouth full.

"What did he do?" I asked. "Who was it?"

Laurie thought. "It was Charles," he said. "The teacher spanked him and made him stand in a corner. He was awfully fresh."

"What did he do?" I asked again, but Laurie slid off his chair, took a cookie and left while his father was still saying, "See here, young man!"

The next day Laurie remarked at lunch, as soon as he sat down, "Well, Charles was bad again today." He grinned enormously and said, "Today Charles hit the teacher."

"Good heavens," I said, mindful of the Lord's name. "I suppose he got spanked again?"

"He sure did," Laurie said.

"Why did Charles hit the teacher?" I asked.

"Because she tried to make him color with red crayons," Laurie said. "Charles wanted to color with green crayons. The teacher said nobody should play with Charles but everybody did."

The third day Charles bounced a seesaw on the head of a little girl and made her bleed, and the teacher made him stay inside all during recess. Thursday Charles had to stand in a corner during story time because he kept pounding his feet on the floor. Friday Charles was deprived of blackboard privileges because he threw chalk.

On Saturday I remarked to my husband, "Do you think kindergarten is too unsettling for Laurie? All this toughness, and bad grammar, and this Charles boy sounds like such a bad influence."

"It'll be all right," my husband said reassuringly. "Bound to be people like Charles in the world. Might as well meet them now as later."

On Monday Laurie came home late, full of news. "You know what Charles did?" he demanded. "Charles yelled so in school they sent a boy in from first grade to tell the teacher she had to make Charles keep quiet, and so Charles had to stay after school. And so all the children stayed to watch him."

"What did he do?" I asked.

"He just sat there," Laurie said, climbing into his chair at the table. "Hi, Pop, y'old dust mop."

"What does this Charles look like?" my husband asked Laurie.

"He's bigger than me," Laurie said. "And he doesn't have any rubbers and he doesn't ever wear a jacket."

Monday night was the first Parent-Teachers meeting, and only the fact that the baby had a cold kept me from going; I wanted passionately to meet Charles's mother. On Tuesday Laurie remarked suddenly, "Our teacher had a friend come to see her in school today. A man who came and made us do exercises; we had to touch our toes. Look." He squatted down and touched his toes. "Like this," he said. He got solemnly back into his chair and said, picking up his fork, "Charles didn't even *do* exercises. The teacher's friend told Charles to touch his toes like I just did and Charles kicked him."

"What are they going to do about Charles, do you suppose?" Laurie's father asked him.

Laurie shrugged elaborately. "Throw him out of school, I guess," he said.

Wednesday and Thursday were routine: Charles yelled during story hour and hit a boy in the stomach and made him cry. On Friday Charles stayed after school again.

With the third week of kindergarten Charles was an institution in our family: the baby was being a Charles when she cried all afternoon; Laurie did a Charles when he filled his wagon full of mud and pulled it through the kitchen; even my husband, when he caught his elbow in the telephone cord and pulled telephone, ash tray and a bowl of flowers off the table, said, "Looks like Charles."

But during the fourth week it seemed that a reformation was taking place in Charles; Laurie reported grimly at lunch one Thursday, "Charles was so good today the teacher gave him an apple."

"What?" I said, and my husband added warily, "You mean *Charles?*"

"Charles," Laurie said. "He gave the crayons around and he picked up the books afterward and the teacher said he was her helper."

For over a week Charles was the teacher's helper; each day he handed things out and he picked things up; no one had to stay after school.

"The PTA meeting's next week again," I told my husband one evening. "I'm going to find Charles's mother there."

"Ask her what happened to Charles," my husband said. "I'd like to know."

On Friday of that week things were back to normal. "You know what Charles did today?" Laurie demanded at the lunch table, in a voice slightly awed. "He told a little girl to say a word and she said it and the teacher washed her mouth out with soap and Charles laughed."

"What happened to Charles?" my husband asked.

"Nothing," Laurie said. "He was passing out the crayons."

At the PTA meeting Monday I sat restlessly, scanning each comfortable matronly face, trying to determine which one hid the secret of Charles. None of them looked to me haggard enough. After the meeting I sought out Laurie's teacher.

"I've been so anxious to meet you," I said. "I'm Laurie's mother."

"We're all so interested in Laurie," she said.

"Well, he certainly likes kindergarten," I said. "He talks about it all the time."

"We had a little trouble adjusting the first week or so," she said primly, "but now he's a fine little helper. With occasional lapses, of course."

"Laurie usually adjusts very quickly," I said. "I suppose this time it's Charles's influence."

"Charles?"

"Yes," I said, laughing, "you must have your hands full in that kindergarten with Charles."

"Charles?" she said again. "We don't have any Charles in the kindergarten."

ᘐ Arthur Godfrey claims that, when he was a boy, his father had an ingenious system for teaching him to save. It involved three boxes. One was a yellow box for pennies. When Arthur had saved five pennies, his father would give him a nickel, which he would put into a blue box. When he'd saved five nickels, his father would give him a quarter, which he would put into a red box.

Arthur says he was 12 before he discovered that the red box was the gas meter. *Wit and Humor*, quoted in *The Link*

THE
WILD WHEEL

Garet Garrett

THE
WILD WHEEL

ONE SUNDAY in 1914, when the prevailing minimum wage for factory workers in this country was a little over $2 a day, news came from Detroit that rocked industry to its heels: Henry Ford had announced a minimum wage of $5 a day and cut the working day from nine hours to eight.

Immediately it was prophesied that Detroit would be ruined by an exodus of employers; that those who remained and tried to meet the new Ford wage scale would go bankrupt; that the Ford company would fall; that Ford employes would be demoralized —they wouldn't know how to spend the money.

When asked about it Ford said, "If the floor sweeper's heart is in his job he can save us $5 a day by picking up small tools instead of sweeping them out."

Later he wrote: "The real progress of our company dates from the time we raised the minimum wage to $5, for then we increased the buying power of our own people, and they increased the buying power of other people, and so on. Behind the prosperity of this country is the enlargement of buying power by paying high wages and selling at low prices."

Five years later when he increased the minimum to $6 a day he said, "Paying $5 for an eight-hour day was one of the finest cost-cutting moves we ever made, and the $6 day is cheaper than the $5 day."

He defined proper wage and price this way: "The right price is not what the traffic will bear, and the right wage is not the lowest sum a man will work for. The right price is the lowest an article can steadily be sold for. The right wage is the highest an employer can steadily pay."

Henry Ford was the supreme practitioner of free enterprise, a credo and a system that grew to full size in the American environment and nowhere else. It was founded on the doctrine that the individual businessman, freely pursuing his own ends in producing things for others, was bound to serve the common good whether he consciously intended to or not. The system was cruel in the way that nature is cruel to weak and marginal things—*but it worked*. It produced in this country the most fabulous material achievement in the history of the human race.

Let us look at this system through the eyes and accomplishments of Henry Ford, a kind of divine mechanic who, by instinct and intuition, acted on the world with ruthless and terrible energy—a man who thought with his hands.

BEFORE Ford, the automobile had been a plaything for the rich. His public announcement of the Model T read: "I will build a motorcar for the multitude. It will be large enough for the family, but small enough for the individual to take care of. It will be constructed of the best materials, by the best men to be hired, after the simplest designs that modern engineering can devise. But it will be so low in price that no man making a good salary will be unable to own one and enjoy with his family hours of pleasure in God's great open spaces."

As Ford saw it, the Model T had but four essentials—power plant, frame, front axle and rear axle—all so designed that no special skill and no great expense would be required to repair or replace them. Those who can remember their Model T days will recall how they used to take the car apart with a monkey wrench and pliers, put the used or damaged parts in a gunny sack and take the sack to the nearest Ford station—where it would be filled with new parts in exchange for the old, plus a slight difference to pay. Then home to put the whole business together again, with an absurd sense of ego satisfaction. More Model T's were rebuilt in barns and sheds and under the shade tree than were ever sent to garage mechanics.

It is impossible for members of this generation to know what a displacement the Model T had in the lives of their fathers. It was a mechanical animal such as never existed before and will never be seen again. It changed the folkways of a nation. In 19 years Henry Ford made 15 million of them, and he brought the price down from $1200 to $295.

From the beginning of the Ford company, there were other and better cars. There was no new principle in the first Ford that other car makers did not already know, nor any new basic principle in the millions of Fords that followed. What set the company apart was the way it went about its work.

Ford's enthusiasm for cutting the price kept his engineers and managers in a state of delirium. Sometimes he would set the price of a Ford below cost, just to see if his men could work it out. They always did.

For the grand mechanics—Ford and his engineers and production men—work was play. If it hadn't been, it would have killed them. They were as men possessed. They often forgot to eat. They drove the workers, but they drove themselves much harder, and they drove the machines until the metal ached.

Once some builders were called in by the Ford factory to bid on a special machine. The specifications called for a speed that could produce 200 finished parts an hour. The builders said, "You've made a mistake. You must have meant 200 a *day*."

The Ford engineer who made the design said, "There's no mistake. Two hundred an *hour*."

"No machine can do that," said the machine builders.

The engineer said, "Before asking you to make these machines we made one for ourselves to see if it would work. It's working now—come see it."

For a new machine that did something better or a new wrinkle that saved time, the glee of Henry Ford and his engineers was like that of children with a wonderful toy. If the idea had come from a foreman or worker, Ford would stuff the man's pocket with money on the spot. Yet immediately they all tried to think of ways to make it work still better, and if anyone could do that, the wonderful toy was broken up for scrap.

When theirs was the wonder plant of the world for doing impossible things in unheard-of ways, these men were so sure they could improve on any given operation that anybody was welcome to come and look—even rival car makers.

All this could happen because Ford did not believe in experts. "Our new operations are always directed by men who have had no previous knowledge of the subject and therefore have not had a chance to get on familiar terms with the impossible," he said.

One of his illustrations was glass. He thought plate glass could be made continuously in a big ribbon with no handwork at all. The glass experts of the world said that this had been tried and could not be done. Ford gave the task to men who had never been in a glass factory. They did it with such marvelous success that now all plate glass is made that way.

The grand mechanics could do anything. To uproot an entire tractor plant and set it down in Ireland was a mere chore. Once the government wanted some anti-submarine boats, provided they could be built in a hurry without interfering with Ford's other war work. Within 120 days, at River Rouge, Ford's geniuses created a building a third of a mile long, 350 feet wide and 100 feet high, and inside it Eagle Boats—stamped out of sheet steel like automobile bodies—were being engined and equipped. And this was the work of men who had never before built a boat!

Foremost of Ford's right-hand men was Charles E. Sorensen— the "Magnificent Dane"—who began as a pattern maker in the Ford shop at $3 a day and became the great production genius of his time. Shortly before we entered World War II Sorensen went to California to see how they made airplanes there, because the Ford company was going to make planes, too. To a California manufacturer he said, "I don't understand why you first build the body of the plane and then drag everything into it through little holes."

"How would you do it?" they asked him.

"I'd build it in four sections," he said, "then stuff the sections and put them together."

That changed the method of airplane construction. It was Sorensen who built the Willow Run plant, which eventually produced a bomber an hour.

THE famous Ford assembly line—first of its kind ever installed in the world—revolutionized industrial methods. The idea came in a general way from the overhead trolley that Chicago meat packers use in dressing beef, where a butcher cuts off one part of the carcass, then pushes the carcass on to the next butcher, who takes another part, and so on. What made the Ford method epochal was the imagination, ingenuity and total logic with which assembly-line principles were applied.

Of general principles, Ford said he knew only two: A man should never have to take more than one step if it could be avoided (which meant that the man should stand still and the work come to him), and no man should have to waste time and energy stooping over (which meant that his work should be brought to him waist-high).

"Save ten steps a day for each of 12,000 employes and you will have saved 50 miles of wasted motion and misspent energy," he said. "The undirected worker spends more of his time walking about for materials and tools than he does in working. Pedestrianism is not a highly paid line!"

It all came down to one principle: *Overcome time.*

Moving the work to the man, and from one machine to another, by gravity slides and conveyor belts was first tried by Ford on what are called sub-assemblies. The engine is an example of sub-assembly—its several hundred parts are always assembled before the engine is put on the chassis. In the old way, one man assembled the Ford engine, walking around and around it until it was finished. This job was now broken down into 84 separate operations, and one man, standing still, was assigned to each operation as the engine came to him. The result: whereas previously 84 men assembled 84 engines in a given period of time, now in the same amount of time 84 men assembled 252 engines.

The first result of speeding up sub-assemblies in this manner was to produce confusion. Each sub-assembly line was a rising stream, and there was no river to take the flood. There stood the chassis, unmoving, in the middle of the floor, with people bringing engine, magneto, transmission, and so on to it. Then a thought presented itself: *The chassis had to move.* At that moment the last secret of mass production was discovered.

First Ford got a windlass and 250 feet of rope, and dragged the chassis slowly along. Everything had been timed and arranged beforehand, with sub-assemblies and parts piled along the way so that each would be within arm's reach just as the chassis arrived. The workers either walked with the chassis or rode it, doing their work as it moved, keeping their tools in their hands. Never before had a car been assembled in less than 12 hours and 28 minutes. The first one pulled along by the rope was assembled in five hours and 50 minutes.

Later the windlass and rope were thrown away and a power-driven endless conveyor belt was installed, flush with the floor, like a flat escalator. It was wide enough to hold the chassis and workers on both sides so that workers and car moved together, each man doing his assigned bit, then stepping back a few paces to repeat it on the next car.

The belt moved, at six feet a minute, past 45 stations. At each station something was added to the car. At station 45 the engine was started and the car moved away under its own power. On that first conveyor belt the time required to assemble an entire automobile was reduced from almost six hours to 93 *minutes.*

"FORTUNATELY we inherited no traditions, and we are not founding any," Ford said once. Nevertheless he *was* founding one, and on second thought he added, "If we have a tradition it is this: Everything can always be done faster and better."

No superintendent had to think of anything else but that. He would be wasting his time if he did. At the end of each day he divided the output of his department by the number of workers in it, and that was his department's score. If the score was good, everything else would come out right.

Ford's feud with time was relentless. "Time waste is the

easiest of all waste," he said, "and the hardest to correct because it does not litter the floor."

As some people can see four-leaf clovers in the grass at a glance, so in his marginal vision as he walked through the shop he could see waste of labor, energy and materials—all representing valuable time. Once he was passing a group of men testing an engine on a block before installing it in a car. "Why do we do that?" Ford asked—talking mainly to himself.

Ford went straight to his engineers. "The only reason we make a trial run of the engine is that we are not sure we made it right. Let's make sure of *that,* and stop wasting time and money on this testing." They made sure—and stopped testing.

As Ford looked further about him, he perceived that the time cost in manufacturing began the moment raw materials were separated from the earth and continued until the finished product was delivered to the consumer. Scanning his sources of supply, all he could see was a chaos of waste. Nobody doing anything the Ford way.

So the Ford Motor Company became a vast integrated manufacturing empire, getting ore from its own iron mines, fuel from its own coal mines, wood from its own forests, rubber from its own plantations, chemicals from its own vats, fabrics from its own looms. Although it continued to buy enormously from suppliers and contractors when there was advantage in it, the company made some things just to learn how, in case the suppliers should begin to charge too much, or as insurance against suppliers' failure.

A fleet of Ford boats brought iron ore from the head of the Great Lakes to the docks at Fordson on the River Rouge. Held to schedule like a railroad passenger train, a Ford ship was limited to 24 hours in port. Finding that $200 million of capital was tied up in stockpiles and warehouses, Ford abolished these sources of waste. The elapsed time from the moment the ore was separated from the earth at the mine to the appearance of the finished automobile had now been reduced from 14 days to three days and nine hours. And a Ford car could be turned out *every ten seconds!*

In shipping out finished automobiles by rail, Ford had originally followed the same procedure as other car makers, putting them aboard a freight car whole, seven to a car. But the first time he made 1000 cars in a day and tried to ship them this way, he created the worst traffic jam Detroit had ever seen. What would it be like when he wanted to ship twice that many?

So he began to ship them knocked down, to be assembled at branch plants; that way he could get 130 in one freight car. He went much further; more and more the branch plants all over the country assembled the cars and also did some manufacturing, so that only the sub-assemblies and bits and pieces went out from Detroit, and these packed with such geometric precision that a loaded freight car was as full as an eggshell.

He created a traffic department that became the day-and-night torment of the railroad people. At the moment a car of Ford freight started from anywhere, a Ford man wired in its number. At the first junction or breaking point there was another Ford man to check its arrival, see that it got on its way again, report it by wire. And so at the next point and the next one, until it arrived at its destination—and there again was a Ford man to see it to the unloading platform. If anywhere on the map a car loaded with Ford freight was an hour late, the Ford traffic department knew it and there was hell to pay.

When Ford finally had the opportunity to look back at the pattern he had established and to rationalize it and find clear words for it, he said: "The new *method* must produce the profit. Never cheapen the product. Never cheapen the wage. Never overcharge the public. Put brains and still more brains into the *method*."

This was the secret of the greatest profit maker of his age, and of any age so far.

I ONCE asked Ford where ideas come from. There was something like a saucer on the desk in front of him. He flipped it upside down, tapped the bottom with his fingers and said: "You know that atmospheric pressure is hitting this object at 14 pounds per square inch. You can't see it or feel it, but you know it is happening. It's that way with ideas. The air is full of them. They are knocking you on the head. You only have to know what you want, then forget it and go about your business. Suddenly the idea you want will come through. It was there all the time."

One day I saw this work. At lunch, Ford was talking to me and William J. Cameron, who did the company's radio broadcasts, when his tall body stiffened; the expression of his face, which had been lively, changed to that of a sleepwalker, and he said to no one in particular, "Ah-h! I'm not really thinking about that at all!"

With no other word he rose and walked rapidly away. An idea he had been wanting had come through, and he had gone to do something about it. Cameron said, "That happens often. We may not see him again for a week."

One day in the engineering laboratory Ford and I happened to pass through his private shop—a mechanic's dream. He dragged out his most precious relic. "That's it," he said.

It was the first Ford car—a small buggy box mounted on four bicycle wheels, with some tiny machinery over the rear axle. He was seven years of nights making it, while holding a job as engineer in the powerhouse of the Edison Illuminating Company of Detroit. As he identified the bits and pieces of scrap it was made of—engine cylinders from a steam exhaust pipe, wheel hubs from railroad washers, and so on—he told me of driving it for the first time by the light of a lantern on a rainy night. He could go only forward, but it got him home, where Mrs. Ford was waiting with an umbrella.

He related how he had got from the mayor of Detroit a permit to appear on the streets with it in daylight. And how when it stalled, as it sometimes did, he would chain it to a lamppost for fear someone would make off with it before he could get back with repairs. "It would run now," he said, "if they hadn't taken souvenirs from it."

Ford was persuaded by someone to set up a statistical department. A year later he ruthlessly abolished it. He found it had grown to a huge bureau—and he knew the nature of bureaus. They grow like demon weeds. If you cut one down to half size, a year later it will be twice as big. The only way to control it is to kill it.

He said that statisticians' facts are dead before they are written down, and that by the time a large collection of facts on any subject has been assembled their value has so changed that they are a record of the past and are useless, even dangerous, as guides to the future. The only facts he cared about were the ones he found as he moved forward.

JUST BEFORE Ford brought out the Model A, which succeeded the Model T, I said to him: "Now you and General Motors and Chrysler are going to make all the Fords and Chevrolets and Plymouths you can and add them to the market. Yet the total number of cars the market can absorb in a year is some definite quantity. Why can't you and they determine what that quantity is, and govern yourselves accordingly?"

"You want to take all the fun out of the game," he said.

"No," I replied, "I'm only thinking it might be possible to bring some kind of stability into the motor industry."

"Stability!" he said, as if he would bite the word. "Stability is a dead fish floating downstream. The only kind of stability we know in this country is change."

"What about unemployment from overproduction?" I asked.

"Overproduction is a false word," he said. "When you say a thing is overproduced, all you mean is that it is wrong in price or in time. I suppose today you could make too many buggies at any price. They would be wrong in time."

Ford constantly dispraised the profit motive. When business thought only of profit for the owners, "instead of providing goods for all," it frequently broke down—so frequently that scientists had invented what they called "business cycles." But a properly conducted business could not fail to return a profit. "A business absolutely devoted to service will have only one worry about profits: they will be embarrassingly large."

His company had grown from a rude frame building where a few mechanics assembled about ten cars a day to a mammoth empire capable of producing two million cars a year. All this had been paid for out of earnings. The company's total original capital was $28,000—invested by 12 individuals, all of whom were eventually bought out by Ford—and not once did the company have to borrow. Each year there had been a profit. Nearly all of it had gone back into the business to provide further means of reducing the cost of a car.

As the public, having confidence in Ford, bought his product, so it provided his capital. He felt he had no right to charge the public interest on its own money. When earnings were used to buy a mine, for example, the profit from the mine belonged to the public. "A business that makes too much profit," he said, "disappears almost as quickly as one that operates at a loss."

His way with profits seems to have proceeded at first from intuition. The theory came later. It was this: If an article costs a dollar less to produce, and you cut a dollar from the price, the result is that more people are able to buy. More buyers make a still larger business, which still further reduces the cost, which in turn increases the business again.

If on the other hand the one dollar saved is added to the manufacturer's profit, the price to the consumer remaining the same, there will be no change in the volume of business. If the dollar saved is added to wages, there will be no change in the volume of business. But when you share the profit with the public, prices go lower, business increases, more men are employed, wages increase, profits rise.

His return to the public for providing him with capital was in the lowered price of the car. When the Model T sold at $295, it was certainly the cheapest satisfaction of a material want that ever appeared in the world.

Ford pointed out that there was a difference between hard work and work well done. Men can work very hard with their hands and never create the amount of goods the world needs, and therefore not enough to exchange for the goods they themselves need. Work well done was the creation of something that satisfies a human want—and sells at a price everybody can afford. That demands production in great quantity. Men working with their hands can never produce that result.

Here, of course, is where the machine comes in. By the mechanical extension of the man the productive power of labor was enormously increased. Ford placed machines closer and closer together—"We put more machinery per square foot of floor space than any other factory in the world," he said. (The room a machine worker needed had been calculated to the inch; also the cubic air space above him, so each worker got the necessary amount of oxygen, and no space wasted.)

If you built skill into machines and caused materials to flow continuously through them, you made it possible for even unskilled workers to earn high wages. And with the product you satisfied otherwise unsatisfiable human wants. That was the pattern. Ford went so much further and faster with it than anyone else that it came to be known as the Ford Idea.

Some said he had taken skill out of work. His answer was that by putting higher skill into planning, management and tool building he made it possible for skill to be enjoyed by the man who was not skilled. And if the machine enslaved this man for eight hours a day, it also enabled him to go home earlier, to have a house such as no other unskilled worker had ever been able to afford, and to own an automobile. The machine organization, for all its hardness, did multiply the wealth and leisure of society, and increase the satisfaction of everyday living in a fabulous manner.

Henry Ford's feeling for the machine was a passion. In his philosophy, the machine was an elemental force, blindly creative, like nature. How to release this force was man's greatest discovery. The consequences were social and tremendous, and might bring many new problems, but these would be problems accompanied by hitherto-unimagined plenty, and you might trust them to solve themselves in time.

DURING the decade between the Depression and World War II the relations between government and people in this country were fundamentally altered. The welfare of the people became a direct responsibility of the government, and people became willing to surrender personal freedoms and to endure compulsions in exchange for security.

Suddenly there died the song of the wild wheel—the unrestrained, magnificently productive organism that Ford and other enterprisers had built. In place of it was heard a mighty chorus demanding that wheels be tamed—planned and governed. The delusion was that the wild wheel had caused the Depression by producing more than could be consumed, thereby causing unemployment and want.

This popular delusion seized the majority of men in business, who were willing to agree with government to limit production, regulate prices and put competition more or less in a strait-jacket. Ford rejected it completely. What he would not, or could not, see was that a world was passing.

The benefits of mass production cannot be realized unless management and labor are both free. So long as that freedom existed in the motorcar industry, the cost of an automobile went lower and lower until it became, pound for pound, the cheapest manufactured thing in the world—not only the Ford car but all American cars. And at the same time American automobile labor was the highest paid in the world.

It was estimated that one year the Model T generated, directly and indirectly, a payroll of one billion dollars, and in that year the car sold for 20 cents a pound. That could not happen again in a world of tame wheels. If the political and social conditions that exist today had existed in 1900, the American motorcar industry as we know it could not have been created.

Wholly free enterprise did not survive Ford. It was stoned to death by the multitude and buried with hymns of praise for the easier life. The obsequies were performed by the government, which assumed ultimate responsibility for the national economy; by the government's tax collector, who was to become insatiable; by organized labor, whose economic power against that of the employer was increased by law, deliberately, on the ground of social policy.

Many people like it better this way. I do not intend to argue the issue. Let me say only this: If private enterprise had not begotten the richest world that ever existed, there would have been much less for the Welfare State to distribute.

ૐ The worst thing about history is that every time it repeats itself the price goes up. *Pillar*

The Power
Men Have Over Women

Marya Mannes

[June 1964]

THE POWER men have over women is that they wear neckties, use shaving cream, and are usually bigger than we are. They are not necessarily brighter, but they usually have us where they want us. Like a man with a dog.

The cocker spaniel (or poodle or basset hound) sits at the feet of the man, waiting for three things: a look, a touch and a word. He wants these more than a bowl of dog food; he'll do anything for them.

Now, the dog is no more a slave than we women are. Like some of us he can be very independent indeed, leaving home for the day to chase rats or rabbits, quite able to feed himself and to survive the rough-and-tumble world outside. But his disposition—like ours—his well-being, his sense of security, still depend on the look in the eye, the touch of the hand and the sound of the voice of the man he returns to at night.

But the silly male fool is often unaware of how much a look, a touch, a word, can hold for a woman. Nor does he seem to have any idea at all of the degree to which their absence can make her cross, resentful, tiresome.

Let's take the eye first. Why should I look at you? the husband says; there isn't anything I don't know about you, there's nothing to look at. He does not mean it unkindly: it's just a married fact of life. You live with a woman or a picture for ten years or more, and how often do you look—really look—at that woman or picture? And yet the female is starved for more recognition: the direct glance that says, I know who you are; you are there.

It's not a question of ardor (although the warm eye is certainly preferable to the fish eye); it is a direct engagement, forging an intangible bond between man and woman. If you want to know what tragedy is, and the death of love, look at the countless married couples sitting in public places, their eyes never meeting. Not because the woman does not look at the man—she searches, hoping against reality—but because the man does not look at her. The engagement is broken. Each sits alone, encased in a plastic bag of indifference.

It is clearly easier for a man to look at something that is beautiful and new and exciting than at something that is familiar and possibly fading. But he forgets that the familiarity and the fading are, in part, of his doing, and that a woman is invested with beauty and excitement by his attention. We bloom under it; we die without it.

Now for the hand. A woman who is not touched may exist as a person but not as a woman. Here again I am not talking of ardor. It is the exceptional man who, after 15 years of marriage and a long day at the office, can lunge at his wife and cover her with passionate kisses. No, women—even the most spirited—are much humbler than that. An occasional hand placed fondly on the shoulder, an arm in arm, a brief kiss on the cheek; things like these make us so happy that we wonder why some men forget them. Are they really that much trouble and effort? We are lovable if we are loved, and part of loving is touching.

We need words, too. Not only the comfortable exchange of thoughts and gossip, cozy and welcome as that is, but once in a while words beamed (like the look) directly at us.

Gentlemen, you have heard it before and you shall hear it again: when we wear a new dress and you notice it, say *something*. One phrase will do: "Nice color," or "Not bad," or "Wow!" If you don't say anything, we count it a failure. You don't know what power this silence has over us. We brood. It doesn't matter how good we think our taste is, how sure we are of our fashion sense; your silence can shatter our confidence. We would rather have you say, "Isn't that a little too tight?" than nothing at all. We'd rather be mad than ignored. There is nothing in the world that makes a woman walk more proudly and gaily than the verbal pat. Wise men know this.

The men who have wit must know what power this, too, can exert on a woman. Make her laugh and you've made her helpless. Women are far more likely to be enslaved on a long-term basis by a homely man who is funny than by an Adonis who isn't. In fact, the higher the sights of a woman, the freer her intelligence, the more she values intelligence in men. It exerts a compelling fascination that many men are still slow to recognize, since they confuse it with rivalry or competition. It is woman asking the most of man so that she can pay him homage. The strong silent man is powerless beside the witty articulate man. The right word is a mighty weapon.

Of course, all these powers of men over women emanate from one premise: caring. If men don't care, they don't look or touch or speak. And if they don't look or touch or speak, they shouldn't be living with us anyway.

But here we come, I think, to the old and lingering inequity between the sexes. Everything in the long history of the male has conspired toward his self-assurance as a superior being. Everything in the long history of the female has conspired toward her adaptability to him, whether as wife, lover or mother. We are bred to care for what he thinks, feels and needs more than he is for what we think, feel and need.

There is no valid comparison between a man's economic support of a woman and her hourly involvement in caring for him. We worry more when he looks seedy than he does when we do, because we notice him more. We concern ourselves daily with what he would like to eat, whom he would like to see, where he would like to go.

And this remains true even now, with all this talk of equality and emancipation, and in spite of the very real evolution of women into complete human beings. For there can be no love without this caring and catering by women. The only difference now is that it is voluntary when it used to be obligatory: no longer the price of room and board, but the tender of love, freely given.

*   *   *

In response to the above article, more than 1500 readers wrote to the Digest to express themselves on the converse theme, the power women have over men. Fortunately, many men and women have a sense of humor about the battle of the sexes. "May it never turn into a cold war," wrote one. Another summarized it all: "The power of women over men is 'NO!' "

A woman wrote: "In a room full of people, it is neither the most beautiful woman nor the most brilliant who is remembered. It is the woman who yields a warmth that lets others know she is interested, and who thereby encourages a shy man to talk, a talking one to think, a thinking one to inquire. I have seen stone men melted by graciousness and strong men flattered limp; stupid men made brilliant, brilliant men shattered—and shattered men made whole again—by a responsive woman."

One important aspect was mentioned frequently: sex. "We men are physiologically committed to the pursuit of love. This is the force which attracts mates and forms a cornerstone for the man-woman relationship. Women possess the magnetic charm and the inborn knowledge of when and how to activate the magnet. Herein lies the power of women over men. We cannot live without you. How we live *with* you has become the concern of the clergy, marriage counselors and bartenders."

A man: "During the Depression of the 1930s, I met a girl—small, slender, perhaps a hundred and ten pounds. Some said she was beautiful. I could not tell. For you see, I was in love. For nearly a year she played the line deftly, surely, keeping the slack reeled in, never applying enough tension to break the silk; then one quick sweep of the net, and I was caught.

"Now, six babies and half as many decades later, she is pudgy and graying. Some might say she is dowdy. I cannot tell. You see, I am in love. For 30 years she has played the line deftly, surely, keeping the slack reeled in, never applying enough tension to break the silk; and heaven holds the sweeping net."

Secrets of a Soviet Assassin

Isaac Don Levine

[January 1960]

"I PUT MY raincoat on the table
so that I could take out the *piolet* [ice ax] in the pocket. When
Trotsky started to read my article, I took the ax and, closing my
eyes, gave him a tremendous blow on the head.

"The man screamed in a way that I will never forget—
Aaaaa! . . . very long, infinitely long. He got up like a madman,
threw himself at me and bit my hand—look, you can still see the
marks of his teeth. Then I pushed him, so that he fell to the
floor."

With these words the most mysterious assassin of our time—
the man who calls himself Jacques Mornard—described his
murder of Leon Trotsky, exiled patriarch of Bolshevism. It took
place on August 20, 1940, inside the steel-shuttered walls of
Trotsky's heavily guarded villa on the outskirts of Mexico City.
"Mornard" was convicted and sentenced to 20 years in the
Mexican Federal Penitentiary.

In August 1960 this man will be freed. For all this time he
has resolutely refused to disclose his identity, motives or political ties. Despite the mask, his true identity has gradually been
pieced together over the years. He is Ramon Mercader del Rio,
a Spaniard now 46 years old, Moscow-trained in the art of
murder. He killed Trotsky on the orders of the world's most
fearsome secret-police organization, the Soviet State Security,
then called the NKVD. But his stubborn refusal to admit his

397

identity has enabled the organizers of the crime to disavow any connection with it.

When he was arrested, the police found on him a three-page statement typewritten in French, dated and signed at the last moment in pencil. It stated that he was the son of "an old Belgian family," that he had been caught up in the Trotskyite movement while studying journalism in Paris. He had met Trotsky and become disenchanted, and finally moved to kill him when the old Bolshevik tried to force him to go to the Soviet Union to organize an assassination plot against Stalin.

These claims, and amplifying details the prisoner gave after his arrest, were quickly proved absurd: the people, schools and addresses he mentioned were nonexistent or totally unlike his descriptions. But no logic could make him change his story.

For six months "Mornard" was given an intensive psychological examination by Dr. José Gomez Robleda, head of the department of medical-biological studies at the National University of Mexico, and Dr. Alfonso Quiroz Cuaron, professor of criminology. The doctors found the killer an extraordinary man. He was fluent in several languages. Attractive to women, he could be ingratiating to men and would pass for a gentleman anywhere. He had superior intelligence, remarkable self-possession, a gift for acting. He displayed a marked interest in gambling, mountain climbing, small-craft sailing. His coördination, dexterity and mechanical aptitudes were unusual: given a Mauser rifle, he proceeded to dismantle it in the dark and put it back together in less than four minutes.

His responses to word-association tests showed the prisoner to be deeply indoctrinated in Stalinist views, and he betrayed his Moscow training on several occasions. At one point, for example, he made a passing reference to a man named Kamo—a figure almost unknown in the West but a hero within the NKVD, whose history is taught in Soviet schools for infiltration and sabotage. A test of "Mornard's" pronunciation showed that his "native French," although excellent, bore traces of a Spanish accent, and he showed a striking familiarity with anything Spanish. The evidence suggested a Spanish communist background.

But it was not until September 1950 that Dr. Quiroz Cuaron found the proof in police archives in Madrid: the fingerprints of a man named Ramon Mercader, arrested in Barcelona in 1935 as a communist youth organizer, tallied with those of "Mornard." So did pictures.

Don Pablo Mercader Marina, a tall elderly man now living in retirement in Barcelona, took a good look at a photograph of the Trotsky killer. "Yes," he said, "that's my son." Don Pablo did not know of his son's crime. Long removed from the family, he did not want to re-establish contact with any of them.

Since then, further revelations by ex-communists have established additional facts in Mornard-Mercader's strange history. This is the story:

Ramon Mercader was born in Barcelona in 1913, the second child of Caridad del Rio Hernandez and Don Pablo, a conservative gentleman of good but not too prosperous family. Ramon's mother, a spirited young society matron, was a strikingly attractive woman, quick-tempered and unpredictable, who at the dangerous age of 33 developed a compulsion to adventure. She began to associate with bohemians and revolutionaries, and in 1925 she moved to France. Here she joined the Communist Party, had numerous love affairs with French communist leaders, and worked as an underground courier.

Ramon, who lived part of the time with his mother, part with his father, worshiped his mother and was soon drawn into her communist associations. When the Spanish Civil War started in 1936, he and his mother were among the first to volunteer to fight Franco.

At this point a new love entered the life of Caridad Mercader: Leonid Eitingon, a general in the NKVD who, under the name of General Kotov, was organizing Loyalist commando and sabotage units in Spain. One of his students was Ramon Mercader. What neither Ramon nor Caridad may have known at this time was that Eitingon was also a leading officer of a special NKVD division in charge of liquidating Soviet political enemies on foreign soil. Their No. 1 target: Trotsky.

Lev Davidovich Bronstein, known to the world as Leon Trotsky, had designed and engineered with Lenin the Bolshevik Revolution of November 1917. Stalin was at that time a semi-obscure henchman of Lenin's, but after Lenin's death he maneuvered to isolate Trotsky politically, and in 1929 expelled him from the Soviet Union. Since then Trotsky had lived the life of a hunted man, pursued by Stalin's killers from one place to another. One by one his retinue was picked off: his secretary was killed in Spain; his son died suddenly in Paris, apparently poisoned. Finally in 1937 Trotsky sought refuge in Mexico.

Caridad and Ramon were now in Moscow with Eitingon, and Ramon was receiving highly specialized training in the arts of terror. Plans for the great assassination were already being laid. What kind of man was needed to deal with Trotsky in Mexico? Spanish-speaking Ramon Mercader must have seemed an obvious choice.

In the Byzantine way of the Soviet secret police, it was decided that Mercader should ingratiate himself with the Trotsky household by seducing one of its female couriers, Sylvia Ageloff, a young American social worker and loyal member of the U. S. Trotskyite group. The NKVD arranged for Ramon to meet Sylvia "by chance" in Paris in the summer of 1938. Young, personable, well-supplied with money, he became her constant companion.

Ramon followed Sylvia to New York on a false passport issued in the name of Frank Jacson. (Embarrassingly, Soviet documentation experts had misspelled "Jackson.") Sylvia and he took a temporary apartment in Greenwich Village. Then "Jacson" announced that he had been offered a job in Mexico City, and in January 1940 Sylvia followed him there. Eitingon was in Mexico to supervise the assassination, and with him was Caridad Mercader.

Ramon's role at this point, Caridad had assured a friend, was solely that of a spy—to find out the nature of the security system at Trotsky's villa at Coyoacán, a Mexico City suburb. Through Sylvia he gained entree. During visits there, although he did not at first meet Trotsky, Ramon roamed through the house, snapping pictures with a concealed camera but relying on his photographic memory for most of the details. His material was sent to Moscow and placed in a special dossier of the

NKVD. (A Soviet intelligence officer who defected in Australia in 1954 saw this dossier in 1948. It contained "complete documentation of Trotsky's life right up to his last days.")

In the early-morning hours of May 24, 1940, the Soviet spy command in Mexico tried an audacious frontal assault on the Trotsky dwelling. A group of 20 men, dressed in Mexican police and army uniforms, drove up to the residence, stormed through the gate, and delivered murderous submachine-gun fire into the bedrooms where the Trotskys and their 11-year-old grandson were sleeping. Amazingly, all three survived—by throwing themselves under their beds. After a month's investigation by the Mexican police, some two dozen persons were arrested. Ramon Mercader, however, remained above suspicion.

Only four days after the armed attack, Mercader offered to drive Mrs. Trotsky to Vera Cruz with some mutual friends. It was on this occasion that Ramon first met his future victim. He entered the villa's courtyard and chatted briefly and courteously with Trotsky. He gave Trotsky's grandson a small glider as a present. Only a man of iron nerve could have carried on with such an assignment so soon after an attempted assassination which he had helped to stage.

Moscow now decided on a single-handed attempt. "Jacson" stepped up his infiltration program. During the last three weeks in July he paid the Trotskys five visits, never neglecting such friendly little gestures as bringing candy for Mrs. Trotsky.

On August 17 Ramon visited the master with the outline of an article he was writing. Trotsky had agreed to check it over. The two men spent 11 minutes alone in Trotsky's study. Trotsky remarked to his wife afterward that the young man's behavior had seemed strange. That visit was the "dress rehearsal."

At 5:20 on August 20 Ramon Mercader showed up at the Trotsky villa with his completed article to show Trotsky. He was carrying a khaki raincoat. Sewn into it was a long dagger, and in one pocket he carried the ice ax, its stock cut down for easy concealment. In the back pocket of his trousers he carried a .45-caliber automatic. He hoped to accomplish his mission with a single crushing blow of the ax, and get away quietly.

If any mishap should occur, he would shoot his way out.

The guards recognized him and opened the double electric doors of the fortress villa without hesitation. One guard led him to Trotsky, who was feeding his pet rabbits in the courtyard, and obviously did not want to tear himself away. But finally he took off his working gloves and walked into the house. Ramon followed him to the study, where Trotsky closed the door and sat down at his worktable. A few inches from his hand was a loaded .25-caliber automatic. Ramon stood at his left side, blocking off the switch to the house alarm system.

Trotsky took the article and started to read. At that exact moment Ramon seized the ice ax and, closing his eyes, smashed it down on his victim's skull, penetrating almost three inches into the brain.

With a fearful cry, Trotsky threw himself at the killer and grappled with him. Mrs. Trotsky rushed to the study to find her husband stumbling dazedly from the room. "See what they have done to me!" he said, and slumped to the floor.

Trotsky's bodyguards swarmed into the room and began to hammer away at Ramon. Mrs. Trotsky addressed a curiously detached question to her still-conscious husband. "What about that one?" she asked, gesturing toward the assassin. "They will kill him."

"No . . . impermissible to kill," Trotsky said slowly. "He must be forced to talk." Rushed to the hospital, Trotsky was operated on, but he died 26 hours later.

A block away Caridad was sitting in a chauffeur-driven car, a bizarre parody of the anxious mother waiting for her son to come home from work. General Eitingon was waiting in another car nearby. When the police alarm sounded and an ambulance came through the streets, they realized that Ramon had not got away. Caridad drove immediately to the airport, and with a forged passport flew to Cuba. Eitingon drove all night to Acapulco, where he boarded a waiting Soviet freighter.

Some weeks later Caridad rejoined Eitingon in Moscow. There Lavrenti Beria, head of the NKVD, himself presented her to Stalin. She received the Order of Lenin—communism's highest decoration—and her son was cited as a Hero of the

Soviet Union. To a friend in Moscow she proudly spoke of these honors.

Caridad spent the war years in the Soviet Union, receiving assurances from her lover Eitingon and his Kremlin superiors that an operation to rescue her son would be launched. Stalin proved reluctant to redeem the pledge but eventually allowed her to try to organize an escape. She arrived in Mexico City in March 1945 but was unable to achieve her objective—or even to see her son, so ironclad was the regime imposed on her by the NKVD to ensure the secrecy of the assassin's identity.

Now 67 and white-haired, Caridad lives in Paris amid disillusionment. The years in the Soviet Union served to cure her of some of her communism. "You are right," she said in Moscow to an intimate Spanish comrade of independent views. "We have been deceived. This is not paradise. It is hell."

Sylvia Ageloff, when she learned that her lover had killed Trotsky, went into a nervous collapse from which it took years to recover. She finally married and is now living quietly in New York City. Trotsky's widow still lives in the same house in Coyoacán. Eitingon is dead, a victim—with his master, Beria —of the 1953 purges after Stalin's death.

Mercader became Mexico's model prisoner. Since 1952 he has run the penitentiary radio-repair shop, a small but profitable business. He is comfortable, having taken advantage of the lenient Mexican prison regulations to ensure special food, books—and the regular visits of a girl named Roquelia Mendoza, a Mexico City nightclub performer. (Prisoners are permitted conjugal visits from wives or common-law wives.)

Now double-chinned and corpulent, Ramon Mercader looks like a relaxed bourgeois businessman. He has few friends inside prison, but he operates his radio shop with cool efficiency, reads fitfully—and through underground channels he keeps in touch with the communist network outside.

He has never stopped giving his name as Jacques Mornard.

*　　*　　*

Upon release from prison in 1960, Mercader went to Cuba. Fifteen days later he flew to Prague, then to Moscow. He is believed to be working in the U.S.S.R. under some other name.

The Fraudulent Ant

Mark Twain

[July 1943]

I T SEEMS to me that in the matter of intellect the ant is strangely overrated. During many summers I have watched him, when I ought to have been in better business, and I have not yet come across a living ant that seemed to have any more sense than a dead one. I refer to the ordinary ant; I have had no experience of those wonderful Swiss and African ones which vote, keep drilled armies, hold slaves and dispute about religion. Those ants may be all that the naturalist paints them, but I am persuaded that the average ant is a sham. I admit his industry, of course; he is the hardest-working creature in the world—when anybody is looking. But his leather-headedness is the point I make against him.

He goes out foraging, he makes a capture, and then what does he do? Go home? No, he doesn't know where home is. It may be only three feet away, no matter, he can't find it. His capture is generally something which can be of no use to himself or anybody else; it is usually seven times bigger than it ought to be; he hunts out the awkwardest place to take hold of it; he lifts it bodily in the air, and starts—not toward home, but in the opposite direction; not calmly and wisely, but with a frantic haste; he fetches up against a pebble, and instead of going around it, he climbs over it backward dragging his booty after him, tumbles down on the other side, jumps up in a passion, kicks the dust off his clothes, moistens his hands, grabs his property viciously, yanks it this way, then that, shoves it ahead of him a moment, lugs it after him another moment, gets madder and madder, then presently hoists it into the air and goes tearing away in an entirely new direction.

At the end of half an hour of rustling about, he fetches up within six inches of the place he started from and lays his burden down. Now he wipes the sweat from his brow, strokes his limbs, and then marches aimlessly off, in as violent a hurry as ever. He traverses a good deal of zigzag country, and by and by stumbles on his same booty again. He does not remember that he ever saw it before; he looks around to see which is not the way home, grabs his bundle and starts; he goes through the same adventures he had before.

Finally he stops to rest, and a friend comes along. Evidently the friend remarks that a last year's grasshopper leg is a very noble acquisition, and contracts to help him freight it home. They take hold of opposite ends of that grasshopper leg and begin to tug with all their might in opposite directions. Presently they take a rest and confer together. They decide that something is wrong, they can't make out what. Each accuses the other of being an obstructionist. The dispute ends in a fight. They lock themselves together and chew each other's jaws for a while; then they roll and tumble on the ground till one loses a horn or a leg and has to haul off for repairs. They make up and go to work again in the same old insane way, but the crippled ant is at a disadvantage; tug as he may, the other one drags off the booty and him at the end of it.

By and by, when that grasshopper leg has been dragged all over the same old ground once more, it is finally dumped at about the spot where it originally lay. The two perspiring ants inspect it thoughtfully and decide that dried grasshopper legs are a poor sort of property after all, and then each starts off in a different direction to see if he can't find something else that is heavy enough to afford entertainment and at the same time valueless enough to make an ant want to own it.

Just today I saw an ant go through such a performance as this with a dead spider of fully ten times his own weight, which he finally left in the middle of the road to be confiscated by any other fool of an ant that wanted it. I measured the ground which this ass traversed, and arrived at the conclusion that what he had accomplished inside of 20 minutes would constitute some such job as this—relatively speaking—for a man; to wit: to strap two 800-pound horses together, carry them 1800 feet, mainly over (not around) boulders averaging six feet high, and in the course of the journey climb up and jump from the top of one precipice like Niagara, and three high steeples; and then put the horses down, in an exposed place, without anybody to watch them.

Science has discovered that the ant does not lay up anything for winter use. He is a deceiver who does not work, except when people are looking, and only then when an observer has a green, naturalistic look and seems to be taking notes. He cannot stroll around a stump and find his way home again. This amounts to idiocy. His vaunted industry is but a vanity, since he never gets home with anything he starts with. This disposes of the last remnant of his reputation and wholly destroys his main usefulness as a moral agent.

It is strange, beyond comprehension, that so manifest a humbug as the ant has been able to fool so many nations so many ages without being found out.

Mother's Moments

⧉ "I have the kind of boy," says a Washington mother, "who nearly drives you crazy when you try to get him to carry out the garbage, and then on the way back he'll bring you a flower."

Marjorie Holmes in Washington *Star*

⧉ My four-year-old sister went to where my mother was at work in the kitchen, looked up at her adoringly and exclaimed, "Mother, I like you better than any other leading brand!" Kerry Klein

⧉ Eight-year-old's essay on "What a mom means to a kid": "A mother is a person who takes care of her kids and gets their meals, and if she's not there when you get home from school you wouldn't know how to get your dinner and you wouldn't feel like eating it anyhow."

Executives' Digest

Nightmare of Dust

Avis D. Carlson

[June 1935]

IN THE western half of Kansas, spring is a time of flowing green wheat fields, of wild-plum thickets foaming into whiteness, of anemones and wild verbena, of blue-blue skies washing into infinity, of sweet, clean curtains, of hope and joy stored against the scorching summer to come.

But this is the spring of 1935. Nothing is as usual. It is like a long nightmare from which we cannot get free. Even a shower brings no lift of spirit. For until it rains, and rains all along that mighty strip of drought-baked prairie running from Canada to the Gulf and reaching to the feet of the Rockies, our own showers are futile. Once we had a rain that lasted all day. Hope stirred. But that night the northwest wind came up. In the morning dust lay thick and brown over everything.

Even the storms are losing their drama. They are simply something that must be endured. Sometimes they strike in the night. Only if we are brave and the stars are bright at bedtime do we open a window. We sleep with ears set to catch the first rattle of window panes, the first bang of the garden gate. If we do not hear these warnings the dust comes in upon us. It drifts in like snow. It settles upon the blankets. It is drawn into our noses and lungs. It creeps into our dreams. Deeper and deeper into our helpless bodies it burrows until finally it wakes us.

Noses burning, throats raw, we run to the window. Bare toes strike into the plushy dust-drifts on the floor. Fumbling hands

LET THERE BE RAIN

O Lord, in Thy mercy grant us rain and by that we don't mean a shower. We want to go out and watch the lightning rip across the southwestern sky in hot blue forks as the fat clouds roll in on us. We want to hurry home to close the house, with the first fat drops the size of marbles, on a suddenly rising wind, chasing us and plunking on the car hood. We want to scramble all over the house, just as the first few sheets descend, frantically slamming down the windows.

O Lord of hosts, we want to look out the windows and watch the regiments of close-packed raindrops march diagonally down. We want to hear the gurgle of the gutters under the eaves, and then the sputter of the downspout.

God of Israel, Isaac and Jacob, let it come down so hard, let the drops dance so high that the streets and sidewalks seem covered with a six-inch fog of spatter-drops. Then let it just keep up for a while, and then begin to taper off, and then turn right around and get a lot worse, swishing, pounding, splattering,

send an acrid shower fuming out of the curtains. The window is bolted down now. But the air inside the room, the air we must breathe, is thick. A wet bath towel flapped about collects some of the dust. A few flaps and it is black. A trip for water to rinse the grit from our lips. And then back to bed with wet washcloths over our noses. We try to lie still because every turn stirs the dust on the blankets.

The day storms are worse because then we cannot lose ourselves in sleep. They come in various ways. Sometimes, after raging and roaring all night, the wind dies down in the early morning. But the dust it has whipped thousands of feet into the air still hangs over us. It must fall, all of it—from the height of a mile, of two miles. It falls slowly because it is incredibly fine. Sweeping it from the porch is like sweeping the finest talc.

Strange world. The dawn is not coming today. The quiet is

pouring, drenching, the thunder coming—crackity-BAM!—and the lightning flashing so fast and furious you can't tell which flash goes with which peal of thunder. So that all the women will get scared and climb on top of the beds and scream at you not to get too close to that window.

And then, O jealous God, repeat the whole act about three times, and in the middle of the second time we will climb the attic stairs and put the wash pan under that tiny leak in the roof which usually you can't even notice in an ordinary rain. And after a couple of hours kind of taper it down, O Lord, to a good steady rain—not a drizzle but a businesslike one that keeps up until just about dawn and then spits a few drops occasionally during the morning from a gray sky.

Kansas is indeed the Promised Land, O Lord, and if it gets a break it will flow with milk and honey. But we can't live much longer on promises. So in Thine own way and in Thine own time, make up Thy mind, O Lord, and we will bow before Thy judgment, and praise Thine everlasting name. Amen.

William L. White, Emporia *Gazette*, 1935

spectral. Even the children are awed. No dawn, no schools, no traffic, almost no work. The boss phones not to try to come down, there's no business anyway.

It is hell for housewives. They wash the kitchen stove, wash the worktable, wash each cooking utensil as they use it. Breakfast is ready at last. When robins should be foraging on the lawn and lilacs purpling by the kitchen window, breakfast by lamplight has an unearthly quality. Dust everywhere, a brown layer of it thickening on all the furniture, creeping into every crevice, befouling every dear possession.

At last the air thins somewhat, and lighted automobiles begin to crawl along the highway. No speeding now. Even the lackwit driver creeps cautiously, worming his way along a highway banked with snow fences drifted level full. Slowly, slowly, the pall lifts and eyes resume seeing. An apple tree buried to the crotch in red sand makes a pitiful attempt to bloom. It cannot quite forget spring. A farmhouse has been sunk to the windows. Fields are bare as the desert floor. Quiet everywhere.

Or the storm may be dramatic. A black or yellow or copper-brown cloud pokes its head over the horizon. It rises slowly at first, then swiftly. It marches angrily, blotting out the world as it comes. Children scurry like chickens to their mother's wing. With a howl the storm bursts upon us. The impact is like a shovelful of fine sand flung against the face. People caught in their own yards grope for the doorstep. Cars come to a standstill, for no light in the world can penetrate that swirling murk.

Dust masks are snatched from pockets and cupboards. But masks do not protect the mouth. Grit cracks between the teeth, the dust taste lies bitter on the tongue, grime is harsh between the lips.

The house rocks and mumbles. Dust comes in, driven somehow through bolted windows, even through windows sealed with adhesive tape. It seems to sift through the very walls. The family huddles together. If quiet storms excite brooding anxiety, this one is pure terror even to plains people hardened to the wind. The darkness is like the end of the world.

In time the fury subsides. If the wind has spent itself the dust will fall silently for hours. If the wind has only settled into a good steady blow the air will be thick for days. During those days, as much of the living as possible will be moved to the basement, while pounds and pounds of dust sift into the house. It is something, however, to have the house stop rocking.

The nightmare is deepest during the storms. But even on the occasional bright day and the usual gray day we cannot shake free from it. We live with the dust, eat it, sleep with it, watch it strip us of possessions and the hope of possessions. Life is a blank like the coppery darkness outside. We wait, simply wait, while the dust falls. The idle hours drag on. All the sadness humanity has ever known distills itself into these hours of waiting. Foreboding gnaws at the soul. The old racial sense of utter helplessness in a hostile universe returns. The poetic uplift of spring fades into a phantom of the storied past.

The nightmare of dust is becoming Life.

Facts Behind
the Cigarette Controversy

Lois Mattox Miller and James Monahan

The Reader's Digest has been a major force in alerting people to the risks in cigarette smoking. The magazine's dozens of feature articles on the subject have exerted, the American Cancer Society notes, a "profound influence on public awareness." In the 1950s and '60s Roving Editors Lois Mattox Miller and James Monahan wrote a newsmaking, award-winning series on those risks. This article was first in the series.

A sidelight: From the time it began to take advertising, the Digest has refused all tobacco ads. The income thereby relinquished amounts, by conservative estimate, to some 60 million dollars thus far.

[July 1954]

LATE in 1953 tobacco advertisers were noisily hawking cigarettes that were milder, safer, freer from harsh ingredients than competing brands. New brands with filter tips made the din more deafening by boasting about the harmful tars and nicotine they removed. Then the ballyhoo backfired with a bang.

An impressive number of medical scientists agreed with the ads that there was indeed something noxious in cigarettes which ought to concern every smoker. And that unidentified factor, they said, was related somehow to the alarming rise in deaths from lung cancer. Investigators at the Memorial Center for

Cancer and Allied Diseases in New York, and the Washington University School of Medicine in St. Louis, announced that they had positively induced epidermoid cancer in mice merely by painting the animals' backs with tar derived from cigarette smoke.

That was the beginning of the current cigarette controversy. Since then the issue has been clouded with countercharges and recriminations. The increase in lung cancer has been called more apparent than real. Statistical studies have been challenged, and the relevance of the mouse-cancer experiments minimized. What are the facts?

Before World War I, lung cancer was rare. But after 1920, U. S. doctors began to encounter it more and more frequently and there was a sharp uptrend in deaths: 3400 in 1933, 8800 in 1942, 22,000 in 1952. Dr. E. Cuyler Hammond, chief of statistical research for the American Cancer Society, declares: "The trend shows every indication of continuing." The future implications make cancer specialists shudder.

Is the increase, as some claim, merely the result of improved diagnostic methods? Few responsible authorities think so. The American Cancer Society states: "Part may be, but it is now generally agreed that most of the increase is real."

Lung cancer is predominantly epidermoid cancer, which unlike other types seems to be influenced by an external carcinogen or cancer-producing agent. So when scientists began their search for the lung carcinogen they looked for some factor increasingly present in our environment during the past half century—preferably something inhaled into human lungs.

Obviously, the very air we breathe has become increasingly polluted with smoke, soot, chemicals, fumes from gasoline and fuel oils. Some of these contain recognized carcinogens. So air pollution is getting careful study. But this theory stumbles over one fact—men and women breathe the same air about equally; yet lung cancer is eight times more prevalent among males than among females. Hence, if the major cause of lung cancer is something inhaled, the inhalant must be something that figures differently in the habits of males and females.

Suspicion of tobacco was inevitable. And when researchers

412

compared the sales figures for cigarettes and the statistics for lung cancer they noticed a remarkable parallel. *On the charts the rising lung-cancer curve bears a striking resemblance to the curve which plots the cigarette sales.*

Lung cancer usually occurs in men over 45. There is good reason to believe that there is a time lag of 20 years or more in its development. Hence doctors saw a link between rising cigarette consumption in 1920–30 and mounting lung-cancer deaths in 1940–50. If the relationship is real, the booming cigarette sales of 1940–50 indicate a soaring death rate in 1960–70.

What about women? They took up smoking slowly during the 1920s, and the habit became widespread after 1930. Even today there are fewer women than men smokers, and fewer still are heavy smokers. Yet the lung-cancer death rate among women has increased in proportion to their consumption of cigarettes, and is still rising.

Could this be mere coincidence? At Washington University young Dr. Ernest L. Wynder won approval for an ambitious research project from his chief, Dr. Evarts A. Graham, distinguished professor of surgery who performed the first successful removal of a cancerous lung. Wynder proposed to shelve the "circumstantial evidence" of the statistics and to study the tobacco-lung-cancer relationship at firsthand.

In a dozen states he enlisted the coöperation of hospitals that had many patients with lung cancer and many more without. Staff interviewers carefully took down each patient's age, personal history, smoking habits, etc. The Wynder-Graham studies, published in 1950, showed that of 650 men with lung cancer, 95 percent had been smoking for 20 years or more. The doctors observed: "The occurrence of carcinoma of the lung in a male nonsmoker is a rare phenomenon." They concluded: "Excessive and prolonged use of tobacco, especially cigarettes, seems to be an important factor in the induction of bronchiogenic carcinoma (lung cancer)."

The report created quite a stir in the medical profession. Some doctors flatly refused to recognize tobacco as the culprit. Dr. Wynder told the Cancer Prevention Committee: "Those physicians who were hardest set against believing that tobacco might play a role in the etiology of lung cancer were heavy smokers themselves. It is only human for one not to believe that harm can come from something one likes."

But more evidence was on the way. From 1948 to 1952 Drs. Richard Doll and A. Bradford Hill interviewed nearly 5000 patients in British hospitals. Out of 1357 men with lung cancer, *all but seven* were smokers. Doll and Hill concluded: "Smoking is an important factor in the production of cancer of the lung."

To date, 13 independent studies of the tobacco-cancer relationship have been made in five different countries. While the findings differ in degree, all these investigators come to the same conclusion: lung cancer occurs more frequently among smokers than among nonsmokers.

The relationship is recognized today by most authorities. The American Cancer Society now takes the official position "that evidence to date justifies the suspicion that smoking does, to a degree not yet determined, increase the likelihood of developing lung cancer."

Why, then, don't all or most cigarette smokers develop the disease? The theory has been offered that everyone inherits either a constitutional susceptibility or an immunity to cancer-causing agents. This gives the smoker poor consolation—who knows whether he is among the lucky or the unlucky?

What is the particular agent in tobacco smoke that causes lung cancer? Drs. Wynder and Graham and Dr. Adele Croninger have recently proved beyond doubt that there is something within tobacco tar which can cause cancer in mice. To produce the tar, the doctors rigged up an apparatus that puffed 60 cigarettes at once. The smoke was drawn into glass condensing flasks. After the tar was extracted it was painted on the shaved backs of mice three times each week. After an average of 71 weeks, about half of a mouse life span, 44 percent of the tarred mice developed cancer—epidermoid cancer, the type that occurs in human lungs.

Obviously, mouse skin is not human lung tissue. But the point of the experiment was simply to establish, using a test animal, that there is a carcinogen in tobacco tar. The next step is to determine which fraction of tobacco tar is the carcinogen.

That work is now under way at the Institute of Industrial Medicine at the New York University Postgraduate Medical School. There tobacco tar goes through an endless fractionation process. Then each fraction must be tested separately on mice.

But every tar fraction in turn contains an enormous number of chemical compounds. Coal-tar research has proved that some of these—particularly the hydrocarbons formed when any organic substance burns at high temperature—can cause cancer. Are such carcinogenic hydrocarbons formed in a burning cigarette? That's one big question they are trying to answer.

In 1953 a German scientist, Dr. H. Druckrey, performed a startling demonstration, since repeated by others. It is based on the fact that certain chemical compounds, including the hydrocarbons, show a fluorescence when exposed to ultraviolet light.

Druckrey had his students smoke cigarettes and—without inhaling—blow the smoke into a flask of purified benzene. Then the flask was exposed to ultraviolet light; the intensity of the glow was measured with a spectrograph. By chemical analysis Druckrey identified more than 50 percent of the fluorescent material as "higher aromatic hydrocarbons." The most dramatic phase came next. Druckrey now had his subjects smoke another cigarette and *inhale the smoke* before blowing it into the flask. Measurements showed that virtually all the fluorescent materials —including the hydrocarbons—*remained in the lungs.*

"With inhalation," he reported, "more than 90 percent of the fluorescent materials was retained. So in the course of a lifetime the bronchial tract would be systematically tarred. Therefore, the cancer risk from tobacco smoke is incurred especially by inhaling."

Can the tars be filtered from the smoke? Druckrey investigated various cigarette filters and generally confirmed the findings of the investigation made in 1953 by the American Medical Association. The most efficient tips and holders absorbed only 50 percent of the tars; some filter tips screened out less than ten percent. And how about the potentially most dangerous fractions of the tars? "The investigated filters," Druckrey reported, "offer no protection against the higher aromatic hydrocarbons." So, if filtration is the protection of the future, the tobacco companies will have to produce a more efficient filter than any they offer today.

The U. S. Public Health Service is now canvassing the smoking habits of more than 80,000 World War I veterans who are in the age brackets most likely to show lung cancer. And the American Cancer Society, through its volunteer field workers, has tabulated the smoking habits of 204,000 men between the ages of 50 and 69. These men are followed up annually. When one dies the cause of death is determined, and if it is cancer the medical records are studied carefully. These studies are likely to confirm the findings of previous surveys. Dr. Hammond cites another possibility: "It may turn out that cigarette smoking not only greatly increases the probability of lung cancer but also markedly increases the death rate from other causes."

Investigators outside the cancer field—particularly those concerned with heart and vascular diseases—agree. They feel that the lung-cancer problem has diverted needed attention from tobacco's effects on other vital organs.

That's where we stand now. The final answer must come from chemical, biological and clinical studies now under way in many research institutions. Meanwhile, cigarette smokers should weigh the available evidence and ask themselves: Are the psychological pleasures of the habit worth the possible risks involved? Each individual must answer for himself.

---

§➤ The new math? Well, here's a bit which was new more than a thousand years ago when introduced by a Moroccan genius whose work was the first to be called algebra. According to Mrs. Abdelkri Boujibar, director of the Museum of Morocco, this genius conceived

the figures 0 through 9 which we know today as Arabic numerals, and he shaped them so that each contained an appropriate number of angles, as shown in the illustration. His figure 1 contains one angle, his 2 two angles, 3 three angles, etc. Zero, signifying nothing, had no angles. Charles McHarry, Chicago Tribune-New York News Syndicate

The Twins
Who Found Each Other

Bard Lindeman

[*August 1964*]

O N A January night in 1963 a tall, handsome man of 24 from Binghamton, N.Y., stepped from a jetliner at Miami International Airport. Masking his excitement, he called to the man waiting nervously for him. "Hi," he shouted. "I haven't seen you in 24 years!"

The other man, also 24, had been planning this occasion for three months. But now he did not know whether to hug the newcomer or shake his hand.

For Tony Milasi, of Binghamton, and Roger Brooks, of Miami, are identical twins. Yet, incredibly, they were meeting for the first time. Separated soon after birth, they had been raised in homes more than a thousand miles apart. At the airport they finally shook hands. "I can't believe it," Tony said.

In many ways the story of the twins who found each other *is* hard to believe. The story starts on May 28, 1938, in Binghamton City Hospital. At 8:31 and 8:36 p.m., Dr. Vincent M. Maddi delivered twin boys, born to a young Italian mother. But the normally happy event was in this case a cause of anguish, because the parents were not married to each other. The father, who was Jewish, was the young woman's lover; her husband was in jail. And she already had two children. Tearfully the mother explained that she could not possibly keep the babies.

417

Dr. Maddi remembered that a neighbor had begged for a child to adopt. He mentioned the twins to her, but she was neither young enough nor strong enough to raise both boys; she had to choose between them. And so "Baby B," the smaller twin, came into the lives of Mr. and Mrs. Joseph Milasi. He was christened Anthony Joseph.

The Milasis lived in an apartment above their small grocery and meat market in Binghamton's predominantly Italian seventh ward. Young Tony attended Catholic schools, was an altar boy at St. Mary's of the Assumption Church, and was graduated from Binghamton Central High School. When he was 12, one of the neighborhood children hurled an accusation which hurt and confused him: "You don't look Italian like the rest of us. Your real father must have been a Jew."

That night Pauline Milasi told the boy the full story. She showed him his adoption papers. As to his twin, she said, Dr. Maddi believed he had died in infancy.

In fact, "Baby A's" chances for life had not been good. When he was three months old the city's public welfare department placed him in a boarding home. There he was badly burned when his crib mattress caught fire. After being hospitalized for almost a year, he was transferred to an orphans' home.

In 1942 Mrs. Mildred E. Brooks, a practical nurse, learned of the sickly, unhappy child. She took the boy, called Roger, to live with her and her husband, Jules Brooks, in Syracuse, N.Y. A year later the couple separated. With 5-year-old Roger, her 11-year-old son and her mother, Mrs. Brooks moved to Miami. There she supported the family by operating a beauty parlor.

Roger knew he was not the true son of Mildred Brooks, but that was all he knew about his origin. Because the Brookses were Jewish, he sang in the choir at the temple and was introduced to Judaism. When he was 15, a friend of the Brooks family told him that he was a twin. Roger was curiously thrilled. He had once dreamed he had a twin, but Mildred Brooks told him to put it out of his mind. "I felt he'd never find his brother," she explains, "so why give him something else to worry about?"

In August 1955, at age 17, Roger enlisted in the Air Force. His school grades had not been good, and he thought the service might give him a fresh start. More important, he believed that he might somehow find his brother in the armed forces.

One night in Japan a soldier approached Airman 2/C Brooks and told him, "I saw you playing basketball for St. Mary's in Binghamton." Roger excitedly wrote down the address of St. Mary's Church and sent his photograph there, with a letter telling about his search for his twin.

Three weeks later a heavy brown business envelope arrived from Binghamton. But the contents proved a disappointment. "They couldn't help me," he says. "But they told me to pray for my lost brother and sent me rosary beads!"

When he left the Air Force in 1959, Roger went home to Miami and took a job as an office worker with an aircraft manufacturer. In three years he worked his way up from $67 to $107.50 a week.

Meanwhile, Tony Milasi's life had paralleled his twin's in a curious way. The same month that Roger enlisted in the Air Force, Tony had joined the Navy. On several occasions during his four-year enlistment GI's stopped him to ask, "Haven't I seen you around Miami?" Tony began to wonder if his twin might not be alive.

Back home in Binghamton in the summer of 1959, he went to the Bureau of Vital Statistics and asked for information about his brother. The registrar told Tony that, because he was adopted, his file was sealed. "That really put me down," he says.

In January 1962 Tony became a book salesman in Buffalo, and soon was promoted to sales manager. One of the door-to-door salesmen he hired that summer was an eager young Bostonian, Mark Frattalone, who worked only a short while before resuming his studies at the University of Miami.

Some weeks later, Roger Brooks stopped at a roadside restaurant near Miami. As he ate, one of the busboys approached his table and said, "Tony?"

"I'm sorry," Roger said. "You've got me confused with someone else."

The busboy explained that he had recently worked in Buffalo, N.Y., for a fellow named Tony Milasi, "who looks *and sounds* just like you." The busboy was Mark Frattalone.

"He was excited," Roger remembers. "If I moved my hands when I spoke he'd say, 'Tony does that! Tony does that!' I made a date to see him the following morning."

Next day, Roger disclosed that he had a twin whom he had never seen. "I'm positive Tony is your brother," Frattalone said. Roger, afraid of being disappointed again, suggested that Mark call the book company in Buffalo and ask when Tony Milasi was born. He pushed a handful of change across the table. Minutes later Mark came out of the phone booth and said, "Tony Milasi was born May 28, 1938."

"That's the day I was born," Roger Brooks said.

The two drove downtown to the Miami office of the book company. In a copy of the monthly newsletter Mark found a picture of Tony Milasi. Without a word he handed it to Roger.

"In that moment," Roger says, "I think I knew this was my brother. I was proud. But I was afraid, too, that something might go wrong, to keep us from meeting."

Roger turned for help to the Family Service Association. There a social worker explained that they must first be certain not only that Roger and Tony were twins, but that Tony Milasi knew he was adopted, and was interested in a reunion.

A letter was sent to the Family and Children's Society of Broome County in Binghamton. The letter arrived October 15, and from then on things moved quickly. Tony was informed. He couldn't wait to hear from his brother.

It was arranged that Roger Brooks would telephone at 6 p.m. on October 19. When his telephone rang that night, Tony grabbed it on the first ring. The operator said, "Long distance calling for Anthony Milasi." Then another voice: "Tony?"

"Roger?"

"I don't know what to say." An awkward pause, then, "How tall are you?"

"How tall are *you?*"

With this they both began to laugh. They discovered they were both six-foot-three. Roger, at 209 pounds, was a pound lighter. Both wore size-13 shoes and had blue eyes and brown hair parted on the left.

After the preliminaries, there was only one point to settle—

where to meet. "I'll come down there," Tony volunteered. "Your weather is better."

Roger took a week's leave from his job. After the first constraint of their meeting at the Miami airport, the brothers found no difficulty in talking. They were fascinated—and amused—by the extent of their physical likeness. And they were even more delighted at their unexpected similarities of taste and habit.

Both smoked the same brand of cigarettes. Both used the same after-shave lotion and—more amazingly—the same kind of toothpaste, an obscure brand made in Denmark. And both were fast eaters, long sleepers and light drinkers.

Tested by a Miami psychologist, the two were found to have almost identical I.Q.'s and great aptitude for clerical work. In personality, however, Tony was much more extroverted and self-assured; Roger was more sensitive and impressionable.

With 24 years to catch up on, the time for Tony to leave came all too soon. In March, Roger visited Tony and the Milasis in Binghamton for 12 days. "Every meal was a Roman banquet," he says. "And I must have met a hundred members of the Milasi family. Tony's friends showed me a kind of friendship I'd never known."

The story of the twins quickly spread through Binghamton. When the boys walked downtown, people called, "Which twin is the Tony?" One woman came up to them and said, "When I read in the paper how you found each other, I cried."

In June, Roger Brooks decided to leave his own familiar world and move to Binghamton. In February 1964, when Tony married a Binghamton girl, Roger was best man.

But the central fact of the lives of both Tony and Roger is that they have succeeded in finding each other. And in doing so, each, in a sense, found a missing part of himself.

&❧ Three distinguished, elderly women were talking to my six youngsters waiting in the car. As I approached, one of the women asked, "Are all these beautiful children yours?" When I replied that they were, she said admiringly, "My goodness, you do nice work!"

John R. Adams

The Day the Bears Go to Bed

Jean George

[October 1966]

H ER GRAVE face turned into the wind, the female grizzly jogged swiftly through a lonely lodgepole-pine forest in Yellowstone National Park. Snow was gusting around her that November 5, 1963. As she reached her den at the base of a fir tree, the behemoth hesitated; then she pushed her head beneath the fir roots and shuffled in.

Sinking down on a bed of boughs she had gathered days before, she fitted her back into the rounded earth, rolled her nose into her belly and covered her head with her paws. Her body relaxed, she growled softly and began to pass into the deep and mysterious sleep that would lower her temperature and slow down her heartbeat and breathing. In hibernation, a state devised by nature for protection, she could live through Yellowstone's cold and foodless winter.

Unknown to the grizzled sleeper, a small radio transmitter in a yellow-plastic collar around her neck beeped on. Following the beeps, three scientists trudged up the steep slope in the spinning snow. Then the signal weakened; it could barely penetrate the earth from the den. Dr. Frank Craighead, Jr., president of Environmental Research Institute, grinned at his snow-covered companions, Dr. John Craighead and Maurice Hornocker. "She's in. The old gal's gone to bed!" Years of work had come to a climax. For the first time in history a grizzly bear had been successfully tracked into its hibernation den by radio.

Frank scanned the blue-white wilderness near Trout Creek. What signs had told the bear that tomorrow's dawn would rise on a snow-locked world that would not release its grip until spring? Although the snow was whiting out the canyons and forest that day, and the great gray owl huddled somewhere against a tree, these signs of winter had come before during Yellowstone's erratic autumn. Each time the signs said "winter" to the men—but not to the bears, who stayed up, knowing by some mysterious sense that these preliminary snows would soon melt and the air would warm above freezing.

But today, the Craighead brothers knew from previous years, all the grizzlies on the Yellowstone plateau—hundreds of them—would go to bed. When darkness came this night, every grizzly bear in the Park would be snowed in under the roots of some lonely tree. Yet the country looked for all the world like any other snowy day in autumn. Why had the bears chosen *this* day? And which of the components of the day—temperature, barometric pressure, vanishing food supply, snow—had triggered the biological clock in each and every bear? Now, on the final day of the fifth year in a seven-year study of the grizzly bear, *Ursus horribilis,* the Craigheads felt they could at last answer some of these questions.

Sons of a naturalist, the Craigheads grew up in a family of naturalists and gravitated toward a joint career in wildlife research. In the 1950s, having learned that the grizzly was vanishing from the West, they decided on a comprehensive study of the bears in Yellowstone. The National Geographic Society, the National Science Foundation, Philco Radio Corporation and the U.S. Fish and Wildlife Service were persuaded to help; the aid of doctors, physicists, engineers and biologists was enlisted. The information they uncovered is now being used to give the grizzly the kind of help and management he needs for survival under today's special conditions.

The Craigheads were among the first to employ the new space science of bio-telemetry, gathering information on distant animals through radio transmitters. "The bears wander far into inaccessible country," says Frank, "and they are most active at night. We could not follow or consistently observe them without radio."

Even with bio-telemetry, it was not easy. The bears first had to be trapped, anesthetized and tagged for identification—by snapping numbered plastic tags of different colors into each ear. The enormous animals then had to be weighed, measured, sexed. Finally, several were fitted with collars carrying transmitters. These pulsed at a different rate for each individual.

Four of the instrumented bears were monitored from the laboratory in Canyon Village, where the radio beeps could be picked up, from as far as 12 miles distance, 24 hours a day. The others could be monitored at will by receivers in the field. When a transmitter began to give off odd sounds, the Craigheads would take compass bearings and hike—sometimes ten miles—into the dense forests to see what the sounds meant. An on-off signal was found to be a bear digging or entering a den. An irregular signal indicated walking and moving around. A continuous rhythmic beep was a nap.

A strong trap made from heavy steel sewer piping, and a dart that injected a drug, were used to capture the bears. The anesthetic had to be carefully administered: there were no known dosages for bears. Once when a cub got too much, John had to give him artificial respiration. (There were radio troubles too: one bear sat down in a stream and shorted her transmitter.) Eventually, some 300 grizzlies coöperated by walking into traps.

One summer day I drove with the Craigheads toward a bear that had just been trapped. He was put to sleep, then lifted out of the trap by four men and placed in a cargo net. When he was cranked up for weighing, the scale read 500 pounds. "Just a little one," Frank said. They tagged the bear, measured his ears and body length, and took a blood sample. Meanwhile, the crew was making imprints in plastic of the bear's glistening teeth and paws. (A technique was developed to determine from these imprints the animal's age.)

Then Bear 114's eyes opened! In a few minutes he sat up, shook his head and arose. Some bears would charge the team of men. But this one just gave us a bored glance and hurried off.

In the laboratory in Canyon Village, bear-paw imprints, maps and radios lay on the long tables. A map for each bear hung on the wall. As the men tuned in on the bear, its location was marked on the map. In this way the home range of each animal was eventually determined. Some bears had a large range, four-by-fourteen miles. One bear, No. 40, required only a three-by-five-mile area in which to eat and nap.

By 1965 the Craigheads were on their way toward understanding the secrets of pre-hibernation. They knew that the bears went off to bed simultaneously, but on a different calendar day of each year studied: October 21-22 in 1961, November 5 in 1963, and November 11 in 1965. All were days of storm, cold and low barometric pressure.

The dens were warm and ingeniously chosen. Some were located on slopes that could be death traps to humans when the snow came; some were on canyon walls. All were on slopes facing north, exposures that would not thaw during the brief warm spells. All were dug by the bears themselves under the roots of big trees. No den found was ever used the following season.

All dens were lined with pine and fir boughs, the region's best insulation, raked down by the bears and carried to their dens in their teeth. It seemed that expectant females fashioned deeper and softer bough beds than did barren females and boars. And the cubs, conceived in June, were born in December to a drowsy mother who may have snoozed through the process.

The bears know that the day of retirement is coming and

prepare their cavities many weeks ahead of the last storm. Then they all wait for that final trigger.

In the last autumn of the study, a series of unusual weather conditions unlocked some answers to the question of what the final trigger was. Until then, winter had always come to Yellowstone gradually, in snows and thaws and slowly increasing cold before the final blow. But that September 15, while chopping wood, Frank noticed that the temperature was dropping swiftly. The thermometer registered 12° F.—unusual for September, and even more so when the cold stayed for eight bitter days. The bears, however, did not move from their summer areas.

October 15 was another unusual day. The morning dawned warm and sunny. Birds sang, rivers ran free. At noon, however, it grew cloudy and Frank flipped on the laboratory receiver. He and assistant Bob Ruff were startled by what they heard. No. 202 had left his Sulphur Mountain summer bedding area and was clipping along Elk Antler Creek.

John tuned in on other bears. They were all on the move. 181 was splashing across the Yellowstone River; 65, a barren female, was trotting toward a canyonside. At four o'clock that afternoon snow dropped silently on Yellowstone.

But though the bears had gone to their dens, they did not go inside. Some were digging, a thing they never did on hibernating day. Perplexed, the brothers waited all night while the transmitters sang on. Three days later the sun came out and the snow melted.

From that day to hibernating day was a lonely vigil in the Yellowstone wilderness. Frank tracked a sow and saw her sitting on her big haunches on an isolated ledge, desperately fighting sleep. He had never seen this before. The lethargy of hibernation had set in, but she would not den. John found that her son, 202, was also having trouble. The receiver beeped as he went into his den and came out, went in and came out—waiting for something, he knew not what.

Finally, on November 11, 1965, a storm rode into Yellowstone. When Frank flipped on the receiver, erratic beeps came from the bear radios. One was giving the weak signal that meant the bear had denned. 202, however, was some little distance from his den. Frank set out to find him. As he fought his way for six miles through dense timber, he watched the ground for tracks. 202, the receiver indicated, was close by, but Frank could not see his tracks.

Then at last he spotted 202, just ahead of him, marching hard. Frank watched his feet. Now he was certain of what the bears were instinctively waiting for—a drifting, blowing storm that would cover their tracks as they hurried to their dens. By morning the radios were all transmitting their "underground" signals. And there was not one paw print to tell which way the bears had gone.

In the laboratory the Craigheads put some of the facts together and speculated. The cold snap of September 15 had set off the first bell—drowsiness. A month later the second bell went off—the urge to be alone. That day grizzlies had gone off to their dens in the canyonsides and forests. They had not denned up, for the final alarm had not yet sounded—the drifting, blowing snow that erased their footsteps and sealed the plateau until spring.

As Frank looked out at the white wilderness, he thought that even though he and John and their colleagues had taken many secrets from the bears, the most awesome one remained unknown—the "feel" of that final storm that would bind the lakes in ice, slow the rivers and close the roads until spring. Perhaps that secret was theirs forever, buried in instinct and old bear wisdom from millions of years of listening to the murmurs from the earth.

&~ *Easy Rider.* A matron in an Oregon suburban community tells about her rather regal Airedale who likes to go exploring. He has a collar which notes his address and the fact that he likes to wander. Anyone who finds him is asked to send him home in a cab. During a violent rainstorm, the woman was caught downtown without her car and she took a bus which dropped her off near her home in the downpour. As she puffed and paddled her way uphill to her house, she noticed a passing cab containing—comfortably ensconced on the back seat—her relaxed, dry pooch.   Peter Thompson in Portland *Oregon Journal*

Quite Immaterial

Alexander Woollcott

A celebrated personality, storyteller and wit, Alexander Woollcott started as a drama critic and columnist. He is perhaps best remembered as radio's "Town Crier," and original of "The Man Who Came to Dinner" —a role he also played on the stage. At his death in 1943 he was a Digest Roving Editor.

[July 1959]

GIVE YOU this story as it first came to me—as something that befell a young woman from Catonsville, Md., while on her honeymoon in France, her first trip abroad. For convenience let me call her Mary.

As she and her husband were motoring from Beaune to Bourges, this thing happened. On the edge of a small village they passed a modest estate—a shabby house of cream-colored plaster standing some distance back from the highway. Midway was an oval fountain in which goldfish disported themselves. Mary caught at her husband's arm and asked him to stop and let her out. He watched while she ran to the high iron fence and stood peering between the palings, studying the large gate and the drive which led up past the garden. When she came back she was visibly shaken. "My dear," she said, "it's my house. The same in every particular."

She didn't have to explain. For years the family had been teasing Mary about her house. In her dreams she'd find herself in the same place—a house she'd never seen in a land she didn't know. She'd never once supposed there was such a place. She'd thought of it purely as a creation of her own subconscious. And now, driving along a road in France, she had come upon it and was seeing it with her open eyes.

After the first shock, Mary was delighted. She was all for exploring the place at once. Why, it might even be possible to rent it for a week or two—to bring her husband to her dream house and actually spend her honeymoon there!

As they approached the gate, a young priest was coming out. In her Catonsville French, Mary started to ask if the family was at home. The priest stared at her incredulously, then crossed himself and hurried down the road in the direction of the village.

Her husband, skeptical about the whole adventure, was delighted with the effect on the holy man of his bride's Maryland French. In hilarious mood they pushed open the gate and walked toward a gardener who was pruning the shrubbery. *"M'sieu, est-ce que vous pouvez me dire . . . ?"* But she got no further. Straightening up to answer her, the gardener took one look, dropped his shears and ran as if the devil were after him.

This was discouraging. But they pushed on to the house. At closer range a hundred details convinced her. It *was* her house. That row of oriel windows under the eaves, the Latin inscription over the door. The same. She was shaking with excitement as her husband gave a pull on the doorbell. They could hear the faint jangle in the distance. Then footsteps and the rattle of a bolt. The door was opened by an elderly woman in cap and apron. Before they could get three words out she bent forward, stared at Mary as at some monster, and slammed the door. They heard the bolt clang back into place.

With a mixture of irritation and bewilderment our friends went back to their car, relieved to find that it hadn't turned into smoke and drifted off over the treetops. "My dear," said the bridegroom, "they don't seem to like us."

At the village they found a promising inn. The innkeeper was an affable soul and they soon were pumping him about the house on the edge of town. Whose was it? Who lived in it? How old was it? Was it possible to rent it?

On the latter score he was doubtful. They mustn't quote him, but it was common talk in the village that the house was haunted. Off and on for the past ten years, the family, the workers on the place and even visitors, like M. le Curé, had seen a silent spirit roaming there. Funny that they should be asking about it at that moment, because he'd just heard that the place was in a turmoil. The ghost was walking again—in broad daylight and no longer silent. His own cook's son was the gardener there and even now was down in the kitchen drinking his head off and shaking like a leaf. He'd seen the ghost. Only an hour before, while he was pruning the syringa by the drive, it had appeared and it had spoken to him—the ghost of a young woman, accompanied this time, he said, by the ghost of a young man.

Well, there's the story. A few years ago it appeared as a work of fiction by André Maurois, but before that I had already heard it by word of mouth. I think it likely that it really happened sometime . . . to somebody . . . somewhere.

Audience Reaction

୧୬ The Laff Box is a machine which dubs electronic laughter into the sound tracks of TV comedy shows. There's a "titter key" and a "chuckles reel," reports *TV Guide*. There's an "anticipation reel" where everybody in the audience says "oh, oh." There's an "intake reel" for surprise reaction, with everybody gasping. There are separate keys for cheering, applause, men laughers only, women laughers only. One key activates "sharpies": those snorts you often hear prior to the main audience roar. There's a "funny-laugh key" for a single idiosyncratic kook laugh—which proves that even maverick individualism can be canned.

୧୬ There is a TV commercial which shows a certain floor wax removing dirt with just one swish of the mop. Recently the company got this letter: "Dear Sirs, I have been using your floor wax for some time, and as a steady customer I feel you owe me a favor. Sell me that mop."   Bill Kennedy in Los Angeles *Herald-Examiner*

Lincoln Goes to Gettysburg

Carl Sandburg

[July 1936]

WHEN Governor Curtin of Pennsylvania set aside November 19, 1863, for the dedication of a National Soldiers' Cemetery at Gettysburg, the only invitation President Lincoln received to attend the ceremonies was a printed circular.

The duties of orator of the day had fallen on Edward Everett. An eminent figure, perhaps the foremost of all American classical orators, he had been governor of Massachusetts, ambassador to Great Britain and president of Harvard. There were four published volumes of his orations. His lecture on Washington, delivered 122 times in three years, had in 1859 brought a fund of $58,000, which he gave for the purchase of Mount Vernon as a permanent shrine.

Serene, suave, handsomely venerable in his 69th year, Everett was a natural choice of the Pennsylvania commissioners, who gave him two months to prepare his address. The decision to invite Lincoln to speak was an afterthought. As one of the commissioners later wrote: "The question was raised as to his ability to speak upon such a solemn occasion; the invitation was not settled upon until about two weeks before the exercises were held."

In these dark days Lincoln was far from popular in many quarters. Some newspapers claimed that the President was going to make a stump speech over the graves of the Gettysburg dead as a political show. Thaddeus Stevens, Republican floor leader in the House, believed in '63 that Lincoln was a "dead card" in the political deck, and hearing that Lincoln and Secretary of State Seward were going to Gettysburg, he commented, "The dead going to bury the dead."

On the day before the ceremony a special train decorated with red-white-and-blue bunting stood ready to take the Presidential party to Gettysburg. When his escort remarked that they had no time to lose, Lincoln said he felt like an Illinois man who was going to be hanged, and as the man passed along the road on the way to the gallows the crowds kept pushing into the way and blocking passage. The condemned man at last called out, "Boys, you needn't be in such a hurry; there won't be any fun till I get there."

Reaching Gettysburg, Lincoln was driven to a private residence on the public square. The sleepy little country town was overflowing. Private homes were filled with notables and nondescripts. Hundreds slept on the floors of hotels. Bands blared till late in the night. When serenaders called on the President for a speech, he responded: "In my position it is sometimes important that I should not say foolish things." (A voice: "If you can help it.") "It very often happens that the only way to help it is to say nothing at all. Believing that is my present condition this evening, I must beg of you to excuse me from addressing you further." The crowd didn't feel it was much of a speech. They went next door with the band and blared for Seward.

Beset with problems attendant on the conduct of the war, Lincoln had had little time to prepare his address. About ten o'clock he sat down in his room to do more work on it. It was midnight or later when he went to sleep.

At least 15,000 people were on Cemetery Hill for the exercises next day when the procession from Gettysburg arrived afoot and horseback. One of the commissioners, riding just behind the President, noted that he sat erect and looked majestic to begin with, and then got to thinking, so his body leaned forward, his arms hung limp and his head bent far down.

The parade had begun to move at 11, and in 15 minutes it was over. But the orator of the day had not arrived. Bands played till noon. Mr. Everett arrived. On the platform sat state governors, Army officers, foreign ministers, members of Congress, the President and his party.

When Edward Everett was introduced, he bowed low to Lincoln, then stood in silence before a crowd that stretched to limits that would test his voice. Around were the wheat fields, the meadows, the peach orchards, and beyond, the contemplative blue ridge of a low mountain range. He had taken note of these in his prepared and rehearsed address. "Overlooking these broad fields now reposing from the labors of the waning year, the mighty Alleghenies dimly towering before us, the graves of our brethren beneath our feet, it is with hesitation that I raise my poor voice to break the eloquent silence of God and nature."

He proceeded: "It was appointed by law in Athens—" and gave an extended sketch of the manner in which the Greeks cared for their dead who fell in battle. He outlined how the war began, traversed decisive features of the three days' battles at Gettysburg, denounced the doctrine of state sovereignty, and came to his peroration quoting Pericles on dead patriots: "The whole earth is the sepulcher of illustrious men." He spoke for an hour and 57 minutes. It was the effort of his life.

When the time came for Lincoln to speak he put on his steel-bowed glasses, rose, and holding in one hand the two sheets of paper at which he occasionally glanced, he delivered the address in his high-pitched and clear-carrying voice. A photographer bustled about with his equipment, but before he had his head under the hood for an exposure the President had said "by the people and for the people," and the nick of time was past for a photograph. The nine sentences were spoken in five minutes, and the applause was merely formal—a tribute to the occasion, to the high office, by persons who had sat as an audience for three hours.

That evening Lincoln took the train back to Washington. He was weary, talked little, stretched out on the seats and had a wet towel laid across his forehead. He felt that about all he had given the audience was ordinary garden-variety dedicatory remarks. "That speech," he said, "was a flat failure, and the people are disappointed."

Much of the newspaper reaction was more condemnatory. The *Patriot and Union* of nearby Harrisburg took its fling: "The President acted without sense and without constraint in a panorama that was gotten up more for the benefit of his party than for the honor of the dead. . . . We pass over the silly remarks of the President; for the credit of the nation we are willing that the veil of oblivion shall be dropped over them and that they shall no more be repeated or thought of." And the Chicago *Times* fumed: "The cheek of every American must tingle with shame as he reads the silly, flat and dishwatery utterances of the man who has to be pointed out to intelligent foreigners as the President of the United States." Wrote the correspondent of the London *Times,* "Anything more dull and commonplace it would not be easy to produce."

A reporter for the Chicago *Tribune,* however, telegraphed a prophetic sentence: "The dedicatory remarks of President Lincoln will live among the annals of man." The Philadelphia *Evening Bulletin* said thousands who would not read the elaborate oration of Mr. Everett would read the President's few words, "and not many will do it without a moistening of the eye and a swelling of the heart." And a writer in *Harper's Weekly:* "The oration by Mr. Everett was smooth and cold. . . . The few words of the President were from the heart to the heart. They cannot be read, even, without kindling emotion. 'The world will little note nor long remember what we say here, but it can never forget what they did here.' It was as simple and felicitous and earnest a word as was ever spoken."

Everett's opinion of the speech, written in a note to Lincoln the next day, was more than mere courtesy. "I should be glad if I could flatter myself that I came as near to the central idea of the occasion in two hours as you did in two minutes." Lincoln's immediate reply: "In our respective parts you could not have been excused to make a short address, nor I a long one. I am pleased to know that, in your judgment, the little I did say was not entirely a failure."

ૐ Prayer is reversed thunder.   George Herbert

LAUGHTER,
THE BEST MEDICINE

ON THE wall of a building near his residence, movie producer Mike Nichols noticed a chalk inscription one morning: I LOVE GRILS. The next morning a line had been drawn through this and a new line printed below: I LOVE GIRLS. The third day that line had been crossed out too, and a third line substituted—in letters twice as large. It read: WHAT ABOUT US GRILS?

Bennett Cerf

SAN FRANCISCO *Chronicle* columnist Herb Caen concocted a game which he calls "Punny Farm," to which readers contribute inspired names for animal pets and acquaintances. Some of the entries are: a white mouse called Mousey Tung; a collie, Flower; a rabbit, Transit; a donkey, Shane. A pigeon is called Toad; a frog, Horn; a horse, Greeley; and a rooster, Shire Soss. And how about a gopher named Broke; a crow, Magnon; a kitten, Kaboodle? Reversing the order, a rat is named Frank Lloyd; a collie, Melon; and a pair of egrets, Miss Otis.

A MARRIAGE counselor began to question a woman concerning her disposition: "Did you wake up grumpy this morning?"
"No," she replied. "I let him sleep."

W. C. Hultgren, quoted by Troy Gordon in Tulsa World

WHEN Congress was discussing federal salary increases it reminded Congressman Tim Lee Carter of Kentucky of an old Kentuckian who thought he was dying. He called his wife to his bedside and instructed her to go down to the old trunk in the basement and get a bottle of fine old bourbon out of it.
"Yes, John," she said. "What then?"
He told her to fill a glass with finely crushed ice, to bruise some mint, and to stir it up in the glass with just a pinch of

sugar. Then she was to pour the bourbon liberally over the concoction, decorate it with sprigs of mint, and set it aside until frost formed on the outside of the glass. "And then, Mary," gasped the old man, his voice all but extinct, "bring it up here to me, and when you bring it, no matter what I say or do, Mary, make me take it."

Congressional Record

AFTER seeing a Sophia Loren movie, I said to my husband, "You wouldn't trade me in for Sophia Loren, would you?"

He deliberated a few seconds, then replied, "No, I wouldn't trade you in for Sophia Loren. I'd keep you for a spare."

Mrs. J. D. Murray

SANDY MACPHERSON, a Nova Scotia deer hunter, was being kidded by a crony about missing a shot at a fast-traveling buck. "Whut's the matter, Sandy?" his heckler inquired. "Were he runnin' too fast fer ye?"

"Runnin'!" Sandy snorted. "That critter weren't runnin' at all! He were only puttin' a foot down here an' there to steer hisself by!"

Fred Boutillier

TOM BAHTI of Tucson offers an All-Purpose Political Speech for Any Audience. Its opening paragraph:

"These are perilous times. We stand at the crossroads of decision, the frontier of destiny. Years ago this was not as true as it proved to be later on. But today there is an increase of 23 percent in the national index alone! Mental illness accounts for an appalling three percent. Every penny of the rest goes for taxes."

Jack Guinn in Denver Post

A MINISTER says that when a man is in love his heart swells and often moves him to unusual acts of generosity. To illustrate he tells about the day he performed the marriage of a shy young farmer and a pretty country girl. When the ceremony was over, the farmer drew four bright silver quarters from his pocket. Extending them to the minister in his palm, he said feelingly, "There you are, sir. Just help yourself until you're satisfied."

Memphis Commercial Appeal, quoted in The Ohio Motorist

How to Swallow a Sword

The Great Zadma, as told to Jule Junker Mannix

[*May 1945*]

I SHALL never forget the first
time I swallowed a lighted, two-foot neon tube. The tube was
a bootlegged one, like all neons used by sword swallowers at that
time, because the electrical companies wouldn't allow anyone
to buy a tube if they knew he intended to swallow it. Several
sword swallowers had been killed by the tubes breaking inside
of them, and the companies felt it was bad publicity.

Neon swallowing really has a lovely effect. All the lights are
turned off except the tube itself, and then the artist, stripped to
the waist, swallows it to the hilt. There the light is, glowing
out through his body. The effect is indescribably weird. Some
people faint, and this makes the trick very popular.

I wanted desperately to be a neon swallower. At the time, I
was working with a carnival and living in the sideshow's truck
with Flamo, the fire eater. One night while we were playing
Trenton, N. J., he located an electrician who said he would
make me up a couple of tubes. With neons you must have an
electrical connection at both ends of the tube before the gas
inside will light. For swallowing, therefore, the tubes are
U-shaped and the ends stick out of your mouth. This means
swallowing a double tube, which is naturally much harder than
swallowing a slender sword blade, so the tube has to be as
thin as possible. The thin tubes are brittle and likely to break.

Flamo and I picked up the tubes one evening after our last

show. But when we had them lighted and ready to swallow I got nervous. "Flamo, I'm getting scared," I told him.

We had just been reading in *The Billboard* of the death of Prince Neon, the first neon swallower. The tube had broken inside him. The Human Electric Light Bulb, who had followed him, had got a short circuit somehow and died before he could be carried off the platform. The game hardly seemed worthwhile.

"Well, if you're scared, kid, I wouldn't swallow 'em," Flamo urged. "Your throat'll tighten up and snap the tube."

I knew if I were going to swallow them I'd have to do it at once, before they got too hot. A hot tube will stick to your insides and you can't withdraw it. So I picked up a tube and wiped it.

I stood with my head thrown back and the tube held straight up from my lips with my right hand. With my cupped left I guided it down my throat. The principle of sword swallowing is to establish a straight line from the throat to the stomach. As the tube slid down, it was pleasantly warm, unlike the chill of steel, but terribly wide.

I felt it strike my breastbone. This is always a creepy feeling. It sends a shudder all through you. Then the tip of the tube slipped off the bone and glided down smoothly until my right hand touched my lips.

I withdrew the tube and turned to Flamo. "Did it shine through my chest?" I asked eagerly.

"Son, you shone like a jack-o'-lantern," he assured me respectfully. "It's a wonderful act. I was darned near taken sick myself."

The next night I performed with the neon tube, and the act was a sensation. Two women had to be carried out, and the parents of a child who had been frightened into hysterics sued the show. My reputation was made.

Most sword swallowers were once "carny punks"—young boys who have run away from home to join a traveling carnival. For a while a punk hangs around the lot, running errands for the performers, helping the joint men set up their concessions. Soon he wants to learn an act. He can't be a freak. He can't afford the elaborate apparatus for an aerial act. He hasn't the ability to be a talker or a gambler. So he becomes a sword swallower.

I have often been asked why anyone wants to be a sword swallower. Well, in a carnival a sword swallower is an artist who is properly respected. It is an art which everyone would like to know but few have the patience to learn.

The performer's swords cost him only $15 or $20, and if he doesn't like the carnival he can tuck them under his arm and hop a freight to the next show. Or he can give shows in barrooms or on street corners for dimes. He is absolutely free and can always get a pocketful of change for a few minutes' work.

Learning to be a sword swallower takes about three or four months of hard practice. First, find out how long a sword you are able to swallow. Swallow a very long sword slowly and carefully until you feel the tip touch the pit of your stomach. Stop there. Feeling the blade touch is a sensation difficult to describe, but you'll know when it happens. Then mark the blade just above your teeth. Withdraw it, cut it off right there, and you have your sword. When you start the sword down your throat for the first time, you will probably be sick. This will keep up for several months until your throat gets used to the feel of cold steel.

Naturally a tall man can swallow a longer sword than a short man. Being quite tall, I held the American record for the longest sword swallowed (26 inches) for many years. The record was taken from me by a shorter man who resorted to the device of eating a heavy meal just before the test, which weighed down his stomach the additional few inches he needed to win. I leave it to the reader to decide whether such a trick is legitimate.

No one knows who was the first to discover he could swallow a sword, but he must have been an unusual personality with a flair for experimentation. Traveling jugglers performed the trick for the Pharaohs, and Agrippa mentions seeing it in ancient Rome.

Sword swallowing first became famous in America at the Chicago World's Fair in 1893. For years afterward it was being "exposed" in newspapers and magazines. The usual explanation was that the sword folded up into its hilt. I used to carry around a straight blade without a hilt and swallow that to convince people. This blade was finally broken by a young man in his efforts to find something wrong with it. Later I heard him say, "That sword folded up. I coulda found out how, but it busted on me."

There are several variations to the regular routine. One friend of mine swallows red-hot swords by first swallowing an asbestos scabbard. But the presence of the scabbard is a secret and it is surprisingly difficult to walk around with a scabbard inside of you without looking awkward.

In the last few years there has been an epidemic of female sword swallowers. I don't approve of it. Women are likely to take chances. I saw a girl who swallowed a sword with a tin blade and then twisted around until the blade was bent inside her before she withdrew it. I don't care if she was drawing down $20 a week for this act. It was dangerous.

A girl who featured neon swallowing appeared in Ripley's Believe It or Not show at the New York World's Fair. She performed on a revolving stage, and I was surprised that she dared to swallow the tubes, as even slight vibrations of the stage might crack one. After going through the usual routine, she produced a tube mounted on the stock of a rifle. She swallowed the tube halfway and then fired off the rifle, so that the kick of the gun drove the neon the rest of the way down her throat.

I rushed out of the hall in a panic while the audience howled with laughter at me. As I staggered past the last row a man stopped me. "I guess you think that girl really swallowed them tubes, don't you?" he said. Then in a low voice he added, "I'll tell you a secret. Them tubes are faked. They fold up into the handles."

᠍᠍᠍ *Firing Line.* My first job in Albuquerque was getting new accounts for the Citizens National Bank. They were paying me $50 a month, and I suggested a raise. Albert Simps, the president, asked if I'd feel bad if I didn't get it, and I said I would. He then fired me, saying that he couldn't stand an unhappy face around the office.   Kyle Crichton, *Total Recoil* (Doubleday)

The Continents Are Adrift!

Ronald Schiller

[April 1971]

$\mathcal{S}$OMEWHERE on the high seas the ship *Glomar Challenger* is, at this moment, logging a voyage of exploration as important as any undertaken since Columbus sailed in 1492. Her scientist crew is drilling the ocean bottoms, examining sedimentary mud and rocks millions of years old. Each time they pull up her three-and-a-half-mile-long drill pipe, they confirm one of the most astonishing scientific discoveries of our time: the world's continents are adrift on the pliable mantle of inner earth.

This revolutionary concept, known as "global-plate tectonics," has challenged all traditional views that rest on the concept of a stable planet. It pictures instead a turbulent, dynamic world in which, during its 4.6-billion-year geologic history, oceans have opened and closed like accordions and continents have been buffeted around like hulks on a stormy sea. It also answers riddles that have baffled man since the dawn of natural science: how the continents, oceans, mountains and islands were formed; the reasons for volcanoes and earthquakes; and why marine fossils are embedded on Himalayan peaks.

Admittedly, some of the pieces of the puzzle are missing, and scientists do not agree on all details. But the general outlines have been verified—and accepted by most scientists as geologic truth. "Global-plate tectonics can no longer be referred to as a mere theory," says Maurice Ewing, dean of American oceanog-

441

raphers. "Scientifically, it is as significant as Darwinian evolution or Einstein's laws of energy and motion—and as important to mankind."

The concept advances these views of the geologic process:

1. Far from being the solid, indestructible shell once imagined, the earth's crust consists of separate plates (ten major ones, subdivided into varying sizes), made of rock 40 to 60 miles thick, which float on the hot, viscous mantle beneath them.

2. The earth's land surfaces rest on these plates (as do the oceans), and were once welded together in a single continent. Some 200 million years ago this super-continent began to split up, eventually forming the seven continents and the major islands we now know, and were rafted to their present positions like packages on a moving conveyor belt.

3. These plates, whose edges are being built up by molten rock welling up from deep fissures in midocean, are being propelled across the globe by forces of undetermined origin, in various directions, at geologically wild speeds of from one-half inch to six inches a year.

4. Phenomenal things occur as the plates jostle one another for room: When a moving plate bearing land (mainly granite) meets an ocean-bearing plate (consisting of dense, less-buoyant basalt), it rides over it like a titanic bulldozer, scraping up the sediment deposited on the sea floor over millions of years, along

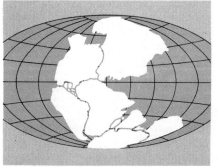

The landmass, 200 million years ago

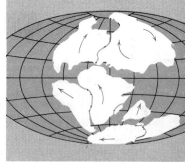

After 20 million years of drift

with slices of the crustal rock. The debris piles up along the edge of the land like a rumpled blanket to form mountain ranges. The ocean-bearing plate, forced down at a steep angle into trenches under the land slab, melts from the heat of the friction, forming deep underground pockets of white-hot lava. The trapped lava is forced up through crevices, erupting on the surface as inland volcanoes. The collision, separation and shearing of the plates also create the seismic disturbances that we call earthquakes.

How did geologists arrive at this fantastic conclusion? For generations, schoolchildren studying their maps have noticed that if South America and Africa were brought together and twisted slightly they would fit like pieces of a jig-saw puzzle. In 1912, German geologist Alfred Wegener theorized that the continents actually *were* once joined. He pointed out that the rock formations along the bulge of Brazil and Africa's Gulf of Guinea are enough alike in age and structure to have been torn from the same geologic flesh, and that identical fossil plants and freshwater animals, which could not have survived a trip across thousands of miles of saltwater, have been found in South America, Africa, Australia and even distant India. But the idea was discredited because no one could conceive of any mechanism that could propel vast continents through the earth's solid crust. Moreover, such moving landmasses would have left behind gigantic wakes of displaced rock on the sea floors, and despite

After 135 million years

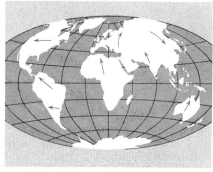

The continents today—still moving

intensive search no ripple of such disturbances was apparent.

A second mystery was the strange sparsity of sediment on the ocean floors. Sediment formed by microscopic marine organisms and dust blown or washed into the sea should have blanketed the ocean beds over the ages to a uniform depth of at least 12 miles. Yet there is practically no sediment in the center of the Atlantic and only a half-mile veneer near the borders. In the late 1850s, telegraph engineers laying the transatlantic cable found submerged mountains in midocean. Similar ridges were later found in the Pacific and elsewhere.

Then in the late 1950s, oceanographers discovered that these ridges form a continuous 40,000-mile chain that winds through all the oceans like the seam on a tennis ball. And down the center run deep, hot rifts, oozing lava. It seemed as though the ocean floors were splitting apart and that lava welling up from the ridges was forming new ocean-floor material as it hardened. Scientists speculated that the crust might be moving ever farther from the ridge, eventually plunging into the deep troughs bordering the land.

This startling idea received support in 1963 from a dazzling piece of deduction by F. J. Vine and D. H. Matthews of England's Cambridge University. Geologists had first discovered that many times in earth's history the magnetic poles had reversed polarity—instead of pointing north, during certain ages the iron particles in rock pointed south. What caused this phenomenon is not yet known; but by measuring the extent to which the radioactive elements in the rock have decayed, and by determining the age of fossils embedded in them, geologists have learned to date and read these magnetic reversals like rings in a tree. (The last flip-over occurred 700,000 years ago.) If the ocean floors actually were born in lava and were spreading apart, reasoned the Cambridge scientists, there should be an identical series of magnetic reversal bands on either side of the mid-oceanic ridges.

When oceanographers took to the sea in ships, towing magnetometers, they found the magnetic reversal bands exactly as predicted. Since scientists know when each reversal occurred, they are able to determine not only the age of any particular segment of ocean floor but the direction and speed at which it is moving. They learned, for instance, that the Atlantic Ocean floor is widening, pushing Europe and North America apart, at the rate of one inch a year!

With the announcement of these findings many mysteries were solved: why there is a mountain chain under the sea, why undersea cables would snap, and why there was so little sediment on the ocean bottoms (the sea floor was moving too fast to allow it to accumulate to any great depth before plastering it up against the continents or carrying it down into the trenches). And by tracing the movement of the sea floors back in time, oceanographers were able to figure out where the continents had originally started.

Still needed to reconstruct the history of our planet was the precise sequence of events, to be obtained only by digging into the ocean floors, recovering sediment and crustal rock and determining their composition and ages. Five American institutes, headed by California's Scripps Institution of Oceanography, have banded together in this brilliant scientific effort aboard the *Glomar Challenger,* one of the strangest craft ever to put to sea. A 142-foot-high oil derrick sits amidships, and a 20-foot-wide hole extends through the bottom—through which the miles-long drill string of steel pipes is lowered. Since anchors are useless at the enormous depths where the *Challenger* drills, position over the selected site is maintained by means of twin screws aft and a total of four lateral thrusters—placed on either side of the bow and stern—which allow the vessel to move sideways when necessary. The ship's thrusters are commanded by computers which, by reference to sonar beacons on the ocean floor, can hold the ship within 40 feet of the drillsite in the roughest seas.

It used to be that once the *Challenger's* drilling bit wore out, a hole would have to be abandoned. But now, thanks to newly developed underwater sensors, motors, and a wide-mouthed metal funnel placed on the sea bed, the drillers are able to pull up the string of pipes, screw on a fresh bit, and find their way back into the same ten-inch-wide hole miles below the surface to continue drilling! This incredible feat has been likened to standing on top of the Empire State Building and inserting the end of a 1250-foot straw into the neck of a soda bottle on the sidewalk below—in a high wind.

Since August 1968, the *Challenger* has been crisscrossing the world's oceans, drilling some 250 holes, the deepest of which reached 3334 feet, pulling up long cores of bottom mud and bedrock—some of it 160 million years old. As each core reaches the deck it is sliced into five-foot lengths, then photographed, X-rayed, metered for radioactivity and analyzed for age, before being packed in plastic and sent to refrigerated vaults in the United States for further study. Excitement runs high. Says the project's scientific manager, Melvin N. A. Peterson, "You feel like an explorer rummaging through the ruins of a civilization lost to time."

Although details of the earth's past must be revised each time the *Challenger* returns to port with new core reports, most geologists agree that the land surfaces were joined 200 million years ago in a single landmass, which they call *Pangaea* (Greek for "all lands"). The heart of this motherland appears to have been located on the equator in what is now the South Atlantic. Japan lay near the North Pole, India near the Antarctic. According to the reconstruction made by geologists Robert S. Dietz and John C. Holden, the first separation was a gigantic east-west crack in the earth's crust, and a rift that appeared between the South American-African mass and Antarctica-Australia. India was liberated and started bolting north. The 200 million years it took the plates to sever and to reach their present positions comprise a phenomenally short time from the geologic point of view—a little over an hour, if the earth's history were compressed into a 24-hour day.

North America sailed northwest. The Eurasian plate, twisting 20 degrees clockwise, moved to the north, pursued by Africa which turned counter-clockwise. South America broke loose and headed west, while Greenland and Northern Europe parted. The last two continents to separate from each other were Antarctica and Australia, the latter migrating to warmer climates. The most spectacular of all was India, which once it tore loose from Africa and Antarctica raced 5500 miles north in 180 million years to ram under the belly of Asia, pushing up the Himalayas ahead of it like a bow wave. (Thus climbers who reach the top of Mount Everest stand on the former ocean floor!)

Almost as violent were the happenings in the Mediterranean, where the African plate bashed into Europe. The collision produced the Pyrenees, Apennines and Alps in Europe. On the other side of the globe the Americas, Asia and Australia plowed toward each other across the vast Pacific. The sea-floor sediment piled up on shore to form the Andes of South America, the ranges of western North America, the island arcs of the Aleutians, Japan and the other archipelagos of the western Pacific.

How often in the past oceans have opened and closed, continents collided, split asunder and welded together again, geologists are still trying to determine. But about the future they speculate with more confidence. Assuming the plates continue in their present directions, they predict that the Atlantic will continue to widen while the Pacific shrinks. With Africa again charging Europe, the Mediterranean seems doomed to become a glorified duck pond. The Himalayas will grow, and India will tire of burrowing under Asia and will slide eastward. Australia, rocketing northward at two inches a year, will sideswipe Asia.

North and South America will still voyage westward, but part company as Panama and Central America retreat northward. The peninsula of Baja California and a sliver of the California coast west of the San Andreas Fault, which lie on a separate plate, will tear away from the mainland and head northwest.

But Los Angeles residents should be in no hurry to pack their bags. It will take ten million years more for the city to sail past San Francisco, and another 50 million years before it slides into the Aleutian trench.

ε➤ *Shockproofing.* I recently purchased a wig from a mail-order house, and when it arrived the following note was enclosed: "Due to the possibility that this wig may slip off your head, do not wear it to bed. Many husbands have been frightened by the sudden awareness of a strange, furry animal under the blankets and have been known to damage the merchandise."   Barbara L. Cabot

"A Troublesome Boy"

Winston S. Churchill

[*August 1949*]

I was on the whole considerably discouraged by my school days. All my contemporaries seemed in every way better adapted to the conditions of our little world. They were far better both at the games and at the lessons. It is not pleasant to feel oneself completely left behind at the very beginning of the race.

I was first threatened with school when I was seven years old. At the time I was what grown-up people in their offhand way called "a troublesome boy." Although much that I had heard about school had made a disagreeable impression on my mind, an impression thoroughly borne out by the actual experience, I thought it would be fun to go away and live with so many other boys, and that we should have great adventures. Also I was told that "school days were the happiest time in one's life." All the boys enjoyed it. Some of my cousins had been quite sorry—I was told—to come home for the holidays. Cross-examined, the cousins did not confirm this; they only grinned.

It was a dark November afternoon when the last sound of my mother's departing carriage died away and I was taken into a Form Room and told to sit at a desk. All the other boys were out of doors and I was alone with the Form Master. He produced a thin, greeny-brown-covered book.

"This is a Latin grammar." He opened it at a well-thumbed page. "You must learn this," he said, pointing to several words in a frame of lines. "I will come back in half an hour and see what you know."

Behold me then on a gloomy evening, with an aching heart, seated in front of the declension of *mensa*.

What on earth did it mean? It seemed absolute rigmarole to me. However, there was one thing I could always do: I could learn by heart.

In due course the Master returned.

"Have you learned it?" he asked.

"I think I can *say* it, sir," I replied. And I gabbled it off.

He seemed so satisfied with this that I was emboldened to ask a question.

"What does it mean, sir?"

"It means what it says. *Mensa*, a table."

"Then why does *mensa* also mean O table," I inquired, "and what does O table mean?"

"*Mensa*, O table, is the vocative case," he replied. "You would use that in speaking to a table."

"But I never do," I blurted out in honest amazement.

Such was my first introduction to the classics from which, I have been told, many of our cleverest men have derived so much solace and profit.

Flogging with the birch was a great feature in the curriculum. Two or three times a month the whole school was marshaled in the Library, and one or more delinquents were haled off to an adjoining apartment and there flogged until they bled freely, while the rest sat quaking, listening to their screams. How I hated this school and what a life of anxiety I lived there for more than two years! I made very little progress at my lessons and none at all at games. The greatest pleasure I had was reading. When I was nine and a half my father gave me *Treasure Island*, and I remember the delight with which I devoured it. My teachers saw me at once backward and precocious, reading books beyond my years and yet at the bottom of the Form. They were offended. They had large resources of compulsion at their disposal, but I was stubborn.

Where my reason, imagination or interest was not engaged, I would not or I could not learn. In all the 12 years I was at school no one ever succeeded in making me write a Latin verse or learn any Greek except the alphabet. To stimulate my flagging interest they told me that Mr. Gladstone read Homer for fun, which I thought served him right.

I had scarcely passed my 12th birthday when I entered the inhospitable regions of examinations. These were a great trial to me. The subjects which were dearest to the examiners were almost invariably those I fancied least. I would have liked to have been examined in history, poetry and writing essays. The examiners, on the other hand, were partial to Latin and mathematics. Moreover, I should have liked to be asked to say what I knew. They always tried to ask what I did not know. When I would have willingly displayed my knowledge, they sought to expose my ignorance. This sort of treatment had only one result: I did not do well in examinations.

This was especially true of my entrance examination to Harrow. The Headmaster, Dr. Welldon, however, took a broadminded view of my Latin prose; he showed discernment in judging my general ability. This was remarkable because I was found unable to answer a single question in the Latin paper. I wrote my name at the top of the page. I wrote down the number of the question: 1. After much reflection I put a bracket round it thus: (1). But thereafter I could not think of anything connected with it that was either relevant or true. Incidentally there arrived from nowhere in particular a blot and several smudges. I gazed for two whole hours at this sad spectacle and then merciful ushers collected my piece of foolscap. It was from these slender indications of scholarship that Dr. Welldon drew the conclusion that I was worthy to pass into Harrow. It is very much to his credit. It showed that he was a man capable of looking beneath the surface of things: a man not dependent upon paper manifestations. I have always had the greatest regard for him.

I was in due course placed in the lowest division of the bottom Form. I continued in this unpretentious situation for nearly a year. However, by being so long in the lowest Form I gained an immense advantage over the cleverer boys. They all went on to learn Latin and Greek and splendid things like that. But I was taught English. We were considered such dunces that we could learn only English. As I remained in the Third Fourth three times as long as anyone else, I had three times as much of it. I learned it thoroughly. Thus I got into my bones the essential structure of the ordinary British sentence—which is a noble thing. And when in after years my schoolfellows who had won prizes and distinction for writing such beautiful Latin poetry and pithy Greek epigrams had to come down again to common English to earn their living or make their way, I did not feel myself at any disadvantage.

It was thought incongruous that, while I apparently stagnated in the lowest Form, I should gain a prize open to the whole school for reciting to the Headmaster 1200 lines of Macaulay's "Lays of Ancient Rome" without making a single mistake. I also succeeded in passing the preliminary examination for the army while many boys far above me failed in it. I also had a piece of good luck. We knew that among other questions we should be asked to draw from memory a map of some country or other. The night before, by way of final preparation, I put the names of all the maps in the atlas into a hat and drew out New Zealand. I applied my good memory to the geography of that Dominion. Sure enough the first question in the paper was: "Draw a map of New Zealand." Henceforward all my education was directed in the army class to passing into Sandhurst. Officially I never got out of the Lower School at Harrow.

It took me three tries to pass into Sandhurst. There were five subjects of which mathematics, Latin and English were obligatory, and I chose in addition French and chemistry. In this hand I held only a pair of kings—English and chemistry. Nothing less than three would open the jackpot. I had to find another useful card. Latin I could not learn. French was interesting but rather tricky. So there remained only mathematics. I turned to them—I turned on them—in desperation.

Of course what I call mathematics is only what the Civil Service Commissioners expected you to know to pass a very rudimentary examination. Nevertheless, when I plunged in I was soon out of my depth. I was soon in a strange corridor of things called Sines, Cosines and Tangents. Apparently they were very important, especially when multiplied by each other or by themselves! They had also this merit—you could learn many of their evolutions off by heart. There was a question in my third and last examination about these Cosines and Tangents in a highly square-rooted condition which must have been decisive upon the whole of my after life. But luckily I had seen its ugly face only a few days before and recognized it at first sight.

I have never met any of these creatures since. With my third and successful examination they passed away like the phantasmagoria of a fevered dream. I am assured that they are most helpful in engineering, astronomy and things like that. I am glad there are quite a number of people born with a gift and a liking for all of this; like great chess players, for example, who play 16 games at once blindfold and die quite soon of epilepsy.

The practical point is that, if I had not been asked this particular question about these Cosines or Tangents, I might have gone into the Church and preached orthodox sermons in a spirit of audacious contradiction to the age. I might have gone into the City and made a fortune. I might even have gravitated to the Bar and persons might have been hanged through my defense who now nurse their guilty secrets with complacency.

In retrospect my school years form the only barren and unhappy period of my life. Actually, no doubt, they were buoyed up by the laughter and high spirits of youth. But I would far rather have been apprenticed as a bricklayer's mate or run errands as a messenger boy. It would have been real; it would have been natural; it would have taught me more; and I should have done it much better.

Road to the Orient

৪০ Translated, one of China's road signs reads as follows: "Go soothingly on the greasy mud, for therein lurks the skid demon."

L. M. Boyd, Chicago Tribune-New York News Syndicate

৪০ A warning sign on a narrow winding road in Okinawa: "Caution Forward, More Curves Curly."

Marilyn K. Bryan

The 100-Percent American

Ralph Linton

[March 1938]

D ESPITE the average American's pride in things American, some insidious foreign ideas have already wormed their way into his civilization.

Thus dawn finds the unsuspecting patriot garbed in pajamas, a garment of East Indian origin, and lying in a bed built on a pattern which originated in either Persia or Asia Minor. On waking he glances at the clock, a medieval European invention, uses one potent Latin word in abbreviated form, rises in haste and goes to the bathroom.

Here he must feel himself in the presence of a great American institution—until he remembers that glass was invented by the ancient Egyptians, the use of glazed tiles for floors and walls in the Near East, and porcelain in China. Even his bathtub and toilet are copies of Roman originals. The only purely American contribution is the steam radiator, against which our patriot very briefly and unintentionally places his posterior. In the bathroom the American shaves (a rite developed by ancient Egyptians), washes with soap, invented by the ancient Gauls, and dries himself on a Turkish towel.

Returning to the bedroom, this unconscious victim of un-American practices puts on garments whose form derives from the skin clothing of ancient nomads of the Asiatic steppes, and fastens them with buttons whose prototypes appeared in Europe at the close of the Stone Age. This costume, appropriate enough for outdoor exercise in a cold climate, is quite unsuited to American summers, steam-heated houses, and Pullmans. Nevertheless foreign ideas and habits hold the unfortunate man in thrall. He puts on his feet stiff coverings made from hide prepared by a process invented in the ancient Near East. Lastly he ties about his neck a strip of bright-colored cloth— a vestigial survival of the shoulder shawls worn by 17th-century Croats. He gives himself a final appraisal in the mirror, an old Mediterranean invention, and goes down to breakfast.

Here his food and drink are placed before him in pottery vessels, the popular name for which—china—betrays their origin. His fork is a medieval Italian invention and his spoon a copy of a Roman original.

If our patriot adheres to the so-called American breakfast, his coffee (descendant of an Abyssinian plant) will be accompanied by an orange, domesticated in the Mediterranean region. He will follow this with a bowl of cereal, made from grain domesticated in the Near East. Then waffles, a Nordic invention, with plenty of butter, originally a Near Eastern cosmetic.

Breakfast over, he places on his head a molded piece of felt, invented by the nomads of Eastern Asia, and sprints for his train—the train, not the sprinting, being an English invention. If it looks like rain he takes an umbrella, invented in India. At the station he pays for his newspaper with coins, invented in ancient Lydia. On the train he settles back with a cigarette, invented in Mexico, or a cigar, invented in Brazil.

Meanwhile our American reads the news of the day, imprinted in characters invented by the ancient Semites by a process invented in Germany upon a material invented in China. As he scans the latest editorial pointing out the dire results to our institutions of accepting foreign ideas, he will not fail to thank a Hebrew God in an Indo-European language that he is a 100-percent (decimal system invented by the Hindus) American (from Amerigo Vespucci, Italian geographer).

ᚠᛞ America is the kind of place where Jewish merchants sell Zen love beads to agnostics for Christmas. John Burton Brimer

How We Trapped Capone

Frank J. Wilson, as told to Howard Whitman

[July 1947]

WHEN my wife and I left Baltimore for Chicago in 1928, all I said was, "Judith, I'm after a fellow named Curly Brown." If I'd told her that Curly Brown was an alias of Scarface Al Capone, she'd have turned the car right around and made me take up some respectable trade like piano tuning.

I was with the intelligence unit of the Bureau of Internal Revenue and my assignment was to find proof of income-tax evasion by Capone. In previous years he had either filed no tax return or had reported insignificant income.

Art Madden, our Chicago agent-in-charge, told me that hanging an income-tax rap on Alphonse Capone would be as easy as hanging a foreclosure sign on the moon. The Grand Panjandrum of the checkered suits and diamond belts had Cook County in the palm of his hand. He did all his business anonymously through front men. To discourage meddlers, his production department was turning out 50 corpses a year.

For a base of operations the government gave me and my three assistants an overgrown closet in the old Post Office Building with a cracked glass at the door, no windows, a double flat-topped desk and peeling walls.

I spent months in fruitless investigation through banks, credit agencies and newspaper files. I prowled the crumby streets of Cicero, but could get no clue to show that a dollar from the big gambling places, the horse parlors, brothels or bootleg joints ever reached Capone. Jake Lingle, a Chicago *Tribune* reporter, had been seen with Capone in Chicago and Miami, and from the tips I got he wasn't just writing interviews. So I saw the *Tribune* boss, Robert R. McCormick, and told him Lingle's help would be appreciated by the U. S. government. "I'll get word to Lingle to go all the way with you," said McCormick. Lingle was assassinated next day, right in the busiest part of the city.

I was stuck, bogged down. Two frustrating years dragged by. Capone was all over the front pages every day. It was common talk that he got a cut on every case of whiskey brought into Cook County; that he ran a thousand speakeasies, a thousand bookie joints, 15 gambling houses, a string of brothels; that he controlled half a dozen breweries. He had bought a Florida palace on Palm Island and was spending $1000 a week on banquets. He tore around in 16-cylinder limousines, slept in $50 pajamas, and ordered 15 suits at a time at $135 each. His personal armed forces numbered 700, equipped with automatic weapons and armored automobiles. But evidence of lavish living wasn't enough. The courts had to see *income*.

One night, in a desperate mood, I decided to check over all the data my assistants and I had piled up. By one o'clock I was bleary-eyed, and while gathering up my papers I accidentally bumped our filing cabinet. It clicked shut. I couldn't find the key. "Now where'll I put this stuff?" I wondered. Just outside, in a storeroom, I found an old filing cabinet full of dusty envelopes. "I can lay this old junk on the table," I figured. "I'll put my own stuff in overnight."

In the back of the cabinet was a heavy package tied in brown paper. Just out of curiosity I snipped the string and found three ledgers, one a special-column cashbook. My eye leaped over the column headings: "Birdcage," "21," "Craps," "Faro," "Roulette," "Horse bets." Here was the diary of a big operation, with a take of $20,000 to $30,000 a day. Net profits for 18 months (the books were dated 1925-26) were upward of half a million.

"Who could have run a mill that size?" I asked myself. The answer hit me like a baseball bat; only three people—Frankie

Lake, Terry Druggan or Al Capone! But I had already cleaned up the Druggan-Lake case. Two from three leaves one.

The ledgers had been picked up in a raid after the murder of Assistant State's Attorney William McSwiggin in 1926. They came from one of the biggest gambling palaces in Cicero, The Ship, where diamond-studded crowds from Chicago laid down $3 million a year in wagers. A record of *income!* If I could hang it around the neck of Al Capone we'd have a case at last.

Scarface must have known we were closing in. On the inside of the gang I had one of the best undercovermen I have ever known, Eddie O'Hare. One afternoon, word reached me that Eddie wanted to see me at once. When we met, he was red-faced and excited. "You've got to move out of your hotel, Frank. The big fellow has brought in four killers from New York to get you. They know where you keep your car and what time you come in and go out. You've got to get out this afternoon!"

"Thanks, Eddie," I replied. So I phoned Judith I had a surprise for her—we were moving to the Palmer House where she had once said she'd like to live. I left word at my hotel we were going to Kansas and drove to the Union Station—but right on through and around to the Palmer. Judith was completely confused. I hoped Al's torpedoes were too.

Later Eddie met me with another report: "The big fellow's offering $25,000 reward to anybody who bumps you off!"

When the story broke in the papers that Capone had put a price on my head, Judith took it with amazing calm. She simply said, "We're going straight home to Baltimore!" I finally won her over by promising she could be with me as much as possible. Women always think they're bulletproof.

Meanwhile I was working on the handwriting in the ledgers of The Ship. I think we must have collected handwriting samples of every hoodlum in Chicago—from voting registers, savings accounts, police courts. The painful process of elimination finally left me with a character named Lou Shumway, whose writing on a bank deposit slip was a dead twin to that in the ledgers. I found out from a tipster that Shumway was in Miami, probably working at Hialeah or the dog tracks. All I had to go on was a description: "Shumway is a perfect little gentleman, refined, slight, harmless—no racetrack sport at all."

In February 1931 I stood by the rail at Hialeah looking at the man I had been stalking for nearly three years. Scarface Al Capone sat in a box, with a jeweled moll on either side of him, smoking a long cigar, greeting a parade of fawning sycophants who came to shake his hand. I looked upon his pudgy olive face, his thick pursed lips, the rolls of fat descending from his chin—and the scar, like a heavy pencil line across his cheek. When a country constable wants a man, I thought, he just walks up and says, "You're pinched." Here I am, with the whole U. S. government behind me, as powerless as a canary.

Two nights later I spotted the "perfect little gentleman" my tipster had described, working at a dog track. I tailed him home, and picked him up next morning as he was having breakfast with his wife. He turned pale green. When I got him to the Federal Building I said cold-turkey, "I am investigating the income-tax liability of one Alphonse Capone."

Gentleman Lou turned greener yet, but he pulled himself together and said, "You're mistaken. I don't know Capone."

"Lou," I said, "if you refuse to play ball with me I will send a marshal to look for you at the track, ask for you by name and serve a summons on you. You get the point, Lou. As soon as the gang knows the government has located you, they will probably decide to bump you off so you can't testify.

"If you don't like that idea, Lou, come clean. Tell the truth about these ledgers. You were bookkeeper at The Ship. You can identify every entry in these books—and you can tell who your boss was. I'll keep everything secret until the trial. You will be guarded day and night, and I'll guarantee that Mrs. Shumway will not become a widow."

Gentleman Lou quivered like a harp string but he finally gave in. I spirited him out of Miami and hid him in California.

But we still had to show that that *income* actually reached the pockets of Al Capone. A painstaking checkup on all the recorded money transactions in Cicero finally showed that one "J. C. Dunbar" had brought gunnysacks full of cash to the Pinkert State Bank and bought $300,000 in cashier's checks.

Agent Nels Tessem and I caught up with "Dunbar," whose

real name was Fred Ries, in St. Louis. We tailed a messenger boy who carried a special-delivery letter and slapped a subpoena in Ries's palm. He was annoyed, especially since the letter was from Capone's headquarters telling him to flee to Mexico. He wouldn't talk at first. But after a week in a special vermin-ridden cell we picked out for him in a jail—we knew he had a pathological fear of bugs—Ries cried uncle. He'd talk if we'd only get him away from the bedbugs. We sneaked him before a Chicago grand jury in the middle of the night. His testimony put the profits of The Ship squarely in the pockets of Scarface Al! I packed Ries off to South America—with government agents to guard him until we needed him in court.

In the autumn of 1931, two weeks before the Capone trial, Eddie O'Hare reported to me: "Capone's boys have a complete list of the prospective jurors. They're fixing them one by one—passing out $1000 bills, promising political jobs, giving donations to churches. They're using muscle too, Frank."

Eddie handed me a list of ten names and addresses. "They're right off the jury list—names 30 to 39!"

Next morning I went with U. S. Attorney George E. Q. Johnson to the chambers of Federal Judge James H. Wilkerson, who was to sit in the Capone trial. There was reassurance in just looking at the judge. Somehow he seemed like a match for Scarface Al. Sure enough, the ten names Eddie had given me tallied with names 30-39 of the judge's list. But the judge didn't seem ruffled. He said calmly, "Bring your case into court as planned, gentlemen. Leave the rest to me."

The day the trial started I fought my way through reporters, photographers and sob sisters. Al Capone came into the court-room in a mustard-colored suit and sat down at the counsel table just a few feet from me. Phil D'Andrea, Al's favorite bodyguard, sat beside him; fawning over Al, he adjusted Capone's chair, plucked a thread from his shoulder.

As Judge Wilkerson entered in his black robe, Capone seemed to be snickering over the jury of "friends" and intimi-dees who'd soon send him back to the overlordship of Chicago.

Judge Wilkerson called his bailiff to the bench. He said in crisp, low tones, "Judge Edwards has another trial commencing today. Go to his courtroom and bring me his entire panel of jurors. Take my entire panel to Judge Edwards." The switch was so smooth, so simple. Capone's face clouded with the despair of a gambler who had made his final raise, and lost.

The trial marched on. My gems, Gentleman Lou Shumway and the bug-bedeviled Ries, stood their ground on the witness stand though Capone and Phil D'Andrea were staring holes through them the entire time.

I kept my eyes on D'Andrea. When he got up to stretch during a recess I could have sworn I saw a bulge in his right hip pocket. But no, I thought, there wasn't a crumb in the world who would dare to bring a gun into federal court. I saw him stretch again. I had word sent in that a reporter wanted to see him. I followed him out of the courtroom. Nels Tessem and Jay Sullivan, my colleagues, led him down the corridor. As we passed Judge Wilkerson's chambers I shoved him inside.

"Give me that gun!" I snapped. D'Andrea handed it over.

"Give me those bullets!"

He ladled out a handful of ammunition from his vest pocket.

Judge Wilkerson interrupted the trial to cite D'Andrea for contempt and send him away for six months. Capone growled, "I don't care what happens to D'Andrea. He's a damn fool. I don't care if he gets ten years." Al was cracking.

The trial wound up in mid-October. As the jury returned from its deliberations I felt sure we had won. "Gentlemen," intoned Judge Wilkerson, "what is your verdict?"

"Guilty!"

The courtroom broke up. Reporters ran. Lawyers ran. Mobsters ran. Everybody seemed to be running but Scarface Al Capone. He slumped forward as if a blackjack had hit him.

When I got home Judith cried, "You did it! I knew you were going to do it all the time!" Then she sighed, "Now can we go back to Baltimore?"

❦ *Sobering Thought.* A man came into a bar with a bad hangover. "If I'd known I was going to live this long," he groaned, "I'd have taken better care of myself." Earl Wilson, Publishers-Hall Syndicate

You Never Stop Learning

James A. Michener

[December 1962]

THE WAR had passed us by on Guadalcanal in 1945, and we could see certain victory ahead. Relieved of pressure, our top officers in the South Pacific Force could have been excused if they loafed, but the ones I knew well did not. One carrier admiral used his free time to study everything he could get on tank warfare. The head of our outfit, Vice Adm. William Lowndes Calhoun, spent six hours a day learning French.

I asked him, "Admiral, what's this big deal with French?"

"How do I know where I'll be sent when the war's over?" he replied.

A few nights later someone asked, "By the way, Michener, what are you studying?" The question, though probably an idle one, stunned me, and the challenge touched off a profound response. That very night I started work on an idea that I had been toying with for months. In a lantern-lit, mosquito-filled tin shack, I began writing *Tales of the South Pacific*.

The good work of the world is accomplished principally by people who dedicate themselves unstintingly to the big, distant goal. Weeks, months, years pass, but the good workman knows he is gambling on an ultimate achievement, one which cannot be measured in time spent. Responsible men and women leap to the challenge of these jobs that require years to fulfill, and are happiest when so involved. But this means that if they hope to make a real contribution, they must *re-educate* themselves periodically. Otherwise they are doomed to mediocrity.

In the United States the average man (leave out doctors and specialized scientists) can expect to work in three radically different fields before he retires. The lawyer is dragged into a business reorganization, and winds up a college president. The engineer uses his slide rule for a while, then finds himself a sales expert, and ends up in labor relations. The schoolteacher becomes a principal, later on heads an automobile agency.

I have been typical in that I have had widely scattered jobs: teacher, businessman, soldier, traveler, writer. No college education could give me specific preparation for any of these jobs. But by fantastic luck, I got to Swarthmore College just as it was launching an experiment. At the end of my sophomore year, the faculty told a group of us, "Life does not consist of taking courses in small segments. We are going to turn you loose on some huge tasks. Let's see what you can do with them."

We were excused from all class attendance and were told, "Pick out three fields that interest you." I chose logic, English history and the novel. "Go to the library and learn what you can. At the end of two years, we'll bring in some experts from Harvard and Yale and they will determine whether you have educated yourself."

What followed was an experience in intellectual grandeur. The Swarthmore professors, realizing that my testing would be a test of them, too, helped me gain as thorough a knowledge of those three fields as a young man could absorb. When the two years ended, the visiting experts for a week queried, probed and heckled. At the end, one of the examiners said to me simply, "You have the beginnings of a real education."

He was right: it was only the beginnings. Nothing I studied in college has been of direct use to me in my various occupations. But what I *did* learn was *how* to learn, how to organize, how to educate myself. And since then, experience and observation have taught me that it is not so much the original education that counts: it's the re-education—the self-discipline that keeps a man driving toward hard and distant goals, the human values he believes in.

Specialization is not enough. For the big jobs—historically, culturally, morally—what the world needs is well-rounded *human* beings.

I remember a day in 1942 when the U.S. Navy was hungry for talent. Four of us would-be officers were shivering in our shorts in a small room. A grim-faced selection committee asked, "What can you do?" and the first man replied, "I'm a buyer for Macy's, and I've trained myself to judge very quickly between markets and prices and trends." The board replied, "Can't you do anything practical?" And they shunted him off to one side.

The next man was a lawyer. He had to confess, "I can weigh evidence and organize information." He was rejected.

I was third and when I answered, "I know language and a good deal of history," the board groaned and I went shivering away.

Then the fourth man said boldly, "I'm a college-trained engineer, and I can overhaul diesel engines." The committee practically embraced him, and made him an officer on the spot.

But this is not the end of the story. When the war was over, the Macy's buyer was assistant to the Secretary of the Navy, in charge of many complex responsibilities requiring instant good judgment. He had given himself courses in Naval management and government procedures and had become a top expert. The lawyer wound up as assistant to Admiral Halsey, and in a crucial battle deduced logically from intelligence reports just where the Japanese fleet *had* to be. He came out covered with medals.

I got the job of Naval secretary to several Congressional committees who were determining the future of America in the South Pacific.

What was the engineer doing at the end of the war? He was still overhauling diesel engines.

ॐ Do little boys still get crushes on their teachers? A fourth-grade teacher in San Juan Capistrano handed out valentines to her pupils, signed "Love, Mrs. Jean Sharke." After school one small boy came up to her desk, stood there a moment, then shyly asked, "Mrs. Sharke, did you put 'love' on all of them?" Laguna Beach, Calif., *Pilot*

The Basque Sheepherder
and the Shepherd Psalm

James K. Wallace

[June 1950]

O LD Ferando D'Alfonso is
a Basque herder employed by one of the big Nevada sheep
outfits. He is rated as one of the best sheep rangers in the state,
and he should be, for back of him are at least 20 generations of
Iberian shepherds.

But D'Alfonso is more than a sheepherder; he is a patriarch
of his guild, the traditions and secrets of which have been
handed down from generation to generation, just as were those
of the Damascus steel temperers and other trade guilds of the
pre-medieval age. Despite a 30-year absence from his homeland
he is still full of the legends, the mysteries, the religious fervor
of his native hills.

I sat with him one night under the clear starry skies, his sheep bedded down beside a pool of sparkling water. As we were preparing to curl up in our blankets, he suddenly began a dissertation in a jargon of Greek and Basque. When he finished I asked what he had said. In reply he began to quote in English the Twenty-third Psalm. There on the desert I learned the shepherd's literal interpretation of this beautiful poem.

"David and his ancestors," said D'Alfonso, "knew sheep and their ways, and David has translated a sheep's musing into simple words. The daily repetition of this Psalm fills the sheepherder with reverence for his calling. Our guild takes this poem as a lodestone to guide us. It is our bulwark when the days are hot or stormy; when the nights are dark; when wild animals surround our bands. Many of its lines are the statements of the simple requirements and actual duties of a Holy Land shepherd, whether today or 6000 years ago. Phrase by phrase, it has a well-understood meaning for us."

The Lord is my shepherd; I shall not want.

"Sheep instinctively know," said D'Alfonso, "that ere they have been folded for the night the shepherd has planned out their grazing for the morrow. It may be that he will take them back over the same range; it may be that he will go to a new grazing ground. They do not worry. His guidance has been good in the past and they have faith in the future because they know he has their well-being in view."

He maketh me to lie down in green pastures.

"Sheep graze from around 3:30 in the morning until about 10 o'clock. They then lie down for three or four hours and rest," said D'Alfonso. "When they are contentedly chewing their cuds the shepherd knows they are putting on fat. Consequently the good shepherd starts his flocks out in the early hours on the rougher herbage, moving on through the morning to the richer, sweeter grasses, and finally coming with the band to a shady place for its forenoon rest in fine green pastures, best grazing of the day. Sheep, while resting in such happy surroundings, feel contentment."

He leadeth me beside the still waters.

"Every shepherd knows," said the Basque, "that sheep will not drink gurgling water. There are many small springs high in the hills of the Holy Land, whose waters run down to the valleys only to evaporate in the desert sun. Although the sheep need water, they will not drink from these fast-flowing streams. The shepherd must find a place where rocks or erosion have made a little pool, or else he fashions with his hands a pocket sufficient to hold at least a bucketful."

He restoreth my soul; He leadeth me in the paths of righteousness for His name's sake.

"Holy Land sheep exceed in herding instinct the Spanish Merino or the French Rambouillet," went on D'Alfonso. "Each takes his place in the grazing line in the morning and keeps the same position throughout the day. Once during the day, however, each sheep leaves its place and goes to the shepherd. Whereupon the shepherd stretches out his hand, as the sheep approaches with expectant eyes and mild little baas. The shepherd rubs its nose and ears, scratches its chin, whispers affectionately into its ears. The sheep, meanwhile, rubs against his leg or, if the shepherd is sitting down, nibbles at his ear and rubs its cheek against his face. After a few minutes of this communion with the master, the sheep returns to its place in the feeding line."

Yea, though I walk through the Valley of the Shadow of Death, I will fear no evil. . . . Thy rod and Thy staff they comfort me.

"There is an actual Valley of the Shadow of Death in Palestine, and every sheepherder from Spain to Dalmatia knows of it. It is south of the Jericho Road leading from Jerusalem to the Dead Sea and is a narrow defile through a mountain range. Climatic and grazing conditions make it necessary for the sheep to be moved through this valley each year.

"The valley is four and a half miles long. Its side walls are over 1500 feet high in places and it is only 10 or 12 feet wide at the bottom. Travel through the valley is dangerous because its floor, badly eroded by cloudbursts, has gullies seven or eight feet deep. Actual footing on solid rock is so narrow in many places that a sheep cannot turn around, and it is an unwritten law of shepherds that flocks must go up the valley in the morning hours and down toward eventide, lest flocks meet in the defile. Mules have not been able to make the trip for centuries, but sheep and goat herders from earliest Old Testament days have maintained a passage for their stock.

"About halfway through the valley the walk crosses from one side to the other at a place where the path is cut in two by an eight-foot gully. One section of the path is about 18 inches higher than the other; the sheep must jump across it. The shepherd stands at this break and coaxes or forces the sheep to make the leap. If a sheep slips and lands in the gully, the shepherd's rod is brought into play. The old-style crook is encircled around a large sheep's neck or a small sheep's chest, and it is lifted to safety. If a more modern narrow crook is used, the sheep is caught about the hoofs and lifted up to the walk.

"Many wild dogs lurk in the shadows of the valley looking for prey. After a band of sheep has entered the defile, the leader may come upon such a dog. Unable to retreat, the leader baas a warning. The shepherd, skilled in throwing his staff, hurls it at the dog and knocks the animal into the washed-out gully where it is easily killed. Thus the sheep have learned to fear no evil even in the Valley of the Shadow of Death, for their master is there to aid them and protect them from harm."

Thou preparest a table before me
in the presence of mine enemies.

"David's meaning is a simple one," said D'Alfonso, "when conditions on the Holy Land sheep ranges are known. Poisonous plants abound which are fatal to grazing animals. Each spring the shepherd must be constantly alert. When he finds the plants he takes his mattock and goes on ahead of the flock, grubbing out every stock and root he can see. As he digs out the stocks, he lays them upon little stone pyres, some of which were built by shepherds in Old Testament days, and by the morrow they are dry enough to burn. In the meantime the sheep are led into the newly prepared pasture, which is now free from poisonous plants, and, in the presence of their deadly plant enemies, they eat in peace."

Thou anointest my head with oil; my cup runneth over.

"At every sheepfold there is a big earthen bowl of olive oil and a large stone jar of water. As the sheep come in for the night they are led to a gate. The shepherd lays his rod across the top of the gateway just higher than the backs of his sheep. As each sheep passes in single file he quickly examines it for briers in the ears, snags in the cheek, or weeping of the eyes from dust or scratches. When such conditions are found he drops the rod across the sheep's back and it steps out of line.

"Each sheep's wounds are carefully cleaned. Then the shepherd dips his hand into the olive oil and anoints the injury. A large cup is dipped into the jar of water, kept cool by evaporation in the unglazed pottery, and is brought out—never half full but always overflowing. The sheep will sink its nose into the water clear to the eyes, if fevered, and drink until fully refreshed.

"When all the sheep are at rest, the shepherd lays his staff on the ground within reach in case it is needed for protection of the flock during the night, wraps himself in his heavy woolen robe and lies down across the gateway, facing the sheep, for his night's repose.

"So," concluded D'Alfonso, "after all the care and protection the shepherd has given it, a sheep may well soliloquize in the twilight, as translated into words by David: *Surely goodness and mercy shall follow me all the days of my life; and I will dwell in the house of the Lord forever.*"

❧ *Muddling Through.* Sergeant to recruits: "Okay, men, line up alphabetically according to height" (Bill Vaughan) . . . Man studying plans for a public building: "It has all the earmarks of an eyesore" (Herb Caen) . . . Helpful sales clerk: "If you see something that isn't there, we probably have more in the back" (David A. Cowdrick, Jr.)

QUOTABLE QUOTES

A LOT OF today's frustration is caused by a surplus of simple answers, coupled with a tremendous shortage of simple problems.   Paul Sweeney in *The Quarterly*

THE DEVIL does a nice business for such a lousy location.
                                                            Dan Bennett

TACT IS the ability to make a person see the lightning without letting him feel the bolt.   O. A. Battista in *Family Digest*

A PINCH of probably is worth a pound of perhaps.
                    James Thurber, *Lanterns and Lances* (Harper & Row)

DO NOT expect a woman to honor your privacy. She is liquid and, unless your resolution is well calked, she will seep through.
        Nicholas Samstag, quoted by Robert Fearon in *Madison Avenue*

A SUCCESSFUL man is one who has the horsepower of an optimist and the emergency brakes of a pessimist.
                            "A Line O' Type or Two," Chicago *Tribune*

SOME PEOPLE would not hesitate to drive up to the gate of heaven and honk.   John Andrew Holmes, *Wisdom in Small Doses* (University)

ONE MAN'S remorse is another man's reminiscence.
                            Gerald Horton Bath in *The Little Gazette*

WE COME late, if at all, to wine and philosophy; whiskey and action are easier.   Mignon McLaughlin, *The Neurotic's Notebook* (Bobbs Merrill)

ADVICE is like snow: the softer it falls, the longer it dwells upon and the deeper it sinks into the mind.
                                            Samuel Taylor Coleridge

The Private Life of Adolf Hitler

Heinz Linge

[*February 1956*]

A<small>T EXACTLY</small> ten minutes to four on the afternoon of April 30, 1945, a whiff of acrid pistol smoke told me that Adolf Hitler had ended his life. I was standing outside the map room of the bunker, 30 feet below the ruins of the Reich Chancellery in Berlin.

Then the silence in the shelter was broken by the rumble of Russian artillery. There was no time to lose. I nerved myself to walk into the map room. There, almost upright in a sitting position on a couch, was the body of Adolf Hitler.

A small hole the size of a German silver mark showed on his right temple and a trickle of blood ran slowly down over his cheek. His uniform, which as his valet I had carefully laid out for him a few hours earlier, was scarcely crumpled. One pistol, a 7.65 Walther, lay on the floor where it had dropped from his right hand. A yard or so away lay another gun.

The body of Eva Braun was by his side. I believe she died a few minutes before the Führer. No mark showed on her face; it was as though she had fallen asleep. She had swallowed a capsule of poison.

Earlier that day my master had his favorite Alsatian dog, Blondi, destroyed. Two other dogs belonging to the household had been shot. Hitler was very fond of dogs.

Five days earlier I had been summoned to the map room which served as Hitler's headquarters, chart room, communications room—the focal point of the disintegrating government. He had used it almost all the time since the Russians had menaced Berlin. Small and simply furnished, it was in the greatest contrast to the vast chambers of the now-shattered Chancellery. A door on one side led to the Führer's bedroom; a door on the other side opened into Eva Braun's room. My own quarters opened off apartments occupied by the Goebbels family.

Hitler was standing like a statue by his table when I entered. His face was white; his eyes were grave and cold. After an exchange of salutes he looked straight at me, and those strange hypnotic eyes seemed to bore into me.

"Linge," he said, "I want to release you from my service—you can break out and rejoin your family."

"*Mein Führer*," I said, "I have been with you in the great days. I will stay with you whatever the future holds."

He half-raised his hand. "I did not expect it otherwise." Then in brisk matter-of-fact tones he added, "Now I have a special order for you.

"I have decided with Fräulein Braun that we will die together. Your duty—and my order to you—is to see that our bodies are burned. No one must recognize me after my death. Get a supply of gasoline ready. Wrap our bodies in blankets, soak them in the gasoline and burn them. Then go back to my room and collect everything I could be remembered by after death. Take everything—uniforms, papers, everything I've used; anything that people could say belonged to the Führer. Take it outside and burn it all. You understand, Linge?"

"Yes, *mein Führer*. I will carry out your orders."

I had long guessed that Hitler intended to die in Berlin rather than try to escape. He had a fear that he would be captured by the Russians, or that they would find his body and something like what had happened to the bodies of Mussolini and his mistress might happen to him.

"If they get hold of me dead or alive, they'll take me to Moscow," he mumbled. "They'll put me on public exhibition—I shall be like a dummy in a waxworks."

His voice rose hysterically: "It must not happen, I tell you. It must never, never happen!"

IN THE ten days before the lights went out forever for Adolf Hitler, the underground bunker was the scene of two parties. The first was on April 20, when Hitler celebrated his 56th birthday. He was unusually gay and lighthearted. Goering, Ribbentrop, Keitel, Bormann and other high-ranking officers came to the bunker to pay their respects.

"Faithful to the end" was the party's theme. Hitler drank cup after cup of tea—not easily procured in those days, even for him. It was his favorite and invariable drink. Coffee and champagne were served to the others and Eva proposed a birthday toast.

I remember how concerned the Führer grew for Eva Braun's health as they lived out their curious underground existence. By his orders I often accompanied her on a walk amid the rubble of Berlin. We were good friends, and once near the end she turned to me and said, "If no miracle happens to save us, it is my greatest wish that when I die with the Führer it will be as his legal wife." Her voice broke. It was an emotional moment but there seemed no comment that I, the valet, could make.

I remembered her remark when Hitler sent for me on the morning of April 29. In silence we walked to the bunker room where many momentous war conferences had taken place. Then he told me to prepare the room for his marriage to Eva Braun. "We will sit at this table with my witnesses, Bormann and Goebbels," he said. "We have sent for Walter Wagner, who married Doctor and Frau Goebbels."

The wedding was to have taken place during the afternoon, but owing to the difficulty of finding Wagner it was at midnight that Hitler and Eva finally became husband and wife.

Then once again in the map room there was a small party with champagne—and tea—to celebrate. Everyone seemed gay, determined to ignore the menace around Berlin. There was great competition, I remember, to kiss the bride's hand. I had known her a long time, but never had I seen her look so happy. I don't think many of the guests realized just how soon death would claim the bride and bridegroom.

I WRAPPED the bodies in thick blankets carefully, so no one could look on the face of the dead Hitler. Two Commandos helped me carry the body into the open. Eva Braun was carried out by Major Guensche, adjutant of the personal staff. She was wearing a dark-blue polka-dot dress, light-brown Italian shoes and nylon stockings. On her wrist was the only jewelry she regularly wore, a platinum wristwatch studded with diamonds. It was a gift from Hitler many years before.

Then came the gasoline. I poured tin after tin on the bodies, helped by Guensche and other officers. And now to the noise of shellfire was added, time and time again, the chatter of machine guns. I knew we had little time to lose. I touched off the gasoline-soaked blankets, and there was a tremendous flash as the vapor went up. It burned brilliantly—a blinding funeral pyre. But it died almost as quickly as it had flared.

I remembered Hitler's wish that only ashes were to be left. Even in that awful moment as I struggled with my grim problem, I wondered why we had not thought of using slow-burning kerosene. It would have worked better. With other members of the small group who stood watching I began to realize that we would never reduce the bodies to ashes. Hitler's uniform was destroyed and so was Eva's simple polka-dot dress. But the Führer and his bride still were recognizable.

It was then that Bormann took charge. He had received private orders, though what they were I never knew. It was less than an hour since I had bid farewell to Hitler. Goebbels, Bormann, and Axmann, leader of the Hitler Youth, were standing near the bodies under the graying and shell-lit sky.

I turned away to begin my second task, to destroy every one of Hitler's personal possessions. When hours later I re-emerged from the bunker, I was told that Hitler Commandos had taken the bodies to a spot nearby and buried them.

I was captured by the Russians and held in a concentration camp for 10½ years. It comes as a surprise to me, since my release in October 1955 and my return to freedom, to find people still asking whether Eva Braun was Hitler's "mistress," and if so for how long.

I can answer that question straightaway. Eva and Hitler were together when I joined his staff in 1935. And all through the war years, until they died together in the bunker, they lived whenever possible in what you might call a love nest.

Eva Braun was the daughter of a Munich schoolteacher. When she was a slim girl of 19 she went to Salzburg as the secretary of Heinrich Hoffman, the photographer, who always was fairly close to Hitler. In some casual way the Führer met her and became interested in her. She was simple and unsophisticated—a "girl of the people," he always called her.

She certainly was not the first woman in Hitler's life. But from that time no other woman ever shared his leisure hours so fully. As early as 1936 he started redesigning his retreat at the Berghof, near Berchtesgaden, with a suite of four rooms for Eva and himself which could be isolated from the rest.

I had a room nearby and I always knew when Hitler had been joined in his study by Eva. It was his invariable practice to walk to the door of his study and lock it from the inside, so from that moment no one could enter the suite. There was one occasion when he forgot and I entered the room to find Eva in his arms. Hitler was furious with me, and I might have fared worse but for Eva. She liked me and looked on me as the man closest to the man she loved.

Was Hitler mad? I've seen a great deal written suggesting that he flew into uncontrollable tempers and ended up biting the rug or tearing curtains to pieces. All I can say is that I never saw him in such a mood, and for many years I was seldom more than a few yards away from him.

Most of his manifold gestures in speaking had been carefully rehearsed in advance. Usually it took Hitler two days and nights, with a relay of secretaries in constant attendance, before he was satisfied with the draft of an important speech. When the draft was ready he would rehearse the speech before a mirror with stopwatch in hand. He studied each gesture carefully, and tried it over and over in front of the mirror until he was satisfied.

Throughout the ten years I was his valet, he had to use glasses to read ordinary print. He had a horror of being seen in them, however. "A Führer cannot wear glasses," he would say.

A special typewriter with extra-large letters was built, on which all his speeches were typed, so that he could read his notes easily in public without glasses. But habit died hard and every time he worked himself up while speaking he would instinctively pull his glasses out of his pocket and hold them in his hand behind his back. Almost invariably, when he reached the high point of his speech he would clench his fist involuntarily and smash his glasses. Hitler never conquered this habit, and I always had to have an extra pair of glasses available.

Another habit that may have given rise to those carpet-biting stories was his use of colored pencils. On his desk Hitler always had three pencils—red, green and blue. "The red one, Linge," he once told me, "I use when I am writing to an enemy. The green one I use when making notes about a friend. I use the blue one when I feel I should be cautious." When he was aroused these usually were the objects he would seize and throw on the desk with such force that they broke. But that is about all I can recall in the way of heated emotion.

As the world began to collapse I watched Hitler become despite his years an old man; a man broken in health. Few in Germany knew—great care was taken to see they should not know—that the Führer was by that time dragging his left leg; that his left eye had developed a ceaseless twitch; that he couldn't see well; that his hair was graying from a life that was now being lived almost entirely underground.

In these straits the Führer turned for help, as he had for so many years, to his physician, Dr. Theo Morell. Morell came on the scene in 1936 and soon exerted an almost hypnotic influence over Hitler. He prepared a special medicine with which the Führer was extremely pleased. "Morell is my man," he told me. "He has saved me from my pain."

In addition to stomach pains, Hitler suffered from insomnia, and he had about a dozen different kinds of sleeping pills which he used in rotation. Under Morell's direction Hitler took injections before any important public occasion. He was afraid his stomach pains would start up in the middle of a big speech. One injection was given to prevent that, and another to step up his energy—perhaps to counteract the deadening effect of the first.

These injections became more and more frequent, and toward the end, speech or no speech, Hitler was receiving jabs with the needle every second day.

In addition to all these medicines, the Führer would take still more. He had a violent reaction to any thought that he was putting on weight. His method of slimming was to take a powerful laxative, followed by opium to quiet the stomach. Then immediately after the opium he would take yet another medicine, to kill any germs that might be accumulating in his body.

Notwithstanding the doctor's early success, the Führer's stomach pains returned, and he became obsessed with the idea that they would cease if only his food were suitable. He caused his vegetables to be grown specially for him in earth which had been fumigated and into which only selected manure had been mixed. From time to time samples of this soil were tested. So was the water in which the vegetables were cooked.

When the war started to go badly for him, Hitler's nerves began to suffer, and belladonna was prescribed regularly to quiet him. Despite this, his left hand began to shake—this was about the time of Stalingrad—and he found difficulty in controlling its tremor. If you examine any pictures of Hitler taken then or later, you will notice that he always had his left hand pressed against his body or clasped in his right hand in front of him. Only thus could he prevent it from shaking violently.

As the Allies closed in, Hitler spent more and more time in the bunker. People who came to see him after an absence were shocked at his appearance. He was looking like an old man now, and I think he began to realize it. "I do not have the enemy to thank for my gray hairs," he would say. "I have to thank my generals, who have let me down."

AFTER my capture by the Russians, I was taken back to that grim spot, the bunker, to show where I thought Hitler was buried. But so closely and so frequently was I questioned subsequently that I am satisfied the body was never found. I have a theory—it can never be more than a theory—that the Commandos buried Hitler and his bride in a common grave near the Chancellery. There they probably lie to this day.

The Wonder of Wood

Donald Culross Peattie

[January 1948]

Wood is man's best friend. Most versatile of all living substances, it held him in his cradle; was the frame of the bed he came to rejoicing; and will make him his last long home. It was the murmuring tree above his childhood play, and the roof over the first house he called his own. It is even the page he is reading at this moment.

Living, a tree sweetens the air where it breathes. It lays the dust and tempers the wind. When it is felled, sawn and seasoned, it lays bare the hidden beauty of its heart, in figures and grains more lovely than the most premeditated design.

Touch any object made of wood—the table top of bright maple, the chopping bowl of cleanly birch, a paneled wall of knotty pine, the lean strength of an ash rake-handle, a basket of woven willow splits, or a tobacco pipe of brier. Pass your fingers sensitively over this wood, then press your full palm upon its firmness. Compared with metal or clay or stone it seems warm still, still living out its useful days.

With its 1000-odd native species of trees, the United States started out with the greatest forest heritage that ever fell to the lot of a lucky people. So wood has gone into the very fiber of our nation. Our first exports back to England from the Jamestown colony came from the forest—black walnut, mighty pines for masts, pitch, turpentine. By the time George Washington inherited Mount Vernon (a wooden house, like millions of

American homes) and planted around it now-mighty elms and tulip poplars, our wood-wise pioneer ways were already 150 years old.

When British shot fell back from the live-oak sides of the frigate *Constitution*, she got her name *Old Ironsides*. When the backwoods boys fought beside Robert E. Lee in their home-spuns dyed with butternut, they were known as Butternuts, and that tree became a synonym for tattered valor. The cabin Lincoln was born in was made of logs of that grand old tree, the American white oak. The rails he split were black walnut.

Wood fired the racing steamboats on the Mississippi, and fed the first railroads. We spanned the treeless plains on ties cut from eastern forests. On rims of hickory and spokes of oak, pioneers rolled west to the Pacific. There new woods came to hand —redwoods and Douglas fir 300 feet high, tremendous sugar and ponderosa pines, gigantic western cedars, timbers such as man had never seen before.

And every kind of tree has its own virtues. Some are perfect in their capacity to absorb sudden shock, like the ash so carefully selected for baseball bats, or the persimmon of golf-club heads. For airplane construction no wood in the world equaled our light Sitka spruce. Most cabinet woods are chosen because they shrink little in seasoning. On the other hand, our ancestors taught us to fit seasoned hickory dowels into chair seats of green sugar maple: when the maple shrinks it clasps the hickory leg in a grip that nothing can loosen.

The same species of wood may have uses ranging from the trivial to the sublime. The little box that holds berries in the market is made of deal. But when you camped beneath its fragrant boughs you called it spruce. Once a year it becomes your Christmas tree. The newspaper publisher calls it pulp and on its macerated fiber he spreads the news for you. When the violinist's bow drops on the strings, the note thrums down through the bridge to the violin's rich, soft belly—made of spruce.

The shingles on your house are probably western red cedar—the same tree the Northwest Indians used for their giant canoes, single logs hollowed out by fire to hold 40 people. The Indians used this wood for their totem poles, too, not only because it endures so well the sun and rain but because the tree grows so high. Western red cedar is a king of the forest, one of the most gigantic growths on the planet.

But of all American woods none has been more significant than white pine. Nowhere else is there a wood so light that grows so tall. Within 30 years of their arrival the Pilgrims were exporting white pine all the way to Madagascar. A single tree made a mast tall as a ship could carry, yet so light it was never top-heavy. When the English navy sailed to some of its greatest victories in the 18th century, it spread its sails on masts and yards of New England white pine. No wonder that the tallest pines on the Crown lands of America were blazed with "the king's broad arrow," to warn the colonists that these were reserved for the Royal Navy. You can imagine how much attention the New England patriots paid to *that!*

White pine built New England's loveliest colonial mansions and churches. A favorite of the carpenter, it works smoothly under the plane, and shrinks or swells little when properly seasoned. Fleets were launched to export it, railroads were bent to great stands of it, mushroom cities rose in its clearings, and it founded great fortunes. Under its boughs evolved the American lumberjack.

For toughness our pioneers turned to hickory. Not steel itself is as shock-resistant. So the Norwegian ski champion wants to know that, when he takes that flying leap, his life is insured by good American hickory under his feet. As a fuel a cord of hickory almost equals in thermal units a ton of anthracite, and epicures will have no smoked hams but those cured over green-hickory coals, so subtle is their aroma.

Every American soldier, from Washington's armies to Eisenhower's, has known the feel of a native black-walnut rifle stock under his palm. Under hard usage walnut does not splinter; instead of growing rougher with handling it becomes smoother. In their increasing scramble for walnut, hardwood buyers now make a farm-to-farm quest. Once the log is at the sawmill it is carefully watched for sign of figured grain. If any turns up, the saws are stopped, and the flitch of wood moved up to the veneer knives. These will pare off sheets less than one 32nd of an inch thick. It is said that a single black-walnut log, one showing a uniquely beautiful figure, sold in the veneer trade for $20,000 wholesale.

And the final gift of wood to us is its sacrifice on our home altars. The companionable whisper of a burning log is the tea-kettle song of the moisture in it; its aroma rises from the rich oils and gases stored up through its living years. Sometimes as the flames penetrate to a hidden storehouse of the wood, the essences ignite in a sudden blue tongue of hissing flame. Gums and resins are driven seething through the cracks in the bark. Slowly into flame go the cellulose, wood oils and gases. The mineral constituents such as potash, silica and calcium remain as ash.

Form and plan are in the very structure of wood from the moment it begins to grow. The tree has the power of reproduction and the power to repair injuries and go on with a stout heart. It can overcome obstacles, split rocks apart, travel far in thirsty search for water. It can adjust to circumstances. It can endure, with an immortality all its own: wooden piles under the streets of Venice have been found intact after 1000 years; white cedar in the swamps of eastern Virginia has lain buried an estimated 3000 years, yet is being dug up today and sawed into boards that may last another thousand.

Each tree, too, is an individual; no two are alike, nor two boards from the same tree. Each piece of wood, with its grain and rings, is as different from the other as your fingerprints are from those of anyone else in the world. Wood reminds us, in its pliancy and resilience, of human flesh and, yes, even human spirit.

Say if you like that wood has no thoughts and no tongue to speak them. But let him who says this look in his own heart and produce for us a thought that will warm the hearth of a friend, or endure 1000 years.

ౠ Put three grains of sand inside a vast cathedral, and the cathedral will be more closely packed with sand than space is with stars.
Sir James Jeans in *Modern Essays* (St. Martin's Press)

Meanest Word
in the Language

H. Allen Smith

[April 1967]

L—ULLABY. Golden. Damask. Moonlight. Do these words seem esthetically attractive to you? They have appeared with some regularity on lists of "the ten most beautiful words in our language." Along with luminous, hush, anemone, mother and various others. But I can't recall ever seeing a list of the ten ugliest words.

Almost everyone has an agglomeration of words that can cause him to wince—such as agglomeration. I lay claim to several hundred of the uglies. Mulcted almost nauseates me. I cringe in the face of albeit, yclept, obsequies, and/or, whilom, and tinsmith. Want to hear a *real* ugly word? Ugly.

But my own nomination for the meanest and low-downest and ugliest word of them all is "Oh." Said twice, with maybe a hyphen, this way: "Oh-oh." In its maximal ugliness, it is customarily spoken softly, with inflections that would curl the toes of a sandy-land mule.

Something is wrong, let us say, with the engine of your car. You take it to the garage. The mechanic lifts the hood and pokes around a bit and then you hear him murmur, "Oh-oh." The wretched creature says it in such a quietly dramatic manner that you know instantly that your whole motor has to be derricked out and thrown away and a new one put in.

Consider our friends, the dentists. Most of them have enough gumption (beautiful word!) to conceal their opinions and judgments, but sometimes you'll run across one who forgets his chairside manner. He'll be inspecting a big molar in the back and suddenly he'll say, "Oh-oh." Or he'll come out of his darkroom carrying an X ray taken a few minutes earlier, and he'll put it up against the light, and he'll look at it briefly, and then his head will give a jerk and he'll say, "Oh-oh." You know at once, without ESP, precisely what is meant. Out. All of them. From now on, plates. No apples. No corn on the cob. No a lot of things.

Physicians as a general thing have schooled themselves carefully to conceal any sinister condition they may find during an examination. Yet I have run across one offender in my checkered medical career. He was giving me the annual checkup. He took my blood pressure and tapped me for knee jerks and scratched me on the bottoms of my feet for God knows what and stethoscoped me front and back and had me blow into a machine to test my "vital capacity" and then he turned the electrocardiograph loose on me. As he studied the saw-toothed dossier on my heart, his brow crinkled and I heard him say, quite softly, "Oh-oh." Everything inside of me suddenly bunched together in one large knot.

"What is it?" I demanded. "Whad you find there?"

"It's nothing, really," he said.

Nothing! Cancer of the heart is *nothing*? It had to be at least that.

"I heard you say 'Oh-oh,'" I told him. "Come on. Tell me. I'm a man. I can take it. Let me have it straight."

"Okay," he said, and I steeled myself and began to turn chicken. "I said 'Oh-oh' because," he went on, "I just happened to think that I haven't made out my tax return yet, and the deadline is tomorrow."

I quit him the next day. I can't use a doctor who is going to say "Oh-oh" in my presence, not unless he has dropped his sphygmomanometer on the floor and busted it. And even in that contingency I think he should employ a more masculine expression. I would.

When Hannah Var
Eight Yar Old

Katherine Peabody Girling

[November 1937]

"WERE you a little girl, Hannah, when you came to America?" I asked.

"No," she replied, letting her sewing fall in her lap as her grave eyes sought mine slowly, "I var a big girl eight yar old."

"Eight years old? Does that seem to you big?"

"Oh, well," Hannah explained, "in Old Country if you are eight yar old and comes younger child'n in familie, you are old woman; you gotta be, or who shall help de moder?"

"Yes? Did your father and mother bring you?" I continued.

"No—fader and moder var daid. My h'aunt, se came for us. I can to tell you how it is I came on Áhmericah, but"—Hannah waited for words to express her warning—"it will make you a sharp sadness."

"Please."

"I don't know if I can tell it to you good, but I tell it so good as I can. My fader he var Swedish fisherman vat h'own his boat and go away by weeks and weeks, and sometimes comes strong wedder and he can't make it to get home quick." Hannah hesitated, and then in lowered tones of soft apology added, "My moder se var a ver' pretty woman. Var t'ree child'n more as me —Olga var six yar old, and Hilda four, and Jens—well, Jens var yust a baby, suppose yar and half. Ve live in a little house close on by de sea. It is yust a little house, but it can to have a shed with a floor of stone. De door of de shed is broken so it is like a window mitout glass.

"De house is close on by a big dock where in somer time comes big excursion steamer mit—suppose hundert tourist people who climb on de mountain up de road. My moder se sell dem hot coffee, also bread and cheese, but it is de big dock is de reason why ve live in de little so lonesome house. My fader he can to come home from late fishings mitout dat he sall walk on de dangersome roads. Ve live dere all somer, but in late autumn my fader he say, 'What about de winter?'

"My moder se say, 'I don't know, but anyway ve try it vonce.'

"Den my fader he go away in his boat and my moder se get bad cold and comes sickness on her, and ven se couldn't to keep care on us se is too weak, se lay on de cot in de kitchen room and vatch on me dat I sall learn to keep care on de child'n."

"But what did you live on? How did you keep warm?"

"Oh—is plenty fuel, and ve make hot stew of dried meat mit rice and raisins.

"One day my moder se say me, 'Hannah,' se say, 'you bain a big girl; I must to tell you sometings. You fader is very late, it seems, and winter comes now. I cannot to wait much more. It is soon I got to go. You mustn't take a fear of me if I come all white like de snow and don't talk mit you any more. De little child'n dey will take a fear and cry. I cannot to bring a fear on my little child'n.'

"So se tell me what I sall do—I sall close bot' her eyes up and tie her hands togeder and lock de shed door."

"The shed door!"

"Ya."

Hannah had resumed her sewing. Her thread fairly snapped as stitch fell by even stitch with monotonous rhythm. In quiet, uneventful tone she continued:

"So one night pretty soon se make dat I sall bring her best nightgown and help her mit to put it on. Den se kiss de little child'n in deir sleepings and se sit on a stool by de fire and say I sall put Jens in her arms. Se try to rock back and fort' and se sing on him a little hymn. But se is too weak, and I must to take him. Den se put on me a shawl and tie it behind under my arms, and se lean heavy on me, and ve go out into de shed. My moder se do her bare feet on de stone floor. Se have yust but her nightgown on, but it is her best one mit crocheted lace at de neck and wrists. Se tell me I sall put de ironing board across two chair seats, but it is too heavy and se sall try to help me, but comes coughing on her and se must to hold on by de shed door. Se look out across de road and de mountain all mit snow white and mit moonlight cold. And blood is on her lips, but se wipe it away. Well, anyway, ve do de ironing board across de seats and I spread a sheet and put a cushion and my moder lie down and I cover her mit other sheet over.

" 'Oh, moder,' I say, 'let me make some warm covering on you.'

" 'No,' se say, so soft dat I listen mit my ear, 'I must to come here while I yet have de stren'th, but I want to go quick away, and in de cold I go more quick. Oh, Hannah!' se say, 'my big daughter! You are so comfortable to me!'

"So I hold my moder's hand. Pretty soon it comes cold. I clap it mit mine, but it comes more cold. I crumple it up and breathe my hot breath in it, but it comes not warm any more. So mit my fader's Sunday handkerchief I bind her eyes like if you play Blindman mit de child'n, and mit an apron string I tie her hands togeder. Den I go back and make my hands warm in de kitchen room, and I go back to my moder mit de comb and make her hair in two braids like as I did all when se was sick. My moder se have very strong hair; it is down by her knees on and so yellow—so yellow as a copper teakettle! Den I lock de shed door and crawl in bed mit de child'n to make me warm.

"Next day I tell de child'n dat moder is gone away. Dey cry some, but pretty soon dey shut up. Anyway, it is so long se haf lain on de cot in de kitchen room dat dey don't haf to miss her.

"So I keep care on de child'n and play mit dem, and some days go by. Comes a stronger wedder mit storms of sleet and snow, and de wind sob and cry. Comes nobody on. At night when de child'n are sleeping I unlock de shed door and go to see if it makes all right mit my moder. Sometimes it is by de moonlight I see on her, but more often it is by a candle glimmer."

Hannah broke the subdued tone of her narrative to add in a lower, more confiding note, "It is mit me now dat when I see a candle on light I haf a sharp sadness.

"Pretty soon de wedder is more better, and comes a man trompling troo de snow to tell my moder dat her husband can't come home—he is drowned in de sea. When he see how it is mit my moder and mit me and de little child'n, de water stands in his eyes—ya. And he go on, troo de snow, t'ree, four mile nearer on de city to de big castle where live de lady vat h'own all de land and se come in sleigh mit four horsen and big robes of fur and yingling bells. Se see on my moder and se go quick away, but so soon as it can, se come again and se do on my moder a white robe, heavy mit lace. And white stockings of silk and white slippers broidered mit pearlen. Se leaf my moder's hair as I fix it, in two braids, but se put a wreath of flowers, white and green, yust like a girl vat gets married should to wear. Den my lady se send her sleigh dat all de people should come see on de brave woman vat couldn't to bring a fear on her little child'n. And de people say it is de prettiest dey ever see it, and make pity my moder couldn't to see it herself." She paused. "I wish se could have to seen dose slippers!"

"And did no one tell you that you were a wonderful little girl?"

"Oh, vell—I var eight yar old."

"But what became of you all?"

"My lady took us home in her sleigh mit—I want to stay mit my moder, but se say I sall come to keep care on de child'n dat dey don't cry. And dey don't cry—dey laugh mit de yingling bells. De need was on me strong, but I don't cry before my lady. Dey do my moder in a coffin and carry her to a little chapel house in cemetaire and in de spring ven de snow is gone dey bury her. My lady se put a white stone mit my moder's name and some poetry—I can't to say it good in English, but it says, 'De stren'th in de heart of her poor is de hope of Sweden.'"

"And then did your aunt come?"

"Ya; my lady se wrote on my fader's broder vat var in Ahmericah. My oncle he send his wife, and ve come back mit her on Ahmericah, und dat is all how I came to be here."

The Wisdom of Wildness

Charles A. Lindbergh

For 50 years The Reader's Digest has been counted among the nation's strongest voices arguing "environmentalist" principles. The magazine has crusaded against careless misuse of the earth's special glories, for preservation of its resources of soil, wildlife, wilderness. Motivated by the same concern, the Digest led all major magazines in advocating birth control and population limitation—long before these became popular causes.

Charles Lindbergh, with a solitary airplane flight in 1927, found himself transformed into a symbol of man prevailing over nature. He is an airman still, but today known as an ardent conservationist.

[April 1968]

THE WILD world is the human world. Having evolved in it for millions of centuries, we are not far removed by a clothing of civilization. It is packed into our genes. In fact, the more power-driven, complex and delicate our civilization becomes, the more likelihood arises that a collapse will force us back to wildness.

There is in wildness a natural wisdom that shapes all earth's experiments with life. Can we tap this wisdom without experiencing the agony of reverting to wildness? Can we combine it with intellectual developments of which we feel so proud, use it to redirect our modern trends before they lead to a worse breakdown than past civilizations have experienced? I believe we can, and that to do so we must learn from the primitive.

My own interest in wildness roots back to early boyhood and stories my father told me about Minnesota's frontier when he was my age. Woods were full of deer, he said; the sky was often black with duck; every lake and river held its fish. Chippewa Indians built their tepees near his home. It was a wonderful place for a boy to grow up.

What changes a single generation brought! I saw no deer around our farm. Virgin forests had been cut. The Chippewa lived on reservations. Even wild duck and fish were scarce.

I envied my father his frontier days; but my generation had compensations—automobiles, airplanes, telephones, thousands of scientific innovations. And still one could reach the wilderness by traveling farther west.

I learned to drive at the age of 11, to fly at 20. I made aviation my profession. Airplanes combined the elements I loved, bringing qualities of science and wilderness together without apparent conflict. Mathematics of engine and airfoil carried me over frontiers wilder and more inaccessible than my father had described. I came to know the world's geography as man had never known it before: great bends of my Mississippi Valley; sweeps of Western plains; Appalachian, Rocky and Sierra ridges, dividing a continent. Looking back in memory, I see caribou on arctic tundra, elephant herds plodding African game trails. Below me are New Guinea jungles, Himalayan peaks, equatorial Pacific islands set gemlike in their reefs—all pieced upon a mental sphere the progress of science has shaped within my mind.

With tremendous effort on the part of increasing thousands of men and women, aviation has developed rapidly. My own lifetime spans the Wright brothers' Kitty Hawk flight and manned spaceships traveling between earth and moon. And scientific progress still rises exponentially. The study of nucleonics places cosmic power in our hands, while cryobiology may suspend the human aging process. We dream of hurtling through galaxies as our ancestors dreamed of imitating birds. Obviously the development potential in all scientific fields is tremendous, extending far beyond our vision. I think the light of science is so dazzling that it can be evaluated only by studying its reflection from the absorbing mirror of life; and life brings one back to wildness.

Looking at the mirror of life first caused me to question our civilization's trends. During years spent flying, I watched changes of shade and texture on the great surface below my wings. Stumplands appeared where forests had been. Lakes climbed mountainsides. Ditches gridded marshlands; dust hazed prairies; highways and power lines kept scarring ground from horizon to horizon. I watched crossroads become villages; villages, towns; towns turn into cities; suburbs spill over hills. Virgin wilderness vanished and wild animals dwindled in numbers.

Now the American eagle is verging on extinction. Even the polar bear on its ice floes has become easy game for flying sportsmen. One of the last known herds of Arabian oryx has been machine-gunned by a sheik. Blue whales have nearly been harpooned out of their oceans. Meanwhile, pollution ruins bays and rivers. Refuse litters beaches. Dam projects threaten Colorado canyons and every place of natural beauty that can be a reservoir for power. Obviously the scientific progress so alluring to me is destroying qualities of greater worth.

Of course virgin wilderness had to retreat as civilization advanced. That was inevitable. But I did not consider its possible *disappearance*. The world seemed so large I had assumed that portions would remain in primitive state, yet attainable. Days spent in laboratories, factories and offices were lightened by intuitive contact with wilderness outside. Had the choice confronted me, I would not have traded nature's miracles of life for all of science's toys. Was not my earth's surface more important than increasing the speed of transport and visiting the moon?

If I were entering adulthood now instead of 50 years ago, I would choose a career that kept me in contact with nature more than science. This is a choice an individual still can make—but no longer mankind in general. Too few natural areas remain. Both by intent and indifference we have insulated ourselves from the wilderness that produced us. Our emphasis on science has resulted in alarming rises in world populations that demand an ever-increasing emphasis on science to improve their standards and maintain their vigor.

I have been forced to the conclusion that an overemphasis on science weakens human character and upsets life's essential balance. Science breeds technology. Technology leads to infinite complication. Examples are everywhere: in the intricacy of government and of business corporations; in automation and labor relations; in war, diplomacy, taxation, legislation, in almost every field of modern man's routine.

From the growth of cities to that of military power, from medical requirements to social-welfare benefits, when progress is plotted against time, exponential curves result with which we cannot long conform. But what action should scientific man prescribe as a result? Suppose technologists conclude theoretically that they are destroying their own culture. Are they capable of taking action to prevent such destruction?

The failures of previous civilizations, and the crises existing for our own, show that man has not evolved the ability to cope with limitless complication. He has not discovered how to control his sciences' parabolas. Here I believe the human intellect can learn from primitive nature, for nature, conceived in cosmic power, thrives on infinite complication. No problem has been too difficult for it to solve. From the dynamics of an atom, nature produces the tranquillity of a flower, the joy of a porpoise, the intellect of man—the miracle of life.

In wildness I sense the miracle of life, and beside it our scientific accomplishments fade to trivia. The construction of an analogue computer is simple when compared to the mixture of space and evolutionary eons represented by a cell. In primitive rather than civilized surroundings I grow aware of man's evolving status, as though I were suddenly released from a hypnotic state. Life itself becomes the standard of all judgment. How could I have overlooked, even momentarily, such an obvious fact?

Walking in the daylong twilight of a high-branched Indonesian jungle, I see grotesquely twisting vines of python-width tangle through multi-trunked trees that have diameters exceeding our largest redwoods. Small birds call constantly. Peacocks screech. Stepping quietly over the soft loam of jungle floor, I watch families of wild pigs trotting, rooting about, and squealing in their quarrels. Monkeys swing overhead. A giant lizard staggers onto a log and gawks. Lying on a sea edge in the evening, I watch flying foxes overhead—giant bats with wingspreads of a yard or more—dozens, sometimes hundreds at a time, flapping slowly against the wind, sometimes dropping low enough to touch the water.

I feel transported from the modern to the Mesozoic era, freed from the blindness caused by our clocked environment. Ages turn to seconds. Man becomes a recent advent among earth's contending forms, with civilization but a flash in the evolutionary process. Surrounded by wildness I become less aware of my individuality. I see animals about me as earthly experiments with life; and so I feel myself. Each of us represents a life stream attempting to survive, to take advantage of every opportunity arising. The heron lengthens its legs to wade. The lion sharpens its teeth to kill. The rhinoceros thickens its skin for protection. Man develops his intellect to gain domination of the earth, and by comparison, the speed with which he has gained this domination is astounding—another of those exponential curves that mount like an explosion.

In civilization's sky-scraping cities I feel my superiority to lower animals confirmed by man's unchallenged rule. I view other creatures with a god's aloofness; for I have intellect, and they, no more than instinct. But surrounded by wildness, I start doubting my superiority. I am struck by the physical perfection of other species in contrast to my own, amazed at the beauty, health and balance nature has achieved through instinct's influence. I ask myself what the intellect has done to warrant its prestige. As earth's most messy, destructive and defective animal, man has a record that gives him little cause for pride. Our present intellectual superiority is no guarantee of great wisdom or survival power in our genes. Homo sapiens may be only an overspecialized branch on the trunk of evolution.

For me, wildness brings out nature's basic wisdom in relationship to man's. I see the control of populations, the encouragement of co-existence, the superb juxtaposition of unity and diversity to form life's character. Above all I see an ability to choose the better from the worse that has made possible life's progress.

In wildness, as in no other environment, elements of body, mind and spirit flux and fuse. Released from artificial influence, one's sensations change, and with them one's appraisals. The importance of accomplishment gives way to values of awareness. The smell of earth, the touch of leaves, sounds of animals calling, myriad qualities interweave to make one not only aware but aware of one's awareness. With stars above, a planet below, and no barrier between or after, intuition reaches out past limits of the mind into a mysticism at which man shies the name of "God." Then I think of listening to an African tribesman describe his people's culture: "We believe God is in everything," he said. "He is in the rivers, the grasses, the bark of trees, the clouds and mountains. We sing songs to the mountains because God is in them."

The primitive emphasizes factors of survival and the mysteries beyond them. Modern civilization emphasizes increasing knowledge and the application of technology to man's way of life. The human future depends on our ability to combine the knowledge of science with the wisdom of wildness.

Letters From Camp

. . . Dear Dad, Remember when my counselor came to visit us in the city before camp started and he said he liked little boys like me. Well, he doesn't. John

. . . Dear Folks, Look what they wrote about me in the camp newspaper. I am also the editor of the camp newspaper. Love and XXX, Evelyn

. . . Dear Mom and Dad, I have joined the boxing club. This morning I had my first fight. I don't think I will need braces for my teeth any more. Love, John

. . . Dear Folks, Yesterday our counselor told us all about where babies come from. You lied to me. Love and XXXXXX, Margaret

. . . Dear Parents, You don't have to meet me at the bus station. My counselor said they are going to bring me home in a special car so I can lie down. Jason   Bill Adler, *Letters From Camp* (Chilton)

I Am Joe's Foot

J. D. Ratcliff

The writer whose work has appeared most often in the Digest is J. D. Ratcliff, with some 200 articles to his credit—many of them on medical subjects— since 1936. This is one of an unusually popular, continuing series that began with "I Am Joe's Heart."

[September 1970]

Joe, 47, is a typical American man. Though somewhat awed by his heart, liver, lungs and other organs, he tends to regard me as an ungainly, trouble-causing nuisance. I am Joe's left foot. I've been described as everything from an architectural nightmare to an anatomical wonder. The latter, I think, is closer to fact.

Joe has no idea what a complex piece of machinery I really am. There he stands, gazing out a window, his mind pretty much a blank. Yet a great deal is going on inside *me*. In effect, through the intricate interaction of my 26 bones (one fourth of all Joe's bones are in his feet), 107 ligaments and 19 muscles, I am balancing a six-foot, 180-pound pile of flesh and bone. Try balancing *anything* that size on an area no larger than the soles of two feet! It's a tricky business. Messages fly back and forth to and from the brain. Sensor spots in my soles report that pressure is growing in one area—it means Joe is tilting slightly. Back come orders: tighten this muscle, relax that one. It would take a good-sized computer to handle a balancing act like that.

Walking is even more complex. My heel takes the initial shock load which is then transmitted along my five metatarsal bones to the ball of Joe's foot, just behind the toes. Finally, with the big toe, I give a forward thrust. This keeps me quite busy.

But Joe pays more attention to the tires of his car than he does to me. He punishes me unmercifully, then gets annoyed when I hurt. He simply cannot understand it. Let him walk down a sidewalk at a comfortable 100-steps-a-minute pace. That means I'm hitting cement with a 180-pound jolt 50 times each minute, and my partner to the right is doing the same. In his lifetime Joe will walk something like 65,000 miles—which means tens of millions of jolts for me.

For the first million years or so that Joe's ancestors were on earth, things were fine for feet. Everyone walked barefoot (later on, they would wrap their feet in animal skins) on yielding, uneven terrain—the finest possible exercise for feet. Then came shoes, cement sidewalks and hard floors. I begin to hurt just thinking about them!

When Joe was a baby his parents, without knowing it, piled punishment on me. They did not realize that my bones were soft and rubbery (I wouldn't be a finished product until Joe was about 20 years old). They tucked crib sheets tightly enough to produce mild deformities in me and crammed me into shoes and socks, both short enough to do further damage.

Like all young parents they were anxious for Joe to take his first wobbly steps, and tried to help him. I was still a little bag of pretty soft jelly, not yet ready for walking. It would have been better if they had let Joe decide when he was ready to walk by himself—and left him barefoot until then, or even later.

As a child Joe got regular checks of heart, lungs and other organs that are rarely defective in the young. But I, a big trouble-causer, was ignored. By the time Joe was four, a podiatrist—foot specialist—would have seen immediately that I needed help. By the time Joe was six, real trouble was under way—as in 40 percent of all kids. My partner and I were going flat, and there were the beginnings of toe deformities, caused mainly by heredity and by shoes.

Joe got lessons in tooth brushing, hair grooming and ear washing, but no one thought to give him walking lessons—mainly, to walk with toes straight forward. He walked with toes out. Also, his parents bought him shoes that would last—

the worst possible thing. Up to age six Joe should have had his feet measured every four to six weeks, and new shoes when necessary—four times a year by age 12.

I can cause symptoms far removed from me: backache, headache, leg cramps and such. Mainly, these troubles trace to Joe changing posture and gait to spare one of my sore spots. I might add that these things have an emotional as well as a physical impact. Sore feet: sour disposition.

By all rights Joe's wife's foot should be telling this story, since women have four times as much foot trouble as men. High-heeled shoes are to blame. They pitch weight forward where it doesn't belong, shorten calf muscles, throw the spine out of balance. That's why women have so many back and leg pains. And why they kick off shoes at every opportunity. They'd do better to throw them away.

There are some 50 things that can go wrong with me. The most common: corns. When a shoe produces a pressure spot on one of my toes I respond by piling up protective tissue. Soon there is a pile of dead cells—high enough to put pressure on a nerve below and cause pain. Joe trims his corns with a razor blade and uses acid corn removers. Both can lead to infection. What he should do is apply a moleskin plaster to ease immediate pain, then get shoes that fit.

Bunions come when my big toe folds under the second toe. This, in males, is mostly a hereditary deformity, but shoes aggravate it. I respond by building a pad of protective tissue. Usually the problem can be alleviated by a specially designed splint or sling or other mechanical appliance used in the shoe. If not, surgery to straighten the big toe may be the only answer.

Calluses, usually on the ball of the foot, are sometimes painful pressure spots. Trimming by a foot doctor helps, but wedges, lifts and appliances to produce better balance are the best answer.

Athlete's foot is caused by fungi. These are always present on me, but they cause no harm until they develop and multiply in a moist skin crack or crevice. The best prevention is to keep me dry—not easy, since sweat glands are more numerous on my sole than in any other part of the body except the palms of the hands. If Joe would give me a good wash twice a day, an alcohol rubdown and frequent dustings with powder, the problem would be kept under control. If these things fail, there are always the new anti-fungus pills.

As for ingrown toenails, best treatment is: clean the corners and put a pellet of medicated cotton under the nail. Still better is prevention—trim the nail straight across, and not too short.

Lately Joe has had a few bouts of coldness and numbness in me—due to poor circulation, a part of the aging process. Get the blood moving faster and the trouble goes away. Tepid baths help to dilate blood vessels and improve circulation. Propping feet up on a desk or hassock also helps. As does a walk.

The very best exercise Joe can give me is walking barefoot, as his ancestors did, *over uneven terrain*. But on hard surfaces I do need shoes for support. And though Joe imprisons me in these leather cells for two thirds of his life, he still doesn't know how to buy a decent pair. In fact he spends more time selecting a necktie. Occasionally when I am giving him a hard time he may buy a pair of "health" shoes. There is no such thing, any more than there are "health" eyeglasses or "health" dentures. Either a shoe fits or it doesn't.

Joe should buy shoes in the late afternoon—when I've swollen to my largest size of the day. He should insist that the salesman measure *both* me and my partner (often one foot is slightly larger than the other) while Joe is standing.

Shoes should be at least half an inch longer than the longest toe. And forget about "breaking in" shoes. If a pair isn't comfortable when bought, it's going to cause me—and Joe—trouble. Too-short socks are almost as bad toe-crampers as shoes. Joe should particularly watch those stretch ones.

One final thing—and I am threatening Joe here, so he had better pay heed. Ahead lies old age. The great majority of older people have ailing, painful feet from years of misuse. This is one of the main reasons they spend so much time in rocking chairs and on park benches at the very time of life when they are most in need of mild exercise and stimulating activities.

In this sense, I can actually shorten life. If Joe is to avoid this, he had better start giving me the *serious* attention I deserve.

84, CHARING CROSS ROAD

Helene Hanff

84,

🎀🎀🎀🎀🎀 CHARING CROSS ROAD 🎀🎀🎀🎀🎀

Marks & Co.   14 East 95th St.
84, Charing Cross Road   New York City
London, W.C. 2, England   October 5, 1949
Gentlemen:

Your ad in the *Saturday Review* says that you specialize in out-of-print books. The phrase "antiquarian booksellers" scares me somewhat, as I equate "antique" with expensive. I am a poor writer with an antiquarian taste in books and all the things I want are impossible to get over here except in very expensive rare editions, or in grimy, marked-up schoolboy copies.

I enclose a list of my most pressing problems. If you have clean secondhand copies of any of the books on the list, for no more than $5 each, will you consider this a purchase order and send them to me?

Very truly yours,
(Miss) Helene Hanff

Miss Helene Hanff   Marks & Co., Booksellers
14 East 95th Street   84, Charing Cross Road
New York 28, New York   London, W.C. 2
U.S.A.   25th October, 1949
Dear Madam,

In reply to your letter of October 5th, we have managed to clear up two thirds of your problem. We are sending nice copies of the Hazlitt essays and the Stevenson by Book Post. Our invoice is enclosed.

The Leigh Hunt essays are not going to be so easy but we will see if we can find an attractive volume. We haven't the Latin Bible you describe but we have a Latin New Testament, also a Greek New Testament, ordinary modern editions in cloth binding. Would you like these?

Yours faithfully,
FPD
For Marks & Co.

November 3, 1949

Gentlemen:

The books arrived safely, the Stevenson is so fine I'm almost afraid to handle such soft vellum and heavy cream-colored pages. I never knew a book could be such a joy to the touch.

A Britisher whose girl lives upstairs translated the £1/17/6 for me and says I owe you $5.30 for the two books. I hope he got it right. I enclose a $5 bill and a single. Please use the 70¢ toward the price of the New Testaments, both of which I want.

Will you please translate your prices hereafter? I don't add too well in American; I haven't a prayer of mastering bilingual arithmetic.

Yours,

Helene Hanff

I hope "madam" doesn't mean over there what it does here.

9th November, 1949

Dear Miss Hanff,

Your six dollars arrived safely, but we should feel very much easier if you would send us your remittances by postal money order.

We are very happy you liked the Stevenson so much. We have sent off the New Testaments, with an invoice listing the amount due in both pounds and dollars, and we hope you will be pleased with them.

Yours faithfully,

FPD

For Marks & Co.

November 18, 1949

WHAT KIND OF A BLACK PROTESTANT BIBLE IS THIS?

Kindly inform the Church of England that they have loused up the most beautiful prose ever written. Whoever told them to tinker with the Vulgate Latin? They'll burn for it, you mark my words.

It's nothing to me. I'm Jewish myself. But I have a Catholic sister-in-law, a Methodist sister-in-law, a whole raft of Presbyterian cousins (through my Great-Uncle Abraham who converted) and an aunt who's a Christian Science healer, and I like to think *none* of them would countenance this Anglican Latin Bible if they knew it existed.

I enclose $4 to cover the $3.88 due you; buy yourself a cup of coffee with the 12¢. There's no post office near here so I am not running all the way down to Rockefeller Plaza to stand in line for a $3.88 money order. If I wait till I get down there for something else, I won't have the $3.88 anymore. I have implicit faith in the U.S. Airmail and His Majesty's Postal Service.

Have you got a copy of Landor's *Imaginary Conversations?*
Helene Hanff

26th November, 1949

Dear Miss Hanff,

Your four dollars arrived safely and we have credited the 12 cents to your account.

We happen to have in stock Volume II of the *Works & Life of Walter Savage Landor,* not very handsome but well bound and a good clean copy, and we are sending it to you today.

I am sorry we made the mistake with the Latin Bible and will try to find a Vulgate for you. Not forgetting Leigh Hunt.
Yours faithfully,
FPD
For Marks & Co.

December 8, 1949

Sir:

(It feels witless to keep writing "Gentlemen" when the same solitary soul is obviously taking care of everything for me.)

Savage Landor arrived safely. I do love secondhand books that open to the page some previous owner read oftenest. The day Hazlitt came he opened to "I hate to read new books," and I hollered "Comrade!" to whoever owned it before me.

I enclose a dollar which Brian (British boy friend of Kay upstairs) says will cover the /8/ I owe you. You forgot to translate it.

Now then. Brian told me you are all rationed to 2 ounces of meat per family per week and one egg per person per month and I am simply appalled. He has a catalogue from a British firm here that flies food from Denmark to his mother, so I am sending a small Christmas present to Marks & Co. I hope there will be enough to go round.

I'm sending it c/o you FPD, whoever you are.

Noel.

Helene Hanff

20th December, 1949

Dear Miss Hanff,

Just a note to let you know that your gift parcel arrived safely today and the contents have been shared out between the staff. Mr. Marks and Mr. Cohen insisted that we divide it up among ourselves and not include "the bosses." I should just like to add that everything in the parcel was something that we either never see or can only be had through the black market. It was generous of you to think of us in this way and we are all extremely grateful.

We all wish to express our thanks and send our greetings and best wishes for 1950.

Yours faithfully,

Frank Doel

For Marks & Co.

March 25, 1950

Frank Doel, what are you DOING over there, you are not doing ANYTHING, you are just sitting AROUND. Where is Leigh Hunt? Where is the *Oxford Verse*? Where is the Vulgate? You leave me sitting here writing long margin notes in library books that don't belong to me; some day they'll find out I did it and take my library card away.

I have made arrangements with the Easter bunny to bring you an Egg. He will get over there and find you have died of INERTIA.

I require a book of love poems with spring coming on. *No Keats or Shelley;* send me poets who can make love without slobbering. Just a nice book, preferably small enough to stick in a slacks pocket and take to Central Park.

Well, don't just sit there! Go find it! i swear i don't know how that shop keeps going.

7th April, 1950

Dear Miss Hanff,

I have to thank you for the very welcome Easter parcel which arrived safely yesterday. We were all delighted to see the tins and the box of shell eggs, and the rest of the staff joins me in thanking you.

I am sorry we haven't been able to send you any of the books you want. About the book of love poems, now and then we do get such a volume as you describe. We have none in stock at the moment, but shall look out for one for you.

Again, many thanks for the parcel.

Faithfully yours,
Frank Doel
For Marks & Co.

7th April, 1950

Dear Miss Hanff,

Please don't let Frank know I'm writing this but every time I send you a bill I've been dying to slip in a little note and he might not think it quite proper of me.

We all love your letters and try to imagine what you look like. I've decided you're young, very sophisticated and smart-looking. Old Mr. Martin thinks you must be quite studious-looking in spite of your wonderful sense of humor. Why don't you send us a snapshot?

If you're curious about Frank, he's in his late 30s, quite nice-looking, married to a very sweet Irish girl. I believe she's his second wife.

Everyone was so grateful for the parcel. My little ones (girl 5, boy 4) were in Heaven—with the raisins and egg I was actually able to make them a cake!

I do hope you don't mind my writing. Please don't mention it to Frank.

With best wishes,
Cecily Farr

P.S. I shall put my home address on the back in case you should ever want anything sent you from London.

April 10, 1950

Dear Cecily—

And a *very* bad cess to Old Mr. Martin. Tell him I'm so unstudious I never even went to college. I just happen to have peculiar taste in books. And I'm about as smart-looking as a Broadway panhandler. I live in moth-eaten sweaters and wool slacks; they don't give us any heat here in the daytime. It's a five-story brownstone and all the other tenants go out to work at 9 a.m. and don't come home till 6—and why should the landlord heat the building for one small script-reader/writer working at home on the ground floor?

Poor Frank, I give him such a hard time, I'm always bawling him out for something. I'm only teasing, but I know he'll take me seriously. I keep trying to puncture that proper British reserve. If he gets ulcers I did it.

Please write and tell me about London, I live for the day when I step off the boat-train and feel its dirty sidewalks under my feet.

Regards—
Helene Hanff

20th September, 1950

Dear Miss Hanff,

It is such a long time since we wrote to you I hope you do not think we have forgotten your wants.

We now have in stock the *Oxford Book of English Verse,* printed on India paper, a good secondhand copy, price $2. Some time ago you asked us for Newman's *Idea of a University.* Would you be interested in a copy of the first edition? We have just purchased one. Price—$6.

In case you would like them, we will put both books on one side until you have time to reply.

Yours faithfully,
Frank Doel
For Marks & Co.

September 25, 1950

(he has a first edition of Newman's *University* for six bucks,
do i want it, he asks innocently.)

Dear Frank:

Yes, I want it. I won't be fit to live with myself. I've never
cared about first editions *per se,* but a first edition of THAT
book—!

oh my. i can just see it.

Send the *Oxford Verse,* too. Enclosed please God find $8.
Did I tell you about Brian? He buys physics tomes from a technical bookshop in London; he's not sloppy and haphazard like
me. He bought an expensive set and went down to Rockefeller
Plaza and stood in line and got a money order and cabled it or
whatever you do with it. He's a businessman, he does things
right.

The money order got lost while in transit.

Up His Majesty's Postal Service!

H.H.

4th April, 1951

Helene dear—

Your marvelous Easter parcels arrived safely and everyone is
upset because Frank left the city on business for the firm the
next morning and so hasn't written to thank you, and of course
no one else quite dares to write to Frank's Miss Hanff.

My dear, the *meat!* I really don't think you should spend your
money like that. It must have cost a packet! Bless your kind
heart.

Love,
Cecily

Earl's Terrace
Kensington High St.
London, W. 8
5th April, 1951

Dear Miss Hanff,

This is just to let you know that your Easter parcels to
Marks & Co. arrived safely a few days ago but have not been

acknowledged as Frank Doel is away from the office on business for the firm.

We were all quite dazzled to see the meat. And the eggs and tins were so very welcome. I did feel I must tell you how exceedingly grateful we are for your kindness and generosity.

We all hope that you will be able to come to England one of these days. We should do our best to make it a happy trip.

Sincerely,
Megan Wells

Tunbridge Road
Southend-on-Sea
Essex
5th April, 1951

Dear Miss Hanff:

For nearly two years I have been working as a cataloguer at Marks & Co. and would like to thank you very much for my share-out in the parcels which you've been sending.

I live with my great-aunt who is 75, and I think that if you had seen the look of delight on her face when I brought home the meat and the tin of tongue, you would have realized just how grateful we are. It's certainly good to know that someone so many miles away can be so kind to people they haven't even seen, and I think that everyone in the firm feels the same.

If at any time you know of anything that you would like sent over from London, I will be most happy to see to it for you.

Sincerely,
Bill Humphries

9th April, 1951

Dear Miss Hanff,

I expect you are getting a bit worried that we have not written to thank you for your parcels and are probably thinking that we are an ungrateful lot. The truth is that I have been chasing round the country in and out of various stately homes of England trying to buy a few books to fill up our stock. My wife was starting to call me the lodger who just went home for bed and breakfast, but of course when I arrived home with a nice piece of MEAT, to say nothing of dried eggs and ham, then she thought I was a fine fellow and all was forgiven.

We should all like to express our appreciation in some way or other, so we are sending a little book which I hope you will like.

Yours faithfully,
Frank Doel
For Marks & Co.

Card enclosed with *Elizabethan Poets:* To Helene Hanff, with best wishes and grateful thanks from all at 84, Charing Cross Road, London. April, 1951.

April 16, 1951

To All at 84, Charing Cross Road:

Thank you for the beautiful book. I've never owned a book before with pages edged in gold. Would you believe it arrived on my birthday? I wish you hadn't been so courteous about putting the inscription on a card instead of on the flyleaf. It's the bookseller coming out in you: afraid you'd decrease its value. You would have increased it for the present owner.

And why didn't you sign your names? I expect Frank wouldn't let you. He probably doesn't want me writing love letters to anyone but him. Thank you again.

Yours,
Helene Hanff

Backstage
London
September 10, 1951

Dearheart—

It is the loveliest old shop straight out of Dickens. You would go absolutely out of your mind over it.

It's dim inside. You smell the shop before you see it; it's a lovely smell, I can't articulate it easily, but it combines must and dust and age, and walls and floors of wood. The shelves go on forever. They go up to the ceiling and they're very old and kind of gray, like old oak that has absorbed so much dust over the years they no longer are their true color. There's a long print table with those wonderful English caricaturists and illustrators that I'm not smart enough to know a lot about, and there are some lovely old illustrated magazines.

I stayed about half an hour hoping your Frank or one of the girls would turn up. But I gather they were all out to lunch.

As you see, the notices were not sensational but we're told they're good enough to assure us a few months' run, so I went apartment-hunting yesterday. I don't have the address here. I'll send it or you can call my mother.

Love,
Maxine

September 15, 1951

Maxine, bless your golden heart, what a peachy description. I don't like to sound bitter, but I would like to know what YOU ever did that the good Lord lets YOU browse around MY bookshop while I'm stuck on 95th St. writing the TV "Adventures of Ellery Queen."

xxxx
hh

October 15, 1951

Frank:

This is not pepys' diary, this is some busybody editor's collection of EXCERPTS from pepys' diary. i could just spit.

where is jan. 12, 1669, when his wife chased him out of bed and round the bedroom with a red-hot poker?

i enclose two limp singles, i will make do with this thing till you find me a real Pepys. THEN i will rip up this ersatz book, page by page, AND WRAP THINGS IN IT.

HH

P.S. Fresh eggs or powdered for Xmas? I know the powdered last longer but "fresh farm eggs flown from Denmark" have got to taste better. You want to take a vote on it?

20th October, 1951

Dear Miss Hanff,

First of all, let me apologize for the Pepys. I was honestly under the impression that it was the complete Braybrooke edition and I can understand how you must have felt when you found your favorite passages missing. I promise to look at the next reasonably priced copy that comes along.

I am glad to say I have managed to dig out a few books for you from a private library that we have just bought. There is a Leigh Hunt which includes most of the essays you like, also a Vulgate New Testament which I hope will be O.K.

About the eggs—I have talked to the rest of the inmates here and we all seem to think that the fresh ones would be nicer. As you say, they would not last so long but they would taste so much better. With best wishes.

Yours sincerely,
Frank Doel
For Marks & Co.

November 2, 1951

Dear Speed—

You dizzy me, rushing Leigh Hunt and the Vulgate over here whiz-bang like that. You probably don't realize it, but it's hardly more than two years since I ordered them. You keep going at this rate you're gonna give yourself a heart attack.

That's mean. You go to so much trouble for me and I never even thank you. I just needle you. I really am grateful for all the pains you take for me. I enclose three dollars. I'm sorry about the top one; I spilled some coffee on it and it wouldn't sponge off but I think it's still good. Is your name Welsh?

HH

7th December, 1951

Dear Miss Hanff,

You will be glad to know that the two boxes of eggs and the tins of tongue have all arrived safely and once again we wish to thank you most sincerely. Mr. Martin, one of the older members of our staff, has been on the sick list for some time and we therefore let him have the lion's share of the eggs, one whole boxful in fact, and of course he was delighted to get them.

We are sending you a little gift for Christmas. It is linen and we do hope you will not have to pay any duty on it. Anyway, we hope you will like it and accept it with our sincere best wishes for Christmas and the coming year.

My name is certainly not of Welsh origin. As it is pronounced to rhyme with the French word "Noel," I think there may be a possibility that it originated in France.

Yours faithfully,
Frank Doel
For Marks & Co.

Card enclosed with hand-embroidered Irish linen tablecloth:

Christmas Greetings
and
All Good Wishes for the
New Year
from

Geo. Martin   Megan Wells
W. Humphries
Cecily Farr   Frank Doel
J. Pemberton

37 Oakfield Court
Crouch End
London, N. 8
20-1-52

Dear Miss Hanff:

For a long time I wanted to write to you to thank you for my family's share in the wonderful food parcels you've been sending to Marks & Co. Now I have an excuse as Frank tells me you want to know the name and address of the old lady who embroidered the linen tablecloth. It was beautiful, wasn't it? Her name is Mrs. Boulton and she lives next door at No. 36. She was thrilled to know that her cloth had crossed the Atlantic.

Our oldest girl was 12 last August—Sheila, who, by the way, is my ready-made daughter, as Frank lost his first wife during the war. Our youngest, Mary, was four last week. Last spring, Sheila announced at school that she was sending Mummy and Daddy an anniversary card and told the nuns (it's a convent) that we had been married four years. It took a bit of explaining as you can imagine.

I will close this with all good wishes for the New Year and especially that we may see you in England one of these days.

Sincerely,
Nora Doel

February 9, 1952

Now listen, Maxine—

You took two dozen pairs of nylons over there, so do me a favor. Take four to the bookshop, give them to Frank Doel and tell him they're for the three girls and Nora (his wife).

Wait'll you see what the shop sent me for Christmas. It's an Irish linen tablecloth, hand-embroidered in an old-fashioned pattern of leaves and flowers, every flower worked in a different color and shaded from very pale to very deep.

Ellery raised me to $250 a script, if it keeps up till June I may get to England and browse around my bookshop myself. If I have the nerve. I write them the most outrageous letters from a safe 3000 miles away. I'll probably walk in there one day and walk right out again without telling them who I am.

xxx
h. hanff

14th February, 1952

Dear Helene,

I quite agree it is time we dropped the "Miss" when writing to you. I am not really so standoffish as you may have been led to believe, but as copies of letters I have written to you go into the files the formal address seemed more appropriate. But as this letter has nothing to do with books, there will be no copy.

We are quite at a loss to know how you managed the nylons which appeared this noon as if by magic. All I can tell you is that when I came back from lunch they were on my desk with a note reading "From Helene Hanff."

I don't see how we can ever repay you for your many kind gifts. All I can say is, if you ever decide to make the trip to England, there will be a bed for you at 37 Oakfield Court.

With best wishes from us all,
Frank Doel

DO YOU MEAN TO SIT THERE AND TELL ME
YOU'VE BEEN PUBLISHING THESE MAMMOTH
CATALOGUES ALL THESE YEARS AND THIS IS THE
FIRST TIME YOU EVER BOTHERED TO SEND ME
ONE? THOU VARLET?

Don't remember which restoration playwright called everybody a Varlet; I always wanted to use it in a sentence.

As it happens, the only thing which MIGHT interest me is
the Catullus.

I shall be obliged if you will send Nora and the girls to
church every Sunday for the next month to pray for the continued health and strength of the messrs. gilliam, reese, snider,
campanella, robinson, hodges, furillo, podres, newcombe and
labine, collectively known as The Brooklyn Dodgers. If they
lose this World Series I Shall Do Myself In and then where
will you be?

Have you got de Tocqueville's *Journey to America?* Regards
to Megan. And what's become of Cecily?

h.h.

13th December, 1955

Dear Helene,

I feel very guilty for not writing to you before this, but you
can put it down to a dose of 'flu which kept me away from the
shop for a couple of weeks.

About the Catullus in our catalogue. This was already sold,
but I have sent you another edition, printed in large type, for
$3.78. We have no edition of de Tocqueville but will keep
looking for one.

Megan is still here but planning to go to South Africa to
live. We are all trying to talk her out of it. We have heard nothing from Cecily Farr since she went out to the East to join her
husband, though they were only to be gone a year.

I shall be only too pleased to root for the Brooklyn Dodgers
if you will reciprocate with a few cheers for The Spurs (the
Tottenham Hotspur Football Club to the uninitiated), who are
at present languishing next to the bottom of the League.

Nora and all here join me in sending our best wishes for Christmas and the New Year.

Sincerely,
Frank Doel

June 1, 1956

Dear Frank:

Brian introduced me to Kenneth Grahame's *Wind in the Willows* and I have to have it—but don't mail it; hold it for me till September, then mail it to the new address.

The sky fell on us in this cozy brownstone. We got eviction notices. I decided the time had come to get me a real apartment with real furniture, and shaking all over I went around to the construction site of a new building going up over on 2nd Avenue and signed a lease on a 2½-room apartment that isn't even there yet. I am now racing around buying furniture and bookshelves and wall-to-wall carpet with all my England money, but all my life I've been stuck in dilapidated furnished rooms and cockroachy kitchens and I want to live like a lady even if it means putting off England till it's paid for.

3rd May, 1957

Dear Helene,

Prepare yourself for a shock. ALL THREE of the books you requested in your last letter are on the way.

Two of your friends dropped in to see us a few days ago and now I have forgotten their names—a young married couple and very charming. Unfortunately they only had time to smoke a cigarette as they were off again on their travels next morning.

With best wishes from us all,
Frank

Stratford-Upon-Avon
May 6, 1957

Helene—

You might have warned us! We walked into your bookstore and said we were friends of yours and were nearly mobbed. Your Frank wanted to take us home for the weekend. Mr.

Marks came out from the back of the store just to shake hands with friends-of-Miss-Hanff and everybody in the place wanted to wine and dine us. We barely got out alive.

Love,
Ginny and Ed

August 15, 1959

sir:

i won it. i won a $5000 Grant-in-Aid off CBS. It's supposed to support me for a year while I write American History dramatizations. I am starting with a script about New York under seven years of British Occupation and i MARVEL at how i rise above it to address you in friendly and forgiving fashion. Your behavior here from 1776 to 1783 was FILTHY.

Is there such a thing as a modern-English version of the *Canterbury Tales?* Love to Nora.

h.h.

2nd September, 1959

Dear Helene:

We were all delighted to hear that you've won a Grant-in-Aid. We will be broadminded about your choice of subject matter, but I must tell you that one of the young inmates here confessed that until he read your letter he never knew that England had ever owned "the States."

I am trying to find a nice secondhand copy of Chaucer.

Sincerely,
Frank

9th November, 1963

Dear Helene,

Some time ago you asked me for a modern version of Chaucer's *Canterbury Tales.* I came across a little volume the other day which I thought you would like. It is not complete by any means, but as it is quite a cheap book and seems to be a fairly scholarly job I am sending it by Book Post today, price $1.35.

Love from us all here,
Frank

Saturday

All right. Enough Chaucer-made-easy, it has the schoolroom smell of Lamb's *Tales from Shakespeare*.

I'm glad i read it. i liked reading about the nun who ate so dainty with her fingers she never dripped any grease on herself. I've never been able to make that claim and I use a fork. Wasn't anything else that intrigued me much. Now if Geoffrey had kept a diary and told me what it was like to be a little clerk in the palace of Richard II—THAT I'd learn Olde English for.

i enclose two bucks for the chaucer, that leaves me a credit with you of 65¢ which is larger credit than i have anywhere else.

xx
h

4th October, 1965

Dear Helene,

It was good to hear from you again. Yes, we're still here, getting older and busier but no richer.

We had just managed to obtain a copy of E. M. Delafield's *Diary of a Provincial Lady,* in an edition published by Macmillan in 1942, a good clean copy, $2. We are sending it off to you.

We had a very pleasant summer with more than the usual number of tourists, including hordes of young people making the pilgrimage to Carnaby Street. We watch it all from a safe distance, though I must say I rather like the Beatles. Nora and the girls send their love.

Frank

September 30, 1968

Still alive, are we?

I've been writing American history books for children for four or five years. Got hung up on the stuff and have been buying American history books—in ugly, cardboardy editions, but somehow I didn't think the stately homes of England would yield nice English editions of Madison's stenographic records of the Constitutional Convention or T. Jefferson's letters to J. Adams.

I introduced a young friend of mine to *Pride & Prejudice* one rainy Sunday and she has gone out of her mind for Jane Austen. She has a birthday round about Hallowe'en; can you find some Austen for her?

Best to Nora and anybody else around

Helene

8th January, 1969

Dear Miss,

I have just come across the letter you wrote to Mr. Doel on the 30th of September last, and it is with great regret that I have to tell you that he passed away on Sunday the 22nd of December. The funeral took place last week on Wednesday the 1st of January.

He was rushed to hospital on the 15th of December and operated on at once for a ruptured appendix. Unfortunately peritonitis set in and he died seven days later.

He had been with the firm for over forty years and naturally it has come as a very great shock to Mr. Cohen, particularly coming so soon after the death of Mr. Marks.

Do you still wish us to try and obtain the Austens for you?

Yours faithfully,
p.p. Marks & Co.
Joan Todd (Mrs.)

29th January, 1969

Dear Helene,

Thank you for your very kind letter. Nothing about it at all offends me. I only wish that you had met Frank and known him personally. He was the most well-adjusted person with a marvelous sense of humor, and now I realize such a modest person.

I have had letters from all over to pay him tribute and so many people in the book trade say he was so knowledgeable and imparted his knowledge with kindness to all and sundry. If you wish it I could send them to you.

At times I don't mind telling you I was very jealous of you, as Frank so enjoyed your letters and some were so like his sense of humor. Also I envied your writing ability. Frank and I were so very much opposites, he so kind and gentle and me always fighting for my rights. I miss him so, life was so interesting, he always explaining and trying to teach me something of books.

My girls are wonderful and in this I am lucky. I suppose so many like me are all alone. Please excuse my scrawl.

With love,
Nora

I hope some day you will come and visit us, the girls would love to meet you.

April 11, 1969

Dear Katherine—

I take time out from housecleaning my bookshelves to scrawl you a Bon Voyage. I hope you and Brian have a ball in London. He said to me on the phone: "Would you go with us if you had the fare?" and I nearly wept.

But I don't know, maybe it's just as well I never got there. I dreamed about it for so many years. I used to go to English movies just to look at the streets.

The blessed man who sold me all my books died a few months ago. And Mr. Marks who owned the shop is dead. But Marks & Co. is still there.

If you happen to pass by 84, Charing Cross Road, kiss it for me? I owe it so much.

Helene

Kittens to Spare

⊱ Mary Hydeberg in Williamsburg *Virginia Gazette:* "What's a good toy for a child of any age? We recommend a piece of string. To activate the string you will need a kitten, which may be obtained at the Shelter. This same 'motor' will operate a paper bag or ball to the satisfaction of the entire family. If you'd like something with a little more power, we have ten dogs."

⊱ Front-page notice in the Rocky Ford, Colo., *Gazette:* "To the person who dumped a cat at the Ernie Campbell farm recently— Your kittens are ready!"

"Stand By to Launch Aircraft"

Hugh Mulligan

[*January 1967*]

Night was falling fast on the South China Sea. The flight deck of the aircraft carrier *USS Independence,* three football fields long, had just come alive with hundreds of tiny figures in "Mickey Mouse" noise-attenuator hats and bright-colored jerseys. Pilots in red-lensed glasses, going through "night-adaptation" procedures, moved out of the ready rooms and down narrow passageways softly lit with red bulbs. Deck crews pushed the big Vigilante reconnaissance bombers into line on the darkened flight deck.

One hundred miles off the coast of South Vietnam, the "Big I," recently arrived for combat duty as part of Task Force 77, was clearing her decks for another night launch, another series of bombing attacks and strafing runs against Vietcong positions below the 17th parallel.

As her skipper, Capt. John E. "Blackjack" Kennedy, watched the deck from his high-backed leather "throne," loudspeakers barked, "Stand by to launch aircraft." Captain Kennedy ordered the carrier turned into the wind, and Comdr. Jack Waits, the navigator, plotted the new course on his charts. The engines of the Vigilantes, poised on the steaming catapults, glowed like huge acetylene torches in the gathering gloom.

The tail end of a typhoon sweeping toward Japan curled the sea into skittish whitecaps. The two destroyers riding the carrier's wake to pick up downed planes in the event of a launch or recovery accident were taking green water over their bows; but the *Independence* plowed stolidly into the wind at 14 knots, her velvety wake stretching like a wide question mark for nearly a mile across the angry water.

Aft of the bridge and two decks below, Comdr. John Barlow stood at the green-glassed windows of primary flight control, known simply as pri-fly. "Launch the Vigilantes," he said softly but authoritatively into the loudspeaker system. In the soft amber glow of the instrument panels, his deeply lined face reflected an anxiety not betrayed in his calm voice. The bold inscription "Air Boss," stenciled on his yellow jersey, somehow seemed to belong more to college week in Fort Lauderdale than to a war zone in Vietnam.

In the cockpit of his 40-ton Vigilante reconnaissance bomber, Lt. Comdr. James Bell gave a thumbs-up sign. In the flight officer's seat, Lt. Comdr. William "Moon" McKenna adjusted his oxygen mask and braced himself for the shock of being hurled into the air like a pebble from a giant slingshot.

After the last of the Vigilantes had been fired, a flight of sleek Phantom jet fighters rolled into position. When these had been catapulted into the dusk, massive Sky Warriors were moved up. Next came the Intruders, then the Sky Raiders.

When the *Independence* had launched more than 25 of her 92 aircraft, she resumed her northward course and an ammunition ship came alongside to deliver bombs and rockets. In one and a half hours, proceeding at 12 knots, the carrier took on more than 200 tons of explosives, swinging them across from the ammunition ship on cables operated by winches. Twice during the "unrep" (underway replenishment), Comdr. Joseph H. Cheshure, the supply officer, went over to the ammo ship on a high-line bosun's chair to check storage problems with her supply officer.

The ammo ship had hardly cast off her lines when the Air Boss's voice sounded again on the flight deck loudspeaker: "Prepare to recover aircraft." The carrier turned once more into the wind. A moon was coming up and riding into the rigging. Taking his station at the big green window, Barlow eyed it with satisfaction. "Tonight we have a commander's moon," he said.

"They'll have no trouble finding the deck." A moment later the loudspeaker crackled again, "Eight miles, eight miles." Barlow's birds were coming home to roost.

Eight miles out, each returning plane, Indian-file fashion, flies into a "radar window" 10,000 feet wide and 675 feet high. Here a pilot comes under the electronic guidance of the highly trained technicians in CCA—Carrier Control Approach. It is like flying into a funnel. By following each green blip on his radar screen and talking to the pilot by radio, the final controller, AC1 Joseph Boggs, Jr., is able to keep each returning plane within 15 feet, up or down, left or right, of the perfect glide path to the flight deck.

Now, five decks below, the radar consoles in CCA were picking up the first of the returning birds and a controller at his microphone was nudging the green blip on the screen into the glide path. When the plane reached a point one third of a mile from the carrier, radar control ceased.

Only two men could wave the pilot off—the Landing Signal Officer on the little catwalk just off the stern end of the runway, and the Air Boss in pri-fly. In the early days of carrier flying, the LSO would be out on deck wagging a set of wooden paddles. Today gadgetry has taken over, and his job is safer; but there is still a mesh circus net extending out from the hull of the ship for him to jump into in case the oncoming plane smashes into the stern.

The first fast-approaching plane roared toward the deck. Never taking his eyes off the aircraft, seldom altering the pleasant tone of his voice, the Air Boss issued a series of calm, decisive orders to the deck teams and plane handlers. The Vigilante hit the deck in a shower of sparks and jolted to a stop as the plane's tail hook caught the second of the four arresting wires stretched taut across the flight deck. The Air Boss sighed in relief. "Those boys are so big, they scare me every time they come in."

In the next eight minutes, three more Vigilantes thundered onto the deck. Then the deck controllers set the gear on the arresting wires to take the flight of Phantom fighters. (The wires must be adjusted to handle the gross weight and landing speed of each of the nine types of aircraft carried by the *Independence*.) Four Phantoms landed on schedule; then one came in too high. The jet touched the deck, missed all four wires, and roared off again out over the sea, its engines glowing in the darkness.

"We call them bolters," explained Barlow. "Have you ever seen a horse bolting for the barn? That's why these boys always go to full power when they hit the deck. If they miss the wires, they're ready to roar off again. If they lost power, they'd wind up in the South China Sea."

That night one rookie pilot bolted six times before finally getting on deck on his seventh try. He had to be refueled aloft by a huge tanker plane. Still, in less than half an hour, 26 planes from six squadrons landed on the *Indy's* flight deck.

Then suddenly Barlow's voice lost its customary cheerful tone. "We've got an Intruder with a nose gear stuck. Wave him off. We'll take him last."

Four other planes landed while the Intruder in trouble circled slowly beneath the pale stars off the port beam. Then Barlow said, with a trace of anxiety in his voice, "502 still reports a stuck gear. We'll take him in the net."

A hundred figures in variously colored jerseys swarmed across the deck, like groundskeepers at a baseball stadium rolling out the infield tarpaulin in a sudden downpour. In less than three minutes the crew had erected an enormous net, 21 feet high, across the flight deck. The Intruder made a long, slow pass over the carrier.

"The warning light on his instrument panel has now gone out," CCA reported. "He may have got that gear down after all." The whole ship murmured the news.

Barlow reacted swiftly. "Get that net down. We'll take him on the deck." Again the army of groundskeepers swarmed across the deck.

As the plane came in, the Air Boss stared anxiously out the green window, but it was too dark to see whether the aircraft had its landing gear down. The worry lines of his face framed the question that seemed to hang over the ship: Should the net have been left up?

The loudspeaker kept up its litany: "One half mile . . . One quarter mile . . ."

The LSO spoke distinctly and calmly into his radio, coaching the plane down onto the deck. "All right now, level off, level off. . . . That's it, that's it. . . . Nose up. . . . Get your nose off that deck. . . . Up, up. . . . Easy now."

The Intruder splashed a wave of sparks across the deck, hung on the fourth wire and jolted to a stop, its nose gear down. "That," said the Air Boss mopping his brow, "is what we call a controlled crash."

When the recovery is over, the Landing Signal Officer shows film tapes of every landing on closed-circuit TV sets in the squadron ready rooms and gives a critique of what each pilot did right or wrong. Television cameras placed at strategic positions around the flight deck record tragedy as well as minor mishaps. One night the pilots watched one of their Vigilantes snap the arresting wire, plunge into the sea and burst into flames. A squadron commander and his flight officer were killed —but the tapes had to be shown so that the other pilots could study the landing and perhaps learn a lifesaving lesson from it.

Now, with the last plane in, Lt. Comdr. Jack Barnes, the aircraft-handling officer, set about bringing order to the clutter of planes spread out on the world's most complicated parking lot. Plane directors in yellow jerseys urged the big silver birds aft with a wave of their lighted red wands; plane pushers in blue jerseys moved the planes into position only inches apart for the next launch; ammunition handlers in red jerseys rolled out the bomb trucks; maintenance crews in green went to work checking the engines.

Above and below decks, life aboard the massive carrier went on. Cooks and bakers prepared meals for the 4500-man crew on a round-the-clock basis. The USS Vega, a refrigerator ship, came alongside to deliver 387 tons of supplies—items from chili powder to kosher pickles. In the Independence's hobby shop, a half-dozen off-duty crew members were inspecting the goods for sale: hand-tooled leather golf bags from the Philippines, black-lace nighties from Hong Kong, etc. In a chapel a Catholic chaplain was conducting a marriage conference, and in the legal office Lt. Richard Slater was helping a burly bosun prepare his income-tax return.

At 10 p.m., when the ship's clock rang four bells, the loud-speakers announced the day's statistics: "Aircraft from the *USS Independence* today flew 92 sorties to fixed targets and in support of ground actions in the 3rd and 4th Corps areas. They expended 98 tons of bombs and 2400 rounds of ammunition. All planes were recovered safely."

In his office on the bridge skipper Kennedy mused on the role of the fleet in the Vietnam conflict. "After every war," he told a correspondent, "the Navy is written off, consigned to mothballs and declared obsolete." But carrier warfare has made a big comeback in this war, where major airports like Bien Hoa in the Saigon area have been wrecked by sabotage despite the tight-est security measures, where sudden monsoon squalls can shut down flight operations. In the Vietnam action, carriers float in a virtual sea of safety.

As the *Independence's* loudspeakers blared, similar progress reports were being broadcast over the speaker systems of the *Midway*, the *Coral Sea*, the *Bon Homme Richard* and other carriers of Task Force 77. And as each prepared to carry on its display of modern air-war techniques, the new day was an-nounced by the familiar "Stand by to launch aircraft."

"Silence more musical than any song."
—Christina Rossetti

THEY WERE sitting high up in the hills overlooking a Mediterranean fishing village. "What a quiet evening it is," he said.

"No," she answered. "There's the chapel bell, and some men shout-ing in the boats down on the quay, and a dog barking, and some ducks in the garden below."

"Not bad! But you've missed about 50 larks in the sky, and the grasshoppers all around us, and a car changing gear on the hill, and the oars in the rowlocks of that boat putting out, and the children playing, and the goat bells on the hill behind us, and far off a smithy. It's so quiet you can hear every sound. Generally there's too much noise for that." Margaret Kennedy, *The Constant Nymph* (Doubleday)

Whatever Is New for Women Is Wrong

Edna Kenton

The first issue of The Reader's Digest appeared in February 1922. The aim of "The Little Magazine," as it called itself, was to publish 31 articles a month, the cream of the current crop: articles "of enduring value and interest—today, next month, or a year hence . . ." Among the original titles was this one. It fulfills the promise by retaining its pungency and relevance 50 years later.

[February 1922]

THE FIRST kindergarten was classed, by then current opinion, with all those innovations that have tended to destroy the home and woman's morality. It "snatched the babe from the mother's breast," thus "weakening maternal love." Hardly less dangerous were the first perambulators, in 1850. "Since it is easier to wheel a child than to carry it, what will prevent a mother from wandering from home many hours every day?" asked the *Lady's Newspaper*.

When the first Women's Rights convention was held, in 1848, the *Albany Register* said: "unsexed women." "Wild women," remarked the *Saturday Review*. The convention in 1852 was "The Tomfoolery Convention." "The Shrieking Sisterhood" was another phrase widely used.

In 1874 the British magazine *Queen* said: "Out of 100

Englishmen, 99 refuse to allow their womenkind to belong to a ladies' club," as being in their minds too mixed up with female suffrage, lady doctors, and other too liberal opinions. Yet by 1890 restaurants as well as clubs for women abounded.

As far back as 1732 the *Spectator* spoke of "masculine females" when women began to ride in regulation habits.

Female "doctresses" were new, therefore condemned. "A woman may give her leisure to literature, but let her once set foot within the pale of professional life and she is practically unsexed," said *Queen* in 1860. Again, ten years later, speaking of women demanding admittance to the professions: "It is time to condemn every step taken toward the individualization of women, lest their children become gamins of the gutters."

"He-girls," shrieked the journals of the 1870s, referring to young women seeking co-education. "Manly women," screamed the journals of the '80s, when the shortened skirt and shirtwaist and women's athletics began to be.

In 1790, when obstetrics began to pass under the control of male physicians and away from women tenders, the change was "unsexing" for women. But then in 1860, when women sought admission to the medical schools to take back obstetrics, the demand was heralded as the most "vulgar," "impudent" and "unsexed" one ever made by women.

A woman of the 18th and early 19th century, bereft of husband and desirous of not starving to death, could sew, teach (for almost nothing a year), or slave in kitchens and in a few mines and factories—nothing else. But women were beginning to read and write. Those mannish females who could spell and pronounce three- and four-syllable words were "apes of men." The "Ladies' Revival of Learning" infuriated men: women— women!—were preparing to write books. "Warlike women, learned women and women who are politicians, they abandon the circle which nature has traced about their sex, and convert themselves into men." Dancing, walking, drawing, the harp and sewing, these were genteel, womanly ways of wasting time. And gardening for women was ever feminine.

What are women coming to? Well, they are coming closer to life, with every generation of them since 1700.

In 1860 the New York *Herald* said: "Thirty years ago it was thought unsafe for a lady to visit a public place in the daytime. Now several women in New York whose social position secured them from criticism have already taken the freedom of attending the theater alone at night."

Queen said hopelessly in 1894: "The Ideal is now a strong, athletic, breezy womanhood, which has no tenderness and no reserve—which talks slang and smokes—which is out in all weathers and all day long, which hunts, fishes, shoots, cycles, goes to its club, gives dinners to male friends, and is something of a boy itself with its comrades. It has no fears, no sense of shyness. To it a man and woman are interchangeable terms: what one does, the other may do also."

In 1890 *The Nation* said: "One would expect these bold innovators would have to go through a long period of probation. But no such thing has taken place. The sweet girl graduates have quietly glided in among us and become familiar figures. They seem to find lovers and husbands in the ordinary course of nature, and among men who are not looked upon as visionary or eccentric."

Modern dances are today in disrepute. Those who first did the turkey trot were depraved beings, and conservatives sighed for the discarded waltz. They forget that the waltz when new was not considered nice—nor were the "modern" and therefore "scandalous" dances of 1860.

Harper's Bazaar was sternly criticized in the late 1860s for "exposing women's faces in public prints." There was excitement over "lady acrobats" in 1870; over the first suggestion of coöperative homes and kitchens and "flats" in 1873; over women ushers in theaters in 1884: "men find the seats sooner."

And so most of the old bogies, tested out, disappear; and new ones take their place. But today, as in every decade since 1700, the home and marriage and the child and female delicacy are still in imminent peril—"endangered as never before."

℘ "I realize it takes all kinds of people to make a world," said the young lady, "and I'm glad I am not one of them."   *The Far East*

The Turning Point of My Life

A. J. Cronin

[May 1941]

I WAS 33 at the time, a doctor in the West End of London. I had been lucky in advancing through several arduous Welsh mining assistantships to my own practice—acquired on the installment plan from a dear old family physician who, at our first interview, gazed at my cracked boots and frayed cuffs, and trusted me.

I think I wasn't a bad doctor. My patients seemed to like me —not only the nice old ladies with nothing wrong with them, who lived near the Park and paid handsomely for my cheerful bedside manner, but the cabbies, porters and deadbeats in the mews and back streets of Bayswater, who paid nothing and often had a great deal wrong with them.

Yet there was something . . . though I treated everything that came my way, read all the medical journals, attended scientific meetings, and even found time to take complex postgraduate diplomas . . . I wasn't quite sure of myself. I didn't stick at anything for long. I had successive ideas of specializing in dermatology, in aural surgery, in pediatrics, but discarded them all. While I worked all day and half of most nights, I really lacked perseverance, stability.

One day I developed indigestion. After resisting my wife's entreaties for several weeks, I went casually to consult a friendly colleague. I expected a bottle of bismuth and an invitation to bridge. I received instead the shock of my life: a sentence to six months' complete rest in the country on a milk diet. I had a gastric ulcer.

The place of exile, chosen after excruciating contention, was a small farmhouse near the village of Tarbert in the Scottish Highlands. Imagine a lonely whitewashed steading set on a rain-drenched loch amid ferocious mountains rising into gray mist, with long-horned cattle, like elders of the kirk, sternly munching thistles in the foreground. That was Fyne Farm. Conceive of a harassed stranger in city clothes arriving with a pain in his middle and a box of peptonizing powders in his suitcase. That was I.

Nothing is more agonizing to the active man than enforced idleness. A week of Fyne Farm drove me crazy. Debarred from all physical pursuits, I was reduced to feeding the chickens and learning to greet the disapproving cattle by their Christian names. Casting around desperately for something to do, I had a sudden idea. For years, at the back of my mind, I had nursed the vague illusion that I might write. Often, indeed, in unguarded moments, I had remarked to my wife, "You know, I believe I could write a novel if I had time," at which she would smile kindly across her knitting, murmur, "Do you, dear?" and tactfully lead me back to talk of Johnnie Smith's whooping cough.

Now, as I stood on the shore of that desolate Highland loch I raised my voice in a surge of self-justification: "By Heavens! This is my opportunity. Gastric ulcer or no gastric ulcer, I will write a novel." Before I could change my mind I walked straight to the village and bought myself two dozen penny exercise books.

Upstairs in my cold, clean bedroom was a scrubbed deal table and a very hard chair. Next morning I found myself in this chair, facing a new exercise book open upon the table, slowly becoming aware that, short of dog-Latin prescriptions, I had never composed a significant phrase in all my life. It was a discouraging thought as I picked up my pen and gazed out the window. Never mind, I would begin. Three hours later Mrs. Angus, the farmer's wife, called me to dinner. The page was still blank.

As I went down to my milk and junket—they call this "curds" in Tarbert—I felt a dreadful fool. I felt like the wretched poet in Daudet's *Jack* whose immortal masterpiece never progressed beyond its stillborn opening phrase: "In a remote valley of the Pyrenees . . ." I recollected, rather grimly, the sharp advice with which my old schoolmaster had goaded me to action. "Get it down!" he had said. "If it stops in your head it will always be nothing. Get it down." And so, after lunch, I went upstairs and began to get it down.

Perhaps the tribulations of the next three months are best omitted. I had in my head clear enough the theme I wished to treat—the tragic record of a man's egoism and bitter pride. I even had the title of the book. But beyond these naïve fundamentals I was lamentably unprepared. I had no pretensions to technique, no knowledge of style or form. I had never seen a thesaurus. The difficulty of simple statement staggered me. I spent hours looking for an adjective. I corrected and recorrected until the page looked like a spider's web, then I tore it up and started all over again.

Yet once I had begun, the thing haunted me. My characters took shape, spoke to me, laughed, wept, excited me. When an idea struck me in the middle of the night I would get up, light a candle, and sprawl on the floor until I had translated it to paper. At first my rate of progress was some 800 labored words a day. By the end of the second month it was a ready 2000.

Suddenly, when I was halfway through, the inevitable happened. Desolation struck me like an avalanche. I asked myself: "Why am I wearing myself out with this toil for which I am so preposterously ill-equipped?" I threw down my pen. Feverishly, I read over the first chapters which had just arrived in typescript from my secretary in London. I was appalled. Never, never had I seen such nonsense in all my life. No one would read it. I saw, finally, that I was a presumptuous lunatic, that all I had written, all that I could ever write was wasted effort, sheer futility. Abruptly, furiously, I bundled up the manuscript, went out and threw it in the ash can.

Drawing a sullen satisfaction from my surrender or, as I preferred to phrase it, my return to sanity, I went for a walk in the drizzling rain. Halfway down the loch shore I came upon old Angus, the farmer, patiently and laboriously ditching a patch of the bogged and peaty heath which made up the bulk of his hard-won little croft. As I drew near, he gazed up at me in some surprise: he knew of my intention and, with that inborn Scottish reverence for "letters," had tacitly approved it. When I told him what I had just done, and why, his weathered face slowly changed, his keen blue eyes scanned me with disappointment and a queer contempt. He was a silent man and it was long before he spoke. Even then his words were cryptic.

"No doubt you're the one that's right, doctor, and I'm the one that's wrong. . . ." He seemed to look right to the bottom of me. "My father ditched this bog all his days and never made a pasture. I've dug it all *my* days and I've never made a pasture. But pasture or no pasture," he placed his foot dourly on the spade, "I canna help but dig. For my father knew and I know that if you only dig enough a pasture can be made here."

I understood. I watched his dogged working figure with rising anger and resentment. I was resentful because he had what I had not: a terrible stubbornness to see the job through at all costs, an unquenchable flame of resolution brought to the simplest, the most arid duties of life. And suddenly my trivial dilemma became magnified, transmuted, until it stood as the timeless problem of all mortality—the comfortable retreat, or the arduous advance without prospect of reward.

I tramped back to the farm, drenched, shamed, furious, and picked the soggy bundle from the ash can. I dried it in the kitchen oven. Then I flung it on the table and set to work again with a kind of frantic desperation. I lost myself in the ferociousness of my purpose. I would not be beaten, I would not give in. I wrote harder than ever. At last, toward the end of the third month, I wrote *finis*. The relief, the sense of emancipation, was unbelievable. I had kept my word. I had created a book. Whether it was good, bad or indifferent I did not care.

I chose a publisher by the simple expedient of closing my eyes and pricking a catalogue with a pin. I dispatched the completed manuscript and promptly forgot about it.

In the days which followed I gradually regained my health,

and I began to chafe at idleness. I wanted to be back in harness.

At last the date of my deliverance drew near. I went around the village saying good-by to the simple folk who had become my friends. As I entered the post office, the postmaster presented me with a telegram—an urgent invitation to meet the publisher. I took it straight away and showed it, without a word, to John Angus.

The novel I had thrown away was chosen by the Book Society, dramatized and serialized, translated into 19 languages, bought by Hollywood. It has sold millions of copies. It altered my life radically, beyond my wildest dreams . . . and all because of a timely lesson in the grace of perseverance.

But that lesson goes deeper still. Today, when the air resounds with shrill defeatist cries, when half our stricken world is wailing in discouragement: "What is the use . . . to work . . . to save . . . to go on living . . . with Armageddon round the corner?" I am glad to recollect it. The door is wide open to darkness and despair. The way to close that door is to go on doing whatever job we are doing, and to finish it.

The virtue of all achievement, as known to my old Scots farmer, is victory over oneself. Those who know this victory can never know defeat.

Clarifications

༞ As children reach a certain age, they begin to get curious about what brought their parents together. One day, a wife had been crabbing freely at her husband. In the evening, when the two of them were sitting sipping something cool but smoldering with ill humor, their six-year-old son asked, "Daddy, how did you meet Mother?"

"I took a thorn out of her paw," the father growled.

George Dolan in Fort Worth *Star-Telegram*

༞ During a downpour, the policeman directing traffic near a popular Dallas restaurant was wearing a bright-yellow slicker heavily labeled with the Dallas Police Department insignia. At a particularly busy moment, a woman ran up. "Are you a policeman?" she asked.

"No, lady," said the officer patiently. "I am a giant canary."

Frances Balch, quoted by Paul Crume in Dallas *News*

How to Lose Weight— And Stay Thin

Theodore Isaac Rubin, M.D.

[September 1966]

BEING fat is a sickness, whether you are mildly sick (three or four pounds overweight) or deathly sick (75 pounds overweight). Spread all over your body, extra fat strains the heart, blocks the arteries, raises the blood pressure and shortens life. Moreover, this condition is destructive to one's psychic and social life.

If you are overweight and would like to reduce, your first step is to admit you are sick. This is crucial. Only when you admit that overeating is an obsession, a compulsion, can you begin to cure yourself.

If you feel sorry for yourself, fine. But don't let pity turn to hate. Self-hate is the biggest enemy of the fat man, since it results in pain requiring sedation in the form of food. Only by accepting yourself, whoever and whatever you are, will you be able to change.

Hopelessness, the deep-down conviction that you can't get well, is your second-biggest enemy. It is used again and again as justification for overeating. The fact is that your illness *can* be cured. But you must be utterly realistic; it's going to be a long, hard struggle.

It is imperative that you realize that *you*—not your glands— are responsible for your excess weight. Again and again we hear how some lucky people can eat tremendous amounts of food and not gain weight because they burn it up quicker—whereas we poor fat types, cursed with slow metabolism, are natural fat-manufacturing plants. Well, it simply isn't so. Most people are perfect in the metabolic department. If your doctor has not put you through the various tests for thyroid function (basal-metabolism rate, blood iodine, blood cholesterol), it is because he believes you are a self-made fatty.

The origin of your sickness is simple: for your size and physical output of energy, you have been taking in too many calories. The cure is equally simple: you must eat food that contains fewer calories—and eventually balance your calorie input with your energy output.

There are many good diets, and practically all of them work. See a doctor in whom you have faith, and ask him what is safe for you. Ask him if a crash diet of a week's duration is compatible with your state of health. The quick loss of a few pounds can be a good morale booster. But use no pills, no "medical aids." You need self-esteem; you need to know that the results come from you alone.

In setting goals for your diet, be realistic. Discouragement, especially early in the game, can be devastating. So if you are 30 pounds overweight, don't think about your diet in terms of losing 30 pounds. Instead, think in terms of, say, a loss of ten percent of the total weight you want to lose. When you reach that goal, set a new one that you can attain.

A warning: big changes don't occur immediately—not even with complete starvation. An initial weight loss will probably be the result of an early loss of water, not fat. Later on, depending on water intake, your weight may go up and down quite a lot until progress becomes steady.

Since it is too much for you to hope to succeed in eating your three daily diet meals and nothing else, always keep a supply of ammunition foods in the house—foods you can eat in any quantity. These include radishes, celery stalks, broccoli, asparagus, sauerkraut, spinach, watercress, tomatoes, lettuce, cucumbers, cauliflower.

Also keep on hand some emergency foods—for days when

things are tough, and you *must* have something sweet. Have some low-calorie chocolate pudding and low-calorie cream whip —a total of 65 calories. Or have half a cantaloupe, or tea and animal cookies (six—no more). If more solid food is necessary, have a hamburger patty or a small steak.

If you feel an overpowering urge to go on a binge, quick! drink two glasses of seltzer, tea, low-calorie soda, black coffee, bouillon, or just plain water. Now eat two large pickles and a whole medium-sized cantaloupe. Then do something very hard: get out of the house and walk—away from the place where you got fat in the first place.

Don't be impatient with your progress. It will take time—it *should* take time—to become thin. This gives your body an opportunity to acclimate itself to its new dimensions; the stomach has a chance to shrink, the skin to tighten.

It will be best, in fact, if you segment your dieting. That is, if you are 40 pounds overweight, diet it off in units of 10 pounds at a time, and take a 30-day vacation after each unit, eating a maintenance diet that will produce neither gain nor loss. Why not go the whole distance in one long burst? Isn't it more difficult to diet, vacation from dieting, and then go back to dieting? Perhaps—but in learning that it can be done, you will improve your morale and your self-control. More important, these vacations get your body and psyche used to a maintenance diet, one that you will ultimately follow for the rest of your life.

The day you start dieting ought to be chosen with care. Begin on a morning when you are well-rested and fairly busy. Ordinary workdays are fine—usually much better than vacation days or weekends.

If possible, eat in pleasant surroundings and in congenial company. Eat slowly, and enjoy whatever you are eating. The mood created by food taken graciously will give more satisfaction than you think possible in sustaining you to the next meal.

If your diet and scruples permit, I see no reason not to have a highball in the evening. This can be something to look forward to, and can make life a little easier.

It is well to be aware of the side reactions and complications associated with dieting. Most diets will result in a sharp decrease in food intake and a consequent decrease in food fluid; these, as well as fat depletion, make constipation a common problem. Unless contra-indicated by your diet or doctor, drink plenty of water—at least six glasses a day. Eat plenty of low-calorie green vegetables—lettuce, kale, beet ends, spinach—and two whole *raw* apples a day. If constipation is chronic, ask your doctor's advice.

Headache, fatigue, mild depression, weakness, listlessness and insomnia are all common initial symptoms. All can be both psychological and physiological in origin. All these symptoms, though, are transient.

Whenever you open the refrigerator or sit down at table, there will be foods there that have always tempted you. And there will be force-feeders, friendly enemies who pressure you with, "Go off your diet just once, just for a little while," and "Don't be so hard on yourself." Or, "I liked you better the other way. You looked more jolly." Or, "You are so irritable—eat and be happy." They will make every effort to keep you fat, for the simple reason that nearly all people dislike the unfamiliar and resist the possibility of any change in their associates.

Remember that your first duty is to yourself. You have to be with yourself all the time—and wouldn't it be nice if your constant companion were thin, healthy, attractive?

When you reach your goal—congratulations! But remember that as a formerly fat person you are something like a former alcoholic. The fat is gone, but your sensitivity to food will always exist. Be aware of it!

During your maintenance period—the rest of your life—the scale will be your most reliable instrument in determining success, danger and potential maintenance failure. Watch it consistently, heed its warnings, and you will never get back into serious trouble. Eventually you will become so stabilized that there will be practically no weight fluctuations at all.

ॐ Overheard in a women's dress shop: "My measurements are small medium and large—in that order." Troy Gordon in Tulsa *World*

LIFE IN THESE UNITED STATES

THE ENGINEERING department of a large oil company is known for its good-looking secretaries. Their motto: "Hire 'em—we'll teach 'em to type." One day a handsome young man came in seeking a job. During the interview, a secretary slipped a note to the manager. It read: "Hire him—we'll teach him engineering."   Mrs. J. F. Miller, *Des Plaines, Ill.*

MY EIGHT-YEAR-OLD son is a terror to shop with, his energy matched only by a flair for trouble-making. Imagining the havoc he'd create in the glassware department where I was headed, I stationed him at a hardware counter with a stern warning about any misbehavior. In 15 minutes I returned. He was waiting quietly. I was about to praise him-- then saw on the counter, in a neat row, 25 mousetraps all set to go off at the slightest touch.   Mrs. E. DeStefano, *Apollo, Pa.*

ON SMALL farms in Virginia, hams are still smoked as they have been for centuries. The meat is hung in a small hut, a fire is built on the floor, and soon the tantalizing odor of hickory smoke and ham kindles the appetite.

My husband asked our venerable neighbor how his smoked hams were coming along. "Lawd-a-mercy," he replied, "when the wind is right, all you need is two pieces of bread and you've got a sandwich."   Mildred A. Williams, *Richmond, Va.*

WHEN my wife and I moved into a sixth-floor apartment, I decided on a "shape-up" program. Each day after work I would spurn the elevator and jog up the stairs. Since my business clothes made me too warm, as I went up I'd shed my coat and tie and begin unbuttoning my shirt. One day on the third-floor landing I met an elderly couple. As I went by, the man turned to his wife and, nodding knowingly, said, "Newlyweds."   Frank Russell, *Anchorage, Alaska*

A DEDICATED second-grade teacher was riding with her daughter, who had just earned her driver's license. "Barbara," she admonished, "if you want to turn left at the next corner, you must get over into the hundreds column."

Virginia Opocensky, *Lincoln, Neb.*

ONE of my techniques as a personnel manager, in interviewing prospective salesmen, was to hand them my cigarette lighter and say, "Sell me this." And the applicant would stumble through an impromptu pitch. But one day a bright young man surprised me. He picked up my lighter, looked at it, then put it in his pocket and said, "For ten dollars you can have your lighter back."

L. N. Bradford, *Hopkins, Minn.*

MY DAUGHTER and her husband delight me with their efforts to live up to each other's expectations. He doesn't especially approve of TV watching. So one day when he was home and working in the basement, she turned on the vacuum before sitting down to watch her show. Then, hearing hammering, she peeked into the basement. There he sat, abstractedly pounding hammer on floor while he browsed through old auto-racing magazines.

Mrs. Earl L. Davis, *Minneapolis, Minn.*

As WE approached Los Angeles airport on a flight from Denver, the man next to me suddenly jumped up and began peering out the plane's windows, first on one side, then the other. What was the problem? "Oh, nothing's wrong," he said. "I was just checking the freeways for traffic jams, to see which one to take home."

Bert Du Mars, *Fullerton, Calif.*

STANDING in line at a supermarket checkout, I listened to the woman ahead of me. She was tearing into the checkout girl on all matters pertaining to the store—prices, arrangement of goods, etc. Yet when my turn came, the checker greeted me with a smile. Gesturing toward the departing fussbudget, I said, "Don't you sometimes get tired of people?"

"Oh, no," she answered with a twinkle. "I'm people, too."

Charles E. Thompson, Jr., *Torrance, Calif.*

The Night the Stars Fell

Arthur Gordon

[October 1964]

ONE SUMMER night in a seaside cottage, a small boy felt himself lifted from bed. Dazed with sleep, he heard his mother murmur about the lateness of the hour, heard his father laugh. Then, with the swiftness of a dream, he was borne in his father's arms down the porch steps, out onto the beach.

Overhead the sky blazed with stars. "Watch!" Incredibly, as his father spoke, one of the stars moved. In a streak of golden fire it flashed across the astonished heavens. And before the wonder of this could fade, another star leaped from its place, then another, plunging toward the restless sea. "What is it?" the child whispered. "Shooting stars. They come every year on certain nights in August. I thought you would like to see the show."

That was all: just an unexpected glimpse of something haunting and mysterious and beautiful. But, back in bed, the child stared for a long time into the dark, rapt with the knowledge that all around the quiet house the night was full of the silent music of the falling stars.

Decades have passed, but I remember that night still, because I was the fortunate seven-year-old whose father believed that a new experience was more important for a small boy than an unbroken night's sleep. No doubt I had the usual quota of childhood playthings, but these are forgotten now. What I remember is the night the stars fell. And the day we rode in a caboose, the time we tried to skin the alligator, the telegraph we made that really worked. I remember the "trophy table" in the hall where we children were encouraged to exhibit things we had found—snake skins, seashells, flowers, arrowheads, anything unusual or beautiful.

I remember the books left by my bed that pushed back my horizons and sometimes actually changed my life. Once my father gave me *Zuleika Dobson*, Max Beerbohm's classic story of undergraduate life at Oxford. I liked it, and told him so. "Why don't you think about going there yourself?" he said casually. A few years later, with luck and a scholarship, I did.

My father had, to a marvelous degree, the gift of opening doors for his children, of leading them into areas of splendid newness. This subtle art of adding dimensions to a child's world doesn't necessarily require a great deal of time. It simply involves doing things more often *with* our children instead of for them or to them. One woman I know keeps a "Why not?" notebook, and in it scribbles all sorts of offbeat and fascinating proposals: "Why not take kids police headquarters get them fingerprinted?" "Why not visit farm attempt milk cow?" "Why not arrange ride tugboat?" "Why not follow river dredge and hunt for fossilized shark's teeth?" And so they do.

I asked her where she got her ideas. "Oh," she said, "I don't know. But when I was a child, I had this wonderful old ne'er-do-well uncle who—" Who used to open doors for her, just as she is opening them now for her own children.

Aside from our father, we had a remarkable aunt who was a genius at suggesting spur-of-the-moment plots to blow away the dust of daily drudgeries. "Can you stand on your head?" she would ask us children. "I can!" And, tucking her skirt between her knees, she would do so. "What shall we do this afternoon?" she would cry, and answer her own question instantly: "Let's go pawn something!" Or, "There's a palm reader on the edge of town. Let's have our fortunes told!" Always a new dimension, always a magic door opening, an experience to be shared. That's the key word: we *shared*.

The easiest door to open for a child, usually, is one that leads to something you love yourself. All good teachers know this. And they know the ultimate reward: the marvelous moment when the spark you are breathing on bursts into a flame that henceforth will burn brightly on its own. At a United States Golf Association tournament a few years ago, a pigtailed ten-year-old played creditably in the junior girls' championship. "How long have you been interested in golf?" someone asked her. "I got it for my ninth birthday," she said. "You mean your father gave you a set of clubs?" "No," she said patiently, "he gave me *golf.*"

The possessor of a wonderful realm had wanted his child to share the magic kingdom. No doubt it took some time and effort, some patience, some mystical transference of enthusiasm. But what a reward for both of them! And it might equally well have been music or astronomy or chemistry or collecting butter-flies—any world at all.

Children are naturally inquisitive and love to try new things. But someone must offer them the choices. Years ago, when the Quiz Kids were astonishing American radio audiences with their brilliance, a writer set out to discover what common denominators there were in the backgrounds of these extraordinary children. He found that some were from poor families, some from rich; some had been to superior schools, some had not. But in every case investigated there was at least one parent who shared enthusiasms with the child, who watched for areas of interest, who gave encouragement and praise for achievement, who made a game of searching out the answers to questions, who went out of his way to supply the tools of learning. No doubt the capacity for outstanding performance was already there, but it took the love and interest and companionship of a parent to bring it out.

I have a friend, a psychiatrist, who says that basically there are two types of human beings: those who think of life as a privilege and those who think of it as a problem. The first type is enthusiastic, energetic, resistant to shock, responsive to challenge. The other type is suspicious, hesitant, withholding, self-centered. To the first group, life is hopeful, exciting. To the second, it's a potential ambush. And he adds, "Tell me what sort of childhood you had and I can tell you which type you are likely to be."

The real purpose, then, of trying to open doors for children is not to divert them or amuse ourselves; it is to build eager, outgoing attitudes toward the demanding and complicated business of living. This, surely, is the most valuable legacy we can pass on to the next generation: not money, not houses or heirlooms, but a capacity for wonder and gratitude, a sense of aliveness and joy. And for those of us who care what becomes of our children, the challenge is always there. None of us meets it fully, but the opportunities come again and again.

Many years have passed since that night in my life when the stars fell. But the earth still turns, the sun still sets, night still sweeps over the changeless sea. And next year, when August comes with its shooting stars, *my* son will be seven.

Driven to Distraction

In a hilly Cleveland suburb, a woman parked her car and got out to mail a letter. While she was at the mailbox, the car took off across an intersection, a sidewalk and a field—landing in a small ravine. Asked by police why the emergency brake hadn't been set, she retorted that she certainly did not consider mailing a letter an emergency.
Cleveland *Sun-Press*

Friends of mine were planning to attend a meeting in downtown Miami. One woman offered to drive her car, but said they would have to go via the old route, as she couldn't drive on the expressway. Asked why, she replied, "I can't *merge!*"
R. Wilson

Two busy mothers, driving their children to school, collided. They got out and inspected the damage, but not really having time for a wreck right then, they agreed to meet later. That afternoon each woman drove to the scene of the accident, maneuvered her car into the exact position of the accident, and *then* they called the police.
Frankie Peterson in Austin, Texas, *American-Statesman*

On a Virginia turnpike a toll collector, walking back to his booth with a cup of coffee, stopped to let a car pass through—then watched in amazement as the woman driver smiled warmly at him and dropped her quarter into his coffee.
The Insider's Newsletter

My Most
Unforgettable Character

Betty MacDonald

[*July 1949*]

I'M SURE no woman ever enjoyed the attentions of a more lovable or more unusual suitor than Mike Gordon. Instead of flowers or candy Mike would send me such gifts as a side of beef; 24 boxes of apples; four dozen pairs of nylons, slightly irregular as to size and color; 288 cans of split-pea soup; six handmade Tyrolean sweaters all exactly alike and all the wrong size; 200 ears of corn; a dozen hams; 367 bars of scented soap.

The stone that dislodged this avalanche of gifts was a casual introduction at a lunch in 1934. Even though I had been married and divorced and had two children, I was only 26; and since Mike was somewhere between 70 and 100, it never occurred to me that he would consider himself my suitor and endeavor during the next eight years to outsuit anyone else.

Mike looked like a jolly little troll. He was not quite five feet tall, had a slight fringe of yellowish-white hair, small sparkling blue eyes, fat red cheeks, and a round little stomach always liberally sprinkled with cigarette ashes. He spoke with an odd accent which bore traces of Swedish, Scottish, Greek and Dead-End Kid.

Mike and I discovered that we were both from Butte, Mont., on that first day at lunch while our mutual friend was getting his coat. I lived with my mother and sisters in Seattle then. Mike said he was originally from Butte, and I told him my father had been a mining engineer there. When our friend came back Mike calmly said, to my amazement, "I've known Betty since she was a baby. Knew her mudder and fadder well. Very wealty and prrrominent man."

I found out later that Mike was like a child about the truth. He considered strict adherence to it a sign of weakness, like being afraid of mice. He said whatever came into his head; he then believed it himself. Further, all Mike's friends had to be "wealty" or "prrrominent." People who weren't his friends were "damn appleknockers."

Mike's home and prosperous lumber business were located in a small town in the heart of the apple country in eastern Washington. September is the peak of the apple harvest, and September 1934 marked the entrance into the lives of my family of an endless procession of Railway Express trucks bearing gifts from Mike. The first truck brought 24 boxes of apples. Each apple was about six inches in diameter. We learned then that Mike always bought not only the most but the biggest. From that day on for years our house smelled like a cider press and buzzed like a beehive with children dashing to the basement for apples.

That first load of apples established Mike in the hearts of my daughters, Anne and Joan, who were five and six. There were many times later on when Mike irritated me, but not once did the children's adoration of him waver. No wonder; his "most and biggest" was the answer to every child's dream.

"I just love grapes," Anne mentioned to Mike one day. The next week the expressman delivered two 25-pound lugs of them. "Cherries are my favorite fruit," said Joan, so every week every year in cherry season Mike sent a ten-pound box of enormous hand-packed cherries.

His gifts were the one thing Mike's friends dreaded about him. If someone mentioned that he liked a certain kind of potato, next day Mike would have a ton of some other kind dumped in his front yard. Someone else would admit to a taste for a variety of ham, and would immediately receive ten of a kind that Mike fancied. Someone else would show Mike a Cape

Cod lighter he had bought, and Mike would get 90 and distribute them by the half-dozen, even to people who had no fireplaces. And Mike was like a child with his gifts—demanding that you *like* them, forcing you to open, while he stood by beaming, a box containing 144 jars of Indian chutney.

I surmise that Mike's obsession for wealth and prominence was an effort to obliterate a humble beginning, but I'm not sure, for neither I nor any of his many friends ever had the slightest idea what his background had been. Once he told me that his father had been a British sea captain and his mother a Russian. Then all of Mike's wealty prrrominent friends began shouting about communism, and Mike dropped that story like a hot rock. When I reminded him of it he denied ever having said it.

"My mudder was Swedish," he said. "My fadder died when I was a baby so I don't know what he was."

Mike drove a car as he did everything else, in superlatives—the worst and the fastest. Fortunately his car was bright red and when people saw him coming they could pull off into the brush until the comet had gone by. His method of driving was to climb behind the wheel, jam the accelerator clear to the floor, and call everyone who got in his way a damn appleknocker.

Two weeks before the first Christmas after we met, Mike dropped in to find out what gifts my children wanted. He said, "I know Santa Claus very well." Joan said, "Of course—you're old enough!" Mike laughed delightedly and got out his notebook and pen. Anne said that she wanted a baby doll, a doll buggy, a toy sewing machine and "ball berrian" roller skates. Joan said that she wanted a bicycle, an electric train, a BB gun and "ball berrian" roller skates.

I said, "I also know Santa Claus, and he happens to be working for the government this year at a very bum salary and you'd better cut down those lists right now before he notices what little pigs you are." The children gave me dirty looks and changed their lists.

Three days before Christmas the Railway Express delivered what seemed to be the entire toy section of the Sears, Roebuck catalogue. Christmas morning Anne and Joan were completely overcome. Mike had proved that he knew Santa Claus.

Mike's entertaining was in perfect character—the biggest and most. He lived in an apartment located under his lumber-mill offices, and furnished in a style recognizable to my family as pure Butte. Everything in Mike's apartment was red, everything was monogrammed, and the place was heated to 80 degrees. In his bathroom were red velvet draperies with huge gold monograms, scented toilet paper, monogrammed soap, an Oriental rug, and a shelf full of bottles of expensive perfumes. The other rooms, also magnificently overdressed, contained such unusual bric-a-brac as a lamp composed of a semi-nude harem beauty gazing into a lighted crystal ball. Mike's chinaware was Tower-pattern Spode, which he called "Spud."

A delightful host, he knew the formula for a successful party: good food, good wine and congenial people. Any occasion was the signal for a party at Mike's, and people drove hundreds of miles over the mountains to attend. He drank very little himself but often mixed for his guests concoctions that would roll back the scalp. At one of his parties he had fruits and flowers frozen into each corner of a 200-pound block of ice, the center of which was hollowed out to form a punch bowl.

Mike was a superb cook and had trained his Filipino houseboy to assist in producing a gourmet's delight, but his meals were so enormous they made eating seem futile. I remember one picnic he gave. The eight of us in my family were instructed by Mike to be at the appointed place on the Skykomish River at two o'clock; we were to bring nothing but ourselves. When we got there Mike had already arrived; he had unloaded and spread under the trees 25 pounds of fried chicken; ten pounds of hamburgers made of beef tenderloin; ten pounds of weenies; eight cases of pop and beer; a vat of potato salad; pickles, olives, hard-boiled eggs; and a gallon of cocktails. Mike, who never ate during the day, didn't eat a mouthful; but he complained bitterly because we didn't completely demolish those mountains of food.

The one trait of Mike's which I found almost unbearable was the one which endeared him the most to the children. This was his bossiness and the "prrrogrrrams" he imposed on his guests. When Mike planned a party or a trip he planned it down to the last split second, and his guests did what he wanted them to, when he wanted them to, or else!

When we went to visit him by train he would meet us at the station and hustle us to the car, outlining "de prrrogrrram" as we went. "De first stop," he would say, "is for lunch. Don't eat much. I am giving a dinner tonight and I want you to save your appetites. After lunch we visit Margaret, den Corinne, den Berle, den Marguerite, den Bea, den doctor's wife, den home to rest up for dinner. I'm having ten couples but I've told dem dey can't stay late because we have to get an early start in de morning to drive to Lake Chelan. We'll stop dere for a minute while you look at de view, den on to Coulee Dam, about ten minutes will cover dat, den on to Moses Lake." He was true to his word, too. It makes me tired and mad just to write about it, but the children loved it.

Another thing they loved about those visits was the fact that Mike got up at four, and when they came pattering down at five, instead of being batted back to bed as was the habit at home, they were greeted cordially and given coffee and leftover desserts for breakfast.

Children were the true love of Mike's life and he always treated them with dignity and courtesy. No matter how busy he was, he would listen gravely to stories of crabby teachers, unfair mothers, cheating playmates, interesting dreams and exciting movies. Mike had no sense of humor according to my standards, but no child's joke was ever too shopworn or obvious to go unapplauded.

Mike had a stock phrase for anything he liked: "Beautiful, beautiful, beautiful!" He applied it to the singing of John Charles Thomas (whom Mike admired tremendously and called John Charlie Thompson), autumn leaves, a plate of fudge, a child's new shoes, a load of lumber. As long as we live, members of our family will, when we see autumn leaves, echo Mike's "Beautiful, beautiful, beautiful, just like gold!"

When I married Donald MacDonald, after being courted by Mike via the Railway Express for eight years, I thought with relief that at last the deluge of presents would stop. It didn't. Mike and Don met, and the admiration was mutual. Don thought Mike was amazing, amusing and very dear. Mike referred to Don as "a great big handsome fellow—a Scotchman just like me." The presents continued but took a new form. Little motors, 50 gallons of antifreeze and cases of Scotch replaced the nylons and soap. The fruit continued. Mike was courting us both.

During all the years I knew him, I tried to think of things to do for Mike, of ways to repay his generosity. I made him sketches, I sent him pictures, I was always on the lookout for something I could afford that he didn't already have 60 of. Then Don and I together took up the cause, but it was a losing game: every time we sent Mike a present he sent one back that was twice as big and eight times as expensive.

It was a problem that loomed bigger with the years until in 1945 I wrote *The Egg and I* and suddenly became, to my surprise, both "wealty and prrrominent." I couldn't have done anything that would have repaid Mike more fully. He carried dozens of copies of the book in his car and tossed them at people with: "Sold ten million copies—biggest thing since the Bible."

When Mike died a year ago, his many friends outdid themselves in giving him a lavish funeral. Usually I avoid funerals, considering them outmoded and barbaric rites, but this one was just what Mike would have wanted. The altar and even the walls of the church were blanketed in flowers, and the coffin was entirely covered with orchids. "Beautiful, beautiful, beautiful!" he would have said.

The minister gave a short eulogy on Mike, his kindness and generosity, his love of children, and ended with the assurance that the deceased had entered the kingdom of heaven. I hoped the minister was wrong, for I knew that Mike would much prefer to be with all the "wealty prrrominent" people.

&≥ *Local Color.* A union movement among Catholic priests has been called, by Washington wags: "National Association for Advancement of Collared People" (Gerald Grant in Washington *Post*) . . . Notice in a California bar: "We reserve the right to toss you out because of your rage, choler or greed" (Neil Morgan in San Diego *Tribune*)

Are You Alive?

Stuart Chase

[September 1922]

I HAVE often been perplexed by people who talk about "life." Americans, they tell me, do not know how to live, but the French—ah, the French! Or the Hungarians, or the Poles, or the Patagonians. When I ask what they mean by "life" they are no help.

What do social prophets mean when they promise a new order of life? Obviously not a new quality of life never before enjoyed by anyone; rather, an extension of vitality for the masses of mankind in those qualities of life hitherto enjoyed only by a few individuals normally, or by large numbers rarely.

What is it which is enjoyed? What *does* it mean to be alive, to live intensely? I want to tell you the facts as I have found them. I do not know what "living" means to other people but I do know what it means to me, and I have worked out a method of measuring it.

I get out of bed in the morning, gulp coffee and headlines, demand to know where my raincoat is, start for the office—and so forth. These are the crude data. Take the days as they come, put a plus beside the living hours and a minus before the dead ones; find out just what makes the live ones live and the dead ones die. Can we catch the verihood of life in such an analysis? The poet will say no, but I am an accountant and only write poetry out of hours.

My notes show a classification of eleven states of being in

which I feel I am alive, and five in which I feel I only exist. These are major states. In addition, I find scores of sub-states too obscure to analyze. The eleven plus reactions are:

- I seem to live when I am creating something—writing this article, for instance; making a sketch, working on an economic theory, building a bookshelf, making a speech.
- Art certainly vitalizes me. A good novel, some poems, some pictures, operas, many beautiful buildings and particularly bridges affect me as though I took the artist's blood into my own veins. There are times, however, when a curtain falls over my perceptions which no artist can penetrate.
- The mountains and the sea and stars—all the old subjects of a thousand poets—renew life in me. As in the case of art, the process is not automatic—I hate the sea sometimes—but by and large, I feel the line of existence below me when I see these things.
- Love is life, vital and intense. Very real to me also is the love one bears one's friends.
- I live when I am stimulated by good conversation, good argument. There is a sort of vitality just in dealing in ideas that to me at least is very real.
- I live when I am in the pressure of danger—rock-climbing, for example.
- I feel very much alive in the presence of a genuine sorrow.
- I live when I play—preferably out-of-doors. Such things as diving, swimming, skating, skiing, dancing, sometimes driving a car, sometimes walking.
- One lives when one takes food after genuine hunger, or when burying one's lips in a cool mountain spring after a long climb.
- One lives when one sleeps. A sound healthy sleep after a day spent out-of-doors gives one the feeling of a silent, whirring dynamo. In vivid dreams I am convinced one lives.
- I live when I laugh—spontaneously and heartily.

In contradistinction to "living" I find five main states of "existence" as follows:

- I exist when I am doing drudgery of any kind—adding up figures, washing dishes, answering most letters, attending to money matters, reading newspapers, shaving, dressing, riding on streetcars or up and down in elevators, buying things.
- I exist when attending the average social function—a tea, a dinner, listening to dull people talk, discussing the weather.
- Eating, drinking or sleeping when one is already replete, when one's senses are dulled, are states of existence, not life. For the most part I merely exist when I am ill.
- Old scenes, old monotonous things—city walls, too familiar streets, houses, rooms, furniture, clothes—drive me to the existence level. Sheer ugliness, such as one sees in the stockyards or in a city slum, depresses me intensely.
- I retreat from life when I become angry. I exist through misunderstandings and in the blind alleys of "getting even."

So, in a general way, I set life off from existence. It must be admitted of course that "living" is often a mental state quite independent of physical environment or occupation. One may feel—in springtime for instance—suddenly alive in old, monotonous surroundings. Then even dressing and dishwashing become eventful and one sings as one shaves. But these outbursts are abnormal. By and large there seems to be a definite cause for living or for existing. So it is with me at any rate. I believe that I could deliberately "live" twice as much—in hours —as I do now, if only I would come out from under the chains of necessity—largely economic—which bind me.

I have indeed made some estimates of the actual time I have spent above and below the "existence" line. For instance, my notes show that in one week, of the 168 hours I "lived" only about 40, or 25 percent of the total time. This allowed for some creative work, a Sunday's hike, some genuine hunger, some healthy sleep, a little stimulating reading, two acts of a play, part of a moving picture, and eight hours of interesting discussion with various friends.

It may be that the states of being which release life in me release it in most human beings. Generally speaking, one's salvation is bound closely with that of all mankind.

Things You Learn
at the Grand Canyon

Wolfgang Langewiesche

[*February 1957*]

The GIGANTIC thing is hidden, so you come on it suddenly. You are in high country, but on a flat plain covered with nice-smelling pine woods. Today, of course, you know what's coming. But 100 years ago a man might have camped in these woods only a few hundred feet from it and never suspected anything. Then one evening he walks in that direction, and there . . . the earth opens up.

Right at your feet is a gash a mile deep, 4 to 18 miles across, 217 miles long. And this is one of the peculiar things about the Canyon: its bigness shows. With a mountain, if you get close enough to make it seem big you also have to look up at it slant-wise, and that makes it seem small. With the Canyon, when you stand on one rim and look squarely across you see a mile-high precipice of rock, and it looks gigantic!

A million people a year visit the Canyon. Some of them look a while, but you can see it doesn't take. "Terrific, yes. But what does it *mean?*" They know they're missing something.

Other people—I am one—try to find the missing thing by leg-work. I have walked down into it and what's more, up out of it again. Main thing I found down there: it's hot! I've flown over the Canyon and down into it. Main finding: scary. In the end, I found that all this poking around is unnecessary. The best way to see the Canyon is to do exactly what most people do: walk over to the rim and look.

Look at what? At the interior of the earth. When you stand there at the rim looking down you see two things. One: the hole, which is an odd, terrific, scenic thing—unique. The other: what you see through the hole. And this, by contrast, is not unique; it is a typical cross section of the earth's crust. If you could cut the earth open in France or England, Texas or Arabia, you would see much the same sort of thing.

But the Canyon is such an odd and violent sight that you look at the hole rather than at what it shows. At best, one asks: "What happened? What made this hole?" Well, never mind that for the moment. Look at what it shows.

The earth's crust is built up of layers of different rocks. At the Canyon one can clearly see 12 major layers, some red, some gray, some brown. Many of them are so regular, clear-cut, neat, they look almost artificial.

These layers are the stuff that settled out of the water of ancient seas. If you let muddy water stand in a glass, the water clears and the mud collects at the bottom. The same thing happens in a sea. The rivers bring sand and mud which settle and form thick layers. In deeper seas, the skeletons of fish and the shells of tiny sea animals sink to the bottom and, mixed with mud, clay and sand, form deep layers. These layers, through millions of years under their own weight, turn into rock. Sandstone is sand cemented grain-to-grain. Shale is former mud. Limestone is former seashell and other material.

These Grand Canyon layers prove that this region, now a mile and a half above sea level, was under the sea not only once but several times. At one time the river brought red mud. At another time the sea was deep, and limestone formed. At still another time it was a river mouth, and sand bars and beaches formed.

If you look down into the deepest part of the Canyon where the Colorado River is cutting a V-shaped gorge, you see the rock is dark and quite different in texture from all the other layers. That's the original land that went under the sea. Geologists call it the "basement."

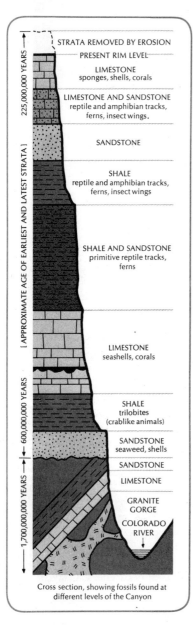

225,000,000 YEARS

[APPROXIMATE AGE OF EARLIEST AND LATEST STRATA]

600,000,000 YEARS

1,700,000,000 YEARS

STRATA REMOVED BY EROSION

PRESENT RIM LEVEL

LIMESTONE
sponges, shells, corals

LIMESTONE AND SANDSTONE
reptile and amphibian tracks,
ferns, insect wings.

SANDSTONE

SHALE
reptile and amphibian tracks,
ferns, insect wings

SHALE AND SANDSTONE
primitive reptile tracks,
ferns

LIMESTONE
seashells, corals

SHALE
trilobites
(crablike animals)

SANDSTONE
seaweed, shells

SANDSTONE

LIMESTONE

GRANITE
GORGE

COLORADO
RIVER

Cross section, showing fossils found at
different levels of the Canyon

The interesting thing is that this is not a local Arizona circumstance. It is worldwide. Most parts of the world have been under water at least once, and have come up again encrusted with marine deposits. Why lands sink under the sea and rise again nobody knows. But there is a regular pattern to it just as there is a pattern to thunderstorms or volcanoes. Only this thing happens slowly, through the ten-thousands of years.

And the process is going on right now! The United States' west coast is slowly rising, the southeast coast sinking. Scandinavia is tilting, the northern part going up, the southern part going down. The Netherlands is sinking an inch per century.

Just south of Texas, temporarily submerged by the Gulf of Mexico, is the well-known (to geologists) country of Llanoria. The Mississippi River is now spreading mud on it. In some far future Llanoria may be high country again. Somebody may then point to a layer of rock and say, "This was once mud. It must have been brought by some river from a land that is supposed to have existed north of here." That would be us.

As you stand at the Canyon rim looking at the stack of rock

552

layers formed in the sea, there's a big idea waiting to be seen. It is this: when each layer was formed, the layer underneath it *was already there.* Of two such layers, the lower one is older. It's obvious; it's hardly worth saying—but it was a terrific discovery. It makes the stack of rock layers into a calendar. As you go down into the earth you go down into the past. Look at the basement rock of the Inner Gorge and you're looking back through 2000 million years. That's 10,000 centuries for every single year since the time of Christ!

And now another vast perspective opens: buried in the rocks of each time are signs of the life of that time. Most of them are marine life, but you find also ferns, trees, insect wings. Covered more and more deeply through the years, these things petrify; the organic matter is replaced, cell by cell, with mineral matter. So fossils remain for us to study—a rock image of the once-living thing. An expert can look at a chip of rock under the microscope and date it by certain characteristic fossils, the way you might date an old photograph by the year models of the automobiles you see in it.

So now the rock calendar becomes also an illustrated history of life on this planet! The basement rock down there contains no signs of life. Was there no life then? Have all its traces been destroyed? Nobody knows. Next layer up, scientists recognize algae, one of the simplest forms of life. Next layer up, a leading citizen of the world was a crablike water creature known as the trilobite. Next, strange fish with rigid shells instead of skins. Then, in most of the Canyon, there comes a big gap in the calendar; millions of years are unaccounted for.

When the story resumes something big has happened: life has come out of the sea onto the land. The living creatures have now learned how to breathe air. They are still only lizardlike amphibians, but their tracks have been found, complete with where the little fellow dragged his tail on a mudbank. At the Canyon that's where the story stops, because even the topmost layer here is very old.

To the experts, then, the Canyon's layers of rock are like pages of a picture book, depicting the past. But the Canyon itself, this astounding piece of scenery: how was it made?

A farmer recognized the cause right away when he saw the Canyon: "Golly," he said, "what a gully!" It's erosion, all right. But there's a difference. On eroded farmland a stream forms and digs its way down, down, down. Here at the Canyon the river was there first. And then the country rose up, up, up.

How do we know? John Wesley Powell, ex-Civil War major and the first scientific explorer of the Canyon, tells us. He had only one arm and only half a scientific education, but he went through the Canyon in a boat, and in the intervals between almost drowning and almost starving he looked at the stony puzzle and solved it.

The puzzle was of the kind: "What's wrong with this picture?" The river seems to have picked its course with complete disregard for the terrain. The Grand Canyon region is a plain. But this plain is really the flat top of a huge dome, a mountain-like upland raised thousands of feet above the surrounding country. The river comes out of lower country, flows in a narrow cut right through the high country and comes out into low country again. It should have flowed *around* the high country. Powell's explanation: the river must have been there first, at a time when all this was lowland. The country must have risen later, and the river stayed in its groove and sawed its way down as the land rose.

One night down in the granite gorge, I heard the river working. It is a peculiar sound you hear through the hiss and rush of the water—a sound like the clinking of marbles. That's boulders and pebbles, the river's cutting tools, rolling along the river floor with the current. That way the river has cut through a mile of rock. The time it must have taken! Yet this cutting was a quickie job compared to what went before—the laying down of all that rock in the first place, a grain at a time.

That's the big thing you see at the Grand Canyon: time, how much time there is. The thing we Americans feel we have the least of, there's the most of. It calms you down.

ᘒ A dinosaur is just an ordinary lizard, the way the government would hatch it.   Weldon Owens in Dallas *Times Herald*

Clear the Road for Nancy!

Jim Bishop

[August 1969]

Everything was right for
Nick. He had a house (with a mortgage); a tall, blond wife
named Nancy who thought he was the greatest man in the
world; he had Vicky, age 12, growing up as stately as her
mother. Then there was that healthy, running, jumping terror
of the schoolyard, James Robert Nickerson, eight years old.
Nick himself was a sergeant of police in the Dade County
Public Safety Department, working out of the Perrine, Fla.,
substation, at $10,800 a year.

Nick was 35, six-feet-two-inches lean, with ruddy face and
black hair. He was easy-moving, modest, a sweet-talking cop
who couldn't be tough unless he was goaded. Everything was
right for Sergeant Nickerson. The right job; the right woman;
the right children.

Under the tall modesty of the man he not only loved the
serene blondness of Nancy; he admired her for having the
things he didn't. She was outgoing. She bowled with him and
sometimes beat him. She worked as a volunteer at the John
Knight Children's Center for Retarded Children. She brought
in $50 a week extra working as a barmaid at a local club.

Maybe it was too good. Some couples become alarmed when
the road is smooth over a long period of time. Nick felt no
alarm, Nancy felt no elation—this is the way it was meant to be.

In early March she was behind the bar at the club and she

picked up a can full of empties and fainted. A friend of Nick's ran around to lift her. Nancy said she was sorry. It was nothing. The perspiration on her forehead and upper lip was cold. The friend had to argue to drive her home.

Nick said he would call the family physician. No, Nancy said. It was just one long lousy headache.

A week later she was in the kitchen at 2 a.m. and fell. Nick no longer listened to Nancy. He phoned an internist, who thought the symptoms seemed akin to polio and said to take her to the hospital. He'd meet them there.

The big attractive girl—just 29—said that everyone was making a fuss about nothing. Two doctors worked up an assortment of tests. It wasn't polio. It wasn't a cerebral hemorrhage. It wasn't a brain growth. It wasn't heart. What was it? Nancy was sent on to Baptist Hospital for a brain tracing. Both arms were punctured, and the doctors watched the flight of the injected fluid through the arteries, up behind the shoulders and, climbing the neck, into the brain, and then the rapid crisscross of the lighted substance through the road map of the mind. The arteries, illuminated by the white substance, looked like strands of spaghetti. Suddenly both lights seemed to fall into a lake.

The doctors tried the test again. Nancy had an artery with a weakened wall which, like a blister on the inner tube of a tire, was stretching.

"She has an aneurysm, Nick," a doctor said. "We've got to go in, now."

"What's an aneurysm?" Nick asked. The doctor drew a diagram. "We're going into the brain and we're going to clamp off that weakened artery." No one had to tell Sgt. James Nickerson that it was going to be a delicate job, for several doctors and for God.

He insisted that he be the one to explain it to Nancy. Her blond hair was a long pale flame on a white pillow. He told her. She told him, holding his big hand in hers, that she was in such pain that the doctors could start right away. But first Nick brought in the children to see her, and Nancy came up off the pillow and hugged them tight.

The children were waxen with fright. She smothered them

to her breast and said, "It's nothing. Be good until I get home."
They promised. Nick took them home and then visited a
church. He prayed in a whisper.

There was a team of five doctors. At Baptist Hospital on
March 17, Nancy, softly sedated, was wrapped in a cooling
blanket to lower her temperature to 80 degrees, then taken into
the operating room. The beautiful long blond hair had been cut
off, and the face was bland as the masked men began to drill
holes in the skull and to saw through the bone between them.

A big piece of skull was lifted out and the dome of diffused
light overhead showed the pulsing aneurysm on the brain. The
doctors worked silently and carefully as if they were defusing a
time bomb.

But the aneurysm burst. Blood began to pulse out. Transfusions had been made ready and two doctors with sponges began
to sop up the blood to find the rupture. From noon until 9 p.m.
the doctors worked on Nancy and put 12 pints of blood into her
to replace losses. They found the rupture and sealed it, and two
neurosurgeons wheeled her to intensive care.

One of the doctors saw the police sergeant. "Nick," he said,
"she hasn't got much of a chance. Everything went wrong."

Nick trotted alongside the cart as though love itself could
restore consciousness. "Nancy!" he said. The tired girl surprised
everybody. She opened her eyes and said, "Hi, honey!" Then
she lapsed into a coma.

For 18 days Nick came to sit beside his sleeping Nancy three
times a day. She had bandages around her head and green
plastic tubes everywhere. On April 4, Good Friday, he thought
her eyes followed him around the room. "Honey," he said, "do
you know me?" She had a tracheotomy tube in her throat, and
talking was a chore. "Yes," she said, and smiled real big. "You're
my Nickerson." Then she lapsed back into the deep sleep.

Nick began to hope. He drove to the Church of the Little
Flower and began to make all the promises no man can keep.
God kept putting a thought into his mind that Nick didn't want
to remember. A year ago Nancy had said, "I've been reading
about these heart transplants. Nick, if anything happens to me,
let me help somebody else." He shut it out.

Nancy went into cardiac arrest. An oscillating machine with a greenish wavy line began to order her heart to beat. At 5:30 a.m. a doctor phoned. "Nick," he said. "Get over here quick." The big man hurried to his wife's side and her eyes were open and unblinking.

"The damage is irreversible," a doctor told him. "Would you agree to a heart transplant?"

Nick stayed with the question until 4:30 p.m., then he said yes and his head fell between his knees. He was giving his wife away.

The oscillating machine kept Nancy's heart going on the 20-mile ambulance ride to the Miami Heart Institute. She was taken to a big squarish room with little curtained booths. In one was a 55-year-old man, dying for want of a heart. "Your wife," a doctor said, "is clinically dead." Nick looked at the green face of the heart machine and saw no wavy lines, just a straight one. Sixteen doctors waited to give a man her heart. Another patient, in another curtained booth, was dying for want of a kidney. A blind woman, age 65, needed one eye. So did another, 35.

The man dying of heart disease could not wait. He died. Another man got Nancy's heart, and it functioned for a while in his chest. A second patient got a kidney from Nancy. The two women each received an eye. Sergeant Nickerson had given his Nancy away, and now the salt tears came. They had loved together and laughed, and now she was a cold shell without eyes or heart or kidney.

At the funeral, 60 policemen showed up in uniform. There were 12 motorcycles. One of the men said, "Sergeant, what can we do for you?" He asked them the same thing he had asked God: "Just clear the road for my Nancy."

8&» *Soil Bank.* A real gardener does not cultivate flowers; he cultivates soil. He is a creature who digs himself into the earth and leaves the sight of what is *on* it to us gaping good-for-nothings. He lives buried in the ground and builds his monument in a heap of compost. If he came into the Garden of Eden he would sniff excitedly and say, "Good Lord, what humus!" Karel Capek, *The Gardener's Year* (Putnam)

But Fish Can't Even Read

Donald Hough

[June 1940]

TEN MILLION people are plan-
ning to go fishing this summer. One million of them are already spending many hours over the selection of fancy lures,
lines and rods, or exhausting themselves learning how to drop
a fly lightly in the water so that it won't sink.

When they actually go fishing they will probably have no
luck until they get a snarl in their line. While they are un-
snarling it the fly will sink and a three-pound trout will grab
the fly and catch himself. This will disconcert the angler, who
thinks fish ought to play according to the rules.

An additional five million anglers are pondering the colors of
their casting plugs and arguing about the tints that fish like
best. But fish are color-blind.

Millions of fishermen are examining flies under magnifying
glasses to be sure they are exact replicas of living flies. More
are testing plugs in the bathtub to find one that has the closest
possible approach, in action, to the movements of the fish it is
supposed to represent.

But fish bite best on flies that have no counterpart in nature,
and the deadliest casting lure ever invented is the common
spoon hook, which looks like nothing on earth—or in its waters
—other than a spoon hook.

Anglers are prone to regard fish as their mental superiors, and
in this way the lives of innumerable fish are saved. The expres-

sion in a fish's eyes is no smoke screen hiding a Harvard intellect. Anglers now planning their scientific campaigns would do well to spend a few hours in a fish market, looking at the fish. They are just as dumb as they look. When treated as a fish, the fish is easy prey.

A fellow I know once caught a big trout which lay in a creek directly under a bridge. My friend first drifted a dry fly under the bridge, then a wet fly. He caught a grasshopper and tried that. No luck. Then the doughty angler figured that he had been drifting his lures downstream and the trout could see the line. So he performed the difficult feat of casting beneath the bridge, the lure striking the water just in front of the trout. But the trout paid no attention. As the angler cast again, his reel dropped off and sank to the bottom. Quick as a flash the fish turned, swooped down on the reel and grabbed it. My friend nearly landed him before he let go.

If you really want to be a smart angler, be dumb like a fish.

In every stream there is a deep pool in which lives a legendary fish, regarded as a combination of heavyweight champion and Rhodes scholar. His name is Old One Fin, Old Spotted Tail, or Old Something Else. Every week some leading local angler tries his luck—and an infinite variety of scientific lures—with him. Sometimes the fish is hooked and lost. Sometimes he won't bite. You can see him down there reading Shakespeare, but he is too "wary," too smart to be caught.

Sometimes this grandpapa of all the fishes disappears. That is a sure sign that some kid has come along with a bunch of big angleworms or a chunk of bacon on a hook big enough to catch Moby Dick, and has hauled him out.

Old Spotted Tail has a good reason for not biting on fancy flies. It takes about as much energy for a large fish to rise to the surface of a pool and return to its depths as a single fly supplies. A six-pound fish that kept chasing No. 16 flies would soon be a four-pound fish. To put it another way, a man who walked a block every day to eat a peanut would die of exhaustion quicker than one who just sat on the curbstone and ate nothing.

The kid comes along with a hunk of bacon. Old Split Fin is

lying deep in the pool because he is interested in food that is heavy enough to sink. He never saw a piece of bacon before, but it is his size and he goes for it.

Men have too much imagination to be good fishermen. They place themselves in the position of the fish and select lures they would go for if they were fish. It irks them to look upon fishing as a simple exercise undertaken by simple men and simpler fishes. They like to feel that when they have caught a fish they have overcome tremendous obstacles.

Try to look at the fish as he really is. He has just sufficient brain power to open his mouth when he sees something to eat, and to swallow it if it turns out all right, or to wiggle his tail away from there if it does not. He does not know what a fishhook is, or a line, or a leader. He is color-blind—scientifically established—and he will bite on anything that moves and on most things that stand still. When you come home with a big string of fish, don't swell with pride. You have not caught the fish; they have caught themselves.

Native Tongue

❧ Discussing a woman who spent money faster than her husband made it, a gal told her friend, "She cuts a wide peel from a small potato."   Toronto, Kan., *Republican,* quoted in Topeka *Capital*

❧ The doctor in a Black Mountain, N.C., clinic asked the weather-beaten mountaineer how he was feeling. "It's like this," drawled the man from the hills after a few seconds of silence. "I'm still kickin', but I ain't raisin' any dust."   Werner G. Marx

❧ When a retired sea captain said he was going to become an Episcopalian, his Congregationalist friends asked, "How do you know when to kneel or stand or sit down?" He replied, "I just sit in the stern and rise and fall with the tide."
Western Massachusetts Pastoral Staff

❧ Returning to our summer home in northern New Hampshire, we learned that the old farmer who used to do odd jobs for us was dead. As his widow put it: "Pa, he didn't winter well."
Lavina C. Tomb

Abe Lincoln's Second Mother

Bernadine Bailey and Dorothy Walworth

[February 1945]

HE BRIDE rode with her husband on the high front seat of the jolting wagon. She was 31 years old, and in 1819 that was middle-aged, for most pioneer women died early. It was a December day, cold for Kentucky, and they were headed north toward forest country. "I reckon it'll be fine weather," she said, for she was the sort to make the best of things.

Yesterday Tom had arrived on horseback, all the way from his Indiana farm, at her house in Elizabethtown. He had come straight to the point: "Miss Sally, I have no wife and you no husband. I came a-purpose to marry you. I knowed you from a girl and you knowed me from a boy. I've no time to lose. If you're willin', let it be done straight off."

That morning they had been married at the Methodist parsonage. The preacher wrote down that she, Sarah Bush Johnston, had been three years a widow and Tom's wife had died last winter. The horses and wagon Tom had borrowed waited outside. The wagon was piled high with her household goods, so there was scarcely room for her three children. Tom had two children of his own; he hadn't told them he would be bringing back a new mother. There was a shadow in Sarah's steady blue-gray eyes when she thought about that. Maybe they'd feel she didn't belong.

A raft ferried the wagon across the half-frozen Ohio River.

The air sharpened; the wheels sank to their hubs in snow. After five days they came to a log cabin in a small clearing on Little Pigeon River. It had no windows and the door was only a deerskin-covered opening. A stick chimney plastered with clay ran up the outside.

Tom hallooed and a little boy ran out the door. He was thin as a scarecrow and wore a ragged shirt and tattered deerskin pants. But it was the look in his eyes that went to Sarah's heart, although it was a look she couldn't put a name to. She got down from the wagon, opened her arms like a couple of wings, and folded him close.

"I reckon we'll be good friends," she said. "Howdy, Abe Lincoln."

Sarah had never been in the wilderness before; she had known small-town comfort. This was a one-room cabin with no real floor, only packed dirt. The bedstead was a makeshift of boards laid on sticks against the wall, with a mattress of loose cornhusks. The bedcovers were skins and cast-off clothing. Ten-year-old Abe and his 12-year-old sister had always slept on piles of leaves up in the loft, to which they climbed by pegs fastened to the wall. The furniture was some three-legged stools and a table axed smooth on top, bark side under. Dennis Hanks, an 18-year-old orphan cousin of Tom's first wife, Nancy Hanks, was living with the family and had been trying to cook with the help of a Dutch oven, one battered pot and a couple of iron spoons. Although she must have expected a place far better than this, all Sarah said was, "Tom, fetch me a load of firewood. I aim to heat some water."

This new stepmother with the rosy face and the bright curly hair wasted no time. As soon as the water steamed, she brought out of her own belongings a gourd full of homemade soap. Then in front of the hot fire she scrubbed Abe and his sister and combed their matted hair with her own clean shell comb. When the wagon was unpacked, little Abe, who had not said a word, ran his bony fingers over such wonderful things as a walnut bureau, a clothes chest, a loom and real chairs. And that night when he went to bed in the loft, he did not find the leaves; she had thrown them outdoors. He had a feather mattress and a feather pillow, and enough blankets so he was warm all night.

In a couple of weeks a body wouldn't have known the place. Sarah had what folks called "faculty"; she worked hard and she could make other people work too. Even Tom, who meant well but was likely to let things slide. She never said he must do thus and so; she was too wise and too gentle. But somehow Tom found himself making a real door for the cabin and cutting a window like she wanted. He put down a floor, chinked up the cracks between the logs, whitewashed the inside walls. Abe couldn't get over how sightly it was. And she made Abe shirts out of homespun cloth, coloring them with dye she steeped out of roots and barks. She made him deerskin breeches that really fit, and moccasins, and a coonskin cap. She had a mirror and she rubbed it bright and held it up so's he could see himself—it was the first time he had ever seen himself—and he said, "Land o' Goshen, is that *me?*"

Sometimes in the early mornings, when Sarah laid a new fire in the ashes, she got to thinking it was queer how things come about. When Tom Lincoln had courted her 14 years ago, she turned him down for Daniel Johnston. Tom had been 12 years married to Nancy Hanks, who died so sudden from the "milk sick." And now after all these years, Tom and she were together again, with his children and hers to feed and do for.

The cabin was 18 feet square and there were eight people under its flimsy roof. Sarah must take what was left of two households and somehow make them into a family of folks who loved each other; she wanted them to feel like they had always been together. There was plenty of chance for trouble, what with the two sets of young'uns who had never laid eyes on each other till now, and all the stories Abe and his sister had heard folks tell about stepmothers. Those first weeks Sarah felt mighty anxious. Especially about Abe, though he did what she said and never answered her back. Once she saw him looking at her real serious when she was putting some johnnycake into the oven. "All my life I'm goin' to like johnnycake best," he said suddenly, and then scooted through the door. You couldn't figure him out. As Dennis said, "There's somethin' peculiarsome about Abe."

Maybe, if it hadn't been for her, he wouldn't have lived to be a man. He had always grown so fast and never had enough to eat. But now, when he had eaten enough johnnycake and meat and potatoes that were cooked through and not just burned on top, he stopped looking so pinched and putty-color. And now he had some flesh on his bones, he wasn't solemn. Why, he was fuller of fun than anybody. He learned to tell yarns, like his father, but he tried them out on Sarah first, and she laughed in the right places. She stood up for him too, when he'd laugh out loud all of a sudden at things nobody else could understand, and Tom thought he was being sassy. "Abe's got a right to his own jokes," Sarah said.

Sometimes Sarah thought, all to herself, that she loved Abe more than her own children. But she didn't really. It was just that she knew, deep down in her heart where she told nobody but God, that Abe was somebody special who didn't belong to her but was hers to keep for a while.

When Abe was little, Tom hadn't minded his walking nine miles to the "blab school" where the scholars learned their letters by saying them over and over out loud. But now Abe was older and stronger, Tom didn't see why he shouldn't stay home and chop down trees and cradle wheat or hire out to the neighbors for husking corn at 30 cents a day. Of course he felt kind of proud when the neighbors came to have Abe write their letters with the pen he had made out of a buzzard's quill and the brier-root ink. But Abe was "reachin' too fur" when he kept reading books instead of clearing swamps; Tom told Abe you didn't need to know so almighty much to get along.

If Sarah hadn't taken Abe's part against his father, Abe wouldn't have got as much schooling as he did, though goodness knows it wasn't much. He learned, as the folks said, "by littles." But through the years she held out against Tom, no matter if Tom said she was plumb crazy.

Abe would rather read than eat. He'd read in the morning soon's it was light enough to see; he'd read in the evening when the chores were done; he'd read when he plowed, while the horse was resting at the end of the row. He walked 17 miles to borrow books from Lawyer Pitcher at Rockport. *Aesop's Fables. Robinson Crusoe. Pilgrim's Progress.* Shakespeare. *The Statutes of Indiana.* When his borrowed Weems' *Life of Washington* got rained on, he worked three full days to pay for it. Once he gave a man 50 cents for an old barrel and found Blackstone's *Commentaries* at the bottom of it, and you'd think he'd found a gold mine. He began reading late at night by the fire, and when Tom complained, Sarah said, "Leave the boy be." She always let him read until he quit of his own accord, and if he fell asleep there on the floor she would get a quilt and wrap it gently around him.

He did his ciphering on a board, and when the board got too black he'd plane it off and start again. If he read something he liked a lot he'd write it down. He was always writing and was most always out of paper. He'd put charcoal marks on a board, for a sign of what he wanted to write, and when he got paper he'd copy it all down. And he'd read it out loud to Sarah by the fire after Tom and the rest had gone to bed. "Did I make it plain?" he always asked her. It made her real proud when he asked her about his writing, and she answered him as well as anybody could who didn't know how to read or write.

They told each other things they told nobody else. He had dark spells when nobody but her could make him hear. Spells when he thought it was no use to hope and to plan. Abe needed a lot of encouraging.

In 1830 Tom decided to look for better farmland in Illinois, and the family moved to Goose Nest Prairie, Coles County. There Abe helped his father build the two-room cabin where Sarah and Tom were to spend the rest of their lives. The place was hardly built when the day came that Sarah had foreseen, the day when Abe would leave home. He was a man grown, 22 years old, and he had a chance to clerk in Denton Offut's store over in New Salem. There was nothing more she could do for Abe; for the last time she had braved out Tom so's Abe could learn; for the last time she had kept the cabin quiet so's Abe could do his reading.

At first he came back often, and later on, after he got to be a lawyer, he visited Goose Nest Prairie twice a year. Every time Sarah saw him it seemed like his mind was bigger. Other folks' minds got to a place and then stopped, but Abe's kept on growing. He told her about his law cases, and as time went on, he told her about his going to the state legislature and his marrying Mary Todd. After Tom died in 1851, Abe saw to it that she didn't want for anything.

When she heard Abe was going to Charleston for his fourth debate with Stephen A. Douglas, she went there too, without saying a word to Abe. It would be enough—it had always been enough—just to watch him. She was one of the crowd on the street as the parade went by. There was a big float, drawn by a yoke of oxen, carrying three men splitting rails, and a big sign, "Honest Abe, the Rail Splitter, the Ox Driver, the Giant Killer." Was that her Abe? And now here he came, riding in a shiny black carriage and tipping his tall black hat right and left. Was that her Abe? She tried to make herself small, but he saw her and made the carriage stop. Then right in front of everybody, he got out of the carriage and came over and put his arms around her and kissed her. Yes, that was her Abe.

She wasn't the crying kind, but she cried when he was elected President. Alone, where nobody could see her. In the winter of 1861, before he went to Washington, he crossed the state to see her, coming by train and carriage in the mud and slush to say good-by. He brought her a present, a length of black alpaca for a dress; it was really too beautiful to put the scissors into; after Abe went, she'd just take it out and feel of it once in a while.

Abe looked tired and he had a lot on his mind, but they had a fine talk. Even when they were silent they still said things to each other, and he still set store by what she thought. When he kissed her good-by, he said he'd see her soon, but she knew somehow that she would not see him again.

Four years later, they came and told her he was dead. The newspapers wrote the longest pieces about his real mother, and that was like it should be, but some folks came and asked her what sort of boy Abe had been. And she wanted to tell them, but it was hard to find the words. "Abe was a good boy," she said. "He never gave me a cross word or look. His mind and mine, what little I had, seemed to run together." And then she added, "He loved me truly, I think."

Often during the four years that remained to her, she would sit of an evening and think of Abe. Being a mother she did not think about him as President, as the man about whom they sang, "We are coming, Father Abraham, three hundred thousand strong." She remembered him as a little boy. She was baking johnnycake for him; she was weaving him a shirt; she was covering him with a blanket when he had fallen asleep over his books, trying, as long as she could, to keep him safe from the cold.

*   *   *

Sarah Bush Lincoln was buried beside her husband in Shiloh Cemetery. Her death on December 10, 1869, passed unnoticed by the nation. For many years she was not even mentioned by historians and biographers. Not until 1929 was Sarah and Tom's Goose Nest Prairie home site made into a state park, with a reproduction of the two-room cabin which Abraham Lincoln helped to build. And only in recent years have Americans come to know that, when Abraham Lincoln said, "All that I am I owe to my angel mother," he was speaking of his stepmother.

ॐ Asked to define peace, a seven-year-old girl in New Delhi, India, wrote: "Peace is when frogs sleep on water lilies."   AP

HUMOR IN UNIFORM

IT WAS the first day of basic training, and a coarse-voiced first sergeant was giving the troops an indoctrination. "First thing I want to say," he growled, "is that there will be no, I repeat, *no* demonstrations or indications of bias, bigotry or prejudice in this man's Army. Every man here is equal, and any man who acts different will be severely disciplined—especially you nuts from California."
Roland C. Rusich

As YOU came through the gate of the outer perimeter of Duc Lap Special Forces Camp in South Vietnam, there was a sign: REMEMBER THE ALAMO! A hundred meters down the road was another sign: REMEMBER THE MAINE! As the road wended its way up the hill toward the inner perimeter, there was yet another reminder: REMEMBER THE PUEBLO! As you entered the inner perimeter, the final sign read: TRY NOT TO THINK ABOUT DUC LAP.
1st Lt. Thomas J. Garvey

WHILE driving through a Navy installation recently, I listened to the base's radio station in my car. At one station break the announcer said: "It is now eight bells." A brief pause. "For you Air Force personnel, that is 1600 hours." A longer pause. "And for you Marines, the big hand is on . . ."
B.D.R.

A GROUP of new arrivals at Itazuke Air Base in Japan were given a fatherly talk by the first sergeant. Included was his sage advice that it would be very unwise to marry Japanese girls. He said, "You'll take them back to the United States, they'll break down, and you won't be able to get new parts for them."
Milton F. Cragg

THE MESS sergeant was among the Army's best. His kitchen was a model of cleanliness and efficiency, and inspections never made him nervous. One day he was stirring up a concoction calling for lots of fresh eggs, adding them six at a time. He took three in each hand, broke them on the side of the pot with one crack, shook them into the mixture, and tossed the shells over his shoulder.

The inspecting officers happened to arrive just at this time and, after watching with great interest, one of them asked, "Sergeant, what if you get hold of a bad egg?"

Without missing a motion, the sergeant replied, "A bad egg, sir? In the *Army*, sir?"   Marjorie Mason

A NAVY admiral in full uniform, attending a social function, was approached by a stranger who'd had a few cocktails too many. The civilian draped his arm around the admiral's shoulder, saying he'd been in the Navy too. Then his eyes gradually focused on the mass of gold braid on the admiral's sleeve. He stopped in mid-sentence and exclaimed, "Gad! You're in this thing pretty deep, aren't you?"   C. Kennedy in *Quote*

AT A U.S. Naval Amphibious Base, a Marine tech sergeant was putting a platoon of recruits through their paces. After several shaky column and flank movements, the sergeant brought the group to a halt. "Man!" he shouted. "What a sorry bunch of left-footed boneheads you guys are."

Then the veteran's grimace gave way abruptly to a look of almost loving tenderness as he said, "Gentlemen, I'm sorry. I forgot. We don't have any left-footed boneheads in the Marine Corps anymore." The recruits' short-lived grins faded as he continued, "But you guys—you sure remind me of the left-footed boneheads we used to have!"   Jon E. Curtis

WHILE serving in Southeast Asia, I wrote my wife of the long evenings, the shortage of books and music, and the abundance of winsome lasses. I mused that I might fill the lonely hours learning to play a harmonica, if I had one. By return mail came a harmonica.

When I finally returned home, I was met at the airport by my wife, who said, "All right, first things first. Let's hear you play that harmonica!"   Capt. Bruce Simnacher

The Day the Atomic Age Was Born

Herbert L. Anderson, as told to J. D. Ratcliff

[*March 1969*]

O F THE events that have changed man's destiny—the invention of the stone ax, the discovery of fire, the drift into the Industrial Revolution—few can be pinpointed in time. But one, possibly the greatest of all, can be timed to the minute. At 3:36 p.m. on December 2, 1942, the world entered the Atomic Age. And I was one of 40-odd witnesses.

The setting was hardly auspicious: a bleak, drafty, dimly lighted squash court under the abandoned and crumbling stadium at the University of Chicago's Stagg Field. There, within a pile of uranium and graphite bricks the size of a small house, neutrons were being born by the billion each second and hurled out at velocities of 18,000 miles a second. Every one that hit the heart of another uranium atom shattered that atom to produce *two* neutrons. Thus, every few minutes the silent, violent storm was doubling itself, in history's first nuclear chain reaction.

We were too awed to speak. The silence was broken only by the staccato rattle of counters keeping track of neutron production. All our advance reasoning indicated that we were safe. Yet we were pushing into territory never before explored. There was at least a chance that the pile would get out of control; that we would be destroyed and a large, thickly settled portion of Chicago would be converted into a radioactive wasteland. Would this, in fact, be doomsday?

Science sometimes moves at a plodding pace. But with atomic fission, events had moved at breakneck speed. Only four years before, at Kaiser Wilhelm Institute for Chemistry in Berlin, nuclear chemist Otto Hahn and his young assistant, Fritz Strassmann, had bombarded uranium with neutrons from an external source. Afterward, chemical analysis showed that something extraordinary had happened. Barium and other substances not there before had appeared as from nowhere and were now mixed with the uranium! But if the two experimenters thought they had split the heavy uranium into barium and other lighter elements, they weren't prepared to say so.

Interpretation fell to a former Hahn colleague, Lise Meitner, who because of her Jewish blood had fled from Hitler's Germany to Sweden. There during the Christmas holidays of 1938 she and her nephew, Otto Frisch, discussed Hahn's data. Possibly, their two brilliant minds concluded, these findings weren't so mysterious after all. Their friend Niels Bohr, the great Danish physicist, had visualized the nucleus of an atom as a liquid drop. If bombardment added an extra neutron to the nucleus, it might become unstable, elongate and divide. The electric repulsion between the two new droplets would be enormous. Within days, Frisch was putting these ideas to experimental test and finding them to be accurate.

When each heavy uranium atom split into lighter atoms, there was a fantastic release of power—200 million electron volts! By itself this was not enough to tickle a mosquito, but if multiplied by trillions it meant a power yield in quantities undreamed of before. The world might no longer have to depend on the fossil fuels alone—coal, oil, natural gas—and face an energy famine when they were gone.

Still, big questions remained if power was to be coaxed from the atom. Could you smash an atom with one neutron and get a yield of *two* neutrons which would go along to smash again and produce four, eight, and so on? That would be a chain reaction. Moving slowly, such a reaction would produce heat which could be converted into power. If the reaction proceeded fast enough, you would have a behemoth of a bomb.

A fear was with all of us. The German pioneers in the field had almost certainly foreseen the possibilities of such a bomb. If the Nazis got it first, other countries would be at their mercy. This was therefore a race we in the United States had to win. We had to find out if a chain reaction was possible.

Most of the work on "The Metallurgical Project" (our code name) would be concentrated at the University of Chicago. Arthur Holly Compton of that institution would head it, and refugee scientist Enrico Fermi would be charged with building CP-1—Chicago Pile No. 1. Fermi had arrived in the United States from Italy in January 1939. (He and his wife and children had gone from Rome to Stockholm to receive a Nobel Prize, and kept right on going.)

As we started work on CP-1 we had no blueprint, only question marks. We knew that natural uranium spontaneously emits a few neutrons. But they travel too fast to cause fission—like a fast-moving golf ball that skims over a cup, where a slow-moving one would drop in. We had somehow to slow down these neutrons. Graphite seemed to offer the best available means: perhaps arranged in some sort of lattice—bits of uranium surrounded by graphite? Then neutrons from one bit of uranium would pass through the graphite, slow down, strike into atoms in another bit of uranium and cause fission?

There were catches in the process. Any impurities in the graphite would act as neutron sponges and put out any atomic fire. And there was no graphite as pure as we needed anywhere —and we'd want it in 100-ton lots. The problem with uranium, which we'd want by the ton, was much the same.

Industry and universities threw themselves with admirable energy into making the absolutely pure stuff, although we couldn't tell them *why* it was so urgent. By the spring of 1942, driblets of uranium metal, uranium oxide and graphite began to arrive. Pile building began: to get basic and needed data, we were to build 30 experimental piles preliminary to the big one. I was 28 years old and had recently earned my doctorate in physics when Fermi selected me to help with the job.

The work crews—mainly graduate students—had one of the world's dirtier jobs. Hands and faces became smeared with greasy graphite. Heavy graphite bricks were slippery, and our fingers were inevitably caught between them when we turned bricklayers.

Finally, on November 7, Fermi indicated that we were ready for the big challenge. Enough graphite, uranium metal and uranium oxide had been accumulated for the big pile. Work was blocked out. Walter Zinn bossed the day shift. They would plane and shape the 40,000 graphite blocks—some of these drilled to contain slugs of uranium metal or uranium oxide. I headed the night shift. We would lay the slippery bricks in exact patterns just as fast as they could be produced.

Preliminary calculations indicated that the most effective shape for our pile would be a sphere 24 feet in diameter. The most active uranium we had—the metal—would be in the center, with the less active oxide farther out. The great sphere began to grow: a layer of graphite, then a layer of graphite bricks containing uranium, and so on.

For safety controls we relied principally on three wooden rods, each with strips of cadmium metal tacked on it, running through the pile. Cadmium, the best of neutron sponges, would dampen any atomic conflagration. One rod would be controlled electrically. A second, the "zip" rod, had to be pulled out of the pile by rope; release the rope and it would zip in. The third was for fine control, and would be hand-operated. Any one of the three rods would quench the atomic fire—unless something unforeseen happened.

As a final precaution, three men would be stationed atop the wooden scaffolding surrounding the pile—a "suicide squad." They would have great flasks of cadmium solution to quench a runaway reaction. "If things get away from us," Fermi told them, "break the flasks. But watch me, and don't do it until I drop dead. If you do it before, I'll use a sledgehammer on you!"

By the time my shift took over on December 1, we were at the 48th layer. Fermi had calculated that layer 51 would complete the job—and he read what was on my mind. There would be the greatest temptation to pull out the control rods and be the first in the world to observe a chain reaction. "When you have finished layer 51," he directed, "lock those rods in place. Everyone be here at 8 tomorrow morning."

A few hours later we completed the final layer. Somewhat reluctantly I followed directions, padlocked our 550-ton monster for the night, and went home.

Morning dawned chill and gray with a dust of snow on the ground. General Eisenhower had launched his North African campaign. The battle for Guadalcanal was in its final victorious phases. Work was already under way on super-secret atomic-bomb plants, on the faith that a chain reaction was possible. If our reactor worked, then, it had the potential not only for death, but for ending a nightmarish war and saving millions of lives.

By 8, we had all filed in and taken our places. I was at a control panel to record instrument readings. Zinn was to pull out the zip rod. George Weil manned the all-important hand rod. The suicide squad was at the ready. Observers stood on a small balcony where spectators had formerly watched squash games. The great show was about to begin.

At 9:45, Fermi, speaking in his quiet voice, ordered the electrically controlled rod out. There was a slight whirring of motors, and the clicking of counters could be heard. Neutron activity was rising. Fermi's mild gray eyes were on the pen as it moved upward on a piece of graph paper before leveling off. Hardly aware of the presence of others, he manipulated a slide rule. Everything was going according to plan.

At 10, he ordered Zinn to pull out the zip rod. There was another increase in neutron production—but again nothing massive.

At 10:37, Fermi directed Weil: "Pull the hand rod out to 13 feet." The counter began to roar. Anxious faces looked at the pen sweeping upward. Fermi indicated that it would level off at a certain point, and it did. From time to time he ordered Weil to pull the rod out another few inches. Each time there was an upsurge of neutron activity, and our tension rose proportionately—to a point almost unbearable.

Then the spell was broken. "Let's go to lunch," said Fermi. It was like Wellington suggesting a lunch break at the Battle of

Waterloo. All rods went back in, and counters fell silent except for an occasional feeble click. Even at rest the pile produced 100,000 neutrons a second.

At 2, we began again, moving more rapidly this time. At 3, the counters had to be recalibrated—slowed down to dampen the rattle and give meaning to their sounds. Further, the pen was going off the graph paper. At 3:19, Fermi ordered the hand rod withdrawn another foot. He glanced at the graph, consulted his slide rule, then turned to Compton standing beside him. "The next foot should do it," he said. At 3:36, the hand rod was withdrawn a final foot. And, minutes later, he spoke again: "This time it won't level off. The curve is exponential" —*i.e.,* the activity would go on doubling and redoubling.

For 17 agonizing minutes the atomic storm raged, growing increasingly violent. The pile was heating up. The first chain reaction was under way. In ominous silence mankind was entering a new age. Fission, we knew, would create new radioactive elements—and with the greatest rapidity. Our pile could be safe one moment and deadly shortly afterward. Understandably, worry was written on many faces. Radiation meters showed we were rapidly approaching danger levels.

At 3:53 Fermi turned to Zinn. "Zip in," he said. As the rod slipped into the pile, activity diminished rapidly. The great drama was coming to an end. We had made a safe journey into the unknown.

On that bitter, blustery winter afternoon in 1942, history was changed. Possibly it was for the worse. We can only hope that time will prove it was for the better.

ᘓ "How much does the earth weigh?" asked a second-grader. The teacher could only respond, "That's a very interesting question. Let's see who can find the answer by tomorrow."

That night she made a beeline for the local library, and after considerable effort came up with the answer. The next day, filled with pride, the teacher announced the results of her research.

The class pondered. Then the same small boy raised his hand and asked, "Is that with or without people?"   David R. Krumboltz

Forgiveness:
The Saving Grace

John Kord Lagemann

[March 1961]

NE OF the great prison wardens of the West, Kenyon J. Scudder, often told this story of a modern-day miracle: A friend of his happened to be sitting in a railroad coach next to a young man who was obviously depressed. Finally the man revealed that he was an ex-convict returning from a distant prison. His imprisonment had brought shame on his family, and they had neither visited him nor written often. He hoped this was only because they were too poor to travel, too uneducated to write. He hoped, despite the evidence, that they had forgiven him.

To make it easy for them, however, he had written them to put up a signal for him when the train passed their little farm on the outskirts of town. If they had forgiven him they were to put a white ribbon in the big apple tree near the tracks. Otherwise, he would stay on the train, go wherever it took him.

As the train neared his hometown his suspense became so great he couldn't bear to look out the window. His companion changed places with him and said he would watch for the apple tree. In a minute he put his hand on the young ex-convict's arm. "There it is," he whispered, his eyes bright with sudden tears. "It's all right. *The whole tree is white with ribbons.*"

In that instant all the bitterness that had poisoned a life was

577

dispelled. "I felt as if I had witnessed a miracle," the other man said. "Perhaps I had."

There is *always* something miraculous about the way forgiveness reconciles the irreconcilable. My father called forgiveness "the saving grace." Essentially it is a religious concept: "Forgive us our trespasses as we forgive those who trespass against us." Modern psychiatry teaches, as Dr. Earl Loomis of St. Luke's Hospital in New York told me recently, that "the experience of forgiving and accepting forgiveness is a prime characteristic of the happy, creative personality."

In the give and take of everyday existence, people are bound to rub us the wrong way occasionally, to hurt our pride, to take unfair advantage, to be thoughtless or ungrateful. The minor irritations we can usually take in stride. But the serious hurts—betrayal or rejection by someone close to us—fill us with the blind urge to return hurt for hurt. Without the saving grace of forgiveness, injury begets injury until revenge has run its course in mutual destruction.

It very nearly happened to two businessmen in a town where I once lived. P.J. and Jim were lifelong friends and partners in a manufacturing concern. One day P.J. learned that Jim had secretly made a deal to join a competing firm. The betrayal was all the more bitter because P.J. had been approached first and had indignantly refused. Vowing revenge, P.J. risked bankruptcy trying to drive Jim's new firm out of business. Jim retaliated by using political influence to raise P.J.'s property assessment. His daughter broke her engagement to P.J.'s son.

At this point P.J.'s wife stepped in and said to her husband, "What did it mean when Jim sold out and you didn't? Simply that you were stronger than he. And what are you proving by taking revenge? Simply that you are weak after all!" At her invitation the two families got together and made their peace. Today the two men are friends once more, despite their keen rivalry as businessmen—and now as grandfathers.

Often we think of forgiveness as a form of charity. We forget that the benefits extend both ways: it is as beneficial to forgive as to be forgiven. This is not a formula, but a spirit which can bring out the best in people and illuminate every moment of living. It is one of the happy paradoxes of human behavior that the readier we are to forgive, the less we are called on to forgive.

"If I had my way," a wise old lawyer said to me, "I'd change the marriage vow to, 'love, honor and forgive,' as a healthy reminder of the power that could save many marriages."

The healing of forgiveness often takes time and effort, as one young couple found out. John and Julia had been married two years when Julia discovered from letters in John's suitcase that he had been unfaithful to her. She kept her knowledge secret, but the longer she suppressed her resentment the more it grew. She began to drink too much and to neglect her appearance.

One day while looking for a safety pin, John found one of his letters hidden in Julia's sewing basket. With no more reason for deception, he confessed what he had done and asked to be forgiven. Julia agreed to let bygones be bygones—but the past kept coming up in bitter quarrels, and husband and wife grew farther apart.

A marriage counselor made them see their mistake: "Instead of forgiving, you have tried to pretend there was nothing to forgive." Julia had to experience all over again the hurt John had caused her. John had to relive his shame. And as Julia's resentment, so long suppressed, came pouring out, love flooded back into her life. Forgiveness created a new situation in which she could once more trust the man who had wronged her. For forgiveness does not undo what has already been done; it enables us to accept what has been done—and to go on from there.

As we proceed along life's journey we must learn when and how to cast off our *own* mistakes and shortcomings, too. Most of us at times blunder into accidentally hurting someone. If it's merely a case of hurt feelings we can usually straighten out the difficulty. But if a physical hurt is involved we find it hard to forgive ourselves.

For years Tom Anderson's life was blighted by the memory of his part in a fraternity escapade that resulted in the death of a classmate. He floundered from one job to another. He and his wife separated after six years of marriage. Then the news about

Tom changed. His wife came back; he won a fine position. One day he told me what had changed his life.

"I used to think, 'Nothing can undo what I have done.' The thought of my guilt would stop me in the middle of a smile or a handshake. It put a wall between Betty and me. Then I had an unexpected visit from the person I dreaded most to see—the mother of the college classmate who died.

" 'Years ago,' she said, 'I found it in my heart, through prayer, to forgive you. Betty forgave you. So did your friends and employers.' She paused, and then said sternly, 'You are the one person who hasn't forgiven Tom Anderson. Who do you think you are to stand out against the people of this town and the Lord Almighty?'

"I looked into her eyes and found there a kind of permission to be the person I might have been if her boy had lived. For the first time in my adult life I felt worthy to love and be loved."

It is only through forgiveness of our mistakes that we gain the freedom to learn from experience. But forgiving our shortcomings doesn't mean denying that they exist. On the contrary, it means facing them honestly, realistically.

Can a person be all-forgiving and still be human? A scientist I know spent four years as a slave laborer in Germany. His parents were killed by Nazi street bullies; his younger sister and older brother were sent to the gas chambers. This is a man who has every reason to hate. Yet he is filled with a love of life that he conveys to everyone who knows him. He explained it to me: "In the beginning I was filled with hatred. Then I realized that in hating I had become my own tormentor. Unless you forgive, you cannot love. And without love, life has no meaning."

Forgiveness is truly the saving grace.

ᒼ᠊ᢣ *Eyewitness.* Perry Como explained why he was wearing mod glasses—which, he said, he only needs in order to see. "Things were beginning to look a little hazy so I went to an eye doctor," said Perry. "He asked me, 'How old are you?' 'None of your damn business,' I replied. 'Yes, that's just about the age,' he said."

Mary Wood in Cincinnati *Post and Times-Star*

Why Did They Call It <u>That?</u>

Gary Jennings

[December 1961]

T HE ENGLISH who scratched out
the early settlements on the eastern rim of this continent—my
own ancestors among them—all seem to have been hungry,
thirsty, weary or peevish. It shows in the place names they
foisted on us. Witness the several Bread Loaf and Sugar Loaf
mountains, Martha's Vineyard, Cape Comfort, Troublesome
Creek. Stingray Point got its name when Capt. John Smith
foolishly picked up a live stingray—and regretted it. The colonists were plain people, and given to plain juiceless names like
Skinquarter and Mulch (in Virginia), Buzzard's Bay, and
mountains called Pignut, Wart and Pimple.

Other expatriate Englishmen, knowing which side of the
ocean their bread was buttered on, named settlements for kings,
queens and princelings—or creditors. Still others, homesick,
used the names of the towns they had left. Norfolk, New
Castle, Southampton—all yearningly face namesakes across the
water.

Many an American community still wobbles under the weight
of an erroneous or ambiguous appellation. Massachusetts owes
its Marblehead to some marblehead who couldn't recognize the
rock as granite. In Iowa there is a little town called Mystic.
Nothing occult about it, just a tidied-up rendition of the remark
made by the first migrants who came there to work the coal
mines: "This is a *mistake.*" The harbor city of Newport News,

Va., whose name puzzles everybody, was originally the new (or second) port founded by the brothers Newce.

Stephen Vincent Benét, who wrote, "I have fallen in love with American names, the sharp names that never get fat," had to delve deep inland to find sharp names like Medicine Hat, Deadwood and Lost Mule Flat. The trappers, traders, scouts and prospectors who escaped westward from the sissy East called a spade a spade, and a mountain shaped like an outhouse, Outhouse Mountain. To them we owe Death Valley, Hungry Horse, Massacre Rocks, Gouge Eye, Rum River, Gunsight Hills. Yet not all of their names were riproarers; some have the ring of discovery, or the reminiscence of a lifesaving oasis, or the serenity of the whispering wilderness—Bonanza, Eureka, Sweetwater, Sweetgrass, Ten Sleep, Sleepy Eye and Dreaming Creek.

Inevitably the civilizers and the nice-namers moved in, and some sharp names got jettisoned for the sake of "progress." Scranton doesn't sound like much of a refinement unless you know that it once suffered under the rousing cognomen of Skunk's Misery. Portsmouth, N.H., before it genuflected to the original in England, was Strawberry Bank. But Marthasville, Ga., didn't lose anything when the Western & Atlantic Railroad picked it for a terminus and insisted it adopt the coined name of Atlanta. And New York's Storm King Mountain certainly sounds more rugged and Peer Gyntish than it did as Butter Hill.

Recently the crossroads hamlet of Tightsqueeze, Va., changed its name to Fairview. The citizens, thrilled at having got into the news for probably the first time in history, immediately switched the name back to Tightsqueeze and thereby got into the news again.

Toward the close of the 19th century, when the pesky Indians had all but vanished, America suddenly decided that their venerable languages would make splendid new place names. But these tongues feature thorny hedges of consonants separated by gutters of grunts. The noble Red Man would never recognize some of the "Indian" names on the map today.

Translating the original lingo into such license-plate poetry as Land of the Sky-Blue Waters calls for considerable contortions, because the Indian words seldom meant anything poetic. Mississippi means not Father of Waters but only Big River; Chesapeake means the same; both Ohio and Allegheny mean simply Good Waters. The Ojibwa's word *she-ka-gong,* or Chicago, meant Stinking River. If the Indian words had any semantic virtue, it lay in their occasional portmanteau capacity. For instance, Stuykson (Tucson) somehow managed to mean Village of the Shaded Spring at the Foot of the Mountains.

More evocative than the English are the mellifluous names of the French-explored fringes and the far Southwest where the Spanish settled. A French trapper could be confronted by a forbidding escarpment of Wyoming crags and somehow be reminded of his mistress's grand *tétons*—while one of Shakespeare's countrymen, roaming the gentle Blue Ridge, could come upon a truly lovely-shaped hill and see only a Hogback. Where the Franciscan would find an *arroyo,* or the Jesuit a *coulée,* the Puritan espied a plain gully. If the Spanish had not inspired the sonorous name, Grand Canyon, we would probably be calling it today That Ditch.

Of course the conquistadores and missionaries weren't infallibly imaginative. Both French and Spanish explorers were wont to name a new place for the saint on whose day it was discovered. But under the sun of southern California those soft Sans and Santas—Ynez, Ysabel, Juan de Capistrano—seem irreplaceably right. When our third-largest city was just a flyspeck on the map, it bore the wonderfully resounding title of El Pueblo de Nuestra Señora la Reina de Los Angeles de Porciúncula— The Town of Our Lady the Queen of the Angels of the Little Allotment of Land. And now we clip it in the slothful modern manner to a contemptuous L.A.!

A French or Spanish place name in America, though it may be simply descriptive, has a glamour lacking in its English counterpart. Prairie du Chien is a much swanker address than would be Dog Field, Wis. The Malheur River is more inviting than it would be as the Bad Luck River. Boca Raton, however it got the name, is easier for the Florida Chamber of Commerce to promote than Mouse Mouth would be.

In some places, a foreign name has stuck unrecognized. Ozark is simply a phonetic spelling of Aux Arks—a clipped French expression meaning "at the place of the Arkansa tribe." And the Lemon Fair River was named by a Vermonter trying to pronounce Les Monts Verts.

A handful of Dutch place names around Nieuw Amsterdam, or New York, still glitter with originality: the Murderkill River, memorializing an Indian fight; Hell Gate, or Hellegate; and Spuyten Duyvil Creek, where a Hollander swore he would swim the dangerous crossing "in spite of the devil."

By way of contrast, consider the prosaic names inflicted in more "enlightened" times—from Ada, Okla., to Zook, Kan. Pennsylvania has enshrined the sooty god Industry in such towns as Trucksville and Factoryville. The demon Yaketty-Yak is evidently worshiped in both Telegraph and Telephone, Texas. And in 1950, Hot Springs, N.M., convulsed itself into Truth or Consequences.

The logical conclusion is that we might improve the whole map by wiping it clean and starting over. Perhaps hold contests for the best name to replace Ho-ho-kus, N.J., or Weed, Calif. And yet . . . and yet there are at least a couple of classic, high-sounding names worth preserving. In the course of my research for this article, I found there is a community named Gary in each of six states and a Jennings in eight.

Night Comes Up

>> It was never a pilot who started the idea that night falls. A pilot knows that it does not. It oozes up out of the ground, fills the hollows and low places with purple pools of shadow that spread and rise to the tops of the trees and the houses. Long before the sky has darkened, the world below is swimming in night. And then finally darkness begins washing up over the sky from the east, climbing over the zenith, closing down at last over the final gleams of the sunset. Here and there stars begin to prick through, larger and more liquid than ever seen from the ground, and the moon, big and white, outlines the earth. Below the plane, lights map the towns, race along the roads, accenting but not relieving the blackness, for darkness clings to the ground. Whatever light there is clings to the sky to the last.

Alma Heflin, *Adventure Was the Compass* (Little, Brown)

Children of the Shadows

Paul de Kruif

Among medical reporters, Paul de Kruif long held No. 1 ranking. He was a brilliant young bacteriologist at the Rockefeller Institute—then collaborated with Sinclair Lewis on the novel "Arrowsmith," and went on to write a dozen books of his own. One of these was the classic "Microbe Hunters." More than 100 articles by him were published in the Digest, for which he wrote as a Roving Editor. Paul de Kruif's zeal to make the best medical science available to all—early, not late—got him into controversies. But few crusading journalists have achieved more positive results.

[May 1935]

I T'S NO FUN to look myself in the face and know that I'm co-guilty in the matter of the needless, uncalled-for, inexcusable dying of thousands of American children.

I used to be a microbe hunter. Cozy in my laboratory, insulated from human suffering, I then laughed at any theory except that it was microbes chiefly that sickened children. But now I've returned from Cincinnati, from the excitement of seeing a stranger, more stirring fight against death than any that goes on in a laboratory. The fighters themselves never so much as peep through a microscope; yet their pioneering is as fundamental as the microbe hunting of Pasteur. It is fundamental because it proves that microbes are not so malignant as men. Slums can kill more children than germs.

To watch this fight we went down into the valley part of

Cincinnati by the Ohio River. If you have the bad luck to be born in that basin, you have less than half the chance to live to be one year old that a baby has who's born in the hills. That is the terrible fact which has been proved by Dr. Floyd Allen, associate secretary of the Cincinnati Public Health Federation, and his boss Bleecker Marquette, an expert in municipal dinginess, a gadfly stinging well-fed Cincinnatians—who pay him to do it!—into dissatisfaction with their city's filth and squalor.

It must be driven home here that this contrast between poverty and prosperity could have been made with similar embarrassing results in any other big city. There are two distinct Cincinnatis, just as there are two different New Yorks, Chicagos, Philadelphias and San Franciscos. The one Cincinnati is what you see in the rotogravures, the city of typical American homes, the Cincinnati of the hills. But let's go with Marquette and Allen to the other city, lying low by the Ohio River. Let it typify the slum blight of every big city in our land.

This is the basin where in many a block nearly 200 people live jammed on 200 square feet of the ground of this our spacious America. This is the Cincinnati where little boys' and girls' skins stay pale in the summer because the playgrounds, if used by all the children at once, would be peopled with 5000 youngsters to the acre.

Such is the Cincinnati of what Dr. Allen calls the lowest economic hundred thousand. To see the dolorous events in this sad laboratory, I was turned over to the visiting nurses.

We start toward these deadly houses of the shadows. We hurry, red-faced at our own prosperity, past people who've forgotten how to smile. We dodge past cats, dogs, an occasional rat, and we recall the words of Bleecker Marquette: "The great bulk of these slum dwellers are honest, respectable people trying under adverse conditions to give their children a chance to live."

We have stumbled up stairs whose dirtiness is hidden by darkness to the two-room home of a Negro mother with eight children. Her husband, hard-working, earns five dollars a week, and no help from welfare. The winter sunlight comes pale through a clean little window onto three pickaninnies dressed in clean but ragged coats to keep them warm. Answering his mother's call, a five-year-old boy came in the door, rocking to-ward us on rickety legs. "No, ma'am. I can't get milk every day. If I has milk every other day I does well."

Out of this darkness, away from this excellent mother with her one quart of milk every other day for eight children, we stumbled into the clean air of America, where dairy herds must be cut down because there's too much milk. We remembered the life-giving science of the late great baby specialist, Alfred Hess, who knew that sunlight not only prevented but actually cured rickets. No child should be deprived of it, said Hess. Then we laughed at the innocence of Hess. Sunlight pouring through sun-swept houses costs money!

This day is one long, black flight of stairs after another. Now we walk into the three-room "home" of a white mother of six children. Five of these are with their mother, crowded around a feeble cookstove in the one room that's heated at all. Flies hover around the face of the baby and crawl over its dirty, thin hands as it lies on a bed of rags, and—"Oh, no, ma'am, it's not three months old; it's eight months old."

The other children, in filthy rags and ragged shoes without laces, peer at us out of blue-lidded eyes. It is intolerable to look at them. Welfare? "Oh, no, ma'am." Their father was working. He made seven dollars a week. Yes, the children should cer-tainly come to the clinic. But how could you leave the baby when he was so sick? No, she sure didn't want them to catch what their 14-year-old sister died of last summer, TB of the spine. . . .

The great sun doctor, Rollier, told how, of all diseases, TB is pre-eminently the one to which resistance can be built up in youngsters by the rays of the sun so that they never get it at all. Yes, but don't forget that there is a tax on humanity's in-come of sunlight!

Now a frail old woman of 30 opens her door to let us into a clean room with two double beds and a single bed in it. There's no other furniture but one chair. A large picture of Rock of Ages covered by cracked glass stands on the floor for this woman's consolation. On one of the beds, without a mat-tress, lies a girl of 12 sick with a sore throat. There are three other children, including a bright boy of four, eating a dish of cold boiled beans.

Yes, this woman's husband had worked in one place for 12 years. They'd got along good till the job went. They'd had nice furniture, almost paid for, but it was gone now.

When the nurse had completed examination of the sick girl's throat—looking for another case of diphtheria—we got ready to leave. Now the little boy tugged at the nurse's skirts.

"Please gimme your gloves," he begged.

"But if I do, my hands'll freeze," she said.

The little boy looked up at her very long and very solemn. "But *you* got pockets, ain't you?" he said.

When we'd left, the nurse confided that her hardest job, something she absolutely couldn't get used to, was to resist the children. Yes, in this land of superabundance we have to resist the children of the shadows, even to the point of their dying. That's the discovery our death fighters have made in their tragic laboratory of the lowest economic hundred thousand. Poverty is a chief cause of children's dying.

Driving away from it all, I had a vision. It was of that greatest of men against death, Louis Pasteur, come back to life today in America's slums. Long ago Pasteur turned his true prophet's look toward the future and said: "It is in the power of man to make parasitic maladies disappear from the face of the globe." Pasteur made no distinction between saving children of high or low degree. The very first child he saved from rabies was a poor boy whose parents could never have paid for the vaccine. He knew he was leaving a heritage for all of us.

Now imagine Pasteur alive again in New York, Chicago or Los Angeles. "Master," he is told, "your gifts to humanity are working wonders among the children of the prosperous who can pay for them. To those with no money they're denied. . . ."

We know, along with city officials who have been ready for years with practical and beautiful plans for a new Cincinnati of the basin, that we *can* build limitless houses to hatch husky child life. Nor is there any question about the existence of a veritable glut of bricks, mortar, glass, steel, concrete—and space where all children may have their heritage of happiness in clean air and sunlight. But the estimates of Cincinnati's housing authority show that to demolish the tenements and build the fine new apartments would require one hundred and fifty millions of dollars.

As a citizen of this country I am co-responsible with all citizens for children's wholesale dying because of a miserable lack of dollars. What is my duty, as I sit at my worktable before the fire, and glance over my shoulder out the window, and see the ghosts of thousands of raggedy children moving by in a horrid procession . . . when I hear the ghosts of their voices calling to me: "Paul, you are strong, can't you help us?"

What I can do is to offer the chief men of our government this challenge:

Let them leave their bountiful tables and well-heated offices. Let them go into the stinking, tuberculous, pneumonic warrens of humanity in any big city of their choosing. Let them look into the big eyes of the little child who wouldn't ask for gloves if he only had pockets. Let them talk to the undernourished mother whose peaked 11-month-old boy is fumbling at her breast for milk that's no longer fit to feed him. They can find such cases by the thousands if they have the nerve to look.

If our chief men would do that, would they give a clear, unequivocal answer to the question asked by a wise friend of humanity: "What else is money but the lifeblood of society?"

My duty is to keep asking over and over again this last question: Why is it, since our nation's wealth in materials, brains and willing hands to build houses, to produce good food and medical care, is so limitless—Why is it that we do not find wise, conservative men who could so order our system that, in exchange for the work our people are willing and able to do, they would receive the modest wherewithal that would give all their children a chance for life?

ৡ *Guide Posts.* Near Gulph Mills, Pa., is a big sign: "YOU ARE LEAVING UPPER MARION TOWNSHIP. COME AGAIN SOON. HAVE A SAFE TRIP, AND GOD'S SPEED." Five feet past that sign is this one: "GOD'S SPEED: 35 MILES PER HOUR." James A. Grady, Jr.

But I <u>Like</u> to Fight
With My Wife

Robert Thomas Allen

[*September 1950*]

E VERY time I pick up a magazine I read about some marriage counselor having a phony conversation with a babe named Mrs. X. The counselor says, "What makes you think your husband doesn't love you, just because he chases you around the house with an ax?"

The woman looks up and says, "You mean, doctor, this is just a normal adjustment of our personality patterns?"

"Exactly." He tells her about the five phases of love, that she must give a lot of thought to making her marriage work.

Until my wife started reading this sort of thing our marriage worked fine. We separated every Sunday. We would storm around pointing trembling fingers at each other and shouting, "I WARN YOU, I HAVE JUST ABOUT REACHED THE END OF MY TETHER!" I would order my wife out of the house. My wife would order me out of the house.

I'd peer balefully through my glasses, thinking, "This is what I get after 15 years of fighting finance companies and waiting outside of grocery stores." I'd tell her she should have married a man who'd have given her a licking every day. My wife would say she wished she had married a man who *could* lick her. I'd say, "Is that so! IS THAT SO!"

We'd take deep breaths and thumb through the phone book looking for the numbers of divorce lawyers. When we had finished we'd feel a fine healthy glow. One of our kids would come in hollering that someone had hit her over the head with a wind-up toy or we'd suddenly remember that we had company coming. We'd pick up our marriage as if nothing had happened. And we might have gone on this way until we had to be propped up in our wheelchairs, if the experts hadn't started telling my wife how to bring harmony into the house.

For the past six months I've done everything to get her to fight but sneak up and cut the ends of her permanent and yell, "My old man can lick your old man!" And all she does is smile patiently and say, "Don't you think, dear, we could talk it over more sensibly in the morning?"

I don't want to talk it over in the morning. I want to kick her around tonight. No man can stand great stifling gobs of harmony. Domesticity is not a natural condition for a normal male; he was trapped into it about 10,000 years ago. The best he can do now is to thump around the house in his pajamas and a foul mood, swatting kids and yelling, "Who's been stealing my razor blades?" Take that away from him and what has he got?

Some of the best fights my wife and I used to have were during motor trips. We'd get out the maps. I'd say, "We should take No. 6." My wife would say, "We should take No. 33A." I'd say, "I think you're confusing No. 33A with that two-lane highway through Lettuceville, dear." My wife would say,

591

"I don't think so, dear." Then I'd say, "All right! All *right!* We'll do it your way, and end up in a swamp."

We never ended up in a swamp. We would cut five miles off the route and strike a fine motel with a dining room where they served hot toddies. My wife would feel so good about being right that she wouldn't bring up my behavior until Christmas.

But lately, just as I'm getting ready to turn where my wife tells me to, she gets that Am-I-showing-him-enough-affection look and says, "You are probably right, dear. Let's try it your way." And we *always* end up in a swamp.

Most marriages are something like used cars—leave them alone and they will perk along fine in spite of loose rings, noisy tappets and miscellaneous knocks. But the minute you start fixing one thing everything else is thrown out of alignment.

Occasionally my wife and I would entertain our friends by getting into fights while they sat around peering happily at their sandwiches. They'd think, "Well, we might have our troubles, but I guess we get along pretty good compared to some people. Bob certainly had no reason to get so sore, but on the other hand *she's* got a temper, *that* one! I think it's six of one and half a dozen of the other."

Now it's just six of one. We get whipping up a good scene when suddenly my wife thinks, "Is he overly tired? Am I *really* being an understanding wife?" She leaves me talking in a voice three octaves higher than normal while she smiles meekly, turns to a guest and says, "Tell us about your trip to Bermuda."

When our friends go home they say, "I know what I'd do with *him*. That poor woman, how she puts up with him . . ."

Since science turned its restless microscopes and inexhaustible vocabulary on marriage it has been coming out with a lot of right answers to the wrong problems. It would do better to keep on making things out of plastic and leave well enough alone.

All over the continent men and women are throwing ash trays, referring in scathing terms to each other's lineage, sitting in frigid, harrowing silence broken only by the tick of a clock or the snick of knitting needles. It's an old marriage custom. They'll make out all right as long as they don't start viewing marriage as another PROBLEM OF TODAY!

How to Protect
Your Family From Fire

Paul W. Kearney

[June 1946]

F IREMEN have always said that "a good house is one you can get out of." It might well be added that a good householder is one who knows *how* to get out.

If this sounds trite, consider the case of two teen-age boys in a western town who died just outside their bedroom door when their home caught fire. From their second-floor bedroom they had only to step out on a porch roof, then drop safely to a garden below. But in their sudden panic they did what practically everybody does under the same circumstances: they started for the main stairway—and never made it.

Three quarters of our dwelling-fire deaths occur *upstairs* from *downstairs* fires, simply because heat rises. When a fire gets under way, superheated air and combustion gases, ranging from 800 degrees to 1000 degrees in temperature, quickly flood the upper hall of a house. People, roused from their sleep, who dash excitedly into that hall from their bedrooms are often felled in their tracks, dead long before the actual flames reach them.

A little advance thought and training would save countless lives. If you wake up and smell smoke, don't jerk open the bedroom door. First, put the palm of your hand on the door panel above your head. If the wood is hot, *don't open that door:* it is too late. The hot wood (or even a hot doorknob) means that the hall beyond is charged with lethal heat and you can't possibly make the stairs.

Instead, leave the door closed; escape by a window, if possible; or at least yell for help from the window. With a closed door between you and the fire, you have every chance of surviving until rescue comes.

If the door isn't hot, open it cautiously. Brace your hip and foot against it, to be prepared in case you have to shut it quickly. Put the palm of your hand across the crack above your head. Then open the door an inch or so. If there is any pressure against the door—or if you feel an inrush of heat on your hand— slam it shut and take to the window.

Next to the knack of opening doors properly in a burning building is the business of *closing the door*. Time and again, the person who discovers a fire rushes off in a frenzy of excitement, leaving the door of the room wide open. The accumulating heat and fumes are then free to sweep upward through the rest of the house, unimpeded. If that door were instantly slammed shut, the fire and its advance guard of heat and gases would be bottled up for quite a few minutes, and perhaps the house could be saved.

The classic case in point is that of the young housewife who tried to pep up the coal fire in her kitchen range with some kerosene; the vapors exploded, blowing fire all over the room.

By the time she regained her wits the whole kitchen was in flames. Her first thought was for her baby, asleep upstairs, so she tore out of the kitchen to the nursery, grabbed the child, and started back downstairs.

Meanwhile neighbors had telephoned an alarm. The fire department responded promptly from a station less than a mile away, but when they arrived they found mother and baby dead in the upstairs hall.

Surviving the blast, which went off virtually in her face, she was killed by the lethal fumes which raced up the stairs—*because she didn't close that door behind her*.

Firemen agree that thousands of householders would still be alive if they had but known and practiced these simple techniques of opening—and closing—doors.

A String of Blue Beads

Fulton Oursler

Newspaper reporter, music and drama critic, editor of magazines, playwright, crime expert, novelist— Fulton Oursler pursued many careers, often simultaneously. He wrote 30 books, ranging from mysteries (signed Anthony Abbot) to religious works like "The Greatest Story Ever Told." As a Senior Editor of the Digest from 1944 to 1952, he was one of the magazine's most prolific and popular authors.

[December 1951]

PETE RICHARDS was the loneliest man in town on the day Jean Grace opened his door. You may have seen something in the newspapers about the incident at the time it happened, although neither his name nor hers was published, nor was the full story told as I tell it here.

Pete's shop had come down to him from his grandfather. The little front window was strewn with a disarray of old-fashioned things: bracelets and lockets worn in days before the Civil War, gold rings and silver boxes, images of jade and ivory, porcelain figurines.

On this winter's afternoon a child was standing there, her forehead against the glass, earnest and enormous eyes studying each discarded treasure, as if she were looking for something quite special. Finally she straightened up with a satisfied air and entered the store.

The shadowy interior of Pete Richards' establishment was

even more cluttered than his show window. Shelves were stacked with jewel caskets, dueling pistols, clocks and lamps, and the floor was heaped with andirons and mandolins and things hard to find a name for.

Behind the counter stood Pete himself, a man not more than 30 but with hair already turning gray. There was a bleak air about him as he looked at the small customer who flattened her ungloved hands on the counter.

"Mister," she began, "would you please let me look at that string of blue beads in the window?"

Pete parted the draperies and lifted out a necklace. The turquoise stones gleamed brightly against the pallor of his palm as he spread the ornament before her.

"They're just perfect," said the child, entirely to herself. "Will you wrap them up pretty for me, please?"

Pete studied her with a stony air. "Are you buying these for someone?"

"They're for my big sister. She takes care of me. You see, this will be the first Christmas since Mother died. I've been looking for the most wonderful Christmas present for my sister."

"How much money do you have?" asked Pete warily.

She had been busy untying the knots in a handkerchief and now she poured out a handful of pennies on the counter.

"I emptied my bank," she explained simply.

Pete Richards looked at her thoughtfully. Then he carefully drew back the necklace. The price tag was visible to him but not to her. How could he tell her? The trusting look of her blue eyes smote him like the pain of an old wound.

"Just a minute," he said, and turned toward the back of the store. Over his shoulder he called, "What's your name?" He was very busy about something.

"Jean Grace."

When Pete returned to where Jean Grace waited, a package lay in his hand, wrapped in scarlet paper and tied with a bow of green ribbon. "There you are," he said shortly. "Don't lose it on the way home."

She smiled happily at him over her shoulder as she ran out the door. Through the window he watched her go, while desolation flooded his thoughts. Something about Jean Grace and her string of beads had stirred him to the depths of a grief that would not stay buried. The child's hair was wheat yellow, her eyes were sea blue, and once upon a time, not long before, Pete had been in love with a girl with hair of that same yellow and with eyes just as blue. And the turquoise necklace was to have been hers.

But there had come a rainy night—a truck skidding on a slippery road—and the life was crushed out of his dream.

Since then Pete Richards had lived too much with his grief in solitude. He was politely attentive to customers, but after business hours his world seemed irrevocably empty. He was trying to forget in a self-pitying haze that deepened day by day.

The blue eyes of Jean Grace jolted him into acute remembrance of what he had lost. The pain of it made him recoil from the exuberance of holiday shoppers. During the next ten days trade was brisk; chattering women swarmed in, fingering trinkets, trying to bargain. When the last customer had gone, late on Christmas Eve, he sighed with relief. It was over for another year. But for Pete Richards the night was not quite over.

The door opened and a young woman hurried in. With an inexplicable start, he realized that she looked familiar, yet he could not remember when or where he had seen her before. Her hair was golden yellow and her large eyes were blue. Without speaking she drew from her purse a package loosely unwrapped in its red paper, a bow of green ribbon with it. Presently the string of blue beads lay gleaming again before him.

"Did this come from your shop?" she asked.

Pete raised his eyes to hers and answered softly, "Yes, it did."

"Are the stones real?"

"Yes. Not the finest quality—but real."

"Can you remember who it was you sold them to?"

"She was a small girl. Her name was Jean. She bought them for her older sister's Christmas present."

"How much are they worth?"

"The price," he told her solemnly, "is always a confidential matter between the seller and the customer."

"But Jean has never had more than a few pennies of spending money. How could she pay for them?"

Pete was folding the gay paper back into its creases, rewrapping the little package just as neatly as before.

"She paid the biggest price anyone can ever pay," he said. "She gave all she had."

There was a silence then that filled the little curio shop. In some faraway steeple a bell began to ring. The sound of the distant chiming, the little package lying on the counter, the question in the eyes of the girl and the strange feeling of renewal struggling unreasonably in the heart of the man, all had come to be because of the love of a child.

"But why did you do it?"

He held out the gift in his hand.

"It's already Christmas morning," he said. "And it's my misfortune that I have no one to give anything to. Will you let me see you home and wish you a Merry Christmas at your door?"

And so, to the sound of many bells and in the midst of happy people, Pete Richards and a girl whose name he had yet to learn walked out into the beginning of the great day that brings hope into the world for us all.

Percentage Play

〰️ A baseball manager with an ulcer was in his physician's office for a checkup. "Remember," the doctor said, "don't get excited, don't get mad—and forget about baseball when you're off the field." Then he added, "By the way, how come you let the pitcher bat yesterday with the tying run on second and two out in the ninth?"

Chicago News, quoted by M. Dale Baughman in *Educator's Handbook of Stories, Quotes and Humor* (Prentice-Hall)

〰️ Once when the Chicago Cubs had been in a long losing streak, a scout phoned manager Charlie Grimm excitedly from the hinterlands. "Charlie!" he shouted. "I've just seen the greatest young pitcher in the country. He pitched a perfect game: 27 strikeouts. No one could even hit a foul off of him until there were two out in the ninth. I've got him here now. What should I do?"

"Sign the guy who got the foul," said Grimm. "We need hitters."

John Dobina in *Coronet*

"... And God Created
Great Whales"

Peter Matthiessen

[April 1971]

AWAKE aboard the whale-catcher *W-29*, get out of the berth and pitch onto the deck, where the dawn wind strikes me in the face. A first bird, the sooty shearwater, slides like a shadow in the trough of the unlit sea. The wind is out of the southwest at ten knots, but there are mare's tails, and the day will freshen. The harpoon gun mounted in the bow, rising and falling as the boat slices through the heavy surge, is a hard black silhouette against the sun that rises from the far austral reaches of the Indian Ocean.

A sailor climbs the rigging to the crow's nest. We are 30 miles due east of Durban, Natal, on the east coast of Africa, headed toward the 1000-fathom shelf at 14.5 knots. *W-25* is off to port, and to starboard, spread out three miles apart, are *W-17*, *W-16*, *W-26*, *W-18*. These are the only whale-catchers now operating in the fleet of the Union Whaling Company. Indeed, the great whales of the seven seas are today so depleted that Japan and Russia alone among the nations of the world are still engaged in large-scale open-ocean whaling. Already the blue whale is practically extinct, with the right whales and humpbacks close behind. The large whales that still survive in any numbers are the finback and sperm whales; hunted in every ocean, they could disappear in the next decade.

Using light aircraft to spot their prey, whale-catchers like these move ponderously about the oceans, killing ever larger numbers of ever smaller whales. The relentless waste of life is barely profitable, since almost every whale product is more readily available from other sources; the whaling industry is dying of consumption. Still, there is no better use for these fleets of ships—and no better use for whales, to judge from the apathy with which their slaughter has been met. "Overhead" is the sole excuse for man's persistence in the destruction of the whales, and in the name of this small economy the mightiest animals that ever existed will pass from the earth forever.

A radio call: the spotter plane has located whales—two pods, several miles apart, headed slowly south. Capt. Torbjorn Haakestad heads for the bridge; he is catch leader of the fleet, responsible for its positioning. At 8:15, W-25 is broadside on the horizon, blunt black on a silver sun. She has just killed a sperm whale. A second whale blows near the yellow-and-green flag that marks her first kill; in the morning wind the bright flag snaps on a bamboo pole that rises 12 feet from the buoy float. Fixed to the pole is a radio transmitter so the whale may be located from a distance, even after dark.

In the old days radios were unnecessary: the ships did not have to wander far to find another whale. Even five years ago, the season's catch of sperm whale out of Durban was 2435 animals; by 1970, the number of whale-catchers in use had to be cut from 13 to 6, and 1824 whales were caught.

At W-29's approach the whale has sounded. A few minutes later the mate reports that he has located it with his sonar. The captain grunts something at the helmsman, who alters course and signals the engine room to halve speed. The gunner (captains prefer to be called gunners) walks the long sloping catwalk to the bow platform, sits patiently by the gun. The boat slows to a hum and glides forward in strange stillness, the slosh of water audible along the hull.

The whale remains a thousand feet below, pushing through the dark, driven by the relentless ping of the sonar that can track it a half-mile down. The steel boat waits above, rolling heavily in the monotony of seas. "With us they stand no chance," the mate says quietly, a trace of weariness in his tone.

The sperm whale can submerge for an hour or more, but this time is rapidly decreased by panic when the animal is pursued. Peering down into the silent sea, I wonder what sort of awareness tuned the minds of those great shapes so far beneath. The sperm whale has a bigger brain than any other animal that has ever evolved, and doubtless it is communicating its alarm with *clicks* that may carry enormous distances.

These *clicks* are the only sound known to be made by the sperm whale—unlike the humpbacks, who sing like the horns of paradise. Cosmic sounds, electronic sounds, the music of the spheres shimmer through the soft gurgle of the sea with the resonance of an echo chamber, and with them soft bell notes and sweet bat squeaks, froggish bass notes, barks, grunts, whistles, oinks and elephantine rumblings. No word conveys the eeriness of whale song, tuned by the ages to a purity beyond refining, a sound that man should hear each morning to remind him of the morning of the world.

W-29 rolls and wallows. The man in the crow's nest swings in crazy arcs. The mate, reappearing, shrugs: the whale has vanished into the abyss. Descending at least 3000 feet, this one has escaped the sonar.

The plane, circling like a black hornet on the sun, has dropped a dye marker where the pod was first sighted, and an unnatural bright stain of plastic green rises and falls on the blue. A mile farther, the ship comes upon the whales, porpoising strongly through the choppy seas. There are more than 20 in the pod, and the family groups remain tight together, swimming abreast. On every rise, the sea pours off the glistening black backs; then the mist of their breathing disappears in an explosion of white water. When the whales blow, a rainbow appears in the fine mist as it drifts downwind.

On the bow, the harpoon gun swings from port to starboard, searching for the biggest whale. The bow cuts the pod in half, and the whale shapes slide like cloud shadows beneath the sea. The gunner raises one hand almost casually to point; he bends to his gun as the ship surges. A loud thump on the wind, muffled and ear-stunning.

Oddly, the shot has missed; the gunner sits down heavily as the mate reloads. From the foredeck a sailor lugs a slotted red harpoon, four feet long, weighing 165 pounds, and with the help of the mate jams it into the muzzle. The mate sets the explosive grenade that detonates in the whale's body three seconds after impact, and with a few turns of light lanyard secures the harpoon against sliding out of the tilted muzzle. Then the human silhouettes retire from the bow, all but the form of the seated gunner, as black as the gun itself on the sparkling sea.

Plowing and blowing, the whales in flight leave a white wake in the blue, backs gleaming like smooth boulders of obsidian in a swift torrent. As the ship heels into position, the whole pod broaches in one mighty burst of mist and spray. The ship rides herd on the black backs, the harpoon still seeking a big whale. Suddenly, a series of explosions: the shot, the muffled boom in the whale's body, and the jolt of a huge spring belowdecks. The nylon harpoon line, with a breaking strength of 19¼ long tons, shivers spray as it snaps taut; the whole ship quakes from the impact of the dying whale's first thrash. The white of the toothed lower mandible flashes in the light as the beast rolls, and the first well of its blood spreads on the surface. With her winch, the ship is warped alongside, and the mate puts a killer harpoon—a grenade carrier with no line attached—into the thrashing hulk as the crewmen jump to dodge the wall of spray. Now the whale is still; only the pectorals twitch as the last life ebbs out of her.

Already a long pole has been used to jam a hose tube into the carcass, and air is pumped in to make sure the whale will float. At the same time the sailors rig a heavy noose around the base of the fluke, which in turn is secured to the big float of the marker buoy. With a flensing knife lashed to the end of a long pole, the mate, doubled up over the gunwale, cuts the harpoon line where it is spliced to the embedded missiles, and the ship backs off from the buoyed whale. The harpoon gun has already been reloaded, and a new line spliced to the harpoon. Eleven minutes have passed since the first iron struck life out.

The inflated whale lies on her side, washed by red waves of her own blood. Already the bright stain on the bright sea is huge and thick, as if it would never wash away. The blood spurting from the wounds is a deep mammalian red, but on the surface of the sea it turns red red, as vivid as a dye, and the amount of it is awful.

By EARLY afternoon the six boats had harpooned but six whales among them, and since W-29 was short two men on its crew, Captain Haakestad decided to tow the six whales into port. The other boats would hunt all afternoon and, if weather permitted, lay to at sea until next morning.

In the late afternoon W-29 collected her last whale and headed west on the long voyage to Durban. She was slowed by the dragged carcasses, which writhed and twisted in the wash and sea surge as if come to life. Crashing together, their graceful flukes cropped, jaws slack, they looked damned.

The infernal atmosphere as twilight came was not lessened by the clank of the rough chains that sawed the hides, nor the din of the sea's rush against the carcasses, nor the rank wake that washed out of them into the darkening blue-turquoise of the water. During the harvest of the whales the ship had collected attendant albatrosses, and the giant birds wheeled up and down, wings motionless, stooping now and then to pluck a scrap, then climbing again until the wind seized them.

Sometime after midnight the W-29 was off the slipway, where each whale is loaded onto a flatcar and trundled by rail a few miles to the shore station. Here, in a bedlam of chains and machinery, six-inch-thick blubber is hauled off in whale-length strips. The meat is stripped next, then the jaws, which are snaked away to power-driven crosscut saws to be cut into manageable pieces for the huge cooking vats buried in the concrete platform. The meat extract is sold to soup and packaged-food industries as a flavoring concentrate. The one to two tons of meal derived from the meat and bone of sperm whales is 75-percent protein, and is used in cattle and chicken feeds. The oil, after processing, is used in the manufacture of additives for lubricating oils, and the teeth are saved for the fashioning of ivory trinkets.

Nothing is wasted but the whale itself.

POINTS TO PONDER

The Irish Digest:
Reforms always come from below. No man with four aces asks for a new deal.

Arthur Somers Roche:
Worry is a thin stream of fear trickling through the mind. If encouraged it cuts a channel into which all other thoughts are drained.

Robert Louis Stevenson:
I never weary of great churches. It is my favorite kind of mountain scenery. Mankind was never so happily inspired as when it made a cathedral.

C. S. Lewis:
No man who says, "I'm as good as you," believes it. He would not say it if he did. The Saint Bernard never says it to the toy dog, nor the scholar to the dunce, nor the pretty woman to the plain. What the claim to equality expresses is the itching, smarting awareness of an inferiority which the patient refuses to accept. *The Saturday Evening Post*

Ouida:
Familiarity is a magician—cruel to beauty, kind to ugliness.

Robert Southey:
To be pungent, be brief. For it is with words as with sunbeams—the more they are condensed, the deeper they burn.

Henri Frédéric Amiel:
Tell me what you feel in your room when the full moon is shining in upon you and your lamp is dying out, and I will tell you how old you are, and I shall know if you are happy.

"Charlie Would Have Loved This"

J. P. McEvoy

S HE WAS sitting beside me on the beach at Waikiki. Sounds romantic, doesn't it? But it wasn't really. There were many ladies just like her—tourists from everywhere—white-haired, restless, lonely. On a small stage flaming with tropical flowers, a colorful group of Hawaiian singers and dancers were broadcasting their weekly sunkissed program of synthetic romance to the frostbitten unfortunates on the Mainland.

"This is your Isle of Golden Dreams, calling to you from across the sea," crooned the announcer. His assistant ran a few yards down to the lapping waves with a microphone.

"Listen, folks! The waves of Waikiki. Can't you see the surfboard riders? Can't you just picture those hula girls swaying under the palms?"

The white-haired lady beside me said, "Charlie would have loved this. It's just like we used to hear it on the radio back in Illinois. Saturday nights when Charlie came in from the fields, he'd turn on this program 'Hawaii Calls' and we'd listen, and Charlie would say, 'Mary, we're going there someday,' and I'd say, 'When?' and he'd say, 'Soon as we've saved up some money and get some time,' and I'd say, 'You've been saying that for years, Charlie, but every time we get a little money ahead you buy another 40 acres. Are you trying to buy up the whole state of Illinois?' That was a joke we had, and Charlie would laugh and say, 'No, I just want the piece next to me.' So Charlie never did get out here."

"You are listening to the Singing Surfriders," purred the announcer, "but unfortunately you cannot see the lovely Lani dancing her famous hula under the palms. She is wearing a green ti-leaf skirt and a red hibiscus in her long black hair."

The little white-haired lady said, "We had such good times together. If only Charlie was here with me now."

Every Sunday night, in the High Talking Chief's Long House on Waikiki Beach, Don the Beachcomber puts on a luau for the tourists. This is a Polynesian-type clambake where only the barbecued pig comes fully dressed, while the guests sit on the floor, kick off their shoes, drape leis of white gardenias or pink carnations around their necks, and the ladies stick a red hibiscus over their ear—the right ear if they have a man, the left if they want one.

Tourists milled around the bar, carrying bamboo tubes filled with rum concoctions playfully labeled Missionary's Downfall, Cobra's Fang and the Vicious Virgin. I spotted my white-haired friend, timid and alone, but bravely sporting a man's aloha shirt that looked like an explosion in a paint factory. But the conventional black skirt and high-heeled shoes were definitely out of place in this technicolor jungle of muumuus, holokuus, sarongs, bare torsos and coconut hats.

I walked over and said, "Are you with anyone?"

"No," she said. "Is it all right to come alone?"

"You're not alone," I told her and hung a flower lei around her neck and kissed her cheek. "Let's go sit down. They're bringing in the barbecued pig."

I introduced her to my party and they moved over to make room for her as she looked around a bit helplessly. "But everybody's sitting on the floor."

"That's right," I said. "Those creaking noises you hear are just old Mainland joints like yours and mine." She sat down beside me. "Now kick off your shoes and dive in."

Wooden platters were set before each guest but no knives

or forks. My friend watched as we old-timers dug in with bare hands and licked our fingers. Then she followed suit, embarrassed at first, but quickly getting into the spirit of the occasion.

"What are we eating?" she asked. "Not that I care," she added quickly.

"This is pig baked underground with heated rocks. And this is laulau—butterfish wrapped in ti leaf. And this," I said, dipping it up with my fingers, "is the poi they sing about. It looks and tastes like paperhanger's paste. If you can scoop it up with one finger, it's one-finger poi. If you need two fingers, it's two-finger poi."

Don came over and tucked a red hibiscus into my friend's white hair over her right ear. I explained the difference and she moved it to her left ear.

"Charlie would have loved this," she said.

And then the jungle drums started and a beautiful young Polynesian typhoon, wearing a crown of plumeria blossoms and a grass skirt, exploded into a dance.

"Wouldn't it be wonderful if people could live like this all the time," my friend said. "Kick off your shoes and sit on the floor and eat with your fingers and wear flowers in your hair and listen to music like that and watch dancers like what's-her-name there."

"Johnny," I said. "She comes from Pukapuka."

"Charlie always wanted to go there," she said. "There was a book, *White Shadows in the South Seas*. He used to read it aloud to me and once we saw a movie by the same name and he said, 'Someday I'll take you there.' But he kept putting it off. And when he died I wouldn't have been able to make this trip if it hadn't been for the insurance money he left."

A troupe from Samoa took the floor and did a dazzling fire dance. My friend sighed.

"I guess we waited too long." She shook her head a little, bewildered. "There's something wrong somewhere. What's the use of working yourself to death if you don't live to enjoy it?"

"Maybe we don't have to," I said. "When we want homes we don't wait until we're too old to get them. We borrow the money and live in the houses while we pay it off. Lots of us do the same about cars. Suppose Charlie had added a few hundred more to the mortgage and brought you out here years ago. Wouldn't that have made a lot more sense than buying another 40 acres? Practical people would be a lot more practical if they were just a little more dreamy. Then they wouldn't put off living until they were dead. Someday we may even be practical enough to invest in our dreams first."

"Aloha!" cried Don the Beachcomber. "Let's sing the song we all know—

> *One fond embrace*
> *Before we now depart,*
> *Until we meet again. . . ."*

There's no sweeter, sadder song. Even in broad daylight you feel like crying like a baby when perfect strangers sing "Aloha" and wave farewell to you from Honolulu piers and airports. As the party ended we started out into the street in our bare feet.

The little white-haired lady from Illinois had forgotten her shoes under the table, but her red hibiscus dangled jauntily over her left ear, and there was a brave swing to the flower lei around her neck.

"You know what?" she said.

"Yes," I said. "Charlie would have loved this."

"That's for sure," she said, and she walked across the street to her lonely hotel room.

Holding Action

৪ In the Middle East there is a legend about a spindly little sparrow lying on its back in the middle of the road. A horseman comes by and dismounts, and asks the sparrow what on earth he is doing lying there upside down like that.

"I heard the heavens are going to fall today," said the sparrow.

"Oh!" said the horseman. "And I suppose your puny little legs can hold up the heavens?"

"One does what one can," said the sparrow. "One does what one can."   William A. Jenkins in *English Journal*

Beyond
Fame or Fortune

Lawrence Elliott

Beyond
Fame or Fortune

They came on a night when the wind shrieked and lashed the land. Moses Carver heard the pounding of their horses and knew at once that they were night riders, the masked bandits who terrorized Missouri in that bitter winter of civil war, stealing livestock and spiriting slaves south where they could be sold at swollen wartime prices. Only weeks before they had raided his farm, and while his wife watched in helpless anguish they had wired his thumbs and strung him up on a tree.

"Where's your niggers?" they bawled, and then they whipped him and burned his bare feet with coals. But he had not told them that his single slave, a young widowed woman named Mary, was hidden in a cave with her children. Now, on this bitter winter night in 1862, the riders were coming back.

"Run to the cave!" Carver shouted to his wife and, hobbling on blistered feet, he stumbled into the night. The horsemen had not yet turned into the farm, and for a moment he thought there might be time for Mary to hide again. But when he flung open the door of her one-room shanty he found her standing motionless by the fire, rooted in fear. Her young daughter Melissa clung to her nightdress. Her little son Jim was asleep in bed. And in her arms she held a baby boy.

"In the name of heaven, girl, move!" Carver cried. "They'll be here in another minute."

He snatched up Jim and started for the door. "Bring the girl and the baby," he called. "And stay right behind me!"

But she did not follow him. From the day he was born her infant son had been sick with a rasping cough, and now, as the blustering wind tore into the room, Mary looked for warm clothing to cover him. While the clatter of the horses grew louder, she ran to one corner searching for a blanket, then to another—until finally the masked men bounded into the cabin and wrenched the baby from her arms.

Swiftly they tied her wrists, dragged her outside and shoved her up on a horse. Trembling in the cold, she begged, "Please cover my babies!" but there was no answer—only the harsh breathing of men in a rush to be mounted and gone—and in another moment the horses were pelting down the dark road.

"Lord forgive me!" Carver whispered to his wife. "They've got her." Susan Carver held Jim close, and began to weep.

Moses Carver had always been opposed to slavery. He did not own a field hand, as other Missouri farmers did, and it was only after the long years had begun to tell on his wife—after Susan had begged him to get her a girl to help with the chores, and to ease the loneliness when he was in the fields—that he had bought Mary from his neighbor for $700. She had lived with them happily for six years, but Moses had never been wholly at peace with his conscience. Now he knew that if he could not get Mary back, he would live with guilt for the rest of his days.

The following morning, trailing a racehorse, he rode into Diamond Grove, the settlement nearest his farm, and sought out a man named John Bentley. According to rumor, this man had once ridden with the night riders.

"They took Mary and two of her young ones," he told Bentley. "I'll pay you to go after them. Pacer is one of my best horses. Take him and ransom her. And if you bring her back I'll give you 40 acres of timberland." Bentley rode south that afternoon, and Carver went home to wait.

Six days later, in a cold, driving rain, Bentley rode into the farmyard with Carver's racehorse behind his own. He appeared to be alone, but when he entered the house he took a damp and dirty bundle from under his coat. "It's all I've got," he said. "I don't know whether it's alive or dead."

"The baby!" Susan cried. She took the filthy parcel, fumbled with the rags and peered down at the pinched, dark face of Mary's child. The boy lay still like a newborn sparrow that had died in the nest. She ran to heat milk, then knelt with the child by the fire, stripping the wet homespun from his tiny body. Moses brought her the milk, with a pinch of sugar, and she held a spoonful to the infant's lips. At first the milk trickled down his chin. Then he choked, cried feebly, and sucked for more.

"At least he's alive," said Susan.

John Bentley jerked his thumb at the wheezing child. "Reckon I couldn't take your timberland for just *that*."

"You did your best," Moses said. "Keep the horse."

Bentley nodded, satisfied. Then he told them how he had followed the gang all the way to the high hill country of Arkansas before he had lost the trail. The men were riding hard for the Mississippi, he said, and he was sure they were going to sell Mary and her daughter downriver.

"And this one?" asked Carver. "Where did you find the boy?"

"Oh, they just give him to some womenfolk down by Conway," said Bentley. "He ain't worth nothin'."

HE WAS called George, Carver's George, and all his first years were a struggle for survival. He fell victim to every childhood ill, and each one threatened to drag him through death's door. The unending cough tore his vocal cords, so that his voice was like the chirp of a frightened bird, and some traumatic memory knotted his tongue and left him with a pitiful stammer. But through Susan's nursing, and some mysterious toughness within himself, he lived.

The war ended. The burned barns were rebuilt and the fields seeded. "You're free now," Moses told the two boys. "All the slaves are free. You can go any place you like." But George didn't understand, and Jim just grinned. That night they crawled up to the cabin loft and went to sleep on their ticks stuffed with cornhusks just as they'd always done.

Jim was soon husky enough to shear sheep and to help Moses with the haying and milking. George, still fighting for a firm hold on life, rarely strayed far from the kitchen. He followed Aunt Susan the day long and began to help with chores, sweeping and dishwashing. But before long he was learning how to tan hides and spin flax and cure bacon. One day, to Aunt Susan's surprise, he taught himself to knit, using turkey feathers from the yard and an old unraveled mitten. Later when he helped sew a crazy quilt, Susan defied Moses to tell the boy's stitches from hers.

As he grew older, George took to slipping off to the woods, to a secret glade he discovered where nature seemed to parade all her wonders. He poked beneath tree bark and watched the insects crawl. He studied the wildflowers, those that sought the sun and those that managed in shade. He examined beetles, rocks, tobacco worms and lizards, and he felt an urgent longing to understand this magically complex world, to know every single thing about it. What made the rain fall, he would ask, and why were some roses red, others yellow?

He loved the feel of earth in his hands. Years later he would say, "People murder a child when they say, 'Keep out of the dirt.' In dirt there is life!" Thus the leaves and ferns and roots became the toys and friends he never had, and soon, under his touch, the Carvers' flowers flourished.

One summer afternoon when Mrs. Baynham, a next-door neighbor, complained about her roses, George went to her yard and found the trouble at once: the flowers were not getting enough sun. He moved and watered them, and then went into the house to explain what he had done. Standing by the parlor door, he suddenly gasped at an astounding sight: pictures were hung around the room, beautiful paintings of forests and flowers, and portraits of bearded old men.

Mrs. Baynham thanked him and gave him a nickel, but those paintings were all that George thought of as he went home. That evening he squeezed the dark juice from some pokeberries. Then, dipping his finger into it, he drew a circle on a flat rock.

After that he was forever making pictures, scratching faces on stone with a piece of tin, or tracing the outline of a flower in any smooth place on the ground.

Meanwhile, Mrs. Baynham's roses bloomed, and the good lady sang the praises of Carver's George wherever she went. Other neighbors came to him with their garden troubles, and George would pick off sucking mites, and water and mulch the earth. He was still only a boy, but people took to calling him the plant doctor, and for miles around it was said that Carver's George could heal the ailments of anything that grew.

Not far from the farm, in Locust Grove, there was a one-room cabin that served as the community's schoolhouse. One day George ran to find Moses in the field.

"When c-can I g-go to school?" he asked.

The old man wiped sweat from his forehead and searched the blue sky for words. At last Moses Carver held George's shoulders and told him, "They don't allow colored young 'uns in that school."

George was stunned. Never before had being colored meant anything more than that his skin was darker than Aunt Susan's. Now in a sickening rush it came to him that he was different from other people. Stricken, lost, he ran to hide in his secret glade. For a time his mind struggled with this thunderbolt, then he pressed his cheek to the earth and wept.

But he refused to abandon his dream. Aunt Susan dug an old speller from her trunk and taught him his letters. In weeks he had memorized every line in the book and could rattle off the spelling of each word. Aunt Susan guided his fist until, unaided, he could write his name.

Then one fair morning during a visit to Neosho, eight miles away, George made a startling discovery. As soon as he could find his brother, he told him the news in an excited stammer.

"There's a s-school in Neosho, a school for the *colored!* And, Jim, I mean to g-go there."

Jim had never understood his younger brother—not his foolishness over flowers or his preoccupation with the speller. But he knew it was senseless to argue. If George said he was going, he would go.

Moses Carver knew this, too. "I can't stop you," he said quietly when George told him. "But what will you do for food and a place to sleep?"

"I c-can cook and s-sweep and t-tend fires."

Moses nodded solemnly, and it was settled. Aunt Susan made him some dodgers—strips of home-cured fatback between loaves of baked corn bread—and one fall morning, sad and silent, she stood with Moses and Jim and watched the thin boy walk through the gate and out into the wide world. The year was 1875, and Carver's George was 14 years old.

In Neosho, Carver's George found a home with Mariah Watkins, a black midwife and washerwoman. She and her husband Andrew, a hardworking odd-jobs man, had no children of their own, and from the first day she saw him—it was a Saturday, but George was sitting patiently on a fence waiting for the school to open—Mariah was convinced that God had brought him to her.

"That boy told me he came to Neosho to find out what made hail and snow, and whether a person could change the color of a flower by changing the seed," she recalled years later. "I told him he'd never find that out in Neosho. Not in Joplin, either, and maybe not even in Kansas City. But all the time I knew he'd find it out—somewhere."

It was Mariah who changed his name. As he started on his way to school that first Monday morning, she called to him, "You can't go calling yourself Carver's George anymore! You're a person, hear? From now on you're George Carver."

Strange as the name sounded on his tongue, he so reported himself to the young Negro teacher at the tumbledown shack known as Lincoln School for Colored Children. Some 30 pupils were packed tightly in the tiny schoolhouse, and the air soon grew fetid, although in winter the wind knifed through the walls and most of the children wore their coats and mittens the day long. But none of this mattered to George. The days sped by for him, and when he wasn't at school he had his reader propped in front of him, even when he helped Aunt Mariah iron or wash dishes or scrub clothing.

Three times that winter he caught cold, and, unable to go to school, he tormented himself over the work he was missing. Sometimes, to distract him, Mariah would tell about her days as a slave. She had lived on a plantation; of all the Negroes there, only one could read. Frequently, slaves who could read and write were suspect and apt to be sold downriver; but, secretly, those who could taught others their words.

"And that's what you must do," Mariah told George. "You must learn all you can, and then go out into the world and give your learning back to our people."

Another winter came, and again George was ill with a cough that kept him home for days. Not that it mattered now—he had long since learned all there was to learn in the school. From Aunt Mariah he had come to believe in God, but he could not accept the fact that it was God's plan for him to be sick all his life. Maybe if he went somewhere else he would grow and get better—and learn more of the answers to his questions.

Then he heard that a family down the street was moving to Fort Scott, in Kansas, nearly 75 miles away. When he asked them to take him along, they agreed. From the Lincoln School he got a certificate of merit dated December 22, 1876, and on a biting cold morning he said good-by to the Watkinses.

"Get him a good school, Lord," Aunt Mariah prayed softly as she watched him disappear from sight. "Get him a teacher who's right smart, because, Lord, there's an awful lot that boy wants to know."

About ten years George wandered the western country, moving from place to place, doing odd jobs, heading for the nearest school and staying until the school could teach him no more, starting a grade in one town and finishing it in another. For a living and to pay for the next set of schoolbooks he cooked, chopped wood, tended gardens, cleaned rugs, dug ditches, hammered nails, swabbed outhouses, whitewashed fences—whatever anyone wanted done. In Fort Scott he found a place by the stagecoach depot, a decrepit cabin that he could rent for a dollar a week. He spent not much more for food, and not a penny on anything else. All afternoon he studied his lessons from school, and at night, by a single candle, he read everything he could lay hands on—books, pamphlets, old newspapers, circulars.

But there he witnessed a moment of horror. A mob of wild-eyed men built a great bonfire in the village square; then they dragged a Negro from the jail, drenched him with oil and threw him into the leaping flames. That night, still trembling, George gathered his belongings and fled Fort Scott forever.

Wherever he roamed, he always woke in the hour before dawn and walked alone in God's garden. With the sun's first light he would search the woods and the hills, entranced by everything that grew. He studied the black in the forest loam, the red in a field of clay, the dazzling blue of a hillside, and he thought that if only he could take those colors from the ground he could make paintings more glorious than men had ever made before.

During harvest seasons he bound wheat, hiring himself out from farm to farm. And somewhere in his wanderings he lost the stammer forever.

In Olathe, Kan., he was taken into the home of Christopher and Lucy Seymour, an elderly Negro couple. Christopher Seymour was an intensely religious man; each Sunday he went to services in the Presbyterian Church, and he was quietly gratified when George asked to accompany him. George had already committed great segments of the Bible to memory. Now he became a Presbyterian. But all his life, if the door of a church—any church—was open, he went in.

In 1880 the Seymours journeyed west to Minneapolis, Kan., a growing, bustling little town in the Solomon River valley, and there George at last entered high school. It was during this time that he took on a middle name. There was another George Carver in town, and sometimes letters intended for George at the Seymours' didn't reach him. Finally he picked a middle initial at random and once, asked jokingly if the W stood for Washington, grinned and said, "Why not?" But he felt there would be something vainglorious in his use of that name, so his signature was always "George W. Carver," or plain "George Carver."

As he neared the end of high school, a short, painstakingly printed letter came from Aunt Mariah. His brother Jim, she wrote, had died of smallpox and was buried in Seneca, Mo.

George wept, and for a time he felt desperately alone. He knew that now, more than ever—for Jim as well as for himself —he had to find his star. And then another letter arrived, one which filled him with hope.

He had sent an application for admission to a small Presbyterian college called Highland, in the northeast corner of Kansas. For weeks he waited anxiously for a reply. Now on a fine June morning it came. His grades were satisfactory, the letter said. Highland College would be happy to have him in attendance commencing with the fall semester, September 20, 1885. The letter was signed by the Rev. Duncan Brown, D.D., principal.

For the rest of the summer George walked in the warmth of that promise, and late in August he took a train to Joplin, bound south on a sentimental journey to the places of his boyhood. From Seneca, after visiting Jim's grave, he walked the 13 miles to Neosho to bid a last farewell to the Watkinses, and then on to Diamond Grove for a nostalgic visit with the Carvers. Past 70, Uncle Moses still worked the fields, but Aunt Susan had turned frail and seldom left the house. George told them of the places he had been and the things he had seen, and they listened in silent pride.

For four nights he slept in his mother's cabin. On the fifth night, September 20, he took a train to Highland, and walked eagerly to the college campus. Then, in the stillness of the principal's office, surrounded by books and dark polished furniture, he presented himself: "I am George W. Carver, sir."

"Yes?"

"I've come to enroll at Highland."

"There has been a mistake."

A remembered cold touched George Carver's heart. He looked at the pinched and meager face of the Rev. Duncan Brown, D.D., and groped for words. "But your letter said—"

"I don't care what it said. You didn't tell me you were Negro. Highland College does not take Negroes."

HE WAS alone again, and the journey to Highland had left him with almost no money. That night he slept in a barn. In the morning he found work on a fruit farm with a family named Beeler. There, for months, he pruned trees and mended fences, biding time, gathering a new grubstake.

He listened thoughtfully when the family read aloud the letters of young Frank Beeler, who had gone west to homestead on the Kansas plains. There was opportunity on the frontier for anyone who would work, Frank wrote, and in 1886 George followed him.

He filed on a 160-acre homestead, and built a sod house, cutting the virgin buffalo grass into brick-like strips for its walls. Waiting to plant his spring crop, he hired out on a nearby stock farm, and there he passed the first terrible winter. Furious blizzards shrieked down from the north, the snow so dense that a man had to cling to a lifeline to go from house to barn. And when summer came, the corn shriveled in the scorching winds.

For almost two years George fought the blizzards and the burning sun. In a garden by his house, however, he coaxed an array of flowers from the sod, and somehow preserved them through winter in a sort of lean-to conservatory. Visitors would burst in from the blinding cold and open frozen eyelids to see his windowsill and table astonishingly bright with bloom. In the long evenings he crocheted, or sorted the stones and Indian relics he collected on walks.

And, gradually, the passing seasons and the solitude healed his spirit. He began to read again, and to paint. Finally he realized that the prairie had become a hiding place, and that he didn't want to hide anymore. In the early summer of 1888 he mortgaged his homestead for $300 and started east.

He crossed into Iowa, and came to the village of Winterset, where he found a job as cook in a hotel. One Sunday morning a white woman, Mrs. John Milholland, heard his high tenor voice during services at the Baptist Church and asked Dr. Milholland to invite him to their home. Mrs. Milholland was the church choir director, and she offered to give George singing lessons. George went to the Milholland house frequently, and before long it was as much a home as he had ever had.

In the warmth of this new friendship he shed the last of the fears he carried from Fort Scott and Highland. It was ignorance, he decided, and not hate, that was his enemy, and as long as there were white people like the Milhollands he was not alone. However, when Mrs. Milholland suggested that he apply for admission to Simpson College in Indianola, George hesitated. Simpson was a white college with white teachers and students. But Mrs. Milholland persisted. The college had been endowed by and named after a friend of Abraham Lincoln, a firm believer in the equality of all men.

So it was that, on September 9, 1890, George W. Carver arrived at Simpson College. His acceptance there was immediate. "It was in high school that I first learned what it meant to be a human being," he said later, "and at Simpson that I could truly believe I was one."

At Simpson he studied etymology, composition, mathematics and his favorite subject, art. To earn his way he set up a laundry in a small house off campus. Students who came to leave their clothes often stayed to talk with the thin young man whose personal history was so vastly different from their own. Sometimes they listened as he read aloud from a book propped beside the steaming tubs; sometimes they shared his savory biscuits and honey. And always there was the question: "Where will you go from here, George?"

He had no answer for that, but he was soon to hear the same question from his art teacher, Miss Etta Budd. As an exercise, he had painted a picture of a cactus-grafting experiment he had devised, and though Miss Budd seemed much taken with it, she did not return it for a long time. When she did, it was with a plainspoken challenge that was to orient George Carver's life: "What are your plans for the future?"

"To be an artist," he replied, "if you think I'm good enough."

"Oh, you're good enough," she told him. "You have great talent. But—George, I showed your picture to my father. He's a professor of horticulture at the Iowa Agricultural College at Ames. I told him about your skill with plants. He thinks you should be studying agriculture at Ames."

If Miss Budd had never spoken, he might have gone on

basking in Simpson's warmth, continuing to paint, and enjoying his friends. But now the specter of tomorrow haunted him. It was 1891; he was past 30. He could not forever remain a student. What *should* he do?

Then one spring night, as he sat on his doorstep and watched the stars, the image of Aunt Mariah Watkins sprang suddenly to his mind's eye, and her voice was in his ear. *You must go out in the world and give your learning back to our people.* And George knew he would go to Ames.

THERE WAS excitement afoot at Ames. It was a time when the craft of agriculture was at last about to become a science, and the educators gathered at the Iowa State College of Agriculture and Mechanic Arts (known today as Iowa State University of Science and Technology) were beginning to transform the old techniques of farming. Two faculty members were to become Secretaries of Agriculture in the years ahead, and the first, James G. Wilson, welcomed George Carver to the college with an extraordinary gesture of friendship.

George had arrived in May, an inauspicious time. The college year followed the planting season, February to November, and with the semester well begun, no one seemed to have an available room for the new student.

"Send him to me!" Professor Wilson said. "I have a room."

Whereupon he swept the papers off his desk, moved up to the second floor, and ordered a cot and chest brought to his old office. This, the most spacious room in North Hall, became the quarters of the astonished and thankful newcomer.

But this kindness was overshadowed by an incident that occurred shortly afterward. George was told that he could not eat in the dining hall; he would have to take his meals in the basement with the kitchen help and field hands. Hurt, he nevertheless agreed to this without objection, reasoning that if the whites upstairs weren't better than he was, neither was he better than the help who ate in the basement.

Professor Budd wrote about the affair to his daughter at Simpson, and George's friends there were furious. One of them, Mrs. Arthur Liston, took the next train to Ames. Surprised, George spent the day showing her about and introducing her to his teachers. Then, at dinnertime, Mrs. Liston insisted that she meant to eat in the basement with her friend.

"But, madam," the dining-hall director pleaded, "what will the dean say?"

"You ought to have considered that when you arranged Mr. Carver's dining facilities," she snapped back. "And please bear in mind that I expect to be visiting here again."

At breakfast next morning George was invited to join the students at Table 6.

He was a favorite from the start. Within a week he had devised a table game that swept the dining hall and remains an institution at Ames to this day. Each dish had to be asked for by its scientific name. If a student remembered *Triticum vulgare,* he could fill up on bread, but if he forgot the words *Solanum tuberosum,* he would not get potatoes—unless he sat next to George Carver. "What's the formula for sugar, George?" a boy would ask after poking at his tasteless oatmeal. And George would whisper, "C twelve, H twenty-two, O eleven."

His list of courses was imposing. Conscious of the fleeting years, he enrolled for botany, geometry, chemistry, zoology, bacteriology and entomology. As always, he worked to support himself—as a janitor in North Hall, waiter, greenhouse-and-laboratory caretaker—but he still found time for extracurricular activities, winning a place on the college quartet, serving as the official trainer and masseur for the athletic teams.

When winter vacation arrived, he rushed back to Simpson to spend a few days in Miss Budd's art class. He had not touched a paintbrush for almost a year, but he now created some of his most memorable canvases—a yucca plant he remembered from his desert wanderings, a vase of roses, peonies.

Back at Ames in February, he plunged again into the hectic work schedule, but the grinding pace took its toll. In the fall he became ill with anemia, and the doctor ordered him to remain on campus during the Christmas holidays.

One afternoon he met Professor Budd, who told him that the Iowa State Teachers Association was meeting in Cedar Rapids between Christmas and the New Year, with an all-Iowa art exhibit to be an important part of the program. Did George plan to show any of his paintings?

"I'm afraid I can't afford the trip."

"That is too bad," the professor replied. "My daughter tells me that you are the finest painter in Iowa."

On the day after Christmas, George was in his room. A wreath in his window marked the holiday season, but he wore his patched and tattered work clothes: he was to earn some money that afternoon by helping to clean a faculty member's house. Then a sleigh filled with students pulled up outside.

"Climb aboard!" the driver yelled to George. "We'll take you where you want to go." But it was soon clear that the sleigh was bypassing faculty row and bound for town. "You'd better let me off!" George shouted. The students took no notice. Instead they burst into chorus after chorus of "Jingle Bells," until the sleigh stopped in front of a men's clothing store.

Struggling, George was all but carried inside, swiftly divested of his trousers, and buttoned into a handsome gray suit. Next he was fitted with hat, shirt, tie, gloves, shoes and socks. Finally he was helped into a new black overcoat, and then the whole band stormed out to the sleigh again, George's questions drowned in still another wave of "Jingle Bells."

The next stop was the Wilson house, and once again George was whisked inside. There in the parlor stood professors Wilson and Budd, and for the first time, George gained someone's full attention. "Sir," he said carefully to Professor Wilson, "I'm supposed to be working this afternoon."

"Nonsense, you're going to Cedar Rapids," the professor replied. "We are determined that Iowa Agriculture shall be properly represented at the art exhibit. Here is your ticket to Cedar Rapids, and here are the paintings that Professor Budd spirited from your quarters—with his daughter's counsel."

Numbly, George took the envelope and the canvases.

"But the money—how will I ever repay it?"

"You have already repaid it." Professor Wilson clamped a hand on George's frail shoulder and said, "The small sum each of your classmates and teachers contributed is little enough for the honor of your friendship. We believe in you."

Iowa Agriculture's faith was not misplaced. At the exhibit, all four of George's pictures were awarded prizes, and "Yucca gloriosa" was chosen to be shown the following summer at the World's Columbian Exposition in Chicago. There, in competition with the work of professionals from all over the world, it won honorable mention, and newspapers across Iowa took note of George Carver's triumph. But the prizes and the sudden spurt of fame did not move him nearly so much as that moment of comradeship in Professor Wilson's parlor.

GEORGE graduated in 1894, his long-sought Bachelor of Science degree won with a thesis entitled *Plants as Modified by Man*. Mrs. Liston came to the graduation exercises from Indianola. She brought a bouquet of red carnations, a gift from Miss Budd and George's former classmates at Simpson. Much moved, he put one of the blooms in his lapel, and, to the best of anyone's knowledge, he wore a flower—a rose, or a sprig of evergreen, even a weed—every day of his life thereafter.

A few days later Dr. Louis H. Pammel, a professor at Iowa State and one of the country's eminent botanists, sent for him. George had applied for a job as an assistant botanist at the college's experiment station. He would not let himself hope he would get the job, for there had never been a Negro on the faculty, but he hurried to the professor's office. "Well, sir," Dr. Pammel greeted him. "What are your plans?"

George took this as a polite dismissal. "I hadn't thought," he mumbled. "Perhaps some small school would take me."

"Take you? You're already taken!" Pammel roared. "You are my new assistant, and I want to know what plans you have. Would you like to take over the greenhouse?"

So George Carver became, at last, a scientist, concentrating on mycology, the branch of botany which deals with fungus growths. Soon his collection consisted of some 20,000 specimens, and his skill at hybridizing rendered whole families of fruits and plants resistant to fungus attack. Scientific papers began to cite G. W. Carver as their authority.

In 1896 George received his master's degree in agriculture and bacterial botany. He had never been more content—and yet he was sometimes disturbed by his happiness. He was a Negro, and across the land millions of his people, starved and stultified, yearned for a place in the sun. Did he serve them best as an example of what a man—any man—could achieve by unending effort? Or did he belong *among* them, sharing the knowledge he had come by with such labor and pain?

About this time, 800 miles away in the Alabama town of Tuskegee, the acknowledged spokesman of the Negro race, Booker T. Washington, was struggling to achieve his dream of a black people's institute of learning. One overwhelming problem confronted him. "These people do not know how to plow or harvest," he wrote. "I am not skilled at such things. I teach them how to read, to write, to make good shoes, good bricks, and how to build a wall. I cannot give them food."

Washington became convinced that his most urgent need was someone who could teach his people to farm. He had heard that there was a noted agriculturist, a colored man, at a school in Iowa, and on April 1, 1896, Washington sat down and wrote him a letter:

"I cannot offer you money, position or fame. The first two you have. The last, from the place you now occupy, you will no doubt achieve. These things I now ask you to give up. I offer you in their place work—hard, hard work—the task of bringing a people from degradation, poverty and waste to full manhood."

One morning four days later, as the tall young scientist read the letter, his blood raced and his heart beat fast. God had revealed His plan for George Carver.

HE WOULD never forget the trip to Tuskegee. After a farewell party at Ames, during which Professor Wilson presented him with a magnificent microscope, he boarded a train and sped south. The rich midwestern plains and prairies fell behind, and soon he was entering the realm of King Cotton. Nothing he had ever studied could have prepared him for the staggering impact of what he saw.

It was harvesttime. Men, women and children—all who had strength to raise a hand—were in the fields picking cotton.

They straightened for a moment to watch as the train raced by, their black faces bereft of hope, and then they stooped again to pick some more. These were the people he had come to help. His heart sank at the enormity of the work ahead, for he knew that what he saw was no different from what he would see if he traveled hundreds of miles east or west or south.

The cotton was planted up to the very doorways of their sad, unpainted shanties. Hardly a tree or a flower or a vegetable garden could be seen, for cotton—every bale of it—brought cash, and nothing else mattered to the white landlord, or to the rare Negro who owned his own few acres. So cotton had ruled in the South for a century, and year by year it had drained the good from the soil, producing an ever smaller yield, so that more ground had to be planted and great forests had to be felled to make room for still more fields. Without the trees, topsoil was washed off by the rains and blown by the winds, until un-counted millions of tons of eroded earth were gone forever.

George arrived at Chehaw, a railroad spur some four miles north of Tuskegee, early in the morning of October 8, 1896. A boy from the Institute met him with a buggy, and as they rode past the cottoned-out farms and propped-up cabins, Carver was anxious for his first view of the school. He imagined it an oasis in this wasted land, a place of order and green fields.

When the buggy finally pulled into the grounds of the Tuskegee Normal and Industrial Institute, he could not believe he had reached his destination. In all directions there were only sand and bare yellow clay, scarred by rain gullies so deep that a man—a horse!—could be lost in them. Numbly, he walked down the main road. It lay ankle-deep in dust and would, he knew, run with a river of mud whenever it rained. Here and there neatly lettered signs warned "Keep Off the Grass"—but nowhere was a blade of grass to be seen.

He passed a pathetic collection of shacks, an occasional larger building, and one of brick, called Alabama Hall. In the sky behind it vultures circled. Each took its turn swooping down on the kitchen garbage, which had been flung into a ditch. There was no sewage system.

Carver was shown into the principal's office, a plain, sparsely furnished room. Booker T. Washington rose to greet him. "What do you think of our school?" he asked.

"There seems much to be done," was Carver's reply.

Washington told him that a site had been chosen for the agriculture building, but for now he could be spared only a single room, which would have to serve, as well, for his living quarters. "Your department exists only on paper," Washington said. "And your laboratory will have to be in your head."

"I will manage," said Carver. He set to work.

THERE WERE 13 students in Carver's first agricultural class, and early one morning he led them to the school junk heap. There he directed the reclamation of a startling array of bottles, rusted pans, fruit-jar lids, saucepan handles, wire and odd bits of metal. No one had the vaguest notion of what this unaccountable teacher was about, but when they had exhausted the possibilities of the school dump, the students moved on to the town, scavenging rubbish in back alleys and knocking on doors to ask for rubber, old kettles and china jars.

When at last the entire collection had been brought to the Institute, 13 pairs of skeptical eyes watched as Carver pointed to the odds and ends. "Now all this may seem junk to you," he said. "But it is only waiting for us to apply our intelligence to it. Let's get to work!"

Before their eyes the students saw a heavy, broken-handled teacup become a mortar, a rounded stub of drapery rod the pulverizer. An ink bottle with a string stuck through the cork for a wick served as a Bunsen burner. Into carefully labeled fruit-jar lids went an assortment of chemicals. Chipped bottles were cut down to size, to become beakers and retorts. Pieces of tin, holes punched in them with nails, turned into strainers through which soil samples could be accurately graded.

The boys watched in awe as a makeshift laboratory took shape. And this first lesson was perhaps the most valuable of all: in years to come, when Tuskegee's graduates went out to impoverished farms, they were armed with the knowledge that elaborate equipment was not a prerequisite for success.

But the students had seen only the first of the wonders their new teacher was to perform. In the year that Carver arrived, the 20-acre school farm had yielded five scrawny bales of cotton, 120 bushels of sweet potatoes, and a cup of strawberries a day. "They told me it was the worst soil in Alabama," George said later. "And I believe them."

Day after day Carver went out with his boys, dividing the 20 acres into plots, emphasizing the urgency of precise measurement. He had no use for the word "about," he told them. "Jumping *about* four feet across a five-foot ditch will earn you a mud bath!" He prevailed on Washington to ask an Atlanta fertilizer company for several hundred pounds of phosphates to start what was to be a three-year agricultural experiment. When the phosphates were spread, the students were ready to plant a crop—but the teacher was not.

Other fertilizers were needed, he announced, and they could find them—right here on campus. He led them to another trash mountain, a dump for the bulkiest kitchen waste, and the students brought back buckets of vegetable peelings, barn sweepings and such until they had made a great compost heap. In the spring, when it had rotted to a rich black humus, they spread it on their 20 acres.

Of course, from the first, the students had expected to plant cotton on each square foot they had labored so hard to make arable. They were stunned when George decreed that their first crop was to be cowpeas. *Cowpeas!* All that backbreaking work for something fit to be thrown to the hogs? But cowpeas it was. Most plants drain lifegiving nitrogen from the soil, the teacher patiently explained, and cotton was among the worst consumers. But legumes such as cowpeas absorb nitrogen from the air and *feed it back to the soil.* So an essential fertilizer ingredient, worth 17 cents a pound commercially, could be gained at no cost.

At the end of that first year, the farm, having provided for the Institute dining room well into November, showed a profit of $4 an acre. In the spring Carver had his boys plant sweet potatoes, and experimented with other legumes. The second-year production was 265 bushels of sweet potatoes to the acre, more than six times the usual harvest.

When finally Carver did plant cotton, farmers, black and white, came to the experiment station and stared in wonder. The yield was an incredible 500-pound bale per acre! So rich a crop had never been grown in that part of the land. How could a Northerner who had never *seen* cotton until he was a grown man best those who had devoted a lifetime to raising it?

George's answer was always the same: A plant needs certain things, the soil has certain things to give, and it is the farmer's job to make the right adjustment between them.

THESE WERE Tuskegee's great growing years, and somehow, after Carver's arrival, chores not clearly marked for some other department wound up in his hands. Carver found himself designing the inside of the new agriculture building, testing wellwater, measuring rainfall and sending daily reports to the Montgomery weather bureau.

Inevitably, he landscaped the campus, grading and terracing, planting young shade trees, shrubbery, grass and flowers, so that, in time, the once barren fields would have the look and mood of a great natural park. He kept up with his own researches as well, contributing more than 100 specimens for a nationwide collection of grasses being assembled by the Department of Agriculture. And when the new agriculture building was completed he persuaded his old friend Professor Wilson, now Secretary of Agriculture, to come and dedicate it.

His students were amazed at his uncanny ability to identify anything that grew, but they were just youthful enough to keep hoping that sometime they would stump him. Once they fabricated a bizarre creature from the body of a beetle, the legs of a spider and the head of an ant. Barely able to suppress their laughter, they thrust it at Carver and said, "Look at this weird bug we found, Professor. What is it?"

Carver took one look and said, "Why, this is what we call a humbug!"

Always, in class and out, he was teaching. He was not there to contribute to their individual gain, he told the boys, but to help them lead their people forward. "*That* will be the mark of your success—not the clothes you wear, or the money you put in the bank. It is only service that counts." Again and again he stressed: "Learn to do the common things uncommonly well."

During his years of wandering Carver had learned to play the piano, and now each Sunday night he would sit down at the ancient upright in Alabama Hall. Boys and faculty members would stop by and listen as he played "Swing Low, Sweet Chariot," Handel's "Largo" and the plantation melodies. It became a school tradition, and one spring Sunday the school treasurer suggested a money-raising concert tour.

Carver laughed. But for five weeks in the summer of 1899 he toured cities and hamlets in Alabama, Georgia, Louisiana and Texas, playing in barns, in public buildings and private homes. And when he returned to Tuskegee he had several hundred dollars with which to add 15 acres to the school farm. For years the full-dress concert suit hung in his closet, never again to be worn. Asked about it, he would chuckle and say, "Oh, that was from my career as a piano player."

During the tour Carver had seen again the squalid homes and grinding lot of his people. He pondered the awful irony of the South. The soil was scorched and spent, but it could be made rich. The despotism of King Cotton could be ended. There could be good food for his people, and opportunity for their children—if only they could be shown!

The Farmers' Institute was a beginning. On the third Tuesday of each month, farmers from the nearby countryside, only a few at the start, shuffled into the immaculate new agriculture building. For two hours, or for as long as he could hold their attention, Carver would talk to them about their land. He urged them to plant a kitchen garden. Fresh vegetables would break the tyranny of the three M's—meat, meal and molasses, the time-rooted southern diet that had made pellagra a deadly caller in almost every home.

Dramatically he would cut into a ripe red tomato—generally regarded as poisonous—and, to the accompaniment of horrified gasps, eat it with obvious relish.

"You will please notice that I have not died," he would say, and then go on to explain that tomatoes could act as a prime protection against scurvy.

In time, the handful of farmers who came to the Institute grew to 25, 50, even more. But out where the roads ended, in the thickets and the swamps, were thousands of Negroes who had never even heard of Tuskegee, and Carver was determined to reach them.

He wheedled a wagon and a mule and, with a few tools, seed packets sent down by Secretary Wilson, and some boxed demonstration plants, set forth after classes. Every weekend, every moment he could spare, he rode the jolting wagon up and down Macon County, seeking out isolated farmers, cornering groups at fairs and on street corners.

Some men were skeptical—"How come you're smarter'n me? You just as black"—but others listened and asked questions. He pressed them to save five cents every working day. At the end of a year they would have $15.65—enough to buy three acres of land and leave a reserve fund of 65 cents. There was no other way to break the grip of the landlord or the plantation commissary, Carver said. Before long, all over the county, nickels were being hoarded in jars, tins and hollow stumps.

Slowly, doggedly, he began to change the eating habits of the South. He taught the farmers how to cure hog meat so that even in the hottest weather it wouldn't spoil. Long before the medical profession understood the value of raw fruit as a safeguard against nutritional diseases, Carver was advocating that wild plums and apples be made a part of the daily diet. He handed out seed packets, but getting the men to plant vegetables was only half the job: their wives had only the most meager idea of what to do with the harvest. So with sleeves rolled up, he went to their stoves and showed them how to flavor and cook the greens and beets and potatoes.

Waste was a foe in every yard and kitchen, and Carver turned on it all his awesome ingenuity. Enough hog fat was thrown away to keep each family in soap through the year, he explained. Sweet potatoes too stringy to eat could be grated into superior starch. Pine needles, cheesecloth and burlap could be woven into mats and coverings. He handed out azalea slips and pansy seeds and said, "Plant these in your dooryard. A flower is God's silent messenger." And he rode on.

As word about the Tuskegee wagon spread, Carver began attracting Saturday-afternoon crowds to the town squares. At first the whites were uneasy with such an arrangement, and some broke up the meetings. "We don't want uppity niggers around here," they said. What they meant was that they did not want colored farmers outproducing the white ones.

Like Washington, Carver believed devoutly that "you can't keep a man in a ditch unless you're willing to get in with him" —and it proved so. Before long, the white men quit grumbling and edged closer to hear what the "nigger teacher" was saying. And Carver was gratified to have them. Blacks and whites in the South had the same problems, the same needs. He was dropping a stone into a vast sea of darkness, and the more people, black or white, he could help to a better life the farther the ripples would spread.

To his dying day Carver would believe that the wagon school was his most important work. It started a revolution in soil conservation, all but eradicating the curse of pellagra, and went on to become a worldwide institution. The first rickety mule-drawn cart evolved into the Jessup Agricultural Wagon, a traveling experiment station with funds donated by Morris K. Jessup, a New York philanthropist. In 1918 the state of Alabama provided a huge truck, and later the farmers of Macon County put up $5000 to equip an even larger school on wheels.

Meanwhile requests from other communities poured in on Tuskegee for assistance in launching their own movable schools, and inevitably the idea spread overseas. Visitors came to the Institute from Russia, China, Japan, India, Africa and South America. All listened as the lanky, unassuming professor recounted his experiences in the rural South and suggested techniques for putting them to use abroad.

THROUGHOUT these years Carver had continued to plead with farmers to plant a variety of crops. He urged the cowpea and sweet potato on them, but with little success. He entered on experiments with the soybean, but, though it was easily transformed into flour, meal, even milk—and, thanks to these early efforts, would someday become a southern staple—he soon saw that the time had not come when cotton acreage would be given to this unfamiliar plant.

Ironically, it was a plague, one of the most devastating agricultural scourges of modern times, that forced the farmers to listen to Carver. For years he had warned that the insidious spread of the boll weevil, a rapacious beetle that feeds on cotton, could not be stopped. By 1915 the weevil was ravaging cotton fields across Louisiana, Mississippi and Alabama, its annual toll exceeding $100 million, driving thousands of farmers to bankruptcy and despair.

By this time Carver had begun to examine an odd little vine that produced something called a peanut or, more often, goober. It, too, was considered worthless, but at least a few farmers had patches of peanuts, mostly because their children liked to crack the double-humped shells and eat the nuts.

"Burn off your infested cotton," Carver now told the stricken farmers. "Plant peanuts!"

To dramatize his campaign, he persuaded Washington to invite nine influential Macon County businessmen to lunch at the Institute. The meal, prepared under Carver's direction, consisted of soup, mock chicken, a creamed vegetable, bread, salad, ice cream, candy, cookies and coffee. The businessmen noted that each dish had a unique and zesty flavor, and when Carver informed them that they had eaten nothing but peanuts prepared in nine different ways, they broke into applause.

Slowly, pushed by the weevil and pulled by Carver, the people began to do as he said. Where there had been random peanut patches, 20- and then 40-acre fields began to bloom with the shy white flowers of the velvety plant. In time, whole communities abandoned cotton, and peanuts became one of the most important crops in a great farming belt that ran from Montgomery to the Florida border.

Then—calamity. It came this time in the seemingly innocent question of an old woman who knocked on Carver's door one October afternoon. She was a widow, she told the professor, but she had followed his counsel and turned the farm to peanuts. There had been a bumper crop, and, after setting aside all the peanuts she could use in the year ahead, she still had hundreds of pounds left over. "Who will buy them?" she asked.

Carver had no answer. He had been so engrossed in breaking the one-crop system, and so successful in promoting the peanut, that almost alone he had created a monster as cruel as the weevil itself. One hasty trip into the countryside, and his blunder glared back at him from every farmyard. Barns were piled high with the surplus, and peanuts were rotting in the field.

He returned racked with guilt, tormenting himself that he had thought the problem only halfway through. Years later Carver told the story of how, groping for solace, he had walked through the predawn darkness of his beloved woodlands and had cried out, "Oh, Mr. Creator, why did You make this universe?"

"And the Creator answered me. 'You want to know too much for that little mind of yours,' He said. 'Ask me something more your size.'

"So I said, 'Dear Mr. Creator, tell me what man was made for.'

"Again He spoke to me: 'Little man, you are still asking for more than you can handle. Cut down the extent of your request and improve the intent.'

"And then I asked my last question. 'Mr. Creator, why did You make the peanut?'

" 'That's better!' the Lord said, and He gave me a handful of peanuts and went with me back to the laboratory, and together we got down to work."

Inside the laboratory, Carver closed the door, pulled on an apron and shelled a handful of peanuts. That whole day and night, he literally tore the nuts apart, isolating their fats and gums, their resins and sugars and starches. Spread before him were pentoses, pentosans, legumins, lysin, amido and amino acids. He tested these in different combinations under varying degrees of heat and pressure, and soon his hoard of synthetic treasures began to grow: milk, ink, dyes, shoe polish, creosote, salve, shaving cream and, of course, peanut butter. From the hulls he made a soil conditioner, insulating board and fuel briquettes. Binding another batch with an adhesive, he pressed it, buffed it to a high gloss—and had a light and weatherproof square that looked like marble and was every bit as hard.

For two days and two nights he worked, dismissing the worried students who tapped at his door—"Are you all right, Professor?" "Yes! Yes! Please let me be." He felt himself to be in God's hands, the mortal instrument of a divine revelation.

Later he would say, "The great Creator gave us three kingdoms—the animal, the vegetable and the mineral. Now He has added a fourth—the kingdom of synthetics." And years afterward, when the new science of chemurgy had been defined as an attempt to create wealth from the dormant power of the soil and air and sun, men would say that George Washington Carver had been a chemurgist before the word was invented.

But none of these lofty considerations even occurred to Carver on that October night in 1915 when he finally sagged back on his workbench, trembling with fatigue. He knew only that with God's guidance he had made it possible for men to use every peanut harvested, and that if the crop trebled—as it was to do in a scant four years—every farmer would still find a ready buyer in the marketplace. Wearily he walked out into the chill sunrise to offer his devout thanks.

BY THE END of World War I the infant peanut industry was worth $80 million a year. Eager to protect this sudden boom, southern planters banded together and formed the United Peanut Associations of America. Then, quick to seize opportunity, Chinese planters began to flood the United States with millions of bushels of Oriental peanuts. The southern planters decided to plead their cause at a tariff hearing before the House Ways and Means Committee, and in January 1921 they sent Carver an urgent telegram: "Want you in Washington. Depending on you to show possibilities of the peanut." Carver replied that he would be there.

The outlook was far from encouraging when the time came for the peanut planters to present their case. The Congressmen had heard arguments in favor of protection for rice, meat and a variety of other products; the hearing room was stuffy with smoke, and tempers had become ragged. It was past 4 p.m. on Friday, January 21, when the first peanut spokesman was summoned. He spoke for nearly 50 minutes, and adjournment had been set for five o'clock. Then the clerk called the name of George W. Carver.

Every head turned, eyes staring at the gray-haired black man lugging two heavy suitcases toward the speaker's stand. In the sudden hush, someone snickered, "Reckon if he gets enough peanuts, he's a right happy coon."

Carver heard it clearly, but he had heard worse and he didn't turn a hair. Then as he reached the stand and began unpacking his cases, Chairman Joseph Fordney announced that he would be given only ten minutes. Carver's heart sank. Nevertheless, he continued with his unpacking, groping for a way to begin.

"What do you know about the tariff?" Rep. John Garner challenged.

"Not a thing," Carver said quietly. "I came to talk about peanuts." And he began to exhibit a dazzling array of products. He showed the Congressmen a peanut substitute for quinine, peanut foods for livestock, mock oysters and 30 different dyes. By now his time was up, but the Congressmen quickly voted him unlimited time to continue. So for nearly two hours he held the committee spellbound as he showed still more of his products—vanishing cream, rubbing oils, milk flakes—and answered questions about the peanut.

Representative Barkley: How is it in punch? (Laughter)

Carver: Well, I'll give you some punches!

Voices: Good! Attaboy! (Laughter)

Carver: Here is one with orange, one with lemon and one with cherry. Here is instant coffee, which already has in it cream and sugar. Here is buttermilk, Worcestershire sauce, pickles—all made from the peanut.

Barkley: Where did you learn all this?

Carver: From a book.

Barkley: What book?

Carver: The Bible. In Genesis we are told: "Behold, I have given you every herb that bears seed on the face of the earth, and every tree bearing seed. To you it shall be meat."

When at last the Congressmen let him go, every member of the committee rose and applauded him, and in the following year a tariff was placed on all imported peanuts.

Meanwhile Carver kept adding to the remarkable roll of products made from the peanut. By the time he died there were well over 300; scores of factories had been built to make them; and their range staggered the mind—mayonnaise, cheese, chili sauce, shampoo, bleach, axle grease, linoleum, metal polish, wood stains, adhesives, plastics.

Today peanuts are our sixth most important agricultural product. The two billion pounds harvested each year are worth close to $300 million to the farmer and another $200 million to industry.

WHEN Booker T. Washington died on November 14, 1915, he was mourned throughout the land. To Carver the loss seemed almost unbearable. He and Washington had been close friends for almost 20 years, and he sought to fill the incalculable void with work, the only solace he had ever known.

His experiments were entering a new and exciting stage. Five years earlier the Tuskegee trustees had voted to establish a Department of Agricultural Research, with Carver in charge. Relieved of all but a few classes, he was free to concentrate on what he called the creative sciences. He continued to contribute to a broad spectrum of human knowledge—in agronomy, nutrition, chemistry, genetics, mycology, plant pathology—but more and more his interests were turning to the creation of useful materials from the waste products of agriculture and industry.

There are those who feel that this concept, still the subject of widespread research, was Carver's most important gift to humankind. Never before had anyone advocated the use of agricultural products for anything but food and clothing. Carver, however, saw that in everything that grew was locked the chemical magic that men could forge to their use, not only for food but perhaps for all their earthly needs.

Some of his ideas took decades to materialize. He made paper from the southern pine—and 25 years later his process led to a major new paper industry. He made synthetic marble from peanut hulls and food wastes, and these efforts presaged the fabrication of plastics from all sorts of vegetable matter. Substituting cellulose for steel, automobile makers would in time be building 350 pounds of agricultural products into every car.

Working with the sweet potato—from which he devised 118 products, ranging from wartime flour to inexpensive mucilage for postage stamps—he laid the groundwork for still another industry. During World War I, Carver discovered that he could reduce 100 pounds of sweet potatoes to a powder that fitted in a compact carton, kept indefinitely and could be instantly reconstituted by the addition of water. Today the dehydrated-food industry is worth hundreds of millions of dollars, as are frozen foods, a first cousin.

There seemed to be no limit to Carver's interests and activity. From the fruit of the Osage orange he extracted a juice that tamed the toughest piece of chuck—one of the first meat-tenderizers. A weed, to Carver, was "a vegetable with concealed promise." Farmers ranted at the giant thistle, but Carver showed that it contained medicinal properties, as did 250 other weeds he examined.

When chemists learned to synthesize rayon and other artificial fibers, the time when southern farmers could sell every bale of cotton they raised seemed at an end. But Carver began seeking new uses for the crop, and in a few years the farmers were flourishing again, their markets spurred by the use of cotton in plastics, paving blocks for roads, tires and fertilizer.

Carver had long since learned to extract paints and color washes from the clay hills, and one paint he developed was used at 14 Tennessee Valley Authority sites as an object lesson in home beautification at nominal cost. Another Carver experiment led to the now-standard use of soybean oil as the base for automobile spray paints, and during World War II his work with camouflage paint was consolidated with a massive camouflage program then being conducted at Fort Myer, Va.

Any one of his achievements could have made Carver a man of fabulous wealth. But all his life he refused to accept payment for a single discovery. Actually he had not the slightest regard for money. He never accepted a raise in salary. "What would I do with more money?" he once asked. "I already have all the earth." Forty years after his arrival at Tuskegee he was still earning the $125 a month that Washington had first offered him.

Even then, the harried treasurer had to plead with him to cash his paychecks, which were always stuffed in pockets or dresser drawers, so the school's books could be balanced. When Carver did dig them out, it was usually to give them away. There is no way of knowing the number of boys, white as well as black, whose bills he paid in their time of need. Virtually everyone who knew him remembers at least one such instance.

He was constantly besieged with offers of money from businessmen willing to pay almost any sum for his advice. A group of peanut planters in Florida sent a check for $100 and a box of diseased specimens; if the professor could cure their crop they would put him on a monthly retainer. Carver sent back a diagnosis of the disease, and the check. "As the good Lord charged nothing to grow your peanuts," he wrote, "I do not think it fitting of me to charge anything for curing them."

When a dyestuffs firm heard that he had perfected an array of substitute vegetable dyes, the owners offered to build a laboratory for Carver, and sent him a blank check. He mailed back the check, and the formulas for the 536 dyes he had found to date. When he declined a princely sum to join another company (which had adopted his process for making lawn furniture out of synthetic marble), the company literally came to him—moving factory and machines to Tuskegee—and got the benefit of his regular counsel at no cost at all.

Thomas Edison once invited him to come work with him in the Edison laboratories in Menlo Park, N.J., at a minimum annual salary of $100,000. Carver declined the offer, as he had all the others, and seemed astonished that anyone expected him to claim rewards from the gifts God had given him.

"But if you had all that money," he was once challenged, "you could help your people."

"If I had all that money," Carver replied, "I might forget about my people."

By now Carver's reputation had spread across the world, and so much mail poured into Tuskegee—a considerable portion of it addressed simply to The Peanut Man—that the substation of the post office at the Institute was swamped. Some 150 letters a day were dumped on Carver's desk, and he answered each in meticulous detail. A steady stream of visitors asked to see him, and his door remained open to all. Farmers came to question him about their seeds, townsfolk about their gardens, and boys in the dormitories thought nothing of asking him for help with their homework.

He was, of course, a revered campus character. He often wore the suit he had been given at Ames four decades before, and his neckties, which he knitted from cornhusks, always flaunted the garish colors of whatever dye he happened to be testing. Despite increasing demands on his time he started a painting class, teaching students to mix an astonishing array of colors from the native clays, and to make canvases from the pulp of peanut shells. And although his genius as an artist had been recognized by the famed Luxembourg Gallery in Paris, where his exquisite work, "Four Peaches," was exhibited, he was quick to give his paintings to anyone who admired them.

Over the years Tuskegee boys had taken to coming to Carver's room on Sunday afternoons, to hear him talk of the relationship between science and the Scriptures. In time the group swelled until finally it became so large that the informal discussions were scheduled as regular classes and shifted to the assembly room in the Carnegie Library. It was a rare week when all 300 seats were not filled.

Waiting, watch in hand, Carver would begin precisely at six. His lessons were vivid and sometimes startling. Once, describing the wickedness of Sodom and Gomorrah, he climaxed the tale by suddenly touching off some chemicals in a great cloud of fume and flame. The boys leaped to their feet, gasping with shock and smoke. Never had religion seemed so close or so real.

It was to this "Bible class" that Carver spoke some of his most pungent aphorisms:

On cigarettes: "If God had intended the human nose to be used for a chimney, He would have turned our nostrils up."

On nature: "I love to think of nature as an unlimited broadcasting system through which God speaks to us every hour, if we will only tune Him in."

On death: "One of the things that has helped me as much as any other is not, 'When am I going to die?' but 'How much can I do while I am alive?'"

Because of their abiding trust in him, students often came to Carver when they were suffering from the rankling hurts of discrimination and prejudice. "You must never let the haters of this world divert you from the path of your own duty," he told them. "For the time will come when the haters will have been consumed by their own hatred, and the ignorant will have learned the truth. And then, if you are prepared for it, you will walk the earth as free men, the equal of any other man."

To a class of seniors he said, "You may have to go into areas where the invisible Not Wanted sign is up. But remember that this has happened before. It happened to a man called Jesus when He went to Galilee."

Nor would he ever let the white man's bigotry serve as a handy excuse for those who grumbled, "Well, what's the use? A Negro can't . . ." "A Negro *can!*" he always shot back, and once told a group, "Not long ago an important businessman said to me that he wished he knew a man who could find oil. He didn't specify white, black or yellow—just a *man!*"

Carver himself was not spared the wounds of bigotry, even after his fame was celebrated in every part of the world. Yet as long as he was able to travel, he never refused to go any place where he might cast light into darkness. He believed that a racist was to be pitied for his blind brutality, and he said, as Washington had often said before him, "No man can drag me so low as to make me hate him."

CARVER had already won the friendship of three Presidents— Theodore Roosevelt, Calvin Coolidge and Franklin Delano Roosevelt—and in the last years of his life kings and princes journeyed to see him. The crown prince of Sweden studied with him for three weeks, gleaning information on the use of agricultural wastes. In an extended correspondence with Gandhi, Carver prescribed a vegetable diet for the Indian leader, and detailed the food values in plants that could easily be grown by the Mahatma's starving people.

Ralph Bunche, then an instructor at Howard University, never forgot the experience of meeting Carver. "I came away thinking about the respect he was winning from all people, and I was convinced—for the first time, I think—that the barriers of race in America were not insuperable."

Carver's most frequent and best-known guest was Henry Ford. They met in 1937, became fast friends and agreed to get together at least once a year thereafter. In the beginning Carver went to Ford's home in Dearborn, Mich., or to his Georgia plantation. Later, when the professor's health began to fail, Ford came regularly to Tuskegee.

Carver's most significant work with Ford was in the fabrication of rubber. Fields of goldenrod covered the Georgia plantation, and from this unlikely harvest Carver extracted a milky liquid that could be synthesized into a material with rubberlike characteristics. Thus an exciting start was made in the long search for a synthetic that would free the nation from total dependence on far-off sources of rubber.

Ford also built and equipped a Dearborn laboratory for Carver; and, nearby, he constructed a nearly precise duplicate of Carver's mother's old cabin in Diamond Grove. But Carver was nearly 80 years old now, and wearying. Moved to tears by his first view of the cabin, he was fated not to see it again.

Though none of the Tuskegee presidents who served during his 46-year tenure could persuade Carver to accept a salary increase, the last one, Dr. Frederick D. Patterson, was determined that the venerable professor must have an assistant. A parade of hopefuls tapped meekly at the professor's door, and at last Austin W. Curtis, Jr., a young Cornell graduate, won the job.

Carver had never married—"How could I explain to a wife that I have to go out at four o'clock every morning to talk to flowers?" he once said—but Curtis was to become almost the son he never had.

During the fortieth-anniversary year of Carver's arrival at Tuskegee, it was Curtis who suggested that Carver's work be commemorated by an exhibit. And so the records of a lifetime's achievement—thousands of products shaped from peanuts, sweet potatoes and weeds—were gathered into a display that was later made permanent in a separate building called the George Washington Carver Museum.

Early in 1940 Carver told Curtis that he wanted to bequeath his savings—which, thanks to his fantastic frugality, amounted to more than $33,000—to Tuskegee, not after his death but now, when he might have a hand in how the money was used. Soon the George Washington Carver Foundation was signed into being, to provide facilities for young Negroes engaged in scientific research. In ensuing years additional funds were contributed, and today the Carver Foundation, housed in a $2-million building, is a center for advanced studies in botany, creative chemistry, mycology, plant genetics and agronomy.

During these years when the museum and foundation were being started, it was clear that Carver's health was weakening. In 1937 he was hospitalized for pernicious anemia. Toward the end of 1942, when he fell ill again, he refused to see a doctor. "There is nothing to be done," he said.

He was right as usual. He was past 80 years old, and the body that housed the great spirit was wearing out. He remained alert, reading the frayed leather Bible that Mariah Watkins had given him long ago. But on January 5, 1943, when his dinner was brought to him, he took nothing except a few sips of milk. "I think I'll sleep now," he whispered—and sometime in the next hours the valiant heart stopped beating.

The sad news was announced that evening, and soon messages from the great men of the world began to pour in. President Franklin D. Roosevelt wrote that he counted it among his great privileges to have known Carver. Vice President Henry Wallace said, "The United States has lost one of its finest Christian gentlemen."

For days, long lines of mourners moved past his bier in Tuskegee's chapel. They came by car and bus and on foot for this final farewell, from the nearby hills and swamps, and from the far reaches of the land. On the fourth day he was buried on the rise where Dr. Washington had rested for 27 years.

Before long a Congressional bill was introduced by Sen.

Harry S. Truman of Missouri, providing for the establishment of the George Washington Carver National Monument on the site of the original Moses Carver farm near Diamond Grove. It was passed without a single dissenting vote, and when the monument was dedicated the New York *Herald Tribune* wrote: "Dr. Carver was, as everyone knows, a Negro. But he triumphed over every obstacle. Perhaps there is no one in this century whose example has done more to promote a better understanding between the races. Such greatness partakes of the eternal."

Thousands of tributes, from world leaders, from businessmen, scientists and artists, and from the humble people for whom he labored, were received at Tuskegee. But there remain no more eloquent words to describe the meaning of Carver's life than the simple epitaph on his grave: *He could have added fortune to fame, but caring for neither, he found happiness and honor in being helpful to the world.*

ROAD SONG OF A 13TH-CENTURY PAGE

By William Alexander Percy

Jesu,
If Thou wilt make
Thy peach trees bloom for me,
And fringe my bridle path both sides
With tulips, red and free,
If Thou wilt make Thy skies as blue
As ours in Sicily,
And wake the little leaves that sleep
On every bending tree—
I promise not to vexen Thee
That Thou shouldst make eternally
Heaven my home;
But right contentedly,
A singing page I'll be
Here, in Thy springtime,
Jesu.

Acknowledgments

BOLD MEN, BOLD DREAMS (page 15), by Catherine Drinker Bowen, condensed from *Sports Illustrated*, © 1962, Time Inc. MAN'S EPIC FIRST FLIGHT TO THE MOON (20), cond. from *Time*, © 1968, Time Inc. BROTHERS IN THE ETERNAL COLD (25), by Archibald MacLeish, from *New York Times*, © 1968, The New York Times Co. Reprinted by permission. GOD AND MY FATHER (27), by Clarence Day, cond. from *The Best of Clarence Day*, copyright © 1931, 1932 and renewed 1960, Mrs. Katherine B. Day. Reprinted by permission of Alfred A. Knopf, Inc. Originally appeared in *Harper's Magazine*.

GOOD-BY, AMERICA! (34), by Henry W. Nevinson, cond. from *Farewell to America*, copyright © 1922, B. W. Huebsch, Inc. Reprinted by permission of The Viking Press, Inc. THE SECRET WORLD OF THE UNBORN (37), by Margaret Liley, M.D., with Beth Day, cond. from *McCall's*, © 1965, The McCall Publishing Co. DEATH IN DALLAS (42), cond. from *Time*, © 1963, Time Inc. MAKING HABITS WORK FOR YOU (49), by William James, cond. from *Psychology: Briefer Course*, Holt, Rinehart and Winston, Inc., Publishers. THE DESERT, LAND OF SURPRISES (59), by Edward Abbey, cond. from *Desert Solitaire*, copyright © 1968, Edward Abbey. Reprinted by permission of McGraw-Hill Book Co. Originally appeared in *Harper's Magazine*. THE DISROBING OF FLAPPER JANE (65), by Bruce Bliven, cond. from *The New Republic*. CAN A SCIENTIST BELIEVE IN GOD? (75), by Warren Weaver, cond. from *Look*, © 1955, Cowles Communications, Inc. HIPPIE OR SCHOOLGIRL—WHICH WAS "THE REAL LINDA"? (83), by J. Anthony Lukas, cond. from *New York Times*, © 1967, The New York Times Co.

Reprinted by permission. THE VIOLENT SUN (90), by Herbert Friedman, cond. from *National Geographic*, © 1965, National Geographic Society. THE SECRET LIFE OF WALTER MITTY (94), by James Thurber, cond. from *My World—and Welcome to It*, copyright © 1942, James Thurber, and renewed 1970, Helen W. Thurber and Rosemary Thurber Sauers. I AM FIFTY —AND IT DOESN'T HURT (99), by Dorothy Canfield Fisher, cond. from *The American Magazine*. WHEN THE DOCTOR EXAMINES YOU (105), by Warren R. Young, cond. from *Life*, © 1962, Time Inc. THE LONGEST DAY (115), by Cornelius Ryan, cond. from the book, copyright © 1959, Cornelius Ryan. Reprinted by permission of Simon & Schuster, Inc. THE SHOCK OF HAPPINESS (150), by George Kent, cond. from *Christian Herald*, © 1966, Christian Herald Assn., Inc. I REMEMBER HYDE PARK (157), by Eleanor Roosevelt, cond. from *McCall's*, © 1963, The McCall Publishing Co. PRAY FOR BARBARA'S BABY (172), by Kristin Hunter, cond. from *Philadelphia Magazine*, © 1968, Philadelphia Magazine.

"GOLFERS, QUIT ALL THAT THINKING!" (179), by Sam Snead, cond. from *Life*, © 1959, Time Inc. SLAVES OF THE MACHINE? (183), by Stuart Chase, cond. from *Harper's Magazine*. THERE IS NO DEATH (189), by Norman Vincent Peale, D.D., cond. from *The Power of Positive Thinking*, copyright © 1952, Prentice-Hall, Inc. RIDDLE OF THE QUICK-FROZEN MAMMOTHS (193), by Ivan T. Sanderson, cond. from *The Saturday Evening Post*, © 1960, The Curtis Pub. Co. MOSCOW REVISITED (198), by John Gunther. Brief portions are cond. from *Inside Russia Today*, copyright © 1957, John Gunther. Used by permission of Harper & Row, Publishers. JUMPED OR

ILLUSTRATIONS